The Economics of Natural Hazards
Volume I

The International Library of Critical Writings in Economics

Series Editor: Mark Blaug

Professor Emeritus, University of London, UK
Professor Emeritus, University of Buckingham, UK
Visiting Professor, University of Amsterdam, The Netherlands
Visiting Professor, Erasmus University of Rotterdam, The Netherlands

This series is an essential reference source for students, researchers and lecturers in economics. It presents by theme a selection of the most important articles across the entire spectrum of economics. Each volume has been prepared by a leading specialist who has written an authoritative introduction to the literature included.

A full list of published and future titles in this series is printed at the end of this volume.

Wherever possible, the articles in these volumes have been reproduced as originally published using facsimile reproduction, inclusive of footnotes and pagination to facilitate ease of reference.

For a list of all Edward Elgar published titles visit our site on the World Wide Web at
www.e-elgar.com

The Economics of Natural Hazards
Volume I

Edited by

Howard Kunreuther

Cecilia Yen Koo Professor of Decision Sciences and Public Policy
Wharton School
University of Pennsylvania, USA

and

Adam Rose

Professor of Energy, Environmental and Regional Economics
Pennsylvania State University, USA

THE INTERNATIONAL LIBRARY OF CRITICAL WRITINGS IN ECONOMICS

An Elgar Reference Collection
Cheltenham, UK • Northampton, MA, USA

Published by
Edward Elgar Publishing Limited
Glensanda House
Montpellier Parade
Cheltenham
Glos GL50 1UA
UK

Edward Elgar Publishing, Inc.
136 West Street
Suite 202
Northampton
Massachusetts 01060
USA

A catalogue record for this book is available from the British Library

Library of Congress Cataloguing in Publication Data

The economics of natural hazards / edited by Howard Kunreuther, Adam Rose.
    2 v. ; cm. — (The international library of critical writings in economics ; 178) (An Elgar reference collection)
    A collection of journal articles and book chapters previously published.
    Includes bibliographical references and indexes.
    1. Natural disasters—Economic aspects. 2. Natural disasters—Planning. 3. Emergency management. 4. Disaster relief. 5. Insurance, Disaster. 6. Risk (Insurance) 7. Regional economics. I. Kunreuther, Howard. II. Rose, Adam Zachary. III. Series. IV. Series: An Elgar reference collection

HC79.D45E25 2004
363.34—dc22

                                                                                              2004047955

ISBN   1 84064 815 5 (2 volume set)

Printed and bound in Great Britain by MPG Books Ltd, Bodmin, Cornwall

Contents

Acknowledgements

The editors and publishers wish to thank the authors and the following publishers who have kindly given permission for the use of copyright material.

American Association for the Advancement of Science for articles: Ronald A. Howard, James E. Matheson and D. Warner North (1972), 'The Decision to Seed Hurricanes', *Science*, **176** (4040), 16 June, 1191–202; Stanley A. Changnon, Jr., Barbara C. Farhar and Earl R. Swanson (1978), 'Hail Suppression and Society', *Science*, **200** (4340), 28 April, 387–94; Paul Slovic (1987), 'Perception of Risk', *Science*, **236** (4799), 17 April, 280–85.

American Economic Association for article: Mary F. Kokoski and V. Kerry Smith (1987), 'A General Equilibrium Analysis of Partial-Equilibrium Welfare Measures: The Case of Climate Change', *American Economic Review*, **77** (3), June, 331–41.

American Society of Civil Engineers for article: Gary R. Webb, Kathleen J. Tierney and James M. Dahlhamer (2000), 'Businesses and Disasters: Empirical Patterns and Unanswered Questions', *Natural Hazards Review*, **1**, May, 83–90.

Blackwell Publishing Ltd for articles: Richard W. Ellson, Jerome W. Milliman and R. Blaine Roberts (1984), 'Measuring the Regional Economic Effects of Earthquakes and Earthquake Predictions', *Journal of Regional Science*, **24** (4), November, 559–79; Sam Cole (1995), 'Lifelines and Livelihood: A Social Accounting Matrix Approach to Calamity Preparedness', *Journal of Contingencies and Crisis Management*, **3** (4), December, 228–40; Adam Rose, Juan Benavides, Stephanie E. Chang, Philip Szczesniak and Dongsoon Lim (1997), 'The Regional Economic Impact of an Earthquake: Direct and Indirect Effects of Electricity Lifeline Disruptions', *Journal of Regional Science*, **37** (3), August, 437–58; Lester B. Lave and Tunde Balvanyos (1998), 'Risk Analysis and Management of Dam Safety', *Risk Analysis*, **18** (4), August 455–62; Sungbin Cho, Peter Gordon, James E. Moore II, Harry W. Richardson, Masanobu Shinozuka and Stephanie Chang (2001), 'Integrating Transportation Network and Regional Economic Models to Estimate the Costs of a Large Urban Earthquake', *Journal of Regional Science*, **41** (1), February, 39–65.

Elsevier for articles: Tracy Lewis and David Nickerson (1989), 'Self-Insurance against Natural Disasters', *Journal of Environmental Economics and Management*, **16** (3), 209–23; Richard L. Bernknopf, David S. Brookshire and Mark A. Thayer (1990), 'Earthquake and Volcano Hazard Notices: An Economic Evaluation of Changes in Risk Perceptions', *Journal of Environmental Economics and Management*, **18** (1), January, 35–49; Jason F. Shogren and Thomas D. Crocker (1991), 'Risk, Self-Protection, and Ex Ante Economic Value', *Journal of Environmental Economics and Management*, **20** (1), January, 1–15; Anthony Fisher,

David Fullerton, Nile Hatch and Peter Reinelt (1995), 'Alternatives for Managing Drought: A Comparative Cost Analysis', *Journal of Environmental Economics and Management*, **29**, 304–20.

Kluwer Academic/Plenum Publishers for article: Baruch Fischhoff, Stephen R. Watson and Chris Hope (1984), 'Defining Risk', *Policy Sciences*, **17**, 123–39.

MIT Press and the President and Fellows of Harvard College for articles: Richard R. Nelson and Sidney G. Winter, Jr. (1964), 'A Case Study in the Economics of Information and Coordination: The Weather Forecasting System', *Quarterly Journal of Economics*, **LXXVIII**, 420–41; Charles W. Howe and Harold C. Cochrane (1976), 'A Decision Model for Adjusting to Natural Hazard Events with Application to Urban Snow Storms', *Review of Economics and Statistics*, **58**, 50–58.

Natural Resources Journal for article: Ian Burton and Robert W. Kates (1964), 'The Perception of Natural Hazards in Resource Management', *Natural Resources Journal*, **3**, January, 412–41.

Public Policy for article: Linda Cohen and Roger Noll (1981), 'The Economics of Building Codes to Resist Seismic Shock', *Public Policy*, **29** (1), Winter, 1–29.

RAND Corporation for article: Jack Hirshleifer (1966), 'Disaster and Recovery: The Black Death in Western Europe', *RAND Corporation Memorandum RM-4700-TAB*, February, 1–31.

RFF Press/Resources for the Future, Inc. for excerpt: Gilbert F. White (1966), 'Optimal Flood Damage Management: Retrospect and Prospect', in Allen V. Kneese and Stephen C. Smith (eds), *Water Research*, Chapter 12, 251–69.

Sage Publications, Inc. for article: Carol T. West and David G. Lenze (1994), 'Modeling the Regional Impact of Natural Disaster and Recovery: A General Framework and an Application to Hurricane Andrew', *International Regional Science Review*, **17** (2), 121–50.

Transactions – Wisconsin Academy of Sciences, Arts and Letters for article: Arthur A. Atkisson, William J. Petak and Daniel J. Alesch (1984), 'Natural Hazard Exposures, Losses and Mitigation Costs in the United States 1970–2000', *Transactions – Wisconsin Academy of Sciences, Arts and Letters*, **72**, 106–12.

University of Chicago Press for articles: Isaac Ehrlich and Gary S. Becker (1972), 'Market Insurance, Self-Insurance, and Self-Protection', *Journal of Political Economy*, **80** (4), July/August, 623–48; David S. Brookshire, Mark A. Thayer, John Tschirhart and William D. Schulze (1985), 'A Test of the Expected Utility Model: Evidence from Earthquake Risks', *Journal of Political Economy*, **93** (2), April, 369–89.

University of Wisconsin Press for article: Clifford S. Russell (1970), 'Losses from Natural Hazards', *Land Economics*, **46**, 383–93.

Water Resources Research and Copyright Clearance Center for article: M. Elisabeth Paté-Cornell and George Tagaras (1986), 'Risk Costs for New Dams: Economic Analysis and Effects of Monitoring', *Water Resources Research*, **22** (1), January, 5–14.

Every effort has been made to trace all the copyright holders but if any have been inadvertently overlooked the publishers will be pleased to make the necessary arrangement at the first opportunity.

In addition the publishers wish to thank the Marshall Library of Economics, Cambridge University, the Library of the University of Warwick and the Library of Indiana University at Bloomington, USA for their assistance in obtaining these articles.

Introduction

Howard Kunreuther and Adam Rose

I.   Framework for Analysis

The economic impact of natural disasters is a subject of interest not only to researchers in the social sciences, but also to those affected directly or indirectly by these untoward events. Until the 1990s, natural hazards received relatively little attention from legislators and regulators except in the immediate aftermath of a catastrophic event. The reason for increased interest today was succinctly summarized by two US congressmen in a column in the *Washington Post*, in 1995, entitled 'Natural Disasters: A Budget Time Bomb':

> Over the past five years the cost of natural disasters has been rising at an alarming rate. In that time, 11 catastrophes have cost the nation more than $1 billion each. Hurricane Andrew and California's Northridge earthquake together cost more ($28 billion) than what the government spends annually on running the federal court system, aiding higher education and pollution control, combined (Emerson and Stevens, 1995, p. 1913).

Figures 1(a) and 1(b) depict the losses due to *great natural catastrophes* from 1950 to 2002 throughout the world. A 'great natural catastrophe' is defined as one where the affected region is 'distinctly overtaxed, making interregional or international assistance necessary. This is usually the case when thousands of people are killed, hundreds of thousands are made homeless, or when a country suffers substantial economic losses, depending on the economic circumstances generally prevailing in that country' (Munich Re, 2002, p. 15). These figures reflect the overall economic and insured losses worldwide (in 2002 dollars) from earthquakes, floods, windstorms, volcanic eruptions, droughts, heat waves, freezes and cold waves.

Systematically investigating the economic aspects of natural hazards requires input from other disciplines. Engineering and the natural sciences provide data on the nature of the risks associated with disasters of different magnitudes and the uncertainties surrounding them (*Risk Assessment*). Geography, organizational theory, psychology, sociology and other social sciences provide insights on how individuals, groups and organizations perceive the risk and make decisions (*Risk Perception and Choice*). Risk and policy analysts examine alternative strategies for both reducing future losses and for dealing with recovery problems (*Risk Management*).

Risk Assessment

The field of risk assessment encompasses studies that estimate the chances of specific events occurring and their potential consequences. Scientists and engineers provide a picture of what we know regarding the nature of a particular risk and the degree of uncertainty surrounding these estimates. Experts in the field need to take special care to minimize the imposition of their subjective values in providing these estimates.

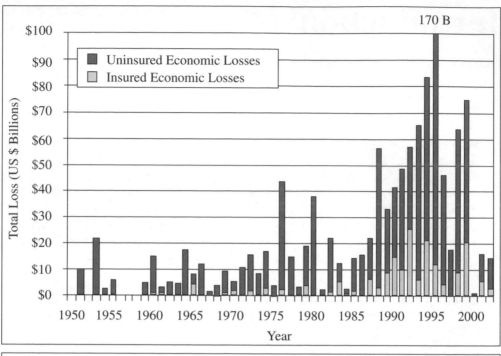

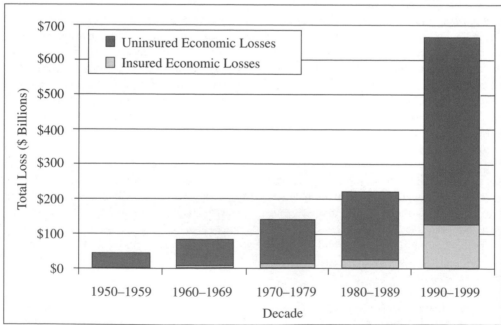

Figure 1.   *Losses due to great natural catastrophes worldwide: (a) by year; and (b) by decade (Munich Re, 2002)*

It is not uncommon for the public to hear Expert 1 say that there is 'nothing to worry about' regarding a particular risk, while at the same time learning from Expert 2 that 'this risk should be on your radar screen'. There may be many different reactions to these conflicting reports. One layperson may decide that she cannot rely on the judgment of any expert. Another individual may decide to focus on the expert supporting his or her own view of the risk. Someone else may seek out the views of other experts to see if there is a degree of consensus on the nature of the risk.

Here are a few questions to ponder with respect to the uncertainties of the following extreme events:

1.   What are the chances that the Los Angeles area will have an earthquake of Magnitude 7.0 or greater next year, and what will be the resulting property damage and direct and indirect business interruption losses?
2.   What is the likelihood of a severe nuclear power accident somewhere in the United States and what would be the results?
3.   What is the probability that an airplane will crash into the Sears Tower in the next year, and how serious would the consequences be?
4.   What are the chances that there will be a terrorist-induced smallpox epidemic in the United States in the next five years, and how many people would be affected?

When experts are asked to answer these questions, they are likely to respond by requesting more precise information to help define the event. Take the question related to the chances of an earthquake of Magnitude 7.0 or greater in the Los Angeles area. The experts will normally require more precise information to define the event. They are likely to ask: 'What is the geographic area that defines Los Angeles?' 'What do you mean by next year (i.e. starting today or on 1 January 2005)?' 'What is an indirect loss?' To obtain more accurate and useful risk assessments, the terms of the analysis need to be defined precisely, so that experts know what to do and users know what they have received.

For many years, the focus of hazard loss estimation was confined to property damage and loss of life. Both of these are stock measures pertaining to a definite point in time (e.g. the period of ground-shaking or above a flood height threshold level). However, there are also flow measures that can extend over long periods of time, such as interruption of business activity and stress caused by disaster losses. Thus, the definition of hazard losses has broadened significantly and its assessment has become much more difficult and uncertain.

Risk Perception and Choice

Traditional risk assessment focuses on losses that are often measured in monetary units. Risk perception is concerned with the psychological and emotional factors that have been shown to have an enormous impact on behavior. In a set of path-breaking studies begun in the 1970s, Paul Slovic, Baruch Fischhoff and other psychologists measured laypersons' concerns about different types of risks.

These studies showed that hazards where a person had little knowledge and experience were also highly dreaded and perceived as being the most risky ones. For some technologies (e.g. nuclear power) and activities (e.g. storing radioactive waste), there was a wide disparity between the general citizenry and the experts' view of the risk. The general finding that laypersons see the world differently from the scientific community also raises a set of questions as to the nature of the decision-making process for dealing with risks.

For a long time the scientific community felt it was appropriate to ignore the public's perception of the risk if it differed significantly from their own estimates. The public often did not believe the experts' figures because they were not communicated very well, the assumptions on which they were based were not well stated, and there was little understanding as to why experts disagreed with one another.

The situation has changed in recent years where there is increased sympathy for incorporating psychological and emotional factors as part of the risk assessment process. Rather than basing one's choices simply on the likelihood and consequences of different events, as normative models of decision-making suggest one does, there is now a recognition by the social science community that individuals are also influenced in their choices by emotional factors such as fear, worry and love.

The problems associated with risk perception and choice are compounded because of the difficulties individuals have in interpreting low probabilities when making their decisions. In fact, there is evidence that people may not even want data on the likelihood of an event occurring even when it is available to them. A recent study of several hypothetical risky managerial decisions shows that when individuals are required to search out their own information, they rarely ask for any data on probabilities. One group was given a minimal description and the opportunity to ask questions. Only 22 per cent of these respondents asked for probability information, and not one of them asked for precise probabilities. Another group of respondents was given precise probability information, and less than 20 per cent of these respondents mentioned the word 'probability' or 'likelihood' in their verbal protocols (Huber *et al.*, 1997).

If people do not think probabilistically, how do they make their choices? There is now a large body of evidence that individuals' risk perceptions are affected by judgmental biases (Kahneman *et al.*, 1982). The *availability heuristic* is one of the most relevant ones for dealing with extreme events such as large-scale natural disasters. Here people estimate the likelihood of an event by the ease with which they can imagine or recall past instances. In cases where the information on an event is salient so that individuals fail to take into account the base rate, there will be a tendency by many to overestimate the probability of the event occurring. Following the terrorist activities of September 11th, many people refused to fly because they perceived the chances of being on a hijacked plane to be extraordinarily high, even though it could be argued that the likelihood of such events occurring in the future were extremely low given increased vigilance and added protection by the federal government.

More generally, in the case of low probability events, there are often two extreme reactions to risks, either 'it will either happen to me' or 'it won't happen to me'. These responses are influenced unduly by personal experience or media events and compounded by other constraints. With respect to natural disasters, there is a general lack of interest by most people in voluntarily purchasing insurance and investing in loss protection measures because these individuals often underestimate the probability of the event occurring and the losses, they are myopic with respect to planning for the future and/or they have budget constraints. An increase in the demand for protection normally occurs following disasters when it is too late. Only then is the event salient in people's mind. For example, most homeowners in California purchase earthquake insurance only after experiencing a quake. When asked whether the probability of a future quake is *more likely, the same or less likely than before the disaster*, most people respond by saying 'less likely' (Kunreuther, 2002).

Risk Management Strategies

In developing risk management strategies for reducing losses from natural disasters and other extreme events, there is a need to incorporate the data from risk assessment studies and the factors that have been shown to influence risk perception and choice.

NEED FOR IMPROVED FORECASTING

The heightened awareness of defining losses more broadly to include direct impacts of a disaster (e.g. physical damage, injuries and loss of lives), as well as indirect losses over time (e.g. business interruption, stress), has now made forecasting a more difficult process than in the past.

Kates (1971) refers to disasters as 'joint-interaction phenomena' – a combination of a physical stimulus and the human settlement system. Both features and their interactions must be incorporated in a forecast. One must also examine feedback effects, such as the extent to which economic development increases water runoff and hence flood damage potential, and/or the extent to which better mapping of earthquake zones alters the spatial pattern of development.

Improved forecasting accuracy can prevent future disasters, as well as reduce losses from those events that occur. For example, improved weather forecasts may reduce the number of deaths or injuries by evacuating residents from threatened areas prior to the onset of a storm. The forecasts may also eliminate unnecessary evacuations if there is knowledge that the storm will not affect specific areas that were previously in danger.

COMMUNICATING INFORMATION ON THE RISK

A number of studies indicate that people have difficulty processing data regarding low probability events. Most people feel small numbers can be easily dismissed, while large numbers get their attention. By stretching the time-frame over which the probability of an extreme event is presented, one may be able to force people to pay attention to an event that they would otherwise ignore. If a company is considering flood protection over the life of its plant, managers are far more likely to take the risk seriously if a .01 probability of a severe flood next year is converted to a longer time horizon so that one is now told that you have a one in five chance of experiencing at least one severe flood of this magnitude occurring during a 25-year period.

USING ECONOMIC INCENTIVES

One can utilize both positive and negative economic incentives to encourage individuals to take protective measures. Here, again, the way people process information on the costs and benefits of reducing the risk plays an important role in their decision on whether or not to adopt protective measures. Suppose that one provides premium reductions on insurance policies for those who undertake loss reduction measures (e.g. strengthening their house against natural disasters, installing dead-bolt locks to ward off criminals). If people think only about the potential benefits of these protective measures in reducing risk over the next year or two, then they are unlikely to view these measures as financially attractive should there be a large upfront cost associated with the protective measure. Had they considered a long time period when evaluating the protective measure, the investment might well have been viewed as worth while.

Fines, coupled with specific regulations or standards, can also be used to encourage protective measures, but there has to be a sufficiently high probability that the negligent individual or firm will get caught. Otherwise the person or manager is likely to play a different game than intended – i.e. ignore the regulation. If the probability is sufficiently low and/or the fine is not very large, then it may pay in the long run not to take protective action. The behavior, in such cases, is not all that different from the decision *not* to put a quarter into the parking meter because one feels that there is a small chance of getting a ticket, and/or the fine if one is caught is small.

PRIVATE–PUBLIC PARTNERSHIPS

There is a need to bring together interested parties from the private sector, representatives from public interest and citizen groups and leaders from governmental organizations to deal with risk management strategies. This type of private–public partnership is likely to be more successful than working independently with each of the above groups.

Long-term Loans, Private Insurance and Building Codes.   To illustrate how such a partnership could work consider the challenges associated with getting individuals or firms to adopt cost-effective measures to reduce losses from hazardous events. Suppose an industrial firm can spend $15,000 to make its plant more earthquake resistant, so that it will save $200,000 in property damage from a severe quake that has an annual probability of one in 100. The firm might have trouble justifying the decision in the short run, even if it received a premium reduction from its insurer. In this case, the expected reduction in annual damage from the investment is $2,000 (i.e. $1/100 \times \$200,000$), so that an insurer could reduce its premium to the firm by approximately this amount. The $15,000 investment would not pay for itself in the two to five-year payback period often required by the firm's management.

How could one encourage the managers of the firm to make this investment? Insurers and banks can work together to offer incentives in the form of disaster mitigation loans. By providing a 20-year loan with an interest rate of 10 per cent, the firm would now face an annual loan payment of $1,700. Combining this payment with an annual $2,000 reduction in its insurance premium, the firm comes out ahead by $300 per year. The bank earns a reasonable interest rate and the insurers have a reduced chance of experiencing large claims from disasters by encouraging their policyholders to adopt loss reduction measures. Everyone is a winner (Kleindorfer and Kunreuther, 1999)!

Even with these financial incentives, there may be a need for government regulations and standards. Building codes may be desirable when property owners would otherwise not adopt cost-effective mitigation measures because they either misperceive the benefits from them and/or underestimate the probability of a disaster occurring. When a building collapses, it may create externalities in the form of economic dislocations and other social costs that are beyond the economic loss suffered by the owners. Losses from these and other *externalities* would not be covered by the firm's insurance policy. A well-enforced building code would help reduce these risks and obviate the need for financial assistance to those who would otherwise suffer uninsured losses.

Catastrophe Bonds and Government Pooling Arrangements.   The shortage of reinsurance following Hurricane Andrew in 1992 and the Northridge earthquake in 1994 led financial institutions to market new instruments for providing protection against mega-disasters. These catastrophe bonds were offered at sufficiently high interest rates to overcome investors' qualms about the likelihood of losing their principal should a major disaster occur. Despite the considerable resources allocated by the private sector in developing and promoting these instruments, the market has been relatively thin, with $4.3 billion in catastrophe bonds outstanding at the end of 2003 (Swiss Re, 2004).

If the private sector feels that it cannot provide insurance protection against losses from catastrophic events, then one may need some type of government pooling arrangement to cover these losses. The Florida Hurricane Catastrophe Fund was established by the state following Hurricane Andrew, when a number of insurers claimed that they could not include windstorm in the future as part of the standard homeowners' coverage. After the Northridge earthquake, insurers had a similar reaction to providing earthquake coverage in California. In 1996 the state formed the California Earthquake Authority that offers homeowners earthquake coverage as a separate policy. There may also be a role for federal reinsurance to cover catastrophic losses from large-scale disasters.

Resiliency and Sustainability

The resilience of a community after a disaster and its sustainability over the long run have important ramifications for estimating the extent of hazard damage and developing risk management policies. Resilience refers to the ability of a business, household or community to cushion potential losses through inherent or explicit adaptive behavior in the aftermath of a disaster and through a learning process in anticipation of a future one (see Tierney, 1997; Bruneau *et al.*, forthcoming; Rose and Liao, forthcoming). Examples include businesses and households conserving water and finding substitutes for electricity.

Resilience also includes the inherent ability of the economy to reallocate resources to the highest value use through changes in price signals in the market. The jury is still out as to whether resilience has increased or decreased over time. More advanced economies become increasingly dependent on sophisticated inputs, especially lifeline services (e.g. electricity, internet communication), that are highly vulnerable and for which substitution is difficult. However, researchers can help by identifying increased opportunities to promote resilience, such as the establishment of an information clearing-house in a given region for suppliers without customers, and customers without suppliers.

Sustainability refers to the long-run viability and self-sufficiency of the community in the face of hazard threats. The more general definition of the term emanates from economic development and stipulates that decisions taken today should not diminish the productive capacity, broadly defined to include natural resources and the environment of a community in the future (Solow, 1992; Costanza, 1992). In the case of natural hazards, sustainability implies that land-use decisions made today should not place the community in greater jeopardy in the future so that it becomes dependent on external disaster assistance to survive. Sustainability emphasizes the importance of integrating mitigation measures into overall economic development policy and eliminating practices that increase the community's vulnerability (Mileti, 1999).

II. Themes of Hazard Research

Research on the economics of natural disasters has raised a set of issues and challenges with respect to the following areas: risk assessment, risk perception and choice, risk management strategies for reducing losses, recovery from a disaster and achieving long-term sustainability. These areas form the basis for the collection of papers in these two volumes. Key themes from these papers are highlighted in this section.

Risk Assessment

NEED TO EXAMINE DIRECT AND INDIRECT IMPACTS FROM DISASTERS

The most obvious direct impact of a disaster is physical damage to structures, but there are a host of other types of losses, such as business interruption, social impacts and regional impacts. An example of indirect effects is when a factory shuts down because firms damaged by an earthquake cancel orders for its products. Moreover, this is only the first link of a chain of ripple or multiplier effects throughout the economy.

CHALLENGES IN FORECASTING HAZARD RISK

Natural disasters are low-probability/high-consequence events, so there is a need to supplement limited historical data with scientific models. One of the key issues is how to combine these data in a systematic way, particularly if experts disagree on the nature of the risk.

ACHIEVING INTEGRATED ASSESSMENT OF HAZARDS

Programs for managing disasters require the use of hazard assessment models that can then suggest risk management strategies. There is a need for a well-articulated methodology for linking science, engineering, economics, sociology and policy in a consistent manner, including various feedback mechanisms.

Risk Perception and Choice

PEOPLE MISPERCEIVE THE RISK

People exhibit a set of systematic biases in estimating the likelihood and consequences from low-probability events and making their choices. These include the availability bias: it cannot happen to me (prior to the disaster), and it will happen to me again (after experiencing a loss).

INDIVIDUALS DO NOT WANT TO INVEST IN RISK REDUCING MEASURES

Prior to a disaster, individuals are reluctant to invest in cost-effective mitigation measures. There is a need to understand why such behavior differs from what normative models of choice would predict, and how one can develop meaningful strategies for encouraging people to adopt such loss reduction measures.

DISASTER INSURANCE IS NOT A BEST-SELLER

Even when premiums are highly subsidized, as in the National Flood Insurance Program, residents in hazard-prone areas are reluctant to purchase policies. People view insurance as an investment rather than as a contingent claim. Insurers also face the problem of adverse selection where only those who face the highest risk purchase a policy. In this case, insurers are in danger of suffering potentially large losses because their premiums are under-priced.

Risk Management

STRUCTURAL MITIGATION MEASURES MAY LEAD TO ILLUSIONS OF SAFETY

There has been a long history of public sector investments in structural measures such as flood control projects, and dams for reducing losses. The use of these funds may actually lead to catastrophic losses due to what Burton and Kates (1964) termed as the *levee effect* – i.e. individuals and businesses locate in flood-prone areas because they falsely believe that a flood control project or a dam will provide them with complete safety. A major disaster may cause these structural measures to fail and result in catastrophic losses because of economic development in the area. A clear example of this phenomenon is the 1993 Midwest floods.

BUILDING CODES NEED TO BE ENFORCED

Although building codes may be on the books, they may not be enforced. For example, following Hurricane Andrew it was estimated that over 30 per cent of the damage could have been averted if building codes had been enforced. Much of the damage and fatalities from the 1999 earthquake in Turkey could have been prevented had houses been constructed according to the existing codes.

CATASTROPHE BONDS REQUIRE LOWER INTEREST RATES

To justify the risks of losing their principal and/or interest, those considering investing in catastrophe bonds have demanded a significant rate of return. As a result of the high interest rates on these catastrophe bonds, there has been limited demand by insurers and reinsurers for protection. The challenge facing the financial community is to develop capital market instruments that are more attractive to both buyers and sellers than products that are currently on the market.

Resiliency and Sustainability

RECOVERY PROCESSES PRODUCE SURPRISES

Disasters normally bring out the best in human behavior such as concern for one's fellow citizen and neighbor. To illustrate, following the Alaska earthquake of 1964, supermarkets decreased their food prices, and residents in Anchorage voluntarily limited their purchases of products in short supply such as orange-juice (whose demand increased because of contamination of the water supply). A disaster also stimulates innovations because of special needs facing the stricken community or region. In Anchorage, Alaska, the construction industry draped plastic covering over structures damaged by the earthquake, so they could restore these buildings during the winter months. This material had been available for several years prior to the 1964 earthquake, but it took a disaster to extend the length of the construction season (Dacy and Kunreuther, 1969).

THE CHALLENGE FOR THE TWENTY-FIRST CENTURY: SUSTAINABLE COMMUNITIES

The trend in recent years has been to encourage communities to invest in hazard mitigation measures, so that they can be sustainable after the next major disaster. The Federal Emergency Management Agency (FEMA) in the US has made the development of a hazard mitigation plan a precondition for many types of disaster assistance. Due to FEMA prompting and local initiatives, some communities have adopted such plans, but these efforts have only scratched the surface. Mileti (1999) has provided scenarios for how this might be accomplished; for example, San Francisco could become a more disaster-resilient community by integrating energy and transportation systems into broader development plans.

EMERGING ECONOMIES FACE SPECIAL CHALLENGES IN DISASTER MANAGEMENT

Developing countries are highly vulnerable to disasters because of low-quality structures, poor land-use planning, hazard perception problems and inadequate emergency response. Moreover, they are subject to political instability in the aftermath of a major disaster. These countries do not have the infrastructure and institutions that we take for granted in formulating risk management strategies for the United States. In addition, these countries face extreme poverty, so that equity considerations need to be taken into account when considering alternative disaster management plans.

III.   Summary of Papers

The papers in these two volumes provide considerable insight into the questions and issues raised above. Below, we summarize key points from each of the articles in this collection.

Volume I, Part I: Foundations

Although the topic of disasters has been treated as part of the subject-matter of economics ever since Adam Smith, the first economist who seriously studied the topic was Jack Hirshleifer. He wrote several papers and monographs in the 1950s and 1960s at the RAND Corporation as a way of providing insights into the possible consequences of thermonuclear war.[1] These studies inspired a number of other economists (including both of us) to pursue research in this area. We have initiated this collection with Hirshleifer's (1966) study 'The Black Death in Western Europe'. It provides a systematic analysis of the short- and long-term economic impacts of the great pandemic of 1348–50 in Western Europe.

Gilbert White, Ian Burton and Robert Kates are geographers who did pioneering work on assessing the risk and reducing losses from natural disasters. Much of their research has focused on the strategies of individuals at risk and policy-makers in coping with hazards. Their work has been especially instrumental because it emphasized the design of programs for reducing future economic losses that takes into account people's decision processes and current institutional arrangements. White began his career in the early 1930s when he spent time working with Congressional Committees on appropriate policies for dealing with flood damage. His doctoral dissertation in 1945, emphasizing non-structural adjustments to floods, earned him the designation as the father of social science research on natural hazards. White's (1966) 'Optimal Flood Damage Management: Retrospect and Prospect' provides insight into the range of choice open to flood plain users and the lessons of three decades of experience and research on these issues with respect to designing flood plain management strategies.

Burton and Kates's (1964) 'The Perception of Natural Hazards in Resource Management' provides data on the magnitude and frequency of disasters in the United States and the differences in how technical-scientific personnel and resource users perceive hazards.

The final paper in this part of Volume I is Clifford Russell's (1970) 'Losses from Natural Hazards'. Russell develops a model of decision-making to determine the optimal adjustment to a natural hazard by equating the marginal benefits against the marginal costs of specific actions. He then examines the implications of this model for analyzing alternative public and private strategies for reducing losses in the future.

Part II: Risk Perception and Its Economic Impact

This part of Volume I contains articles exploring how individuals' perceptions of risks affect their behavior and economic well-being. Psychologists have been interested in characterizing risk more broadly than just probability and outcome. Paul Slovic's (1987) 'Perception of Risk' is a systematic treatment of the factors that characterize people's judgments in evaluating hazardous activities and technologies. Through the use of psychophysical scaling and multivariate analysis techniques, he provides quantitative representations of risk attitudes and perceptions. He shows that *riskiness* means more to individuals than simply the expected number of fatalities and that other factors, such as dread and catastrophic potential, must be taken into account when developing risk communication and risk management strategies.

Building on Slovic's work on risk perception, Baruch Fischhoff, Stephen Watson and Chris Hope (1984) explore ways to incorporate the many dimensions characterizing risk for aiding the choice process in their paper 'Defining Risk'. They show how one can construct a risk index by characterizing the relative importance of different attributes with respect to a particular hazard or technology. Through an illustrative example they demonstrate how such an index can be useful to decision-makers in evaluating the relative riskiness of alternative options for addressing a specific problem.

The other two papers in this part focus on whether the risk associated with a particular hazard is captured in people's choices and is reflected in the value of their property. David Brookshire, Mark Thayer, John Tschirhart and William Schulze's (1985) 'A Test of the Expected Utility Model: Evidence for Earthquake Risks' shows that the prices of homes in parts of California are consistent with a model of expected utility maximization by consumers. Safer homes with identical characteristics command higher prices. The authors did not study the actual decision-making processes of individuals, but used hedonic models to estimate the relative importance of site-specific characteristics, including location relative to an active earthquake fault, on property values.

In 'Earthquake and Volcano Hazard Notices: An Economic Evaluation of Changes in Risk Perceptions', Richard Bernknopf, David Brookshire and Mark Thayer (1990) examine the impact of US Geological Survey earthquake and volcano hazard notices on recreational visitation patterns and property values in the Mammoth Lakes area of California. Utilizing a stock adjustment investment model and secondary data sources, they conclude that recreation activity was largely unaffected by the notices, but that property values in the area were adversely affected due to a change in risk perceptions.

Part III: Direct Losses and the Distribution of Impacts

Losses from major disasters are dramatic and have left indelible impressions on society. The first level of analysis is to measure direct losses, that until recently has been confined to evaluating property damage, and was primarily the purview of the insurance industry and the engineering community. A major contribution of economists has been to broaden the focus to include the direct loss of the flow of goods and services stemming from damaged capital stock, now referred to as *business interruption losses*.

Several attempts have been made to survey the terrain of actual and potential losses in the United States and throughout the world. The 1984 paper by Arthur Atkisson, William Petak and Dan Alesch 'Natural Hazard Exposures, Losses and Mitigation Costs in the United States 1970–2000' provides insight into the enormity of the hazard threat and of the challenges in estimating it accurately. They develop a computerized probabilistic risk analysis model to estimate the annual expected losses for the major categories of natural hazards and conclude that economic damage from natural hazards exceeded all other categories of accidents, crime and pollution in 1970.

A major focus of research by economists has been to establish a solid empirical foundation for loss estimation. Carol Taylor West and David Lenze, (1994), in 'Modeling the Regional Impact of Natural Disaster and Recovery' examine how standard economic models must be modified, and how to use available data to do so. Although the analysis is performed in the broader context of a regional econometric model, the focus is on the microeconomic foundations of individual decision-making in markets, as illustrated by the economic impact of Hurricane Andrew on the economy of Florida.

Another major contribution first explored in depth by sociologists is that of *business resiliency* to disasters – the ability to cushion losses by adaptive behavior in the short- and long-run aftermath of ground shaking or flood inundation.[2] This research, supported by field surveys undertaken by Kathleen Tierney and her associates in the Disaster Research Center at the University of Delaware, attempts to identify the major sources of business interruption loss and major coping mechanisms. Their findings, summarized in Gary Webb, Kathleen Tierney and James Dahlhamer's (2000) 'Business and Disasters: Empirical Patterns and Unanswered Questions', indicate that these types of losses can rival property damage in their magnitude.

Another important dimension of losses is their distribution across different socio-economic groups. Hal Cochrane (1975) first explored this issue and formulated some important hypotheses. Distributional issues have historically received limited attention by economists due either to the lack of data and/or the political sensitivity of the issue, so very little progress has been made in this arena. Sam Cole (1995), in 'Lifelines and Livelihoods: A Social Accounting Matrix Approach to Calamity Preparedness', shows how a social accounting matrix can serve as both a useful organizing framework and a database for evaluating aspects of disaster preparedness and recovery strategies. The breadth and disaggregated features of the framework are especially well suited for studying the distribution of impacts of alternative policy objectives across socio-economic groups.

Part IV: Regional and Economy-Wide Impacts

Another dimension of flow measures of losses is that they can be transmitted beyond the area directly affected by the physical shock via multiplier or general equilibrium effects. The advantages of using an econometric model to trace these impacts can be seen in the 1984 paper by Richard Ellson, Jerome Milliman and R. Blaine Roberts 'Measuring the Regional Economic Effects of Earthquakes and Earthquake Predictions'. At first glance, it would appear that econometric models might be ill-suited because they are based on time-series data that are unlikely to include any hazard experience. However, the authors point out that all exogenous shocks except the very largest disasters are likely to fall within the normal range of major variables (e.g. housing starts). In addition, econometric models can readily incorporate supply constraints and are superior to other models in incorporating economic growth to establish an appropriate baseline by which to measure hazard impacts.

Input–output models have dominated the regional impact analysis literature. Adam Rose, Juan Benavides, Stephanie Chang, Philip Szczesniak and Dongsoon Lim, in their 1997 paper 'The Regional Economic Impact of an Earthquake: Direct and Indirect Effects of Electricity Lifeline Disruptions', show how such models can incorporate engineering simulations and survey data to better represent hazard conditions. They also demonstrate how considerations of individual behavior and regional resilience can avoid the overestimation of economic losses by assuming decision-makers address disasters differently from how they deal with every-day situations. By formulating their model as a linear program that also includes spatial features, the authors show how regional losses might be significantly reduced if scarce utility resources are rationed in the aftermath of an earthquake through the market or by administrative decree to their highest value use.

The paper by Sungbin Cho, Peter Gordon, James Moore, Harry Richardson, Masanobu Shinozuka and Stephanie Chang (2001), 'Integrating Transportation Network in Regional Economic Models to Estimate the Cost of a Large Urban Earthquake', shows how infrastructure performance, transportation network and multi-regional input–output (I-O) models can be combined to more accurately measure hazard impacts. The authors find that the significant amount of highway/road system redundancy is likely to cushion the economic impacts of a Southern California earthquake.

The state of the art in economic impact analysis today is computable general equilibrium (CGE) analysis. In 'A General Equilibrium Analysis of Partial-Equilibrium Welfare Measures: The Case of Climate Change', Mary Kokoski and V. Kerry Smith (1987) examine the applicability of the CGE model to climate change as manifested primarily through economic impacts on agriculture. At present, CGE models are still best suited to problems with longer duration because of the assumptions of full adjustment to equilibrium. However, this paper serves as a solid foundation upon which future research can build.[3]

Part V: Role of Forecasting in Reducing Disaster Impacts

This part of Volume I focuses on the role of forecasting and modification in reducing future weather-related events. The first two papers examine the accuracy of forecasts for undertaking protective decisions, given the tradeoffs between incurring fixed costs to reduce future losses and the potential benefits from this action. The other two papers analyze the decision on whether or not to modify weather by seeding clouds with silver iodine to reduce losses from potential disasters.

In 'A Case Study in the Economics of Information and Coordination: The Weather Forecasting System', Richard Nelson and Sidney Winter (1964) determine the value of information and the optimal form that a weather forecaster should present estimates to determine whether or not to incur the cost of protective measures. They focus on the daily decision taken by the dispatcher of a fleet of trucks on whether to cover the merchandise with a tarpaulin to prevent damage from rain; however, their model has applicability to a wide variety of natural hazards.

Charles Howe and Harold Cochrane (1976), in 'A Decision Model for Adjusting to Natural Hazard Events with Application to Urban Snow Storms', extend the Nelson and Winter model by examining decisions that urban managers should take in response to forecasts of the snow hazard. They show that forecasts will reduce the costs of incurring long-term investments in fixed snow-removal capability by substituting supplemental equipment and crews to deal with a future snowstorm. While they demonstrate there is a range of decisions that cause only small differences in the expected total cost of snow fighting, they also show the large potential benefits from improved accuracy of snow forecasts.

Ronald Howard, James Matheson and Warner North (1972), in 'The Decision to Seed Hurricanes', show how decision analysis can be used to determine whether one should seed a hurricane bearing down on a coastal area to reduce its wind speed. Although the scientific evidence suggests that seeding is far more likely to reduce than increase the hurricane's wind speed, the government is likely to be perceived as being responsible for any damage caused by the disaster. This is one of the principal reasons why hurricane seeding has not been implemented, despite its attractive features with respect to reducing economic losses.

Stanley Changnon, Barbara Farhar and Earl Swanson's (1978) 'Hail Suppression and Society' argues for greater financial support for research over a 20-year period to develop a more effective technology for hail suppression to reduce crop loss and property damage. The paper recommends that regulation of hail suppression activities be undertaken at the state level, but that federal standards for monitoring and evaluation should be developed and incorporated into state regulations.

Part VI: Reducing Risks through Self-Protection

This part of Volume I is comprised of three theoretical papers on incentives for consumers to invest in measures that reduce the likelihood of a disaster occurring and/or the losses resulting from a disaster. Consumers are assumed to maximize their expected utility and have to make tradeoffs between the costs of the protective measure and the expected benefits they will receive from the investment should a disaster occur. The papers raise a set of interesting questions as to when individuals will want to invest in protection and suggest empirical analyses that need to be undertaken for understanding more fully what policies are appropriate for improving social welfare.

Isaac Ehrlich and Gary Becker (1972), in 'Market Insurance, Self-Insurance and Self-Protection', show that market insurance encourages individuals to invest in cost-effective protective measures that reduce the probability of loss if the premiums are based on risk. However, undertaking self-insurance measures that reduce the size of a future loss may lead to moral hazard problems. For example, individuals who invest in seat-belts or fire sprinkler systems will behave more carelessly because they now feel safer.

Tracy Lewis and David Nickerson (1989) examine the extent to which disaster assistance programs discourage investment in protection by individuals. In 'Self-Insurance against Natural Disasters', they propose several public policies, such as well-enforced regulations (e.g. building codes and restrictions on where to build), taxes or subsidies, to encourage investment in protection and the dissemination of more precise information about the risks to those in hazard-prone areas.

In 'Risk, Self-Protection and Ex Ante Economic Value', Jason Shogren and Thomas Crocker (1991) define self-protection as an investment that can influence both the probability and the severity of the potential loss. An example of this type of measure would be raising one's house on stilts to reduce both the likelihood of the structure being affected by a flood and the damage to the property and contents if the water rose to a high enough level such that it entered the house. They show that individuals with similar wealth levels who are exposed to greater risk do not necessarily want to increase their investment in self-protection.

Part VII: Structural Mitigation Measures

Structural measures are the traditional approach to hazard mitigation. Linda Cohen and Roger Noll (1981), in 'The Economics of Building Codes to Resist Seismic Shock', first explain the rationale for government involvement in setting standards for mitigation – the fact that the building owner is unlikely to consider the full social costs of the collapse of the structure and that recourse by injured parties through liability rules is also unlikely to be effective. The authors show how the framework utilized for minimizing the costs of long-lived capital investments can be used to devise an optimal building code. Based on this model, they indicate the type of information required to estimate the frequency of earthquakes of different magnitudes and the resulting damage from different codes in place.

In 'Alternatives for Managing Drought: A Comparative Cost Analysis', Anthony Fisher, David Fullerton, Nile Hatch and Peter Reinelt (1995) utilize a simulation model of the East Bay Municipal Utility District (EBMUD) water system of San Francisco Bay to determine how a large urban water district should best respond to a drought. They find that a combination of conjunctive use and water market pricing is far superior to the standard structural approach of increasing storage capacity. The results are, in large part, due to the permanence of the investment in constructing storage capacity versus the intermittent application of the non-structural alternatives as the need arises.

There has been considerable resistance to the use of cost–benefit analysis (CBA) and risk–benefit analysis in hazard mitigation policy. The last two papers in Volume I show how these approaches can be applied to dam safety problems. M. Elisabeth Paté-Cornell and George Tagaras (1986), in 'Risk Costs for New Dams: Economic Analysis and Effects of Monitoring', develop a joint probability model to analyze the interdependence of dam failures in the context of risk–benefit analysis. They apply their methodology to three case studies and show that a previous decision to accept a project may be reversed when one considers the value of human safety and cascading failures from upstream dams to downstream dams.

In 'Risk Analysis and Management of Dam Safety', Lester Lave and Tunde Valvanyos (1998) contend that CBA can be used effectively as a risk management tool because hydrologists have the data and methodology to accurately estimate the peak-flow distribution of floods. They then show that, with limited available resources, society would be better served by using more of the available funds to design or retrofit dams to reduce losses from small- or medium-sized floods than extremely rare large floods.

Volume II, Part I: Role of Disaster Insurance

Disaster insurance can be viewed as a policy tool that complements structural mitigation measures, in the sense that those who purchase coverage pay lower premiums if they and/or their community invests in protection that reduces the frequency and/or magnitude of losses from future disasters. The principal function of insurance, however, is to transfer a financial risk from one party, such as a business firm (the insured), to a specialized insurance company.

In this first part of Volume II, Kenneth Arrow's (1971) 'Insurance, Risk and Resource Allocation', examines the limitations of insurance in shifting risk. He shows that insurance permits individuals to engage in risky activities they would otherwise not pursue. However, complete insurance markets may not exist because of moral hazard problems, whereby the purchase of insurance would lead one to be more careless and hence increase the likelihood and/or magnitude of a loss.

In 'An Economic Approach to Coping with Flood Damage', John Krutilla (1966) argues for a compulsory flood insurance program, so that those residing in hazard-prone areas are charged premiums that reflect not only the risks of their losses, but also the negative externalities they create in the form of additional damage to others from encroaching on the floodway. Such an insurance program can be the basis for evaluating the merits of alternative flood-control measures. One can compare the discounted reduction in insurance premiums to the affected residents over the life of the project with the costs of the project. The measure that yields the highest net discounted benefits should be selected.

Dan Anderson (1976), in 'All Risks Rating within a Catastrophe Insurance System', extends the concepts developed by Krutilla for flood insurance by advocating that all natural hazard risks be included as part of a mandatory homeowners' policy. Under such a program, the insurer can spread its potential loss more broadly while, at the same time, reducing the variability across regions and over time from what it would be if policies were written on a specified peril basis. The private sector would market this insurance but there would be a need for federal subsidies on existing properties in high-hazard areas and for federal reinsurance to cover catastrophic losses that would not be covered by private reinsurers.

The above papers on protection and insurance assume that individuals and insurers are making decisions as if they were maximizing discounted expected utility based on accurate information on the relevant costs and benefits. As Howard Kunreuther (1996) shows in 'Mitigating Disaster Losses through Insurance', residents in hazard-prone areas have limited information on the risk and use highly simplified choice rules. They do not purchase coverage prior to a disaster, but may choose to do so after experiencing a large loss. If they do not make a claim over the next few years, they will cancel their policy, perceiving it to be a bad investment. Insurers offer coverage at premiums that greatly exceed actuarially based rates because of the uncertainty of the risk and the fear of catastrophic losses. Kunreuther proposes a comprehensive disaster insurance program, similar to the one advocated by Anderson, with risk-based rates used to encourage the adoption of hazard mitigation measures.

Part II: Financial Coverage against Catastrophic Losses

This part of Volume II contains a set of articles that examines why insurers and reinsurers have not been able to provide coverage against mega-disasters, thus leading to the emergence of new financial instruments to supplement traditional coverage. Dwight Jaffee and Thomas Russell (1997), in 'Catastrophe Insurance, Capital Markets and Uninsurable Risks', argue that a principal reason that insurers are reluctant to provide coverage against catastrophic risks is that they are required to hold large amounts of liquid capital. They then discuss the role of the capital markets in providing protection against these risks through catastrophe bonds, catastrophe futures and options. They conclude that there is still a need for state and federal involvement in providing protection against very large losses from natural disasters even though these new instruments are available.

David Cummins, Neil Doherty and Anita Lo (2002) address the question as to whether the insurance industry has the financial ability to pay for a mega-catastrophe that could be as high as $100 billion in their paper 'Can Insurers Pay for the "Big One"? Measuring the Capacity of the Insurance Market to Respond to Catastrophic Losses'. They point out that, although it appears that the industry has sufficient capacity to cover disasters of this magnitude, the current configuration by firms in the industry disrupts the market by causing numerous insolvencies.

One way for insurers to obtain more capacity is by purchasing reinsurance. In 'The Market for Catastrophe Risk: A Clinical Examination', Kenneth Froot (2001) provides eight theoretical explanations as to why few insurers turn to reinsurance for protection against catastrophe losses. Based on empirical data, he concludes that reinsurers face financing imperfections and have market power that leads them to charge prices for covering catastrophe coverage that are often considerably higher than the actuarially based values.

If the private insurance and reinsurance market cannot provide protection against catastrophic losses, there may be a need for federal government involvement. In 'The Role of Government Contracts in Discretionary Reinsurance Markets for Natural Disasters', Christopher Lewis and Kevin Murdock (1996) propose that the federal government write and sell excess-of-loss (XOL) contracts to insurance companies, pools and reinsurers to cover industry losses from a disaster in the $25 to $50 billion range. The XOL contracts would complement the new financial instruments and are designed such that the private sector can 'crowd out' the federal government, should it be able to provide protection at this high level of losses.

Some type of index that characterizes the magnitude of a disaster is often utilized in determining when a catastrophe bond will cover losses from hurricanes and earthquakes. Jerry Skees (2000) extends these ideas to the challenges that developing countries face in having sufficient food supplies under drought conditions in his paper 'A Role for Capital Markets in Natural Disasters: A Piece of the Food Security Puzzle'. He proposes that a rainfall contract be designed for making payments to farmers in a specific location if there is a rainfall shortage. The amount of the payment could be a function of the rainfall shortage measured by a credible rainfall index. Skees discusses the advantage of such a financial arrangement over traditional crop insurance programs, while at the same time raising several challenges that must be addressed before rainfall contracts can be introduced.

Part III: Developing Private–Public Partnerships for Managing Disasters

Economists and other social scientists generally agree that on both efficiency and equity grounds one needs to rely on both the private and public sectors in managing the risks from natural disasters. The papers in this part examine alternative private–public partnerships for dealing with catastrophic losses.

In 'The Economics of Catastrophes', Richard Zeckhauser (1996) points out that catastrophes are produced jointly by nature (e.g. an earthquake occurs) and by humans (e.g. structures are built in earthquake-prone areas). Catastrophes are also consumed both before an event occurs in the form of worry and stress, as well as after a disaster through the sharing of losses including empathy for victims. Recognizing that individuals misperceive and misprocess information, and that disasters create negative externalities, Zeckhauser argues for the use of market-based policies, such as insurance and liability, in combination with government regulations for preventing and ameliorating catastrophes.

Peter May (1991), in 'Addressing Public Risks: Federal Earthquake Policy Design', argues for public–private partnerships by emphasizing the difficulty of stimulating protective actions by a public who is unconcerned with the potential consequences of natural disasters. He also notes that the federal government has little influence over state and local policies, so that there is limited implementation of building codes and land-use policies for reducing future disaster losses. He proposes a program whereby communities in moderate- and high-risk areas develop earthquake-risk reduction programs, such as well-enforced building codes and land-use regulations, in return for the federal government making earthquake insurance available to homeowners within participating communities.

The United Nations declared the 1990s as the International Decade for Natural Disaster Reduction (IDNDR) and formed national committees to coordinate federal agency programs and link the public and private sectors. In 'Mitigation Emerges as Major Strategy for Reducing Losses Caused by Natural Disasters', members of the National Research Council Board on Natural Disasters (1999) emphasize the importance of coordinating investment in loss prevention and land-use planning with private-sector programs using insurance premium reductions and economic incentives such as long-term loans for mitigation. The paper argues for those developing nations that are highly vulnerable to natural hazards to implement this type of approach.

In 'The Complementary Roles of Mitigation and Insurance in Managing Catastrophic Risks', Paul Kleindorfer and Howard Kunreuther (1999) provide an empirical analysis of the economic impact of well-enforced building codes coupled with risk-based insurance policies on homeowners and insurers. They construct two model cities, Oakland, CA (earthquake-prone), and Miami/Dade County, Florida (hurricane prone), to evaluate expected and worst-case losses. One of their proposals is that insurance premium reductions be linked with long-term loans as a way of encouraging property-owners to adopt loss prevention measures.

Part IV: Recovery and Reconstruction

Media attention and post-disaster assistance usually focus on the immediate aftermath of a disaster, but very little attention has been paid to whether there are significant long-term economic impacts of disasters. Peter Rossi, James Wright, Sonia Wright and Eleanor Weber-Burdin (1978), in 'Are There Long Term Effects of American Natural Disasters?', examine this issue. By undertaking a statistical analysis of census tract and county data of areas affected by disasters, they show that for the United States there were no discernible impacts on population and housing growth trends during the 1960s. It is important to note, however, that there were major exceptions – e.g. towns near the epicenter of the 1964 Alaska earthquake. The authors were not able to control for the influence of external financial assistance, which several researchers (see e.g. Cochrane, 1997) have suggested is a dominant factor in reducing negative long-term impacts and, in some cases, even produces an artificial economic boom.

In 'Disasters and Charity: Some Aspects of Cooperative Economic Behavior', Christopher Douty (1972) provides a rationale for explaining post-disaster behavior that differed from standard economic theory at the time of the paper's publication. When Douty wrote this paper, economists felt altruistic behavior contradicted the theory of consumer choice and the theory of the firm based on expected utility and profit maximization. Earlier attempts at reconciliation focused on interdependent utility functions and long-term profits. In contrast, Douty emphasizes the importance of the family and the community in impacting individuals' choices. He contends that the occurrence of a disaster forces reassessment of these roles and leads to altruistic behavior not typically witnessed under ordinary circumstances.

In 'Economic Lessons of the Kobe Earthquake', George Horwich (2000) examines the successes and failures of the recovery from the most severe earthquake ever to hit a modern industrial area. Horwich notes that the major factors accounting for the relatively fast recovery in Kobe were the relatively few fatalities and the ability to mobilize the city's intact human capital and price-directed market responses. The major problems in the recovery were attributed to the mismatch in the needs and supplies of outside aid, lack of preparation by regulated utilities and misguided government policy prior to the earthquake – e.g. over-regulation of lifelines and insurance, stifling of private-sector initiatives in mitigation, and fostering unsustainable land-use patterns. Horwich's conclusion that 'privatization and competition, wherever feasible . . . should be central to disaster policy', will not be immediately accepted by all policy-makers, but will at least stimulate a healthy debate that can lead to future policy improvement.

Part V: Integrated Assessment of Hazards

Extreme natural phenomena and their impacts, and how society addresses them, require inputs from the physical sciences, engineering and the social sciences. Economists have typically shied away from interdisciplinary research, so it is not surprising that geographers and engineers who have an interest in economic impacts have made the major contributions to integrated analysis. Robert Kates's (1971) 'Natural Hazard in Human Ecological Perspective: Hypotheses and Models' presents a framework for analyzing adjustments to hazards that incorporates many different disciplines. The human ecological perspective stresses the importance of distinguishing between types of hazards, understanding decision processes and social vulnerability, and making cultural distinctions ranging from risk perceptions to the influence of the stage of economic development (e.g. effectiveness of institutions, availability of capital).

The past decade has seen a boom in integrated modeling most visibly with respect to climate change. Most of these models have a strong resemblance to Kates's framework although they were developed independently. The paper by Hadi Dowlatabadi and Granger Morgan (1993), 'A Model Framework for Integrated Studies of the Climate Problem', is one of the first operational frameworks for the integrated assessment of climate change and is applicable to natural hazards as well.[4] Their model explicitly incorporates uncertainty and informed judgment in a decision-analysis setting, as well as evaluating macroeconomic feedback effects on the earth's climate.

The paper by Robert Whitman, Thalia Anagnos, Charles Kircher, Henry Lagorio, Scott Lawson and Philip Schneider (1997), 'Development of a National Earthquake Loss Estimation

Methodology', provides an overview of HAZUS, originally funded by FEMA through the National Institute of Building Standards. HAZUS combines major principles of engineering and economic loss estimation laid out in a National Research Council (1989) study with a voluminous data set. It is an expert system capable of being used by emergency management practitioners to provide ballpark estimates for recovery in almost real time, as well as accurate estimates for mitigation planning.[5]

Part VI: Sustainability and Disaster-Resistant Communities

The first major assessment of social science research on natural hazards was published in 1975, with Gilbert White and Eugene Haas as lead authors. The book *Disasters by Design* by Dennis Mileti (1999) summarizes the findings from the second major assessment; the key points are found in his 'Summary', reprinted in this collection of papers. Mileti's unifying theme is that hazard mitigation needs to be placed in the broader context of sustainable communities, the ability of an affected geographic area to rebound from hazard losses without significant outside infusion of resources. He contends that we are not making progress in dealing with hazards if communities continue to be bailed out by the federal government following a major disaster. Choices made today impact future generations, thereby underscoring the need to at least maintain the quality of the environment so as not to undercut future economic vitality.

Philip Berke, Jack Kartez and Dennis Wenger (1993), in 'Recovery after Disaster: Achieving Sustainable Development, Mitigation and Equity', examine conditions for sustainability during the period following a disaster. They emphasize that many decisions and actions during that time can not only help the community rebound rapidly from its current state, but also its ability to respond to future disasters. The authors stress the important role of public participation to provide opportunity to improve equity in the recovery process. Three case studies illustrate how the relation between the community's various social units (horizontal integration) and the ties with political, social and economic units outside the community (vertical integration) influence the recovery process.

'Unleashing the Power of Planning to Create Disaster-Resistant Communities', written by a team of planners led by Raymond Burby (1999), identifies the importance of local planning with regard to land use. It emphasizes how the effectiveness of land-use planning could be enhanced by reorienting the federal framework within which it must operate. The authors argue for reducing subsidies that promote risky behavior and increasing support to local government through funding of activities relating to hazard mitigation.

Part VII: Economics of Disasters in Developing Countries

It is well known that vulnerability to disasters rises with economic development. This is due to the increased value of the capital stock, as well as increased self-sufficiency and sectoral interdependence, both of which increase the size of negative multiplier effects on output and employment.

Barclay Jones and William Kandel's (1992) 'Population Growth, Urbanization, and Disaster Risk and Vulnerability in Metropolitan Areas: A Conceptual Framework' traces the exploding trend of urbanization, and its associated concentration of population and assets as yet another dimension of this vulnerability. They point out that features of economic locational attractiveness are correlated with hazardness (e.g. harbor areas). They also express the concern that pressures for development in these locales will lead to sacrifices in hazard safety for expedience. This increases the likelihood of catastrophic losses in developing countries.

In 'Natural Disaster Situations and Growth: A Macroeconomic Model for Sudden Disaster Impacts', J.M. Albala-Bertrand (1993) constructs a macroeconomic model to analyze the effect of sudden, large local natural disasters on national economic growth and development. The application of the model to a sample of Latin American countries indicates that such disasters do not, in fact, have major macroeconomic consequences. One important implication is that relief efforts might better be targeted to those regions and groups incurring losses rather than for more general growth maintenance activities such as deficit reduction and foreign exchange growth.

Developing countries are least capable of coping with disasters with their own resources and thus typically require outside aid. Since 12 per cent of all overseas development assistance is now devoted to this purpose, there is pressure to find other ways to deal with the problem. Paul Freeman (2001), in 'Hedging Natural Catastrophe Risk in Developing Countries', analyzes strategies other than self-insurance, market insurance and relief to deal with the problem – namely, financial instruments (e.g. derivatives) as a hedge against risk. He examines their application to government-owned assets and government's role in facilitating risk transfer among its citizenry, and also government as a protector of the poor. Freeman concludes that hedging can be successful in the former two cases but is unlikely to be so for protecting the poor due to extreme adverse selection and moral hazard problems.

IV. Conclusion

Although we were able to include 52 papers in the two volumes, space constraints prevented us from including other worthy papers. Recent articles by a new generation of scholars, whose contributions to future research and policy cannot be fully ascertained at this early stage, will be appropriate for a future volume in this area. We must also admit to a cultural bias by including papers written primarily by authors from the United States. A growing number of researchers in Europe and other parts of the world are now focusing on natural hazards (see e.g. Van der Veen *et al.*, 2003), so that an international community of researchers is emerging. In the same spirit of globalization, there is increasing attention being paid to natural hazard management in developing countries as evidenced by the formation of the ProVention Consortium at the World Bank several years ago and recent activities at other international organizations.

Finally, we note that natural hazards research is and will continue to be an interdisciplinary field. Although the title of the volume focuses attention on economics, we have included a number of papers by engineers and social scientists from other disciplines. Several of the papers deal with fundamental aspects of risk analysis that are cited or included in compendiums of classics in related fields. Recent events have illustrated the robustness of both theoretical and applied work in this volume to the topics of terrorism and security in the wake of the September 11th attacks. The papers included here provide considerable insight into how to deal with these problems that are now taking center stage in the world.

Notes

Portions of this introduction are based on material that appeared in Kunreuther (2002).

1. Several other economists have written on the subject of war, including Thomas Schelling and Mancur Olson.
2. This concept is being broadened to evaluate several aspects of both the built environment and socio-economic systems by Bruneau *et al.* (2003). See also its application to regional economies by Rose and Liao (forthcoming).
3. Research on adapting CGE models to shorter impact periods is being undertaken by Rose and Liao (forthcoming), who have developed a methodology for recalibrating major parameters (substitution elasticities and productivity terms) in light of simulation and survey data on individual business resiliency to input supply shortages caused by hazards.
4. There is an obvious overlap between the focus on climate change and mainstream hazards research, both in terms of long-term secular warming and short-term climate variability. For example, a scrambling of climatic conditions is seen to both increase and decrease rainfall in different parts of the world, thereby altering drought and flood severity and frequency.
5. Several other contributors to this volume were involved in the development and testing of HAZUS, including David Brookshire, Stephanie Chang, Hal Cochrane and Adam Rose. Also, economists and other social scientists were instrumental in developing an important precursor of HAZUS (see Hirschberg *et al.*, 1978).

References

Bruneau, M., S. Chang, R. Eguchi, T. O'Rourke, M. Sinozuka, K. Tierney and D. van Winterfeldt (forthcoming), 'A Framework to Quantitatively Assess and Enhance Seismic Resilience of Communities', *Earthquake Spectra*, **19** (4), 733–52.
Burton, I. and R. Kates (1964), 'The Perception of Natural Hazards in Resource Management', *Natural Resources Journal*, **3**, 412–41.
Cochrane, H. (1975), *Natural Hazards and their Distributive Effects: A Research Assessment*. Boulder, CO: Institute for Behavioral Sciences.
Cochrane, H. (1997), 'Forecasting the Economic Impact of a Mid-West Earthquake', in B. Jones (ed.), *Economic Consequences of Earthquakes: Preparing for the Unexpected*. Buffalo, NY: National Center for Earthquake Engineering Research, pp. 233–47.
Costanza, R. (1992), 'Three General Policies to Achieve Sustainability', in A. Jansson *et al.* (eds), *Investing in Natural Capital: The Ecological Economics Approach to Sustainability*. Washington, DC: Island Press.
Dacy, D. and H. Kunreuther (1969), *The Economics of Natural Disasters*. New York: The Free Press.
Emerson, B. and T. Stevens (1995), 'Natural Disasters: A Budget Time Bomb', *Washington Post*, 31 October, A13.
Hirschberg, J., P. Gordon and W. Petak (1978), *Natural Hazards, Socio-Economic Impact Assessment Model*. Redondo Beach, CA: J.H. Wiggins Co.
Huber, O., R. Wider and O. Huber (1997), 'Active Information Search and Complete Information Presentation in Naturalistic Risky Decision Tasks', *Acta Psychologica*, **95**, 15–29.
Kahneman, D., P. Slovic and A. Tversky (eds) (1982), *Judgment under Uncertainty: Heuristics and Biases*. New York: Cambridge University Press.
Kates, R. (1971), 'Natural Hazard and Human Ecological Perspective: A Hypotheses Modeled', *Economic Geography*, **47**, 438–51.
Kleindorfer, P. and H. Kunreuther (1999), 'The Complementary Roles of Mitigation and Insurance in Managing Catastrophic Risks', *Risk Analysis*, **19**, 727–38.
Kunreuther, H. (2002), 'Risk Analysis and Risk Management in an Uncertain World', *Risk Analysis*, **22**, 655–64.

Mileti, D. (1999), *Disaster by Design*. Washington, DC: Joseph Henry Press.

Munich Re (2002), *Topics: Natural Catastrophes 2002*. Munich: Munich Re.

National Research Council (1989), *Estimating Losses from Future Earthquakes*. Washington, DC: National Academy of Sciences.

Rose, A. and S.-Y. Liao (forthcoming), 'Modeling Regional Economic Resiliency to Disasters: A Computable General Equilibrium Analysis of Water Service Disruption', *Journal of Regional Science*, forthcoming.

Solow, R. (1992), *An Almost Practical Step Toward Sustainability*. Washington, DC: Resources for the Future.

Swiss Re (2004), *Insurance-Linked Security Quarterly*, New York: Swiss Re Capital Markets Corporation, January.

Tierney, K. (1997), 'Impacts of Recent Disaster on Businesses: The 1993 Midwest Floods and the 1994 Northridge Earthquake', in B. Jones (ed.), *Economic Consequences of Earthquakes: Preparing for the Unexpected*. Buffalo, NY: National Center for Earthquake Engineering Research, pp. 189–222.

Van der Veen, A., A. Arellano and J.-P. Nordvik (eds) (2003), *Proceedings of the Joint NEDIES and University of Twente Workshop: In Search of a Common Methodology for Damage Estimation*. Brussels: Office for Official Publications of the European Communities.

White, G. (1945), *Human Adjustment to Floods*. Research Paper No. 29. Chicago, IL: University of Chicago, Department of Geography.

Part I
Foundations

[1]

DISASTER AND RECOVERY:
THE BLACK DEATH IN WESTERN EUROPE

Jack Hirshleifer

-1-

I. INTRODUCTION

A previous RAND study examined a number of great disasters of
modern times[*][1] in order to explore such questions as: (1) How rapid
and successful were the recoveries from disaster? (2) Which government policies promoted, and which hindered, recovery? (3) To what
extent was the loss due to disaster (or the failure to recover from
disaster) an unavoidable consequence of the narrowed technological
possibilities and resources of the post-disaster society, and to what
extent was it the consequence of organizational failures and mistakes
in the utilization of surviving resources? The major conclusion
arrived at was that, in the instances examined, rather prompt recovery
(say, within four or five years) to pre-disaster levels of well-being
was technologically possible and did, in fact, take place -- with
some "slippage" due mostly to avoidable mistakes in monetary policies.

This, like other related RAND studies,[2] was intended to cast
some light on the aftermath of the great potential disaster of our
age -- thermonuclear war. No disaster of modern times, however,
really compares to a large-scale nuclear war, in geographic scope,
suddenness of impact, and intensity of effect. There are, of course,
a number of historical instances of violent destruction of particular
cities (for example, Hiroshima in World War II). There are also some
examples of substantial population declines over wider areas (for
example, Ireland after the potato famine), but these latter instances
have been more in the nature of slow decay than sudden destruction.
The Black Death of 1348-50 was much closer to a hypothetical nuclear

---

[*]In the body and footnotes to this Memorandum, citations will be
given in abbreviated form. Full descriptions of sources may be found
in the Bibliography attached.

[1]Hirshleifer, RM-3079-PR. Among the large-scale disaster-recovery
experiences investigated were the Southern Confederacy during and after
the American Civil War, Russia under war communism (1918-21), and
Germany and Japan during and after World War II.

[2]Winter, RM-3436-PR; Clark and Bear, P-2093; Clark, RM-1809;
Hirshleifer, P-674.

-2-

war in its geographical extent, abruptness of onset, and scale of casualties. Of course, in other important respects its impact was unlike that of nuclear war; in particular, there was no physical destruction of material property. (Thus, the Black Death is a closer analog to bacteriological than to nuclear war.) And, in addition, the 14th century is so distant in time from the current period as to preclude the drawing of easy parallels. Nevertheless, we may hope that the study of even such a remote historical experience will help provide some depth of understanding as to the human potentialities for recovery from great catastrophes. A point heightening interest in this historical episode is that it has been cited, by at least one author, in the course of a pessimistic evaluation of the prospect for recovery from the potential disaster of atomic war.[1]

Another difficulty in the evaluation of social consequences specific to the Black Death is the fact that the period in which it fell was one of great turbulence in Western Europe. The effects of the pestilence are not easily separable from those of the destructive Hundred Years' War; in addition, the Western European nations and especially England and France suffered also from internal dynastic conflicts, class warfare, and regional separatism. Table 1 provides a chronology of the major events of the period surrounding the Black Death.

Finally, the reader must be warned that any attempt to evaluate the overall lessons to be drawn from complex phenomena such as disaster-recovery experiences must, necessarily, be in large part subjective and impressionistic. In the case at hand the force of this caveat is strengthened by the paucity and defects of the data available, together with all the other problems of comprehending individual and social behavior in a social and historical context very different from our own.

---

[1]Stonier, Nuclear Disaster, Ch. 13 (especially pp. 159-61, 166-67).

-3-

Table 1

CHRONOLOGY[a]

1310-22	Wars of Edward II, King of England, with barons, Scots, Irish.
1324	Fighting with French in Aquitaine.
1327	Revolt in England. Abdication and murder of Edward II, King of England; accession of Edward III.
1328-36	English intervene in Scottish dynastic conflict.
1328	Accession of Philip VI, King of France.
1328	French suppress lower-class insurrection in Flanders.
1336	Beginning of Hundred Years' War.
1337	English support revolt in Flanders.
1341	Fighting in Brittany begins between English and French candidates for dukedom.
1346	English victory over Scots at Neville's Cross, over French at Crecy.
1348-50	Black Death.
1350	Death of Philip VI, King of France; accession of John II.
1356	English victory at Poitiers; John II captured.
1357-59	Near-anarchy in France. Jacquerie suppressed. Dynastic intrigues of Charles the Bad, King of Navarre. Du Guesclin's tactics exhaust English.
1360	Truce of Bretigny.
1360-61	Recurrence of plague.
1364	Death of John II, King of France; accession of Charles V.
1367-69	Fighting in Spain ends in victory of French-backed contender, Don Henry.
1369	Recurrence of plague.
1369-75	Resumption of Hundred Years' War; French successes.
1374	Recurrence of plague.
1375	Truce of Bruges; English retain only Calais and small portion of Gascony.
1376	"Good Parliament" in England; independence of Commons.
1377	Death of Edward III, King of England; accession of Richard II.
1380	Death of Charles V, King of France; accession of Charles VI.
1381	Peasants' Revolt in England.
1382	French crush English-supported insurrection in Flanders.
1399	Revolt in England. Deposition of Richard II, accession of Henry IV.
1402-06	English defeat Scots.
1400-16	Revolt of Welsh suppressed.
1413	Cabochian riots in Paris.
1413	Death of Henry IV, King of England; accession of Henry V. Resumption of war with France.
1415	English victory at Agincourt.
1418	English occupy Paris.
1420	Burgundians ally themselves with English.
1422	Death of Henry V, King of England; accession of Henry VI. Death of Charles VI, King of France; accession of Charles VII.
1429	French victory at Orleans; Joan of Arc.
1429-53	French gradually reconquer national territory.
1450	Jack Cade's Rebellion.
1453	End of Hundred Years' War; English retain only Calais.

Note:

[a]Based mainly on Previte-Orton, *Cambridge History*, Ch. 29, 33.

-4-

II. THE BLACK DEATH

Throughout the historic period, plague has been endemic in
certain permanent centers of infection. Three great outbreaks of the
disease are recorded.[1] The first is the so-called plague of Justinian,
which raged over the known world in the latter half of the 6th century.
After this waned, human plague was for centuries almost unknown to
Western Europe until the great pandemic of 1348-50. (Some maintain
that there was a precursor plague around 1316.)[2] Thereafter, repeated
onslaughts recurred on a gradually diminishing scale; the last London
plague was in 1665, and in Western Europe the last great outburst was
at Marseilles in 1720. The third outbreak began around 1890 in China;
in the West its effects have been held in check by modern sanitary
knowledge.

Plague is primarily a disease of rodents, carried to man by the
flea. Some historians have blamed the plague of 1348-50 upon the
arrival of the rat in Europe, but others disagree.[3] The gradual
decline of the disease over the following centuries has been attributed
to the replacement of the black rat (Rattus rattus) by the brown rat
(Rattus norvegicus). The latter, a better fighter, has driven out
the former except on shipboard and in the vicinity of ports. From the
human point of view the brown rat is a less unpleasant neighbor, as he
prefers to live out-of-doors -- and even more important, his fleas
have more aversion to biting human beings than do those of the black
rat.[4]

Plague in human beings takes two main forms: bubonic and pneumonic
(a third form, the septicemic, is sometimes reported). Bubonic
plague is characterized by swellings (buboes), especially in the

---

[1]Saltmarsh, pp. 30-32.

[2]Slicher van Bath, p. 88.

[3]Langer, "The Black Death," p. 114.

[4]Saltmarsh, pp. 32-34.

-5-

groin and armpits. This is the less fatal form, with a typical
mortality rate of perhaps 50 per cent. It is not infectious from
man to man but requires the intervention of the flea. The pneumonic
form is seated in the lungs; it is extremely infectious and nearly
always fatal. In the bubonic form an outbreak of the disease dies
down in the winter, but in the pneumonic form it will rage more
violently than ever in the cold season. Pneumonic plague is less
common, but when it occurs the mortalities may be enormous; the
Black Death itself was a combined attack of both forms of plague.

There have been some fluctuations of opinion over the years
about the scale of mortality attendant upon the original plague of
1348-50, and the later visitations during the next quarter-century.
The reports of contemporary chroniclers abound with tales of total
or near-total depopulation, often still repeated in non-technical
writings. Generally speaking, however, historians today place a
more moderate estimate on the scale of casualties. Without necessarily dismissing all the early reports as fabulous, it is evident
that there is a tendency for occasional chronicles to record, even
if they do not exaggerate, the extreme and unusual as opposed to the
typical. Modern historians, in contrast, are in a position to base
opinions on spotty but nevertheless rather extensive surviving
manorial, legal, and church documents.[1] The impression one gains
from such records is that the Black Death proper carried off between
a quarter and a third of the population of Western Europe, while the
later attacks -- the Pestis Secunda of 1360-61 and the plagues of

---

[1]The reference here is to mortalities in England and France.
It cannot be definitely determined whether the plague produced
relatively greater casualties in other European countries. As an
example of the sort of disagreement that may arise, a modern art
historian concludes (on the basis of chroniclers' reports) that
"during the summer months of 1348 more than half the inhabitants of
Florence and Siena died of the bubonic plague" (Meiss, p. 65).
Such a conclusion about a particular city or cities is not beyond
the bounds of credibility, but is more likely exaggerated.

-6-

1369 and 1374[1] -- may each have swept away around 5 per cent of the
populations remaining.[2]

Russell's detailed study for England,[3] seemingly the only attempt
to weigh the demographic evidence scientifically, comes to a somewhat
different conclusion (see Table 2). Russell's data tend to discount
the scale of the original Black Death somewhat (in comparison with
the general opinion of scholars), and to magnify the later blows.
The demographic factors, not previously appreciated, explaining the
differences are: (1) making a proper allowance for age-distribution
of the initial populations and of the survivors, rather than simply
averaging the documented mortality rates; and (2) deducting normal
mortality. This latter is especially significant, since the Black
Death extended over a period of about 2-1/3 years. As Russell
estimates the normal annual mortality at 3 per cent, this factor
reduces the observed mortality rate of 23.6 per cent over the Black
Death period to around 16.6 per cent, which may be interpreted as
the proportionate "excess mortality" associated with the disaster.
Table 2 indicates that the 1369 visitation produced an excess mortality of 10.0 per cent in one year, a per annum rate greater than that
of 1348-50. Cumulatively, the later attacks outweighed the Black
Death itself (see also Fig. 1, reproduced from Russell's book).

With respect to overall population trends, Postan (one of the
leading students of this era) argues on the basis of price and
occupancy data that population decline began some thirty years
before the Black Death.[4] (The question of whether the plague
initiated the population decrease of the following century takes on
considerable importance in interpreting the evidence as to the
post-disaster recovery or lack of recovery.) Russell admits some

---

[1] Some sources date this recurrence in 1375.

[2] Saltmarsh, pp. 34-38; Bean, p. 424; Langer, "The Black Death,"
p. 114.

[3] Russell, British Medieval Population.

[4] Postan, "Some Economic Evidence," p. 245.

Table 2

MORTALITY AND POPULATION IN ENGLAND[a]

	Mortality Rate in Period (per cent)	Normal Mortality in Period (per cent)	Excess Mortality in Period (per cent)	Population Remaining	Population Index (1348 = 1)
1348				3,757,500	1.0
Plague periods					
1348-50	23.6	7	16.6	3,127,500	.836
1360-61	18.7	6	12.7	2,745,000	.730
1369	13.0	3	10.0	2,452,500	.657
1374	11.6	3	8.6	2,250,000	.600

Notes:

[a]Data are reproduced as shown in the cited source. There seem to be minor discrepancies in the calculations. Also, the technique of deducting the "normal" 3 per cent mortality is strictly correct only if the population would have been stationary under that mortality rate. (I am indebted to Russell T. Nichols for this point.)

Source:
    Russell, British Medieval Population, p. 263.

-8-

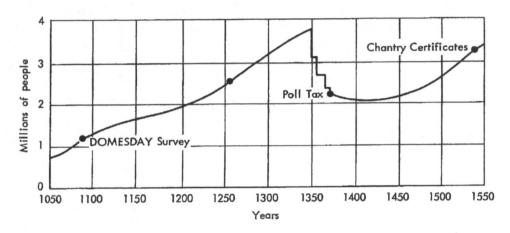

Fig.1—Trends of gross population in England

Source:
       Russell, <u>British Medieval Population</u>, p. 280.

-9-

retardation in the rate of growth before 1348, but nevertheless his
chart (Fig. 1) shows a rising population curve to that date.[1]

The discussion of the Black Death and its aftermath as a disaster-
recovery experience will be divided into two main headings. The first
will take up the real or alleged immediate and relatively early consequences, distinguishing between social and political effects on the
one hand and economic on the other. The time-span considered is up to
perhaps a decade in length; during this period the line of causation,
as to what are properly effects of the plague as such and what are
coincidental consequences of other acting forces, is fairly clear.
The next section will take up a much longer period, up to perhaps a
century, in which long-term effects of the Black Death have been
asserted to play a significant role. In dealing with this latter
topic, the key problem will be to isolate the effects of the initial
plague disaster from those of other events leaving their mark upon
the same period.

---

[1]Russell, pp. 259-60, 280.

-10-

III. AFTERMATH -- THE EARLY PERIOD

There are curious divergences in the contemporary reporting of
social and political events during and immediately after the Black
Death. Some writers describe extremes of socially disruptive behavior
(flagellant cults, massacres of Jews,[1] flight of upper classes), whereas
the reports of other chroniclers emphasize the continuity of established
forms and institutions.[2] That there was some flight from the cities
seems certain, and yet it is clear that government did not collapse.
(One reason, perhaps, is that the disease did not strike a whole nation
at once; in Britain it began in the southeast in the fall of 1348, waxed
greatly while spreading north and west during 1349, and by 1350 was
mostly limited to Scotland.) The following remarks on the enrollment of
wills in London's Husting Court are suggestive of the course of the disease.
They also signify the continuation of this bureaucratic function through
all but a few months:

> Those who died of the plague leaving wills were, of course,
> but a small fraction of the whole mortality; but the wills
> during some eight months of 1349 are ten or fifteen times
> more numerous than in any other year before or after, except-
> ing perhaps the year of pestis secunda, 1361. Starting from
> 3 in November, 1348 (none in December), the probates rise to
> 18 in January, 1349, 42 in February, 41 in March, none in
> April (owing to paralysis of business, doubtless), but 121
> in May, 31 in June, 51 in July, none in August and September,
> 18 in October, 27 in November, and then an ordinary average.[3]

----

[1] Massacres took place primarily in Germany. The Jews had previously been expelled from England and, for the most part, from France.

[2] Boccaccio's Decameron opens with a famous description suggesting
a breakdown of organized society in Florence. Froissart, in his
Chronicles, also comments on the flagellants and the persecution of
the Jews -- but his reports on government and church activities suggest that established institutions continued to function. Froissart
indicates that the Jews were despoiled at the instance of the lords,
and were protected in papal territories. As indicated in a footnote
earlier, it is possible that Florence suffered unusually high mortality.
On the other hand, mortality was certainly high in London (Creighton,
p. 128) where no breakdown occurred.

[3] Creighton, pp. 117-8.

-11-

A similar continuity of agricultural records is shown by Miss Levett,
who accordingly denies the earlier view that anarchy reigned in the
countryside.[1]

The English Parliament was prorogued on account of the plague
several times during 1349; it did not meet again until 1351. However,
a considerable number of ordinances and decrees on economic matters
were issued by the King's Council in 1349 and 1350. The Hundred Years'
War was in a period of truce, but in the last days of 1349 Edward III
led troops in combat before Calais. During 1350 a great feast was
held at Windsor to celebrate the institution of the Order of the
Garter. Also during this year, extensive military and naval preparations were organized, and a Spanish fleet was defeated in a great
engagement. Froissart reports great celebrations in France upon the
accession of John II (1350); the Order of the Star was instituted
about this time. The French parlement, which ordinarily convened only
when the King needed funds, did not meet until 1355. In that year, it
issued large grants for the conduct of the war. Also in 1355 began
the campaign of the Black Prince that ended in the great English
victory at Poitiers (1356). It is evident from this recital that
paralysis of government in England and France, if it occurred at all,
was limited to the period when the plague was actually raging.

Turning to the economic impact of the disaster, traditional doctrine tells us that the equilibrium rate of wages must have risen
consequent upon the new scarcity of labor. And a rapid rise in wages
certainly did occur. The following is illustrative (data refer to
England):

> Threshing will be taken as being the most significant type
> of labor....Up to the time of the Great Plague, threshing
> was paid at steady, and on the whole low, rates. But
> directly afterward the wages were doubled. The increase
> due to the plague is 32 per cent for the threshing of
> wheat, 38 per cent for barley, 111 per cent for oats in

---

[1]Levett, pp. 72, 142-43.

-12-

the eastern counties. In the middle counties the percentages of rise are 40, 69, 111; in the south, 33, 38, 75; in the west, 26, 41, 44; in the north, 32, 43, and 100.[1]

One of the most interesting developments was the Statute of Laborers in England (1351), a Parliamentary enactment that had been anticipated by an ordinance of the King's Council in 1349.[2] The Statute fixed wages at the pre-disaster level, forbade idleness, and required reasonable prices for necessities. It would appear that serious efforts were made for some years to enforce these regulations.[3] The French Statute of Laborers[4] had a similar origin, but seems to have been largely a dead letter. That per capita income of the lower classes (the vast majority, of course) tended to rise is evidenced by innumerable reports of individuals of lower status stepping up to fill vacant places, of remissions and recontracts of feudal dues, as well as by complaints against unwontedly lavish living by "wasters" and nouveaux riches.[5] Correspondingly, however, the scarcity of labor led to falling rents.[6] As a result, high-status individuals tended to suffer diminution of income.

In the aftermath, economic as well as political recovery from the crisis took place promptly. Agriculture was of course the overwhelmingly dominant industry; vacant manorial places were rapidly

---

[1]Robbins, p. 463. Note the seeming inconsistency between the generalization about the "doubling" of wages and the particular percentages shown; the generalization may refer only to "panic" rates in the immediate aftermath. See also Seebohm, p. 269; Creighton, p. 185; Mullett, p. 23; Robbins, p. 470.

[2]Ordinances in the same year forbade migration to Scotland, and taking money out of the kingdom. See Mullett, p. 23.

[3]Robbins, p. 476.

[4]Ibid., pp. 474-5.

[5]Creighton, p. 187; Robbins, p. 450. In England, a Statute of Dress of 1363 forbade the lower classes to imitate upper-class attire. (But even in 1336, it is reported, a law forbade many courses at meals.)

[6]Robbins, pp. 461-2.

-13-

filled by a general up-grading of holdings, with abandonment of some
marginal lands no longer worthy of cultivation by the thinned labor
force. Direct evidence on trade and industry is largely lacking,
but the ability of the English and French kings to call for and obtain
renewed support for military campaigns (see above) seems to deny the
possibility of any but short-lived paralysis in the non-agricultural
sectors. It appears that competition was lively between country and
town for scarce labor, newly "mobilized" by the widened opportunities
everywhere.[1]

---

[1]Creighton, p. 197; Robbins, pp. 468-73.

-14-

IV. AFTERMATH -- LONG-TERM

Several authors have asserted that the short-term recovery from
the Black Death, described above, was but temporary or illusory and
that a long-lasting depression set in shortly thereafter.[1] Others,
without necessarily tying the onset of the recession to the event of
the Black Death, have maintained that the century following 1350 was
generally depressed.[2] There are two great questions about this
"economic depression of the Renaissance": First, did it really occur?
And second, if so, was the Black Death its cause?

There has been a lively controversy among economic historians as
to whether the century following the Black Death was in actuality a
period of economic recession. In view of the reduced population, that
aggregate production was on the whole lower in 1350-1450 than in 1250-
1350 is obvious but hardly relevant; the question at issue is whether
there was a depression in the sense of impoverishment -- whether per
capita production fell. Historians writing on this topic have, regret-
tably often, been unable to keep these two questions apart and may thus
have debated at cross-purposes.[3] The following points, however, can
be regarded as established in comparing the century after 1350 with
the century before. (1) A great increase in real wages and the standard
of life of the laboring classes, both rural and urban, took place;[4]

---

[1] Saltmarsh, pp. 25-26; Langer, "The Black Death," p. 118.

[2] For example, Postan ("Some Economic Evidence," p. 245) and
Slicher van Bath (pp. 89, 132) suggest that the depression was a natural
reaction to excessive agricultural expansion in the previous centuries
(see below).

[3] For example, Lopez and Miskimin, among the leading proponents of
the "depression" hypothesis, show only that aggregate production fell
and state their inability to draw conclusions as to per capita income
(p. 410). Cipolla, an "anti-depression" scholar, does not deny the
fall in aggregate production but argues that per capita income rose
(pp. 523-24).

[4] Cipolla, pp. 523-24; Postan, "Some Economic Evidence," pp. 225-
29; Beveridge, pp. 164-65; Slicher van Bath, pp. 137-40. War-ravaged
France may have been an exception to the general European picture,
however (ibid., p. 139).

-15-

(2) A very considerable <u>decline</u> in rents, and therefore in the incomes of the propertied classes, also occurred.[1] In short, the long-term effects paralleled the short-term ones with respect to the relative position of the two great social classes.

The first of these points and, by implication, the second are illustrated by the English data in Table 3 showing wage indexes in nominal monetary units, in grains of silver, and in wheat. Postan remarks, in a footnote, that the figures probably understate true wages in the period during which the Statute of Laborers was effective (presumably, the first decade or two after 1350) -- as the Bishop tended to make a show of conformity while actually evading the law.

The fall in the price of wheat relative to wages, that provides quantitative support for the innumerable reports of declining land rents, is also displayed by the data in Table 4. Note that the wheat price indexes also reach a peak in the 1301-50 period, falling steadily thereafter until 1500.

Among the points that may be regarded as still in doubt are the <u>overall</u> behavior of per capita income when rising wages and falling rents are considered together. There is another interesting question, the relative prosperity of towns versus countryside, on which the historical authorities seem hopelessly divided. Langer argues that a depression in agriculture took place first, leading to a massive movement of rural population to the towns.[2] Postan denies that any net movement took place; also, he indicates that urban and rural wages rose in about the same proportion.[3] Creighton emphasizes disparities from one town to the next.[4] Robbins draws a contrast between an

---

[1] Postan, "Some Economic Evidence," p. 237, "The Fifteenth Century," pp. 161-62; Robbins, pp. 461-62.

[2] Langer, "The Black Death," p. 118.

[3] Postan, "Some Economic Evidence," pp. 231-34.

[4] Creighton, pp. 195-97.

-16-

Table 3

DAILY WAGES OF AGRICULTURAL LABOR ON THE
ESTATES OF BISHOPS OF WINCHESTER

Years	Index of Wages in Silver Pence	Index of Wages in Grains of Silver	Index of Wages in Wheat
1300-19	100	100	100
1320-39	124	125	140
1340-59	133	117	148
1360-79	169	142	154
1380-99	188	153	235
1400-19	189	143	210
1420-39	189	130	200
1440-59	189	125	236

Source:

Postan, "Some Economic Evidence," p. 226. The index in grains of silver has been calculated from other data in the source.

-17-

Table 4
WHEAT PRICES AND REAL WAGES

Years	Index of Wheat Prices, France (1721-45 = 100)	Index of Wheat Prices, England (1721-45 = 100)	Index of Real Wages, England[a] (1721-45 = 100)
1201-50	41.9	35.8	--
1251-1300	51.5	47.8	110.0
1301-50	75.9	53.1	115.7
1351-1400	65.4	43.9	145.7
1401-50	61.7	36.1	182.9
1451-1500	31.8	27.7	170.0
1501-50	57.8	30.0	182.9[b]

Notes:

[a]Threshing labor, piecework.

[b]This figure is perhaps a typographical error. Other sources agree that real wages were significantly lower for this period.

Source:

Slicher van Bath, pp. 326-27.

-18-

urbanization trend in England, and urban depopulation due to war and
brigandage in France.[1] Herlihy reports a greater decline of the rural
than the urban population of Pistoia in Italy.[2]

In the hundred years 1350-1450 on a priori grounds there would
have been considerable reason to anticipate a rather definite increase
in per capita income overall. First, the short-term aftermath of the
disaster in all probability led to a jump in real per capita wealth
-- recovery from the crisis was associated with a general upgrading
of holdings. Since population did not increase rapidly thereafter
(see Fig. 1), the continuing long-term trend of improvement in technology, plus the possibilities for reallocating resources in line with
the changed availabilities of land and labor, could operate without
encountering increased numbers of mouths to feed. Leaving aside the
question of whether an overall reduction in per capita income may have
taken place, it would appear that failure to achieve a marked increase
in this period may have been a significant development lending some
support to pessimistic views of the ability of societies to recover
from massive disasters.

A number of hypotheses have been put forward to explain what seems
to be a lagging pace of economic development in Western Europe during
the hundred years after 1350. Hypotheses involving forces other than
the Black Death will here be considered first, after which an attempt
will be made to place the role of the Black Death in its proper
perspective.

Apart from the plague, war is the most obvious factor damaging
the Western European economies during this period. England was heavily
burdened by wars with Scotland, Spain, and the Hanseatic League, and
rebellions in Ireland and Wales in addition to the conflict in France;
furthermore, the final outcomes were mainly adverse for her. But
France was even more severely affected by the repeated ravages of the

---

[1]Robbins, pp. 471-73.

[2]Herlihy, p. 231.

armies of England and her separatist allies, not to mention recurrent
class conflicts and periods of near-anarchy. The evidence that most
strongly suggests the impact of war is the comparative fate of
urbanization in England and France during this period. For England
the records of city growth in the century after 1350 are very uneven;
some towns, and especially Norwich (previously the second city in the
kingdom), declined sharply,[1] while others including Bristol and Coventry
definitely grew. London is reported as "no less populous."[2] By way
of contrast, the French territory involved in the Hundred Years' War
was largely depopulated, and Paris itself seemed almost deserted in the
15th century.[3] One author contrasts the war-caused destruction in
France with an asserted rapid growth of urbanization and industrializa-
tion in England.[4]

A second economic drag upon the recovering society has been
emphasized by several authors: The _continuing_ drain represented by
the onslaughts of plague following the Black Death itself.[5] The

---

[1]Creighton, pp. 193-4. But on Norwich compare Mullett, p. 26.

[2]Creighton, p. 195.

[3]Robbins, p. 454 n.

[4]Ibid., pp. 478-9. The plague in France is described as
"almost incidental," "an aggravation of an already desperate situation," whereas in England the disorder attendant upon the pandemic
provided an opportunity for the villein to desert the manor for the
growing towns.

[5]Saltmarsh, _passim_. In a critique of Saltmarsh's thesis, Bean
has argued that the fall in England's population probably terminated
by about 1400, around which date the rise in agricultural wages
stopped (see Table 3 above) and in urban wages slowed down (Bean,
pp. 435-36). This is an assertion about the date at which the
Malthusian forces -- tending to bring about an increase in births in
response to the high level of wages -- began to overcome the direct
and indirect effects of the plague.

-20-

great pandemics of 1361, 1369, and 1374 have already been mentioned;
and recurrences of considerable magnitude continued, on a gradually
declining scale, for centuries. The impact of this upon levels of
per capita well-being (limiting the discussion to the purely material
elements of loss) would be due primarily to the wholly or partially
wasted investments in child-rearing, and in education and training.[1]
It is true that the impact of early mortalities is less in an
agricultural society than it would be in an industrial community,
because of the lesser degree of training involved as well as the
earlier start of productive contributions on the part of the child.
Even so, the loss must have been very considerable. A further
point worth noting is that recurrences of plague disproportionately
attacked the young, presumably because older individuals tended to
possess some degree of natural or acquired immunity.

A third independent cause of decline has been suggested: that
there may have been an adverse climatic change in Western Europe
beginning in the 14th century.[2] There is indeed some evidence that
a cooler, wetter phase set in about this time in the North Atlantic
area. The climate of Greenland and Iceland definitely deteriorated.
As for England, cultivation of vineyards for wine was still at its
height in the 13th century, but had disappeared by 1400.[3] (As an
incidental point of interest, it is possible that the onset of
plague in the 14th century and its decline in later centuries were
ecologically connected with such changes in climatic conditions.)
It might be argued, however, that the same climatic change ought to
have been beneficial for countries like Italy and Spain, and there
is no clear evidence for this. Furthermore, some sources maintain

---

[1] A discussion of such losses in a different historical context
appears in Hansen, "The Cost of Children's Mortality."

[2] Utterstrom, "Climatic Fluctuations."

[3] Ibid., p. 10.

-21-

that climate in the prosperous 1150-1300 era was worse than the
climate in the following centuries.[1] But perhaps the chief argument
against the climate theory is that the period from 1300 on was
characterized by falling wheat prices (see Table 4), suggesting good
harvests rather than bad.[2]

Finally, there is still another view holding that a level of
over-population had been attained by 1300, not permanently maintainable with the available resources and technology:

> As long as the colonization movement went forward and new
> land was taken up, the crops from virgin lands encouraged
> men to establish new families and settlements. But, after
> a time the marginal character of marginal lands was bound
> to assert itself and the honeymoon of high yields was
> succeeded by long periods of reckoning, when the poorer
> lands, no longer new, punished the men who tilled them
> with failing crops and with murrain of sheep and cattle.
> In these conditions a fortuitous combination of adverse
> events, such as the succession of bad seasons in the
> second decade of the fourteenth century, was sufficient to
> reverse the entire trend of agricultural production and to
> send the population figures tumbling down.[3]

Thus, Postan and a number of other authors contend that population
decline and/or economic "depression" began well before the Black
Death.[4] At least in the Malthusian form put forward by Postan and
Slicher van Bath, however, the argument is vulnerable to the same
criticism these very authors levy against the climatic theory.
Over-population relative to the long-term capacity of the soil
should have led to a period of failing harvests and low real wages

---

[1] Slicher van Bath, p. 161.

[2] Ibid.

[3] Postan, "Rapport," p. 235.

[4] Postan, "Some Economic Evidence," pp. 245-46; Lopez and Miskimin,
p. 412; Slicher van Bath, p. 89. Florence suffered a profound
economic crisis beginning about 1340; the King of England, because
of reverses in the Hundred Years' War, defaulted upon enormous loans
contracted from the great Florentine banks (see Meiss, pp. 61-62,
Burckhardt, p. 50).

until the population fell to a maintainable level. But, from Tables
3 and 4, it is evident that the period 1350-1400, during which the
bulk of the decline in population took place (see Fig. 1), was a
period of relatively low wheat prices (good harvests) and high real
wages.

Integrating some portions of the different theories outlined
above, the following is put forward as a hypothesis consistent with
the main body of evidence as to economic phenomena in the period under
consideration. The initiating, autonomous cause of a break in economic
trends was the onset of plague -- a source of ecological pressure upon
the human population beginning with the Black Death of 1348-50 (or,
beginning some 30 years earlier, according to some authors). The
sudden population decline due to the arrival of the plague, with
material property left essentially unaffected, raised overall per
capita wealth in the short-term while drastically shifting relative
returns and incomes in favor of the laboring and against the property-
owning classes. In terms of price statistics, the short-term effects
included a rise in wages and fall in wheat prices.[1] Under normal
circumstances, Malthusian forces would then be expected to operate to
increase population once again -- if so, the longer term aftermath
would have been associated with rising population, falling real wages,
and a recovery in wheat prices. But in this special situation the
corrective forces were inhibited by the <u>continuing</u> plague now endemic,
and recurrently breaking out in great attacks. Not only did the plague
directly wipe out substantial fractions of what would have been a
recovering population, but it reduced incentives to bear children and
raise familes. Consequently, population continued to fall throughout
the 14th century, leading to further declines in wheat prices and

_____

[1]Wheat production is the resultant of property inputs (land,
primarily) and labor inputs. With labor suddenly more scarce, but
land as available as before, wheat production would tend to decline
but <u>in lesser proportion</u> than the decline in labor input. Hence,
there would be relatively good harvests in a per capita sense, and
low wheat prices.

-23-

increases in wages. Secondary effects included shifts to less labor-
intensive crops; tillage often gave way to pasture.[1] Furthermore,
it is plausible to argue that whereas agriculture benefited by being
able to abandon marginal lands, industry (being subject to increasing
returns with respect to population size) suffered a loss of relative
position.[2] Eventually, with the attenuation of the pressure of plague,
the Malthusian forces began to assert their dominance; thus, in the
latter part of the 15th century real wages decline once again.

The explanation offered above ascribes primary responsibility
for the lag in aggregate recovery to plague recurrences. The alternative explanation of war need not be entirely rejected, especially
in relation to stricken France. A high rate of real daily or hourly
wages could have been in effect whenever conditions were peaceful
enough to permit work -- but, with armies and marauders often about,
the opportunity to engage in productive work may have been severely
limited, quite apart from actual destruction. Thus, war tends to
engender high wage rates but lower labor income (and per capita
production). The third explanation mentioned, over-population
entailing a natural self-corrective reaction, does not appear to be
defensible.[3]

The explanations considered above were all in the nature of
alternatives to a hypothesis that specifically relates the long-term
depression to the shock engendered by the Black Death as a unique
event -- comparable in some ways to the possible shock of a nuclear
war.[4] Langer's analysis outlines the supposed mechanism in economic

---

[1]Slicher van Bath, p. 142.

[2]As indicated above, however, the data are inconclusive as to
the relative contraction of the rural and urban populations.

[3]Still other, less cogent, explanations of the recession or
lagging recovery have been offered, including an autonomous slowdown
in technological advance, and reduced supplies of gold and silver.

[4]Stonier's discussion (pp. 160, 165) suggests this hypothesis,
though it is not explicitly stated therein.

-24-

terms: The great contraction of population, by reducing aggregate
demand, led to a semi-permanent state of depression -- only relieved
when population growth began once more.

> For a short time the towns and cities experienced a flush
> of apparent prosperity. Many survivors of the epidemic
> had suddenly inherited substantial amounts of property and
> money....The rural areas, on the other hand, virtually
> collapsed. With fewer people to feed in the towns and
> cities, the farmers lost a large part of the market for
> their crops. Grain prices fell precipitately...the rural
> population fled to the cities en masse....And of course in
> the long run the depression of agriculture engulfed the
> cities in depression as well.[1]

Langer clearly has in mind depression in the sense of _impov-_
erishment -- decline in per capita income -- and he is evidently
referring to impoverishment of the mass of the population. But
although the course of _overall_ per capita income may be in doubt, it
is substantially certain, as we have seen, that per capita income for
the mass of the population _rose_ considerably (except possibly in war-
torn France).[2] It is true that "farmers" (lords?) lost a large part
of their markets, but surviving farm tenants were able to extend and
up-grade their holdings, and farm laborers were able to command higher
wages. Labor in _both_ city and countryside was scarce relative to the
demand; far from there being flight en masse to the cities, it remains
in doubt whether there was any substantial net shift of population at
all. Leaving aside what seems (to the present author) to be very dubious
reasoning about the economic mechanism of the supposed downward spiral,
Langer's picture of events is not consistent with the evidence reviewed
earlier.

The same author has also emphasized the psychological consequences
of the Black Death: the interest in death and the macabre, the

---

[1]Langer, "The Black Death," pp. 118, 121.

[2]Perroy, writing specifically of France, presents data casting
considerable doubt upon earlier conclusions that real wages tended to
rise in that country after 1350. He also remarks, however, that in this
period we must _not_ conclude that the wage-earners led a miserable
life (p. 235).

-25-

intensification of religious feeling, and the tendency toward licentious yet guilt-ridden behavior.[1] The view that there were such effects appears to have considerable justification.[2] An argument might conceivably be offered that this psychological transformation was associated with the economic depression, perhaps by leading to a withdrawal from worldly economic activities to otherworldly religious ones. But the evidence of the chronology in Table 1 suggests that, when we leave the economic sphere and turn to government and politics, the period was characterized by normal and even hyper-normal levels of energetic worldly activity. Nor was all this activity of a destructive nature. In England, for example, the same period saw significant developments in the direction of national unification and parliamentary independence.[3]

Turning to long-term socio-political effects, one question is the bearing of the Black Death upon the decline of the feudal system in Western Europe. Since the manorial system was decaying in any case, the plague catastrophe was more of an auxiliary force than an underlying cause of the great social change. The feudal system was, of course, status-oriented and tradition-bound. Although there seems to be great disagreement about the progress of commutation of personal services by the time of the Black Death,[4] there nevertheless was enormous ridigity in the established terms of economic relationships. The system was ill-adapted to cope with the pressures for changes in these terms dictated by the new scarcity of labor relative to land. Hence the complaints about flight of labor, vagrancy, and the like, and legislative attempts (for example, in the Statutes of Laborers)

---

[1] *Ibid.*, p. 121. See also Meiss, *passim*.

[2] Not entirely dissimilar phenomena occurred in the **pre**-Black Death period, however. The flagellant cult began earlier, for example as did expulsions and massacres of Jews. The Children's Crusade of 1212, and the "dancing manias" beginning in the 13th century might also be cited.

[3] *Cambridge History*, pp. 895-96.

[4] For a view of this question as it concerns England, see Miss Power's study. Evidently, in England commutation had progressed considerably though unevenly before 1350.

-26-

to reverse by fiat the concessions granted perforce by individual lords.
On this hypothesis, outbursts like the Peasants' Revolt in England (1381)
were caused basically by attempts to insist upon and enforce feudal dues
and rights or status relationships no longer economically maintainable
in the changed circumstances.[1] (The immediate cause of the Peasants'
Revolt was the imposition of a severe poll tax, highly oppressive to
the lower classes.) The pressure of labor scarcity contributed to the
decay of the vestiges of serfdom, and a shift toward a contractual
form of employment relationship.[2]

---

[1]It is suggestive that the burden of villein services was heavy
in a number of the countries where the Revolt was most violent.
Power, p. 115.

[2]Seebohm, p. 277; Creighton, p. 192, Robbins, pp. 468-69.

-27-

V. CONCLUSIONS

1. The Black Death of 1348-50 swept away perhaps one-fourth of
the population of Western Europe, though the "excess mortality" was
somewhat lower. Among all recorded catastrophes, it is the one most
comparable in suddenness, geographical scope, and scale of casualties to a hypothetical thermonuclear war. On the other hand, in contrast with war, there was no direct destruction of material property.

2. Although there are literary reports of organizational breakdowns in cities during the period when the plague was at its height,
it is evident -- from records of governmental proceedings, and the
fact of large-scale military and naval activity -- that the mechanisms
of government did not collapse. It should, of course, be appreciated
that "government" in the 14th century was a simpler and more limited
activity than government today. (And, indeed, it might be conjectured
that the socio-political structure of the 14th century had evolved so
as to be particularly resilient to disaster.)[1]

3. The short-term economic aftermath of the Black Death was very
much in line with what economic theory would predict: a rapid rise in
wages and per capita incomes of the laboring classes, and downward
pressure on rents and the incomes of the propertied classes. The
attempt to stem these pressures by government fiat (Statutes of
Laborers) had only limited success. Economic recovery from this
initial blow was rapid.

4. The century following the Black Death is usually considered
by historians to be a period of depression, and some authors have
attributed the depression to the Black Death. Review of the evidence
indicates that it remains questionable whether the period saw an
actual decline in per capita well-being in comparison with the level
prevailing before the Black Death. And the century was a prosperous
one for the laboring classes, the mass of the population. But

---

[1]This point was suggested to the author by Michael Arnsten.

-28-

economic improvement was less than might have been expected, especially
as population was relatively stable. The stagnation of this century
appears to have been mainly due to the continuing recurrences of
plague, secondarily to the effects of war (the latter applying
especially for France).

    5. The Black Death accelerated the decline of feudalism and the
shift to modern contractual economic relationships. Although this
development was proceeding in any case, the suddenly changed relative
scarcities of labor and land dictated a "new deal" that the tradition-
bound feudal system was unable to provide.

    6. Direct inferences can hardly be drawn from this 14th-century
catastrophe as to possible consequences of thermonuclear war. But we
can state the negative conclusion that this historical record provides
no support for contentions that social collapse or an economic downward spiral are necessary or likely consequences of massive disasters.

-29-

BIBLIOGRAPHY

1. Bean, J. M. W., "Plague, Population, and Economic Decline in England in the Later Middle Ages," The Economic History Review, 2nd Ser., v. 15 (April 1963).

2. Beveridge, W. H., "The Yield and Price of Corn in the Middle Ages," The Economic Journal (Economic History Series No. 2), May 1927, pp. 155-67.

3. Boccaccio, Decameron.

4. Burckhardt, Jacob, The Civilization of the Renaissance in Italy (Phaidon Press, Oxford, 1945).

5. Cipolla, Carlo M., "Economic Depression of the Renaissance?" The Economic History Review, 2nd Ser., v. 16 (April 1964).

6. Clark, Paul G., Vulnerability and Recuperation of a Regional Economy: A Study of the Impact of a Hypothetical Nuclear Attack on New England, The RAND Corporation, RM-1809 (October 1956).

7. Clark, Paul G. and D. V. T. Bear, "The Importance of Individual Industries for Defense Planning," The RAND Corporation, P-2093 (September 1960).

8. Creighton, Charles, A History of Epidemics in Britain, v. 1 (Cambridge, 1891).

9. Froissart, Sir John, Chronicles of England, France, and Spain, tr. Thomas Johnes.

10. Hansen, W. Lee, "A Note on the Cost of Children's Mortality," Journal of Political Economy, v. 65 (June 1957).

11. Herlihy, D., "Population, Plague and Social Change in Rural Pistoia, 1201-1430," The Economic History Review, 2nd Ser., v. 18 (1965).

12. Hirshleifer, Jack, "Some Thoughts on the Social Structure After a Bombing Disaster," The RAND Corporation, P-674 (August 1955).

13. -----, Disaster and Recovery: A Historical Survey, The RAND Corporation, RM-3079-PR (April 1963).

14. Langer, William L., "The Next Assignment," The American Historical Review, v. 63 (January 1958).

15. -----, "The Black Death," Scientific American (February 1964).

-30-

15. Levett, A. Elizabeth and A. Ballard, The Black Death, Oxford
    Studies in Social and Legal History, v. 5, Paul Vinogradoff, ed.
    (Oxford, 1916).

17. Lopez, R. S. and H. A. Miskimin, "The Economic Depression of the
    Rennaissance," The Economic History Review, 2nd Ser., v. 14
    (1961-62).

18. Meiss, Millard, Painting in Florence and Siena after the Black
    Death (Harper Torchbooks: Harper & Row, New York, 1964).

19. Mullett, Charles F., The Bubonic Plague and England (University
    of Kentucky Press, 1956).

20. Perroy, E., "Wage Labour in France in the Later Middle Ages,"
    The Economic History Review, 2nd Ser., v. 8 (1955).

21. Postan, M., "Revisions in Economic History: IX -- The Fifteenth
    Century," Economic History Review, 2nd Ser., v. 2 (1949-50),
    pp. 160-67.

22. -----, "Some Economic Evidence of Declining Population in the
    Later Middle Ages," The Economic History Review, 2nd Ser.,
    v. 2 (1950).

23. -----, "Moyen Age: Rapport," in Rapports du IXe Congres
    International des Sciences Historiques, I, pp. 225-41.

24. Power, E. E., "Historical Revisions: VII -- The Effects of the
    Black Death on Rural Organization in England," History, New
    Series, v. 3 (1918), pp. 110-16.

25. Previte-Orton, C. W., The Shorter Cambridge Medieval History
    (Cambridge University Press; Cambridge, 1953), v. 2.

26. Robbins, Helen, "A Comparison of the Effects of the Black Death
    on the Economic Organization of France and England," Journal of
    Political Economy, v. 36 (August 1928).

27. Russell, Josiah Cox, British Medieval Population (University of
    New Mexico Press, Albuquerque, 1948).

28. Saltmarsh, John, "Plague and Economic Decline in England in the
    Later Middle Ages," Cambridge Historical Journal, v. 7 (1941).

29. Seebohm, F., "The Black Death, and Its Place in English History,"
    Fortnightly Review, v. 2 (1865) [in two parts].

30. Slicher van Bath, B. H., The Agrarian History of Western Europe,
    A. D. 500-1850 (Edward Arnold; London, 1963), Olive Ordish, tr.

-31-

31. Stonier, Tom, <u>Nuclear Disaster</u> (Meridian Books: World Publishing
     Co.; Cleveland, 1963).

32. Utterstrom, Gustaf, "Climatic Fluctuations and Population Problems
     in Early Modern History," <u>The Scandinavian Economic History
     Review</u>, v. 3 (1955).

[2]

Optimal Flood Damage Management: Retrospect and Prospect

Gilbert F. White*

In the worldwide struggle to manage water resources for human good the gap between scientific knowledge of optimal methods and their practical application by farmers, manufacturers, and government officials is large and generally widening. Man's ability to forecast streamflow, to store water and transport it long distances, to alter its quality and extract it from great depths is growing more rapidly than his skill in putting the improved technology to earthy, daily use. This gap between the desirable and the actual is especially dramatic where peasant societies are exposed to new agronomy and water technology, but the contrast is hardly less striking in sectors of United States production where we often think of new techniques as being avidly embraced. Farmers who over-irrigate, manufacturers who neglect tried water conservation devices, and officials who misuse measures of economic efficiency testify to the difficulty.

At times we placidly accept this gap, as when a projection of future national water needs assumes that industry will not increase the adoption of new technology [ref. 1]. At other times we confidently ignore it, as when economic justification for a flood protection scheme assumes all the farmers will change their farming system to take advantage of new conditions [ref. 2]. When the failure to employ economically optimal management practices is frankly confronted, it often is charged off to cultural lag, or ignorance, or inept social organization.

* Professor of Geography, University of Chicago. The author is indebted to Robert W. Kates and W. R. D. Sewell for their helpful criticism of an early draft of the paper.

OPTIMAL FLOOD DAMAGE MANAGEMENT

In a broad sense we are dealing with the basic and immensely intricate problem of how social change takes place non-violently, and we must recognize it has strong and diverse components of customary cultural behavior, organized social action, and natural environment. A soothing and academically safe observation is to say we need more research on why the optimum is not achieved. Clearly this is true, but I feel uncomfortable about even that platitude because some of the research on both technology and analytical methods seems to have widened rather than narrowed the gap in the field of water resources. And the gap promises to widen still further if I read correctly the lessons to be drawn from the American encounter with water resources and the shape of federal programs to come. There is reason to suspect that concentration of analysis on testing for economically efficient solutions may have impeded attainment of the efficiency goal. To modify Voltaire's observation, perhaps the search for the best has been, in these instances, the enemy of the good.

The United States' attempt to manage flood damage over more than three decades illustrates the point. From experience with the planning, construction, and study of the national flood protection efforts, beginning with the massive public works projects of 1933, a few conclusions emerge. That record of natural catastrophe, far-flung surveys, and gigantic expenditures suggests that similar though less grandiose events may well unfold on the flood plains of other developing lands. It also suggests that some portion of the myopic view of remedies, of the failure to understand how choices are made, and of the difficulty in interpreting scientific findings—troubles which have dogged federal flood activities to date—may trip up such growing programs as pollution abatement, water supply, and recreation.

I shall try to review the experience with management of flood losses in several steps. In beginning, a confession must be made of our confusion concerning optimal management. Next, the state of our knowledge about the human use of flood plains is summarized. That is sharpened by pointing out those findings that seem sufficiently valid to warrant recommendation for public policy. The obverse, of course, is admitting what we do not know, thereby outlining major research needs. Both knowledge and ignorance are stated more concretely in reference to the Denver flood of June 1965. Finally, what we have learned that may be of value in other sectors of resources management is the subject of a concluding section.

Were this a review of works of art rather than of engineering construction, public policy, and geographic studies it might be called program notes on a retrospective show. I do not attempt to appraise all the

GILBERT F. WHITE

thinking which has bloomed in the muddy wake of U.S. floods. It has been summarized elsewhere [ref. 3, 4, 5, 6]. The emphasis here is on what some of us associated with University of Chicago studies have learned that commends further public action, and on the lessons that may be relevant in distant flood plains or in broader fields of water management.

CONCEPTS OF THE OPTIMUM

If the optimum management of flood damage is taken as that form of flood plain use that is most satisfactory and desirable in yielding the largest net social benefits over an investment period, it must be admitted at the outset that there are pitifully few grounds for judging where it has been achieved. This is because the methods of assessing optimal use are still crude and have been tried in only a few areas. It is difficult to tell whether a given reach of a valley will best serve the needs of the community in one use rather than any other. Rare is the community that is able to define its land needs clearly. Even if methods were established and readily applied, the political task of using the results in urban planning is fraught with complications. When faced with the question, it is common for agencies to follow a greatly simplified process of judgment, such as that embodied in the Milwaukee and Detroit municipal policies of buying up valley bottoms for recreational use without attempting to weigh the alternatives, or the implicit decision in Los Angeles that any land which can be protected from floods at reasonable cost should be used for residential, commercial, and industrial purposes. In some of these cases and in certain clearly warranted protection projects, the present use no doubt is optimal.

If, on the other hand, optimal management is taken as that combination of adjustments to flood hazard for any given use that yields the largest net social benefits, the task is much simpler. At hand are relatively satisfactory methods of comparing the social costs of protection or flood proofing or insurance with the ever available alternative of simply bearing the loss. [Ref. 3, pp. 83–92.] Not that there are no differences of professional judgment; there are, as is shown later, but that major definition and approach seem valid.

The federal policy, freely translated and omitting numerous details, is that flood damage is undesirable, and that the government is prepared to prevent it by feasible engineering or watershed treatment so long as the benefits to whomsoever they may accrue exceed the costs and so long as local interests contribute to the costs of non-reservoir projects. Surveys

253

OPTIMAL FLOOD DAMAGE MANAGEMENT

by the Corps of Engineers and the Soil Conservation Service character-istically assess costs and benefits for one or more engineering schemes for loss reduction. As economic critics have pointed out, these comparisons do not select the optimum: they may ignore incremental analysis, and discount practices are in question [ref. 7, 8]. Thousands of completed survey reports give benefit-cost findings and their implicit forecasts as to what the future will bring.

Inherent in those surveys are a pair of ambiguities. One hinges on the obvious fact that what is optimal for the community may not be optimal for individual managers of flood plain land, depending upon arrange-ments for sharing costs and benefits. A second is the policy of cost sharing. The Corps sometimes counts benefits from land value enhance-ment resulting from more intensive use only if necessary to obtain a favorable benefit-cost ratio, and then seeks to recover part as local contribution; the Soil Conservation Service counts them but has no au-thority to require reimbursement for them. The Corps is not expected to seek reimbursement for the cost of protection from reservoirs. A change in one of these policies by the Congress or a change in the social arrange-ments for providing technical assistance to individual managers would alter the estimated optimum.

It must be admitted, then, that hortatory declarations as to the proper national policy for making wise use of flood plains can only come to grips at long distance and in a shadowy way with the question of wisest use. They really are addressed, for the most part, to the more limited question of whether or not, given a particular use, the adjustment selected is optimal.

However, there are several bits of evidence that the uses prevailing in United States flood plains in the 1960's are less than optimal. In the more limited goal of federal legislation, we have not been doing well. It is clear that the mean annual toll of flood losses has been rising for half a century [ref. 9]. This in itself would not be evidence of less than optimal use, for it might be that rising total losses would be a character-istic of wise use. Such a conclusion is thrown into doubt by the wide-spread attempts of flood sufferers to avoid future losses through flood protection works, and by the inability of the federal government, in its expenditure of more than $7 billion since 1936 on protection works, to curb the volume of flood losses. Further scepticism is induced by the readiness of some managers to change their uses of flood plains when presented with new information and opportunities, and by the growing recognition by the Corps of Engineers, itself, that engineering works alone are not fully serving their intended aim.

We know a little about the over-all shift in use of flood plains in the

GILBERT F. WHITE

United States. Corps of Engineers studies show that encroachment continues to be rapid in most sections of the nation. The invasion is predominantly urban, and in many areas consists in enlargement of existing commercial and industrial uses or the expansion of urban uses along new highways [ref. 10]. Loss potential mounts vigorously in reaches where partial protection is offered by dams or levees.

Two aspects of rural flood plain use seem clear from sample studies. One is that the major encroachments of loss potential upon rural flood plains are for new urban use rather than for agriculture [ref. 11]. The second is that in selected places where additional protection against flooding has been provided by watershed protection works there has not been rapid intensification of cropping. (See Burton [ref. 2].) Insofar as the latter relation is true, it challenges the assumption underlying much of the Watershed Protection program that decreases in flood frequency and magnitude will lead to prompt increases in intensity of farm use. It also appears from Burton's work that where parts of a farm are protected, there is a tendency for farmers to gamble on higher risks in unprotected lands [ref. 2, pp. 39–41].

In general, the primarily urban protection programs are running fast to keep up with further encroachments; and the agricultural program is failing to satisfy its promise for farmland use changes, and increasingly is protecting or promoting urban invasion of flood plains. Individual managers of the flood plain are working over large areas at cross-purposes with stated federal aims.

How much do we now know as to why and how these managers—both public and private—behave as they do in the face of floods?

KNOWLEDGE OF FLOOD PLAIN USE

My first preoccupation with American flood problems was with the primitive methods of economic justification practiced by public agencies thirty years ago. When the first national Flood Control Act was passed in 1936, the simple and in many respects more comprehensive comparison of land values that had been used to justify local drainage and Miami Conservancy investments was being replaced by the more complicated but narrowed benefit-cost computations used in the 308 Studies. From my appraisal of the situation came probably the first and certainly the worst paper ever published on the subject in an academic journal [ref. 12]. There also emerged the recognition that engineering protection works are only one of the several adjustments which a flood plain manager may make to flood hazard.

OPTIMAL FLOOD DAMAGE MANAGEMENT

Very slowly it became evident in subsequent years that a benefit-cost calculation has little meaning in seeking optimal solutions unless it predicts with modest reliability the streams of gains and losses that probably will flow from the area in the future. To do this requires sufficient understanding of the behavior of flood plain managers to discern how they may be expected to respond to whatever conditions are postulated for the future. Is a dam likely to reduce net losses downstream? How would a shopkeeper be inclined to use a new map showing his hazard from flooding? Would a change in cost sharing alter a farmer's view of his feasible alternatives? Seeking answers to questions such as these leads to examination of what managers in fact see as their range of choice, how they evaluate the flood hazard, what they regard as available technology for adjusting to floods, what appears to be the economic efficiency of each available technique, and how they are encouraged or constrained by social action. We cannot realistically assume these people to be uniformly well-informed, rational optimizers, nor can we dismiss them cavalierly as stupid, pigheaded, or knaves. More will be said later about models of flood plain behavior.

How Much Choice?

The range of choice open to flood plain users in dealing with flood hazard was outlined systematically in 1942 and has not changed greatly since. [Ref. 13, Table 2.] It was apparent then, as now, that the heavy federal emphasis on full support of reservoir projects and partial support of other engineering protection encouraged both public agencies and individual property managers to think of their choice as being between bearing the loss or enjoying federal protection. The early Tennessee Valley Authority program and the Department of Agriculture Watershed Protection program reinforced this view. Emergency evacuation, while facilitated by Weather Bureau river forecasts, was not specifically organized. Structural adjustments and land elevation were not canvassed in federal studies, and were not promoted by federal or other public agencies. Relief was available principally for extreme hardship. Insurance was lacking in all but a few special cases. Change in land use rarely was considered; a reduction in intensity of use was presumed to meet invariably with local opposition (a presumption later shown to be false). Prediction of enhancement in land value by changing to a more intense use was avoided for a long time, because of fear of open involvement with speculative land development, and the extreme option of relocation of entire communities was so abrupt, radical, and lacking in implementation that it was practical in only a few instances.

It now appears in hindsight that the 1942 typology of human adjust-

GILBERT F. WHITE

ment to floods was misleading and that, while showing principal alternatives, it set back thinking about solutions. The fault lay in two aspects of the classification of adjustment. One was the inclusion of social guides to adjustment as though they were in themselves adjustments. For example, land use regulation was listed as an alternative public measure, whereas we now recognize it as being a possible guide to any adjustment or use. Second, a change in land use was listed as one alternative adjustment. This is true for any given situation of land use, but as stated it carried the implication that a change in use excludes other adjustments. A more accurate way of stating the range of choice would be to show seven different adjustments for each of all possible land uses, as indicated in Table 1, and to omit any mention of the various social actions which might be taken to affect the choice.

The effect of the earlier classification, which still appears in discussions of zoning ordinances or flood plain information studies, is to imply that the range of adjustments applies only to the current use, and that any change in use will mean reduction in intensity. As a result, the possibility of a different use or of use regulation often is ruled out of consideration before it is canvassed: a town rejects zoning on the ground it would automatically prevent commercial uses; a property owner opposes land use studies because he thinks they surely will lead to his relocation or to downgrading of land value. They may, but they do not necessarily have that effect.

Moreover, we have come to recognize that the process of choice is dynamic rather than static. To think of there being a decision only when a major project is under consideration is to ignore the variety of paths along which adjustments move. [Ref. 3, pp. 18–21.] When attention is focused on these diverse paths, then more importance is attached to critical times of decision and to methods of planning for changing and flexible adjustments. [Ref. 3, pp. 17–18; and ref. 14.]

TABLE 1.

Typology of Range of Choice in Adjustments to Floods

1942	1965
Land elevation	Land use A—
Flood abatement	Bearing the loss
Flood protection	Protection
Emergency measures	Emergency measures
Structural adjustments	Structural, including land elevation
Land use	Flood abatement
Crops	Insurance
Urban relocation	Public relief
Public measures	Land use n—
Public relief	Bearing the loss
Insurance	etc.

OPTIMAL FLOOD DAMAGE MANAGEMENT

How Is the Hazard Perceived?

One of the comforting explanations for apparently less than optimal use of flood plains is that there is lack of information as to flood hazard. The obvious corrective—making the information available—was slow in coming in the form of flood hazard maps, and when the first map appeared, it failed to yield the expected results. The U.S. Geological Survey map of Topeka in 1959 did not have a prompt, significant effect upon the thinking of people in Topeka [ref. 15]. Experience there and in the Tennessee Valley pointed out the need for understanding how people habitually perceive hazard and for designing means by which hazard information may become meaningful to flood plain dwellers.

Kates's study of LaFollette and five other communities indicates that perception of flood hazard is a function of direct flood experience and of outlook toward nature, and that the mere supply of information, as to where the water reached and when, does not necessarily lead to more precise recognition of the probability and magnitude of floods [ref. 5]. He shows how the ambiguity of flood risk and the difficulty of facing uncertainty foster a division between flood plain dweller and the scientist in recognizing the hazard for what it is to each of them [ref. 16].

The pioneering flood reports of TVA [ref. 17] and the wide experimentation of the Northeastern Illinois Metropolitan Area Planning Commission with USGS maps have begun to point out specific steps, such as distribution of hazard reports to financial agencies, which will enhance their reception. Regional studies by the USGS of flood frequency are making possible more reliable estimates of hazard. From the burgeoning number of Corps of Engineers flood plain information reports new experience is accumulating but has not been assessed in detail.

We still have only a rudimentary knowledge of how man perceives the risk and uncertainty of a flood or any other natural disaster [ref. 18] and, until this is refined, the judgment of what information in what form will be useful to him will be largely pragmatic.

What Technology Is Available?

It early became apparent that many flood plain managers, while vaguely aware of the possible range of choice and of the flood risk, did not understand the techniques of certain adjustments such as emergency evacuation, structural change, and insurance. From the LaFollette study there is evidence that those who have lived longest on the flood plain are more aware of alternatives, that those most recently flooded perceive emergency action more acutely, and that the times of construction, normal renovation, or disaster repair are more propitious for adoption of

GILBERT F. WHITE

alternatives than are other times. Sheaffer's study of flood proofing in Bristol, Tennessee-Virginia showed systematically for the first time the potentialities of combining emergency and structural measures [ref. 19]. This led to TVA and state discussions with local authorities and those, in turn, to a significant deviation from usual federal flood control policy. At Bristol and White Oak, the TVA authorized federal contributions to partial engineering works on condition that local government regulate further encroachments, flood-proof its own buildings, and take responsibility for advising property managers as to flood proofing of the other structures which would enjoy only partial protection under the feasible engineering works [ref. 20].

Emergency evacuation measures have received little detailed study other than at LaFollette and Bristol, and it is only in recent months that the Weather Bureau has begun to go beyond mail questionnaires to ask how its forecasts are used.

Notwithstanding elaborate engineering studies of flood control spillway and channel design, there is no significant research under federal or any other auspices on methods of using plastics, temporary barriers, electronic control, and similar devices to prevent flood losses, and nothing since 1936 on means of rehabilitating damaged property. Expert services are poured into specifications for a dam, but it still is impossible to get from a federal agency the simplest advice as to technology for flood proofing. This lack becomes especially critical when it is recognized that the number of places receiving unfavorable reports from the Corps of Engineers on local protection projects probably equals those receiving favorable reports; that among the authorized projects more than 200 have not been undertaken because of local complications; and that even where comprehensive reservoir programs have been authorized and are under construction, it may be years before the full effect of protection will be felt. Recently, unfavorable reports have tended to include more references to possible alternatives to protection.

Insurance, while a practicable alternative for the few managers who know how to obtain special coverage for flood-proofed property, or who fortuitously are covered by an all-purpose auto policy, is closed to most others. Partly as a result of caution on the part of the insurance companies and partly the consequence of inept beginnings by the administration of the authorized but abortive Federal Flood Insurance Agency, there has been no systematic experimentation with this device. Were the recent explorations by an industry committee to be extended with Housing and Home Finance Agency encouragement and, using the full technical advice of federal agencies, to offer limited coverage in sample areas, it would be practicable to find out precisely how much could be indemni-

OPTIMAL FLOOD DAMAGE MANAGEMENT

fied at costs and in circumstances that would supplement or substitute for protection and other alternative measures. Insurance may well have its most influential uses in being available as a substitute where protection and structural adjustments are not feasible, or in covering the hazard during a period when old uses are phased out.

Is It Economically Efficient?

Although public approaches to flood problems have centered upon benefit-cost analysis of protection projects, little attention has been paid to the economic efficiency of other adjustments and, particularly, to the efficiency of choices by private managers. As a result, we still have only a sketchy knowledge of how far individuals seek to optimize their uses, and what they would choose if they were to do so rationally using their preferred criteria. It is plain that differences in time horizon, discount rate, perceived benefits, and, most of all, direct costs give many individual managers a view of alternatives that would favor federal reservoir projects and would discourage an alternative such as insurance so long as existing federal policy prevails.

By assuming that managers are both rational and subject to the same efficiency criteria as public agencies, the federal programs predict changes which do not materialize—as with the Soil Conservation Service anticipation of intensification of agricultural land use—and fail to predict other changes that do materialize—as with earlier Corps of Engineers disregard for continued encroachment into valleys partially protected by new reservoirs. Economic research has contributed notably to refinement of public analysis without confronting these problems. The recent study of industrial losses in the Lehigh shows that loss and benefit estimates may be sharpened by improved methods, but that a more important step is to recognize differences in the economic stance of an industrial plant versus its region versus the nation [ref. 21].

How Are Other Places Affected?

A principal deficiency of most economic efficiency analysis has been the handling of external economies and diseconomies. In physical terms, little attempt has been made to assess the full physical consequences of changing the regimen of a stream or altering its channel. These go largely unmeasured [ref. 22]. In economic terms, the impacts of a change in land use upon other parts of the same community and region are rarely and imperfectly traced. It is much easier to compare possible adjustments for a store in the Dallas flood plain than to estimate what would be the effects upon Dallas of sharply or progressively shifting that use to recrea-

260

GILBERT F. WHITE

tional or residential. Hopefully, the current Pittsburgh study will throw some light on this. And analysis, such as that attempted at Towson, Maryland [ref. 23, 24], of the social costs of alternative uses will help make choices in the light of impacts upon the whole community.

The early studies of flood plain adjustments tended, as Kates has pointed out, to attribute much of the behavior of flood plain dwelling to ignorance, cupidity, or irrationality [ref. 16]. We took a long time—far too long—to begin to test these riverside opinions as to motives and as to the decision process itself. Perhaps we lacked a handy model of how decisions are made if they are not made by rational, economic men. Perhaps the relative simplicity of manipulating a benefit-cost ratio fascinated us. Perhaps we had too much faith that if a government commission charted a path, both property owners and government officials would follow it sheepishly. At any rate, we went many years aiming at what people should do about floods without trying to deepen our understanding of the different paths which people actually take in living with floods.

To do this requires a much more complex model of human behavior than the optimization model. It must be a model which takes sufficient account of differences in perception, decision criteria, and the effect of social guides to permit a reasonably accurate description of what and how people decide to cope with flood hazard.

How Does Society Guide the Choice?

The role of social guides in constraining or encouraging the flood plain manager has been noted at several points. More is known about how public managers respond to pressures [ref. 25, 26] than about how individual managers respond to public guidance. We have just begun to identify the ways in which federal policies of flood control, flood forecasting and urban renewal, state regulatory action on stream channels and highway location, municipal building codes, urban plans and renewal programs, and financing agency policy can be integrated to promote maximum choice in adjusting to flood hazard and in use of flood plains. We have learned, for example, that while a flood hazard map alone may have little influence upon the decision of a property owner to build in a flood plain, it becomes powerful when placed in the hands of a professional appraiser who has been instructed in its use, and even more powerful when mortgage insurance officers in the Federal Housing Administration and Veterans Administration are instructed to look for it and use it. We have learned that a cost-sharing requirement for a protection project may change a manager's view not only of the project, but of the alternatives open to him. Reactions to enforcement of encroachment lines, zoning ordinances, and subdivision regulations are better

OPTIMAL FLOOD DAMAGE MANAGEMENT

known. The legality of setting encroachment lines now appears well established, but no solid test yet has been made of restrictive zoning of the plain above [ref. 27] the channel, or of the liability of a property owner who knowingly exposes others to the damages of flood.

Perhaps the most baffling single problem in achieving any significant advances in public action with respect to flood loss reduction is the set of mind and institutional position of public agency personnel. To ignite the field staff of an agency like the Corps of Engineers or the Bureau of Reclamation with a new approach in contrast to a new technique is like setting fire to a pile of soggy newspapers—time, patience, and systematic ventilation are required. And a new organization can mismanage a promising innovation, as in the case of flood insurance. But there are exciting exceptions, as in the Tennessee Valley Authority where one man gave the leadership for a new federal-state-local co-operative approach to flood loss reduction.[1]

Basic to the action of the administrators and the public pressures they feel are the attitudes toward nature, water, and floods which they and other resource managers share. The sense of man as a conqueror of nature, the view of access to water as a divine right, these and other attitudes combine to condition the position of a city manager who argues that restriction on channel encroachment is a denial of a right to share nature's largess, or of an engineer who after daily travelling a hazardous expressway to his office concludes that the only suitable engineering works are those promising virtually complete safety from loss of life.

Unlike the larger enterprise of river basin development, difficulties in flood loss management cannot be charged primarily to splintering of responsibility among agencies operating under divided congressional authority. True, the number of federal, state, and local agencies having a hand in guiding decisions about floods is large, but they now have little conflict or duplication—except where the Soil Conservation Service bumps into the Corps of Engineers as it moves downstream with larger dams and smaller local requirements—and the greatest opportunity for co-ordination appears to rest in the application of an integrated federal approach within existing legislative policy.

Side Effects of Normative Analysis

Emphasis upon normative economic analysis by federal agencies and their academic reformers may have retarded the attainment of optimal goals. Refinement of the benefit-cost practices has directed attention to

---

[1] The work which has been carried out under the leadership of James E. Goddard is reported briefly in two papers [see ref. 28, 29].

GILBERT F. WHITE

what should be engineering investment in flood plains rather than to explaining their present use. While there is much room for improvement and while benefit-cost analysis would be enhanced by insight into managerial behavior, it detours the realistic prediction of future use. By assuming the managers of flood plain property are either optimizing, rational men, or narrow, inflexible men, it avoids difficulties that would arise were account taken of information lacks; interpretation of information; differing perception of hazard, technology, and efficiency; differing decision rules; and inconsistent social guides. Having prescribed a simple cure, there is little incentive for the government doctor to return to the bedside to find out what happened to the patient. Public doubts about economic justification are soothed by B/C ratios exceeding unity while public side-effects are largely ignored. It should not be abandoned, but the weight of its authority should not be carried unless it is used to help explain the vital question of what will be the future use if a given adjustment or use is adopted.

One day a short, sturdy Maine blacksmith, after long wooing the willowy village belle, won her consent to marriage as they talked in his shop. Enthusiastically, he jumped onto the anvil and kissed her. Then they walked hand in hand out across the meadows. "Shall we kiss again?" he asked. "Not yet," she said. Farther on he again put the question. "But why do you keep asking?" she replied. "Because," he said, "if there isn't going to be any more kissing, I'll stop carrying this anvil." Normative economic analysis is an anvil that can serve several important uses, including intangible aesthetic ones, but there isn't much point in carrying its weight unless it is used properly.

WARRANTED PUBLIC ACTION

Given optimal use as our distant aim, what do we know sufficiently well to warrant immediate prescription of public program? I think we know enough about human use of flood plains to assert that if the burden of annual losses is to be reduced without concomitant expenditures for engineering works, federal policy and program must be revised and supplemented in several ways. These would help to see to it that managers of flood plain land are supplied with full information, in intelligible form and at the right times, as to the range of choice in use and adjustment open to them in using the flood plain. This means piecing together a genuine program from diverse parts.

Solid data on flood losses would help. There are grounds for believing that sufficient research has been done to enable us to design and carry

OPTIMAL FLOOD DAMAGE MANAGEMENT

out a new system for collecting flood loss data which would substitute synthetic for reported losses, estimate the degree to which potential losses are averted, and rely upon a stratified, systematic set of samples [ref. 3, pp. 111–14]. We ought to end our unhappy plight of having to say that mean annual flood losses are "in the neighborhood of $300–900 million."

Technical studies on flood proofing and insurance and on relationships between flood characteristics and flood losses should be pushed, and their results disseminated where and when people will use them.

A profound change in approach would result if the Corps of Engineers were to exercise its present authority to require, as a condition of further construction, state agencies to regulate encroachments upon stream channels, and to require local agencies to regulate land uses in reaches of streams where federal protection is to be provided.

Perhaps more important is the opportunity for the Corps of Engineers and the Soil Conservation Service, in collaboration with the appropriate federal agencies dealing with urban problems, to encourage local communities to assure that consideration of flood hazard enters into public and private planning decisions [ref. 3, p. 124]. This would include expansion of reports on flood areas and frequencies, interpretation of the results to interested managers and key people such as architects and mortgage officers, stimulation of flood-forecasting and warning systems, dissemination of information on alternative measures for loss reduction, promotion of improved land use regulations, and support of selective public acquisition of hazard areas. Reconciliation of cost-sharing policy is in order.

In brief, the chief threats from clearly uneconomic encroachment should be curbed. Next to this, the major opportunity now seems to rest in promoting choice by private managers among combinations of protection, emergency, structural, and insurance measures. In the light of our knowledge of decision making and of a few practical experiments, it seems likely that public action with that aim would improve flood plain use and that it would be politically acceptable. Only a few aspects would require new federal legislation.

In contrast to earlier times when proposals for federal policy, whatever their theoretical merit, fell on inhospitable ground, three aspects of the present scene make action seem more hopeful: (1) There is a rather widespread feeling in both federal and state agencies that engineering works are not enough. (2) At the same time practical experience is building respect for new analytical techniques and for such social guides as flood information reports, mortgage insurance policy, and zoning. (3) The public groups concerned with flood damage management have been expanded significantly in recent years. To the flood sufferers have

GILBERT F. WHITE

been added citizen and government contingents seeking speedy urban renewal and greater open space, and their support for a broadened approach seems assured.

Now let us list points at which understanding is so lacking that it is necessary to be cautious about recommending public action.

While there are rough methods for weighing alternative adjustments for the same land use, such as protection and flood proofing, there is no satisfactory method of comparing the feasibility of different land uses, having in mind the external economies and diseconomies accruing to other parts of the same urban area. Until this is achieved the public choice of alternative uses in hazardous areas, a choice which at best is subject to highly political pressures, is bound to be vague.

In the case of both urban and rural reaches, much more needs to be known about the precise factors affecting individual choice, particularly the managerial perception of uncertainty and of economic efficiency. Without such refinement of relationships, U.S. Department of Agriculture's predictions of flood plain land use in Watershed Protection projects, and Corps of Engineers' estimates of urban land use changes will remain speculative. We need to find out precisely how many alternatives people can consider and in what conditions.

DENVER AS AN EXAMPLE

With the June 1965 disaster in Denver in mind [ref. 10, pp. 127–33], how would these conclusions apply to that inundated South Platte flood plain as its residents dug out of the mud and repaired their bridges behind them? After Red Cross and federal disaster assistance had been assured and people began to look to the possibility of future floods (including some which, they have been told for many years, will bring a flow twice as large as that of 1965), a program of the type suggested could have affected the city in the following fashion.

The Corps of Engineers, while open to discussion about getting funds for an upstream dam, would announce that no federal funds would be available for protection until the state took steps to curb further encroachment on stream channels. Any further protection for Denver would also be contingent upon the city showing it had extended its present regulation of land use from a few of the tributary dry washes to the full South Platte flood plain. Assistance would be offered to the municipal authorities in getting accurate, intelligible reports on the hazard areas and likely frequency of flooding, and in advising them as to how the results could be put in the hands of property managers. Technical assistance would be available to owners, architects, and city officials,

OPTIMAL FLOOD DAMAGE MANAGEMENT

not only on how to speed up appropriations by Congress but on how to save on salvage operations, how to flood-proof existing buildings against future losses, how to improve the flood-warning service, and how to draw up building codes which would prohibit dangerous uses such as flammable gas installations. Highway officials and the Federal Housing Administration and Veterans Administration would be alerted to hazard areas. Appraisers would state flood hazards, like termite infestation, as a routine part of their reports. The new urban affairs agency would offer to collaborate in planning of renewal for part of the area and in preparing schemes for open land reservation and acquisition for other parts of the area. Insurance would be available, perhaps through private companies at rates reflecting the risk, to property owners who already were within the reach of floods and could not be protected or who must wait years for protection.

What would all of this mean in terms of future occupance of the South Platte? As a minimum, the harmful encroachments on natural channels and needlessly hazardous invasion of adjoining flood plains at last would stop. No further increase in damage potential would take place without both property managers and public agencies being aware of the hazard and the possible choices. Emergency damage reduction plans would become a part of industrial and municipal preparations. Structural changes would receive routine consideration in any rehabilitation or construction of buildings in hazard areas. Insofar as renewal or open space schemes were studied, there would be conscious public judgment of the merits of changing existing uses. As a maximum, Denver might find itself after two decades of progressive adjustments with only as much property in the path of floods as city and owners feel warrants the risk. Thus, the optimal adjustments to flood hazard would be approached. The present policy of permitting dangerous invasion of the channel and of restricting many flood plain dwellers to a choice between bearing flood losses or seeking federal aid would be abandoned.

LESSONS FROM THREE DECADES

This rich and partly distilled experience of the United States in coping with the risk and uncertainty of floods is relevant to broader efforts at water management in several ways. Wherever growing cities spread into flood plains and whenever governments feel obliged to curb the losses from inundation there is danger that public investment may take the course which has been etched in buildings, earth, and concrete along American river valleys during the past three decades. This need not be repeated in growing countries with rapid urbanization.

266

GILBERT F. WHITE

Beyond the flood plain, there are three more general lessons that may apply to other sectors of water management. One is to guard against becoming bemused by commitment to a single engineering solution to the exclusion of other alternatives. Just as devotion to dams, channels, and levees obscures the view of possible gains in flood management from changes in emergency action, structures and insurance, or from other land uses, the preoccupation with stream dilution may divert attention from alternative waste treatment, and the search for new water supplies may prevent the exploration of methods of saving water already available.

Another lesson is to beware of easy, unsupported explanations of why people manage resources as they do. Willingness to believe that flood plain dwellers are rational managers who will seek the optimal economic adjustments to floods, can sidetrack our understanding of the complex factors which in fact affect their decisions. In the same way, simple curbstone explanations of manufacturers' preferences may delay measures to improve the efficiency of their water use, and casual assumptions concerning an irrigator's aims may obstruct the public attempts to help him adopt soil- and water-saving practices.

In both the exploration of alternatives and the understanding of the intricate process of resource decisions it is essential, if the results are to be useful, to be continuously alert to ways of reporting and interpreting findings so that they will be employed at the right time by farmer or manufacturer or government official. It is better to know that flood plain dwellers interpret the same sequence of flood events differently than to believe erroneously that a single government statement of hazard will have similar significance to all. It is even more important to learn by both study and trial what form of information will be meaningful to them and in what circumstances decisions will be made. The manager must not only see the choices, but see precisely how he or others can carry out each alternative.

When we address ourselves to lessons such as these, we are confronting—whether in flood plain or upland or city or farm—the fundamental problem of how man, in the face of diverse cultural tradition, social rigidity, and resource disparity, manages peacefully to gain a more fruitful living from the earth.

OPTIMAL FLOOD DAMAGE MANAGEMENT

REFERENCES

[1] Senate Select Committee on National Water Resources. *Report.* 86th Congress, 1st Session, Report No. 29. Washington: U.S. Government Printing Office, 1961, p. 24.

[2] Burton, Ian. *Types of Agricultural Occupance of Flood Plains in the United States.* Department of Geography Research Paper No. 75. Chicago: University of Chicago, 1962.

[3] White, Gilbert F. *Choice of Adjustment to Floods.* Department of Geography Research Paper No. 93. Chicago: University of Chicago, 1964.

[4] Tennessee Valley Authority, Technical Library. *Flood Damage Prevention: An Indexed Bibliography.* Knoxville: Tennessee Valley Authority, 1964.

[5] Kates, Robert William. *Hazard and Choice Perception in Flood Plain Management.* Department of Geography Research Paper No. 78. Chicago: University of Chicago, 1962.

[6] Hoyt, William G., and Langbein, Walter B. *Floods.* Princeton: Princeton University Press, 1955.

[7] Hufschmidt, Maynard M., Krutilla, John V., and Margolis, Julius. *Report of Panel of Consultants to the Bureau of the Budget on Standards and Criteria for Formulating and Evaluating Federal Water Resources Developments.* Washington: U.S. Bureau of the Budget, 1961.

[8] *Policies, Standards and Procedures in the Formulation, Evaluation, and Review of Plans for Use and Development of Water and Related Land Resources.* Senate Document No. 97, 87th Congress (approved by the President on May 15, 1962).

[9] Cook, Howard L., and White, Gilbert F. "Making Wise Use of Flood Plains," *United States Papers for United Nations Conference on Science and Technology,* Vol. 2. Washington: U.S. Government Printing Office, 1963.

[10] White, Gilbert F., et al. *Changes in Urban Occupance of Flood Plains in the United States.* Department of Geography Research Paper No. 57. Chicago: University of Chicago, 1958.

[11] ———. *Rural Flood Plains in the United States: A Summary Report.* Department of Geography (mimeo.). Chicago: University of Chicago, 1963.

[12] ———. "Limit of Economic Justification for Flood Protection," *Journal of Land and Public Utility Economics,* Vol. 12, 1936.

[13] ———. *Human Adjustment to Floods.* Department of Geography Research Paper No. 29. Chicago: University of Chicago, 1945.

[14] James, Douglas. *A Time Dependent Planning Process for Combining Structural Measures, Land Use and Flood Proofing to Minimize the Economic Loss of Floods.* Report EEP-12. Stanford: Stanford University Institute in Engineering Economic Systems, 1964.

[15] Roder, Wolf. "Attitudes and Knowledge in the Topeka Flood Plain," in *Papers on Flood Problems.* Department of Geography Research Paper No. 70. Chicago: University of Chicago, 1960.

[16] Kates, Robert W. "Variation in Flood Hazard Perception: Implications

GILBERT F. WHITE

for Rational Flood-Plain Use," *Spatial Organization of Land Uses: The Willamette Valley.* Corvallis: Oregon State University, 1964.

[17] Senate Select Committee on National Water Resources. "Flood Problems and Management in the Tennessee River Basin," *Committee Print No. 16.* 86th Congress, 1st Session. Washington: U.S. Government Printing Office, 1960.

[18] Burton, Ian, and Kates, Robert W. "The Perception of Natural Hazards in Resource Management," *Natural Resources Journal,* Vol. 3, 1964.

[19] Sheaffer, John R. *Flood Proofing: An Element in a Flood Damage Reduction Program.* Department of Geography Research Paper No. 65. Chicago: University of Chicago, 1960.

[20] *Plan for Flood Damage Prevention at Bristol, Tennessee-Virginia.* Bristol: Bristol Flood Study Committee, 1962.

[21] Kates, Robert W. *Industrial Flood Losses: Damage Estimation in the Lehigh Valley.* Department of Geography Research Paper No. 98. Chicago: University of Chicago, 1965.

[22] Wolman, M. Gordon. "Downstream Changes in Alluvial Channels Produced by Dams." U.S.G.S. Professional Paper, in preparation.

[23] McHarg, Ian, and Wallace, D. A. *Plan for the Valleys.* Towson: Worthington and Green Valley Planning Commission, 1964.

[24] Sutton, Walter G. *Planning for Optimum Economic Use of Flood Plains.* A.S.C.E. Environmental Engineering Conference, Atlanta, 1963.

[25] Maass, Arthur. *Muddy Waters: The Army Engineers and the Nation's Rivers.* Cambridge: Harvard University Press, 1951.

[26] Murphy, Francis C. *Regulating Flood Plain Development.* Department of Geography Research Paper No. 56. Chicago: University of Chicago, 1958.

[27] Beuchert, Edward W. "Recent Natural Resource Cases: Constitutional Law–Zoning–Flood Plain Regulation," *Natural Resources Journal,* Vol. 4, 1965.

[28] Goddard, James E. "The Cooperative Program in the Tennessee Valley," in *Papers on Flood Problems.* Department of Geography Research Paper No. 70. Chicago: University of Chicago, 1960.

[29] ———. "Flood Damage Prevention and Flood Plain Management Improve Man's Environment," *Proceedings American Society of Civil Engineers,* Vol. 89, 1963.

[3]

THE PERCEPTION OF NATURAL HAZARDS IN RESOURCE MANAGEMENT

IAN BURTON* AND ROBERT W. KATES†

*"What region of the earth is not full of
our calamities?"* Virgil

To the Englishman on his island, earthquakes are disasters that happen to others. It is recognized that "while the ground is liable to open up at any moment beneath the feet of foreigners, the English are safe because 'it can't happen here.' "[1] Thus is described a not uncommon attitude to natural hazards in England; its parallels are universal.

Notwithstanding this human incapacity to imagine natural disasters in a familiar environment, considerable disruption is frequently caused by hazards. The management of affairs is not only affected by the impact of the calamities themselves, but also by the degree of awareness, or perception of the hazard, that is shared by those subject to its uncertain threat. Where disbelief in the possibility of an earthquake, a tornado, or a flood is strong, the resultant damages from the event are likely to be greater than where awareness of the danger leads to effective precautionary action.

In this article we attempt to set down our imperfect understanding of variations in the perception of natural hazard, and to suggest some ways in which it affects the management of resource use. In so doing we are extending the notion that resources are best regarded for management purposes as culturally defined variables, by consideration of the cultural appraisal of natural hazard.

It may be argued that the uncertainties of natural hazards in resource management are only a special case of the more general problem of risk in any economic activity. Certainly there are many similarities. But it is only when man seeks to wrest from nature that which he perceives as useful to him that he is strongly challenged by the vagaries of natural phenomena acting over and above the usual uncertainties of economic activity. In other words, the management of resource use brings men into a closer contact with nature (be it viewed as friendly, malevolent, or neutral) where the extreme variations of the environment exercise a much more profound effect than in other economic activities.

---

* Assistant Professor of Geography, University of Toronto.
† Assistant Professor of Geography, Clark University, Worcester, Mass.

1. Niddrie, When the Earth Shook 36 (1962).

I

THE DEFINITION OF NATURAL HAZARDS

For a working definition of "natural hazards" we propose the following: Natural hazards are those elements in the physical environment, harmful to man and caused by forces extraneous to him. According to Zimmerman's view, the physical environment or nature is "neutral stuff," but it is human culture which determines which elements are considered to be "resources" or "resistances."[2] Considerable cultural variation exists in the conception of natural hazards; change occurs both in time and space.

In time, our notion of specific hazards and their causal agents frequently change. Consider, for example, the insurance concept of an "act of God." To judge by the volume of litigation, this concept is under constant challenge and is constantly undergoing redefinition. The "acts of God" of today are often tomorrow's acts of criminal negligence. Such changes usually stem from a greater potential to control the environment, although the potential is frequently not made actual until after God has shown His hand.

In space a varied concept of hazard is that of drought. A recent report adequately describes the variation as follows:

> There is a clue from prevailing usage that the term 'drought' reflects the relative insecurity of mankind in the face of a natural phenomenon that he does not understand thoroughly and for which, therefore, he has not devised adequate protective measures. A Westerner does not call a rainless month a 'drought,' and a Californian does not use the term even for an entire growing season that is devoid of rain, because these are usual occurrences and the developed water economy is well bolstered against them. Similarly, a dry period lasting several years, or even several decades, would not qualify as a drought if it caused no hardship among water users.[3]

This may be contrasted with the official British definition of an "absolute drought" which is "a period of at least 15 consecutive days to none of which is credited .01 inches of rain or more."[4]

Even such seemingly scientifically defined hazards as infective diseases seem to be subject to changes in interpretation, especially when applied to the assignment of the cause of death. Each decennial revision of the International Lists

---

2. Zimmermann, World Resources and Industries (1951); see also Zimmermann's diagram, *id.* at 13.

3. Thomas, The *Meteorological Phenomenon of Drought in the Southwest, 1942-1956*, at A8 (United States Geological Survey Prof. Paper No. 372-A, 1962).

4. Meteorological Office, United Kingdom Air Ministry, British Rainfall, 1958, at 10 (1963). This definition was introduced in British rainfall research in 1887.

of Causes of Death has brought important changes to some classes of natural hazards. Thus, the change from the fifth to the sixth revision found a decrease of approximately twenty-five per cent in deaths identified as caused by syphilis and its sequelae as a result of the new definition arising from ostensibly improved medical knowledge.[5]

The definability of hazard is a more sophisticated form of perceiving a hazard. It is more than mere awareness and often requires high scientific knowledge, *i.e.*, we must understand in order to define precisely. But regardless of whether we describe definitions of drought by western water users or the careful restatement of definitions by public health officials, all types of hazard are subject to wide variation in their definition—a function of the changing pace of man's knowledge and technology.

To complicate the problem further, the rise of urban-industrial societies has been coincident with a rapid increase in a type of hazard which may be described as quasi-natural. These hazards are created by man, but their harmful effects are transmitted through natural processes. Thus, man-made pollutants are carried downstream, radio-active fallout is borne by air currents, and pesticides are absorbed by plants, leaving residues in foods. The intricacies of the man-nature relationship are such that it is frequently not possible to ascribe a hazard exclusively to one class or the other (natural or quasi-natural). A case in point is the question of when fog (a natural hazard) becomes smog (quasi-natural).[6] Presumably some more or less arbitrary standard of smoke content could be developed.

In the discussion that follows, we specifically exclude quasi-natural hazards while recognizing the difficulty of distinguishing them in all cases. Our guide for exclusion is the consideration of principal causal agent.

II

A CLASSIFICATION OF NATURAL HAZARDS

Table I is an attempt to classify common natural hazards by their principal causal agent. It is but one of many ways that natural hazards might be ordered, but it is convenient for our purposes. The variety of academic disciplines that study aspects of these hazards is only matched by the number of governmental basic data collection agencies which amass information on these hazards. The most cohesive group is the climatic and meteorological hazards. The most

---

5. DHEW, Public Health Service, I Vital Statistics of the United States, 1950, at 31 (*Interpretation of Cause-of-Death Statistics*), 169 (*Mortality by Cause of Death*) (1954).

6. Glossary of Meteorology 516 (Huschke ed. 1959), defines "smog" as follows: A natural fog contaminated by industrial pollutants; a mixture of smoke and fog. This term coined in 1905 by Des Voeux, has experienced a recent rapid rise in acceptance but so far it has not been given precise definition.

diverse is the floral group which includes the doctor's concern with a minor fungal infection, the botanist's concern with a variety of plant diseases, and the hydrologist's concern with the effect of phreatophytes on the flow of water in streams and irrigation channels.

TABLE I

COMMON NATURAL HAZARDS BY PRINCIPAL CAUSAL AGENT

Geophysical		*Biological*	
CLIMATIC AND METEOROLOGICAL	GEOLOGICAL AND GEOMORPHIC	FLORAL	FAUNAL
Blizzards & Snow	Avalanches	Fungal Diseases *For example:*	Bacterial & Viral Diseases *For example:*
Droughts	Earthquakes	Athlete's foot	
Floods	Erosion (including soil erosion & shore and beach erosion)	Dutch elm Wheat stem rust Blister rust	Influenza Malaria Typhus
Fog		Infestations	Bubonic Plague Venereal
Frost	Landslides	*For example:*	Disease Rabies
Hailstorms	Shifting Sand	Weeds Phreatophytes	Hoof & Mouth Disease
Heat Waves	Tsunamis	Water hyacinth	Tobacco Mosaic
Hurricanes	Volcanic Eruptions	Hay Fever	Infestations *For example:*
Lightning Strokes & Fires		Poison Ivy	Rabbits Termites Locusts
Tornadoes			Grasshoppers
			Venomous Animal Bites

In a fundamental way, we sense a distinction between the causal agents of geo-physical and biologic hazards. This distinction does not lie in their effects, for both hazards work directly and indirectly on man and are found in both large and small scales. Rather, our distinction lies in the notion of prevent-ability, *i.e.*, the prevention of the occurrence of the natural phenomenon of hazardous potential as opposed to mere control of hazardous effects. A rough rule of thumb is that changes in nature are to be classed as prevention, but changes in man or his works are control.

Given this rule of thumb, it is clear that few hazards are completely pre-ventable. Prevention has been most successful in the area of floral and faunal hazards. Some such hazards (*e.g.*, malaria) have been virtually eliminated in the United States by preventive measures, but they are still common in other parts of the world.

At the present levels of technology, geophysical hazards cannot be prevented, while biological hazards can be prevented in most cases, subject only to economic and budgetary constraints.

We suggest that this is a basic distinction and directly related to the areal dimensions and the character and quantities of energy involved in these natural phenomena. While much encouraging work has been done, we still cannot prevent a hurricane, identify and destroy an incipient tornado, prevent the special concentration of precipitation that often induces floods, or even on a modest scale alter the pattern of winds that shift sand, or prevent the over-steepening and sub-soil saturation that induces landslides. We might again note the distinction between prevention and control: we can and do build landslide barriers to keep rock off highways, and we can and do attempt to stabilize shifting sand dunes.

Despite much loose discussion in popular journals, repeated surveys of progress in weather modification have not changed substantially from the verdict of the American Meteorological Society in 1957, which was that:

> Present knowledge of atmospheric processes offers no real basis for the belief that the weather or climate of a large portion of the country can be significantly modified by cloud seeding. It is not intended to rule out the possibility of large-scale modifications of the weather at some future time, but it is believed that, if possible at all, this will require methods that alter the large-scale atmospheric circulations, possibly through changes in the radiation balance.[7]

The non-preventability of the class of geophysical hazards has existed throughout the history of man and will apparently continue to do so for some time to come. Our training, interest, and experience has been confined to this class of hazards. Moreover, as geographers we are more comfortable when operating in the field of geophysical phenomena than biological. However, we do not know whether the tentative generalizations we propose apply only to geophysical hazards or to the whole spectrum of natural hazards. A priori speculation might suggest the hypothesis that men react to the non-preventable hazard, the true "act of God," in a special way, distinct from preventable hazards. Our observations to date incline us toward the belief that there is an

---

7. Senate Select Comm. on Nat'l Water Resources, 86th Cong., 2d Sess., *Weather Modification* 3 (Comm. Print No. 22, 1960); see also Batton & Kassander, *Randomized Seeding of Orographic Cumulus* (Univ. Chi. Meteorology Dep't Tech. Bull. No. 12, 1958); Greenfield, *A New Rational Approach to Weather-Control Research* (Rand Corp. Memo. No. RM-3205-NSF, 1962).

orderly or systematic difference in the perception of preventable and non-preventable natural hazards.

This arises from the hiatus between popular perception of hazard and the technical-scientific perception. To many flood-plain users, floods are preventable, *i.e.*, flood control can completely eliminate the hazard. Yet the technical expert knows that except for very small drainage areas no flood control works known can effectively prevent the flood-inducing concentration of precipitation, nor can they effectively control extremely large floods of very rare occurrence. On the other hand, in some parts of the world hoof and mouth disease is not considered preventable, although there is considerable evidence that it is preventable when there is a widespread willingness to suffer large economic losses by massive eradication of diseased cattle combined with vigorous control measures of vaccination.

The hiatus between the popular perception of hazard and the perception of the technician scientist is considered below in greater detail.

III

THE MAGNITUDE AND FREQUENCY OF HAZARDS

There is a considerable volume of scientific data on the magnitude and frequency of various hazards. The official publications of the agencies of the federal government contain much of it. Examples of frequency data are shown in Figures 1, 2, and 3. In general, these show spatial variations in the degree of hazard in terms of frequency occurrence. The measurement of magnitude is more difficult to portray in graphic form, but in general it is directly related to frequency. For example, areas with higher frequency of hailstorms are also likely to experience the most severe hailstorms. The magnitude of floods is more complex, and attempts to portray variations in magnitude of floods graphically have generally not been successful.[8] We have attempted to show variation in magnitude of floods for New York (Figure 4).

It is our finding that the variations in attitude to natural hazard cannot be explained directly in terms of magnitude and frequency. Differences in perception mean that the same degree of hazard is viewed differently. Part of this variation is due, no doubt, to differences in damage experienced, or in damage potential. In Tables II and III we have attempted to set out some examples of damage caused by natural hazards. These tables give some idea of the order of magnitude of damages to life and property. The estimates are in most cases crude. The loss figures given in Table II amount to about $12 billion. If we

---

8. See, *e.g.*, the maps prepared by M. Maurice Pardé in Comité National de Géographie, Atlas de France, Sheets 20, 22 (1934).

Figure 1

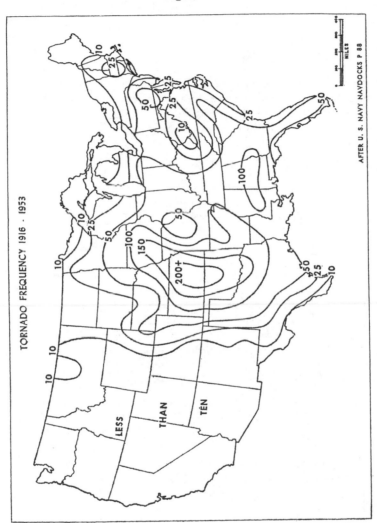

Figure 2

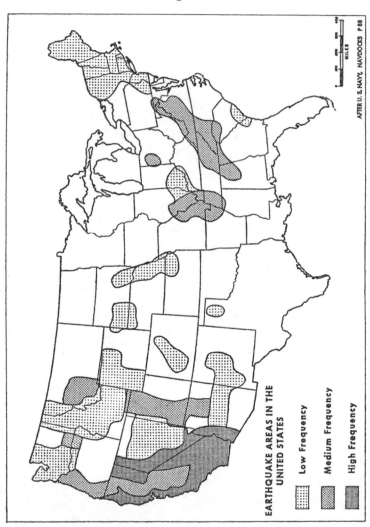

Figure 3

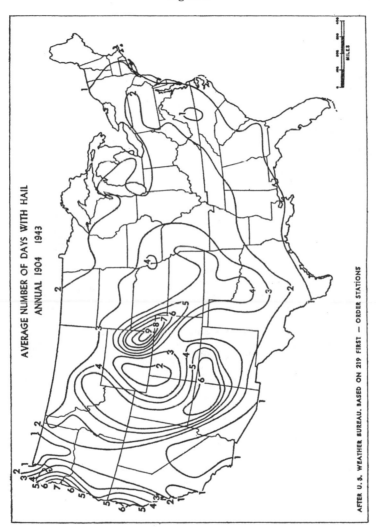

Figure 4

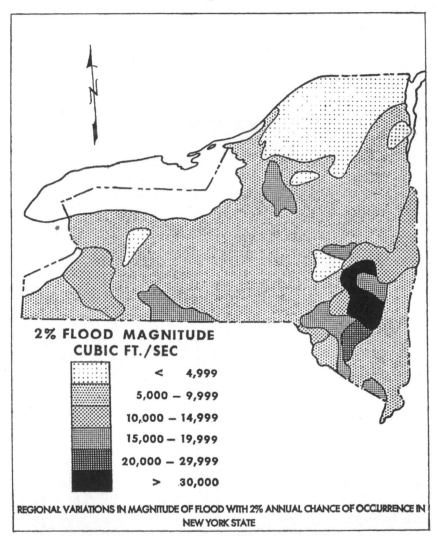

2% FLOOD MAGNITUDE
CUBIC FT./SEC

	< 4,999
	5,000 – 9,999
	10,000 – 14,999
	15,000 – 19,999
	20,000 – 29,999
	> 30,000

REGIONAL VARIATIONS IN MAGNITUDE OF FLOOD WITH 2% ANNUAL CHANCE OF OCCURRENCE IN NEW YORK STATE

add to this the $25 billion which are spent annually for health care,[9] and the large amounts spent for control and prevention of other natural hazards, then

---

9. Mushkin, *Health as an Investment*, 70 J. Political Economy 129, 137 (1962); see also Merriam, *Social Welfare Expenditures, 1960-1961*, 25 Social Security Bull. 3 (No. 11, 1962).

TABLE II

AVERAGE ANNUAL LOSSES FROM SELECTED NATURAL HAZARDS

Floods	$350 M (Million) to $1 Billion[10]
Hail	$53 M[11]
Hurricanes	$100 M[12]
Insects	$3,000 M[13]
Lightning Strokes	$100 M[14]
Plant Disease	$3,000 M[15]
Rats and Rodents	$1,000 M to $2,000 M[16]
Tornadoes	$45 M[17]
Weeds	$4,000 M[18]
TOTAL	$11,648 M to $13,268 M

TABLE III

LOSS OF LIFE FROM SELECTED NATURAL HAZARDS

Cold Waves	242[19]	(1959)
Floods	83.4[20]	Average annual, 1950-1959
Hay Fever	30[21]	(1959)
Heat Waves	207[22]	(1959)
Hurricanes	84.8[23]	Average annual, 1950-1959
Influenza	2,845[24]	(1959)
Lightning Strokes	600[25]	Average annual, Years not specified
Malaria	7[26]	(1959)
Plague	1[27]	(1959)
Tornadoes	204.3[28]	Average annual, 1950-1959
Tuberculosis	11,456[29]	(1959)
Venomous Bites & Stings	62[30]	(1959)
Venereal Disease	3,069[31]	(1959)

10. See notes 32-34 *infra.*

11. Flora, Hailstorms of the United States 3 (1956).

12. Our estimate.

13. Byerly, *Why We Need Loss Data*, Nat'l Academy of Science, Nat'l Research Council, *Losses Due to Agricultural Pests* 3 (Summary of Conference of the Agricultural Bd. Comm. on Agriculture Pests, Nov. 4-5, 1959).

14. Bureau of Yards & Docks, United States Navy, *Natural Disasters* 24 (Navdocks P-88, 1961).

15. Byerly, *op. cit. supra* note 13.

16. *Ibid.*

17. Flora, *op. cit. supra* note 11.

18. Byerly, *op. cit. supra* note 13.

19. DHEW, Public Health Service, II Vital Statistics of the United States 18-36 (1959).

20. Metropolitan Life Ins. Co., Statistical Bulletin, vol. 41, at 9 (April, 1960).

21. DHEW, Public Health Service, *op. cit. supra* note 19.

22. *Ibid.*

23. Metropolitan Life Ins. Co., *op. cit. supra* note 20.

it is clear that our struggle against natural hazards is of the same order of magnitude as the defense budget!

That these estimates are not highly reliable is demonstrated in the wide variation of some of them. Flood damages, for example, are placed at $350 million by the United States Weather Bureau,[32] over $900 million by the United States Army Corps of Engineers,[33] and $1,200 million by the United States Department of Agriculture.[34]

There are partial explanations for the wide discrepencies in these and other similar data. These usually include such questions as definitions used, time period employed, methods of computation, accuracy and completeness of reporting, changing dollar values, and so on. However, even when all these differences are taken into account the perception of natural hazards still varies greatly. There is variation in the resource manager's perception of hazard. Managers as a group differ in their view as opposed to scientific and technical personnel, and the experts, in turn, differ among themselves. These differences persist even when all the scientific evidence upon which conclusions are based is identical. It is to this complex problem of differing perceptions-that we now turn.

IV

VARIATIONS IN PERCEPTION

It is well established that men view differently the challenges and hazards of their natural environment. In this section we will consider some of the variations in view or perception of natural hazard. In so doing we will raise more questions than we shall answer; this is a reflection of the immaturity and youth of this line of research.

Our scheme will be to consider the *within group* and *between group* variation in perception of two well-defined groups: resource users, who are the managers of natural resources directly affected by natural hazards (including of course

---

24. DHEW, Public Health Service, *op. cit. supra* note 19.
25. Bureau of Yards & Docks, *op. cit. supra* note 14.
26. DHEW, Public Health Service, *op. cit. supra* note 19.
27. *Ibid.*
28. Metropolitan Life Ins. Co., *op. cit. supra* note 20.
29. DHEW, Public Health Service, *op. cit. supra* note 19.
30. *Ibid.*
31. *Ibid.*
32. Weather Bureau, Dep't of Commerce, Climatological Data, National Summary, Annual 1961, at 85 (1962).
33. Senate Select Comm. on Nat'l Water Resources, 86th Cong., 2d Sess., *Floods and Flood Control* 5-7 (Comm. Print No. 15, 1960).
34. Senate Comm. on Banking and Currency, *Federal Disaster Insurance*, S. Rep. No. 1313, 84th Cong., 2d Sess., 69-71 (1956).

their own persons),[35] and technical and scientific personnel—individuals with specialized training and directly charged with study or control of natural hazards.

A. *Variation in the Perception of Natural Hazard Among Scientific Personnel*

The specialized literature is replete with examples of differences in hazard perception among experts. They fail to perceive the actual nature of the hazard, its magnitude, and its location in time and space. Technical personnel differ among each other, and the use of reputable methods often provides estimates of hazards of great variance from one another.

Such variation is due in small part to differences in experience and training, vested organizational interest, and even personality. But in a profound and fundamental way, such variation is a product of human ignorance.

The Epistemology of Natural Hazard

We have emphasized the nature of natural hazard as phenomena of nature with varying effects on man, ranging from harmless to catastrophic. To know and to fully understand these natural phenomena is to give to man the opportunity of avoiding or circumventing the hazard. To know fully, in this sense, is to be able to predict the location in time and space and the size or duration of the natural phenomenon potentially harmful to man. Despite the sophistication of modern science or our ability to state the requirements for such a knowledge system, there seems little hope that basic geophysical phenomena will ever be fully predictable. No foreseeable system of data gathering and sensing equipment seems likely to pinpoint the discharge of a lightning bolt or the precise path of a tornado.

Given this inherent limitation, almost all estimation of hazard is probabilistic in content, and these probabilities may be computed either by counting (relative frequency) or by believing in some underlying descriptive frequency distribution. The probability of most hazardous events is determined by counting the observed occurrence of similar events. In so doing we are manipulating three variables: the magnitude of the event, its occurrence in time, and its occurrence in space.

For some hazards the spatial variable might fortunately be fixed. Volcanic eruptions often take place at a fixed point, and rivers in humid areas follow well-defined stream courses. For other hazards there may be broadly defined belts such as storm paths or earthquake regions (see Figure 2). There are no geophysical hazards that are apparently evenly or randomly distributed over

---

35. A definition of "resource manager," as we use the term, is found in White, *The Choice of Use in Resource Management*, 1 Natural Resources J. 23, 24 (1961).

the earth's surface, but some, such as lightning, approach being ubiquitous over large regions.

The size or magnitude of the hazard varies, and, given the long-term human adjustment to many hazards, this can be quite important. Blizzards are common on the Great Plains, but a protracted blizzard can bring disaster to a large region.[36] On great alluvial flood plains small hummocks provide dry sites for settlement, but such hummocks are overwhelmed by a flood event of great magnitude.

Magnitude can be thought of as a function of time based on the apparent truism of extreme events: if one waits long enough, there will always be an event larger than that previously experienced. In the case of geophysical events, waiting may involve several thousand years. Graphically, this is presented for fifty years in Figure 5 for two common hazards.

Most harmful natural phenomena are rare events; if they were not, we humans would probably have been decimated before we became entrenched on this planet. Since the counting of events is the major method of determining probabilities, rare events by their nature are not easily counted. Equally disturbing is the possibility that by climatic change, or improved scientific knowledge, or human interference, the class of natural events may change and create further uncertainties in the process of observing and recording.

Faced with a high degree of uncertainty, but pressed by the requirements of a technical society for judgments and decisions, scientific and technical personnel make daily estimates of hazard with varying degrees of success.

An example of unsuccessful estimating is seen in the case of the San Carlos Reservoir on the Gila River in Arizona. Completed in 1928, this reservoir has never been filled to more than sixty-eight per cent of its capacity and has been empty on several occasions.[37] The length of stream flow record on which the design of the dam was based was short (approximately thirty years), but it was not necessarily too short. The considerable overbuilding of this dam, according to Langbein and Hoyt, was due in part to the failure to take into account the increasing variability of annual flows as indicated in the coefficient of variation. In their view, the San Carlos Reservoir is "a victim of a deficiency in research to develop the underlying patterns of fluctuations in river flow."[38] To our knowledge, this deficiency still exists, and we have doubts as to whether such patterns can actually be determined.

Until recent years, that highly reputable practitioner of actuarial precision,

---

36. Calef, *The Winter of 1948-49 in the Great Plains*, 40 Ass'n Am. Geographers, Annals 267 (1950).

37. Langbein & Hoyt, Water Facts for the Nation's Future 229 (1959).

38. *Id.* at 230.

Figure 5

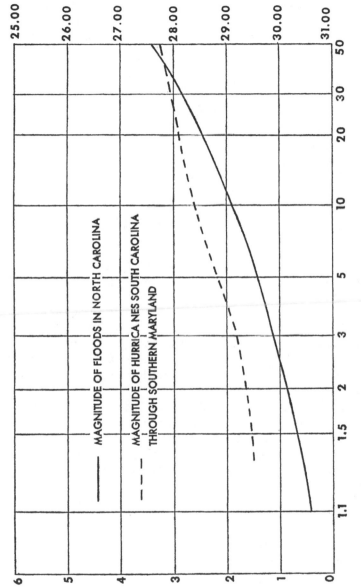

CENTRAL PRESSURE INDEX (Inches)

——— MAGNITUDE OF FLOODS IN NORTH CAROLINA

– – – MAGNITUDE OF HURRICA NES SOUTH CAROLINA THROUGH SOUTHERN MARYLAND

FREQUENCY BY RECURRENCE INTERVAL (Years)

RATIO TO MEAN ANNUAL FLOOD

SOURCE: NATIONAL HURRICA NE RESEARCH PROJECT REPORT NO. 33; FLOODS IN NORTH CAROLINA; MAGNITUDE AND FREQUENCY

the insurance industry, charged rates for hail insurance that were largely a matter of guesswork.[39] Flora notes that

> often in widely level areas, where we now know that the hail risk varies but little over a distance of a hundred miles or more, one county might have several damaging hailstorms while adjacent counties might escape entirely. In such instances, the county which had suffered severe damage would be given a much higher insurance rate than others.[40]

With regard to flood insurance, the industry has long apologized for its unwillingness to even enter the fray, using words similar to these:

> [The insurance company underwriters believe that] specific flood insurance covering fixed location properties in areas subject to recurrent floods cannot feasibly be written because of the virtual certainty of loss, its catastrophic nature and the reluctance or inability of the public to pay the premium charge required to make the insurance self sustaining.[41]

Some hazards have been only belatedly recognized. Langbein and Hoyt cite the fact that in the *American Civil Engineers Handbook*, published in 1930, there are no instructions about reservoir sedimentation.[42]

Public agencies charged with flood control responsibilities have had to make estimates of the long run recurrence of these phenomena. Despite a great deal of work and ingenuity, results are not overly impressive. Three highly respected methods of flood frequency analysis place the long run average return period of the largest flood of record in the Lehigh Valley as either twenty-seven, forty-five, or seventy-five years.[43]

The disparate views and perceptions of technical and scientific personnel are a reflection of our ignorance of the chance occurrence of events, and more fundamentally of our lack of understanding of the physical forces themselves. There is little hope of eliminating this uncertainty, and the technical-scientific community follows the course of recognizing it, defining it, and finally learning to live with it.

---

39. Flora, Hailstorms of the United States 56 (1956).
40. *Ibid.*
41. American Ins. Ass'n, Studies of Floods and Flood Damage 3 (1956).
42. Langbein & Hoyt, *op. cit. supra* note 37, at 232.
43. *Delaware River Basin, New York, New Jersey, Pennsylvania, and Delaware,* H.R. Doc. No. 522, 87th Cong., 2d Sess., VI, Plate 42 (1962).

428   *NATURAL RESOURCES JOURNAL*   [Vol. 3

B. *Variations in the Perception of Natural Hazard Among Resource Managers*

Resource users or managers do not display uniformity in their perception of natural hazard any more than do scientific and technical personnel. Not being experts, they have less knowledge or understanding of the various possible interpretations of data and are often amazed at the lack of agreement among the professionals. Their views may be expected to coincide insofar as the lay managers subscribe to the various popular myths of hazard perception (whether "it can't happen here," or "after great droughts come great rains," or "a little rain stills a great wind"). But in this age of enlightenment, perception is not easily limited to such aphorisms. Differences in perception arise both among users of the same resource and between users of different resources.

1. Perception Among Users of the Same Resource

Urban and rural flood-plain users display differences in the perception of flood hazard. Our own studies of urban[44] and agricultural[45] flood-plain users suggest a greater hazard sensitivity in terms of awareness on the part of agricultural land users. However, the frequency of hazard that encourages certain responses on the part of resource users is approximately equal for both urban and agricultural land users.[46]

The limited work on flood plains in variation of perception between users suggests three explanatory factors: (1) the relation of the hazard to the dominant resource use, including in agriculture the ratio between area subject to flooding and the total size of the management unit, (2) the frequency of occurrence of floods, and (3) variations in degree of personal experience. Interestingly, there seems to be little or no significant effect in hazard perception by the few generalized indicators of level of social class or education that have been tested against hazard perception.

The first factor is essentially a reflection of an ends-means scheme of resource use. We would expect to find a heightened hazard perception in those cases, such as drought in an agricultural region or beach erosion on a waterfront cottage, where the hazard is directly related to the resource use. Where it is incidental, such as lightning or tornadoes, the perception of hazard is variant, vague, and often whimsical.

The second factor suggests that the frequency of natural events is related

44. Kates, *Hazard and Choice Perception in Flood Plain Management* (Univ. Chi. Dep't of Geography Research Paper No. 78, 1962).

45. Burton, *Types of Agricultural Occupance of Flood Plains in the United States* (Univ. Chi. Dep't of Geography Research Paper No. 75, 1962).

46. Kates, *Perceptual Regions and Regional Perception in Flood Plain Management*, Papers of the Regional Science Ass'n (1963). [Ed. note: A volume number has not been assigned to this set of papers.]

to the perception of hazard. Where the events in question are frequent, there is little variation among users in their perception. The same holds true where the event is infrequent, for here the failure to perceive a significant hazard is widely shared. It is in the situation of moderate frequency that one expects to find (and does find) considerable variation among resource users.

The third factor is also related to frequency. One would expect that when personally experienced a natural event would be more meaningful and lead to heightened perception. The limited evidence to date does not clearly bear this out. There is a pronounced ability to share in the common experience, and newcomers often take on the shared or dominant perception of the community. Also given a unique or cyclical interpretation of natural events, the experience of an event often tends to allay future anxiety; this is in keeping with the old adage about lightning not striking in the same place twice. Thus the effect of experience as a determinant of hazard perception is considerably blurred.

2. Perception Between Different Resource Users

Differences in perception are found between coastal and flood-plain land resource users in areas subject to storm damage or erosion. Unfortunately, we cannot say more about hazard perception differences between resource users. To our knowledge, they have never been carefully explored, although such study would undoubtedly throw much light on the problem of comparing the resource management policies of different groups and nations.[47] Some historical comment provides suggestions for the direction that such differences might take.

In a recent article, David Lowenthal notes the changes in our attitude towards wilderness. Once viewed as awesome and tyrannical, nature in the wild is now wonderful and brings us close to the spirit of the Creator. "Our forefathers mastered a continent; today we celebrate the virtues of the vanquished foe."[48] Nature itself has become synonymous with virtue.[49] This subject has been examined in some detail by Hans Huth in his study of the attitudes that led to the establishment of the conservation movement.[50]

The rapid expansion of agriculture in the Great Plains during a relatively humid period by settlers from areas with different environmental experience and background is well known. Unprepared for the climatic hazards they encountered, many settlers "were predisposed to believe that the climate was be-

---

47. For one such attempt see Comparisons in Resources Management (Jarrett ed. 1961).

48. Lowenthal, *Not Every Prospect Pleases—What Is Our Criterion for Scenic Beauty?*, 12 Landscape 19 (Winter, 1962-1963).

49. Lowenthal, *Nature and the American Creed of Virtue*, 9 Landscape 24 (Winter, 1959-1960).

50. Huth, Nature and the American (1957).

coming permanently more humid. In fact, many thought that it was the spread of cultivation that brought about an increase in rainfall."[51]

Study of other hazards suggests that there is considerable difference in the social acceptance of personal injury depending on the kind of hazard that was the causal agent. Edward Suchman notes that "a report of a few cases of polio will empty the beaches, but reports of many more deaths by automobile accidents on the roads to the beaches will have little effect." He suggests that one explanation may lie "in the greater popular acceptance of accidents as inevitable and uncontrollable."[52]

A contrast in awareness of natural hazards is exemplified by a warning sign observed in a coastal location on the island of Hawaii. Affixed to a palm tree in an area subject to *tsunamis* at the front door and the hazard of volcanic eruptions and lava flows at the back door (Mauna Loa volcano), this sign merely advises the reader: "Beware of falling coconuts!"

C. *Variation in Natural Hazard Perception Between Technical-Scientific Personnel and Resource Users*

It is our impression that there is considerable divergence between the perception of natural hazard of technical-scientific personnel and resource users. In the case of floods such divergence is widespread.

Although we have emphasized in the previous section the variation in probability that technical people might assign to a given flood event, these are essentially differences in estimation. Over the past several years we have interviewed or spoken with well over one-hundred technical people concerned with floods, and we have never met one who discounted the possibility of a flood occurring again in a valley that had been previously flooded. By contrast, out of 216 flood-plain dwellers interviewed in a variety of small urban places between 1960 and 1962, all of whom had a measurable flood hazard, some 84 categorically did not expect to be flooded in the future.[53]

Another example of the disparity between the technical and resource user perception is found in the occasional experience of the rejection of plans for protective works by at least part of the resource users, even when the cost of such works directly to the users in monetary terms was nominal or non-existent. In Fairfield, Connecticut some users of waterfront property opposed the construction of a protective dike along the shore, principally on the contention that such protection "would seriously interfere with their view and result in loss

---

51. Thornthwaite, *Climate and Settlement in the Great Plains, Climate and Man*, USDA Yearbook 177, 184 (1941).

52. Suchman, *A Conceptual Analysis of the Accident Phenomenon*, Ass'n for Aid of Crippled Children, Behavioral Approaches to Accident Research 40 (1961).

53. Kates, *op. cit. supra* note 46.

of breeze."[54] Similarly, dune-levelling which is universally condemned by technical personnel as destructive of nature's main protection against the ravages of the sea, is widely practiced (as at West Dennis, Massachusetts) to improve the scenic view or to make room for more buildings.

Is such behavior adopted out of ignorance of the hazard; is it symptomatic of the irrationality of resource users in hazard situations; or is there some other explanation? While there are resource users who act in total ignorance of natural hazards, their number is relatively small. Nor can the difference simply be explained away in terms of irrationality. In our view, the difference arises primarily out of the evaluation of the hazard. We offer the following explanation for divergence in hazard evaluation:

1. For some resource users, the differences in perceiving a natural hazard may be a reflection of those existing among scientific and technical personnel themselves. Given the great uncertainty that surrounds the formulation of an "objective" estimate of hazard, the estimate made by a resource user may be no more divergent than that supplied by the use of a different formula or the addition of more data.

2. For some resource users we suspect the divergence in hazard perception may be as fundamental as basic attitudes towards nature. Technical-scientific estimates of hazard assume the neutrality of nature. There are resource users who perceive otherwise, conceiving of nature as malevolent or benevolent. Our language is full of metaphors and descriptions of "Mother nature," "bountiful nature," or, conversely, of "angry storms." Besides attributing motivation to nature, there is also the distinction of man's relation to nature. One recent anthropological study, using a cross-cultural approach, developed a man-nature classification comprising man over nature, man with nature, and man under nature.[55] Each of these three divergent points of view is represented by the following statement:

> *Man Subject to Nature.* 'My people have never controlled the rain, wind, and other natural conditions, and probably never will. There have always been good years and bad years. That is the way it is, and if you are wise you will take it as it comes and do the best you can.'

> *Man With Nature.* 'My people help conditions and keep things going by working to keep in close touch with all the forces which make the rain, the snow, and other conditions. It is when we do the

54. *An Interim Hurricane Survey of Fairfield, Connecticut,* H.R. Doc. No. 600, 87th Cong., 2d Sess., 14 (1962).

55. Kluckholm & Strodtbeck, Variations in Value Orientations (1961).

right things—live in the proper way—and keep all that we have—the land, the stock and the water—in good condition, that all goes along well.'

Man Over Nature. 'My people believe that it is man's job to find ways to overcome weather and other conditions just as they have overcome so many things. They believe they will one day succeed in doing this and may even overcome droughts and floods.'[56]

Samples of respondents were selected from five different cultural groups in an area of western New Mexico, and their responses were distributed as shown in Table IV.

TABLE IV
VIEWS OF MAN AND NATURE BY CULTURAL GROUPS (in percentages)

View of Nature Cultural Group	Man Subject to Nature	Man with Nature	Man over Nature	Number Interviewed
Spanish-Americans	71.7	10.9	17.4	23
Texans	30.0	22.5	47.5	20
Mormons	25.0	55.0	20.0	20
Zuni Indians	19.0	62.0	19.0	21
Rimrock Navaho Indians	18.2	68.2	13.6	22

Source: Variations in Value Orientations, Appendix 4.

The wide divergence of human views of nature, as illustrated in Table IV, is strong testimony to support our contention that variations in perception are significant and are likely to affect management policies. A society in which belief in the dominance of nature is strong, such as among the Spanish-Americans, is less likely to be conscious of the possibilities of environment control than one in which belief in the dominance of man over nature is more pronounced, as among the Texans.

The belief in technical engineering solutions to problems of hazard is widespread in American society. This belief in the efficacy of man's control over nature is frequently encountered in studies of hazard perception. Thus, it is no longer surprising to find protective powers ascribed to flood control works far beyond their designed capacity. Notable examples are seen in those persons who consider themselves protected by dams downstream from their flood-plain location, or who are satisfied that floods will not occur in the future because a government agency has been established to study the problem.[57]

---

56. *Id.* at 86-87.
57. Such a response was given to Burton during recent field work in Belleville, Ontario. There, two respondents considered that the establishment of the Moira Valley Conservation Authority meant that no more floods would occur. Such is, in fact, far from the case. The Authority has not been successful in its attempts to have protective works constructed.

3. How much of the divergence in hazard perception can be ascribed to fundamental views of nature is speculative. Much more of the divergence is explicable in terms of basic attitudes towards uncertainty.

We are convinced that there is a fundamental difference between the attitudes or values of technical-scientific personnel and resource users towards uncertainty. Increasingly the orientation and formal training of scientific personnel emphasizes an indeterminate and probabilistic view of the world. Common research techniques involve the use of estimates that reflect imperfect knowledge, and stress is placed on extracting the full value of partial knowledge.

We have considerable social science and psychological theory and some evidence that resource users are unwilling or unable to adopt this probabilistic view of the world and are not able to live with uncertainty in such a manner as to extract full value from partial knowledge.

Malinowsky held that every human culture possesses both sound scientific knowledge for coping with the natural environment and a set of magical practices for coping with problems that are beyond rational-empirical control.[58] Festinger describes the role of the concept of "cognitive dissonance" as a motivating force, which may lead to actions or beliefs concerning the state of nature that do not accord with rational or logical expectations.[59] For example, he cites the case of a severe earthquake in India in 1934, in which some people experienced the earthquake but saw no evidence of damage which was quite localized. This situation apparently led to the circulation of rumors which helped to reduce the dissonance created by the fear generated by the earthquake and the absence of signs of damage. People were left in a state of fear but no longer saw reason to be afraid. The rumors that circulated in such a situation have been described by Prasad[60] and include the following:

> There will be a severe cyclone at Patna between January 18th and January 19th. [The earthquake occurred on January 15th.]

> *   *   *   *

> There will be a severe earthquake on the lunar eclipse day.

> *   *   *   *

> January 23rd will be a fatal day. Unforeseeable calamities will arise.

58. Malinowsky, Magic, Science, and Religion in Science, Religion, and Reality (Needham ed. 1925).

59. Festinger, The Motivating Effect of Cognitive Dissonance in Assessment of Human Motives (Lindzey ed. 1960); Festinger, A Theory of Cognitive Dissonnance (1947).

60. Prasad, *A Comparative Study of Rumors and Reports in Earthquakes*, 41 British J. Psychology 129 (1950).

In our experience resource users appear to behave in ways that suggest an individual effort to dispel uncertainty. Among flood-plain users and in coastal areas, the most common variant is to view floods and storms as a repetitive or even cyclical phenomenon. Thus the essential randomness that characterizes the uncertain pattern of the hazard is replaced by a determinate order in which history is seen as repeating itself at regular intervals. Some experiments in the perception of independent events and probability distributions have been conducted by psychologists. The results of such rigorous tests are interesting but are not yet at the level that affords useful generalizations about the real world.[61] Where the hazard is made repetitive, the past becomes a guide to the approximate timing and magnitude of future hazardous events. An historical example of this is documented by Niddrie.[62] A mild earthquake was recorded in London on February 8, 1750. A somewhat more severe earthquake occurred exactly one lunar month (twenty-eight days) later on March 8th. Predictions were made that a third and more terrible earthquake would occur on April 5th. Niddrie describes the events which followed:

> A contagious panic spreading through every district of the town required only the slightest indication that those who could afford to leave the town unobtrusively were doing so, for a wholesale evacuation to begin. The gullible who could not leave bought pills 'which were very good against the earthquake.' As Doomsday came nearer whole families moved to places of safety . . . . By April 3rd it was impossible to obtain lodgings in any neighboring town or village.[63]

When no earthquake occurred on April 5th the prophesies changed to April 8th as though the number eight had some special connotations for earthquakes. Niddrie reports that in fact few of the gentry and well-to-do returned to London until April 9th.

Another view, which is less common, is the act of "wishing it away" by denigrating the quality of the rare natural event to the level of the commonplace, or conversely of elevating it to a unique position and ascribing its occurrence to a freak combination of circumstances incapable of repetition. Either variant has the advantage of eliminating the uncertainty which surrounds hazardous natural phenomenon.

The last alternative view that we can suggest is the completely indeterminate

61. Hake & Hyman, *Perception of the Statistical Structure of a Random Series of Binary Symbols*, 45 J. Experimental Psychology 64 (1953); Cohen & Hansel, *The Idea of a Distribution*, 46 British J. Psychology 111 (1955); Cohen & Hansel, *The Idea of Independence*, 46 British J. Psychology 178 (1955); Hyman & Jenkin, *Involvement and Set as Determinants of Behavioral Stereotypy*, 2 Psychological Rep. 131 (1956).
62. Niddrie, When the Earth Shook 20-34 (1962).
63. *Id.* at 29-30.

position that denies completely the knowability of natural phenomena. For this group, all is in the hands of God or the gods. Convinced of the utter inscrutability of Divine Providence, the resource users have no need to trouble themselves about the vagaries of an uncertain nature, for it can serve no useful purpose to do so.

These viewpoints are summarized in Table V.

TABLE V

COMMON RESPONSES TO THE UNCERTAINTY OF NATURAL HAZARDS

Eliminate the Hazard		*Eliminate the Uncertainty*	
DENY OR DENI-GRATE ITS EXISTENCE	DENY OR DENI-GRATE ITS RE-CURRENCE	MAKING IT DE-TERMINATE AND KNOWABLE	TRANSFER UN-CERTAINTY TO A HIGHER POWER
"We have no floods here, only high water."	"Lightning never strikes twice in the same place."	"Seven years of great plenty . . . . After them seven years of famine."	"It's in the hands of God."
"It can't happen here."	"It's a freak of nature."	"Floods come every five years."	"The government is taking care of it."

1. Divergence of Values

Natural hazards are not perceived in a vacuum. They are seen as having certain effects or consequences, and it is rather the consequences that are feared than the hazard phenomenon per se. Another source of divergence in the perception of natural hazard between technical-scientific personnel and resource users is related to the perceived consequences of the hazard. For very good and sound reasons the set of probabilities related to the occurrence of a natural phenomenon at a given place is not the same as the set of probabilities of hazard for an individual. Given the high level of mobility in our society, the nature of the personal hazard is constantly changing, while the probabilities for a given place remain fixed (although not precisely known).

Thus, the soil erosion that concerns the technicians in Western Iowa, reported in a recent study,[64] is an ongoing continuous long-term hazard. The carefully calculated long-term rates of erosion, however, do not have the same meaning for farmers who averaged only nine years as individual farm managers, or where ownership itself changes hands every fourteen years on the average. Soil losses arise from a series of discrete physical events with intensive rains and high winds acting as the major erosional force. The long-term

---

64. Held, Blase & Timmons, *Soil Erosion and Some Means for Its Control* (Iowa State Univ. Agri. and Home Econ. Experiment Sta. Special Rep. No. 29, 1962).

average of these erosional events may have meaning for the continued occupancy of the agriculture of this area. Hence, the technician's concern for the cumulative soil loss. But given the short average managerial period, the cumulative soil loss seems hardly worth the cost and effort involved in its control for the individual manager.

2. The Case of the Modern Homesteaders

Evan Vogt's study of the "Modern Homesteader"[65] provides a case study that exemplifies the types of divergence that we have been describing.

Homestead, the site of Vogt's studies during 1951-1952, is in his own words "a small dry-land, bean-farming community" of 200 people in western New Mexico.[66] It was founded in the early 1930's by families from the South Plains Region of western Texas and Oklahoma, but prior to the deep drought of 1934-1936. While spurred by low agricultural prices, Vogt felt they migrated for primarily what they perceived as a good farming opportunity, a chance to receive 640 acres for sixty-eight dollars in fees and residential and improvement investments.[67]

By 1932 eighty-one families had obtained sections under what was objectively governmental encouragement to agricultural settlement in an area with an average rainfall of about twelve inches. By 1935 the official perception of the suitability of the natural environment for agriculture had changed drastically. Under the Taylor Grazing Act,[68] all the land in the area which was still in the public domain was classified for grazing, and no additional homestead applications were accepted. The official estimate had changed, but that of the local citizens had not. To this day they perceive of their submarginal farming area as one quite suitable for dry land farming. In so doing, their perception is at considerable variance with that of the governmental technicians in a variety of ways.

As we suggested before, total ignorance of natural hazards is uncommon. While drought and frost are perennial hazards (two decades have provided seven good years, seven average years, and six crop failures), these were not ignorant city folk lured to the Plains by free land. They came from agricultural families in an area of less than twenty inches average rainfall. They do, however, perceive the marginality of the area in their own fashion. So marked is the divergence of this perception that Vogt reports the following:

> But through the critical days of 'battle' with the government, which
> had defined their community as 'submarginal' and unsuitable for

65. Vogt, Modern Homesteaders (1955).
66. *Id.* at 1.
67. *Id.* at 17-18.
68. 48 Stat. 1269 (1934), as amended, 43 U.S.C. §§ 315-315r (1958).

agriculture, there emerged in the Homesteaders a sense of mission
in life: To demonstrate to the experts in the Departments of Agriculture and Interior that the Homestead area is farming country
and that they can 'make a go of it' in this semi-arid land. They point
to the fact that Pueblo Indians made a living by farming in the area
long before the white man arrived. There is a general feeling that
somehow the surveys and investigations made by the experts must
be wrong. They insist that the Weather Bureau has falsified the rainfall figures that were submitted by the Homestead Weather station
in the 1930's, and indeed they stopped maintaining a weather station because they felt that 'the figures were being used against us.'[69]

Vogt mentions in passing another divergence in hazard perception. Homesteaders appear alert to the high westerly wind hazard that erodes the top soil,
and they strip crop and plow across the line of this prevailing wind. In so
doing, they look askance at the elaborate terraces constructed by the Soil
Conservation Service in the 1930's because these terraces are on the contour,
and contour plowing itself inevitably results in some of the rows lying in the
direct path of the westerly winds.[70]

Faced with continued drought, sandstorms, and killing frosts, the "Homesteaders" exemplify much of what has been discussed in this paper. Vogt finds
the predominant attitude as that of nature being something to be mastered and,
arising from this, a heady optimism in the face of continued vicissitudes. He
finds the strong need to eliminate uncertainty to the point of not collecting
weather data as reported above, or through the widespread resort to agricultural magic, involving signs of the zodiac, planting by the moon, and water
witching. It is in this last act, the use of water witching, that we find direct
parallels with the behavior of flood-plain users. The geology of the Homestead
area as it relates to ground water supply is one of considerable uncertainty.
The geological structure generates an uncertainty as to the depth and amount
of water available at a particular point. Faced with such uncertainty, there
was a strong-felt need to hire the local water witch to dowse the wells. While
the performance ratio of successful wells to dry holes appeared equal whether
they were witched or not, Vogt gives a convincing explanation that witching
provides a determinate response to uncertainty where the best that the local soil
conservation geologists could provide was a generalized description of the
ground water situation. Whether, as in Vogt's terms, the motive is to reduce
anxiety, or in Festinger's, to reduce cognitive dissonance, or as we would put
it, to eliminate uncertainty, there is the apparently strong drive to make the
indeterminate determinate.

---

69. Vogt, *op. cit. supra* note 65, at 68.
70. *Id.* at 70.

In conclusion, Vogt emphasizes

> that despite more secure economic alternatives elsewhere, most 'Homesteaders' choose to remain in the community and assume the climatic risks rather than abandon the independence of action they cherish and the leisure they enjoy for the more routinized and subordinate roles they would occupy elsewhere.[71]

3. Levels of Significance in Hazard Perception

There are men who plow up semi-arid steppes, who build villages on the flanks of volcanoes, and who lose one crop in three to floods. Are they irrational? Or, to put it another way, having looked at the variation in hazard perception and speculated on the causes of variation, what can be concluded about the rationality of hazard perception? In general, we find absent from almost every natural phenomena a standard for the objective (*i.e.*, true) probability of an event's occurrence. Even if such existed, we are not sure that man can assimilate such probabilities sufficiently to be motivated to act upon them. If decisions are made in a prohibilistic framework, what level of probability is sufficient for action? In the terms of statistics, what level of significance is appropriate? What amount of hazard or error is tolerable? Science is of little help here, since levels of statistical significance are chosen at ninety-five per cent or ninety-nine per cent primarily by convention.

Despite the impressive growth of game theory, the growing literature of decision-strategies, and some psychological experimentation with perceived probabilities, the artificiality of the game or laboratory seems to provide at best only limited insights into this complex phenomenon. On the other hand, the derivation of empirical observations, *i.e.*, estimates of the perceived frequency of events or perceived probabilities at which decisions are actually made, provides almost insuperable research difficulties.

In the last analysis, we seem destined to judge the rationality of man's actions vis-à-vis natural hazard out of a mixture of hindsight and prejudice. For the successful gambler in the game against nature there are but a few lonely voices crying that the odds will overtake him. The unsuccessful is clearly judged as foolhardy, ignorant, or irrational. Our prejudice expresses itself in our attitudes towards uncertainty, our preferences for certain types of risk, and how we feel about the objects of resource management.

CONCLUSION

There is a wide variation in the day-to-day management practices of resource users, even within culturally homogeneous groups. We believe that the varia-

---

71. *Id.* at 176.

tions in hazard perception reported in this article are an important explanatory variable. Unfortunately, careful studies of variation in resource management practices are few and far between. Some of the recent studies of innovation[72] and the study of farm practices in western Iowa, already cited,[73] approach what we have in mind. To our knowledge there have been no studies which adequately describe variations in management practice and rigorously attempt to assess the role of differing perception.

We can say that there is good reason to believe that variations in perception of hazard among resource managers tends to diminish over time. Those who are unwilling or unable to make the necessary adjustments in a hazardous situation are eliminated, either because disaster overtakes them or because they voluntarily depart. Those who remain tend to share in a uniformity of outlook.

Long-term occupancy of high hazard areas is never really stable, even where it has persisted over time. A catastrophe, a long run of bad years, a rising level of aspiration marked by the unwillingness to pay the high costs of survival—each provides stimulants to change. The "Modern Homesteaders," while determined to stay put and exhibiting a high degree of uniformity in their assessment of the environment and its hazards, may yet yield to a combination of an extended run of drought and frost and the lure of a more affluent society. Long-term occupancy, while potentially unstable, is still marked by a tenacity to persist, reinforced, we think, by the uniformity of hazard perception that develops over time. Thus all of the homesteaders who took jobs elsewhere in the bad drought of 1950 returned to the community. More dramatic is the return of the residents of Tristan da Cunha to their volcanic island home.

We have no evidence of a similar growth in accord between resource users and scientific-technical personnel. Clearly, variations in perception may profoundly affect the chances of success of a new management proposal developed by the experts. Such new programs are constantly being devised, but assessments of past programs are seldom found. George Macinko's review of the Columbia Basin project is a recent welcome exception.[74] Rarely do such studies review programs in terms of divergence of perception. L. Schuyler Fonaroff's article on differences in view between the Navajo and the Indian Service is another exception which proves the rule.[75]

While lacking many detailed statements of this divergence, we can nevertheless state the implication of our findings to date. The divergence in perception

72. See the bibliography in Lionberger, Adoption of New Ideas and Practices (1960).

73. Held, Blase & Timmons, *op. cit. supra* note 64.

74. Macinko, *The Columbia Basin Project, Expectations, Realizations, Implications*, 53 Geography Rev. 185 (1963).

75. Fonaroff, *Conservation and Stock Reduction on the Navajo Tribal Range*, 53 Geography Rev. 200 (1963).

implies limits on the ability of resource managers to absorb certain types of technical advice regardless of how well written or explained. Thus, to expect farmers to maintain conservation practices for long periods of time may be wishful thinking if such practices do not accord with the farmer's view of his resource and the hazards to which it is exposed. Similarly, to expect radical changes in the pattern of human adjustments to floods simply by providing detailed and precise flood hazard information is unduly optimistic. Yet another example is seen in the upper Trinity River area in Texas.[76] To expect farmers to convert flood-plain land from pasture to cotton or other high value cash crops simply because flood frequency is reduced is to assume that he shares the perception of the Soil Conservation Service. Nor is it a strong argument to claim that such changes in land use were indicated as possible by the farmers themselves, if the question was put to them in terms of the technologist's evaluation of the problem. Good predictions of the future choices of resource managers are likely to be based on an understanding of their perception and the ways in which it differs from that of the technologists.

It seems likely that the hiatus between technical and managerial perception is nowhere greater than in the underdeveloped countries.[77] There is good reason, therefore, for further research into this topic and for attempts to harmonize the discrepancies in technical programs wherever possible.

While the study of natural hazard perception provides clues to the ways in which men manage uncertain natural environments, it also helps to provide a background to understanding our national resource policy. Despite the self-image of the conservation movement as a conscious and rational attempt to develop policies to meet long term needs, more of the major commitments of public policy in the field of resource management have arisen out of crises generated by catastrophic natural hazards (albeit at times aided and abetted by human improvidence) than out of a need to curb man's misuse and abuse of his natural environment. Some years ago this was recognized by White: "National catastrophes have led to insistent demands for national action, and the timing of the legislative process has been set by the tempo of destructive floods."[78] It has also been documented in some detail by Henry Hart.[79] The Soil Erosion Service of the Department of Agriculture was established as an emergency agency in 1933 following the severe drought and subsequent dust

76. Burton, *op. cit. supra* note 45, at 59-73.

77. The results of a recent effort to improve communication between technical experts and resource managers are reported in Central Treaty Organization, Traveling Seminar for Increased Agricultural Production, Region Tour (1962).

78. White, *Human Adjustments to Floods* 24 (Univ. Chi. Dep't of Geography Research Paper No. 29, 1945).

79. Hart, *Crises, Community, and Consent in Water Politics*, 22 Law & Contemp. Prob. 510 (1957).

bowl early in the decade. The Service became a permanent agency called the Soil Conservation Service in 1935.[80]

Just as flood control legislation has followed hard upon the heels of major flood disasters, so the present high degree of interest in coastal protection, development, and preservation has been in part stimulated by recent severe storms on the east coast.[81] Such a fundamental public policy as the provision of water supply for urban areas was created partly in response to needs for controlling such natural hazards as typhus and cholera and the danger of fire, as well as for meeting urban water demands.[82] Agricultural and forestry research programs were fostered as much by insect infestations and plant diseases as by the long-range goals of increased production.

Unusual events in nature have long been associated with a state of crisis in human affairs. The decline of such superstitions and the continued growth of the control over nature will not necessarily be accompanied by a reduction of the role of crisis in resource policy. Natural hazards are likely to continue to play a significant role, although their occurrence as well as their effects may be increasingly difficult to separate from man-induced hazards of the quasi-natural variety. The smog of Donora may replace the Johnstown flood in our lexicon of major hazards, and *The Grapes of Wrath* may yield pride of place to *The Silent Spring* in the literature of the effects of environmental hazard, but there will continue to be a pattern of response to crisis in human relations to an uncertain environment. Under these circumstances, understandings of the variations of perception such as we have attempted here are likely to remain significant.

---

80. Buie, *Ill Fared the Land*, USDA Yearbook 155 (1962).

81. Burton & Kates, *The Flood Plain and the Sea Shore: A Comparative Analysis of Hazard Zone Occupance* (Unpublished manuscript, 1963), scheduled for publication in July, 1964 issue of Geographical Review.

82. Blake, Water for the Cities (1956).

[4]

Losses from Natural Hazards[†]

By CLIFFORD S. RUSSELL[*]

IN THE LAST TWO DECADES interest in such natural events as floods, earthquakes and hurricanes, often called natural hazards, has grown more widespread and more intense. This is true in the federal government where, for example, the Small Business Administration and the Civil Defense authorities have extensive responsibilities in an area which once was the preserve of the scientists and engineers of the Geological Survey and the Corps of Engineers. In the academic world, psychologists, sociologists, anthropologists and economists have joined engineers, climatologists, hydrologists and geographers in working on one or another aspect of the problem.[1]

Several reasons for this expanded interest may easily be found. On one level, the ability of television to bring the impact of natural disasters home (literally) to large numbers of people has created a background climate of awareness, sympathy and concern about possible local occurrences of these same disasters. A second spur to natural hazard research activity is the hypothesized similarity, in their impacts on human society, between some of the more violent climatic and geologic crises and a nuclear attack on one or more cities. This line of inquiry has seemed especially interesting to students of the phenomena of leadership, group interaction, etc., in such disciplines as sociology and social psychology, and to those concerned with government policies to assist recovery operations.[2] A third reason for increasing public and private investigation of natural hazards is the feeling that advancing technology will, in the fairly near future, give us some measure of control over a number of presently untamed hazards, such as lightning, tornadoes and even hurricanes.[3]

Finally, and perhaps most important, there has been growing pressure from both inside and outside government for improvement in the criteria on which public expenditure decisions are made. This general reforming trend has implied quickened specific interest in natural hazards, since many governmental projects are designed to protect against or warn of natural events such as flood, drought, hurricane and tornado, and the benefits to be attributed to such projects are the losses avoided over the future. Thus, flood control works are intended to reduce future flood losses; public sur-

† The author is grateful to Professors Robert Kates and David Arey for the initial, stimulating discussions which led to this paper, and to Professor Donald J. Volk for the suggestion that relevant future adjustments were a key to a firm conceptual basis for loss studies. Charles Howe, Blair Bower and John Krutilla made valuable comments on earlier drafts. Remaining inadequacies are, of course, my own responsibility.

* Resources for the Future, Inc.

1 For an introduction to this rapidly evolving field an excellent source is Ian Burton, Robert W. Kates and Gilbert White, "The Human Ecology of Extreme Geophysical Events," (Toronto, Canada: Department of Geography Working Paper Number 2 of the Natural Hazard Research Group, University of Toronto, 1968).

2 See, as examples of the former type of research, M. Wolfenstein, *Disaster: A Psychological Essay* (Glencoe, Illinois: Free Press, 1957); and G. W. Baker and D. W. Chapman (eds.), *Man and Society in Disaster* (New York, New York: Basic Books, 1962). For discussion of recovery and other aspects of governmental policy problems in the area see, D. C. Dacy and H. Kunreuther, *The Economics of Natural Disasters: Implications for Federal Policy* (New York, New York: The Free Press, 1969).

3 For a set of papers relevant to weather control and its impact see, W. R. D. Sewell, *Human Dimensions of Weather Modification* (Chicago, Illinois: Department of Geography Research Paper #105, University of Chicago Press, 1966).

face water supply systems are designed to increase the level of withdrawals possible from a given stream or watershed during a dry spell of a particular severity; hurricane tracking and tornado warning systems are efforts to reduce losses of life and property from these presently uncontrollable events by providing people in the probable path sufficient warning to accomplish some battening down and to evacuate the area if necessary.

It is our aim in this paper to discuss some of the principles and problems associated with the estimation of losses from natural hazards. First, we argue that a particular level or severity of natural event becomes a hazard only in relation to existing human adjustments. There are, then, no strictly physical definitions of what levels of severity of natural events constitute hazards.[4] Actual estimates of losses are always based on a combination of a particular natural event *and* an existing state of human adjustment. It follows that losses are a measure of the relative success of human adjustment to variable nature, and that losses from a natural hazard should, in principle, always be measured with some future adjustment to that hazard in mind.

Now, the fact that we emphasize the central role of human adjustments to natural events in defining hazards and measuring losses suggests that it will be valuable to explore more fully the range of available public and private adjustments and to discuss the relation between the two sets; in particular, this presents the problem of incentives created by public institutions aimed at private decision makers. Here we must also deal with the relation between individual perception of a hazard, private adjustment to it, and prevailing social views of the losses suffered.

Hazards and Events: Natural Forces and Human Adjustments

Nature is always with us in the sense that natural events are always occurring: the sun is shining or the sky is cloudy; streams are flowing at particular rates; the earth's crust is in perceptible motion or it is not. Over a somewhat longer run, an event might be the cumulated precipitation, or the hours of sunshine. Some of these events pass essentially unnoticed; they are merely the backdrops for normal life. Such normal events usually correspond in some way to the long-run average experience of the people and place in question. A few events, on the other hand, are characterized as hazards, disasters or catastrophes, and we should be clear about the ways in which such events differ from normal natural events. In particular, is it possible to characterize hazards purely in terms of the qualities of the events themselves?

At first glance, there would seem to be one clear difference between hazards and non-hazards for a particular time, place and population.[5] That is, hazardous events tend to be extreme events, to be found far out in the tails of the relevant probability distributions. Thus, floods are, in a general sense, characterized by very high streamflows; droughts by extremely low cumulations of precipitation over given periods. But even this line may not be pursued too far; some of the most dangerous snow storms

---

[4] Similarly, there are no purely man-made hazards. Man may opt for (or have forced on him) relatively less adequate adjustments to some natural phenomenon; this will in general increase the frequency and severity of hazard occurrence by lowering the necessary level of severity. Nature still must act, however.

[5] Clearly certain events which would be extreme hazards for one group may be the stuff of normal routine for another. We only need think of ourselves living with the Eskimo or the desert Bedouin to see this.

LOSSES FROM NATURAL HAZARDS 385

in terms of social disruption are very common in terms of the snowfalls involved. This example, indeed, points out to us that hazards can be defined only in terms of impact on human society, and hence that they must be seen as the joint product of the events occurring in nature and the existing human adjustments to those events.[6] Since hazards are so named because they cause economic damage and social disruption, the level and type of economic activity existing in an area, the institutional framework of the society in that area, and the previous decisions about specific adjustments to the natural event in question are all involved in assessing that event's hazardous character.

For example, that streamflow which is exceeded only five per cent of the time (the 20-year flood) will have very different effects in different basins depending on such variables as the degree of channel encroachment and the extent of commercial occupance of the lower levels of the flood plain. A rainfall shortage so severe that only one per cent of such events can be expected to be worse, may well wreak havoc with farmers without irrigation, while scarcely being felt by city people served by a large enough surface water storage system. There is no wind-speed/wave-height combination beyond which a tropical cyclonic storm is inevitably a hazard to us (though there is such a line to separate gale, storm and hurricane). If a most severe storm comes ashore in a relatively deserted area, it need prove a minor inconvenience only, while a far weaker storm hitting a heavily built up and poorly protected resort can do enormous damage. Thus, while we may say that, in the same human setting, a more severe natural event will cause greater damage and disruption, once we allow that set-

ting (the result of past adjustments) to vary, no such simple statement need hold.

If we wish to extend our understanding of natural hazards, it is necessary to introduce the notion of the *relative adequacy* of existing human adjustments. A measure of relative adequacy shows the relation between man's "demands" on nature and his ability to devise a system for serving those demands. For example, in the study of the impact of drought on municipal water supply systems, one possible measure of the relative *inadequacy* of man's existing adjustment is the ratio of potential demand to system safe yield.[7] Potential demand is the amount system customers would (on the average) like to withdraw from the system for given price, etc. Safe yield is the amount the system is able to deliver under all but some small per cent of the possible low flow events (often 5 per cent). Thus, if demand is relatively much greater than safe yield, a low flow event less severe than the 5 per cent will be sufficient to create shortage, and vice versa.

As another example, consider a possible measure of adequacy of adjustment to snow storms. Take a city with M feet of streets of average width W feet. Assume that from historical data it is determined that only 5 per cent of all snowfalls can be expected to be worse than one depositing T tons per square foot per hour. Then the five per cent snowfall event would be one depositing

---

[6] Professor Kates suggested this definition to the author in connection with a study of the recent Northeast Drought. The same idea is clearly at the heart of the flood studies conducted by various of the geographers associated with Gilbert White and the University of Chicago.

[7] Clifford Russell, David G. Arey and Robert W. Kates, *Drought and Water Supply: the Implications of the Massachusetts Experience for Municipal Planning* to be published by Johns Hopkins Press.

M × W × T tons per hour on the city's streets.[8] This becomes a probabilistic reference point analogous to water system safe yield. Here, however, we might say that the aim of adjustments is to keep the roads as free as possible of accumulations of snow, so that M × W × T may be taken as one measure of the city's probabilistic requirement for snow removal service. If the city has, at a given time, the ability to remove (by chemical or physical means) R tons per hour, the ratio of (or difference between) R and M × W × T is a measure of the adequacy of the city's adjustment to the snow hazard.[9] The greater R relative to M × W × T, the less probable a storm severe enough to accumulate snow at a rate greater than the removal capacity of the city (and hence, presumably, to cause traffic delays, accidents, etc.).

Adjustment and Loss: A Model for Decision Making

The above examples should make clear that to attribute losses to a natural event alone is misleading. Loss studies must, at least, recognize explicitly that losses are the *joint* product of man and nature. Thus, though it may be of some intrinsic interest to display losses from some natural event in relation to a measure of the severity of the event's physical impact, it is necessary to be clear that this measure of physical impact reflects *both* the actual severity of the event and the state of human preparation for the event.

It is, however, desirable to go beyond recognition of the general character of the losses measured during and after natural events. Because man decides on the adjustments which affect his losses, the matter of real interest is the future, not the past, and the losses we are after

are those which will be avoided in the future if we make this or that decision now. The purpose of measuring past losses is, then, to estimate the relationship among natural variation, extent (adequacy) of adjustments and resulting losses. The loss estimates, to be of value, must be those relevant to contemplated adjustments, present or future.[10]

A potentially useful framework for the study of the economics of natural hazards is shown graphically in Figure 1. Here the horizontal axis represents the relative adequacy of adjustment (A) to

---

[8] We assume for purposes of our illustration that quantity of snow falling per hour is the only important dimension to the snow hazard. This is not, of course, true. The character of the snow itself (whether it is wet or dry), the air temperature and wind-speed during its fall, the existing snow cover conditions, and the time of day of the storm are some of the other dimensions which will, in fact, be important.

[9] Note that it will not matter, in general, what point on the snowfall probability distribution function we choose for our requirement number. What matters is the underlying distribution itself, for it will determine the expected losses.

[10] The word *contemplated* is to be interpreted in the widest sense to include any conceivable adjustments, not just those now technologically or politically feasible. Clearly loss studies aimed at potential benefits from far out schemes will have much to do with whether or not the schemes become seriously considered.

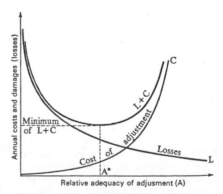

Figure 1. Optimal adjustment to a natural hazard.

LOSSES FROM NATURAL HAZARDS 387

the class of natural events of interest (*e.g.*, the ratio $R/M \times W \times T$ from our snow removal example above).[11] On the vertical axis we measure annual dollar amounts. The curve labelled L represents the expected annual losses from the hazard under study for any particular level of adjustment. The curve C is the annual cost of achieving any given level of adjustment. Losses fall as higher levels of human adjustment are achieved; the costs of achieving successively higher levels of adjustment will, naturally, be in general higher.[12] Clearly, the best level of adjustment is the one at which the *sum* of (adjustment) costs and expected losses is the least. In Figure 1, we show this level of adjustment, A*, as that corresponding to the lowest point on the curve L + C, the vertical sum of the cost and expected loss curves.[13]

The study of losses from a particular class of natural events should, then, be seen as an integral part (at least potentially) of the process of evaluating alternative human adjustments to those events. The point of this statement is not that we should have fewer or even less comprehensive loss studies; it is merely that studies which ignore the role of human adjustment are, at best, of very limited usefulness and at worst may be seriously misleading guides to public expenditure. The most familiar violations are those which purport to tell us the average annual losses from this or that natural hazard suffered by the United States. These studies, appearing both in the popular and professional literature, implicitly assume a stable average correspondence between natural events of particular severities and human adjustments of a particular adequacy. Thus, a study which estimated the average annual losses from snow

falls on the urban areas of the United States for the last 25 years could be using annual loss estimates which reflected trends in the climate (the distribution of snowfall events) or in snow removal capability relative to urban street system size, or in both determinants. Even if there is no reason to suspect a trend in climate or average level of adjustment, however, the reported losses stated in this broad way are relevant only to further adjustments totally ridding the nation of the urban snowfall hazard. This will never be possible for any hazard because there are, in general, no upper limits on the severity of the natural events involved. But, in any case, such efforts would surely be enormously expensive relative to the losses avoided. As we illustrated above, what is important is the point at which it no longer pays to incur costs to avoid losses.

In the flood control field, concentrating attention on the role of high streamflows and ignoring the importance of human adjustments in the creation of losses from flooding have led to an expensive program of public investments accompanied by an escalating total of annual losses. Here the problem seems

[11] We assume that, for any particular study, the region or political entity of interest could be relatively easily identified. This choice, and the related choice of an economic point of view for measuring losses (*e.g.*, national or local) will have significant implications for the actual measurement of losses. See, C. S. Russell *et al.*, *op. cit.*, Chapter 10.

[12] The calculation of annual costs requires the choice of some planning horizon (finite or infinite) and of a rate of discount. For most hazard studies it will be desirable to take account of changing human requirements over time, as in the growth of a street system which requires plowing.

[13] If we graphed *marginal* costs and the negative of *marginal* expected losses against the adjustment level, the level A* would be found at the intersection of the two curves. There is, however, no reason to expect the intersection of the *total* cost and loss curves to occur at A*. This point is sometimes confused.

to have been that general public sympathy for those who suffered in the dramatic floods of the thirties was translated into public investment in reservoirs, flood walls, etc., erected with minimal arrangements for the sharing of costs with those benefitting. These measures have been augmented by public and private relief programs for ex post assistance to flood victims. The combination has been sufficient to encourage rapidly increasing private investment in flood plains, for the costs of such private decisions have, in effect, been publicly borne. Very little has been done by way of flood plain zoning or the provision of incentives for private flood proofing of individual structures.[14] Adjustments to adjustments have thus confounded the original goals of the program by apparently increasing expected annual losses for virtually every basin even while massive structural works have changed the frequencies of occurrence of flooding of key parts of the flood plains. A truly relevant flood loss study would take account of these private adjustments but not just by projecting increased use of protected (or semi-protected) areas and hence raising both the benefits of the structural measures and the expected losses from catastrophic floods. Rather, flood losses should be related to mixes of private and public actions, to private flood-proofing as well as public control reservoirs.[15] Recognizing explicitly that flood losses depend on private decisions and not only on variability in stream-flows might dampen some of the enthusiasm for the programs presently distorting the decision processes of individuals. Discussions of the proper size of and appropriate mechanism for redistribution toward those inhabiting flood plains could be freed from the present rhetoric

about victims who bear losses *for* the rest of society.

Private and Public Adjustments to Natural Events

The adjustments possible in the face of variable, and sometimes hostile, nature may be categorized in any number of ways. Some consist largely of fixed investments (flood control dams), while others involve primarily recurrent expenses for personnel, etc. with only a relatively small capital base (weather forecasting). Some are inherently public (zoning regulations), other private (flood proofing of individual structures). Some involve physical interference with the actual natural events (weather modification), others are merely attempts to smooth out the effects of natural variations (reservoirs), and still others involve only the control of human society (parking regulations for snow storms). As our discussion above has pointed out, one of the key questions to be asked in any natural hazard study is the extent to which contemplated adjustments interact; that is, particularly, the extent to which certain public measures serve as spurs to other private adjustments which may or may not be in the direction of reducing the expected future costs.

There are, however, two other inter-

[14] See, for example, G. F. White, *Papers on Flood Problems*, and *Changes in Urban Occupance of Flood Plains in the U.S.* (Chicago, Illinois: Department of Geography Research Papers Numbers 70 and 57, University of Chicago Press, 1961 and 1958).

[15] L. James, *A Time Dependent Planning Process for Combining Structural Measures, Land Use and Flood Proofing to Minimize the Economic Loss of Floods*, Report EEP-12, Stanford University Institute in Engineering Economic Systems, 1964. For a suggested compulsory insurance scheme to force private decision-makers to face the costs implied by their decisions to occupy the flood plain see, J. V. Krutilla, "An Economic Approach to Coping with Flood Damage," *Water Resources Research*, Vol. 2, No. 2, 2nd Quarter, 1966, pp. 183-190.

LOSSES FROM NATURAL HAZARDS

esting sets of questions concerning adjustments. First, consider the situation in which there are no *justifiable* additional adjustments.[16] What, then, is the conceptual role of an estimate of expected annual losses? What other actions are open to private actors? What should be the public (social) stance? Second, in discussing private adjustments of any sort, it is necessary to keep in mind the conditions under which decisions about such adjustments are made, particularly the private attitudes toward nature and natural variation which may be expected to influence private coping with potentially hazardous natural events.

If, for every level of additional human adjustment to a particular class of natural events, the marginal costs of the available adjustments are greater than the marginal expected losses, then we may say that no adjustments are *justified*. Such a situation may be represented graphically as in Figures 2A and 2B. In Figure 2A, we show a set of marginal cost and marginal loss curves for which no further adjustment is justifiable; the status quo (if that is the way we choose to define the zero adjustment level) is better than any contemplated change. In Figure 2B we show a set of total cost and loss curves which could lead to the situation in Figure 2A. The minimum point on this L + C curve is at A = 0.[17]

What, if anything, remains for the individual to do in such a situation? Essentially, one may suggest that some form of spreading of losses either spatially or temporally will improve individual welfare. Compulsory insurance against the risk, with premiums based on expected losses, would reduce the variance of every individual's income and presumably result in an increase in welfare so long as those involved are

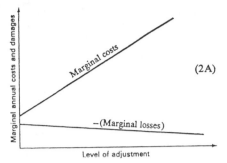

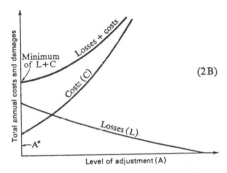

Figure 2. No adjustment justified.

risk averters.[18] If the insurance scheme covered the same risk in widely scattered areas with independent natural events,

[16] For a definition of "justifiable" in the context of our model, see the discussion below.

[17] To say that no adjustment is justified is to say that the damage-cost comparisons for all adjustments lead to the same situation as depicted in Figure 2. Specifically, it will be necessary to consider such alternatives as moving out of the hazard area as well as environmental modification and investment in physical protection. Changing technology will often result in new kinds of justifiable adjustments and so no characterization of hazards according to whether or not adjustments to them are possible will be valid permanently.

[18] And, as Krutilla has discussed (*op. cit.*), such a scheme could serve as the basis for efficient allocation of costs if and when some loss-reducing adjustment did become feasible.

expected value would be a sufficient measure of risk and the overall variance of losses would be reduced. Some provision for insurance might be made even within a single area (e.g. hail insurance in a single county) if sufficient allowance were made for the between-year variance of losses, either in the size of premium payments (e.g. by paying premiums such that the probability of exhausting the insurance fund in any year would be less than or equal to some small number), or establishing a sufficiently large and long-term line of credit to prevent ruin. With the same qualifications, an individual might undertake self-insurance in an attempt to even out his time stream of income.

In such a situation, new decisions about locating in the region should allow for the expected annual losses from the unavoidable hazard. Thus, the proper price to pay for forest or farm land in a region with known precipitation distribution (both inter- and intra-year) would reflect the discounted sum of expected annual earnings *allowing for droughts*.[19] Similar statements would hold for other enterprises (and even for private homes with weather-sensitive lawns) to the extent that they depend on the availability of direct precipitation. The situation changes, of course, when it is justifiable to store and pipe water. These are adjustments which will reduce average annual drought losses and the question becomes one of the proper degree of adjustment. (It may still be worthwhile to insure in some way against residual losses.)

Note that if an insurance scheme is in existence for the area and the risk in question, this expected earnings calculation will be an easy and obvious one for the most hard-headed man of business, for the insurance premiums will be an annual cost of doing business. It is, of course, in situations for which no expert evaluations in the form of insurance policies are available that individual attitudes toward and perceptions of nature become particularly relevant for these will be central to the choice of a risk allowance. Indeed, individual knowledge and perception will be important to every type of private adjustment including those aimed at decreasing future expected losses, so long as the individual is not required to buy a particular expert, actuarial view. Thus, the impact of our remarks below goes far beyond the problem merely of coping with unavoidable losses.

One last matter, however, needs to be cleared up in relation to unavoidable losses. That is, given that private factors have open to them a number of ways of improving the time pattern of such losses, what should be the social view of the losses suffered in any given year? Of the long-run average of such losses? Basically what is important here is the ability of society to transfer real income over time in such a way as to smooth aggregate social welfare, as the insurance-type transfer payments we have discussed smooth the income streams of groups within the society.

At one extreme in this respect, we may conceive of a society in which the unavoidable expected (annual) losses in real outputs are known and which has

---

[19] Allowance for the variance of the return may or may not be necessary, depending on the relative importance for the buyer of the income stream involved. For example, a large paper company with forests all over North America could almost certainly ignore variance. A small lumber firm relying entirely on a single wood lot probably could not. The expected annual earnings would probably be different from the earnings associated with average annual rainfall. If diminishing returns of tree growth to rainfall hold, the expected annual earnings will be less than the annual earnings from average rainfall (all ignoring intra-year distribution).

a system for accumulating stocks of these outputs in good years for use in bad years. The rate of accumulation of these stocks would be a function of the variance of losses, depending on the degree of assurance the society wished to maintain that it would not be ruined, and on the availability of foreign aid. (We note here that Joseph's problem was relatively simple because he was faced with a determinate nature. Our locusts, droughts, floods, earthquakes are less reliable.) In such a society, the relevant indices of economic welfare would be those calculated net of the provisions for future losses for such netting out would reflect the true state of society's relation to nature. Since we have assumed no further adjustments to be possible, such an index could be uniquely defined using the annual product under natural conditions optimal for the *existing* state of adjustment.[20]

At the other extreme, a primitive society with no means of storing its products (*e.g.*, a hunting/gathering society without means of preserving meat) has no particular reason to be concerned with expected losses since it has no smoothing option. Indeed, here the entire concept of loss is of doubtful usefulness. It would seem that concern with losses from natural hazards is something relevant only to groups having at least the option to make allowances in advance for such events.[21]

If a society is in a position to at least anticipate (on the average) the losses it has no economically justifiable way to avoid, then actual year-to-year occurrences of loss should already have been taken into account in the society's evaluation of its welfare position. The level of economic activity enjoyed in a particular year is not so important as the average level sustainable in the face of

nature (for the given adjustments). Indeed, here again, the word losses may not seem very useful as a name for the difference between optimal and actual production. What may very well be discussed as loss (or gain) is the difference between some anticipated stream of production over a relevant planning horizon and the actual results achieved. If, over 50 years, the initial projections of average production prove optimistic, it seems quite natural to say that the society has suffered a loss. To say this, however, in relation to a single year for which the results are worse than average is to imply that gains are made in each year that production is above average, and essentially to ignore the implications of society's self-insurance option.

Perception and Adjustment: Human Views of Nature

For our discussion of the losses attributable to a particular combination of natural variation and human adjustment, two facets of man's general view of nature are of considerable interest. First, since efficient adjustment to nature requires explicit recognition of the random quality of certain natural events, we should like to explore some

---

[20] These observations are relevant to the usual indices of aggregate economic activity such as GNP. Here the problems of dealing with natural hazards are complicated by present conventions which include the investment total for each year as an addition to welfare for that year, and the future streams of production from the investments as additions in the years of accrual. At least, however, it should be recognized that what is of interest is the expected annual level of such an index, net of unavoidable expected annual losses from randomly occurring natural events. Year-to-year fluctuations in GNP due to such events do not reflect corresponding fluctuations in aggregate welfare to the extent that rational provision has been possible.

[21] This observation is of some interest in connection with our discussion below of man's view of his relation to nature. A society without even our "smoothing" option is very much like a part of nature rather than something different from, and partly in control of, her.

common human perceptions of natural randomness. Second, because as we have pointed out, the usefulness and, indeed, the very meaning of losses from events hinges on the ability of society to adjust either to avoid or insure against them, it will be worthwhile to mention certain relevant cross-cultural variations in views of man's relation to nature.

Kates and others, in studying flooding, have found that people living with a natural hazard tend to adopt one or another view of the future denying the randomness of the size and timing of the events.[22] Some adopt the view that the hazard is a repetitive, cyclical event. This implies no need to worry about floods until just before the repetition is due. Others use a naive law-of-averages approach, claiming that the occurrence of a flood in year t reduces the probability of experiencing one in year $t + 1$.[23] This has a similar, if less dramatic, implication for action as the first view. For some time after the occurrence of some bad event, we are relatively safe from its recurrence. Another strategy is to wish away the hazardous character of the event by renaming it or lowering its amplitude to the commonplace. Thus, a flood becomes a spring freshet or just high water. Finally, some residents of hazard areas avoid thinking about the event at all by invoking a higher power — in particular by referring to God's will. It does no good (and may actually do harm depending on one's view of God's resentment over meddling humanity) to attempt to deal rationally with what is clearly part of the unfathomable plan of an infinitely superior mind.

These strategies all work in the direction of discouraging private adjustment to avoid expected losses. Since, in fact, events such as floods do not seem to be cyclical or to behave as the naive law of averages would suggest, those who are anxious to avoid probabilistic views are likely to be caught out time and again. This probably encourages an emphasis on losses, since nature has been more than merely random: it has been actively perverse.

The contributions to American culture of the northern European peoples seem to have included a view of man as a master of nature. There is certainly evidence that such a view tends to be the dominant one among the rural white protestants so important in our agricultural sector.[24] It seems likely that a feeling of mastery over nature is even more highly developed among city-dwellers, whatever their cultural backgrounds, for they are very largely cut off from direct contact with a harsh nature. It may be hypothesized then that most people in our society are, in general, unwilling to see nature as other than man's servant. A stress on losses from natural hazards arises easily from a vague faith in the ability of science to find and apply controls to even the most spectacular events.

On the other hand, a view of nature stressing man's oneness with her forces might be expected to accompany rela-

[22] Robert W. Kates, *Hazard and Choice Perception in Flood Plain Management* (Chicago, Illinois: Department of Geography Research Paper Number 78, University of Chicago Press, 1962); also Ian Burton and Robert W. Kates, "The Perception of Natural Hazards in Resource Management," *Natural Resources Journal*, January 1964, pp. 412-41.

[23] Note that there are hazards f·r which serial correlation of events is important and well established. For example, if streamflows are known to be low in year t, it is more likely that they will be low in year $t + 1$ than we would predict from the long-run percentage of low-flow years. (The Markov properties with positive serial correlation.)

[24] See for example, F. R. Kluckhohn and F. L. Strodtbeck, *Variations in Value Orientations* (Evanston, Illinois: Row Peterson, 1961); also E. Z. Vogt, *Modern Homesteaders* (Cambridge, Massachusetts: Harvard University Press, 1955); and W. Firey, *Man, Mind and Land: A Theory of Resource Use* (Glencoe, Illinois: Free Press 1960).

LOSSES FROM NATURAL HAZARDS   393

tively primitive technology and food-provision systems. As we suggested above, a hunter-gatherer society without the means to store food over seasons or years is, in a very real sense, a part of nature. The more easily the society is able at least to allow in advance for bad years, the less pronounced we should expect this feeling of oneness to become.[25]

It seems reasonable to characterize our society as one in which a view of man as the master, actual or potential, of all of nature, goes hand in hand with a general refusal to think in probabilistic terms about natural events. It is not sufficient that man's adjustments be regarded as changing probability distributions of undesirable events; there is a great need to see these actions as eliminating hazard entirely. Hence, flood works make the protected area *safe*; water systems have *safe yields*; and weather forecasters are urged by the public to say that it either will or will not rain — not that the probability of rain is 4 in 10. The pressures arising from this combination of views seem clearly to favor programs aimed at nature directly rather than at man; indeed, programs which provide no incentive for efficient adjustment by private individuals. These same individuals tend to dismiss their own danger by stressing the "safety" of public adjustments and the predictable nature of extreme natural events. When the unpredicted event occurs or the event more extreme than the adjustments can handle, it is understandable that public sympathy for the losers

is relatively great and that programs of redistribution in favor of these victims are conceived or expanded.

In general, the society's handling of extreme natural events could be significantly improved by an educational campaign stressing the modification of some key ideas. First, it would be an important contribution to more phases of our lives than only our relation to nature if some way could be found of persuading the average man to think rationally about random events. Purging the naive law of averages will not be easy; our tendency to personify inanimate objects (and, of course, nature) encourages us to give memories to coins we are tossing as well as to the forces that spawn hurricanes, floods and earthquakes. If such a purge were to be accomplished, however, we might find the society more receptive to an accurate description of the relative adequacy of existing and projected adjustments. If, in addition, our ideal of mastery over nature could be realistically modified to allow us to admit that some losses will inevitably occur, we might be able to discuss more carefully the desirable level of those expected losses as against the costs of further adjustments to avoid them.

---

[25] The view that man is *under* nature would seem to be related not to the relative ability of society to adjust to nature, but to its view of the personal or impersonal quality of that nature. If a society is convinced that there is some anthropomorphic spirit behind natural events ready to react, perhaps whimsically or perversely, to human adjustments, this would seem to encourage a view of subjection to nature. This view does not, however, so readily fit into our observations.

Part II
Risk Perception and its Economic Impact

[5]

Perception of Risk

PAUL SLOVIC

Studies of risk perception examine the judgments people make when they are asked to characterize and evaluate hazardous activities and technologies. This research aims to aid risk analysis and policy-making by (i) providing a basis for understanding and anticipating public responses to hazards and (ii) improving the communication of risk information among lay people, technical experts, and decision-makers. This work assumes that those who promote and regulate health and safety need to understand how people think about and respond to risk. Without such understanding, well-intended policies may be ineffective.

T HE ABILITY TO SENSE AND AVOID HARMFUL ENVIRONMEN-
tal conditions is necessary for the survival of all living
organisms. Survival is also aided by an ability to codify and
learn from past experience. Humans have an additional capability
that allows them to alter their environment as well as respond to it.
This capacity both creates and reduces risk.

In recent decades, the profound development of chemical and
nuclear technologies has been accompanied by the potential to cause
catastrophic and long-lasting damage to the earth and the life forms
that inhabit it. The mechanisms underlying these complex technologies are unfamiliar and incomprehensible to most citizens. Their
most harmful consequences are rare and often delayed, hence
difficult to assess by statistical analysis and not well suited to
management by trial-and-error learning. The elusive and hard to
manage qualities of today's hazards have forced the creation of a new
intellectual discipline called risk assessment, designed to aid in
identifying, characterizing, and quantifying risk (1).

Whereas technologically sophisticated analysts employ risk assessment to evaluate hazards, the majority of citizens rely on intuitive
risk judgments, typically called "risk perceptions." For these people,
experience with hazards tends to come from the news media, which
rather thoroughly document mishaps and threats occurring
throughout the world. The dominant perception for most Ameri-
cans (and one that contrasts sharply with the views of professional
risk assessors) is that they face more risk today than in the past and
that future risks will be even greater than today's (2). Similar views
appear to be held by citizens of many other industrialized nations.
These perceptions and the opposition to technology that accompa-
nies them have puzzled and frustrated industrialists and regulators
and have led numerous observers to argue that the American
public's apparent pursuit of a "zero-risk society" threatens the
nation's political and economic stability. Wildavsky (3, p. 32)
commented as follows on this state of affairs.

> How extraordinary! The richest, longest lived, best protected, most
> resourceful civilization, with the highest degree of insight into its own
> technology, is on its way to becoming the most frightened.
> Is it our environment or ourselves that have changed? Would people like
> us have had this sort of concern in the past? . . . Today, there are risks from
> numerous small dams far exceeding those from nuclear reactors. Why is the
> one feared and not the other? Is it just that we are used to the old or are some
> of us looking differently at essentially the same sorts of experience?

During the past decade, a small number of researchers has been
attempting to answer such questions by examining the opinions that
people express when they are asked, in a variety of ways, to evaluate
hazardous activities, substances, and technologies. This research has
attempted to develop techniques for assessing the complex and
subtle opinions that people have about risk. With these techniques,
researchers have sought to discover what people mean when they say
that something is (or is not) "risky," and to determine what factors
underlie those perceptions. The basic assumption underlying these
efforts is that those who promote and regulate health and safety need
to understand the ways in which people think about and respond to
risk.

The author is president of Decision Research, 1201 Oak Street, Eugene, OR 97401,
and professor of psychology at the University of Oregon.

If successful, this research should aid policy-makers by improving communication between them and the public, by directing educational efforts, and by predicting public responses to new technologies (for example, genetic engineering), events (for example, a good safety record or an accident), and new risk management strategies (for example, warning labels, regulations, substitute products).

Risk Perception Research

Important contributions to our current understanding of risk perception have come from geography, sociology, political science, anthropology, and psychology. Geographical research focused originally on understanding human behavior in the face of natural hazards, but it has since broadened to include technological hazards as well (4). Sociological (5) and anthropological studies (6) have shown that perception and acceptance of risk have their roots in social and cultural factors. Short (5) argues that response to hazards is mediated by social influences transmitted by friends, family, fellow workers, and respected public officials. In many cases, risk perceptions may form afterwards, as part of the ex post facto rationale for one's own behavior. Douglas and Wildavsky (6) assert that people, acting within social groups, downplay certain risks and emphasize others as a means of maintaining and controlling the group.

Psychological research on risk perception, which shall be my focus, originated in empirical studies of probability assessment, utility assessment, and decision-making processes (7). A major development in this area has been the discovery of a set of mental strategies, or heuristics, that people employ in order to make sense out of an uncertain world (8). Although these rules are valid in some circumstances, in others they lead to large and persistent biases, with serious implications for risk assessment. In particular, laboratory research on basic perceptions and cognitions has shown that difficulties in understanding probabilistic processes, biased media coverage, misleading personal experiences, and the anxieties generated by life's gambles cause uncertainty to be denied, risks to be misjudged (sometimes overestimated and sometimes underestimated), and judgments of fact to be held with unwarranted confidence. Experts' judgments appear to be prone to many of the same biases as those of the general public, particularly when experts are forced to go beyond the limits of available data and rely on intuition (8, 9).

Research further indicates that disagreements about risk should not be expected to evaporate in the presence of evidence. Strong initial views are resistant to change because they influence the way that subsequent information is interpreted. New evidence appears reliable and informative if it is consistent with one's initial beliefs; contrary evidence tends to be dismissed as unreliable, erroneous, or unrepresentative (10). When people lack strong prior opinions, the opposite situation exists—they are at the mercy of the problem formulation. Presenting the same information about risk in different ways (for example, mortality rates as opposed to survival rates) alters people's perspectives and actions (11).

The Psychometric Paradigm

One broad strategy for studying perceived risk is to develop a taxonomy for hazards that can be used to understand and predict responses to their risks. A taxonomic scheme might explain, for example, people's extreme aversion to some hazards, their indifference to others, and the discrepancies between these reactions and opinions of experts. The most common approach to this goal has employed the psychometric paradigm (12, 13), which uses psychophysical scaling and multivariate analysis techniques to produce

quantitative representations or "cognitive maps" of risk attitudes and perceptions. Within the psychometric paradigm, people make quantitative judgments about the current and desired riskiness of diverse hazards and the desired level of regulation of each. These judgments are then related to judgments about other properties, such as (i) the hazard's status on characteristics that have been hypothesized to account for risk perceptions and attitudes (for example, voluntariness, dread, knowledge, controllability), (ii) the benefits that each hazard provides to society, (iii) the number of deaths caused by the hazard in an average year, and (iv) the number of deaths caused by the hazard in a disastrous year.

In the rest of this article, I shall briefly review some of the results obtained from psychometric studies of risk perception and outline some implications of these results for risk communication and risk management.

Revealed and Expressed Preferences

The original impetus for the psychometric paradigm came from the pioneering effort of Starr (14) to develop a method for weighing technological risks against benefits in order to answer the fundamental question, "How safe is safe enough?" His "revealed preference" approach assumed that, by trial and error, society has arrived at an "essentially optimum" balance between the risks and benefits associated with any activity. One may therefore use historical or current risk and benefit data to reveal patterns of "acceptable" risk-benefit trade-offs. Examining such data for several industries and activities,

Table 1. Ordering of perceived risk for 30 activities and technologies (22). The ordering is based on the geometric mean risk ratings within each group. Rank 1 represents the most risky activity or technology.

Activity or technology	League of Women Voters	College students	Active club members	Experts
Nuclear power	1	1	8	20
Motor vehicles	2	5	3	1
Handguns	3	2	1	4
Smoking	4	3	4	2
Motorcycles	5	6	2	6
Alcoholic beverages	6	7	5	3
General (private) aviation	7	15	11	12
Police work	8	8	7	17
Pesticides	9	4	15	8
Surgery	10	11	9	5
Fire fighting	11	10	6	18
Large construction	12	14	13	13
Hunting	13	18	10	23
Spray cans	14	13	23	26
Mountain climbing	15	22	12	29
Bicycles	16	24	14	15
Commercial aviation	17	16	18	16
Electric power (non-nuclear)	18	19	19	9
Swimming	19	30	17	10
Contraceptives	20	9	22	11
Skiing	21	25	16	30
X-rays	22	17	24	7
High school and college football	23	26	21	27
Railroads	24	23	29	19
Food preservatives	25	12	28	14
Food coloring	26	20	30	21
Power mowers	27	28	25	28
Prescription antibiotics	28	21	26	24
Home appliances	29	27	27	22
Vaccinations	30	29	29	25

Starr concluded that (i) acceptability of risk from an activity is roughly proportional to the third power of the benefits for that activity, and (ii) the public will accept risks from voluntary activities (such as skiing) that are roughly 1000 times as great as it would tolerate from involuntary hazards (such as food preservatives) that provide the same level of benefits.

The merits and deficiencies of Starr's approach have been debated at length (15). They will not be elaborated here, except to note that concern about the validity of the many assumptions inherent in the revealed preferences approach stimulated Fischhoff *et al.* (12) to conduct an analogous psychometric analysis of questionnaire data, resulting in "expressed preferences." In recent years, numerous other studies of expressed preferences have been carried out within the psychometric paradigm (16–24).

These studies have shown that perceived risk is quantifiable and predictable. Psychometric techniques seem well suited for identifying similarities and differences among groups with regard to risk perceptions and attitudes (Table 1). They have also shown that the

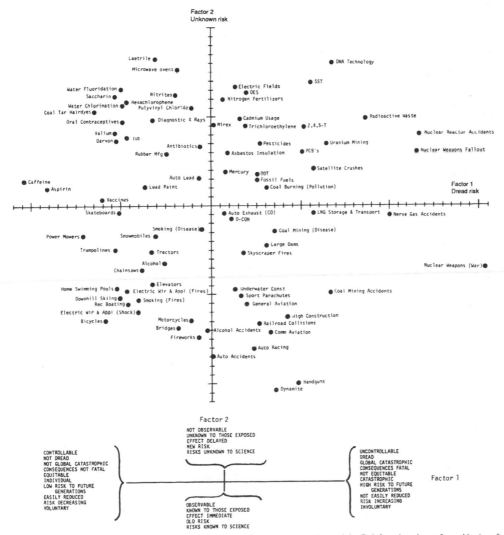

Fig. 1. Location of 81 hazards on factors 1 and 2 derived from the relationships among 18 risk characteristics. Each factor is made up of a combination of characteristics, as indicated by the lower diagram (25).

concept "risk" means different things to different people. When experts judge risk, their responses correlate highly with technical estimates of annual fatalities. Lay people can assess annual fatalities if they are asked to (and produce estimates somewhat like the technical estimates). However, their judgments of "risk" are related more to other hazard characteristics (for example, catastrophic potential, threat to future generations) and, as a result, tend to differ from their own (and experts') estimates of annual fatalities.

Another consistent result from psychometric studies of expressed preferences is that people tend to view current risk levels as unacceptably high for most activities. The gap between perceived and desired risk levels suggests that people are not satisfied with the way that market and other regulatory mechanisms have balanced risks and benefits. Across the domain of hazards, there seems to be little systematic relationship between perceptions of current risks and benefits. However, studies of expressed preferences do seem to support Starr's argument that people are willing to tolerate higher risks from activities seen as highly beneficial. But, whereas Starr concluded that voluntariness of exposure was the key mediator of risk acceptance, expressed preference studies have shown that other (perceived) characteristics such as familiarity, control, catastrophic potential, equity, and level of knowledge also seem to influence the relation between perceived risk, perceived benefit, and risk acceptance (*12, 22*).

Various models have been advanced to represent the relation between perceptions, behavior, and these qualitative characteristics of hazards. As we shall see, the picture that emerges from this work is both orderly and complex.

Factor-Analytic Representations

Many of the qualitative risk characteristics are correlated with each other, across a wide range of hazards. For example, hazards judged to be "voluntary" tend also to be judged as "controllable"; hazards whose adverse effects are delayed tend to be seen as posing risks that are not well known, and so on. Investigation of these relations by means of factor analysis has shown that the broader domain of characteristics can be condensed to a small set of higher order characteristics or factors.

The factor space presented in Fig. 1 has been replicated across groups of lay people and experts judging large and diverse sets of hazards. Factor 1, labeled "dread risk," is defined at its high (right-hand) end by perceived lack of control, dread, catastrophic potential, fatal consequences, and the inequitable distribution of risks and benefits. Nuclear weapons and nuclear power score highest on the characteristics that make up this factor. Factor 2, labeled "unknown risk," is defined at its high end by hazards judged to be unobservable, unknown, new, and delayed in their manifestation of harm. Chemical technologies score particularly high on this factor. A third factor, reflecting the number of people exposed to the risk, has been obtained in several studies. Making the set of hazards more or less specific (for example, partitioning nuclear power into radioactive waste, uranium mining, and nuclear reactor accidents) has had little effect on the factor structure or its relation to risk perceptions (*25*).

Research has shown that lay people's risk perceptions and attitudes are closely related to the position of a hazard within this type of factor space. Most important is the horizontal factor "dread risk." The higher a hazard's score on this factor (the further to the right it appears in the space), the higher its perceived risk, the more people want to see its current risks reduced, and the more they want to see strict regulation employed to achieve the desired reduction in risk (Fig. 2). In contrast, experts' perceptions of risk are not closely related to any of the various risk characteristics or factors derived

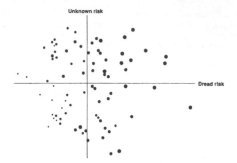

Fig. 2. Attitudes toward regulation of the hazards in Fig. 1. The larger the point, the greater the desire for strict regulation to reduce risk (*25*).

from these characteristics (*25*). Instead, as noted earlier, experts appear to see riskiness as synonymous with expected annual mortality (*26*). As a result, conflicts over "risk" may result from experts and lay people having different definitions of the concept.

The representation shown in Fig. 1, while robust and informative, is by no means a universal cognitive mapping of the domain of hazards. Other psychometric methods (such as multidimensional scaling analysis of hazard similarity judgments), applied to quite different sets of hazards, produce different spatial models (*13, 18*). The utility of these models for understanding and predicting behavior remains to be determined.

Accidents as Signals

Risk analyses typically model the impacts of an unfortunate event (such as an accident, a discovery of pollution, sabotage, product tampering) in terms of direct harm to victims—deaths, injuries, and damages. The impacts of such events, however, sometimes extend far beyond these direct harms and may include significant indirect costs (both monetary and nonmonetary) to the responsible government agency or private company that far exceed direct costs. In some cases, all companies in an industry are affected, regardless of which company was responsible for the mishap. In extreme cases, the indirect costs of a mishap may extend past industry boundaries, affecting companies, industries, and agencies whose business is minimally related to the initial event. Thus, an unfortunate event can be thought of as analogous to a stone dropped in a pond. The ripples spread outward, encompassing first the directly affected victims, then the responsible company or agency, and, in the extreme, reaching other companies, agencies, and industries.

Some events make only small ripples; others make larger ones. The challenge is to discover characteristics associated with an event and the way that it is managed that can predict the breadth and seriousness of those impacts (Fig. 3). Early theories equated the magnitude of impact to the number of people killed or injured, or to the amount of property damaged. However, the accident at the Three Mile Island (TMI) nuclear reactor in 1979 provides a dramatic demonstration that factors besides injury, death, and property damage impose serious costs. Despite the fact that not a single person died, and few if any latent cancer fatalities are expected, no other accident in our history has produced such costly societal impacts. The accident at TMI devastated the utility that owned and operated the plant. It also imposed enormous costs (*27*) on the nuclear industry and on society, through stricter regulation (resulting in increased construction and operation costs), reduced

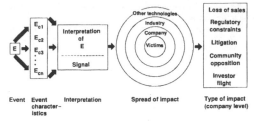

Event   Event   Interpretation   Spread of impact   Type of impact
         character-   (company level)
         istics

Fig. 3. A model of impact for unfortunate events.

operation of reactors worldwide, greater public opposition to nuclear power, and reliance on more expensive energy sources. It may even have led to a more hostile view of other complex technologies, such as chemical manufacturing and genetic engineering. The point is that traditional economic and risk analyses tend to neglect these higher order impacts, hence they greatly underestimate the costs associated with certain kinds of events.

Although the TMI accident is extreme, it is by no means unique. Other recent events resulting in enormous higher order impacts include the chemical manufacturing accident at Bhopal, India, the pollution of Love Canal, New York, and Times Beach, Missouri, the disastrous launch of the space shuttle Challenger, and the meltdown of the nuclear reactor at Chernobyl. Following these extreme events are a myriad of mishaps varying in the breadth and size of their impacts.

An important concept that has emerged from psychometric research is that the seriousness and higher order impacts of an unfortunate event are determined, in part, by what that event signals or portends (*28*). The informativeness or "signal potential" of an event, and thus its potential social impact, appears to be systematically related to the characteristics of the hazard and the location of the event within the factor space described earlier (Fig. 4). An accident that takes many lives may produce relatively little social disturbance (beyond that experienced by the victims' families and friends) if it occurs as part of a familiar and well-understood system (such as a train wreck). However, a small accident in an unfamiliar

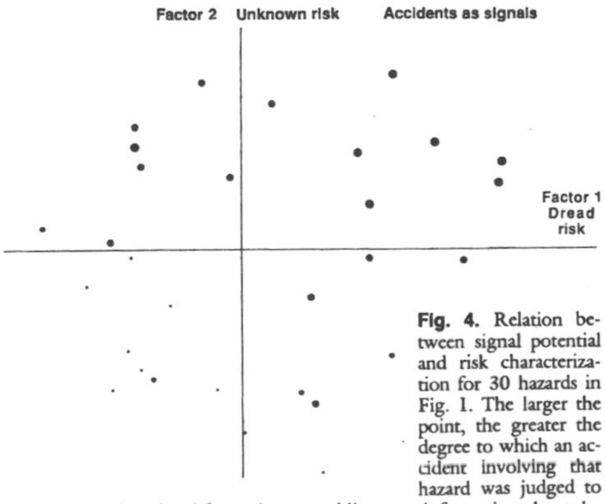

Factor 2   Unknown risk   Accidents as signals

Factor 1
Dread
risk

Fig. 4. Relation between signal potential and risk characterization for 30 hazards in Fig. 1. The larger the point, the greater the degree to which an accident involving that hazard was judged to "serve as a warning signal for society, providing new information about the probability that similar or even more destructive mishaps might occur within this type of activity." Media attention and the higher order costs of a mishap are likely to be correlated with signal potential (*28*).

system (or one perceived as poorly understood), such as a nuclear reactor or a recombinant DNA laboratory, may have immense social consequences if it is perceived as a harbinger of further and possibly catastrophic mishaps.

The concept of accidents as signals was eloquently expressed in an editorial addressing the tragic accident at Bhopal (*29*).

> What truly grips us in these accounts is not so much the numbers as the spectacle of suddenly vanishing competence, of men utterly routed by technology, of fail-safe systems failing with a logic as inexorable as it was once—indeed, right up until that very moment—unforeseeable. And the spectacle haunts us because it seems to carry allegorical import, like the whispery omen of a hovering future.

One implication of the signal concept is that effort and expense beyond that indicated by a cost-benefit analysis might be warranted to reduce the possibility of "high-signal accidents." Unfortunate events involving hazards in the upper right quadrant of Fig. 1 appear particularly likely to have the potential to produce large ripples. As a result, risk analyses involving these hazards need to be made sensitive to these possible higher order impacts. Doing so would likely bring greater protection to potential victims as well as to companies and industries.

Analysis of Single Hazard Domains

Psychometric analyses have also been applied to judgments of diverse hazard scenarios within a single technological domain, such as railroad transport (*30*) or automobiles (*31*). Kraus (*30*) had people evaluate the riskiness of 49 railroad hazard scenarios that varied with respect to type of train, type of cargo, location of the accident, and the nature and cause of the accident (for example, a high-speed train carrying passengers through a mountain tunnel derails due to a mechanical system failure). The results showed that these railroad hazards were highly differentiated, much like the hazards in Fig. 1. The highest signal potential (and thus the highest potential for large ripple effects) was associated with accidents involving trains carrying hazardous chemicals.

A study by Slovic, MacGregor, and Kraus (*31*) examined perceptions of risk and signal value for 40 structural defects in automobiles. Multivariate analysis of these defects, rated in terms of various characteristics of risk, produced a two-factor space. As in earlier studies with diverse hazards, the position of a defect in this space predicted judgments of riskiness and signal value quite well. One defect stood out much as nuclear hazards do in Fig. 1. It was a fuel tank rupture upon impact, creating the possibility of fire and burn injuries. This, of course, is similar to the notorious design problem that plagued Ford Pinto and that Ford allegedly declined to correct because a cost-benefit analysis indicated that the correction costs greatly exceeded the expected benefits from increased safety (*32*). Had Ford done a psychometric study, the analysis might have highlighted this particular defect as one whose seriousness and higher order costs (lawsuits, damaged company reputation) were likely to be greatly underestimated by cost-benefit analysis.

Forecasting Public Acceptance

Results from studies of the perception of risk have been used to explain and forecast acceptance and opposition for specific technologies (*33*). Nuclear power has been a frequent topic of such analyses because of the dramatic opposition it has engendered in the face of experts' assurances of its safety. Research shows that people judge the benefits from nuclear power to be quite small and the risks to be unacceptably great. Nuclear power risks occupy extreme positions in psychometric factor spaces, reflecting people's views that these risks are unknown, dread, uncontrollable, inequitable, catastrophic, and likely to affect future generations (Fig. 1). Opponents of nuclear power recognize that few people have died thus far as a result of this technology. However, long before Chernobyl, they expressed great concern over the potential for catastrophic accidents.

These public perceptions have evoked harsh reactions from experts. One noted psychiatrist wrote that "the irrational fear of nuclear plants is based on a mistaken assessment of the risks" (34, p. 8). A nuclear physicist and leading advocate of nuclear power contended that " . . . the public has been driven insane over fear of radiation [from nuclear power]. I use the word 'insane' purposefully since one of its definitions is loss of contact with reality. The public's understanding of radiation dangers has virtually lost all contact with the actual dangers as understood by scientists" (35, p. 31).

Risk perception research paints a different picture, demonstrating that people's deep anxieties are linked to the reality of extensive unfavorable media coverage and to a strong association between nuclear power and the proliferation and use of nuclear weapons. Attempts to "educate" or reassure the public and bring their perceptions in line with those of industry experts appear unlikely to succeed because the low probability of serious reactor accidents makes empirical demonstrations of safety difficult to achieve. Because nuclear risks are perceived as unknown and potentially catastrophic, even small accidents will be highly publicized and may produce large ripple effects (Fig. 4).

Psychometric research may be able to forecast the response to technologies that have yet to arouse strong and persistent public opposition. For example, DNA technologies seem to evoke several of the perceptions that make nuclear power so hard to manage. In the aftermath of an accident, this technology could face some of the same problems and opposition now confronting the nuclear industry.

Placing Risks in Perspective

A consequence of the public's concerns and its opposition to risky technologies has been an increase in attempts to inform and educate people about risk. Risk perception research has a number of implications for such educational efforts (36).

One frequently advocated approach to broadening people's perspectives is to present quantitative risk estimates for a variety of hazards, expressed in some unidimensional index of death or disability, such as risk per hour of exposure, annual probability of death, or reduction in life expectancy. Even though such comparisons have no logically necessary implications for acceptability of risk (15), one might still hope that they would help improve people's intuitions about the magnitude of risks. Risk perception research suggests, however, that these sorts of comparisons may not be very satisfactory even for this purpose. People's perceptions and attitudes are determined not only by the sort of unidimensional statistics used in such tables but also by the variety of quantitative and qualitative characteristics reflected in Fig. 1. To many people, statements such as, "the annual risk from living near a nuclear power plant is equivalent to the risk of riding an extra 3 miles in an automobile," give inadequate consideration to the important differences in the nature of the risks from these two technologies.

In short, "riskiness" means more to people than "expected number of fatalities." Attempts to characterize, compare, and regulate risks must be sensitive to this broader conception of risk. Fischhoff, Watson, and Hope (37) have made a start in this direction by demonstrating how one might construct a more comprehensive measure of risk. They show that variations in the scope of one's

definition of risk can greatly change the assessment of risk from various energy technologies.

Whereas psychometric research implies that risk debates are not merely about risk statistics, some sociological and anthropological research implies that some of these debates may not even be about risk (5, 6). Risk concerns may provide a rationale for actions taken on other grounds or they may be a surrogate for other social or ideological concerns. When this is the case, communication about risk is simply irrelevant to the discussion. Hidden agendas need to be brought to the surface for discussion (38).

Perhaps the most important message from this research is that there is wisdom as well as error in public attitudes and perceptions. Lay people sometimes lack certain information about hazards. However, their basic conceptualization of risk is much richer than that of the experts and reflects legitimate concerns that are typically omitted from expert risk assessments. As a result, risk communication and risk management efforts are destined to fail unless they are structured as a two-way process. Each side, expert and public, has something valid to contribute. Each side must respect the insights and intelligence of the other.

REFERENCES AND NOTES

1. For a comprehensive bibliography on risk assessment, see V. Covello and M. Abernathy, in *Technological Risk Assessment*, P. F. Ricci, L. A. Sagan, C. G. Whipple, Eds. (Nijhoff, The Hague, 1984), pp. 283–363.
2. "Risk in a complex society," report of a public opinion poll conducted by L. Harris for the Marsh and McClennan Company, New York (1980).
3. A. Wildavsky, *Am. Sci.* 67, 32 (1979).
4. I. Burton, R. W. Kates, G. F. White, *The Environment as Hazard* (Oxford Univ. Press, Oxford, 1978).
5. J. F. Short, Jr., *Am. Sociol. Rev.* 49, 711 (1984).
6. M. Douglas and A. Wildavsky, *Risk and Culture* (Univ. of California Press, Berkeley, 1982).
7. W. Edwards, *Annu. Rev. Psychol.* 12, 473 (1961).
8. D. Kahneman, P. Slovic, A. Tversky, Eds. *Judgment Under Uncertainty: Heuristics and Biases* (Cambridge Univ. Press, New York, 1982).
9. M. Henrion and B. Fischhoff, *Am. J. Phys.*, in press.
10. R. Nisbett and L. Ross, *Human Inference: Strategies and Shortcomings of Social Judgment* (Prentice-Hall, Englewood Cliffs, NJ, 1980).
11. A. Tversky and D. Kahneman, *Science* 211, 453 (1981).
12. B. Fischhoff *et al.*, *Policy Sci.* 8, 127 (1978).
13. P. Slovic, B. Fischhoff, S. Lichtenstein, *Acta. Psychol.* 56, 183 (1984).
14. C. Starr, *Science* 165, 1232 (1969).
15. B. Fischhoff, S. Lichtenstein, P. Slovic, S. L. Derby, R. L. Keeney, *Acceptable Risk* (Cambridge Univ. Press, New York, 1981).
16. G. T. Gardner *et al.*, *J. Soc. Psychol.* 116, 179 (1982).
17. D. R. DeLuca, J. A. J. Stolwijk, W. Horowitz, in *Risk Evaluation and Management*, V. T. Covello, J. Menkes, J. L. Mumpower, Eds. (Plenum, New York, 1986), pp. 25–67.
18. E. J. Johnson and A. Tversky, *J. Exp. Psych. Gen.* 113, 55 (1984).
19. M. K. Lindell and T. C. Earle, *Risk Anal.* 3, 245 (1983).
20. H. J. Otway and M. Fishbein, *The Determinants of Attitude Formation: An Application to Nuclear Power* (RM-76-80 Technical Report, International Institute for Applied Systems Analysis, Laxenburg, Austria, 1976).
21. O. Renn and E. Swaton, *Env. Int.* 10, 557 (1984).
22. P. Slovic, B. Fischhoff, S. Lichtenstein, in *Societal Risk Assessment: How Safe is Safe Enough?*, R. Schwing and W. A. Albers, Jr., Eds. (Plenum, New York, 1980), pp. 181–216.
23. C. A. J. Vlek and P. J. Stallen, *Organ. Behav. Hum. Perf.* 28, 235 (1981).
24. D. von Winterfeldt, R. S. John, K. Borcherding, *Risk Anal.* 1, 277 (1981).
25. P. Slovic, B. Fischhoff, S. Lichtenstein, in *Perilous Progress: Managing the Hazards of Technology*, R. W. Kates, C. Hohenemser, J. X. Kasperson, Eds. (Westview, Boulder, CO, 1985), pp. 91–125.
26. P. Slovic, B. Fischhoff, S. Lichtenstein, *Environment* 21 (no. 3), 14 (1979).
27. Estimated at $500 billion [see *Electr. Power Res. Inst. J.* 5 (no. 5), 24 (1980)].
28. P. Slovic, S. Lichtenstein, B. Fischhoff, *Manage. Sci.* 30, 464 (1984).
29. The Talk of the Town, *New Yorker* 60 (no. 53), 29 (1985).
30. N. Kraus, thesis, University of Pittsburgh (1985).
31. P. Slovic, D. MacGregor, N. Kraus, *Accident Anal. Prev.*, in press.
32. *Grimshaw* vs. *Ford Motor Co.*, Superior Court, No. 19776, Orange County, CA, 6 February 1978.
33. P. Slovic, B. Fischhoff, S. Lichtenstein, in *Advances in Environmental Psychology*, A. Baum and J. E. Singer, Eds. (Erlbaum, Hillsdale, NJ, 1981), vol. 3, pp. 157–169.
34. R. L. Dupont, *Bus. Week*, 7 September 1981, pp. 8–9.
35. B. L. Cohen, *Before It's Too Late: A Scientist's Case for Nuclear Energy* (Plenum, New York, 1983).
36. P. Slovic, *Risk Anal.* 6, 403 (1986).
37. B. Fischhoff, S. Watson, C. Hope, *Policy Sci.* 17, 123 (1984).
38. W. Edwards and D. von Winterfeldt, *Risk Anal.*, in press.
39. The text of this article draws heavily upon the author's joint work with B. Fischhoff and S. Lichtenstein. Support for the writing of the article was provided by NSF grant SES-8517411 to Decision Research.

Policy Sciences 17 (1984) 123–139
Elsevier Science Publishers B.V., Amsterdam – Printed in the Netherlands

Defining Risk

BARUCH FISCHHOFF

*MRC Applied Psychology Unit, Cambridge, Great Britain and Decision Research,
A Branch of Perceptronics, 1201 Oak Street, Eugene, Oregon 97401, U.S.A.*

STEPHEN R. WATSON

Emmanuel College, Cambridge University, Cambridge, Great Britain

CHRIS HOPE

Cavendish Laboratory, Cambridge University, Cambridge, Great Britain

ABSTRACT

Risk is the focal topic in the management of many activities and technologies. For that management to be successful, an explicit and accepted definition of the term "risk" is essential. Creation of that definition is a political act, expressing the definers' values regarding the relative importance of different possible adverse consequences for a particular decision. Those values, and with them the definition of risk, can change with changes in the decisionmaker, the technologies considered, or the decision problem. After a review of the sources of controversy in defining risk, a general framework is developed, showing how these value issues can be systematically addressed. As an example, the approach is applied to characterizing the risks of six competing energy technologies, the relative riskeness of which depends upon the particular definition used.

Defining Risk

Managing the risks of technologies has become a major topic in scientific, industrial, and public policy. It has spurred the development of some industries and prompted the demise of others. It has expanded the powers of some agencies and overwhelmed the capacity of others. It has enhanced the growth of some disciplines, distorted the paths of others. It has generated political campaigns and countercampaigns. The focal ingredient in all this has been concern over risk. Yet, the meaning of "risk" has always been fraught with confusion and controversy. Some of this conflict has been overt, as when a professional body argues about the proper measure of "pollution" or "reliability" for

0032-2678/84/$ 03.00 © 1984 Elsevier Science Publishers B.V.

124

incorporation in a health or safety standard. More often, though, the controversy is unrecognized; "risk" is used in a particular way without extensive deliberations regarding the implications of alternative uses. Typically, that particular way follows custom in the scientific discipline initially concerned with the risk.

However, the definition of "risk," like that of any other key term in policy issues, is inherently controversial. The choice of definition can affect the outcome of policy debates, the allocation of resources among safety measures, and the distribution of political power in society. The present essay begins with an analysis of the key sources of controversy in this definition. It proceeds to advance a highly flexible general approach to defining "risk." Finally, it demonstrates the approach with an analysis of the comparative risks of different energy technologies, showing that the relative "riskiness" of those technologies depends upon the definition used. No definition is advanced as the correct one, because there is no one definition that is suitable for all problems. Rather, the choice of definition is a political one, expressing someone's views regarding the importance of different adverse effects in a particular situation. Such determinations should not be the exclusive province of scientists, who have no special insight into what society should value. As a result, the present approach is designed to offer a way to generate definitions of risk suitable for many problems and value systems.

Dimensions of Controversy

Objectivity. Technical experts often distinguish between "objective" and "subjective" risk. The former refers to the product of scientific research, primarily public health statistics, experimental studies, epidemiological surveys, and probabilistic risk analyses. The latter refers to non-expert perceptions of that research, embellished by whatever other considerations seize the public mind. This distinction is controversial in how it characterizes both the public and the experts.

Although it is tempting (and common) to attribute disagreements between the public and the experts to public ignorance or irrationality, closer examination often suggests a more complicated situation. Conflicts often can be traced to unrecognized disagreements about the topic, including what is meant by "risk." When the public proves misinformed, it is often for good reasons, such as receiving faulty (unclear, unbalanced) information through the news media or from the scientific community (Lichtenstein et al., 1978). In some instances, members of the lay public may even have a better understanding of specific issues (or for the definitiveness of knowledge regarding them) than do the experts (Cotgrove, 1982; Wynne, 1983).

Along with these elements of objectivity in public opinion, there are inevitably elements of subjectivity in expert estimates of risk. Within the philosophy of science, "objective" typically means something akin to "independent of observer." That is, any individual following the same procedure should reach the same conclusion. However meritorious as a goal, this sort of objectivity can rarely be achieved. Particularly in complex, novel areas, such as risk analysis, research requires the exercise of judgment. It is expert judgment, but judgment nonetheless. Even in those orderly areas for which public health statistics are available, interpretative questions must be answered before current (or even historical) risk levels can be estimated: Is there a secular trend (e.g., are we sitting on a cancer time bomb)? Is the effect of predisposing causes (e.g., poor nutrition) underestimated because deaths are typically attributed to immediate causes (e.g., pneumonia)? Are some deaths deliberately miscategorized (e.g., suicides as accidents when insurance benefits are threatened)? Total agreement on all such issues is a rarity in any active science. Thus, objectivity should always be an aspiration, but can never be an achievement of science. When public and experts disagree, it is a clash between two sets of differently informed opinions. Sciences, scientists, and definitions of risk differ greatly in how explicitly they acknowledge the role of judgment.

Dimensionality of risk. The risks of a technology are seldom its only consequences. No one would produce it if it did not generate some benefits for someone. No one could produce it without incurring some costs. The difference between these benefits and non-risk costs could be called its net benefit. In addition, risk itself is seldom just a single consequence. A technology may be capable of causing fatalities in several ways (e.g., by explosions and chronic toxicity), as well as inducing various forms of morbidity. It can affect plants and animals as well as humans. An analysis of "risk" needs to specify which of these dimensions will be included. In general, definitions based on a single dimension will favor technologies that do their harm in a variety of ways (as opposed to those that create a lot of one kind of problem). Although it represents particular values (and leads to decisions consonant with those values), the specification of dimensionality (like any other specification) is often the inadvertent product of convention or other forces, such as jurisdictional boundaries (Fischhoff, in press).

Summary statistic. For each dimension selected as relevant, some quantitative summary is needed for expressing how much of that kind of risk is created by a technology. The controversial aspects of that choice can be seen by comparing the practices of different scientists. For some, the unit of choice is the annual death toll (e.g., Zentner, 1979); for others, death per person exposed or per hour of exposure (e.g., Starr, 1969; Wilson, 1979); for others, it is the loss of life expectancy (e.g., Cohen and Lee, 1979; Reissland and Harries, 1979); for still others, lost working days (e.g., Inhaber, 1979). Crouch and Wilson (1982) have shown how the choice of unit can affect the relative riskiness of technologies; for example, today's coal mines are much less risky than those of thirty years ago in terms of accidental deaths per ton of coal, but marginally riskier in terms of accidental deaths per employee. The difference between measures is explained by increased productivity. The choice among measures is a policy question, with Crouch and Wilson suggesting that, "From a national point of view, given that a certain amount of coal has to be obtained, deaths per million tons of coal is the more appropriate measure of risk, whereas from a labor leader's point of view, deaths per thousand persons employed may be more relevant" (p. 13).

Other value questions may be seen in the units themselves. For example, loss of life

126

expectancy places a premium on early deaths which is absent from measures that treat all deaths equally; using it means ascribing particular worth to the lives of young people. Just counting fatalities expresses indifference to whether they come immediately after mishaps or following a substantial latency period (during which it may not be clear who will die). Whatever individuals are included in a category are treated as equals; these may include beneficiaries and non-beneficiaries of the technology (reflecting an attitude toward that kind of equity), workers and members of the general public (reflecting an attitude toward that kind of voluntariness), or participants and non-participants in setting policy for the technology (reflecting an attitude toward that kind of voluntariness). Using the average of past casualties or the expectation of future fatalities means ignoring the distribution of risk over time; it treats technologies taking a steady annual toll in the same way as those that are typically benign, except for the rare catastrophic accident. When averages are inadequate, a case might be made for using one of the higher moments of the distribution of casualties over time or for incorporating a measure of the uncertainty surrounding estimates (Fischhoff, in press).

Bounding the technology. Willingness to count delayed fatalities means that a technology's effects are not being bounded in time (as they are, for example, in some legal proceedings that consider the time that passes between cause, effect, discovery, and reporting). Other bounds need to be set also, either implicitly or explicitly. One is the proportion of the fuel and materials cycles to be considered: to what extent should the risks be restricted to those directly associated with the enjoyment of benefits or extended to the full range of activities necessary if those benefits are to be obtained? Crouch and Wilson (1982) offer an insightful discussion of some of these issues in the context of imported steel; the U.S. Nuclear Regulatory Commission (1983) has adopted a restrictive definition in setting safety goals for nuclear power (Fischhoff, 1983); much of the acrimony in the debates over the risks of competing energy technologies concerned treatment of the risks of back-up energy sources (Herbert et al., 1979). A second recurrent bounding problem is how far to go in considering higher-order consequences (i.e., when coping with one risk exposes people to another). A third is how to treat a technology's partial contribution to consequences, for example, when it renders people susceptible to other problems or when it accentuates other effects through synergistic processes.

Concern. Events that threaten people's health and safety exact a toll even if they never happen. Concern over accidents, illness, and unemployment occupy people even when they and their loved ones experience long, robust, and salaried lives. Although associated with risks, these consequences are virtual certainties. All those who know about them will respond to them in some way. In some cases, that response benefits the respondent, even if its source is an aversive event. For example, financial worries may prompt people to expand their personal skills or create socially useful innovations. Nonetheless, their resources have been diverted from other, perhaps preferred pursuits. Moreover, the accompanying stress can contribute to a variety of negative health effects, particularly when it is hard to control the threat (Elliott and Eisdorfer, 1982). Stressors not only precipitate problems of their own, but can complicate other problems and divert the psychological resources needed to cope with them. Thus, concern about a risk may hasten the end of a marriage by giving the couple one more thing to fight about and that much less energy to look for solutions.

Hazardous technologies can evoke such concern even when they are functioning perfectly. Some of the response may be focussed and purposeful, such as attempts to reduce the risk through personal and collective action. However, even that effort should be considered as a cost of the technology because that time and energy might be invested in something else (e.g., leisure, financial planning, improving professional skills) were it not for the technology. When many people are exposed to the risk (or are concerned about the exposure of their fellows), then the costs may be very extensive. Concern may have even greater impact than the actual health and safety effects. Ironically, because the signs of stress are diffuse (e.g., a few more divorces, somewhat aggravated cardiovascular problems), it is quite possible for the size of the effects to be both intolerably large (considering the benefits) and unmeasurable (by current techniques).

Including concern among the consequences of a risky technology immediately raises two additional controversial issues. One is what constitutes an appropriate level of concern. It could be argued that concern should be proportionate to physical risk. There are, however, a variety of reasons why citizens might reasonably be concerned most about hazards that they themselves acknowledge to be relatively small (e.g., they feel that an important precedent is being set, that things will get worse if not checked, or that the chances for effective action are great). The second issue is whether to hold a technology responsible for the concern evoked by people's perceptions of its risks or for the level of concern that would be evoked were they to share the best available technical knowledge. It is the former that determines actual concern; however, using it would mean penalizing some technologies for evoking unjustified concerns and rewarding others for having escaped the public eye.

The Nature of Risky Decisions

Although a part of all risky decisions, risk is all of very few. Hazard management would be easy if risk were a substance and a technology could be characterized (and managed) effectively in terms of how much of that substance it contained (Watson, 1981). Risky decisions are, however, not about risk alone. Rather, they are choices among options, each of which has a variety of relevant features, including a level of risk. When a technology is adopted, so is its entire package of features. Thus, it is impossible to infer from its adoption that a technology has an acceptable level of risk (Fischhoff et al., 1981; Green, 1980; Otway and von Winterfeldt, 1982). Those adopting it might prefer much less risk, but be unable to obtain it at an acceptable price. In other decisions (or even in that decision should the possibilities change), they might adopt much less risky options.

From this perspective, the most general role for a definition of risk is to provide a

128

coherent, explicit, consistent expression of one subset of the consequences arising in risky decisions. For deliberative decisionmaking to proceed, it must be complemented by comparable conceptual analyses of the other consequences. With a clear set of concepts, it is possible to begin making the hard tradeoffs between risks and net benefits (which may include any positive value attributed to risk itself due, say, to the thrill or excitement it produces).

There are, however, some reasons for thinking about risks in isolation. One is educating the intuitions. The risks created by many technologies are so diverse that it is hard to think about them all at once. The rem and Sievert, which aggregate diverse radiation doses, attempt to serve this role. A second reason is to summarize the conclusions of policymaking that has considered other factors (Fischhoff, in press). Health and safety standards are often expressed in terms of an "acceptable level of risk," even though nonrisk costs and benefits strongly influenced how they were set (otherwise, they would be set at zero risk). That expression may enunciate a political philosophy ("we care about the public to this extent"), or it may provide an operational rule for the technical staff monitoring compliance, or it may be the only legitimate public conclusion of an agency that is mandated to manage risk (but must, in practice, consider risk–benefit tradeoffs). A third role is providing an explicit criterion for guiding and evaluating an agency's actions. A safety measure, such as a mandatory seat belt law, might have quite a different effect on "risk" if that is defined as deaths, serious injuries, or all injuries. Evaluating it fairly requires knowing what it was intended to accomplish.

Aspects of Risk

The first step in defining "risk" is determining which consequences it should include. Because that determination depends upon the particular problem, some context must be specified in order to produce even a hypothetical example. The context adopted here is evaluating the risks of competing energy technologies, as a component of setting national energy policy. Like any other choice of context, this one renders consequences that none of the competing options create – "unimportant for present purposes" – whatever their overall importance to society. This particular choice means that the selection of consequences (like other aspects of the definition process) should reflect "society's values," rather than those of any single interest. If one wished to revise or criticize this example, that effort, too, should begin with its selection of consequences.

Figure 1(B) shows that selection. Three kinds of risky consequence are included: fatalities, concern, and morbidity. Each is meant to include consequences whose magnitude is known, even though the identity of the casualties is not. For example, fatal accidents are a risk to those exposed to motor vehicles, even though the annual death toll is quite predictable. Each is meant to exclude anything but threats to human health and safety (e.g., accompanying property and financial risks). Actually choosing among energy technologies would require consideration of the broader set of consequences appearing in Fig. 1(A). The general form of Fig. 1(B) takes a position on one of the five

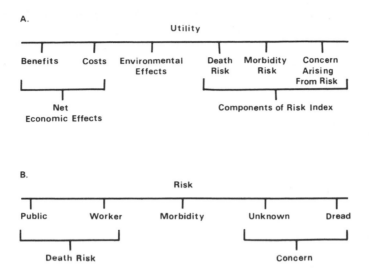

Fig. 1. Possible dimensions of consequence: (A) for decisionmaking, (B) for risk index.

sources of controversy regarding risk, its dimensionality. The specific contents take a position on a second, whether to consider concern a consequence of risk, despite its not having an obvious physical or physiological measure. Positions on the others are taken below in the course of developing a procedure for expressing the risks of the energy technologies.

Figure 1(B) makes two further distinctions. One is between mortal risks to the general public and mortal risks to workers in the technology. Such a distinction is made in many industries, with safety standards for workers being (very) roughly one-tenth as stringent as those for nonworkers (Derr et al., 1983). Making the distinction here allows one to decide whether this common practice should be accepted and enshrined in public policy by assigning a different weight to public and worker deaths. As discussed above, distinctions might also be made on the basis of whether those who die also benefit from the technology, have consented to exposure, or lose their lives in catastrophic accidents.

The second distinction is between two kinds of concern. Studies of lay risk perceptions (Fischhoff et al., 1978; Slovic et al., in press; Vlek and stallen, 1981) have shown that concern about technologies' risks can be predicted quite well by two "subjective dimensions of risk." These dimensions summarize a large number of individual determinants of perceived risk. They may be described as reflecting (a) the degree to which the risk is *unknown* and (b) the degree to which the risk evokes a feeling of *dread*. The former expresses aversion to uncertainty, and thus represents cognitive (or intellectual) aspects of concern, whereas the latter captures a risk's ability to evoke a visceral response. This usage takes these dimensions from the domain of prediction to the domain of prescription, from antici-

130

pating how people will respond to technologies to guiding how those technologies will be shaped.

The morbidity aspect is intended for all nonfatal injury and illness. It would also include genetic damage, whether expressed in birth defects or latent in the population. (The production of spontaneous abortions might appear here or in the previous category.) It should also include the unpleasantness of the period preceding death, which should be negligible for some accidents and considerable for some lingering illnesses.

Constructing Risk Indices

Choosing a set of attributes to describe a risk prospect creates a vector, each element of which expresses one dimension of consequence. The definition process could be terminated at that point, leaving users to integrate the elements intuitively. Alternatively, the elements can be combined into an aggregate measure of risk in order to eliminate the costs, errors, and vagueness that come with intuitive integration. The essence of aggregation is determining the relative importance of the elements. The following is a generalized scheme that can be adapted to the needs of many problems and value systems. It is drawn from multiattribute utility theory, fuller expositions of which can be found elsewhere, for both the theory itself (Keeney and Raiffa, 1976) and its application to risk problems (Ahmed and Husseiny, 1978; Keeney, 1980; Lathrop and Watson, 1982). The present application differs from its predecessors in focussing on risk, emphasizing the full range of options, and offering no opinion as to the correct solution. The logic of such procedures is as follows:

An aggregation procedure for risks should characterize a technology by a single value such that activities having a higher value will be more risky (in the eyes of those whose values the procedure represents). After the components have been selected, the next step is their operationalization. For example, if the consequences are called x_i, then x_1 might be the number of (additional) deaths among members of the general public; x_2, the number of years of incapacitating illness caused; x_3, a measure of public concern, etc. These consequences are often called "attributes"; we will use the terms interchangeably. This operationalization creates a vector of measurements $(x_1, \ldots, x_n)$.

This vector expresses the measure, but not the worth, of those consequences. "Utility" is commonly used as a generalized unit of worth. Utility theory offers a wide variety of procedures for converting each such vector into a single number, representing its overall (un)desirability. These procedures can incorporate highly complex value systems and varying degrees of uncertainty regarding which consequences will, in fact, be experienced. In practice, though, various simplifying assumptions are adopted to render the analysis more tractable. For example, instead of explicitly modeling uncertainty (complete, say, with the elicitation of probability distributions for the values of different parameters), the analyst might treat all results as certainties. However, at the end of the analysis, each parameter will be varied through a range of plausible values to see whether such sensitivity analyses affect the previously reached conclusions.

In order to simplify the exposition, the present example makes two potentially controversial assumptions regarding the value structure. The first of these is *risk neutrality,* meaning, for example, that the certain loss of one life is just as bad as one chance in 10^5 of 10^5 deaths. Although it has been argued that people are particularly averse to losing many lives at once (as opposed to losing as many lives in separate accidents), this tendency appears to be due primarily to the great uncertainty that surrounds technologies capable of producing large accidents. A death is a death, whether it comes alone or with many others (Slovic et al., in press). In this definition, the uncertainty surrounding those deaths can be incorporated in the sensitivity analyses and the first "concern" attribute. The second simplifying assumption asserts that the underlying value structure is not overly complex. It is formalized as the property of *mutual preference independence.* Roughly speaking, two attributes are preference independent of all others if tradeoffs between them do not depend upon the levels of the other attributes.

If either of these assumptions seems wanting, then it is straightforward (if cumbersome) to repeat the analysis with alternative assumptions. If they seem adequate, then it is possible to express the index as

$$R = \sum_{j=1}^{n} w_j y_j \tag{1}$$

where y_j is the expected utility for attribute j and w_j is a weighting factor, expressing its relative importance. "Expected utility" is the product of a consequence's utility and the probability of it being incurred if a technology is pursued. For example, if x_i were the number of public deaths, then y_i would be the expected utility for public deaths, which would consider not only the probability for different losses, but also any changes in the significance of marginal deaths as a function of total deaths.

Risks of Electricity Generation: Different Definitions

Problem Description

Electricity generation is an interesting case for two reasons. One is the evidence that disagreement about the definition of key terms (including "risk") has contributed to the bitterness of many energy debates. The second is that important issues tend to generate research, producing data upon which risk estimates may be more soundly based.

In this analysis, six energy technologies are considered. Five of these, coal, hydropower, large-scale windpower, small-scale windpower, and nuclear power, can increase the supply of electricity. The sixth, energy conservation, can reduce the demand for electricity, thereby freeing existing supplies for use elsewhere.

Attribute Definition

The five attributes of these technologies are those shown in Fig. 1(B). They are opera-

132

tionalized as follows: Both kinds of death are measured in terms of the expected number of deaths per Gigawatt year (GWyr) of electricity generated or saved. Choosing this summary statistic means taking positions on two additional dimensions of controversy regarding the definition of risk: Broad bounds are set on the technologies, so as to attribute to them all casualties incurred in conjunction with generating electricity. Deaths are just tallied, without regard for the number of years taken off each, the extent of each victim's exposure, the distribution of deaths over time, or any of the other features discussed earlier. Morbidity will be measured by expected person-days of incapacity per GWyr of electricity.

The two attributes associated with concern will be specified in terms of the technologies' ratings on the two comparable factors in psychometric studies of perceived risk (e.g., Slovic et al., in press). These studies have produced sufficiently robust results to make reliance on them conceivable; perceptions of risk have proven sufficiently good predictors of attitudes and actions for them to serve as reasonable indicators of level of concern. What is most arguable about such reliance is treating the expression of concern as evidence of adverse consequences. As discussed above, one ground for that claim is that concern itself is an adverse consequence, which should not be imposed upon people without compensating benefit; a second ground is that concern is associated with stress which is, in turn, associated with various physiological effects that are so difficult to measure that it is reasonable to use concern as a surrogate for them.

Evaluating Consequences

Having defined the attributes, the next step is to evaluate each possible outcome on each (e.g., how bad is it to incur 10 or 100 worker deaths). In technical terms, this means defining a utility function for each attribute. A convenient way of doing so, given the assumptions made here, is to use a 100-point scale for each attribute, where 0 represents the least extreme possible consequence and 100 the most extreme possible consequence. (If both good and bad consequences were being considered, then a distinction between positive and negative scores would be necessary. Here, 100 is the worst possible outcome.) Intermediate values are defined appropriately. Although linear scaling is possible, it is not necessary. For example, for most people winning $100 will not be 10 times as satisfying as winning $10. Setting the end points of each scale requires a factual (or scientific) judgment regarding what consequences are possible. Setting the midpoints requires a value judgment regarding how those intermediate consequences are regarded.

A natural zero point for a casualty scale is zero casualties. It will be used here, recognizing that no deaths to workers, no deaths to the public, and no person-days lost are practically unachievable with any energy technology. On the basis of worst-case analyses, scores of 100 on attributes 1 and 2 are defined, respectively, as 10 public deaths and 10 occupational deaths per GWyr of electricity generated or saved. Similarly, 60,000 person-days of incapacity per GWyr would merit a score of 100 on attribute 3. Intermediate scores are assigned linearly (e.g., on attributes 1 and 2, one death receives 10, two

133

TABLE 1

The Components of Attributes 4 and 5

Attribute	Score of 0 implies risk has these properties	Score of 100 implies risk has these properties
4. Unknown risk	Observable	Not observable
	Known to exposed	Unknown to exposed
	Effect immediate	Effect delayed
	Old	New
	Known to science	Unknown to science
5. Dread risk	Controllable	Uncontrollable
	Not dread	Dread
	Not global catastrophic	Global catastrophic
	Consequences not fatal	Consequences fatal
	Equitable	Not equitable
	Individual	Catastrophic
	Low future risk	High future risk
	Easily reduced	Not easily reduced
	Decreasing	Increasing
	Voluntary	Involuntary
	Doesn't affect me	Affects me

Source: Slovic, Fischhoff and Lichtenstein, 1984.

deaths receive 20, etc.), reflecting a desire to assign an equal value to each casualty (as distinct, perhaps, from the decreasing sensitivity to additional casualties that people might actually experience).

Table 1 shows the characteristics that would give a technology scores of 0 and 100 on attributes 4 (unknown risk) and 5 (dread risk). Research has shown that although no technology quite reaches either extreme, mountain climbing and handguns score close to zero on attribute 4 (at least in the U.S.A., as do home appliances and high school football on attribute 5. At the other extreme, DNA research is rated as sufficiently unknown to receive a score in the 90s on attribute 4, while nuclear weapons do likewise on attribute 5.

Making Tradeoffs

The final step in specifying an evaluation scheme is to assign weights reflecting the relative importance of the different attributes. As these weights reflect value judgments, disagreements are legitimate; in the present context, they are to be expected. Table 2 presents four sets of weights, each reflecting a different set of values.

Brief descriptions might help explicate the perspectives that could motivate each set's adoption. The first rejects anything but readily measured physiological effects; treats a death as a death, whether it befalls a worker or a member of the public; views a life as equal to 6000 person-days of incapacity. Set B reflects a belief that concern is a legitimate consequence, that public deaths are twice as important as worker deaths, and that a

134

TABLE 2

Four Possible Sets of Weights for Five Risk Attributes

Attributes	A	B	C	D
1. Public deaths	0.33	0.40	0.20	0.08
2. Occupational deaths	0.33	0.20	0.05	0.04
3. Morbidity	0.33	0.20	0.05	0.40
4. Unknown risk	0	0.10	0.30	0.24
5. Dread risk	0	0.10	0.40	0.24
Sum of weights	1	1	1	1

worker death should be treated as equivalent to the loss of 6000 person-days. As Dunster (1980) argues, "it is not easy to weigh the benefits of reducing anxiety against those of saving life, but our society certainly does not require the saving of life to be given complete priority over the reduction of anxiety" (p. 127). Set C increases the importance ratio for public to occupational deaths and assigns major significance to concern. The specific weights imply a willingness to tradeoff 10 public deaths per GWyr to move from a technology causing extreme dread to one that is about average, perhaps feeling that the toll from concern-generated stress is large or that even minor accidents in a dread technology can cause enormously costly social disruption. The D weights represent a paramount concern with the suffering of the living, whether through injury or anxiety, rather than with the number of deaths.

Whatever one's value system, the weights assigned should be very sensitive to the range of outcomes considered on each attribute. If, for example, 100 on attribute 1 meant 50 public deaths per year (rather than 10), then Set A would have to assign a larger value to attribute 1 to achieve the same effect of weighting a public and a worker death equally.

Scoring Technologies

In order to apply this scheme to technologies, it is necessary to assess the magnitude of the consequences that each produces on each attribute. This is a scientific, not a value question. It should be informed by the best available technical knowledge. However, applying that knowledge in the present case requires the exercise of judgment, to choose, weigh, and extrapolate from existing studies. Despite having a commitment to objectivity, we cannot escape some subjectivity in attempting to derive this sort of policy-oriented advice.

Table 3 provides point estimates roughly summarizing the research reported in the following sources: Baecher et al. (1980), Birkhofer (1980), Bliss et al. (1979), Budnitz and Holdren (1976), Comar and Sagan (1976), Department of Energy (1979), Dunster (1980), Greenhalgh (1980), Hamilton (1980), Okrent (1980), Rogers and Templin (1980), and Slovic et al. (1980, in press). This literature reveals both substantial differences of opinion and substantial areas of ignorance. As two examples: The extreme values for

TABLE 3

The Scores of Six Technologies of Five Risk Attributes by One Expert

Attribute	Coal	Hydro	Large scale wind	Small scale wind	Nuclear	Conservation
1. Public deaths	80	10	20	5	10	5
2. Occupational deaths	30	20	10	30	5	10
3. Morbidity	20	20	40	50	10	40
4. Unknown risk	70	60	90	50	80	40
5. Dread risk	50	50	40	20	90	10

expected occupational deaths from coal were 0.7 and 8 deaths per GWyr of electricity generated. Very few risk data were available for either small-scale wind power or conservation; these scores were liberally adapted from knowledge of other technologies. Where available, the concern scores required the least exercise of judgment. Technologies that have been rated have proven to have rather robust scores on these dimensions, regardless of who does the rating, how the rating is carried out, and what other technologies are in the rating set (Slovic et al., in press). However, several energy technologies have yet to be evaluated in this way. Their scores were derived by conjecture. For example, the scores for conservation on attributes 4 and 5 were averages of those for home appliances and bicycles.

Given the unreliability of these estimates, any attempt to establish the risks of energy technologies would have to address the uncertainty surrounding them, with either sensitivity analyses or explicit assessment of probabilities. Given the illustrative nature of the present example, that exercise will be foregone as misplaced imprecision.

Computing Risk

Using these values and Set A's weights, Expression (1) shows the risk from coal to be $0.33(80) + 0.33(30) + 0.33(20) = 42.9$. Other scores are computed similarly and displayed in Fig. 2. Because the scores are standardized to range from 0 to 100 and the weights to sum to 1.0, it is possible to compare scores across technologies and across weighting schemes. That comparison shows that the riskiness of coal, small-scale windpower, and conservation vary little across these four sets of weights, whilst those for hydro, large-scale windpower, and particularly nuclear power vary greatly. Thus, if one accepts the consequence estimates of Table 3, then the riskiness of these last three technologies depends upon the importance assigned to the different consequences.

Table 4 shows how this sensitivity expresses itself in terms of the relative riskiness of the six technologies. Coal, for example, ranks consistently low, whereas nuclear may be best or worst depending upon the definition used. These enormous variations occur despite complete agreement regarding the magnitude of the consequences. Thus, arguments over relative risk may reflect only disagreements about values.

136

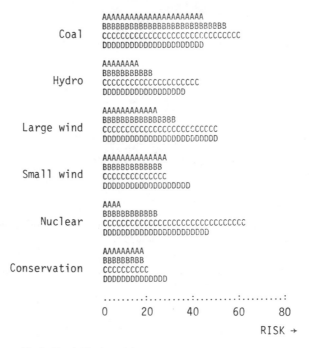

Fig. 2. The risk indices of six technologies on four sets of weights.

Conclusion

An effective decisionmaking process, whether conducted by individuals or societies, requires agreement on basic terms. Without such conceptual clarity, miscommunication and confusion are likely. Definitional ambiguity regarding the term "risk," in particular,

TABLE 4

The Risk-To-Human-Health Rankings of Six Technologies Given Four Sets of Weights on One Set of Five Attributes and the Scores of One Expert

Rank		Set of Weights			
		A	B	C	D
Best	1.	*Nuclear*	Conservation	Conservation	Conservation
	2.	Hydro	Hydro	Small wind	Hydro
	3.	Conservation	*Nuclear*	Hydro	Small wind
	4.	Large wind	Small wind	Large wind	Coal
	5.	Small wind	Large wind	Coal	*Nuclear*
Worst	6.	Coal	Coal	*Nuclear*	Large wind

has spawned needless (and irresoluble) conflict over the relative riskiness of different technologies. At the same time, it has obscured the need for debate over the value issues involved in specifying what "risk" means.

The present analysis presents a framework for defining risk which directly faces those inherent conflicts. Indeed, it forces one to adopt an explicit position on each aspect of the controversy before a workable definition can be created. As a result, the specific indices of risk developed here are controversial by design. However, they are also expendable by design. The general framework is highly flexible, capable of fitting many problems and many value systems. Its use in a particular problem makes possible a diagnosis of the extent to which conflicts reflect disagreements about facts or disagreements about values. In the former case, one can hope that consensus about risk will evolve as scientific research progresses. In the latter case, consensus will only emerge if there is effective public debate about what society should value. That debate can be informed (and spurred) by ethical and policy analyses, but it cannot be resolved by them.

Applying this potentially rich procedure required a series of simplifying assumptions. These included taking only five risky consequences from the vector of possibilities, asserting risk neutrality and mutual preference independence, and representing effect magnitude by point estimates. Despite these restrictions, this illustrative analysis showed that the relative riskiness of different energy technologies is quite sensitive to how risk is defined.

The emphasis here has been on the logic of the analysis, rather than on its content. Making a definitive statement regarding the risks of competing energy technologies would require definitive estimates of both the magnitude and the importance of those consequences for a particular society. Neither was attempted here. An additional caution is that even a definitive statement about risk would have no necessary implications for most policymaking. People do not accept risks, but technologies, one of whose significant features may be their risks. Developing an index of risk allows systematic treatment of one aspect of those decisions, but only one aspect. Analogous treatments of other consequence domains would be needed to complete the picture.

Developing a definition of risk requires a variety of explicit value judgments. Choosing to express risk in a numerical index may itself make a statement of values. The present exposition emphasized the possibilities that an index offers for including different people's values in policymaking. However, it may also be used to exclude the people themselves from the policymaking process, with policy experts serving as self-appointed spokespeople for what the public wants. Even if careful research is conducted to identify the public values that are to be incorporated in society's risk index, such technical recognition need not substitute for active, personal participation. If it is used that way, then the index may be blamed for the faults of a political process that can tolerate public opinion, but not the public.

138

Acknowledgments

This research was supported by the National Science Foundation under Grant PRA-8116925 to Perceptronics, Inc. Any opinions, findings and conclusions expressed in this article are those of the authors and do not necessarily reflect the views of the National Science Foundation. We give our thanks to Vincent Covello, Jack Dowie, Ken Hammond, Paul Slovic, and Ola Svenson for perceptive comments on previous drafts.

Notes

Chris Hope is now at the Department of Fuel Sciences, University of Leeds, Leeds, Great Britain. Requests for reprints should be sent to Baruch Fischhoff, 1201 Oak Street, Eugene, Oregon 97401, U.S.A.

References

Ahmed, S. and Husseiny, A. A. (1978). "A multivariate utility approach for selection of energy sources," *Energy* 3: 669–700.

Baecher, G. B., Pate, M. E. and de Neufville, R. (1980). "Risk of dam failure in benefit–cost analysis," *Water Resources Research* 16: 449–456.

Birkhofer, A. (1980). "The German risk study for nuclear power plants," *IAEA Bulletin* 22 (5/6): 23–33.

Bliss, C., Clifford, P., Goldgraben, G., Graf-Webster, E., Krickenberger, K., Maher, H. and Zimmerman, N. (1979). *Accidents and Unscheduled Events Associated with Non-Nuclear Energy Resources and Technology*. Washington, D.C.: MITRE Corporation for Environmental Protection Agency.

Budnitz, R. J. and Holdren, J. P. (1976). "Social and environmental costs of energy systems," *Annual Review of Energy* 1: 553–580.

Cohen, B. and Lee, I. (1979). "A catalog of risks," *Health Physics* 36: 707–722.

Comar, C. L. and Sagan, L. A. (1976). "Health effects of energy production and conversion," *Annual Review of Energy* 1: 581–660.

Cotgrove, A. (1982). *Catastrophe or Cornucopia? The Environment, Politics and the Future*. New York: Wiley.

Crouch, E. A. C. and Wilson, R. (1982). *Risk/Benefit Analysis*. Cambridge, Mass.: Ballinger.

Department of Energy (1979). *Energy Technologies for the United Kingdom, Vol. I and II*. London: HMSO.

Derr, P., Goble, R., Kasperson, R. E. and Kates, R. W. (1983). "Responding to the double standard of worker/public protection," *Environment* 25 (6): 6–11, 35–36.

Dunster, J. H. (1980). "The approach of a regulatory authority to the concept of risk," *IAEA Bulletin* 22 (5/6): 123–128.

Elliott, G. R. and Eisdorfer, C., (Eds.) (1982). *Stress and Human Health*. New York: Springer Verlag.

Fischhoff, B. (1983). "Acceptable risk: The case of nuclear power," *Journal of Policy Analysis and Management* 2: 559–575.

Fischhoff, B. (1984). "Standard setting standards," *Management Science* in press.

Fischhoff, B., Lichtenstein, S., Slovic, P., Derby, S. L. and Keeney, R. L. (1981). *Acceptable Risk*. New York: Cambridge University Press.

Fischhoff, B., Slovic, P. and Lichtenstein, S. (1983). "The public vs. The experts: Perceived vs. actual disagreements about the risks of nuclear power," in V. Covello, G. Flamm, J. Rodericks, and R. Tardiff (Eds.), *Analysis of Actual vs. Perceived Risks*. New York: Plenum.

Fischhoff, B., Slovic, P., Lichtenstein, S., Read, S. and Combs, B. (1978). "How safe is safe enough? A psychometric study of attitudes towards technological risks and benefits," *Policy Sciences* 8: 127–152.

Green, C. H. (1980). "Risk: Attitudes and beliefs," in D. V. Canter (Ed.), *Behaviour in Fires*. Chichester: Wiley.

Greenhalgh, G. (1980). *The Necessity for Nuclear Power*. London: Graham & Trotman.

Hamilton, L. D. (1980). "Comparative risks from different energy systems: Evolutions of the methods of studies," *IAEA Bulletin* 22 (5/6): 35–71.

Herbert, J. H., Swanson, L. and Reddy, P. (1979). "A risky business," *Environment 21 (6): 28*-33.
Inhaber, H. (1979). "Risk with energy from conventional and nonconventional sources," *Science* 203: 718–723.
Keeney, R. L. (1980). "Evaluating alternatives involving potential fatalities," *Operations Research* 28: 188–205.
Keeney, R. L. and Raiffa, H. (1976). *Decisions with Multiple Objectives. Preferences and Value Trade-offs.* New York: Wiley.
Lathrop, J. W. and Watson, S. R. (1982). "Decision analysis for the evaluation of risk in nuclear waste management," *Journal of the Operational Research Society* 3: 407–418.
Lichtenstein, S., Slovic, P., Fischhoff, B., Layman, M. and Combs, B. (1978). "Judged frequency of lethal events," *Journal of Experimental Psychology: Human Learning and Memory* 4: 551–578.
Okrent, D. (1980). "Comment on social risk," *Science* 208: 372–375.
Otway, H. and von Winterfeldt, D. (1982). "Beyond acceptable risk: On the social acceptability of technologies," *Policy Sciences* 14: 247–256.
Reissland, J. and Harries, V. (1979). "A scale for measuring risks," *New Scientist* 83: 809–811.
Rogers, D. W. O. and Templin, R. J. (1980). "Errors in a risk assessment of renewable resources," *Energy* 5: 101–103.
Slovic, P., Fischhoff, B. and Lichtenstein, S. (1980). "Facts and fears: Understanding perceived risk," in R. Schwing and W. A. Albers Jr. (Eds.), *Societal Risk Assessment: How Safe is Safe Enough?* New York: Plenum.
Slovic, P., Fischhoff, B. and Lichtenstein, S. (1984). "Characterizing perceived risk," in R. W. Kates and C. Hohenemser (Eds.), *Technological Hazard Management*. Cambridge, Mass.: Oelgeschlager, Gunn & Hain, in press.
Slovic, P., Lichtenstein, L. and Fischhoff, B. (1984). "Modeling the societal impact of fatal accidents," *Management Science* in press.
Starr, C. (1969). "Social benefit versus technological risk," *Science* 165: 1232–1238.
U.S. Nuclear Regulatory Commission (1982). *Safety Goals for Nuclear Power Plants: A Discussion Paper.* NUREG-0880. Washington, D.C.: The Commission.
Vlek, C. A. J. and Stallen, P. J. M. (1981). "Risk perception in the small and in the large," *Organizational Behavior and Human Performance* 28: 235–271.
Watson, S. R. (1981). "On risks and acceptability," *Journal of the Radiological Protection Society* 1: 21–25.
Wilson, R. (1979). "Analyzing the daily risks of life," *Technology Review* 81 (4): 40–46.
Wynne, B. (1983). "Institutional mythologies and dual societies in the management of risk," in H. C. Kunreuther and E. V. Ley (Eds.), *The Risk Analysis Controversy*. New York: Springer Verlag.
Zentner, R. D. (1979). "Hazards in the chemical industry," *Chemical and Engineering News* 57 (45): 25–27, 30–34.

[7]

A Test of the Expected Utility Model: Evidence from Earthquake Risks

David S. Brookshire

University of Wyoming

Mark A. Thayer

San Diego State University

John Tschirhart

University of Wyoming

William D. Schulze

University of Colorado

The purposes of this paper are twofold. The first is to demonstrate that the expected utility hypothesis is a reasonable description of behavior for consumers who face a low-probability, high-loss natural hazard event, given that they have adequate information. The second is to demonstrate that in California information on earthquake hazards was generated by a 1974 state law that created a market for safe housing that previously did not exist.

I. Introduction

In a recent survey article on expected utility theory, Schoemaker (1982) describes the theory as "the major paradigm in decision mak-

The research reported here was funded by the U.S. Geological Survey. We would like to give special thanks to Richard Bernknopf, Edward Dyl, James Murdoch, Robert Wallace, Carl Wentworth, and an anonymous referee.

[*Journal of Political Economy*, 1985, vol. 93, no. 2]

ing since the Second World War." But Schoemaker indicates that in field studies the theory has not been supported. In particular, people do not behave as if they are maximizing expected utility for low-probability, high-loss events such as natural disasters. This conclusion is drawn from the work by Robertson (1974), Kunreuther (1976), and others. For example, Kunreuther interviewed homeowners in flood plains and earthquake-prone areas and concluded that the expected utility model "provides relatively little insight into the individual choice process regarding the purchase of [flood and earthquake] insurance."

The results in this paper are more encouraging for expected utility theory. An expected utility model of self-insurance that incorporates a hedonic price function is developed and applied to low-probability, high-loss earthquake hazards. Individuals can self-insure by purchasing houses in areas where the expected earthquake damage is relatively low. Our empirical results establish the existence of a hedonic price gradient for safety in the Los Angeles and San Francisco areas; ceteris paribus, individuals pay less for houses located in relatively hazardous areas. Moreover, the magnitude of the price gradient is consistent with our theoretical results when reasonable estimates of earthquake probabilities and potential damages are used, thereby lending support to the expected utility paradigm.[1]

The existence of a safety price gradient implies that individuals in the Los Angeles and San Francisco areas possess information on the relative danger of different locations. Yet Kunreuther found that Californians residing in earthquake-prone areas did not purchase earthquake insurance, in spite of subjective values on probabilities and magnitudes of potential losses that suggest such insurance may have been desirable. Our empirics show that a 1974 law passed by the state of California provided information that has allowed individuals to self-insure. Essentially, the law's passage created a market for safety that affected housing values.

The paper is organized as follows: In Section II, a simple theoretical model of self-insurance that includes a hedonic price function is developed. Empirical results on the existence of a safety price gradient and the source of safety information are presented in Section III. Section IV demonstrates the applicability of the expected utility model. A review of alternative evidence and qualifications to our analysis follows in Section V.

---

[1] Our approach can be likened to that of Gould (1969), who shows that the expected utility hypothesis cannot be rejected as a description of behavior for consumers purchasing auto insurance.

II. Theory

The theoretical model combines previous work on self-insurance in an expected utility framework with hedonic housing value analysis. Ehrlich and Becker (1972) discuss the acquisition of market insurance as a method of redistributing resources toward the less well-endowed states. They indicate that in lieu of market insurance, individuals may choose to perform a similar redistribution through self-insurance. The latter is therefore seen as a substitute for market-obtained insurance. Familiar examples of self-insurance include procuring a burglar alarm to thwart thieves or wearing a helmet while riding a bicycle. For earthquake hazards, self-insuring would entail, inter alia, locating one's residence in an area of relative safety.[2] If enough consumers possess information on where the relatively safer areas are located, one would expect to see higher housing values in these areas ceteris paribus. Location, with regard to safety, is a housing attribute much the same as other attributes including structural, neighborhood, and community characteristics. Thus, consumers choose a level of self-insurance through their locational choices with respect to earthquake safety.

In order to incorporate housing attributes into the self-insurance model, a hedonic price function similar to the type introduced by Rosen (1974) is utilized. Housing value studies using hedonic prices have proved fruitful for valuing public goods such as clean air (Anderson and Crocker 1971; Harrison and Rubinfeld 1978), social infrastructure (Cummings, Schulze, and Mehr 1978), and noise level (Nelson 1979), as well as estimating prices for more traditional attributes such as square footage, fireplaces, and swimming pools. The safety attribute is novel, however, in that it is random; it enters the consumer's utility function differently depending on the state of the world that prevails. It has a mitigating effect on damage if an earthquake occurs, whereas if there is no earthquake, there is no damage.

The existence of a hedonic price gradient for the safety attribute reveals that information about natural hazards is available and that

---

[2] Ehrlich and Becker (1972) distinguish between self-insurance and self-protection. The former reduces the loss in the event (e.g., earthquake) state whereas the latter reduces the probability that the loss will occur. It might be argued that location away from an earthquake hazard area accomplishes either or both of these objectives. However, reducing the loss in the case of an event rather than reducing the probability of the event and the associated loss seems more plausible. Therefore, we view the location decision as equivalent to the purchase of self-insurance. Although market insurance is available in some areas, few consumers purchase it. Only 4 percent of the structures in Los Angeles are covered by earthquake insurance (*Science*, May 1976).

consumers account for this information in their decision making. In our theoretical development, consumers are assumed to be informed about relatively safe and unsafe locations. The information may be attained by visual inspection, word of mouth, or a government program that delineates relatively unsafe housing locations for home buyers. The empirical results in Section III not only support the contention that information is available and considered in home purchase decisions, they shed light on the source of the information.

The consumer's problem is to maximize expected utility over two states of the world: the earthquake state and no earthquake state, which occur with probabilities ρ and $1 - \rho$, respectively. The consumer pays $p(a, s)$ for a house where $a = (a_1, \ldots, a_n)$ is a vector of n attributes and s is the safety attribute. Specifically, s is the monetary loss that the consumer perceives would be sustained during an earthquake. The function $p(a, s)$ is assumed to be twice continuously differentiable in all arguments with first partial derivatives positive for $i = 1, \ldots, n$. This implies that the n attributes are all desirable; if, for instance, neighborhood crime is considered, the attribute is the absence of crime. The partial derivative of the hedonic price equation with respect to the safety attribute is necessarily negative as shown below.

Expected utility is written as

$$V = \rho U[W(a) - p(a, s) - s] + (1 - \rho)U[W(a) - p(a, s)], \quad (1)$$

where U has continuous first and second partial derivatives. The function $W(a)$ is the wealth equivalent of the bundle of attributes the consumer has in the two states and is also assumed to be twice continuously differentiable. The safety attribute (or the amount of self-insurance) appears in both states as a reduction in the price of the house but appears again in the earthquake state as a damage loss.

The optimum choice of attributes is characterized by the following first-order conditions:

$$a_i: \rho U_e'(W_i - p_i) + (1 - \rho)U'(W_i - p_i) = 0, \quad i = 1, \ldots, n; \quad (2)$$

$$s: -\frac{(1 - \rho)p_s}{\rho(1 + p_s)} = \frac{U_e'}{U'}; \quad (3)$$

where subscripts on W and p denote partial derivatives and the e subscript on U denotes evaluation in the earthquake state. Assuming nonsatiation (U_e', $U' > 0$), condition (2) implies that the ith attribute is chosen where $W_i = p_i$, or its marginal value to the consumer equals its marginal cost in the market. Condition (3) indicates that at the optimum the ratio of marginal utilities in the two states must equal the price ratio of self-insurance where the prices are weighted by the state of the world probabilities.[3] Note also that $-1 < p_s < 0$, or an additional dollar spent on safety must decrease damages by more than a dollar.

Assuming second-order conditions are satisfied, optimum values of a and s solve conditions (2) and (3). Either risk neutrality or risk aversion is compatible with second-order sufficient conditions.[4]

Equation (3) forms the basis for testing the expected utility model. That is, given values for the unknown parameters in equation (3) one can determine whether or not individuals act in accordance with expected utility theory. The empirical analysis presented in the next section is directed at determining both the existence of a price gradient with respect to relative earthquake safety and the magnitude of any price differential (p_s). In addition, the source of this location information is examined. In Section IV the estimated price differential is combined with probability and expected damage estimates to analyze the expected utility model.

III. Empirical Analysis: Hedonic Housing Equations

In the theoretical model it was hypothesized that individuals, acting on hazard information and possessing varying levels of risk aversion, would locate along a hedonic price gradient, with relatively safer homes commanding higher prices, everything else equal. In this section, a methodology that enables this hypothesis to be tested is described. Empirical tests are conducted for both Los Angeles County and the San Francisco Bay Area counties—Alameda, Contra Costa, and San Mateo. Also included is a description of the data base and the test results.

Proximity to earthquake-related hazards is the important variable under study. Relatively hazardous areas have been delineated through research programs conducted by the U.S. Geological Survey and the California Division of Mines and Geology. The outcome of these efforts was the Alquist-Priolo Special Studies Zone Act passed by the California legislature in 1972 and amended in 1974, 1975, and 1976. This act represents an attempt to provide society with information concerning relative earthquake-associated risk.

Special Studies Zones (SSZs) are designated areas of elevated relative risk determined by potentially and recently active earthquake fault traces (surface displacement has occurred in Holocene time, i.e.,

---

[3] See Ehrlich and Becker (1972) for graphical interpretations of a similar result.

[4] One of the sufficient conditions for a maximum is that $V_{ss} = -\rho(U_e''p_s + U_e'p_{ss}) - (1 - \rho)(U''p_s + U'p_{ss}) < 0$. This is satisfied if the marginal cost of safety is increasing, $p_{ss} > 0$, and if either $U'' = 0$ or $U'' < 0$ for risk neutrality or risk aversion, respectively.

over the last 11,000 years). The evidence of faults may be directly observable (ruptured streets, crooked fences, etc.) or inferred (i.e., geomorphic shapes). The length of an SSZ coincides with the fault length whereas the width is generally one-eighth of a mile on each side of the fault.

Within California, the total number of SSZs designated through January 1979 was 251. There are two important ways in which consumers become aware of these. First, when an SSZ is designated, property owners in the zone are notified. Second, consumers selling property in an SSZ are required to notify prospective buyers that the property is in a zone (Alquist-Priolo Special Studies Zones Act 1974). This latter requirement has been implemented by the Department of Real Estate by having agents disclose the information via an addendum to the purchase contract. The buyer is then granted a period to collect additional information or to cancel the sale.

The potential effects of the Alquist-Priolo Act form the basis of a testable hypothesis. The null hypothesis is that consumers respond to the awareness of hazards associated with SSZs with the alternative being that they do not.

Data Specifics

The study areas are Los Angeles County and the San Francisco Bay Area counties, and observations are confined to single family residences. Thus, we do not consider the impact of hazard location on other structures (multiple family dwellings, mobile homes, commercial, etc.) or other ownership types (rental, leasing, etc.). Therefore, within our sample, this research asks if Los Angeles and San Francisco Bay Area households will pay a premium in the form of higher housing values for homes located outside an SSZ and what is the magnitude of that willingness to pay.

The data base was constructed so that hypotheses concerning the impact of SSZ location differences on housing sale price could be tested. The dependent variable in the entire analysis is the sale price of owner-occupied single family residences.[5] The independent variable set consists of variables that correspond to three levels of aggregation: house, neighborhood, and community. The Appendix describes further the data employed in the study.

The housing characteristic data, obtained from the Market Data Center (a computerized appraisal service centered in Los Angeles),

---

[5] Note that sale price or the discounted present value of the flow of rents rather than actual rent is used as the dependent variable. The two are interchangeable given the appropriate discount rate.

pertain to houses sold in 1978 and contain information on nearly every important structural and/or quality attribute. The Appendix provides summary statistics for the housing, neighborhood, and community characteristics used in the hedonic analysis. It should be emphasized that housing data of such quality (e.g., micro level of detail) are rarely available for studies of this nature. Usually outdated data that are overly aggregate (for instance, census tract averages) are employed. These data yield functions relevant for the "census tract" household but are only marginally relevant at the household (micro) level.

The Market Data Center provided computer data tapes listing all houses sold in Los Angeles County and the San Francisco Bay Area counties during the period specified. The number of entries was unmanageably large, so the data set was reduced as follows. First, a data set was constructed that contained houses within SSZs.[6] This was accomplished by first searching the tape for all houses located in census tracts that were wholly or partly in an SSZ. This list was further reduced through a random number matching system. The addresses of the remaining entries were then checked against a detailed map to select those clearly within an SSZ. The numbers of valid Los Angeles County and the San Francisco Bay Area SSZ data points were 292 and 745, respectively.

Second, data sets were constructed that included houses not located in hazard areas. After deletion of incomplete data entries, a random number matching system was utilized to choose sample sizes of approximately five thousand observations in each study area. The safety variable is then represented by a dummy variable that takes on the value one for houses in an SSZ and zero otherwise.

In addition to the immediate characteristics of a home, other variables that could significantly affect its sale price are those that reflect the condition of the neighborhood and community in which it is located. That is, school quality, ethnic composition, proximity to employment centers (and in Los Angeles County, distance to the beach), and measures of the ambient air quality have a substantial effect on sale price. In order to capture these impacts and to isolate the independent influence of location vis-à-vis the SSZs, these variables were included in the econometric modeling.

The data base assembled for the housing value study is appropriate to test the hypotheses outlined above for two reasons. First, the housing characteristic data are extremely detailed at the household level of aggregation and extensive in that a relatively large number of observations are considered. Second, a variety of neighborhood and com-

---

[6] See Hart (1977) for the location of SSZs.

TABLE 1

Estimated Hedonic Equations for Los Angeles County and Bay Area Counties

Variables	Los Angeles County	Bay Area Counties
Site-specific characteristics:		
Sale date	.002	.008
	(17.92)	(8.17)
Age of home	−.002	.0005
	(−11.37)	(2.37)
Square feet of living area	.0003	.00005
	(36.85)	(14.85)
Number of bathrooms	.098	.260
	(11.58)	(40.12)
Number of fireplaces	.124	.188
	(17.90)	(27.86)
Pool	.093	.067
	(8.66)	(4.83)
View	.143	.128
	(11.56)	(12.68)
SSZ location	−.056	−.033
	(−3.76)	(−3.39)
Community characteristics:		
School quality	.020	.012
	(20.72)	(12.85)
Home density	−.00004	−.00002
	(−7.72)	(−14.15)
Percent black	−.006	−.006
	(−33.55)	(−29.91)
Percent greater than 62		
years old	.003	.009
	(6.35)	(18.22)
Air pollution	−.001	−.004
	(−5.01)	(−9.76)
Location characteristics:		
Distance to employment	−2.313	−.401
	(−2.04)	(−.17)
Distance to beach	−.016	N.A.
	(−22.44)	
Alameda County	N.A.*	−.158
		(−15.78)
Contra Costa County	N.A.	−.27
		(−21.20)
Constant	5.003	5.335
	(60.59)	(77.17)
R^2	.79	.69
Residual sum square	281.02	302.570
Number of observations	4,865	5,438

Note.—Dependent variable = ln(home sale price in 1978 $100s); *t*-statistics in parentheses.
*N.A. = not applicable.

EXPECTED UTILITY MODEL   377

munity variables that make it possible to isolate the SSZs' location influence on housing values have been included.

Empirical Results

The underlying structure of the hypothesis test is a single-equation empirical model that attempts to explain the variation in sale prices of houses located in Los Angeles County and the San Francisco counties.[7] The estimated coefficients of these hedonic equations specify the effect a change in a particular independent variable has on sale price. In reference to the SSZ location variable, this procedure allows one to focus on its significance while separating out the influence of other extraneous variables. Therefore, this analysis yields two outputs concerning the relationship of hazard location differentials to housing price. First, the relative significance of location variations is determined and, second, the estimated coefficient pertaining to location implicitly measures its monetary value.

The estimated Los Angeles and San Francisco hedonic gradients that provide the best fit of the data are presented in table 1.[8] A number of aspects of the equations are worth noting. First, as measured by R^2, the nonlinear form is a significant improvement over linear specifications. In addition, a comparison of the log of the likelihood values (semilog to the linear) indicated that the semilog form was a significant improvement at the 1 percent level (see Judge et al. 1980). As Rosen (1974) pointed out, this is to be expected since consumers cannot always arbitrage by dividing and repackaging bundles of housing attributes. Thus, on both theoretical and empirical grounds the semilog specification proved to be a better functional form.

Second, in the semilog equations all coefficients have the expected sign and are significantly different from zero at the 1 percent level. The SSZ dichotomous location variable has the a priori expected relationship to home sale price and is significant at the 1 percent level. This result is invariant with respect to various sample sizes, model formulations (various independent variable sets were tested), and estimated functional form.[9] These results indicate that individuals are

---

[7] See Freeman (1979) and Mäler (1977) for a review of estimates of hedonic housing equations.

[8] The main difference between the Los Angeles and Bay Area analyses is the locational variables. In the Bay Area distance to beach (ocean) is unimportant due to the presence of the bay. In addition, the three Bay Area counties were assigned dichotomous variables to account for county differences. San Mateo County is the excluded group and therefore is included in the constant term.

[9] Since the SSZ location variable is a zero-one variable then our choice set over functional forms was essentially restricted to the linear and semilog forms. Thus, possi-

acting on hazard information when making locational choices, and this action is translated into a measurable hedonic gradient.

Regarding the monetary impact on housing sale price, the nonlinear specification does not allow straightforward interpretation since the effect of any independent variable depends on the level of all other variables. However, the Los Angeles County (Bay Area) results indicate that if all other variables are assigned their mean values, then living outside of an SSZ causes an increase in home value of approximately \$4,650 (\$2,490) over an identical home located in an SSZ. In relative terms the magnitude has approximately one-half the impact of a swimming pool or one-third the value of a view.

In the next section, these monetary figures are used to test the expected utility model. But before proceeding to this analysis, we can confirm the source of the hazard information used by home buyers. As indicated above, the Alquist-Priolo Act was enacted in 1974. Therefore, a pre-1974 analysis of the housing market would yield insight concerning the importance of the act in providing consumers relative risk information.

Housing data for the 1972 time period are used in the test of the Alquist-Priolo Act. Successful enhancement of consumers' awareness by the Alquist-Priolo disclosure provisions would require a change in the hedonic rent gradient over time. This change could take one of two forms: (i) an SSZ location would be an insignificant housing characteristic in 1972 yet significant in 1978; or (ii) the location variable would be significant in both years but its relative magnitude would increase over time. The first type of change could be considered a strong test of the impact of the Alquist-Priolo Act since the act would have filled an existing information void. Thus evidence of a direct market effect would be available. The magnitude change of the SSZ variable would imply a weaker response since it would be evident that consumers had hazard location information from some other source and were already acting on it before passage of the Alquist-Priolo Act.

The relative impact of hazard information independent of the Alquist-Priolo Act is also tested using the pre- and postdata sets; that is, if SSZ location remains a stable (no relative magnitude change), significant determinant of housing price, then consumers are acting on some available information although their preferences have not been enhanced or changed by the public disclosure program.

---

ble forms such as quadratic, log, inverse semilog, exponential, semilog exponential, and the Box-Cox transformation of the SSZ location variable are not available since they inevitably reduce to zero-one or cannot be estimated (e.g., log of zero). Further, a Box-Cox transformation of the dependent variable that is not equivalent to linear or semilog yields difficult to interpret results. Finally, the translog transformation is not available because the objective is to determine the separate influence of SSZ locations.

The 1972 time period results are presented in table 2. The semilog functional form provides the best fit of the data, and all coefficients, with the exception of SSZ location, are significant at the 1 percent level and related to home sale price as expected. However, the most noteworthy aspect of the equations is that the SSZ location variable does not demonstrate significance in 1972, even at the 10 percent level. The combined 1972 and 1978 results indicate that the Alquist-Priolo Act *has* caused a structural change in the hedonic gradient over time. This is evidenced both by the significant monetary impact change over time and by the change in significance. Therefore, in the study areas the Alquist-Priolo Act does pass a strong test of effectiveness, suggesting that the act provided information that consumers used in their market decisions.

IV. Empirical Results: Expected Utility Model

If consumers behave as if they maximize expected utility, then first-order condition (3) must necessarily be satisfied. The terms in condition (3) include the probability of an earthquake, marginal utilities of income, marginal damage to a house, and the marginal change in the house price. Our approach is to solve equation (3) for this latter term by substituting in reasonable values of all the former terms for the Los Angeles region. This provides an analytical solution for the price difference between houses in and out of SSZs. This price difference is then compared to the observed difference in housing prices estimated in the previous section. The two differences are shown to be close, thereby supporting the expected utility paradigm.

In the empirical work, houses were described as either in or out of unsafe areas so that the safety attribute was discrete. In equation (3) the attribute is continuous. Therefore, the partial derivative p_s in (3) is approximated as $\Delta p / \Delta s$, where Δp is the total price difference between safe and unsafe houses, and Δs is the total damage in dollars resulting from an earthquake. Equation (3) can then be rewritten as

$$\Delta p \cong \frac{U_e'}{U'} \left\{ \frac{-\rho \Delta s}{1 - \rho[1 - (U_e'/U')]} \right\} < 0. \qquad (4)$$

The hedonic housing equation provides an estimate of Δp of $-\$4,650$ for an average house worth \$83,153. On an annual basis using the prevailing home mortgage interest rate in 1978 (9.5 percent), this implies a home outside of an SSZ would cost \$442 more per year in mortgage payments than one in an SSZ. One possible assumption is that this is the perceived annual cost of living outside of an SSZ to home buyers, which may be plausible given a home turnover rate of once every 3–4 years in 1978. However, if home buyers properly

TABLE 2

ESTIMATED HEDONIC EQUATIONS FOR LOS ANGELES COUNTY AND BAY AREA COUNTIES

Variables	Los Angeles County	Bay Area Counties
Site-specific characteristics:		
Sale date	.004	.004
	(5.20)	(6.96)
Age of home	−.005	−.002
	(−19.52)	(−15.17)
Square feet of living area	.0003	.0002
	(41.71)	(47.42)
Number of bathrooms	.133	.084
	(19.51)	(15.35)
Number of fireplaces	.091	.103
	(18.10)	(20.52)
Pool	.131	.105
	(14.73)	(9.57)
View	.130	.080
	(10.36)	(10.20)
SSZ location	.0002	−.022
	(.0174)	(−1.44)
Community characteristics:		
School quality	.0098	.003
	(12.44)	(7.34)
Home density	−.000017	−.00001
	(−3.88)	(−8.83)
Percent black	−.0029	−.002
	(−22.64)	(−15.147)
Percent greater than 62		
years old	.002	.004
	(4.83)	(13.25)
Air pollution	−.0018	−.004
	(−6.33)	(−13.18)
Location characteristics:		
Distance to employment	−7.64	−8.113
	(−8.40)	(−4.74)
Distance to beach	−.0095	N.A.*
	(−16.74)	
Alameda County	N.A.	1.020
		(−135.04)
Contra Costa County	N.A.	.233
		(−25.34)
Constant	5.54	6.126
	(82.05)	(170.53)
R^2	.80	.91
Residual sum square	169.44	150.700
Number of observations	4,927	5,460

NOTE.—Dependent variable = ln(home sale price in 1972 $100s); *t*-statistics in parentheses.
*N.A. = not applicable.

perceive the role of inflation and keep their homes for a longer period, then use of the real rate of interest would be more appropriate in calculating the true cost differential for living outside of an SSZ. From the early 1950s up until 1978 the real rate of interest on home mortgages averaged around 3 percent. If we use this rate of interest, we obtain a real cost differential of $140 per year. These figures provide a range for comparison to Δp from equation (4) after substituting in values for $\dot{p}$, Δs, and U'_e/U'.

First, consider a range of values for U'_e/U'. As a lower bound, and to be consistent with second-order maximization conditions, we use risk neutrality where $U'_e/U' = 1$. For risk aversion, however, $1 < U'_e/U' < \infty$. To establish an upper bound we appeal to recent work that employs cross-sectional data on household assets to establish properties of household utility functions. In particular, Cohn et al. (1975) found evidence that the coefficient of relative risk aversion is slightly decreasing in wealth. Friend and Blume (1975) found that "if there is any tendency for increasing or decreasing proportional risk aversion, the tendency is so slight that for many purposes the assumption of constant proportional risk aversion is not a bad first approximation" (p. 915). More recently, Morin and Suarez (1983) found the coefficient to be slightly decreasing for wealth levels up to $100,000, after which it becomes approximately constant. Furthermore, Friend and Blume estimated the market price of risk to determine a value for the coefficient, which they argue is greater than one and may be as high as two. Since we are interested in the ratio of marginal utilities and not the coefficient of relative risk aversion, we cannot use these results directly; but we can explore the implications suggested by this work.

To determine an upper bound, one approach is to examine U'_e/U' for various utility functions that exhibit the properties cited above. The largest upper bound is associated with a utility function exhibiting constant relative risk aversion equal to two; thus, we use $U(A) = -A^{-1}$, where A is total wealth. The denominator of U'_e/U' is evaluated at total wealth, while the numerator is evaluated at total wealth minus the dollar value of earthquake damage. Again, to determine the largest upper bound, we assume the maximum expected damage of about $20,000 developed below. To obtain total wealth we note from Friend and Blume's data (table 3, p. 908) that over their entire sample the market value of a house as a percentage of total wealth averaged 16 percent.[10] Since the average market value of houses in

---

[10] The use of 16 percent as the ratio of market value of houses to total wealth may seem small until one realizes that Friend and Blume (1975) define wealth to include human wealth. The authors regard this as the most appropriate definition; consequently, we use it here.

our sample is \$83,153, we use as an estimate of total wealth $A = \$83,153/.16 = \$519,706$. Finally, using $U(A) = -A^{-1}$, we obtain $U'_e/U' = 519,706^2/499,706^2 = 1.08$ for the largest upper bound.

Another approach for estimating U'_e/U' is to use a linear approximation (first-order Taylor series expansion) for describing changes in U'. Thus, we assume $U'(A) \cong U'(A_0) + U''(A_0)(A - A_0)$, where the Taylor series expansion takes place around the level of wealth A_0. Since the coefficient of relative risk aversion is defined as $c = | U''(A_0)A_0/U'(A_0) |$ we can then rewrite our approximation for $U'(A)$ as

$$U'(A) \cong U'(A_0) \cdot \left[1 - c\left(\frac{A - A_0}{A_0}\right)\right].^{11}$$

If we let A_0 equal the level of wealth before the earthquake and let A equal the level of wealth after the earthquake, dividing the expression above by $U'(A_0)$ gives

$$\frac{U'_e}{U'} \cong 1 - c\left(\frac{A - A_0}{A_0}\right)$$

as an approximation of the ratio of marginal utilities in the two states of the world. This expression does not depend on use of a particular utility function, but rather will be a good approximation for utility functions that have small higher order terms for U''' and beyond. Using the highest estimated value for c of 2 and the highest estimate of damages of about \$20,000 we obtain

$$\frac{U'_e}{U'} \cong 1 - 2\left(\frac{499,706 - 519,706}{519,706}\right) = 1.08.$$

This second approach gives an identical estimate to the first developed above and suggests that risk aversion plays a surprisingly small role in our analysis apparently due to the relatively small changes in lifetime wealth involved.

To estimate the odds of an event in the Los Angeles area, we use two sources. First, Kunreuther et al. (1978) report results of a survey question among California residents on the subjective beliefs concerning the odds of an earthquake. The average perceived odds of an event from that survey are about 2 percent per year.[12] To obtain a more objective estimate of the risk of an event we turn to a report

---

[11] Note that $U''A/U'$ will be a negative number for risk-averse individuals. Thus, we replace $U''A/U'$ by $-c$ in developing this formula.

[12] The average of the perceived odds used here was obtained from fig. 5.7 on p. 96 of Kunreuther et al. (1978) by taking the average of the end point risk of each risk category and multiplying by the reported frequency of occurrence.

issued by the Federal Emergency Management Agency (FEMA 1980), which estimated the odds of a large earthquake to be from 2 percent to 5 percent per year for the Los Angeles area. The upper bound of that range, 5 percent, resulted from scientific concerns over the Palmdale bulge, a temporary uplifting of the desert floor north of Los Angeles that occurred in the late 1970s. The lower bound estimate, which was widely publicized prior to the FEMA report, is based on the historical pattern of large earthquakes that have occurred in the Los Angeles area (Sieh 1978). For the relevant time period for our study, 1972–78, and for the Los Angeles area, there exists a remarkable coincidence between subjective and objective measures of risk of an earthquake. The FEMA lower bound estimate, which is appropriate prior to the occurrence of the Palmdale bulge, and the Kunreuther et al. estimate both imply $\rho = .02$ for estimating Δp in equation (4).

Finally, we need to develop an estimate of earthquake losses or damages associated with residing in an SSZ as opposed to residing outside of an SSZ, defined as Δs in equation (4). Again, we can obtain a subjective estimate of about \$20,000 from Kunreuther et al. (1978) for the average total damage people expect to occur to their homes if an earthquake occurs.[13] As an alternative measure, engineering studies suggest that the *average* damage to a single-story frame house should a great earthquake occur near Los Angeles would be about 5 percent of the home's value (NOAA 1973). This implies a level of damage for the average house in our property value sample (worth \$83,153) of \$4,158. However, homes in areas of maximum ground shaking, such as would occur in an SSZ if the local fault ruptured, would suffer damage equal to about 25 percent of the home's value (NOAA 1973). For the average house in our sample, this implies damages of \$20,788 (for a home in an area of maximum ground shaking). These figures obviously span the Kunreuther et al. estimate, with the upper bound figure quite close, suggesting that households answering the Kunreuther survey may have perceived the question to imply that their home would be located in an area of maximum damage. Note, however, that Δs represents the difference in damages an individual would expect from living in versus outside of an SSZ should an earthquake occur. Thus, as an absolute upper bound, we will use a value of Δs of \$20,000 consistent with a subjective assessment that homes outside of an SSZ will suffer no damage. As a lower bound we will take the difference in the objective engineering assess-

---

[13] Again, this average was obtained by weighting expected damage by frequency of occurrence among the survey respondents from fig. 5.6, p. 94, of Kunreuther et al. (1978).

ments ($20,788 minus $4,158) of $16,630. Thus, the lower bound assumes homes in an SSZ will suffer the maximum level of ground shaking and homes outside an SSZ will suffer average levels of ground shaking.

To obtain an upper bound estimate for the annual value of living outside of an SSZ to an expected-utility-maximizing household, we substitute values of $U''_c/U' = 1.08$, $\rho = .02$, and $\Delta s = \$20,000$ into equation (4). These figures are consistent with the highest observed coefficient of relative risk aversion of 2 and the subjective evidence obtained by Kunreuther et al. on earthquake risk and damages. To obtain a lower bound estimate we assume risk neutrality so $U''_c/U' = 1$ and use scientific-engineering evidence for $\rho = .02$ and $\Delta s = \$16,630$. These assumptions yield a range for Δp of from $333 to $431 per year. In contrast, from the estimated property value equation, the perceived annual cost of living outside of an SSZ ranges from $140 to $440 depending on use of real or nominal interest rates. This evidence suggests that the estimated property value equation for Los Angeles is consistent with utility-maximizing behavior with respect to earthquake risks.

V. Conclusion

Schoemaker (1982, p. 552) summarizes the problems of expected utility theory as follows: "As a descriptive model seeking insight into how decisions are made, EU [expected utility] theory fails on at least three counts. First, people do not structure problems as holistically and comprehensively as EU theory suggests. Second they do not process information, especially probabilities, according to the EU rule. Finally, EU theory, as an 'as if' model, poorly predicts choice behavior in laboratory situations. Hence, it is doubtful that the EU theory should or could serve as a general descriptive model." Our analysis provides only indirect evidence with respect to Schoemaker's first point. However, having demonstrated consistency between our property value market results and the expected utility model for Los Angeles, we can strengthen the argument considerably by briefly considering the San Francisco case.

For San Francisco, home sale prices, damage to homes should an earthquake occur, and, presumably, risk preferences are all similar to the Los Angeles case analyzed in the previous section. However, the probability of a damaging earthquake is considerably less according to available scientific evidence. For example, the FEMA report (1980, p. 3) states: "the current estimated probability . . . is smaller [than for Los Angeles] but significant," and later gives annual odds for a great earthquake on the San Andreas fault near San Francisco as 1 percent.

These are half the odds given for a great earthquake in the Los Angeles area in the same report. Thus, from equation (4) of the previous section one would predict, on the basis of expected utility theory, that the property value differential for houses in SSZs in the Bay Area should be about half that observed in Los Angeles. From the two property value studies the differentials are $2,490 and $4,650, respectively. This successful "prediction" suggests both that individual households process probability information in a reasonably rational and accurate way and that, at least in a market situation with a well-defined institutional mechanism, the expected utility model may perform well in predicting behavior. It should be pointed out that through the decade of the 1970s, the media in California carried an average of two stories per week relating to local earthquake events, actual or possible damages, and probabilities (see, e.g., *Los Angeles Times*, April 7, 1975; April 4, 1976; April 22, 1978). Possible earthquake events are a topic of considerable interest within the state, and the level of awareness among state residents is very high (Turner et al. 1979). The scientific evidence summarized in the 1980 FEMA study used in our calculations was widely publicized throughout the 1970s and may well be responsible for the similarity between the Kunreuther et al. (1978) subjective probability estimates of earthquake risk and more objective scientific assessments.

In summary, the property value studies make a strong case for self-insuring behavior consistent with maximization of expected utility. Further support of this result can be found by comparing the property value studies with surveys (Brookshire et al. 1982). In our survey of homeowners located in SSZs in Los Angeles (Brookshire et al. 1980), when asked how much more they would pay to purchase the same home outside of an SSZ, only 26 percent of respondents were willing to pay anything more. However, the average of all responses (including zero bids) was $5,920, very close to the average sale price differential of $4,650 from the Los Angeles property value study.[14]

Efficient prices should convey information to consumers. We have shown that the property value markets for both Los Angeles and San Francisco convey hedonic price differentials to consumers that correspond closely to expected earthquake damages for particular homes located in SSZs. Although the information provided by the SSZ program is by no means perfect, our results suggest that programs to provide consumers with hazard information may well be effective.

[14] Interestingly, when homeowners located outside of an SSZ were asked how much less expensive their house would have to be to get them to relocate in an SSZ, the average response was $28,250 (see Brookshire et al. 1980). This asymmetry between willingness to accept and willingness to pay measures of value has been demonstrated in a number of studies (see, e.g., Hovis, Coursey, and Schulze 1983).

Appendix

TABLE A1
VARIABLES USED IN ANALYSIS OF HOUSING MARKET

Variable	Definition (Expected Effect on Housing Sale Price)	Units	Source
Dependent			
Sale price	Sale price of owner-occupied single family residences	$100	Market data center
Independent—housing:			
Sale date	Month home was sold (positive)	January 1972 = 1 December 1972 = 12 January 1978 = 1 December 1978 = 12	Market data center
Age	Age of home (negative)	Years	Market data center
Bathrooms	Number of bathrooms (positive)	Number	Market data center
Living area	Square feet of living area (positive)	Square feet	Market data center
Pool	1 if pool, 0 if no pool (positive)	0 = no pool 1 = pool	Market data center
Air conditioning	1 if air conditioned, 0 if not (positive)	0 = no air conditioning 1 = air conditioned	Market data center
Fireplaces	Number of fireplaces (positive)	Number	Market data center
Independent—neighborhood:			
Distance to beach	Miles to nearest beach (negative)	Miles	Calculated
Age composition	Percent greater than 62 in census tract (positive)	Percent	1970 census
Ethnic composition	Percent black in census tract	Percent	1970 census
Distance to employment	Weighted distance to 10 employment centers (negative)	Miles	Calculated
SSZ location	1 if in SSZ, 0 if not (negative)	1 = SSZ 0 = not in SSZ	Fault hazard zones in California (E. W. Hart)
Independent—community:			
School quality	Community's twelfth-grade reading score (positive)	Percent	California Assessment Program (1979)
Housing density	Homes per square mile in surrounding community (negative)	Houses/square mile	1970 census, Southern California Association of Governments, Bay Area Association of Governments
Air pollution (TSP)	Total suspended particulates (negative)		California Air Resource Board

386

TABLE A2

MEANS AND STANDARD DEVIATIONS (in Parentheses) FOR THE VARIABLES USED IN THE HEDONIC HOUSING EQUATIONS

VARIABLE	LOS ANGELES COUNTY		BAY AREA COUNTIES	
	1978	1972	1978	1972
Sale price (1978 dollars)	83,153	64,075	75,650	58,959
	(55,938)	(35,213)	(37,581)	(36,881)
Sale date	5.382	6.61	6.33	6.141
	(2.86)	(3.25)	(3.22)	(3.40)
Age of home	27.57	24.43	25.00	20.159
	(17.09)	(12.91)	(17.69)	(15.64)
Square feet of living area	1,442	1,439	1,430.714	1,494.796
	(642.3)	(626.8)	(994.19)	(531.89)
Number of bathrooms	1.690	1.62	1.670	1.724
	(.71)	(.66)	(.62)	(.61)
Number of fireplaces	.663	.63	.825	.897
	(.62)	(.61)	(.52)	(.50)
Pool	.130	.12	.059	.045
	(.33)	(.32)	(.23)	(.20)
View	.095	.05	.126	.098
	(.29)	(.22)	(.33)	(.29)
SSZ location	.060	.049	.137	.022
	(.24)	(.22)	(.34)	(.14)
School quality	60.83	69.67	63.544	69.810
	(3.70)	(3.70)	(4.19)	(6.41)
Home density	2,213.5	2,262	2,476	2,431
	(731.96)	(697.9)	(2,152)	(2,018)
Percent black	5.47	9.91	6.636	4.603
	(18.00)	(24.5)	(16.37)	(13.17)
Percent greater than 62 years old	10.94	11.69	9.802	10.113
	(7.01)	(7.84)	(7.37)	(7.75)
Air pollution	107.7	106.12	52.319	51.585
	(14.16)	(13.93)	(11.91)	(11.92)
Distance to employment	.0183	.0183	.007	.007
	(.004)	(.004)	(.002)	(.002)
Distance to beach	12.41	11.48		
	(7.69)	(7.48)		
Number of observations	4,865	4,927	5,438	5,460

References

Alquist-Priolo Special Studies Zones Act, Sec. 2621.9, California, 1974.

Anderson, Robert J., Jr., and Crocker, Thomas D. "Air Pollution and Residential Property Values." *Urban Studies* 8 (October 1971): 171–80.

Brookshire, David S.; Schulze, William D.; Tschirhart, John; Thayer, Mark A.; Hageman, Rhonda; Pazand, Reza; and Ben-David, Shaul. "Methods Development for Valuing Hazards Information." Technical Report. Washington: U.S. Geological Survey, 1980.

Brookshire, David S.; Thayer, Mark A.; Schulze, William D.; and d'Arge, Ralph C. "Valuing Public Goods: A Comparison of Survey and Hedonic Approaches." *A.E.R.* 72 (March 1982): 165–77.

Cohn, Richard A.; Lewellen, Wilbur G.; Lease, Ronald C.; and Schlarbaum, Gary G. "Individual Investor Risk Aversion and Investment Portfolio Composition." *J. Finance* 30 (May 1975): 605–20.

Cummings, Ronald G.; Schulze, William D.; and Mehr, Arthur F. "Optimal Municipal Investment in Boomtowns: An Empirical Analysis." *J. Environmental Econ. and Management* 5 (September 1978): 252–67.

Ehrlich, Isaac, and Becker, Gary S. "Market Insurance, Self-Insurance, and Self-Protection." *J.P.E.* 80 (July/August 1972): 623–48.

Federal Emergency Management Agency (FEMA). *An Assessment of the Consequences and Preparations for a Catastrophic California Earthquake: Findings and Actions Taken.* Washington, 1980.

Freeman, A. Myrick, III. "Hedonic Prices, Property Values and Measuring Environmental Benefits: A Survey of the Issues." *Scandinavian J. Econ.* 81, no. 2 (1979): 154–73.

Friend, Irwin, and Blume, Marshall E. "The Demand for Risky Assets." *A.E.R.* 65 (December 1975): 900–922.

Gould, John P. "The Expected Utility Hypothesis and the Selection of Optimal Deductibles for a Given Insurance Policy." *J. Bus.* 42 (April 1969): 143–51.

Harrison, David, Jr., and Rubinfeld, Daniel L. "Hedonic Housing Prices and the Demand for Clean Air." *J. Environmental Econ. and Management* 5 (March 1978): 81–102.

Hart, Earl W. *Fault Hazard Zones in California.* Special Publication 42, rev. Sacramento: California Div. Mines and Geol., 1977.

Hovis, John J.; Coursey, Don L.; and Schulze, William D. "A Comparison of Alternative Valuation Mechanisms for Non-Market Commodities." Unpublished manuscript, Univ. Wyoming, 1983.

Judge, George G.; Griffiths, William E.; Hill, R. Carter; and Lee, Tsoung-Chao. *The Theory and Practice of Econometrics.* New York: Wiley, 1980.

Kunreuther, Howard. "Limited Knowledge and Insurance Protection." *Public Policy* 24 (Spring 1976): 227–61.

Kunreuther, Howard; Ginsberg, Ralph; Miller, Louis; Sagi, Philip; Slovic, Paul; Borkan, Bradley; and Katz, Norman. *Disaster Insurance Protection: Public Policy Lessons.* New York: Wiley, 1978.

Mäler, Karl-Göran. "A Note on the Use of Property Values in Estimating Marginal Willingness to Pay for Environmental Quality." *J. Environmental Econ. and Management* 4 (December 1977): 355–69.

Morin, Roger-A., and Suarez, A. Fernandez. "Risk Aversion Revisited." *J. Finance* 38 (September 1983): 1201–16.

National Oceanic and Atmospheric Administration (NOAA) and Environmental Research Laboratories. *A Study of Earthquake Losses in the Los Angeles,*

California Area. Report prepared for the Federal Disaster Assistance Administration, Department of Housing and Urban Development. Washington: Government Printing Office, 1973.

Nelson, Jon P. "Airport Noise, Location Rent, and the Market for Residential Amenities." *J. Environmental Econ. and Management* 6 (December 1979): 320–31.

Robertson, L. "Urban Area Safety Belt Use in Automobiles with Starter Interlock Belt Systems." Washington: Insurance Inst. Highway Safety, 1974.

Rosen, Sherwin. "Hedonic Prices and Implicit Markets: Product Differentiation in Pure Competition." *J.P.E.* 82 (January/February 1974): 34–55.

San Fernando, California, Earthquake of February 9, 1971. Vols. 1–4. Washington: Dept. Commerce, National Oceanic and Atmospheric Admin., 1973.

Schoemaker, Paul J. H. "The Expected Utility Model: Its Variants, Purposes, Evidence and Limitations." *J. Econ. Literature* 20 (June 1982): 529–63.

Sieh, Kerry E. "Prehistoric Large Earthquakes Produced by Slip on the San Andreas Fault at Pallett Creek, California." *J. Geophysical Res.* 83 (August 10, 1978): 3907–39.

Turner, Ralph H.; Nigg, Joanne M.; Paz, Denise H.; and Young, Barbara S. *Earthquake Threat: The Human Response in Southern California.* Los Angeles: Inst. Social Sci. Res., Univ. California, 1979.

[8]

JOURNAL OF ENVIRONMENTAL ECONOMICS AND MANAGEMENT **18**, 35–49 (1990)

Earthquake and Volcano Hazard Notices:
An Economic Evaluation of Changes
in Risk Perceptions[1]

RICHARD L. BERNKNOPF

U.S. Geological Survey, National Center, MS 922, Reston, Virginia 22092

DAVID S. BROOKSHIRE

Department of Economics, University of Wyoming, Laramie, Wyoming 82071

AND

MARK. A. THAYER

Department of Economics, San Diego State University, San Diego, California 92182

Received February 29, 1988; revised September 12, 1988

Earthquake and volcano hazard notices were issued for the Mammoth Lakes, California area by the U.S. Geological Survey under the authority granted by the Disaster Relief Act of 1974. The effects on investment, recreation visitation, and risk perceptions are explored.

The hazard notices did not affect recreation visitation, although investment was affected. A perceived loss in the market value of homes was documented. Risk perceptions were altered for property owners. Communication of the probability of an event over time would enhance hazard notices as a policy instrument and would mitigate unnecessary market perturbations. © 1990 Academic Press, Inc.

I. INTRODUCTION

The introduction of natural hazards information into a market will potentially alter individuals' perceptions of risk as that risk relates to recreation and investment activities. An exogenous, but temporary, shock to a market such as a hazard notice for an earthquake or a volcano in a particular community should cause a reaction proportional to the level of the risk announced to the public. Market activity should return to pre-warning levels once the announcements are withdrawn and the risk to individuals has subsided. This analysis focuses on a specific market reaction to a low probability, high loss situation when a series of Federal Government notices have been issued to heighten public awareness and to promote hazard mitigation. In particular, we examine the well-publicized impacts of two types of notices concerning earthquake and volcano hazards at the resort community of Mammoth Lakes, California.

Previous studies addressing the impacts of hazards information on markets have concentrated on risks associated with long-term exposure to health hazards that have caused injury or death [10, 26, 11]. In these cases regulations were imposed to protect individuals from the hazards and to promote mitigating behavior. Empirical evidence of consumer responses to government warning programs provide a mea-

[1]This study was sponsored, in part, by the U.S. Geological Survey. We thank John DeYoung, John Filson, Darrell Herd, David Hill, and William Schulze.

35

sure of the value of hazards information associated with a risk to health. Other investigations [13, 7] examine low probability technological risks, acceptable risks, and the role played by compensation.

There are currently no regulations designed to protect individuals from the perils of earthquakes and volcanoes other than the minimum standards contained in the California building code.[2] In order to provide hazards information to the public during a period of elevated risk, provisions of the Disaster Relief Act of 1974 [23] contain responsibilities for the issuance of geologic hazard notices based on scientific investigations.[3] While the legislation provides the authority to issue announcements, there is not a specific mechanism to quantitatively convey the level of risk or the duration of increased hazard. The Mammoth Lakes notices provide an example of how a market responds to qualitative statements about a temporary change in risk.

Mammoth Lakes is on the western edge of an ancient volcano that was the site of a massive eruption 700,000 years ago. Less significant volcanic activity continued in the area up to a few hundred years ago. In the early 1980s, swelling of the crater floor (where the town and resort are located) was detected and intense swarms of earthquakes occurred that may have been caused by the movement of molten rock in the volcano.[4] Because of these events, the U.S. Geological Survey issued an earthquake Hazard Watch for the Mammoth Lakes area in May 1980 [24]. In addition, a Notice of Potential Hazard for volcanic activities was issued in May 1982 [6, 25].

Prior to September 30, 1983, a Hazard Watch and a Notice of Potential Hazard were the middle and lowest stages in a three level hierarchy used by the U.S. Geological Survey when formally notifying the public to express the relative urgency of a potential geologic hazard. In September 1983, the three level system was changed to a single level system termed "Hazard Warning." The current level of activity in the region has been determined not to satisfy the "imminent threat" criteria for an official warning of either a volcanic eruption or a major earthquake [9]. Thus, the notices were subsequently removed, allowing an analysis of risk perceptions, recreation, and investment behavior before, during, and after the issuance of the notices.

---

[2]The Uniform Building Code (UBC) is used throughout California, including Mammoth Lakes. The only special provision for natural hazards in Mammoth Lakes concerns snow accumulation on building roofs. There exist no special provisions to prevent potential earthquake and/or volcano damage.

[3]The Disaster Relief Act of 1974, Public Law 93-288 (88 Stat. 143) [23], charges the Director of the U.S. Geological Survey with the Federal responsibility to issue geologic hazard warnings. These responsibilities and authorities include: (1) identification, assessment, and monitoring of potential geologic hazards; (2) development of capabilities to predict the time, location, and severity of hazardous geologic events; and (3) dissemination of related findings and their implications, including the provision of technical and scientific advice to public officals. Until 1984 the U.S. Geological Survey issued three classes of warnings: (1) Notice of Potential Hazard—the location and possible magnitude or geologic effects of a potential hazardous geologic event; (2) Hazard Watch—information as it develops from a monitoring program from observed precursor phenomena that a potentially catastrophic event of generally predictable magnitude may be imminent with an indefinite time period; (3) Hazard Warning—the time, location, and magnitude of a potentially disastrous geologic event or process.

[4]Prior to the hazard announcements the Mammoth Lakes area was subjected to 64 magnitude 4 (Richter Scale) earthquakes, 4 magnitude 5 earthquakes, and 3 magnitude 6 earthquakes from October 1978 to June 1980. During the interval that the warnings spanned, an additional 37 magnitude 4 earthquakes, 6 magnitude 5 earthquakes, and 1 magnitude 6 earthquake occurred. The area also experienced volcanic activity in the form of an uplift and new fumaroles.

EARTHQUAKE AND VOLCANO HAZARD NOTICES   37

As a result of the hazard notices, our expectation is that nonresident recreationists should not have altered behavior and visitation should not have changed. Based on long-term trends in California and other western states, there is a low joint probability of 0.00003 for incurring an injury (fatal or otherwise) in Mammoth Lakes during a volcanic eruption [9].[5] The corresponding joint probability of suffering an injury from an earthquake in Mammoth Lakes is 0.000002.[6] On the other hand, individuals involved in the real estate market might be expected to react negatively to the notices and property values should fall since there is a relatively higher probability that an event could affect a property over its lifetime. For instance, earthquakes of magnitude 5–6, capable of property damage, have occurred in clusters in 1927, 1941, and 1980 in the Mammoth Lakes region [9].[7] After the notices were rescinded we would expect property values to return to pre-notice levels because there would be a reduction in the threat to the community.

In order to examine the actual behavior of nonresident visitors and resident property owners and their consequent impacts upon recreation and investment/ property values data were collected from both secondary and primary sources. Three hypotheses are tested:

 • Perceptions concerning the risk of dying and the risk to property are constant in the time periods before, during, and after hazard notices;

 • Recreation visitation patterns are constant in the time periods before, during, and after hazard notices;

 • Investment behavior and property values (holding all extraneous variables constant) are constant in the time periods before, during, and after hazard notices.

The first hypothesis, concerning risk perceptions, essentially constitutes a test of the Slovic *et al.* [20] finding that the media are important in forming individual risk perceptions since the hazard notices were issued to the public through the usual media outlets. The second hypothesis tests whether or not recreationists respond to changes in the recreation experience. The existing literature indicates that recreationists are generally quite responsive to environmental effects. Both behavioral changes [21] and willingness to pay/receive to prevent changes in the existing environment have been documented.[8] The final hypothesis examines the role that risk plays in the determination of investment in housing and property valuation. Recent papers by Brookshire *et al.* [1] and MacDonald *et al.* [15] indicate that risk information is capitalized into housing markets.

The results of these hypothesis tests are generally consistent with our expectations. We find that risk perceptions as to the probability of dying or incurring property damage either from an earthquake or volcano appear to be quite volatile

---

[5]Data for the joint probability for a minor eruption of a Mono Crater are based on one event per 500 years [9].

[6]Data for the joint probability of an earthquake of Richter Scale magnitude 6 or greater in Mammoth Lakes are based on historical evidence that six events out of 36,550 measurable earthquakes between 1980 and 1987 exceed magnitude 6 (see USGS earthquake catalog).

[7]The Richter scale magnitude of an earthquake is one of many factors that determine the ultimate damage to single family residences. Other important factors include characteristics of surrounding terrain, shaking intensity, and type of construction (brick or woodframe, with or without fireplace, before or after 1940, etc.). See Brookshire *et al.* [2] for a detailed discussion.

[8]See Cummings, Brookshire, and Schulze [4] for a summary of contingent valuation literature, most of which addresses environmental changes.

over time and consistent with the timing of the hazard notices. Recreation visitation is largely unaffected by the hazard notices and consequent risk perception change. However, investment behavior is affected and a perceived reduction in property values results.

II. RISK PERCEPTIONS

A survey among resident and nonresident property owners provided a means to obtain risk perception information, recreation visitation patterns, and property value data. The survey instrument used followed the total design method (TDM) [5].[9] The primary focus of the survey was threefold. First, the survey gathered information about the respondents' knowledge of the hazard announcements and risk perceptions as to the dangers to life and property before, during, and after the hazard announcements. A second focus of the survey supplied data about the effect of hazard announcements on nonresident property owners recreation visitation patterns. Finally, the survey furnished data necessary to estimate a hedonic price relationship relating house price to the risks involved.[10]

In order to capture changes in risk perceptions over time as well as focus on the risk of dying as separate from the risk of property damage, risk ladders were presented to respondents as a means of conveying relative risk information.[11] The risk ladders were divided into nine rungs along a logarithmic scale in order to represent the probability that various events would occur.

The respondents were asked to choose the letter associated with a rung on the ladder that corresponded to the level of risk they perceived during four distinct time periods: (1) before the Earthquake Hazards Watch on May 27, 1980, (2) after the Earthquake Hazards Watch but before the May 26, 1982, Notice of Potential Volcanic Hazard, (3) after the Notice of Potential Volcanic Hazard but before August 1984, when the hazard announcements were cancelled, and (4) after the hazard announcements were removed.

The results of the survey are presented in Fig. 1 and illustrate the change in risk perceptions over time. Each point along the trend lines represents the percent of respondents choosing the *lowest* risk category.[12] A downward trend from the time period before the hazard announcement of May 27, 1980, indicates that the perceived likelihood of dying or incurring property damage *increased*.

---

[9] The Dillman method achieves an acceptable response rate through careful design, personalization, and enactment of the survey.

[10] The sample from the survey drew upon Mammoth Lakes property owners obtained from Mono County, California, tax records. Eliminating unimproved property and duplicate owners, approximately 4000 property owners remained. A random sample of 1845 property owners was selected, of which a total of 340 were full time residents of Mammoth Lakes. Following the TDM of repeated mailings a 64.5% overall response rate was obtained. That is, 1190 completed surveys form the basis for the empirical analysis. A copy of the survey is available upon request from the authors.

[11] See Thayer and Schulze [22] for a discussion of risk ladders.

[12] Each respondent answered sixteen questions (two hazards, two types of damage, and four time periods). The number that chose the lowest risk category (one in 100,000,000) was converted to percentage terms by dividing the total responding to each question, determined as total questionnaires returned (1,190) minus missing values (generally less than 3%). An alternative approach to the presentation of only one portion of the distribution would be to present the entire distribution of responses for each question. However, this would require the presentation of 16 histogram charts. We have chosen this tactic to minimize space requirements but full distribution details are available from the authors.

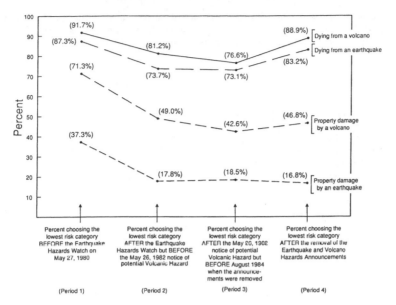

FIG. 1.   Lowest risk perceptions of death or property damage from an earthquake or volcano during four time periods.

A test of means across time periods was conducted for each trend line depicted in Fig. 1. Risk perceptions with regard to dying from a volcano were significantly increased by the earthquake notice (period 2), not affected further by the volcano notice (period 3) and then returned to pre-warning levels (period 4). The risk perception patterns and significance with regard to the prospect of death from an earthquake were statistically identical to those corresponding to death from a volcano. Thus, the Earthquake Hazards Watch issued May 27, 1980, significantly affected the perceptions of the risk of death. Perceptions returned to original levels *after* removal of the notice.

Risk perceptions as they related to possible property damage changed significantly from their levels in the pre-notice time interval as a result of both the earthquake and volcano notices. Risk perceptions returned only to levels resulting from the earthquake warning (period 2) *after* both the earthquake and volcano announcements were lifted (period 4). Thus, to the time of the survey, the perceived risk of damage to property from a volcano was elevated by the hazard notices.

The perceived risk of property damage from an earthquake was increased significantly by the earthquake announcement (period 2), unaffected by the volcano announcement (period 3), *and* remained at the elevated level of periods 2 and 3 even after the removal of the notices. These results suggest a permanent decline in investment and/or property values. This outcome could be due to the immobility of property vis-a-vis earthquake and volcano hazards.

Based upon these results concerning the risk of dying and prospective property damage, we reject the hypothesis that risk perceptions are equal in the time periods before, during, and after the issuance of hazard notices. In addition, since the media were the primary source of information our results confirm the Slovic *et al.* [20] result that the media are important in the formation of risk perceptions.

III. CONCEPTUAL FRAMEWORK

In order to quantitatively assess the extent of the Mammoth Lakes market impacts on changes in recreation visitation and investment behavior over time an economic framework is developed. The model focuses on the dynamic aspects of individuals' behavior in a volatile market when the prospect of low-probability, but possibly damaging, event influences transactions.

To examine the relationships between the hazard notices and the visitation and investment/property value effects, a traditional stock adjustment investment model is utilized [12, 19]. The investment model captures the notion that visitation is affected by the current level of capital stock. Investment is specified as the difference between the desired level of capital stock and the actual capital stock. In this context the term capital stock refers to the housing stock since our empirical estimation utilizes housing stock values as a proxy for the overall social infrastructure. Thus, investment is defined as the annual change in the housing stock.

Let

V = Recreational visitation.

$\mathbf{X}$ = A vector of characteristics of a resort area. These include weather conditions and physical attributes, as well as economic and other conditions.

r = Interest rate.

I = Per capita income.

K = Current level of capital (housing) stock.

K^* = Desired level of capital (housing) stock.

$\dot{K}$ = Investment, equal to the change in the capital (housing) stock over time.

H = Hazard notice.

α = A constant.

Formally, the model is specified as

$$V = V(\mathbf{X}, K, H) \tag{1}$$

$$K^* = K^*(V, r, I, H) \tag{2}$$

$$\dot{K} = \alpha(K^* - K) \tag{3}$$

Equation (1) states that visitation (V) is a function of resort area attributes, the current level of capital stock, and hazard notices. Equation (2) captures the interdependence between the desired level of capital stock and visitation. The desired level of the capital stock is also a function of the interest rate, income in the region, and hazard notices. Equation (3) states that investment in any time period is determined by the difference between the desired capital stock and the actual capital stock.

Substituting Eqs. (1) and (2) into Eq. (3) yields an estimable investment equation:

$$\dot{K} = \alpha\left(K^*\left(V(\mathbf{X}, K, H), r, I, H\right) - K \right). \tag{4}$$

The economic model therefore has two equations to be estimated: the visitation equation (Eq. 1), which relates the attributes of a site to recreational visitation, and the investment equation (Eq. 4), which relates investment to the desired level of capital stock (completely specified as dependent upon visitation, economic parameters, and the hazard notices) and the current level of the capital stock.

Four aspects of the equation system should be noted. First, the hazard notice variable enters both equations in a predictable manner. In the investment equation, the hazard variable appears twice, as it affects the desired capital stock both directly and indirectly through visitation. In each case the expected sign is negative. Second, the actual capital stock enters the investment equation twice. Its effect on the desired capital stock through visitation is expected to be positive. However, the actual capital stock also indirectly enters Eq. (4) negatively. Therefore, the sign on the actual capital stock variable is indeterminate, depending upon the relative strengths of the separate influences. Third, the statistical performance of the model is of interest and can be examined via the current level of capital stock variable. The current level of the capital stock variable should affect visitation in a significant manner. Further, the capital stock variable should be significant yet of indeterminate sign in the investment equation. Finally, the system is completely predetermined; that is, there exists no simultaneity in the system because it is the current capital stock (K) rather than investment ($\dot{K}$) that affects the visitation level.

The data employed to test the specific hypotheses concerning recreation and investment were collected from secondary sources as well as from the survey results. The secondary cross-sectional and time series data were collected for 11 western recreation sites which are predominately winter resorts.[13]

The dependent variable measuring recreational visitation was specified as skiing visitations. The important explanatory variables determining skiing visitation can be grouped into four separate categories: site, economic, size, and location variables as shown in Table I.

Site characteristics variables include the snow conditions and/or the presence of snowmaking equipment. The economic variables include the price of lift tickets and the level of personal income, used as a proxy for the general state of the economy. Each of these measures is deflated to constant dollars. The size-related variables include the population that is within a day's driving distance and the presence of an airport as a proxy for public infrastructure. The locational variables are distance to a major airport, the presence of substitute sites, the state in which the resort is located, and the presence of the hazard notices.

The data required to estimate Eq. (4) include a measure of investment (housing starts) and the set of independent variables (interest rates, income, visitation, capital stock). The interest rate that prevailed in the nearest SMSA is used as an indicator

---

[13] The resorts and years for which the data were gathered are Mammoth Lakes, CA (1974–1984); Lake Tahoe, NV (1978–1984); Park City, UT (1979–1984); Alta, UT (1976–1984); Sun Valley, ID (1974–1983); Apsen, CO (1974–1984); Steamboat Springs, CO (1979–1984); Telluride, CO (1974–1984); Vail, CO (1974–1984); Breckenridge, CO (1975–1984); and Mount Bachelor, OR (1974–1983).

42   BERNKNOPF, BROOKSHIRE, AND THAYER

TABLE I

Summary Statistics—Variables for the Recreation and Visitation Model

Variable	Definition	Mean	Standard Deviation	Minimum	Maximum
Visitation[a]	Number of ski resort visitations per year (#)	478,900.00	314,481.00	8,054.00	1,275,578.00
Investment[b]	Annual housing starts (#)	329.54	428.89	1.00	2,846.00
Interest rate[b]	Prevailing interest rate in the SMSA nearest to the ski resort (%)	11.32	1.99	8.63	15.11
Ski conditions[c]	Amount of snow on the ground as of February 15 each year (inches)	93.28	58.93	5.00	358.00
Snowmaking	1 if resort has snowmaking equipment, 0 if not	.63	.49	0.00	1.00
Price of lift ticket[c]	Price of an adult all-day pass deflated into constant dollars ($)	7.84	1.61	3.74	11.95
Personal income[b]	Per capita personal income for the county deflated into constant dollars ($)	3,736.00	884.90	1,850.00	6,273.00
Population[b]	Population within one day's driving distance of the resort (#)	42,387.00	23,529.00	13,728.00	107,464.00
Housing stock[b]	Housing stock available to visitors (nonlocal) (#)	3,326.93	3,293.30	315.00	13,384.00
Airport[d]	1 if resort has airport, 0 otherwise	.445	.449	0.00	1.00
Distance to airport[e]	Distance to major airport (miles)	84.89	47.68	22.00	196.00
Capacity/distance[e]	Capacity at nearest substitute site weighted by distance to that site (lift lines/distance)	15.64	6.05	6.00	26.00
State: CA, CO, UT, OR, ID	State in which the ski area is located (0 or 1)	N/A	N/A	N/A	N/A
Hazard notice[e]	0 = no hazard; 1 = earthquake hazard; 2 = earthquake and volcanic hazards	.079	.365	0.00	2.00

[a]Source: Ski resort or forest service.
[b]Source: Statistical abstract of the U.S.
[c]Source: Ski resort.
[d]Source: Local Chamber of Commerce.
[e]Source: Calculated.

of the cost of financing, whereas income in the surrounding community accounts for the availability of funds required for investment purposes.

The hypotheses concerning recreation visitation and housing valuation are also tested using data collected from the survey. With regard to recreation visitation, information concerning recreation activity during the time periods before, during, and after the hazard alerts was collected and analyzed. The housing valuation hypothesis was examined using data collected for the purpose of estimating a hedonic price equation.

TABLE II
Estimated Equation for Visitation to Ski Areas—Dependent
Variable = ln(Visits)

Variables	Coefficients	t-Statistics[a]
Site influences		
ln(Snow conditions)	.39	3.73
Snowmaking equipment	1.73	4.93
Economic influences		
ln(Price of lift tickets)	−1.58	−3.08
ln(Personal income)	.82	2.49
Size influences		
ln(Population within one day's drive)	1.59	5.98
ln(Housing stock)	1.83	1.47
(ln(Housing stock))^2	−.15	−1.83
Airport	.73	2.88
Location influences		
ln(Distance to major airport)	−1.00	−5.97
ln(Capacity at nearest site/distance)	−.48	−3.63
Hazard notices	.28	1.69
Constant	−12.20	−1.93
R^2	.69	
Number of observations	101	

[a] Due to the complex form of the estimated equation, significance of the coefficients cannot be determined by simple visual inspection of t-statistics. Except for the airport variable, all are significantly different from zero at the 10% level.

IV. RECREATION VISITATION

The estimated recreation visitation relationship based on secondary data sources, Eq. (1), is presented in Table II. The regression in Table II is the log-linear formulation. Other functional forms, such as linear, semilog, and translog, yielded similar results. The search over functional form presumes nothing about the underlying utility function since Eq. (1) is entirely general.

Excluding the hazard notices variable the coefficients on all independent variables are significantly different from zero and possess the expected relationship to recreation visitation. However, these results are not very stable. In particular, the income variable is especially sensitive to various variable specifications (e.g., inclusion of zero–one variables identifying the state in which the resort is located) and functional forms. The explanation for the performance of the income variable may lie in the nature of the skiing activity. Skiing is a relatively expensive sport so the use of county per capita income may not accurately represent skiing activities.

With regard to the relationship of the capital stock variable to visitation (Eq. 1) it is evident that the housing stock affects visitation in a positive manner only to a point and then the relationship turns negative. Moreover, this result is relatively insensitive to functional form variable specifications. This may result from recreationists' desire to vacation in relatively undeveloped areas, as long as some minimum development is available.

With regard to the recreation hypothesis, the hazard notice variable is significantly different from zero at the 10% level. However, two additional aspects of the hazard notice/visitation relationship should be noted. First, the hazard notice

44   BERNKNOPF, BROOKSHIRE, AND THAYER

TABLE III
Average Recreational Visits Over Time (n = 4884)

Year	Mean	Standard Deviation
1979–1980	5.3563	5.0732
1980–1981[a]	5.5663	4.9836
1981–1982	5.5491	4.9947
1982–1983[b]	5.3501	4.7645
1983–1984	5.1609	4.5631
1984–1985[c]	4.6155	4.1239

[a] First ski season after the earthquake Hazard Watch.
[b] First ski season after the Notice of Potential Volcanic Hazard.
[c] First ski season after cancellation of the hazard announcements.

variable affects visitation in a positive manner instead of the expected negative manner. This is likely the result of spurious correlation rather than anything systematic (i.e., recreationists lured to Mammoth Lakes in anticipation of an earthquake or volcano). Second, the hazard notices variable is extremely unstable ranging from insignificant (negative and positive) to significant (positive only) depending on particular functional forms and variable specifications.[14] The inherent fragility of the hazard notices coefficient, together with the fact that no significant negative relationship could be uncovered during the search process, leads us to conclude that we cannot reject the hypothesis that recreation visitation is constant (with respect to the hazard notices) over time. Any deviation in recreational visitation that occurred at Mammoth Lakes in the time period when the notices were operational must be attributable to factors other than hazard notices.

In addition to examining secondary data for resort areas, an analysis of nonresident survey respondents was conducted. For the portion of the property owner sample that does not permanently reside in Mammoth Lakes, California, data were collected concerning the frequency of yearly trips beginning in 1979 to Mammoth Lakes during the ski season. This included length of stay, type of transportation, and length of trip. Table III presents the mean visitation levels as well as the standard deviations. A test of equality of the means was conducted. The calculated F-statistic of 4.45 indicates that the hypothesis that the means were all equal was rejected. However, the pattern of recreation was inconsistent with the hypothesis that the hazard notices affected visitation; that is, visitation actually increased during the heightened risk time period (possibly due to a growth in the popularity of skiing as a recreational activity). Therefore, it seems that the hazard notices had no effect upon recreation visitation.

---

[14] A point which has been raised in the literature by Leamer [14] and others concerns the stability of the results. A variety of tests on the stability of the results were conducted. The recreation model was estimated by using (1) various samples of recreation areas, (2) various variable specifications, and (3) various functional forms. In no estimated equation was the hazard notice variable both significantly different from zero and negatively related to recreation visitation. For example, the coefficients on the hazard notices variables, with t-statistics in parentheses, for the linear and semilog functional forms (constant independent variable set) were 78,459 (.96) and .069 (.36), respectively.

TABLE IV
Estimated Equations for Investment in Ski Areas (Dependent Variable =
ln(Change in Housing Stock))

Variables	Equation A	Equation B	Equation C
Constant	−.91	−.93	−3.22
	(−.12)[a]	(−.12)	(−.41)
ln(Visitation)	−1.80	−1.75	−1.56
	(−1.73)	(−1.73)	(−1.46)
(ln(Visitation))^2	.077	.075	.067
	(1.77)	(1.77)	(1.47)
ln(Interest rate)	.009	.089	−.16
	(.02)	(.20)	(−.35)
ln(Income)	.94	.89	1.11
	(1.87)	(1.79)	(2.19)
ln(Housing stock)	1.11	1.11	1.12
	(8.63)	(8.71)	(8.61)
Hazard:			
0 for no announcements	−.685	—	—
1 for earthquake warning	(−2.61)		
2 for earthquake and volcano			
announcements			
Hazard:			
0 for years before 1980	—	−1.39	—
1 for years after 1980		(−3.14)	
Hazard:			
0 for years before 1982	—	—	−.63
1 for years after 1982			(−1.34)
R^2	.58	.58	.56
Number of observations	101	101	101
Durbin–Watson statistic	1.88	1.84	1.92

[a] t-Statistic.

Further support of this result can be found in another survey question that asked what most affected recreation visitation plans: general economic conditions, articles in the press on the wonders (dangers) of skiing, articles in the press about Mammoth Lakes, the amount of vacation time, or the hazard notices. Hazard notices were chosen in only 5 out of 964 completed surveys.

V. INVESTMENT AND PROPERTY VALUE RESULTS

The investment equation results, utilizing the secondary data sources, are presented in Table IV. The functional form is log-linear. A variety of other functional forms were estimated with no effect on the results. Further, functional forms such as the translog or quadratic Box–Cox did not significantly improve the fit of the data. With the exception of the interest rate variable, coefficients of all variables are significantly different from zero at the 10% level.[15] The capital (housing) stock variable is significantly different from zero and positively related to investment. The sign implies that the positive effect of the capital stock as an indirect influence

[15]A variety of alternative interest rates (e.g., regional, national, etc.) were utilized and were found to be insignificant.

through the desired capital stock outweighs the expected negative direct effect. The other sign relationships of the independent and dependent variables are as expected.

Three definitions of hazard notices were utilized as variables (see Table IV). In Eqs. (A) and (B), the hazard variables are significantly different from zero and negatively affect investment. The hazard variable in Eq. (C) is not significantly different from zero. In Eq. (C), the hazard notice does not take effect until after the 1982 notice of potential volcanic activity. This is in contrast to Eq. (B), in which the hazard notice takes effect after the 1980 earthquake warning with no additional escalation to include the later volcano notice. This indicates that the earthquake watch contributed to the downturn in investment as early as 1980. Thus, we reject the hypothesis that investment levels were not affected by the hazard notices.

Based on the writings of Rosen [18], Freeman [8], and others, the hedonic price method (HPM) is utilized to determine the effect on property values of individual characteristics for single family residences.[16] Property value information collected from the survey included type of property, date of purchase, square footage, fireplace, bathrooms, view, number of stories, ski in/ski out access, age of property, and knowledge of the hazard announcements at the time of purchase.

The underlying structure of the hypothesis test is a single equation model that attempts to explain the variation in the market value of homes located at Mammoth Lakes. The analysis yields two conclusions concerning the relationship of a hazard notice to market value. The relative significance is determined and the estimated coefficient implicitly measures the monetary value at the margin. The approach is generally viewed as a multi-stage procedure: (1) estimate the hedonic price gradient, which explains the home sale price as a function of its structural characteristics as well as the characteristics of the community and neighborhood in which it is located, and (2) determine the implicit price of the variable of interest leading to estimation of a demand curve. A comparison to the investment model utilizes the first stage estimation results because sufficient information is not available to identify the demand curve in subsequent steps [3, 17].

An important aspect of the property value data relates to the market value, which serves as the dependent variable. Due to the unavailability of actual data including detailed characteristics information, we utilized the stated market value in 1985 instead of actual sales price.[17] Thus, we capture the perceived market value of the homes.

Table V presents two regressions. Nonlinear specifications were utilized following Rosen's [18] notion that consumers cannot always arbitrage by dividing and repackaging bundles of attributes. Approximately 30 to 34% of the variation in market value is explained by the independent variable set. A possible reason for the relatively low R^2 lies in the absence of neighborhood and community variables

---

[16]Not considered is the effect of the hazard announcements upon multiple family dwellings, commercial property, undeveloped property, or alternative ownership patterns.

[17]We were able to obtain data on the number of actual sales and the corresponding dollar value for Mammoth Lakes for the period 1979–1984 (Safeco Title Insurance Co.). In general, Mammoth Lakes sales volume (units sold) closely paralleled trends in San Diego County and California for the same time period. However, Mammoth Lakes dollar value sales declined relatively much more than either San Diego County or California. This latter result would be expected if sellers were forced to discount their homes to offset the risk in nature of their location. We were not able to use these actual sales data in the estimation of the hedonic function since corresponding characteristic data were not available for each home.

EARTHQUAKE AND VOLCANO HAZARD NOTICES   47

TABLE V
Variables and Estimated Equations for Hedonic Price Analysis

Variable	Definition, expected relationship to dependent variable, and units of measure	Eq. 1: semilog dependent variable = ln(stated market value in $100)	Eq. 2: log linear dependent variable = ln(stated market value in $100)
Dependent:			
Market value	Estimated market value as of July 1985 ($)		
Independent:			
Interest rate	Interest rate on home mortgage; negative; percent	−.023 (−3.11)	−.035 (−.99)
View	Home with scenic view; positive; 0 = no; 1 = yes	.12 (3.84)	.12 (3.92)
Stories	Number of stories; positive; number	.043 (1.65)	.085 (1.73)
Fireplace	Number of fireplaces; positive; number	.08 (1.08)	.106 (.95)
Ski in/ski out	Does home possess ski in/ski out attribute; positive; 0 = no; 1 = yes	.14 (4.20)	.15 (4.29)
Bathrooms	Number of bathrooms; positive; number	.185 (7.60)	.40 (8.85)
House age	Age of home; negative; years	.114 (2.85)	−.09 (−3.57)
Living area	Square feet of interior living space; positive; feet	.00018 (7.21)	.121 (5.39)
Home type	Detached or attached; negative; 0 = detached; 1 = attached (condo)	−.10 (−4.19)	—
Date of home purchase	Year in which home was purchased; positive; year	.114 (2.85)	.003 (1.11)
Hazard knowledge	Were hazards considered at time of purchase; negative; 0 = no; 1 = yes if one hazard considered; 2 = yes if both hazards considered	—	−.041 (1.28)
Hazard timing	Was home purchased after earthquake and volcano notices negative; 0 = pre-1980; 1 = 1980–1982; 2 = post-1982	−.057 (−2.14)	—
R^2		.34	.30
Number of observations		868	868

which increase explanatory power. All variables are significantly different from zero at the 5% level and possess the expected sign relationship, except for the fireplace variable.

The two different specifications of the hazard variables—hazard timing and hazard knowledge—are both significantly different from zero and are both related negatively to stated home market value. Interpreting the hazard coefficient in Eq. 1 of Table IV indicates an 11.4% loss in market value, or approximately $13,000 for an average home. Equation 2 suggests an 8.2% loss, or approximately $9,400. Thus, we reject the hypothesis that hazard announcement timing and knowledge of the hazard did not affect the perceived market value of homes. This result is consistent with the estimated results from the investment model and offers further evidence to reject the third hypothesis. In addition, this result is consistent with Brookshire *et al.* [1] and MacDonald *et al.* [15] which demonstrate that risky attributes are capitalized into home value.

VI. CONCLUDING REMARKS

The hazard notices issued for the Mammoth Lakes area contributed to a measurable economic loss in property values as risk perceptions were altered, at least for the short term, with regard to prospective property damage from earthquakes and/or a volcano. Recreation visitation was largely unaffected. The actual risk of death from a natural hazard at Mammoth Lakes has been and remains quite low while the risk to property over a longer period remains. The results reported are quite robust since both secondary and primary data sets produce identical conclusions and the variety of tests conducted to determine stability failed to produce alternative interpretations.

The difference between the results of this paper and the earlier work in this area may be explained by the relative experience and knowledge of natural hazards by the Mammoth Lakes property owners. There were numerous earthquakes before and during the time period of the hazard notices. In addition, Mount St. Helens had erupted on May 18, 1980. There were numerous media stories on natural hazards that also contributed to the information flow.

The importance of this result for public policy is that hazard warnings can alter behavior. Future Notices and Warnings in the Mammoth Lakes region should be quite specific and quantitative in describing the temporal and spatial nature of expected events. Location, magnitude, and time of event are important characteristics that should be defined as precisely as possible. This type of procedure would avoid undesirable behavioral changes.

For the general case of natural hazards the U.S. Geological Survey should distinguish between low probability events with large uncertain time dimensions and emergency situations or predictions. The risks of each hazard should be communicated in commonly understood terms (e.g., cigarette or x-ray equivalents) to prevent any misperceptions of risks. Finally, the removal of any notice should receive the same media attention as the initial warning.

The prescriptions for communication of natural hazards risk also apply to labels for hazardous household products (e.g., cleaning and pesticide products). Labels should contain specific risk information in commonly understood terms. Emergency situations should be clearly identified and distinguished from less life threatening situations. The information should also be presented succinctly to prevent information overload [16].

REFERENCES

1. D. S. Brookshire, M. Thayer, J. Tschirhart, and W. Schulze, A test of the expected utility model: Evidence from earthquake risks, *J. Polit. Econom.* **93**, 369–389 (1985).

EARTHQUAKE AND VOLCANO HAZARD NOTICES   49

2. D. S. Brookshire, W. D. Schulze, J. Tschirhart, M. Thayer, R. Hageman, R. Pazand, and S. Ben-David, "Methods Development for Valuing Hazards Information," Technical Report, U.S. Geological Survey, Reston, Va (October 1980).
3. J. Brown and H. Rosen, On estimation of structural hedonic price models, *Econometrica* **50**, 762–768 (1982).
4. R. G. Cummings, D. S. Brookshire, and W. D. Schulze, Eds., "Valuing Environmental Goods: An Assessment of the Contingent Valuation Method," Rowman and Allanheld, NJ (1986).
5. D. A. Dillman, "Mail and Telephone Surveys: The Total Design Method," Wiley–Interscience, New York (1978).
6. Federal Register, "Revision of Terminology for Geologic Hazard Warnings," Department of the Interior, Geological Survey, Notices, Vol. 49, No. 21 (January 31, 1984).
7. B. Fischhoff, S. Lichenstein, P. Slovic, R. Keene, and S. Derby, "Acceptable Risk," Cambridge Univ. Press, Cambridge (1981).
8. A. M. Freeman, III, Hedonic prices, property values and measuring environmental benefits: A survey of the issues, *Scand. J. Econom.* **81**, 154–173 (1979).
9. D. P. Hill, R. E. Wallace, and R. S. Cockerham, Review of evidence on the potential for major earthquakes and volcanism in the Long Valley-Mono Craters-White Mountains regions of California, *Earthquake Pred. Res.* **3**, 571–594 (1985).
10. P. M. Ippolito, Information and the life cycle consumption of hazardous goods, *Econom. Inquiry* **19**, 529–558 (1981).
11. F. R. Johnson and R. A. Luken, Radon risk information and voluntary protection: Evidence from a natural experiment, *Risk Anal.* **7**, 97–107 (1987).
12. D. W. Jorgenson, Econometric studies of investment behavior: A survey, *J. Econom. Lit.* **5**, 1111–1147 (1971).
13. H. Kunreuther and J. Linnerooth, Low probability accidents, *Risk Anal.* **4**, 143–152 (1984).
14. E. E. Leamer, Let's take the con out of econometrics, *Amer. Econom. Rev.* **73**, 31–43 (1983).
15. D. N. MacDonald, J. C. Murdoch, and H. L. White, Hazards and insurance in housing, *Land Econom.*, **63**, 361–371 (1987).
16. W. A. Magat, W. K. Viscusi, and J. Huber, Consumer processing of hazard warning information, *J. Risk Uncertainty* **1**, 201–232 (1988).
17. R. Palmquist, Estimating the demand for characteristics of housing, *Rev. Econom. Statist.* **66**, 394–404 (1984).
18. S. Rosen, Hedonic prices and implicit markets: Product differentiation in pure competition, *J. Polit. Econom.* **82**, 34–55 (1974).
19. W. M. Scarth, "Macroeconomics: An Introduction to Advanced Methods," Harcourt Brace Jovanovich, San Diego (1988).
20. P. Slovic, B. Fischhoff, and S. Lichtenstein, Facts and fears: Understanding perceived risk, *in* "Social Risk Assessment: How Safe is Safe Enough?" (R. C. Schwing and W. A. Albers, Eds.), Plenum, New York (1980).
21. M. Thayer, Contingent valuation techniques for assessing environmental impacts: Further evidence, *J. Environ. Econom. Management* **8**, 27–44 (1981).
22. M. A. Thayer and W. D. Schulze, "An Economic Evaluation of Hazard Alerts: A Case Study of the Mammoth Lakes Basin, California," Research Report, U.S. Geological Survey, Contract #14-08-0001-20458, Reston, Virginia (May 1986).
23. United States Congress, Disaster Relief Act of 1974, Public Law 93-288 (88 Stat. 143).
24. United States Geological Survey, "Earthquake Activity Could Continue At Mammoth Lakes, Calif.," Reston, Virginia (1980).
25. United States Geological Survey, "Notices of Potential Volcanic Hazard Issued for Eastern California," Reston, Virginia (1982).
26. W. K. Viscusi, W. A. Magat, and J. Huber, Informational regulation of consumer health risks: An empirical evaluation of hazard warnings, *Rand J. Econom.* **17**, 251–365 (1986).

Part III
Direct Losses and the Distribution of Impacts

[9]

NATURAL HAZARD EXPOSURES, LOSSES AND MITIGATION COSTS IN THE UNITED STATES, 1970-2000

ARTHUR A. ATKISSON
Public and Environmental Administration
University of Wisconsin-Green Bay

WILLIAM J. PETAK
Institute of Safety and Systems Management
University of Southern California

DANIEL J. ALESCH
Public and Environmental Administration
University of Wisconsin-Green Bay

This paper presents the major findings of a three-year study of the exposure of United States population and buildings to nine natural hazards: expansive soils, landslide, earthquake, tsunami, coastal storm surge, riverine flooding, hurricane, tornado, and severe wind.[1] The research utilized computerized probabilistic risk analysis methods to determine annual expected losses for each hazard. The losses were calculated on the basis of long-term exposure of geographic areas in the United States to the various hazards, including estimated magnitude or intensity expected for each area. The research includes an examination of the costs and benefits of a wide variety of possible policies to mitigate the effects of the nine natural hazards on life and property, utilizing a variety of discount rates.

THE INCIDENCE AND COSTS OF NATURAL HAZARDS IN THE U.S.

Almost no portion of the planet's surface is free from the risks produced by hazardous natural events. Scattered around the planet are 516 active volcanoes from which eruptions occur approximately once each fifteen days. The global network of earthquake monitoring instruments currently records approximately 2000 tremors beneath the crust of the earth each day and, almost twice each day, earthquakes of a magnitude sufficient to damage buildings and other struc-

tures occur somewhere on the face of the planet. Quakes of sufficient strength to produce widespread damage and death occur fifteen to twenty times each year. Above the surface of the earth, 1800 orbiting thunder storms can be observed at any given time and lightening strikes the planet's outer skin at the rate of 100 times per second. In late summer, 50 or more hurricanes can be observed forming somewhere in the world and, during approximately the same season, from 600 to 1,000 tornadoes strike somewhere in the United States at a rate of four or more per day. Nearly one half billion members of the planet's total population now reside in riverine and coastal flood plains where they produce one third of the world's total products and, on any given day, some fraction of these plains are covered by flood waters.

Many natural events occur only infrequently, but when they do occur, they produce catastrophic results. Natural disasters of major proportions have occurred throughout the history of the United States. Twenty-one years before the adoption of the Declaration of Independence, earthquakes shattered Massachusetts. During the height of the War of 1812, the highest magnitude earthquake in the history of the United States left parts of Missouri and Arkansas permanently sunken. In the immediate post-Civil War years a devastating earthquake struck South Carolina, and, in

1871, a forest fire raged throughout northeastern Wisconsin causing the deaths of more than 1200 persons.

On a single day in 1889, flood waters claimed 2,209 lives in Johnstown, Pennsylvania. Eleven years later, the largest civil disaster in U.S. history occurred when a hurricane pushed the waters of a storm surge over Galveston, Texas, causing 6,000 deaths. Six years later, in 1906, an earthquake rocked San Francisco and, along with the fires produced by the event, caused the deaths of 500 to 700 persons and more than $374 million in property damage. In 1928, a dam collapsed in California, sending a wall of water over an unsuspecting population, sweeping 450 persons to their deaths. Only a few months later a Florida hurricane caused 1833 deaths.

More recently, the Palm Sunday tornadoes of 1965 claimed 271 lives in five states; hurricane Camille (1969) destroyed over $1.4 billion in property and claimed 256 lives; the South Dakota flash flood of 1972 killed 236 persons; the Alaska earthquake (1965) killed 131; and Agnes, the hurricane and tropical storm (1972), caused 118 deaths and property losses in excess of $3.1 billion. On a single day in 1974, separate tornadoes caused the deaths of 318 persons in several southern and midwestern states.

Although less dramatic, a variety of other natural hazards produced considerable damage to property during these same time periods, resulting in substantial annual economic losses. These hazards include expansive soils, land subsidence, landslides, erosion of river and shore banks, periodic droughts, and hail, ice, snow, and rain storms.

The economic losses due to the nine natural hazards considered in this research project are substantial. As shown in Table 1, "Annual Expected Losses from Nine Natural Hazards in 1970, Compared with Annual Value of Other Types of Losses and Events," the annual expected losses from these hazards exceeds all losses from traffic

TABLE 1.   Annual Expected Losses from Nine Natural Hazards in 1970,
Compared with Annual Value of Other Types of Losses and Events

Type of Loss or Event	Value in 1970 (Millions of $)
1. All Property Tax Collections by State and Local Governments	34,054
2. All Accidents	27,000
3. Expected Annual Natural Hazard Losses (2000 Exposure)	17,779
4. All Traffic Accidents	16,200
5. Total Economic Effects of Air Pollution	16,000
6. Health Insurance Premiums	11,546
7. Increase in Annual Expected Losses from Natural Hazards, 1970–2000	9,685
8. Pollution Control Costs (Air, Water, Solid Wastes)	9,300
9. Auto Liability Insurance Premiums	8,958
10. Expected Annual Natural Hazard Losses (1970 Exposure)	8,094
11. Losses from Accidents at Work	8,000
12. Losses from Air Pollution-Related Morbidity and Mortality	6,000
13. Air Pollution Effects on Value of Property	5,200
14. Air Pollution Effects on Materials and Vegetation	4,900
15. Expenditures by All State and Local Police Departments	4,494
16. All Crimes against Property	4,264
17. Investments in Water Pollution Control Facilities	3,100
18. Business Losses Due to Six Types of Criminal Activities	3,049
19. Building Losses Due to Fires	2,209

Source: Petak and Atkisson (1982)

accidents and is approximately half the amount of all property taxes collected by state and local governments.

PUBLIC POLICY AND NATURAL HAZARDS

Many public and private actions have been taken in our efforts to mitigate the effects of exposures to natural hazards. Population warning systems have been placed in operation, rivers have been dammed, deepened, and diked. Coastlines have been equipped with sea walls, storm cellars have been dug in back yards, buildings have been elevated above the level of expected flood heights, and a variety of means have been employed to strengthen structures and reduce their vulnerability to the forces exerted by winds, land movement, and other natural hazards.

Unfortunately, these efforts at mitigating losses due to exposure have produced less than satisfactory results. Construction of flood control facilities has seemed to prompt heavy migration into flood prone areas and has, thereby, escalated the real costs of flood exposures. Governmental provision of disaster relief, low cost loans, and subsidized insurance has seemed to encourage, rather than discourage, private risk-taking activity. A public unwillingness to acknowledge the threat of future loss-producing occurrences in high hazard areas and an accompanying faith that government will somehow protect them, has contributed to a continuing population movement into such high hazard areas as the hurricane and flood prone coastal areas along the Gulf Coast and the South Atlantic. Similar population movements have taken place in seismically active areas and along the shores of rivers and lake subject to periodic flooding. As a result, the United States now faces the probability that one or more major community catastrophes, each far greater in loss of life and property than any which have previously occurred in our history, may occur over the span of the next several decades.

At the same time we have ignored the high risks of natural hazard events, we also face the risk of over-reacting to the threats posed by natural hazards and the related risk of implementing public policies which may result in costs far in excess of the benefits they will yield.

Numerous types of building strengthening, area protection, site development, and other technologies are available for use by those who wish to reduce the risks associated with exposure to natural hazards. Mandatory application of these technologies can be forced through adoption of a wide variety of federal, state, and local public policies. Hazard mitigating amendments to building codes, subdivision standards, and land use regulations can be enacted. Hazard zones can be identified and sanctions employed to prohibit development in such areas. The risk of loss may be spread through use of insurance schemes. The impact of catastrophic events on exposed populations may be reduced through community safety plans, disaster relief, and recovery measures financed by non-impacted parties.

What mix of these measures to employ, when, where, at what cost, and to whom, has become a major public policy question. To assist in resolving this question, the authors have conducted an interrelated set of policy studies of this subject[2] and have anchored these studies on findings from a computer-based study of U.S. population and building exposures to nine natural hazards over the period 1970–2000.[3] The computer models used in the study were based on risk analysis procedures developed to predict annual expected losses arising from the periodic occurrences of these hazards and were supplemented by procedures which permit examination of the relationship between the costs and benefits associated with applying a variety of loss-mitigating measures in the U.S. natural hazard zones.[4]

ANNUAL EXPECTED LOSSES
AND EXPOSED POPULATIONS

Application of risk assessment models resulted in estimates of nationally aggregated annual expected natural hazards losses

TABLE 2.   Expected Annual Losses from Natural Hazard Exposures in the United States By Type of Hazard and Type of Loss, 1970 and 2000

Expected Annual Losses

Hazard	Building Damage* (Millions of 1970$)		Number of Deaths		Housing Units Lost		Person Years of Homelessness		Person Years of Unemployment	
	1970	2000	1970	2000	1970	2000	1970	2000	1970	2000
1. Earthquakes	781.1	1,553.7	273	400	20,485	22,858	736	648	413.5	634.9
2. Expansive Soils	798.1	997.1	—	—	—	—	—	—	—	—
3. Hurricane	1,056.0	3,528.3	62	153	31,885	52,237	34,505	48,271	21,004	58,223.7
4. Landslides	370.3	871.2	—	—	—	—	—	—	—	—
5. Riverine Flooding	2,758.3	3,175.33	190	159	24,521	43,757	7,290	10,330	373.1	850.9
6. Severe Wind	18.0	53.4	5	11	547	748	852	1,014	369.7	1,018.3
7. Storm Surge	641.2	2,342.9	37	103	36,212	52,119	86,122	107,630	57,541.6	146,568.5
8. Tornado	1,656.0	5,219.1	392	920	234	335	345	389	97.5	195.9
9. Tsunami	15.0	40.4	20	44	—	—	—	—	—	—
Totals	8,094.0	17,779.4	979	1,790	113,884	172,084	129,850	168,302	79,799.1	207,492.2

* Includes Contents, Income, and Supplier Loss.

for 1970 and 2000. These data are summarized in Table 2. The study revealed that natural hazard exposures in the year 1970 produced annual expected dollar losses totalling approximately $8 billion and nearly 1,000 annual expected deaths. Approximately 71 per cent of the expected dollar losses for 1970 resulted from building damage, approximately 24 per cent from damage to building contents, and the balance from expected losses sustained by workers and increased costs of transporting goods due to delays and reroutings. The study showed that annual expected natural hazard losses (in 1970 dollars) would rise to approximately $17.8 billion in the year 2000 and that building contents losses will rise to approximately 40 per cent of that total. Annual expected deaths from natural hazard exposures were predicted to increase to 1790 in 2000. Expected annual national losses from exposure to all nine hazards produced per capita losses of $39.76 in 1970 and $69.41 in 2000 (1970 dollars).

MITIGATION TECHNOLOGIES AND COSTS

Seventeen potential loss-reducing strategies were examined in detail, representing five different major approaches to managing natural hazard risks. The five include hazard avoidance, area structure protection, building strengthening, site preparation, and building removal. The seventeen potential strategies are listed in Table 3. Each mitigation strategy is related to the hazards for which it is potentially applicable.

As a result of technology and cost analyses, it became clear that the high levels of hazard exposure the study predicted for the future need not occur; they can be prevented or lessened through use of several types of technologies and through implementation of a variety of public policies. The analysis revealed that building damage losses alone could be reduced by approximately 42 per cent from those projected for the year 2000. However, the study also revealed that no loss-reducing strategy is completely free

TABLE 3. Hazard-Mitigating Technologies, by Type and Applicability to Nine Natural Hazards

Hazard to which applicable

Technology by class and title	Riverine flooding	Storm surge	Tsunami	Hurricane	Tornado	Severe Wind	Earthquake	Landslide	Expansive Soil
1.0 Hazard Avoidance Strategies and Technologies									
1.1 Zero growth on fifty-year flood plains after 1980	●	●							
1.2 Zero growth on 100-year flood plains after 1980	●	●							
1.3 Zero growth on fifty-year riverine flood plains in specified additional numbers of flood-prone cities each year, to 2000	●								
1.4 Zero growth in counties exhibiting high Tornado Strike Risk (greater than 10^{-4} tornado strikes per year per square mile).					●				
2.0 Area Structural Protection Strategies									
2.1 Structural protection (dams, levees, etc.) of cities with riverine flood problems.	●								
2.2 Construction of sea-walls to protect four additional counties per year from 100-year storm surge heights. Construct in order of decreasing damages in affected counties.		●							
3.0 Building Strengthening Strategies									
3.1 Require tie-downs on all mobile homes.				●	●	●			
3.2 Increase designed wind resistance capability of new buildings to level equalling 1.5 x the level specific in the Uniform Building Code (1.5 x UBC)				●	●	●			
3.3 Increase designed wind resistance capability of new buildings to level equalling 3.0 x the level specified in the Uniform Building Code (3.0 x UBC).				●	●	●			
3.4 Increase strength of new buildings to level required in UBC Earthquake Zone #3. (UBC 3).							●		
3.5 Floodproof 2% annually of all structures in fifty-year riverine flood plains to provide zero damage to height of four feet.	●								
3.6 Floodproof 2% annually, of all structures in 100-year riverine flood plains to provide zero damage to height of four feet.	●								
3.7 After 1980, floodproof all new buildings in storm surge areas to height of four feet.		●							
3.8 Modify and retrofit existing buildings in high seismic risk areas to meet seismic safety standards.							●		
4.0 Site Preparation Strategies									
4.1 Require soils testing and improved site grading standards in landslide-prone areas.								●	
4.2 Require soils testing and pre-construction moisture control and/or soil stabilization on construction sites.									●
5.0 Building Removal Strategies									
5.1 Purchase and/or condemn and accelerate removal of high vulnerability structures in high hazard areas.	●	●	●					●	●

Source: Petak and Atkisson (1982).

from economic or social cost and that over-zealous use of some strategies might actually increase total national hazard exposure costs when these costs are defined to include both the losses resulting from hazard exposures and the costs of implementing the mitigations used to reduce such losses.

Examination of the annual amortized costs of implementing each alternative loss-reducing strategy resulted in the finding that many strategies are not cost-effective; their annual principle repayment and annual interest requirements exceed the projected value of their loss-reducing potential. The data generated by this study suggest clearly that imprudent and overzealous application of risk-reducing mitigations could actually increase net annual expected natural hazard costs in 2000 from 38.4 to 90.0 per cent above the levels that would be experienced if current policies remain unaltered.

Not all costs and benefits associated with implementation of mitigation strategies were included in the study. For example, the study did not include estimates of hazard-induced loss of public infrastructure. Perhaps more importantly, the study did not place an economic value on the reduction in human mortality that might result from application of more rigorous hazard management strategies. The authors do not attempt to place economic values on human life; they prefer to analyze the cost required to avert deaths. Such costs are often more meaningful to policy makers.

The procedures used to estimate losses were based on assumed, but empirically-supported, relationships between the magnitude of dollar loss associated with hazardous occurrences and the loss of life associated with such occurrences. This method resulted in annual expected life loss estimates which were substantially greater for 1970 than the annual average life loss from natural hazards actually reported for any of the decades in the current century. Moreover, both hazard-induced death rates and the absolute annual

average number of deaths has been declining rather steadily throughout the century. Thus, even though the estimates of life loss were probabilistically derived and therefore reflect the intermittent and large losses of life which may be expected from major catastrophes, the annual expected estimates of life loss may overstate the consequences of natural hazard exposures. Past mitigations, including installation of warning systems, may be working effectively. On the other hand, since the estimates are probabilistic, and since the events are intermittent and characterized by massive losses, we may simply have been fortunate so far this century.

Even if the expected hazard-induced mortality predicted in the study were to occur, the annual expected estimates of life loss reported in the study are not as impressive as the mortality from other causes in our society. Examination of evidence suggests that the cost per death averted in natural hazard risk reduction programs can well be escalated to levels substantially in excess of those associated with other death and injury reducing programs which currently may be under-funded. Although this inference is not intended to suggest that life loss reduction should not be an objective of natural hazard management programs, neither does it seem appropriate to overstate the benefits and to understate the costs associated with such programs.

NOTES

[1] The studies which resulted in this report were supported, in part, by National Science Foundation Grant Number ERP-09998, and by National Science Foundation Purchase order 78-SP-0620. In a substantially expanded form, the data reported here are also included in William J. Petak and Arthur A. Atkisson, *Natural Hazard Risk Assessment and Public Policy*, New York: Springer-Verlag, Inc., 1982.

[2] See, for example: (1) William J. Petak, Arthur A. Atkisson, Paul H. Gleye. *Natural Hazards: A Public Policy Assessment*. Redondo Beach, California, J. H. Wiggins Company, 1978 NTIS #PB297361/AS A23; (2) Arthur A. Atkisson, William J. Petak, Daniel J.

Alesch, et al, *Natural Hazards and Public Policy: Recommendations for Public Policies to Mitigate the Effects of Natural Hazard Exposures in the United States,* Green Bay, Wisconsin: University of Wisconsin-Green Bay Papers in Public Policy and Administration, 78-2 (December 1978); (3) Arthur A. Atkisson and William J. Petak, *Seismic Safety Policies and Practices in U.S. Metropolitan Areas.* (A Report to the Federal Emergency Management Agency), Redondo Beach, California: J. H. Wiggins Company, January 1981.

³ William J. Petak, Arthur A. Atkisson, Paul Gleye, op. cit.

⁴ J. Hirschberg, P. Gordon, and W. J. Petak. *Natural Hazards: Socioeconomic Impact Assessment Model.* Redondo Beach, California: J. H. Wiggins Company, 1978. NTIS # PB294681/AS A10.

[10]

©*International Regional Science Review* 17, 2: 121–150 (1994)

Modeling the Regional Impact of Natural Disaster and Recovery: A General Framework and an Application to Hurricane Andrew

Carol T. West

David G. Lenze

Bureau of Economic and Business Research
University of Florida
Gainesville FL 32611 USA

Two common features of natural disasters are intense regional impact and the call immediately after the event to estimate the economic impact of recovery and reconstruction. The broad purpose of this paper is to help fill the gap in the regional science literature that addresses this issue. Initially, the impact estimation problem is presented conceptually. Using a general regional model schematic, direct disaster impacts on exogenous variables, endogenous variables, and model linkages are identified. Next, the conceptual problem is adapted for practical application. This translation has two aspects: (1) modifying the direct impacts for a specific model (common variants from the schematic are considered) and (2) estimating those impacts from available data. One component of the latter identifies primary sources of information typically available at the time of a natural disaster and indicates how secondary data may be used to complement, cross-check, and expand those data. A second component identifies areas of no information or high uncertainty and discusses treatment of that information gap in empirical analysis. A final section applies the research to the problem of estimating the impact of Hurricane Andrew on the economy of Florida.

Introduction

Natural disasters occur regularly, if not predictably, and their common characteristic is intense regional economic and social impact. When the acute emergency phase is past, hope and attention immediately focus on the potential "silver lining" of the disaster — the jobs, income, and revenue which will be generated in the region as reconstruction funded by insurance payments and federal aid ensues. The regional economist is the one asked to estimate the brilliance of the silver lining, yet the regional science literature has been surprisingly mute on how to conduct that estimation.

The authors are indebted to the editor and five anonymous referees for insightful suggestions which significantly improved the presentation of the research.

Paper first received June 1993; revised November 1993 and July 1994.

122   INTERNATIONAL REGIONAL SCIENCE REVIEW   VOL. 17 NO. 2

Modeling the reconstruction following a natural disaster presents excep-
tional challenges to regional impact methodologies. First, the size of the
event is not well known. This is in marked contrast to most impact studies
which start with some firm numerical inputs on expenditure, employment,
income, or tax rate changes. Second, natural disasters are not concentrated
sectoral events. Unlike a military base closure or the opening or closing of a
firm in a specific SIC, natural disasters cut a wide swath across a range of
regional economic activities. This makes potential doublecounting of
impacts a problem that requires a careful accounting framework. Third, they
are neither exclusively "supply" nor exclusively "demand" events. Reconstruction is predominantly the latter, but the geographic concentration of
devastation is likely to strain regional capacity, and the exact size of that
capacity is difficult to determine. In addition, direct supply interruptions may
result from the devastation of physical facilities, both business structures and
public infrastructure. Fourth, the reactions of households to the unexpected
destruction of their homes, personal property, and neighborhoods are poorly
understood. It is difficult to distinguish situations that lead to energetic
rebuilding from those that result in permanent population dispersion from
the impacted area. Finally, although broad effects of wealth changes on consumption have been measured, they predominantly reflect modest variations
in financial portfolios and real property values. The applicability of these
estimates to situations in which shelter and personal physical possessions
have been destroyed is not clear.

The detailed, specific numerical input requirements of sophisticated
regional impact models are not readily reconciled with the confusion, uncertainty, and imperfect measurements that often follow in the wake of a natural
disaster. Indeed, analytical techniques used to evaluate disaster losses and
reconstruction gains have become increasingly sophisticated. They have
advanced from descriptive case studies (Haas, Kates, and Bowden 1977) to
formal implementation of regression and time series techniques (Friesema et
al. 1979; Chang 1983) to analysis based on regional simultaneous equation
econometric models (Ellson, Milliman, and Roberts 1984; Guimaraes,
Hefner, and Woodward 1993), input-output models (Cochrane 1992a;
Boisvert 1992; Gordon and Richardson 1992) and most recently, computable
general equilibrium (CGE) models (Brookshire and McKee 1992).

The problem, however, of making the transition from an actual event to
specific exogenous model inputs is highlighted by what these studies omit.
Many use hypothetical, stylized natural disasters and consequently consider
only limited aspects of the complex set of economic events which actually
characterize a natural disaster (e.g., Ellson, Milliman, and Roberts 1984;
Brookshire and McKee 1992). Others analyze historical events but often fail
to quantitatively link total impacts to specific direct impacts. For example,

Chang's (1983) *ex post* analysis of revenue impacts of Hurricane Frederic does not identify the specific spending pattern which generated the enhanced municipal revenues, nor do Guimaraes, Hefner, and Woodward (1993) specify the direct employment and income factors which led to the aggregate income and employment impacts found in their *ex post* analysis of Hurricane Hugo. Given that the direct impact is often a large portion of the total impact, and that much of the apparent multiplier differences between impact models can be due to how the direct impact is measured (Crihfield and Campbell 1991; Grimes, Fulton, and Bonardelli 1992), it is important to devote proportionate attention to its measurement.

That transition from actual event to specific exogenous model inputs is the primary focus of the current research, which develops a systematic framework for analysis. Differences among natural disasters render impossible a uniformly applicable template, but the broad issues to be considered are similar across disasters. The appropriate procedure in any specific instance will necessarily be a modification of experience from other events.

In addition, this article attempts to integrate the regional science and natural disaster literatures to enable better estimation of direct impacts. At present, available data to study the regional impact of natural disasters are not centrally organized, and how secondary data might be used to fill primary data gaps is not systematically discussed. Each disaster brings a flurry of localized regional analysis, which first must organize a scattered literature and even then often proceeds on only partial documentation of the results of earlier, similar work elsewhere.

Specific illustration is drawn from the case of estimating the impact of reconstruction in south Florida following Hurricane Andrew, the costliest natural disaster in U.S. history. The lack of specific documentation on historical efforts to measure the regional effects of natural disasters is not neglected. While major results are summarized here, an unpublished working paper (West and Lenze 1993), available upon request, details the derivation of estimates in the case of Hurricane Andrew.

The first section of this article conceptually outlines the problem of estimating the impact of a natural disaster on a regional economy. It uses a schematic of a regional economy to indicate which endogenous variables, exogenous variables, and linkages are directly impacted. The next section considers empirical application of the conceptual framework. Estimation of direct impacts is one component of that application. Also important are adaptation of the conceptual framework for specific empirical model nuances and treatment of issues not readily resolved with available data and research findings to date. The following section describes application of the results of the first two sections to the problem of simulating the impact of

Hurricane Andrew reconstruction on the Florida economy. Concluding comments in the final section outline an agenda for future research.

The Conceptual Problem

The conceptual problem of disaster impact analysis can be elucidated most readily with the aid of a schematic regional model depicted in figure 1. The small circles labelled E1 through E11 denote factors exogenous to the model. For example, E1 includes legislated minimum wages, E2 includes net migration of military personnel, E6 includes federally legislated transfer payments, E11 includes export demand, and so on. Endogenous variables are depicted by other geometric shapes, and lines denote sectoral linkages which may be either accounting identities or behavioral relationships. Dashed lines indicate the updating of dynamically endogenous, but contemporaneously fixed, stock variables. Behavioral linkages have specific functional forms and parameters which are derived from time series or cross-section estimation or are calibrated based on the results of other research.

A natural disaster potentially directly affects exogenous variables, endogenous variables, and model linkages. Direct exogenous variable impacts include a rise in transfer payments and government grants to the region and a change in net migration due to a change in household perceptions of the region's amenities and disamenities.

Direct endogenous variable impacts are of two types. The first explicitly reflects disaster damages and losses and includes a reduction in the existing private and public residential and nonresidential capital stock and a decline in real income as a consequence of uninsured private losses. The second type derives from the limitations of regional models (and regional data). Specifically, regional models do not explicitly include insurance payments as a determinant of regional spending or asset liquidity constraints and job transfers as determinants of net migration. The disaster induces increased consumption, investment, and government purchases financed by payments received from insurance claims. In addition, an immediate rise in outmigration may ensue as individuals are suddenly released from the liquidity constraint of selling their current homes and as jobs in national firms (or federal government entities) are immediately relocated outside the disaster region.

Major direct impacts on model linkages include (1) a shift in established relationships between local demand and demand for locally produced output, (2) change in the resolution of labor supply and demand imbalances, (3) disruption of the link from income to spending, (4) alteration of the links between stocks and their respective investments, and (5) shifts in the resolution of housing supply and demand. Less clear is (6) a potential alteration

FIGURE 1
Schematic of a Generalized Regional Economy

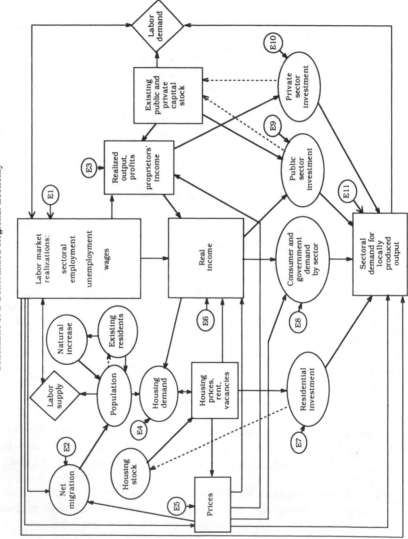

of the link from local labor market conditions to work-force attached migration.

Model linkage impacts (1) and (2) derive from the unexpected suddenness of a natural disaster. Regional purchase patterns will change abruptly as area shortages lead to an unusual rise in the proportion of purchases made outside the region. Similarly, immediate acute shortages of insurance claims adjusters, utility repair crews, and social service workers are met by temporary reassignment of outside labor to the disaster area. In addition, the subsequent spending surge is often outside the model's normal range of "cyclical upturn," resulting in short-term overtime wage increases accounting for a larger-than-usual proportion of the labor market resolution of supply and demand imbalances.

Link disruptions (3) and (4) occur as a consequence of the direct impacts on exogenous and endogenous variables noted above. Most U.S. regional models are based on the Bureau of Economic Analysis (BEA) income definition which includes a (one-time) reduction for uninsured private structural losses. Spending reactions to the reduction in property income from destruction of physical property are unlikely to be explicitly represented in the model, and more basically, are not well understood. Furthermore, the savings rate link between income and spending can be expected to change in the wake of a natural disaster as people deplete their savings to supplement insurance payments for the replacement of damaged goods and structures.

Common specifications of investment demand depict the dynamic accumulation of capital and housing stocks as a partial adjustment process to optimal levels. The disaster suddenly widens the gap between actual and optimal, but it is not closed by the usual adjustment process. The influx of insurance payments effectively speeds up the closure process, bypassing the normal adjustment. Including the direct endogenous spending increase from insurance payments without altering the partial adjustment investment process doublecounts this component of reconstruction.

Link disruptions (5) and (6) occur as a consequence of the impermanence of disaster disruption and reconstruction. If simply presented to the model as a new level of excess demand, the housing market imbalance resulting from sudden destruction of residences would generally yield a rapid run-up in housing prices and rental rates and a rapid decline in vacancies. However, the known short-term nature of the imbalance in the event of a natural disaster likely dampens these responses — i.e., near-term repairs and return to structures is anticipated. This results in temporary housing arrangements (e.g., doubling up with relatives or residing in a camper) which mitigate the impact on prices and vacancies in the housing market. Note that this phenomenon significantly affects the regional price module since regional price variation is closely related to regional housing price variation.

Similarly, jobs generated as part of the reconstruction process are known to be temporary, thereby reducing their attractiveness to potential job seekers and altering the usual relationship between regional employment creation and migration. Offsetting this phenomenon, however, is the fact that the new jobs are concentrated in the construction industry, a sector that has an unusually mobile workforce and in which temporary projects are the norm. A possible outcome is a rise in temporary migrants, persons who move in response to the available jobs but who effect only a partial move of limited time horizon by not purchasing a home, not bringing family, limiting re-spending of wages in the reconstruction area, and so on. The regional impact of such workers is less than that of "permanent" migrants, but regional models (and regional data) do not distinguish work-force attached migrants by their degree of permanence.

Natural disasters are a formidable challenge for impact analysis, as this brief conceptual outline of the problem shows. In practice, analysis is impeded by the lack of data and research on the direct exogenous and endog-enous variable impacts and the disruption to model linkages caused by natural disasters. In addition, general lack of regional data has historically prohibited explicit comprehensive representation in regional models of all figure 1 components.

Empirical Application of the Conceptual Framework

Application of the framework outlined in the previous section requires (1) model adjustments and adaption of the direct impacts to compensate for differences between standard regional models and the schematic of figure 1, and (2) quantitative estimation of the direct impacts.

Adjustments for Model Variations

While adaptation of the conceptual framework to a particular regional model depends on the specific impact model being used, a few of the most common variants can be noted:[1]

Lack of explicit private and public capital stock in the regional produc-tion process. In the conceptual framework, rebuilding of these stocks is treated as a direct impact on spending, and the stock adjustment process must be altered to avoid doublecounting this phenomenon. The same direct spending impact can be entered in a model without explicit capital stocks in the production process.

---

[1] The major variants are discussed in review articles by Bolton (1985) and Richardson (1985).

A new problem arises, however. In the schematic model, the immediate effect of loss of capital stock available to the production process will be to reduce regional output, employment, wage income, and proprietors' income. These losses, which offset reconstruction gains, will not automatically be simulated in the model without explicit capital. Those job and output losses which occur directly as a consequence of the disaster must be estimated and also entered as an immediate exogenous impact. Note that they must also be exogenously restored in conjunction with the time path of capital reconstruction.

Lack of a fully developed housing market and residential investment sector. Like the private and public nonresidential stock, the spending impact is again directly entered, and lack of the explicit stock adjustment process avoids the need for further model adjustments. Unlike with the schematic model, induced impacts on housing prices, rents, and vacancies will be missed, but as noted above, the existing links in the schematic model are likely to be inappropriate in this sector. How to modify them is unclear.

Again, the partial model may introduce a new problem. In particular, the operation of a partial housing sector in the model must be examined to determine if it behaves perversely, either undercounting or doublecounting housing sector impacts. For example, the Florida econometric model used to simulate the impact of Hurricane Andrew has partial housing components, equations for new housing starts that are not imbedded in a complete housing market model such as the one outlined in figure 1. Determinants of starts include changes in households and total starts relative to household growth over a five-year period, the latter specifying over-building in the market. Immediate post-disaster outmigration of households whose homes were destroyed will lower starts within the normal operation of the model both because household growth is reduced and because starts relative to household change over the recent five year period will appear to have risen. The problem is that the model does not look explicitly at total housing stock, so it does not take into account the fact that the household which left also left behind a destroyed housing unit — i.e., there is no reason its departure should alter the basic supply and demand balance (or imbalance) and new starts. This was resolved in simulation by adjusting household growth in the housing start equation to equal change in number of households excluding estimated immediate outmigration of households whose homes were destroyed. The specific details of this example are particular to the formulation of the Florida model, but the broader problem of a partial sector simulating perverse results is likely to be encountered in any other model which does not embody a complete regional housing market specification.

Lack of a regional price module. This is not independent of the previous item since regional price variation is closely related to regional housing price variation. Based on general comparative impacts calculated by CGE models and by models which do not explicitly include price modules, lack of the price module will overstate reconstruction impacts. Some regional impact comparisons from models with and without price modules exist which might be used to crudely adjust final estimates (e.g., Treyz 1993). Their direct relevance to the post-disaster problem is not clear, however, because the price module itself is affected by the disaster.

Lack of detailed (or aggregate) demand output categories. Regional models commonly use aggregate construction, trade, and service sectors. Also common are models which bypass explicit output estimates and focus on the population/labor-market/income interactions of regional economies. Disaster reconstruction activities, however, are concentrated in very specific industries that are often atypical of broader aggregates in their labor utilization. For example, average retail trade is heavily influenced by restaurants and bars, but reconstruction retail expenditures are in the far less labor-intensive categories that sell household goods and automobiles. Similarly, aggregate services is dominated by medical services, but the service components pertinent to reconstruction are automobile and household-goods repair. If extensive industrial detail does not appear in the model, the exogenous demand streams must be translated for simulation into exogenous employment demand and labor payments.

In the case of simulating Hurricane Andrew with the Florida model (which does not have the requisite detail), the following approach was used. Quarterly detailed exogenous demand flows were first converted to exogenous labor payments using the detailed national input-output Make and Use tables. Labor payments were converted to employment using average compensation data, which were derived from Florida-specific average wages in four-digit industries reported in the State Unemployment Insurance (ES 202) data, augmented by national data on compensation relative to wages. Since employment levels respond only gradually to upturns in demand (Hammermesh 1976), especially at a cyclical trough when currently employed labor may be working below capacity, the amount of exogenous labor actually realized as new jobs was gradually increased over time from approximately 25 percent to one. Remaining labor payments were direct additions to wages. From each demand flow there was then an exogenous job flow and an exogenous wage flow which could be directly incorporated into the more aggregated components existing in the model.

Bypassed demand or output levels must also be exogenously augmented (for example, service sector output must be increased *after the simulation* by the amount of service sector output which was directly represented in the model by exogenous labor demand). In addition, however, the model must again be examined to determine if its inherent operation inadvertently over-counts or undercounts disaster impacts, given what has been treated exoge-nously. For example, in the Florida model, a determinant of retail trade activity is residential construction levels reflecting the purchase of household durable goods concomitant with new home construction and home buying. Reconstruction of homes is treated exogenously as is repur-chase of destroyed household goods (including durable goods). Because of its structure, the model will overstate reconstruction impacts if the retail equation is allowed to reflect the exogenous residential construction activity. This outcome is prevented by adjusting the construction level in the retail trade equation to be construction net of the exogenous post-disaster activity. Again, the particulars of this example are specific to the Florida model, but the potential for undercounting or doublecounting is common to virtually all regional models.

Estimation of **Direct** Impacts

Following the conceptual outline, impact analysis requires estimates of (1) losses of existing public and private capital stock, including insurance coverage of these losses, (2) the rise in external transfer payments and grants to the region, (3) the reconstruction spending flows, (4) changes in the reso-lution of labor supply and demand imbalances, (5) disaster-induced changes in net migration, (6) shifts in regional purchasing patterns, (7) changes in the link from income to spending, and (8) shifts in the resolution of housing supply and demand imbalances. In addition, for models without explicit capital stocks in the regional production function, direct impacts include immediate employment and proprietor income losses arising from the destruction of places of work.

All items are not equally amenable to estimation. Emergency aid legis-lation can be used to determine item (2). Data available at the time of the disaster and previous studies permit some quantification of items (1), (3), (4), and direct job losses. Given research to date, estimation of (5) through (8) remains elusive. Recognition of these limitations expands the problem of implementing the conceptual framework. In particular, practical application must address how to treat complete lack of knowledge about some factors and very high uncertainty about others.

Estimation of physical damages. Estimation of physical damages in-cludes loss of existing public and private capital stock (item 1) and provides a basis for determining the reconstruction spending flows (item 3). Primary data collected at the time of the disaster include Property Claim Services

(PCS) estimates of total insured losses, the Red Cross survey of destroyed and damaged housing units, utility company damage estimates, and government agency reports of damage to public buildings, equipment, and infrastructure.[2] Each is of limited coverage and uneven quality, necessitating both augmentation of the primary data with considerable secondary data and extensive cross-checking for plausibility.[3] Property insurance claims and disaster unemployment insurance claims, which are reported to state labor and insurance agencies, provide additional information 1–3 months after the disaster.

The Appendix outlines a process for combining primary and secondary data to establish detailed estimates of damages and their respective insurance coverages. The tabular format summarizes primary data typically available, limitations of those data, how primary data can be augmented with secondary data to improve estimates, and techniques for consistency cross-checking. Major problems of estimation arise from biases derived from over-counting or undercounting primary sources, lack of information on uninsured losses, and lack of detail in damage estimates. Note that estimates from other natural disasters are used with caution and primarily when historical disaster characteristics can be matched with those of the current disaster. For example, Sorkin's (1982) compilation indicates that little can be learned about "insurance coverage" from broad historical summaries.[4]

Estimation of labor market adjustments. Direct labor market impacts include both changes in the resolution of labor supply and demand imbalances and estimation of direct job losses. Hammermesh (1976) presents a range of job and employee-hour responses which allow identification of extreme adjustments that are perhaps more appropriate to the natural disaster situation than average responses. The immediate need for insurance

---

[2] In the case of Hurricane Andrew, which did unusual damage to marine craft, specific estimates of boat damages were also made by insurers specializing in this sector.

[3] The All-Industry Research Advisory Council (AIRAC 1986) has analyzed accuracy of the PCS estimates, and Gillespie(1991) notes limitations of the Red Cross survey.

[4] Sorkin (1982: 125) presents total damage and insured damage estimates for various natural disasters that occurred between September 1954 and September 1979. Among the 12 hurricanes reported, the percent of total damage covered by insurance ranges from near zero in the case of Hurricane Diane (1955) to almost 70 percent in the case of Hurricane Celia (1970). These wide variations reflect, in part, differences in the type of storm. Heavily flooding hurricanes are typified by relatively low insurance coverage since floods are not covered by standard homeowners' policies and the purchase of federal flood insurance is sparse. In addition, differences in aggregate insurance coverage are induced by the nature of the area impacted — insurance coverage of government buildings and agricultural crops is typically poor, yielding a large proportion of uninsured losses when these types of structures and commodities are significant in the disaster region.

132   INTERNATIONAL REGIONAL SCIENCE REVIEW   VOL. 17 NO. 2

adjusters and utility repair crews is typically met by direct transfer of personnel to the impacted region and estimates of these transfers are available
from the industries. Such temporary transfers do not constitute new regional
population or jobs, but transferred workers spend per diem, and that estimated spending stream in turn generates labor demand. Much of their
activity is perhaps technically classified as belonging to the emergency and
restoration phase of the disaster, but complete separation between that phase
and reconstruction is precluded because of their temporal overlap.[5]

No estimates of direct job losses from destroyed places of business are
available in the immediate post-disaster period, although some survey estimates may appear many months later. The most obvious immediate source
of data are unemployment insurance benefits. *Ex post* deviations from the
trend of aggregate unemployment insurance claims underestimate these
losses. As noted by Brady and Perkins (1991), the losses are almost immediately blurred by gains from the initiation of reconstruction. Furthermore, it is
difficult to appropriately isolate that component of total deviations from the
trend which is attributable to cyclical changes in the economy, especially
when the disaster occurs at a cyclical turning point as it did in the case of
Hurricane Andrew.

Direct tracking of Disaster Unemployment Insurance claims provides a
more reliable estimate. Persons not covered in the regular unemployment
insurance system are encouraged to file claims to this special program. Job
losses among these individuals may still be undercounted because required
proof of previous employment often cannot be provided. Alternatively, job
loss estimates may be derived from estimated numbers of workers at commercial establishments suffering major damage or total destruction.[6]

---

[5] Haas, Kates, and Bowden (1977) provide a useful conceptual breakdown of the postdisaster period. The *emergency period* covers the initial clearing of rubble to provide medical care
to victims, finding temporary shelters, locating missing persons, protecting property from
looting, etc. The *restoration period* includes patching structures capable of being restored, re-
establishing utilities, complete clearing of rubble, etc. The *replacement reconstruction period*
consists of rebuilding lost capital stock and replacing or repairing damaged non-structural possessions, and the *commemorative, betterment, and developmental reconstruction period* involves
large projects which may enhance the impacted area beyond its pre-disaster state. While conceptually different, the periods overlap temporally. Haas, Kates, and Bowden (1977) and Brady and
Perkins (1991) illustrate this point, and Cochrane (1992b) discusses it in regard to empirical
benefit-cost analyses of hazard mitigation.

[6] Unpublished data from *County Business Patterns* allow estimation of average employees
per firm in the most intensely impacted subcounty regions, the areas in which major damage or
destruction is concentrated. More difficult to estimate is the number of heavily damaged establishments. An approximation of the latter can be derived from the Red Cross survey of heavily
damaged or destroyed single-family homes coupled with summaries of different relative storm
impacts to single-family homes and commercial buildings (e.g., Friedman 1984).

Uncertain direct impacts. While the direct impact estimates described in the previous two sections are subject to significant measurement error, they are nonetheless appropriately considered "estimates" as opposed to "guesstimates" or "pure speculation." In contrast, available data and research to date provide little basis for quantifying the interrelated issues of migration impacts and translation of estimated losses to reconstruction spending flows. Similarly elusive are shifts in regional purchasing patterns, changes in the link from income to spending, proprietor income losses, and shifts in the resolution of housing supply and demand imbalances.

The need to estimate shifts in regional purchasing patterns can be partially side-stepped by broadening the definition of "region of impact." For example, the impacted county or metropolitan area may abruptly shift regional purchasing patterns, but to the extent the shifts primarily draw upon other regions within the state, analysis with a statewide model may not require adjustment of state purchasing patterns. As noted below, however, broadening the definition of "region" complicates simulation of migration impacts. Other uncertain impacts can only be treated by considering a range of reconstruction scenarios.

Potential migration impacts are three-fold, consisting of immediate population dispersion from the region, long-run impacts on net migration, and short-run changes in the link relating regional labor market conditions to workforce attached net migration. The case studies of Haas, Kates, and Bowden (1977) suggest that the reconstruction period may hasten prevailing predisaster trends in the regional economy, accelerating expansion in growing industries and regions and accelerating decline in stagnant industries and regions. If out-migration has been restrained by the weakness of home sales in a declining area, then lump sum insurance payments for destroyed or highly damaged homes provide unanticipated asset liquidity stimulating movement from the area. Rebuilding in the impacted region is consequently reduced.

Current regional research would also raise the issue of "sense of place" in the reconstruction process. Bolton (1989) and Bartik (1991) have noted the role of this phenomenon in reducing the elasticity of worker migration with respect to wage differentials, and the natural hazards literature has considered it in the form of valuing the "social capital" of a neighborhood (Kling 1992). Theoretically, "sense of place" can hasten the reconstruction process, strengthening community ties and enhancing determination to rebuild the "place." Alternatively, it can be the root of permanent population dispersion from the area as ties to the neighborhood are severed by physical destruction of the "place" and forced temporary moves foster a "sense of place" attachment to new neighborhoods.

Attempts to apply these concepts to a particular situation are thwarted not only by lack of previous quantitative research, but also by a lack of clarity in defining the "region." Subregions within a county or metropolitan area most intensely impacted by the disaster may have been characterized by predisaster trends atypical of the broader region resulting in intraregional population movements.

Immediate population dispersion reduces reconstruction spending relative to estimated losses in the impacted area. The total effect of such population shifts, however, is more complicated if the dispersed population remains within the region of model analysis, an event that becomes more probable as the geographical scope of the model is expanded. Such intraregional shifts create new housing starts or absorb excess supply of housing units outside the immediate area of most intense impact but still within the region of analysis. The phenomenon can be treated in simulation by altering construction and housing start equations so that the dispersed population is depicted in them as "new" population. The total short-term impact is then highly dependent upon the tightness of the regional housing market at the time of the disaster and may range from negligible effect in significantly overbuilt markets to an almost immediate one-to-one increase in housing starts in tight markets.

Like the population dispersion issue, longer-run impacts of natural disasters on population migration to a region are also ambiguous and potentially affect the realized construction. Based on a national cross-section study, Wright et al. (1979) concluded that natural disasters have no significant impact on regional demographic growth trends. Recently, however, these findings have been questioned by the research of Yezer and Rubin (1987), who distinguish between anticipated and unanticipated disasters. Their hypothesis is that "expected" disasters, those occurring at a rate predicted by historical experience in a region, have no impact on migration — such expectations have already been reflected in the trend rate of migration. In contrast, "unexpected disasters," a spate in excess of those predicted by historical experience, discourage migration. Empirical testing that explicitly distinguishes "anticipated" from "unanticipated" supports the hypothesis.

While the literature provides some basis for speculation on the first two migration issues, none addresses the question of the link relating the conditions in the regional labor market to net migration of workforce attached population. Extremes can be examined in simulation by leaving the link unchanged and then completely turning off the labor market-to-migration feedback in a manner similar to previous multiplier decomposition studies (e.g., Charney and Taylor 1986; Treyz 1993).

Assumptions on immediate population dispersion partially link losses to exogenous reconstruction spending. Complete specification of this spending requires assumptions on three further questions: (1) What proportion of losses are replaced by households and businesses choosing not to migrate? (2) How are they replaced — construction, repair, or retail purchase? (3) How much of construction and repair is done by the owner versus contractors? No studies were found that provided insight on these questions, again necessitating assumptions and testing of impact sensitivity to the assumptions.

Resolution of these questions determines the total volume of reconstruction spending but not its time path. The multiplier impact of the reconstruction expenditure, however, is dependent on how it is spent over time. Capacity constraints interact with elasticities that vary between the short and long runs. Given a less than unitary short-run elasticity of employment with respect to output and a lagged relationship between job creation and migration, a moderate direct impact sustained over time yields a larger average multiplier than a comparable impact concentrated into a short period. If the pace of reconstruction is limited only by regional capacity constraints in impacted industries, then the determination of those capacities is central to the impact analysis. The lack of specific data on regional stocks of capital and investment makes estimation of regional capacity difficult for any industry. The problem is exacerbated in the current case because the industry of greatest direct impact is construction, and the concept of regional "construction capacity" is more elusive than that for an industry with immobile plant and equipment.

Although the high mobility of construction workers suggests unlimited regional capacity, even if labor can be rapidly transferred to the region, constraints on financing, licensing, permitting, inspecting, and the distribution network for moving materials to the area are effective limitations. In the cases studied by Haas, Kates, and Bowden (1977), reconstruction required a 2–10 year period, and Guimaraes, Hefner, and Woodward (1993) were surprised at how long the reconstruction stimulus following Hurricane Hugo remained in the South Carolina economy. These observations imply that some capacity constraints do exist in regional construction.

Crude estimation of regional construction capacity may be obtained by first assuming that historical peak volumes of activity reflected full capacity levels and then allowing for expansion (or contraction) of capacity in proportion to aggregate regional growth since the peak. More difficult to account for, however, is the effect of cyclical phase of the national construction industry on regional capacity. If historically observed regional peak levels are correlated with national industry peaks, the former may understate regional capacity at a different phase of the national cycle when there is greater availability of construction labor and capital from outside the region.

Given an estimate of construction capacity, a forecast of construction not related to the hurricane, and a total volume of construction spending for disaster repairs, a time path for reconstruction spending is determined by assuming full capacity operation of the regional industry. The implicit assumption is that disaster-related construction occurs at the rate the capacity constraints can accommodate it given the previously planned non-disaster-related construction. Indeed, the actual pattern may be some temporary postponement of the latter to allow the more urgent disaster repairs, but the realization of the displaced construction at a later period then still remains part of the reconstruction economic impact.

The remaining uncertain issues relate to income and the income-to-spending link. Disaster impacts on proprietors are income losses as opposed to direct job losses. Nonfarm proprietor losses from business interruption may be counterbalanced by increased sales in establishments not closed by the natural disaster. Thus, the net effect on such proprietors' income is unclear when an entire metropolitan area or state is the geographical region of analysis. There are, however, some short-run aggregate losses in categories such as entertainment spending as a consequence of disruption to normal spending patterns. These short-run losses are difficult to measure and remain a controversial issue in the natural hazards literature (Gordon and Richardson 1992).

Finally, research to date provides little guidance on how to treat the income decline which reflects the wealth loss from uninsured property. For large disasters or moderate disasters with low insurance coverage, the impact on measured income can be substantial. For example, in the case of Hurricane Andrew, the estimated $2.1 billion adjustment reduced 1992 real income growth statewide in Florida from 1.8 percent to 1.0 percent, turning stable real per capita income into real per capita income decline. The extent to which this income phenomenon is reflected in spending changes and when the effect occurs is poorly understood. Again, varying assumptions can be examined with alternative impact scenarios.

Specific Application to the Case of Hurricane Andrew in Florida

Estimation of Direct Impacts

Estimates of damage caused by Hurricane Andrew and insurance coverage of those damages based on the methodology outlined above are summarized in table 1. Overall, physical damages were estimated to be near $23 billion with two-thirds, or $15.4 billion, expected to be covered by insurance payments. This constitutes a fairly high proportion of insurance coverage by historical hurricane standards, but is consistent with the nature of the storm, which primarily ravaged by wind and not by flooding. The table also implies

TABLE 1
Hurricane Andrew Damage Estimates for Florida (billions of dollars)

	Total	Insured	Uninsured
Residential structures	10.481	8.253	2.228
Mobile homes	0.289	0.101	0.188
Commercial structures	1.142	1.028	0.114
Residential and mobile homes contents	5.385	3.309	2.706
Commercial contents	1.080	0.972	0.108
Autos	0.473	0.331	0.142
Boats	0.591	0.414	0.177
Airplanes	0.045	0.036	0.009
Utilities	0.420	0.350	0.070
Agriculture	0.455	0.227	0.227
Structures	0.277	0.194	0.083
Equipment	0.048	0.034	0.014
Crops and inventories	0.130	0.000	0.130
Government	2.273	0.409	1.864
State and local	1.122	0.409	0.713
Buildings	0.437	0.224	0.213
Other public works	0.410	0.100	0.310
Equipment	0.275	0.084	0.191
Federal	1.151	0.000	1.151
Homestead AFB	1.007	0.000	1.007
Other nondefense	0.144	0.000	0.144
Structures	0.119	0.000	0.119
Equipment	0.025	0.000	0.025
Nonprofit	0.015	0.005	0.011
Total	**22.649**	**15.435**	**7.214**

Note: Insurance payments exclude $249 million estimated loss-of-use payments. Estimated damages exclude landscaping losses. Components may not sum to total because of rounding.

physical losses were concentrated in residences, an outcome consistent with the fact that a major area of impact was residential suburbs south of downtown Miami. Large industrial facilities analogous to the natural gas pipelines in the Louisiana area of Hurricane Andrew impact did not exist in the Florida area of impact. Estimated direct job losses were 21,000, a figure based on unemployment insurance disaster claims and cross-checked with job loss estimates derived from estimated numbers of workers at commercial establishments that suffered major damage or total destruction.[7]

---

[7] Details of the damage estimates and job loss estimates are available in the appendices to the West and Lenze (1993) study.

Translating damages to reconstruction expenditures required making assumptions on the many issues raised in the preceding section. The only definite information immediately available on population dispersion was the permanent reassignment of Homestead Air Force Base personnel out of the state (a loss of 12,755 persons). Data on changes in enrollment across school districts and post office change of address forms suggested considerably more dispersion away from the area of intense impact, south Dade County, but precise estimates were precluded by lack of historical data on normal levels of such changes. There was ample scope for population dispersion in this case. Approximately 100,000 housing units were destroyed or incurred major damage, providing many households with the unanticipated asset liquidity to permanently relocate. Whether pre-disaster trends encouraged such migration depends on the definition of region. Certainly Dade County overall is a "growth" area, but some of the specific subcounty regions suffering the most severe damage were not. Population shifts from south Dade to northern parts of the county and to adjacent counties existed prior to the hurricane.

Based on the Homestead AFB personnel reassignment and the incomplete (and imprecise) school district and post office data, initial simulations assumed a permanent population dispersion out of the impacted area of 35,000 households with 8,000 of those leaving the state of Florida. No permanent shifts in net migration to Florida were assumed, but the potential for such changes cannot be ruled out. Yezer and Rubin (1987) specifically modeled the expectation of disaster occurrence. Hurricanes are "expected" in south Florida, and there has not been a frequency of such storms in excess of predictions based on historical experience. It is less clear, however, whether a hurricane the *magnitude* of Andrew was "anticipated." Research to date has not explicitly studied the distinction between "unanticipated occurrence" and "unanticipated magnitude." Finally, given the indeterminate theoretical arguments on whether the link from regional labor market to net migration is altered, initial simulations left the link unaltered, but alternatives eliminated the feedback.

The only firm information about replacement of damages was the decision not to rebuild Homestead Air Force Base (except for some runway repairs). The population dispersion assumptions implied that some of the damaged properties outside of the Air Force base would also not be rebuilt. The dispersion reduced total losses considered for rebuilding (or replacing) within the area of impact. This reduction was estimated by (1) assuming that all dispersed population had suffered total or major damage to their homes (so that walking away with the insurance money was an economically viable option), (2) removing a corresponding amount of damage to housing and contents from the damage estimates to obtain a net amount potentially replaced,[8] and (3) assuming that the number of commercial structures that were not replaced was proportionate to population dispersion since most of these were trade and service firms serving the local population.

After adjusting for Homestead AFB and the dispersed population, it was further assumed that (1) all insured and 50 percent of uninsured owner-occupied homes and residential contents are replaced, with the remaining uninsured portion of such housing being repaired by the owner doing home repairs, (2) all commercial structures (and contents), multifamily structures, and government structures are replaced, (3) all auto damage is replaced, (4) all insured and 50 percent of uninsured boat damage is replaced, and (5) the distribution of replacement between repair and purchase is 60/40 for automobiles, 50/50 for boats, and 35/65 for structure contents. These assumptions translate the loss estimates of table 1 into total reconstruction expenditures reported in table 2.

More than 80 percent of potential reconstruction following Hurricane Andrew is in Dade County; hence, Dade County's construction capacity was estimated to determine the time path of reconstruction. That derivation was based on historical peak activity adjusted for aggregate expansion of the county since the peak year (1973) and the difference in cyclical phase of the national construction industry in 1973 and 1992.[9] The resultant $5 billion (1992 dollars) current capacity estimate implies that prior to the hurricane, Dade County construction was operating at approximately 50 percent of capacity. Although some rise in construction levels was forecast without the hurricane, it was very moderate in Dade as a consequence of recent sharp declines in net migration and the recent closure of several large employers. Accommodating both planned "non-hurricane" and "hurricane" construction then implies that $2.5 billion (1992 dollars) in hurricane reconstruction can occur in each year.

Assumed to be primarily completed in a year were construction outside of Dade, purchase of materials for own home repairs, and purchase of commodities to replace home contents, automobiles, boats, and mobile homes. Longer time spans were allowed for repairs, although explicit capacity constraints are more difficult to determine in this case because of the option of shipping or towing damaged goods elsewhere for repair. The resultant trans-

---

[8] The detailed damage estimation procedure disaggregated residential unit damage by extent of that damage. By assuming that the dispersed population was associated with the most severely impacted units, the reduction to potential damage replacement was greater than the proportion of affected households assumed to immediately outmigrate.

[9] National construction capacity was more fully utilized in 1973 than in 1992. Consequently, current county capacity estimates had to allow for greater availability of construction labor and capital from outside Dade.

TABLE 2
Estimated Reconstruction Expenditures (billions of dollars)

Total	**17.313**	
Expenditure to replace damaged structures	10.361	
Single-family housing units		4.949
Condominiums/Apartments		2.746
Government-owned structures		1.032
Nonfarm business structures		0.937
Farm structures		0.277
Utilities		0.420
Expenditure on repair services (nonstructural)	2.015	
Autos		0.284
Boats		0.251
Aircraft		0.024
Other		1.456
Expenditure on new purchases	4.937	
Residential contents		2.704
Commercial contents/vehicles		0.888
Government contents/vehicles		0.300
Agricultural equipment		0.048
Autos (household)		0.189
Aircraft		0.016
Boats		0.251
Mobile homes		0.169
Materials for do-it-yourself house repairs		0.372

lation of total expenditures to a temporal distribution of those expenditures is summarized in table 3.

It was immediately evident that shifts in regional purchase patterns were both significant and difficult to precisely quantify. Even though hurricane damage was concentrated in south Dade County in the Miami metropolitan statistical area (MSA), purchase patterns were affected throughout Florida. For example, sales almost simultaneously surged in the nearby large Ft. Lauderdale MSA, mobile homes traditionally purchased through Miami dealers were purchased directly from central Florida firms, and damaged boats were towed to repair facilities all around the state. The problem of large abrupt shifts in regional purchase patterns was side-stepped by not attempting to estimate the impact with a Miami MSA model. Rather, a statewide model was used.

The Florida model (West, Lenze, and Studley 1992) does not have a structure which admits direct entry of detailed exogenous spending flows. Indeed, most regional models would not, given the very specific categories of impact such as automobile repair and mobile home purchase. Recon-

TABLE 3
Temporal Distribution of Reconstruction Expenditures (billions of dollars)

	1992	1993	1994	1995	1996
Construction	1.371	3.945	2.500	2.500	0.045
Repair services	0.242	1.132	0.596	0.045	0.000
Trade	0.764	2.862	1.186	0.125	0.000
Total	**2.377**	**7.939**	**4.282**	**2.670**	**0.045**

Note: Although results are summarized here in broad industrial categories, detailed
sectors of impact were used in their derivation.

struction expenditures were translated into direct job impacts and direct
wage impacts using the methodology outlined in the previous section. Table
4a reports the resultant direct job impacts. There is not an exact temporal
correlation with expenditures because early in the process much of the
increased labor demand is met by greater utilization of already employed
personnel.

Table 4a is modified in table 4b to include other direct job impacts noted
above — namely, the impact of government expenditure on such things as
emergency and restoration clean-up and protective services, per diem expenditures of personnel temporarily transferred to the impacted area, and most
significantly, estimated direct job losses. The inclusion of estimated direct
job losses transforms a net job gain in 1992 to a net job loss and substantially
offsets the direct effect of reconstruction expenditures on trade and services
in 1993. The persistent loss of government employment shown in table 4b is
the loss of civilian Department of Defense employees coincident with permanent closure of Homestead Air Force Base.

Not all direct impacts are entered as job impacts. Like other regional
models, the employment focus is on nonagricultural civilian jobs, but
income includes farm and military income. Estimated losses in farm and military categories are entered as exogenous direct income impacts in table 4c.
Of larger consequence are the estimated exogenous reduction in personal
rental income resulting from uninsured owner-occupied structural losses,
which dominates direct income effects in 1992, and the exogenous wage and
salary payments which are part of the direct impact of reconstruction expenditures, which dominates in 1993.

It is impossible to express the "direct" impact of population dispersion
throughout the rest of Florida as a direct job or income impact. That population directly reduced the reconstruction expenditures shown in tables 2 and
3 but indirectly raised employment by increasing housing starts outside the
hurricane-impacted area. That dispersion also more generally shifted res-
ident-serving jobs from south Dade County to other parts of Florida, but that
shift is ignored in a statewide model.

TABLE 4
Direct Impacts of Hurricane Andrew[1]

a. Direct job impact of reconstruction expenditures (thousands of jobs)

	1992	1993	1994	1995	1996
Construction	2.751	16.879	18.590	21.564	0.396
Services	0.362	5.271	4.607	0.193	0.000
Trade	0.828	6.715	4.707	0.531	0.000
Total	3.846	28.472	27.904	22.288	0.396

b. Modified direct jobs impact[2] (thousands of jobs)

	1992	1993	1994	1995	1996
Construction	2.751	16.879	18.590	21.564	0.396
Services	−3.511	1.921	4.607	0.193	0.000
Trade	−2.767	2.670	4.707	0.531	0.000
Government	1.952	−0.352	−1.884	−1.884	−1.884
Total	−1.575	21.118	26.020	20.404	−1.448

c. Direct income impacts (millions of dollars)

	1992	1993	1994	1995	1996
Nonagricultural wages and salaries	362.9	940.6	236.2	27.9	0.0
Military income	−26.8	−109.2	−112.7	−116.5	−120.3
Farm income	−187.4	−152.2	−102.6	−76.1	−44.0
Transfer payments	268.0	403.3	0.0	0.0	0.0
Dividends/interest/rent	−2,149.4	0.0	0.0	0.0	0.0
Total	−1,732.7	1,082.5	20.9	−164.7	−164.3

[1] The "direct" impact of population dispersion into other parts of Florida is not well defined. The simulated job impact of this phenomenon was (in thousands of jobs): 0.0 in 1992, 6.0 in 1993, 7.5 in 1994, 3.0 in 1995, and 1.3 in 1996.

[2] Modifications from table 4a include jobs impacts of government expenditure on emergency and restoration and per diem expenditures of temporarily transferred personnel, plus estimated direct job losses.

Note: Although results are summarized here in broad industrial categories, detailed sectors of impact were used in their derivation.

Simulation and Sensitivity Testing of the Direct Impacts

The direct impacts outlined in table 4 were simulated over the period 1992 to 2005. Summarizing effects in terms of jobs, total job loss in 1992 was −13,200 (0.25 percent of the Florida economy total). Positive impacts averaging 69,900 jobs (1.2 percent of the Florida total) characterized the 1993–95 period. Small positive total effects lingered during 1996 and 1997 but turned negative in 1998 and settled at a sustained −11,900, reflecting the impact of permanent losses (the dispersion of population out of Florida and the closure of Homestead Air Force Base).

Given the uncertainties that arose in deriving the direct impacts, a range of scenarios was examined. No explicit allowance was made for short-term price rises, which reduce real impacts, and the Florida model does not contain a regional price module. The extent of this phenomenon is not clear, and even in a model containing such a module, the disaster undoubtedly disrupts the operation of this component. Within the context of this analysis, allowance for price impacts is equivalent to reducing the real stream of reconstruction expenditures, which proportionately reduces the positive real impacts simulated in the 1993–95 period.

More specifically examined were (1) the impact of the 1992 reduction in property income, (2) the assumption of no disruption in the labor market to net migration linkage, (3) the population dispersion assumption, (4) the assumptions on treatment of uninsured losses, and (5) the assumptions on the distribution of reconstruction between repair and replacement through new purchases. Issues (4) and (5) had only modest effects. Assuming only 10 percent, instead of 50 percent, of uninsured losses were replaced reduced the positive 1993–95 impacts by 11 percent and left short-term 1992 impacts and long-term sustained effects unchanged, damage which is partially attributable to the nature of the storm. The type of damage caused resulted in a high proportion of insurance coverage. Treatment of uninsured losses was less significant than it would be in the case of a disaster where losses were less well-covered by insurance. Also important is the fact that estimated uninsured losses were concentrated in mobile homes and household goods. Replacement of these items has less direct impact on the regional economy than restoration through construction. The results of testing assumption (5) also highlighted the dominant role of the construction sector. Assuming that all replaced auto, boat, and structure contents were purchased — instead of a proportion being repaired — reduced positive 1993–95 impacts by 7 percent and again left short-term 1992 and long-term impacts unchanged. Although repair activities generally retain more money for respending in the local economy than new purchases, these changes are small compared with the overall role of construction.

In contrast, simulation outcomes were more sensitive to the first three issues. The 1992 direct job impact of −1,600 (table 4b) mushroomed into a total 1992 impact of −13,200. Virtually all of the latter impact is attributable to the 1992 property income deduction reported in table 4c. The question remains of how that income phenomenon should be treated, and the comparative simulation results emphasize the significance of its treatment.

The question of disrupting the linkage from local labor market conditions to migration has also been raised. In the original simulation reported above, the model link was unaltered. For comparison, and representing an extreme, the link was eliminated so that no feedback of direct reconstruction effects to migration occurred. In the two simulations, immediate short-term 1992 impacts and long-term final impacts were unchanged. Also, *total* net migration to Florida summed over the 1992–2005 period was unchanged between the two simulations. In the original simulation, higher net migration induced by the rise in employment opportunities in the 1993–95 period was offset later in the simulation by lower net migration when the employment opportunities dissipated. However, the effect on intermediary years was substantial. Turning off the migration link lowered job impacts in the 1993–95 period 18 percent. In 1996, the original simulation still had a lingering positive impact, but in the comparison simulation, the long-term permanent negative impact was already evidenced in that year.

Substantial uncertainty surrounded the issue of population dispersion. In the original simulation, 35,000 households were dispersed, nearly one-fourth of them out of Florida. An alternative simulation dispersed 70,000 households, with 22,000 of them leaving the state. In the alternative, the permanent long-run negative impact increased commensurately with the permanent population loss from the state overall. The intermediary 1993–95 impact was reduced 37 percent, reflecting both the increased permanent loss to the state and the fact that population which remained in the state but left south Dade County had less of a reconstruction impact than population which rebuilt in the area of destruction.

Concluding Remarks

Regional science research on economic impact analysis of natural disasters lags engineering and natural science analyses of these events. The lag is peculiar and distressing, given the wrenching regional impact of natural disasters. The present study has raised numerous challenges for such research in the future.

First, natural disaster impact analysis was considered in the context of a schematic regional model. Conceptually, the problem required far more than changing exogenous variables or changing the current state of dynamically endogenous variables — fundamental model linkages were potentially impacted. When a substantial number of such linkages are affected, serious doubts about the appropriateness of the original model for the problem are raised.

New regional models specific to natural disaster impact analysis are needed. As a starting point, further research is required on the linkage issues raised and on the performance of existing types of impact models. Comparative studies of similar models are not uncommon in the regional science literature,[10] but comparisons among different types of impact models remain rare.[11] Hopefully, the data from tables 1–4 will be used by researchers with access to appropriate input-output, econometric, and CGE models to begin understanding why models produce different impacts in the case of complex events such as natural disasters, what their structural biases are, and how the strengths of each might be combined to develop an impact model specific to the problem. Such research must also include non-modeling impact methodologies. Indeed, the uncertainties and complexities of the issue may ultimately yield the outcome that impact techniques derived from adapting historical experience with other natural disasters or using quasi-experimental control group methods yield better projected impacts (e.g., Isserman and Merrifield 1982, 1987; Isserman and Beaumont 1989).

Second, the effort to measure direct impacts highlighted fundamental data deficiencies likely to be encountered in regional impact analysis of natural disasters. Better primary data would reduce uncertainty with respect to the magnitude of the event, but the call for more survey data is likely to be answered with the same silence as the call for more survey data to generate regional input-output tables and regional Social Accounting Matrices.[12] More realistically, we need to develop a systematic body of experience on combining primary and secondary data to generate the detailed economic inputs needed to analyze regional impacts of natural disasters. Without basic model development and improved estimation of direct impacts, a range of reconstruction scenarios must be considered. Even the small set of alternatives considered in the case of Hurricane Andrew illustrated how widely "plausible" outcomes might vary.

Finally, the current research has not considered issues of evaluation. How do we determine whether a model has "correctly" simulated an impact? Theoretically, such evaluation requires *ex post* determination of both the

---

[10] Many such comparative studies of economic base multiplier analysis and regional input-output modeling are referenced in the review article by Richardson (1985), and more recent comparisons of regional input-output models are reported by Brucker, Hastings, and Latham (1990) and Beemiller (1990). Taylor (1982, 1985) provides examples of regional econometric modeling direct comparisons, and Shoesmith (1990) compares time series models.

[11] A recent interesting comparison of multipliers from an econometric model and an input-output model can be found in Conway (1990), and a recent exchange compares REMI and IMPLAN models (Crihfield and Campbell 1991, 1992; Grimes, Fulton, and Bonardelli 1992).

[12] Experience in the wake of Hurricane Andrew, however, does indicate that silence is not always the response. In particular, the state of Florida funded a multi-year survey to collect data on immediate population dispersion from south Dade County. Early results from that study are reported in Smith (1994).

direct and total impacts. At present, most evaluation in regional impact analysis is confined to the fairly simple and non-rigorous step of asking whether the results look "reasonable." This type of evaluation was also carried out in the case of the Hurricane Andrew simulations, but clearly it falls far short of scientific evaluation.[13] Developing techniques for such scientific evaluation is critical in helping direct future research in the field.

References

All-Industry Research Advisory Council (AIRAC). 1986. *Catastrophic losses: How the insurance system would handle two $7 billion hurricanes.* Oak Brook, Ill.: All-Industry Research Advisory Council.

Bartik, T. J. 1991. *Who benefits from state and local economic development policies?* Kalamazoo, Mich.: W. E. Upjohn Institute for Employment Research.

Beemiller, R. M. 1990. Improving accuracy by combining primary data with RIMS: Comment on Bourque. *International Regional Science Review* 13: 99–101

Boisvert, R. N. 1992. Direct and indirect economic losses from lifeline damage. In *Indirect economic consequences of a catastrophic earthquake,* eds. J. W. Milliman and J. A. Sanguinetty. Study conducted by Development Technologies, Inc. for the Federal Emergency Management Agency, pp. 207–65.

Bolton, R. 1985. Regional econometric models. *Journal of Regional Science* 25: 495–520.

Bolton, R. 1989. An economic interpretation of a "sense of place." Williamstown, Mass.: Williams College, Department of Economics, Research Paper No. 130.

Brady, R. J., and J. B. Perkins. 1991. *Macroeconomic effects of the Loma Prieta earthquake.* Oakland, Calif.: Association of Bay Area Governments.

Brookshire, D., and M. McKee. 1992. Indirect loss measurement and computable general equilibrium model. In *Indirect economic consequences of a catastrophic earthquake*, eds. J. W. Milliman and J. A. Sanguinetty. Study conducted by Development Technologies, Inc. for the Federal Emergency Management Agency, pp. 267–325.

Brucker, S. M., S. E. Hastings, and W. R. Latham III. 1990. The variation of estimated impacts from five regional input-output models. *International Regional Science Review* 13: 119–39.

Chang, S. 1983. Disasters and fiscal policy: Hurricane impact on municipal revenue. *Urban Affairs Quarterly* 18: 511–23.

---

[13] In the case of Hurricane Andrew, three types of *ex ante* evaluations were conducted. First, a complete reconstruction scenario was considered. Complete rebuilding should have no long-run effect on the economy and it did not. Second, direct income and population dispersion impacts were converted to estimated job impacts so that at least a crude "multiplier" could be calculated as part of determining model simulation "plausibility." Estimated cumulative multipliers were 1.8 in 1993 and rose to 2.0 in 1994, 2.3 in 1995, and 2.6 in 1996. Again, the results were not "unreasonable" for what amounted to a construction multiplier in a state economy with an integrated construction industry. Third, alternative scenarios were compared for "plausibility" — for example, the comparison of cumulative net migration impacts. *Ex post*, few data are yet available for evaluative purposes. In 1993, employment in Florida surged almost 4 percent over 1992. The simulation results suggest that 25–30 percent of the Florida expansion was attributable to hurricane reconstruction — again, not "implausible." It would have been perhaps "illogical" if the hurricane impact had either accounted for *all* the state growth at the time of a cyclical upturn or had accounted for none of it — something between these broad bounds was implied.

Charney, A. H., and C. A. Taylor. 1986. Integrated state-substate econometric modeling: Design and utilization for long-run economic analysis. In *Regional econometric modeling*, eds. M. R. Perryman and J. R. Schmidt. Boston: Kluwer-Nijhoff.

Cochrane, H. C. 1975. *Natural hazards and their distributive effects: A research assessment.* Washington, D.C.: U.S. Department of Commerce, NTIS PB-262 021.

Cochrane, H. 1992a. *Assessment of damage from Hurricane Hugo and the Loma Prieta earthquake.* Ft. Collins.: Colorado State University, unpublished report.

Cochrane, H. 1992b. Overview of economic research on earthquake consequences. In *The economic consequences of a catastrophic earthquake*, Proceedings of the National Research Council, Committee on Earthquake Engineering, August 1990. Washington, D.C.: National Academy Press.

Conway, R. S., Jr. 1990. The Washington projection and simulation model: A regional interindustry econometric model. *International Regional Science Review* 13: 141–65.

Crihfield, J. B., and H. S. Campbell, Jr. 1991. Evaluating alternative regional planning models. *Growth and Change* 22: 1–16.

Crihfield, J. B., and H. S. Campbell, Jr. 1992. Evaluating alternative regional planning models: Reply. *Growth and Change* 23 (2): 521–30.

Ellson, R. W., J. W. Milliman, and R. B. Roberts. 1984. Measuring the regional economic effects of earthquakes and earthquake predictions. *Journal of Regional Science* 24: 559–79.

Friedman, D. G. 1984. Natural hazard risk assessment for an insurance program. *The Geneva Papers on Risk and Insurance* 9: 57–128.

Friesema, H. P., J. Caporaso, G. Goldstein, R. Lineberry, and R. McCleary. 1979. *Aftermath: Communities after natural disasters.* Beverly Hills, Calif.: Sage Publications.

Gillespie, W. 1991. Economic impact of Hurricane Hugo. Columbia: South Carolina Budget and Control Board, Division of Research and Statistical Services, Office of Economic Research, unpublished report.

Gordon, P., and H. W. Richardson. 1992. *Business interruption effects of a major earthquake in the Newport/Inglewood Fault Zone (NIFZ)*. Report submitted by The Planning Institute, School of Urban and Regional Planning, University of Southern California, to the National Committee on Property Insurance, Boston, Mass.

Grimes, D. R., G. A. Fulton, and M. A. Bonardelli. 1992. Evaluating alternative regional planning models: Comment. *Growth and Change* 23: 516–20.

Guimaraes, P., F. L. Hefner, and D. P. Woodward. 1993. Wealth and income effects of natural disasters: an econometric analysis of Hurricane Hugo. *Review of Regional Studies* 23: 97–114.

Haas, J. E. , R. W. Kates, and M. J. Bowden, eds. 1977. *Reconstruction following disaster.* Cambridge: MIT Press.

Hammermesh, D. S. 1976. Econometric studies of labor demand and their application to policy analysis. *Journal of Human Resources* 11: 507–25.

Insurance Institute. 1990. *Property/casualty insurance facts.* New York: Insurance Institute.

Isserman, A. M., and P. M. Beaumont. 1989. New directions in quasi-experimental control group methods for project evaluation. *Socio-Economic Planning Sciences* 23: 39–53.

Isserman, A. M., and J. Merrifield. 1982. The use of control groups in evaluating regional economic policy. *Regional Science and Urban Economics* 12: 43–58.

Isserman, A. M., and J. D. Merrifield. 1987. Quasi-experimental control group methods for regional analysis: An application to an energy boomtown and growth pole theory. *Economic Geography* 63: 3–19.

Kling, R. W. 1992. What are likely categories of loss and damage? In *The economic consequences of a catastrophic earthquake*, Proceedings of the National Research Council, Committee on Earthquake Engineering, August 1990. Washington, D.C.: National Academy Press.

Richardson, H. W. 1985. Input-output and economic base multipliers: Looking backward and forward. *Journal of Regional Science* 25: 607–62.

Shoesmith, G. L. 1990. The forecasting accuracy of regional Bayesian VAR models with alternative national variable choices. *International Regional Science Review.* 13: 257–69.

Smith, S. K. 1994. Demography of disaster: Population estimates after Hurricane Andrew. Paper presented at the annual meeting of the Population Association of America. Miami, Florida, May 1994.

Sorkin, A. L. 1982. *Economic aspects of natural hazards.* Lexington, Mass.: Lexington Books, D. C. Heath and Co.

Taylor, C. A. 1982. Econometric modeling of urban and other substate areas: An analysis of alternative methodologies. *Regional Science and Urban Economics* 12: 425–48.

Taylor, C. A. 1985. The effects of refining demographic-economic interactions in regional econometric models. In *Population change and the economy: Social science theory and models,* ed. A. M. Isserman. Boston: Kluwer-Nijhoff.

Treyz, G. I. 1993. *Regional economic modeling: A systematic approach to economic forecasting and policy analysis.* Boston: Kluwer.

U.S. Department of Commerce, Bureau of the Census. 1989. *Census of agriculture 1987,* AC87-A-9, vol. 1, Geographic Area Series, Part 9, Florida State and County Data. Washington, D.C.: Government Printing Office.

U.S. Department of Commerce, Bureau of Economic Analysis. 1993. *Fixed reproducible tangible wealth in the United States, 1925–89.* Washington, D.C.: Government Printing Office.

West, C. T., and D. G. Lenze. 1993. Modeling natural disaster and recovery: A general framework for developing direct regional impacts and a specific application to the case of Hurricane Andrew. Gainesville: University of Florida, Department of Economics, Working paper 93-94-13.

West, C. T., D. G. Lenze, and R. E. Studley. 1992. *The Florida long-term economic forecast 1991. Vol. 1: Metropolitan statistical areas.* Gainesville: University of Florida, Bureau of Economic and Business Research.

Wright, J. D., P. H. Rossi, S. R. Wright, and E. Weber-Burdin. 1979. *After the clean-up: Long-range effects of natural disasters.* London: Sage.

Yezer, A. M., and C. B. Rubin. 1987. The local economic effects of natural disasters. Boulder: University of Colorado, Institute of Behavioral Science, Working Paper #61.

Appendix: Summary of Damage Estimation Procedure

A. Residential Structures and Contents

Primary data Red Cross Survey — estimated numbers of housing units impacted, cross-classified by extent of damage (total destruction, major destruction, minor destruction) and type of unit (mobile home, single-family home, apartment/condominiums)

Limitations • Incomplete coverage of impacted units and no estimates of damage to contents
  • No determination of insurance coverage
  • No monetary evaluation of damage

Augmented by • Historical natural disaster information organized into tables relating specific physical characteristics of the storm to expected impacts (Friedman 1984) used in conjunction with Census enumerations to adjust for undercoverage of the survey
  • National insurance industry data on typical relative damage to structures and contents to estimate damage to household contents
  • National aggregates on percent of homeowners carrying insurance and the percent of renters carrying insurance (e.g., Insurance Institute 1990) and insurance coverage surveys of specific historical events which can be identified as similar in nature (e.g., the primarily windstorm loss surveys reported in Cochrane [1975] are similar in nature to Hurricane Andrew) to estimate insurance coverage
  • F. W. Dodge construction data to estimate replacement cost of structural losses
  • National data on the average value of mobile home shipments to estimate value of mobile homes lost

Cross-check Implied number and average value of homeowner insurance claims compared with reported numbers and averages

B. Government Structures and Property

Primary data Government agency damage reports on insured and uninsured losses

Limitations Errors in allocation of losses between structures and contents and mixing of government operating cost increases with physical losses

Augmented by • Reconstruction of the document tables to correct errors and mixes
  • Removal of government-owned housing losses to avoid doublecounting of residential unit losses

Cross-checks • Comparison of estimated distribution of losses between structures and equipment with national data on the distribution of public capital stock between these categories (U.S. Department of Commerce 1993)
  • Estimation of implied percent of total public capital in the region which was lost
  • Comparison of proportion of total losses which are public sector losses with similar historical natural disasters

C. Commercial and Industrial

Primary data Utility company damage estimate reports

Limitations Incomplete coverage of commercial and industrial sector

Augmented by • PCS total insured loss estimates in conjunction with loss estimates of other categories imply the insured commercial and industrial component as a residual
• Data from previous disasters on insured coverage in the commercial sector relative to the residential sector in combination with residential coverage to estimate total losses from insured losses
• National data on the distribution of commercial/ industrial property between inventories, equipment, and structures to distribute losses between these categories

Cross-check Combining commercial/industrial estimates with apartment loss estimates implies number and average value of commercial multi-peril claims which can be compared with reported claims.

D. Agriculture

Primary data County Farm Bureau reports of damage

Limitations • Tendency to overstate losses
• Some doublecounting of losses (e.g., in the case of fruit-bearing trees, counting the value of a destroyed tree as the present value of its future crop yields and also counting the foregone future crops)
• No information on insurance coverage

Augmented by • *Census of Agriculture* (U.S. Department of Commerce 1989) and historical data on cash value of crops to determine reasonable upper bounds on damage
• National data on crop insurance coverage to estimate insured and uninsured losses

Cross-check Data available for cross-checking the original damage reports were used to modify those estimates. Comparison with other disasters is not useful because the type of farming is usually not similar

E. Vehicles

Primary data PCS insured loss estimates, automobile insurance claims filed, estimates of insured losses of marine craft made by boat insurers

Limitations Little information on uninsured losses requiring assumptions on insurance coverage

Cross-check The three primary sources were cross-checked for consistency

[11]

BUSINESSES AND DISASTERS: EMPIRICAL PATTERNS AND UNANSWERED QUESTIONS

By Gary R. Webb,[1] Kathleen J. Tierney,[2] and James M. Dahlhamer[3]

ABSTRACT: Through five systematic, large-scale mail surveys conducted since 1993, the Disaster Research Center has obtained data on hazard awareness, preparedness, disaster impacts, and short- and long-term recovery among 5,000 private-sector firms in communities across the United States (Memphis/Shelby County, Tenn.; Des Moines, Iowa; Los Angeles, Calif.; Santa Cruz County, Calif.; and South Dade County, Fla.). This paper summarizes findings from those studies in three major areas: (1) factors influencing business disaster preparedness; (2) disaster-related sources of business disruption and financial loss; and (3) factors that affect the ability of businesses to recover following major disaster events. Implications of the research for business contingency planning and business disaster management are discussed.

INTRODUCTION

Until recently, the literature on hazards and disasters contained very few references to the ways in which private-sector organizations prepare for, respond to, and recover from disasters. Research in the disaster field has focused almost entirely on units of analysis other than businesses, most notably on families, households, and governmental units, particularly local communities. Studies that have attempted to assess the economic consequences of disasters have tended to concentrate primarily on aggregate-level effects, such as communitywide and regional economic losses, rather than on firm-level impacts [e.g., Rossi et al. (1978); Friesema et al. (1979); Cohen (1993); West and Lenze (1994); Gordon et al. (1995); for a review of the literature on large-scale economic impacts, see Jones and Chang (1995)].

Although there is a long tradition of organizational research in the field of disaster studies, that research has focused overwhelmingly on public sector organizations, such as local emergency management agencies, fire and police departments, and other governmental entities. While interest in private organizations has grown, to date the majority of published material on businesses, disasters, and hazards consists of single-case studies, prescriptive articles that are largely lacking in empirical content, and research that concentrates either on rare catastrophic events [e.g., Perrow's (1984) classic on "normal accidents"], or on atypical types of organizations [e.g., La Porte and Consolini (1991) and La Porte and Rochlin (1994) on high-reliability organizations]. A small number

of studies have attempted to document the hazard- and disaster-related experiences of particular types of firms, such as those involved in the production and transportation of hazardous materials (Quarantelli et al. 1979) and in chemical emergency preparedness (Solyst and St. Amand 1993; Lindell 1994), tourist industry firms (Drabek 1994), and small businesses (Durkin 1984; Kroll et al. 1991). However, systematic studies of groups of typical firms of different sizes representing the full range of economic sectors have been virtually absent from the research literature.

In 1993, the Disaster Research Center (DRC) initiated a series of surveys exploring the preparedness activities and disaster-related experiences of large and representative samples of businesses in communities around the United States. As shown in Table 1, this group of studies, all of which involved large-scale mail surveys, focused on businesses in several different regions of the country, on different types of disaster events, and on different phases in the hazard cycle. The first of these studies, the Memphis/Shelby County project, provided data on earthquake hazard awareness and preparedness among businesses in a nondisaster context. The other studies involved research on businesses in communities that had experienced four of the most severe and costly disasters in U.S. history: (1) the 1989 Loma Prieta earthquake; (2) Hurricane Andrew in 1992; (3) the 1993 Midwest floods; and (4) the 1994 Northridge earthquake. These projects differ from other work that has been undertaken on businesses and disasters in that they focus on large, systematically-selected groups of businesses, employ advanced analytic techniques, and attempt to generate findings that can be generalized to broader populations of businesses. Three of the studies— Memphis/Shelby County, Des Moines, and Los Angeles/Santa Monica—used stratified random sampling techniques to obtain large representative samples of businesses. The samples for all three studies were stratified by business size and by broadly-defined economic sectors. Additionally, the Northridge earthquake sample was stratified geographically by earthquake impact severity using the Modified Mercalli Intensity measure of earthquake shaking intensity. The Loma Prieta and Hurricane Andrew

[1]Postdoctoral Res. Fellow, Disaster Res. Ctr. and Dept. of Sociology and Criminal Justice, Univ. of Delaware, Newark, DE 19716.

[2]Prof. of Sociology and Co-Dir., Disaster Res. Ctr. and Dept. of Sociology and Criminal Justice, Univ. of Delaware, Newark, DE.

[3]Postdoctoral Res. Fellow, Disaster Res. Ctr. and Dept. of Sociology and Criminal Justice, Univ. of Delaware, Newark, DE.

Note. Discussion open until October 1, 2000. To extend the closing date one month, a written request must be filed with the ASCE Manager of Journals. The manuscript for this paper was submitted for review and possible publication on October 14, 1999. This paper is part of the *Natural Hazards Review*, Vol. 1, No. 2, May, 2000. ©ASCE, ISSN 1527-6988/00/0002-0083-0090/$8.00 + $.50 per page. Paper No. 22112.

TABLE 1.   Disaster Research Center Studies on Businesses, Hazards, and Disasters

Community (1)	Year of survey (2)	Event (3)	Sample (4)	N (response rate) (5)	Time (6)	Topics (7)
Memphis/Shelby County	1993	—	Random stratified	737 (40)	Pre-event	Hazard awareness, lifeline criticality, pre-event preparedness
Des Moines	1994	Midwest floods	Random stratified	1,079 (50)	12 months post-event	Losses, disruption, pre- and post-event preparedness, short-term recovery
Los Angeles/ Santa Monica	1995	Northridge earthquake	Random stratified	1,120 (24)	18 months post-event	Losses, disruption, pre- and post-event preparedness, short-term recovery
Santa Cruz County	1997	Loma Prieta earthquake	Population	933 (34)	8 years post-event	Losses, disruption, pre- and post-event preparedness, long-term recovery
South Dade County	1998	Hurricane Andrew	Population	1,078 (27)	6 years post-event	Losses, disruption, pre- and post-event preparedness, long-term recovery

Note: Values in parentheses represent percentage of response rates.

surveys focused on the entire population of currently-existing businesses that had been operating in the areas selected for study at the time those events occurred. The topics addressed in the surveys included proprietors' hazard perceptions, business preparedness, disaster impacts and losses, and short- and long-term business recovery. In all, data have been obtained on nearly 5,000 businesses.

In this paper, we review and summarize selected findings from this body of research, focusing both on explanatory variables that have received considerable empirical support and on areas in which research is contradictory or ambiguous. Our discussion centers on significant research findings in three general areas: (1) factors influencing business preparedness and the adoption of other self-protective measures; (2) disaster-related sources of business disruption and financial loss; and (3) factors that affect the ability of businesses to recover following major disaster events. Each section also highlights questions raised by this group of studies. We conclude by discussing gaps in our current knowledge and posing questions for future research.

BUSINESS DISASTER PREPAREDNESS

Using checklists similar to those employed in studies of household disaster preparedness, DRC surveys have attempted to assess the nature and extent of preparedness activities undertaken by private-sector firms, as well as the factors that affect business preparedness. With respect to the first topic, perhaps the most consistent finding from this group of studies is that the average or typical business places relatively little emphasis on disaster preparedness and other loss-reduction measures. To illustrate this point, Table 2 shows the percentages of businesses in Memphis/Shelby County and in the Northridge earthquake sample that reported engaging in various pre-earthquake preparedness activities. Only one of the measures listed, obtaining first aid supplies, had been carried out by more than half of the businesses surveyed, and one measure, helping employees learn first aid, had been undertaken by about half of the businesses. Adoption of other preparedness

TABLE 2. Pre-Earthquake Preparedness Measures Taken by Businesses in Memphis/Shelby County, Tenn. and Los Angeles and Santa Monica, Calif.

Action (1)	N (response rate) for Memphis (2)	N (response rate) for Los Angeles/ Santa Monica (3)
Attended meetings/received information	729 (39)	1,015 (39)
Talked to employees about preparedness	728 (30)	1,009 (35)
Purchased earthquake insurance	680 (41)	952 (18)
Purchased business interruption insurance	675 (29)	936 (24)
Stored fuel or batteries	725 (22)	980 (29)
Learned first aid	726 (51)	996 (49)
Obtained first aid supplies	728 (60)	1,013 (61)
Developed business emergency plan	723 (22)	1,007 (29)
Developed business disaster recovery plan	721 (13)	978 (14)
Conducted earthquake drills	730 (9)	993 (17)
Involved in earthquake preparedness or response training programs	725 (11)	988 (18)
Arranged to move business to other location	727 (9)	970 (5)
Obtained generator	726 (15)	973 (13)
Braced shelves and equipment	724 (17)	1,003 (26)
Stored water	725 (14)	995 (36)
Had engineer assess building	720 (11)	978 (14)
Stored office supplies	723 (34)	—
Mean number of actions taken	4.1	3.9

Note: Values in parentheses represent percentage of response rates.

measures range from very low, for making arrangements for business relocation (9% in Memphis/Shelby County, 5% for the Northridge sample) and requesting an engineering assessment of the building (11% and 14%, respectively), to moderate for measures such as attending meetings and obtaining earthquake-related information (39% in each community). Overall, mean business preparedness levels were quite low in both communities.

Businesses undertook an average of 4.1 out of 17 measures for which information was requested in Memphis, and 3.9 out of 16 measures in Los Angeles. Our other studies show a similar pattern. In Des Moines, for example, nearly half of the businesses surveyed had not undertaken a single preparedness measure.

This pattern is in line with what other investigators have found. For example, Thomas Drabek found preparedness efforts "unsatisfactory" among the 180 tourist firms he studied, commenting that "less than one-third of the businesses surveyed really measured up" (Drabek 1994), and Mileti et al. (1993) also reported very low levels of preparedness among the businesses they surveyed in the San Francisco Bay Area.

Focusing again on Table 2, businesses also appear to show a preference for particular kinds of preparedness activities over others. Activities that are less complicated and expensive, and measures that provide protection against a range of different types of emergencies, are preferred over technically difficult, more expensive, and time-consuming efforts. Thus, both Memphis and Los Angeles businesses are much more likely to have first aid supplies on hand, have employees with first aid experience, obtain earthquake-related information, and talk with their employees about preparedness than they are to prepare business recovery and business relocation plans, purchase generators for emergency power, engage in extensive employee training and disaster drills, or employ engineering consultants to conduct structural assessments. Relatedly, businesses show a preference for undertaking measures geared toward enhancing life safety in the immediate postimpact period, rather than those aimed at ensuring business continuity. These same general patterns have been observed in DRC's other surveys.

Moving beyond describing what businesses have done to prepare for disasters, DRC investigators have also focused on the development and testing of models explaining business disaster preparedness. These analyses have helped identify which businesses are most likely to prepare for disasters. Overall, the size of a business appears to be the most important factor influencing the propensity of businesses to prepare. In every community DRC has studied, larger organizations have done more to prepare than their smaller counterparts. Both DRC and other researchers [e.g., Mileti et al. (1993); Dahlhamer and Reshaur (1996); Dahlhamer and D'Souza (1997)] have generally interpreted this relationship as a matter of resource availability. Larger businesses are more likely to have staff specifically dedicated to preparing for disasters, and compared with small companies, larger organizations generally have more access to financial resources with which to undertake preparedness.

While the impact of size on preparedness was consistent across various surveys, other factors were also found to affect preparedness, albeit less consistently. In the Memphis and Des Moines surveys, firms that owned their business properties, as opposed to leasing them, were found to be more likely to engage in preparedness activities (Dahlhamer and D'Souza 1997). This may be the case since building owners see themselves as having a greater stake in the survival of their properties. It may also be that ownership of a property makes it more feasible to undertake a greater number of preparedness measures. For example, we would probably not expect a business proprietor who leases space in a larger building to pay to have the property inspected by an engineer or have its foundation strengthened. If leasing, rather than owning the business property, does indeed make a difference in the willingness to prepare, the fact that a substantial majority of business properties around the country are leased rather than owned may well work to discourage business preparedness.

Our data show that it is also quite likely that different types of businesses differ in the emphasis they place on preparing for disasters. The Northridge and Memphis studies found that other things being equal, firms in the finance, insurance, and real estate-sector were generally better prepared than businesses in other sectors of the economy (Dahlhamer and Reshaur 1996; Dahlhamer and D'Souza 1997), a pattern that may be attributable to the higher degree of regulation and overall scrutiny businesses in this sector receive. In contrast, retail and service-sector businesses tend to lag somewhat, which is disconcerting, given the relatively large size of these two sectors.

There is a good deal of evidence in the literature suggesting that disaster experience contributes to higher levels of preparedness at the household- and community-levels, and the studies undertaken by DRC suggest that the same pattern may well hold for businesses. For example, prior experience exerted a positive influence on pre-event preparedness in Memphis, Des Moines, and Los Angeles (Dahlhamer and Reshaur 1996; Dahlhamer and D'Souza 1997). Our surveys also indicate that over the long term, businesses in the areas hard hit by the Loma Prieta earthquake and Hurricane Andrew have improved their preparedness over predisaster levels. Measured several years after those events, the mean number of preparedness measures adopted had risen from 3.5 to 5.6 (out of 17 items on the checklist) in Santa Cruz County and from 6.1 to 8 (out of 19 items on the checklist) in South Dade County.

While disaster experience clearly can have a positive effect, our research also shows that experiencing a major disaster does not necessarily lead to dramatic improvements in preparedness, at least not in the short term. Surveyed 18 months after the Northridge earthquake, for example, the businesses in our sample did improve their preparedness, but almost imperceptibly, from a pre-earthquake mean of 3.9 (out of 16 measures included in the checklist) to a postearthquake mean of 4.0. Moreover, improvements in preparedness did not occur across the board. Rather, improvements were most marked among firms that had experienced business interruption as a result of the earthquake, larger firms, and those that had already been doing more to prepare before the earthquake occurred. In other words, not everyone learns equally from disaster experience, and those organizations that already place a priority on preparing and that have the resources to take action may be the ones that show the most improvement.

SOURCES OF BUSINESS DISRUPTION AND LOSS

Shifting from disaster preparedness to actual disaster impacts, DRC's business surveys have also documented various ways in which businesses are vulnerable to disasters. Although the physical damage disasters produce can have a major negative effect on business operations, our research clearly reveals that direct damage is only one among several factors that contribute to the losses businesses experience in the aftermath of disasters. In particular, damage and disruption to utility and transportation lifelines can contribute significantly to business interruption and subsequent financial losses. In the 1993 Midwest floods, for example, floodwaters inundated the Des Moines Water Works, leaving 300,000 residents without potable water. Electrical power stations were flooded, resulting in power outages that affected 35,000 households and the entire downtown business district. Our Des Moines study found that while only 15% of the businesses surveyed experienced flood damage, 80% of all Des Moines businesses were without water as a result of the flooding, 40% lost sewer and waste water treatment services, 33% were without electricity, and just over 20% lost phone service. Forty-two percent of businesses were forced to close for at least some period of time. Illustrating the importance of off-site lifeline impacts, when asked for reasons why they experienced business interruption, businesses were most likely to cite disruptions to water, electric power, and sewer and wastewater services (Tierney 1997).

The impact of lifeline disruptions on business operations has been documented in other cases as well. In 1992, for example, when the waters of the Chicago River flooded into an underground tunnel system directly below the Chicago Loop, all businesses in that commercial area were unable to operate, not because of flooding but because of the loss of electrical power. In research on the regional economic impacts of the 1994 Northridge earthquake, Peter Gordon and his colleagues (Gordon et al. 1995) estimated that just over one-fourth of the business interruption losses resulting from the earthquake were the result of damage to the region's transportation system. Our own analyses of firm-level losses resulting from the Northridge earthquake suggest that loss of electric power, and, in particular, the duration of power service interruption, were significant contributors to the dollar losses businesses experienced (Dahlhamer et al. 1999).

This series of surveys also found that businesses often have difficulty coping with a range of disaster-induced operational problems that are not necessarily the result of direct property damage at the business site. These problems include disruptions in the flow of supplies and in the ability to ship goods, reduced employee productivity caused by transportation problems and by employee's own disaster-related difficulties at home, and declines in customer traffic and reduced demand for certain kinds of goods and services in the aftermath of a disaster. Owners may find themselves forced to pay less attention to their businesses because of damage to their own homes, or, conversely, to neglect problems at home in order to concentrate on keeping the business up and running. Damage to nearby businesses and residential areas can result in reduced customer traffic. Such problems, which can persist for long periods after disasters, affect even those businesses that escape direct damage. As discussed in the section that follows, these postdisaster operational problems can be a significant impediment to business recovery.

POSTDISASTER RECOVERY

Explaining business disaster recovery outcomes is difficult for a number of reasons. It is often hard to track down businesses that go out of existence following disasters, particularly after time has passed. New businesses are established and others fail on a regular basis, making it hard to determine how disasters affect these ongoing patterns. The fact that normal rates of founding and mortality also differ by business type and size introduces additional complications. The notion of what constitutes a postdisaster business failure can be problematic. For example, after a disaster the owner of a damaged, but potentially viable firm, may make a strategic decision to retire a year or two early rather than go through the effort of restarting the business. Should this be counted as a business failure caused by the disaster? Looking at businesses at only one point in time, as we have in our studies, could present a distorted picture, since a business may do well a short time after a disaster only to flounder later, while businesses experiencing initial difficulties may subsequently become very profitable. Despite the occurrence of a disaster, larger economic cycles continue to exert a very strong influence on the well-being of individual firms, making it difficult to disaggregate macroeconomic and disaster-related effects. With all these caveats in mind, we nevertheless believe that our research has yielded a number of important findings concerning business recovery.

First, although it is commonly assumed on the basis of anecdotal evidence that disasters result in business failures and bankruptcies on a large scale, our research indicates that most businesses, even those that are especially hard hit, do indeed recover following disasters. In the postevent surveys we conducted, business owners were asked for assessments of the financial condition of their businesses at the time of the survey, compared with financial well-being just prior to the disaster event, and to indicate whether the business was worse off, better off, or about the same as it had been. Table 3 summarizes general patterns of reported short- and long-term recovery outcomes

TABLE 3.   Patterns of Short- and Long-Term Business Disaster Recovery

Event (1)	Current Business Condition[a]		
	Worse off (%) (2)	About the same (%) (3)	Better off (%) (4)
Midwest floods (N = 1,017)	12.2	70.0	17.8
Northridge earthquake (N = 1,083)	23.3	52.2	24.6
Loma Prieta earthquake (N = 898)	21.5	41.5	37.0
Hurricane Andrew (N = 1,055)	34.2	34.4	31.4

[a]Measured as comparison between condition of business at time of survey and its condition just before disaster event.

for the Loma Prieta and Northridge earthquakes, Hurricane Andrew, and the Midwest floods. Based on these findings, it is clear that the vast majority of businesses return to predisaster levels, both in the short- and long-term, and that a substantial number of firms also report being better off in the wake of disaster. DRC's study of the Loma Prieta earthquake, for example, found that eight years after the event, 37% of businesses in the sample reported being better off than they had been just before that event.

The data reported in Table 3 also indicate that disasters vary in the extent to which they affect the short- and long-term well-being of businesses. At one extreme, when the survey was conducted in Des Moines one year after the 1993 floods, nearly 88% of business owners indicated that their businesses were functioning at or above predisaster levels. The majority reported being about the same as before the floods, 18% were better off, and only 12% said that their businesses were worse than they had been prior to the disaster. At the other extreme, six years after Hurricane Andrew, about two-thirds of the businesses surveyed can be said to have recovered—if recovery is defined as returning to or exceeding predisaster levels— while one-third reported being worse off than they had been before the hurricane. Businesses in South Dade County fared worse than their counterparts in Santa Cruz County, the other community in which long-term recovery outcomes were assessed, where about one business in five reported being worse off than before the earthquake. Indeed, viewed in another light, these kinds of data on recovery outcomes may serve as proxy measures of disaster severity.

Additional analyses have sought to identify the factors that account for firm-level recovery outcomes. The most thorough analyses conducted to date have focused on businesses affected by the Northridge earthquake (Dahlhamer 1998). In that study, Dahlhamer identified several variables that distinguished between nonrecovered and recovered firms, i.e., businesses that had either returned to or exceeded their predisaster status. As with predisaster preparedness, size proved to be an important predictor of

recovery. Other things being equal, larger firms were more likely to have recovered than smaller ones.

In the preceding section, we pointed to the fact that in addition to direct physical damage and lifeline service interruption, disasters also produce a variety of operational problems for businesses, such as disruptions in supply chains and employee-related problems. Dahlhamer's analyses found that the more of these kinds of problems businesses reported, the less likely they were to recover. Additionally, irrespective of their own levels of damage and disruption, businesses located in areas where the earthquake shaking had been more intense were less likely to recover. Physical damage and business interruption, in and of themselves, were not related to recovery. Rather, the impact of these variables on recovery was mediated by other factors, such as operational disruption and earthquake shaking intensity. These kinds of findings point to the importance of viewing disaster impacts and recovery in a broader ecological context. What happens to an individual business organization depends mainly on how neighborhoods, critical infrastructural systems, and communities are affected by a disaster.

Analyses of survey data have also focused on explaining differential patterns of gains and losses. Nearly 25 years ago, Harold Cochrane (1975) pointed out that disasters have distributive effects. Lower-income groups suffer a disproportionate share of disaster losses, while their better-off counterparts may actually benefit. Earlier, Dacy and Kunreuther (1969) found that because of their ability to tap into postdisaster relief programs, some homeowners victimized in the 1964 Alaska earthquake ended up in better financial condition than nonvictims. Looking specifically at business outcomes, research by Kroll et al. (1991) suggests that particular kinds of businesses, i.e., construction-related firms, experienced gains as a result of the Loma Prieta earthquake.

Our research on short-term recovery following the Northridge earthquake found that some types of businesses experienced financial gains in the aftermath of disasters, while others tended not to fare as well (Dahlhamer and Tierney 1996; Dahlhamer 1998). Consistent with the research by Kroll et al. (1991) construction-related businesses experienced major gains, suggesting that the earthquake gave these firms a needed boost, at least in the short term. Smaller firms were significantly more likely to report being worse off than larger ones, as were businesses that reported being in poor financial condition just prior to the earthquake. These last findings suggest that marginal firms with few resources are particularly ill-equipped to weather a disaster.

Prior disaster experience might be expected to have a positive impact on recovery, since presumably, businesses that have been through other disasters have learned from those experiences and are thus better able to cope. In fact, our research suggests this is not the case. In the Loma Prieta and Andrew studies, experience was unrelated to recovery outcomes, and in the Northridge study, business owners with prior disaster experience were less likely to report that their businesses had recovered. Los Angeles businesses with prior disaster experience were most likely to report having sustained damage in the 1992 riots, which occurred less than two years before the earthquake. It may be that many of these businesses were still dealing with riot-related problems when the earthquake struck and thus found it even more difficult to cope. Businesses with previous disaster experience were also more likely to seek postdisaster aid following the Northridge event, which, as we will see later, may actually have been detrimental to their overall financial well-being.

Some of the most intriguing findings from this group of studies center on the linkage between predisaster preparedness and postdisaster aid and short- and long-term recovery outcomes. We would intuitively expect that good preparedness planning helps businesses to recover more rapidly and completely, but DRC's research suggests that this is not the case. Extensive analyses of the data from Northridge, Loma Prieta, and Hurricane Andrew show no relationship at all between preparedness measures and recovery outcomes. In other words, unprepared businesses were as likely to report positive recovery outcomes as their well-prepared counterparts. In considering why this might be the case, we suggest several possible answers. First, as noted earlier, the vast majority of businesses are quite ill-prepared, and even the best prepared among the businesses we studied had done relatively little to get ready for disasters. There may be a threshold below which self-protective measures do little actual good, and it may be the case that most businesses fall well below that threshold. Second, of the items asked about in our preparedness checklists, the measures that businesses were most likely to undertake were directed much more toward life safety and immediate emergency response than toward longer-term loss containment. Having a first aid kit on hand and providing information about disasters to employees are certainly very helpful should disaster strike, but such measures will not necessarily help a business regain its financial footing in the aftermath of a disaster. Third, the preparedness measures we assessed in our surveys—which are the measures most commonly advocated for businesses—focus primarily on avoiding or handling problems that may occur at the worksite when a disaster occurs, rather than on coping with problems originating off-site, such as transportation system and community-level disruption. Businesses that score high in these workplace-centered preparedness activities may nevertheless find themselves ill-equipped to deal with other sources of disaster-related disruption and loss, including the various kinds of operational problems we described above. Thus, we hypothesize that preparedness has no influence on recovery because businesses have done so little to prepare, because they are preparing to respond, rather than to recover, and because recommended preparedness actions do not address the real recovery-related problems businesses face.

Our findings on the relationship between the use of postdisaster assistance and recovery outcomes are equally counterintuitive and intriguing. Obviously, aid is supposed to facilitate recovery, and it seems fair to assume that the use of outside sources of aid helps businesses, just as postdisaster assistance has been shown to improve recovery outcomes for households (Bolin 1989; 1994). However, in the analyses conducted to date, we have found no evidence that outside aid helps businesses recover following disasters. In the Santa Cruz and Dade County studies, for example, businesses that tried to take advantage of various sources of recovery assistance, ranging from Small Business Administration and bank loans to public disaster assistance, showed no improvement over those that had utilized less aid. Indeed, there was no relationship whatsoever between the number of aid sources businesses relied on during the postdisaster period and the extent to which they had recovered.

DRC's post-Northridge study found that use of disaster aid was associated with recovery, but in the opposite direction. That is, businesses that reported using outside assistance were actually less likely to have recovered and more likely to report being worse off. This pattern seems to be attributable to the fact that the businesses that used external aid were also those that had suffered higher losses and were thus worse off in the first place [for additional discussions, see Dahlhamer (1998) and Dahlhamer and Tierney (1998)].

Another reason outside aid does little to help businesses to recover may lie in the kinds of aid that are available for businesses, as compared with households. While in many cases households can rely on outright grants from programs such as FEMA's Individual and Family Grant Program, direct assistance from agencies like the Red Cross, and insurance, a greater proportion of business recovery aid comes in the form of loans that businesses must repay. Few of the businesses we studied had insurance coverage, and many of those with coverage did not file claims. Many business owners reported using their own personal savings in order to recover. For many businesses, then, recovery assistance brings additional indebtedness and draws down savings. Seen in this light, it is not surprising that recovering businesses see little advantage in the monetary assistance they receive from outside sources.

Finally, there is some evidence to suggest that individual business fates may well be more dependent on larger economic trends than on disaster-related factors. For example, following the Northridge earthquake, businesses in industrial sectors that had been experiencing growth just prior to the earthquake were more likely to recover than businesses in declining industries (Dahlhamer 1998). In our Loma Prieta and Hurricane Andrew studies, owners' assessments of the health of the overall business climate in their communities were strongly associated with their assessments of the extent to which their own businesses had recovered. Economic trends likely have a strong effect on business recovery, independent of how individual firms are affected.

QUESTIONS FOR FUTURE RESEARCH

Although yielding large amounts of data, DRC's business surveys also have a number of weaknesses and shortcomings. Each of the five surveys was cross-sectional, rather than longitudinal, making it impossible to track changes that occurred over time. Despite the fact that virtually identical survey procedures were used in each study, response rates varied from a low of 24% (Northridge) to a high of 50% (Des Moines). Concepts were not always measured consistently across survey instruments. For example, the number and content of items used to assess disaster preparedness varied slightly across the different surveys. Assessments of recovery outcomes were based on self-report measures, rather than on actual business financial data, largely because the latter were judged too difficult to obtain for reasons of confidentiality. The surveys were not timed consistently. Both the short-term recovery studies (Des Moines and Los Angeles) and the surveys assessing longer-term recovery outcomes (Santa Cruz and South Dade Counties) were carried out at slightly different postdisaster time intervals, making cross-event comparisons difficult. The long-term studies focused on business "survivors," i.e., businesses that could be located years after the earthquake and the hurricane occurred. Businesses that were no longer in existence were not part of the study, raising the question of whether long-term impacts were underestimated.

This series of studies raises at least as many questions as it answers. Only a small number of findings, such as those concerning the positive impact of organizational size on preparedness and on recovery outcomes, were replicated across multiple sites, indicating that further research is needed. As we noted in the section above, findings were often contradictory across study sites. For example, while it seems relatively clear that the use of outside postdisaster assistance does little to help businesses recover, the question of whether currently available sources of aid are actually detrimental to businesses remains open. Although similar explanatory models were used in the various studies, relationships among model variables that were found to be statistically significant in some analyses did not achieve significance in others.

Many of the models that were tested in the various analyses associated with the surveys explained relatively little variance in dependent variables such as preparedness, monetary losses, and recovery, indicating that these variables are subject to multiple and complex influences that our models did not capture well. This may be because this series of studies focused primarily on organizational, agent-specific, and community-level variables. Other types of factors not taken into account in this research, such as the behavior and decision processes of individual business owners, also need to be taken into account. As Alesch and Holly (1996) noted in their study of small businesses in

the aftermath of the Northridge earthquake, some owners simply try harder to keep their businesses operational in the aftermath of disasters, and some owners make sounder business decisions than others. These kinds of factors, which undoubtedly affect how well businesses fare when disaster strikes, warrant more extensive study.

New studies are needed that improve upon the approaches described here. There is a need for more longitudinal research on businesses, as well as for studies that explore how business disaster impacts and recovery outcomes vary across different types of disaster agents and different degrees of disaster severity. Researchers should undertake the difficult task of systematically following up on businesses that have ceased operations to find out why they closed, while also examining whether disasters can stimulate the creation of new firms or alter turnover processes in particular business niches.

IMPLICATIONS FOR LOSS-REDUCTION PRACTITIONERS AND BUSINESS OWNERS

Recent years have seen an expansion in interest in advising businesses on how to get ready for, manage, and recover from disasters. Business contingency planning is a growing field, and new journals with titles like *Disaster Recovery* have been established specifically to give advice and assistance to private-sector organizations. The research findings and issues discussed here can provide a more solid empirical basis for such efforts. For example, the data show that businesses are more likely to carry out particular types of preparedness measures while overlooking others, which should provide guidance for practitioners who are trying to encourage more comprehensive planning. These studies also show that certain types of businesses are less able and willing to prepare for disasters than others, even though those same businesses may also be among the most vulnerable. Although educational programs and other strategies are being undertaken to enhance business preparedness, these programs appear to be mainly reaching the largest businesses in particular sectors of the economy, suggesting that more emphasis needs to be placed on targeting smaller firms and less well-prepared sectors.

To improve practice in the area of business disaster management, more information is needed on what kinds of approaches work best in encouraging businesses to undertake loss reduction measures and on what forms of assistance actually help businesses recover when they do experience disasters. The need for better private-sector crisis and recovery management has been recognized, but before advocating particular programs and approaches, it is necessary to document systematically which strategies have proven effective for different types of businesses, in real disaster situations.

This research also indicates that in thinking about disasters, businesses need to look beyond their own doors and to appreciate the extent to which their chances of coping with and recovering from disasters are tied to communitywide loss-reduction activities. Although awareness is certainly growing, more business owners need to recognize that they have a vested interest in promoting higher levels of disaster resistance in their communities. For example, this research shows that businesses are very vulnerable to disaster-related lifeline disruption and other offsite impacts. Concentrating on reducing losses only at the business level will not address those sources of vulnerability. Instead, the business community should understand that making lifelines and other key elements in the civil infrastructure more resistant to disaster-related disruption will help reduce losses to individual businesses by reducing the likelihood of business interruption. Similarly, if a community has an effective plan in place for responding to disasters—containing and assessing damage, cleaning up debris, making emergency lifeline repairs, and undertaking other critical emergency response tasks—businesses will benefit directly, because they can resume operations more rapidly in the event of a disaster. If a community engages in pre-event disaster recovery planning, the businesses in that community will recover more quickly in the event of a disaster. The more businesses work with governmental preparedness organizations in the communities in which they operate to reduce potential communitywide disaster impacts and streamline the recovery process, the more confident they can be that their own disaster-related problems will be less severe.

ACKNOWLEDGMENTS

The research summarized here was supported by two grants from the National Science Foundation, SGER Grant No. 9425810001 and Grant No. CMS-9632779, and by the National Center for Earthquake Engineering Research (now the Multidisciplinary Center for Earthquake Engineering Research) Grant No. 93-6303. The findings and conclusions are those of the writers.

APPENDIX. REFERENCES

Alesch, D. J., and Holly, J. N. (1996). "How to survive the next natural disaster: Lessons for small business from Northridge victims and survivors." *Paper presented at the Pan Pacific Hazards '96 Meeting.*

Bolin, R. C. (1989). "Family in disaster: Theoretical and empirical aspects." *Preparations for, responses to, and recovery from major community disasters.* E. L. Quarantelli and C. Pelanda, eds., Disaster Res. Ctr., University of Delaware, Newark, Dela., 194–208.

Bolin, R. C. (1994). *Household and community recovery after earthquakes.* Inst. of Behavioral Sci., University of Colorado, Boulder, Colo.

Cochrane, H. C. (1975). *Natural hazards and their distributive effects.* Inst. of Behavioral Sci., University of Colorado, Boulder, Colo.

Cohen, M. J. (1993). "Economic impact of an environmental accident: A time-series analysis of the Exxon Valdez oil spill in Southcentral Alaska." *Sociological Spectrum*, 13, 35–63.

Dacy, D. C., and Kunreuther, H. (1969). *The economics of natural disasters.* The Free Press, New York.

Dahlhamer, J. M. (1998). "Rebounding from environmental jolts: Organizational and ecological factors affecting business disaster recovery," PhD dissertation No. 31, Disaster Res. Ctr., University of Delaware, Newark, Dela.

Dahlhamer, J. M., and D'Souza, M. J. (1997). "Determinants of business-disaster preparedness in two U.S. metropolitan areas." *Int. J. Mass Emergencies and Disasters*, 15(2), 265–281.

Dahlhamer, J. M., and Reshaur, L. M. (1996). "Businesses and the 1994 Northridge earthquake: An analysis of pre- and post-disaster preparedness." Preliminary Paper No. 240, Disaster Res. Ctr., University of Delaware, Newark, Dela.

Dahlhamer, J. M., and Tierney, K. J. (1996). "Winners and losers: Predicting business disaster recovery outcomes following the Northridge earthquake." Preliminary Paper No. 243, Disaster Res. Ctr., University of Delaware, Newark, Dela.

Dahlhamer, J. M., and Tierney, K. J. (1998). "Rebounding from disruptive events: Business recovery following the Northridge earthquake." *Sociological Spectrum*, 18, 121–141.

Dahlhamer, J. M., Webb, G. R., and Tierney, K. J. (1999). "Predicting business financial losses in the 1989 Loma Prieta and 1994 Northridge earthquakes: Implications for loss estimation research." Preliminary Paper No. 282, Disaster Res. Ctr., University of Delaware, Newark, Dela.

Drabek, T. E. (1994). *Disaster evacuation and the tourist industry.* Inst. of Behavioral Sci., University of Colorado, Boulder, Colo.

Durkin, M. E. (1984). "The economic recovery of small businesses after Earthquakes: The Coalinga experience." *Paper presented at the Int. Conf. on Natural Hazards Mitigation Res. and Prac.*

Friesema, H. P., Caparano, J., Goldstein, G., Lineberry, R., and McCleary, R. (1979). *Aftermath: Communities after natural disasters.* Sage Publications, Beverly Hills, Calif.

Gordon, P., and Richardson, H. W., Davis, B., Steins, C., and Vasishth, A. (1995). "The business interruption effects of the Northridge earthquake." *Final Report to the National Science Foundation*, Lusk Ctr. Res. Inst., School of Urban and Regional Plng., University of Southern California, Los Angeles.

Jones, B. G., and Chang, S. E. (1995). "Economic aspects of urban vulnerability and disaster mitigation." *Urban disaster mitigation: The role of engineering and technology.* F. Y. Cheng and M. S. Sheu, eds., Elsevier Science, Oxford, England, 311–320.

Kroll, C. A., Landis, J. D., Shen, Q., and Stryker, S. (1991). "Economic impacts of the Loma Prieta earthquake: A focus on small business." Working Paper No. 91-187, Transp. Ctr. and the Ctr. for Real Estate and Economics, University of California, Berkeley, Calif.

La Porte, T. R., and Consolini, P. M. (1991). "Working in practice but not in Theory: Theoretical Challenges of high-reliability organizations." *J. Public Admin. Res. and Theory*, 1, 19–47.

La Porte, T. R., and Rochlin, G. (1994). "A rejoinder to Perrow." *J. Contingencies and Crisis Mgmt.*, 2, 221–227.

Lindell, M. K. (1994). "Are local emergency planning committees effective in developing community disaster preparedness?" *Int. J. Mass Emergencies and Disasters*, 12, 159–182.

Mileti, D. S., Darlington, J. D., Fitzpatrick, C., and O'Brien, P. W. (1993). "Communicating earthquake risk: Societal response to revised probabilities in the Bay Area." Hazards Assessment Lab. and Dept. of Sociology, Colorado State University, Fort Collins, Colo.

Perrow, C. (1984). *Normal accidents: Living with high risk technologies.* Basic Books, New York.

Quarantelli, E. L., Lawrence, C., Tierney, K. J., and Johnson, T. (1979). "Initial findings from a study of socio behavioral preparations and planning for acute chemical hazard disasters." *J. Haz. Mat.*, 3, 79–90.

Rossi, P. H., Wright, J. D., Wright, S. R., and Weber-Burdin, E. (1978). "Are there long-term effects of American natural disasters?" *Mass Emergencies*, 3, 117–132.

Solyst, J., and St. Amand, M. (1993). *Emergency planning and community Right to Know Act: A status of state actions—1992.* National Governors' Association, Washington, D.C.

Tierney, K. J. (1997). "Impacts of recent disasters on businesses: The 1993 Midwest floods and the 1994 Northridge earthquake." *Economic consequences of earthquakes: Preparing for the unexpected.* B. Jones, ed., Multidisciplinary Ctr. for Earthquake Engrg. Res., Report No. NCEER-SP-0001, State University of New York at Buffalo, Buffalo, 189–222.

West, C. T., and Lenze, D. G. (1994). "Modeling the regional impact of natural disaster and recovery: A general framework and an application to Hurricane Andrew." *Int. Regional Sci. Rev.*, 17(2), 121–150.

Lifelines and Livelihood: a Social Accounting Matrix Approach to Calamity Preparedness

Sam Cole*

This paper[1] describes a Social Accounting Matrix (SAM)-based method for evaluating disaster preparedness and recovery strategies. The first section of the paper explains the overall approach and its extension to the evaluation of specific components of lifeline systems in a small Caribbean island. The next section explains the relationship between the physical and economic parameters of the energy-electricity-water lifelines and the tourism sector on the island and describes the construction of the corresponding accounting framework. The diachronic multipliers calculated from this extended matrix are used to determine the impact of potential hazards for tourism and other economic activities on the island. The case of a water storage tank, providing back-up supply to the major hotels, is used to illustrate the approach. In the final sections, the example is elaborated to highlight trade-offs between economic and non-economic costs for particular businesses or households. The events and strategies described then may be combined into an event-based scenario analysis.

Background — lifelines and social accounts

This paper describes a social accounting matrix-based approach to disaster preparedness and recovery planning suitable for small localities, such as islands, rural districts and inner city neighborhoods (NCEER, 1993). The rationale behind the project is essentially as follows. Natural disasters such as earthquakes, cyclones, floods, mud slides and volcanoes disrupt all sectors of an economy and all segments of a population (see NRC, 1989). Even when they are not impacted directly, individuals and businesses may be affected for an extended period through damage to lifelines such as water supply or roads, as well as through indirect effects such as the loss of livelihood or markets (Kreimer and Munasinghe, 1990; 1992; NEHRP, 1992).

A variety of techniques have been used to evaluate losses arising from disasters and the merits of alternative strategies for recovery. This includes input-output methods (Cochrane, 1975; 1992; Boisvert, 1992; West and Lenze, 1993), econometric models (Ellson, Milliman and Roberts, 1984; Guimares, Hefner and Woodward, 1992) and regression and time-series models (Freisema et al., 1979; Chang, 1983). Each approach has its advantages and limitations. The method used in this paper, a variety of input-output tables called a social accounting matrix (SAM), has the particular advantage that, given the requisite data, both the supply and the demand sides of the economy can be described in considerable detail. Input-output tables, in general, provide a means for representing the flows of goods, income and people between businesses, households and public service within an economy, or between neighboring localities and regions, providing a picture of how the different parts of a community are linked together as an productive technological and social network (NCEER, 1993). During a period of disaster, some of these flows are interrupted, with ramifications throughout the economy. With its intrinsic network structure, an input-output model allows the direct and indirect consequences of this damage for various actors in an area's economy to be represented and calculated. Although an input-output table strictly provides only a 'snap-shot' of an economy at a fixed point in time, this may be combined with various assumptions about economic behaviour in order to calculate the overall impacts of a particular event. These calculations may be rather straightforward, as with the conventional Leontief inverse method of solution, or adapted to dynamic analysis (Leontief, 1970), to computable general equilibrium (CGE) methods (Taylor, 1979; Brookshire and McKee, 1992), or to distributed lag methods (Ten Raa, 1986; Cole, 1988).

Disaster assessment models have usually

* Same Cole, University of Buffalo, New York, Departments of Geography and Planning, University at Buffalo, Hayes Hall, Buffalo, NY 14260

been applied at the national or regional level, with some efforts at the county level (Rose and Benavides, 1993; West and Lenze, 1993). However, in the majority of cases, natural disasters have their most severe impacts on isolated localities and small or marginal communities. In the United States, for example, natural disasters are a national problem, experienced at the local level (Berke and Beatley, 1992). At this geographic scale, the details of both the supply and demand-sides of the economy can be quite idiosyncratic and specific — thus it may be necessary to take explicit account of particular businesses and populations, and the trade-offs between their competing interests. The SAM approach is useful here since households and the workforce are sub-divided by attributes such as occupation, education, income, gender and ethnicity. The use of SAM's in national, regional and local planning (Pyatt and Roe, 1977; Taylor, 1979) has been extended to small territories and islands (McCoy, 1990; Cole, 1992), villages (Adelman, Taylor and Vogel, 1988), sub-county (Robinson and Lahr, 1993) and inner-city neighbourhoods (Cole, 1992). The present project extends their use to disaster planning.

The extreme severity of impacts to small localities and marginal populations often can be traced to poverty and inappropriate development, such as inferior infrastructure or housing. In some cases, victims are disadvantaged further by deficient recovery programs (Ebert, 1982; Cuny, 1983). In this sense, disasters may be viewed as failures of development (Jones, 1981; 1989). Thus, while the main priority must be to deal with the immediate consequences of the disaster (such as health and shelter), it is also necessary to devise an economic recovery which improves the quality of development so that hardship from future disasters will be reduced. The specific components of a sensible recovery strategy (such as improvements to lifelines, or other infrastructure) should also contribute to overall development. This is also true of planning instruments such as those described here. In particular, since most disasters occur with rather little specific warning (Jones and Tomazevic, 1981; Cuny, 1983), and small localities usually do not have the necessary planning capability, one need is for tools that can be constructed relatively quickly, so as to assess the economic damage caused by the disaster, but which then may be integrated into in the longer-term recovery and development process. Such techniques must be able to evaluate preparedness measures of various kinds, for example through cost-benefit type analyses of individual

components of a strategy, as well as through investigation of more complex and integrated recovery and development strategies.

The various types of natural and human-made disasters, such as earthquakes, hurricanes and oil spills, have particular types of damage associated with them (Cuny, 1983). Despite this, the actual damage in each disaster varies considerably, depending, for example, on windspeed, location of epicentre, amount of flooding and on the condition of buildings and infrastructure, or the amount of pollutant. In effect, the damage arises from a set of specific events, or combinations of events, each of which may be considered separately, but which may be re-combined into an overall disaster and recovery scenario (NCEER, 1993). Activities aimed at damage mitigation, reconstruction, or recovery too may be considered on an event-by-event basis. Equally, a given type of event could be a component of several quite different disasters or recovery strategies. As part of this overall event-based approach, this paper extends previous work to consider specific components of lifeline systems and strategies connected with them. However, while this exercise focuses on a specific item, it is rehearsed in the context of a broad social and economic framework.

In general, the steps in such cost-benefit type calculations are as follows:

1 Identify the range of events and their probability of occurrence, or specify the actual events resulting from an event such as a hurricane or earthquake, or the hypothesized mitigation strategy;
2 for each event, identify the likely or actual direct losses (or gains) to all activities, including transactions with external actors;
3 estimate the indirect consequences on other production sectors, households and government;
4 check whether it is possible to reallocate resources so as to reduce the overall impact on various selected or community interests;
5 repeat 2 to 4 for all events; and
6 combine events according to the their assessed risk in order to assess the overall value of specific responses and lifeline.

The first items correspond to the steps suggested by, for example, French and Isaacson (1984). In the context of input-output analysis, step 3 is essentially the task of calculating the various multipliers and impacts as performed using the SAM. Step 4 may be improved or elaborated using a variety of scenario, programming and scheduling methods (Ray, 1984), while step 5 may be considered as an aspect of risk analysis (Van der Veen et al, 1994). This paper concentrates on items 3 and 6, focusing on a particular activity, as an illustration of the overall approach to developing and using the relevant sections of the model. Overall, the potential contribution of the methods adopted in this paper are that they extend the possibilities of constructing detailed input-output type models for small localities and for introducing fairly complex disaster and reconstruction scenarios, made up of many events, taking account of changes in the internal structure of the economy as well as the exogenous changes.

Economy and community in Aruba

The subject for the present study is the small Caribbean island of Aruba, until 1986 a member of the Netherlands Antilles. Aruba is some 20 miles long and in 1980 had a population of about 60 thousand. Aruba is less prone to natural disasters than most Caribbean islands. In early 1993 she experienced two minor earth tremors and most recently was a near miss for *Hurricane Brett* (which caused massive damage to favelas in nearby Caracas) and in 1991 suffered a fatal mudslide (Bon Dia Aruba, 1993). The island has a complex geology, lying 20 miles from Venezuela, across an extension of the Oca-Ancon fault (Doukhan and Leon, 1988). Although the island has not suffered a major natural disaster in recent years, Aruba has proved useful as a site for testing the model. This is because of the relatively good availability of data for the construction and testing of the SAM and the cooperation of the local authorities. Most importantly, in the mid-1980s, she experienced a dramatic economic upheaval following the shutdown of her major industry and the rapid expansion of the tourism industry. Over less than a decade, employment in Aruba first fell by over 30 per cent in 1985, and then rose to more than 30 per cent above its original level by 1990, leaving the island with a present population estimated at 75 thousand. In this period, the main 'driving force' of the island's economy shifted from oil refining (located in San Nicolas) to tourism (located in Oranjestad and Noord), which is now the life and livelihood of the island. This shift has changed the geographic, economic and demographic complexion of the community. This series of events afforded an opportunity to assess some details of the forecasts of the SAM model (NCEER, 1993), a significant step, since as West and Lenze (1993) observe, regional impact analysis and regional economic forecasting generally has been exempt from the necessary ex-post testing.

Aruba's history has been marked by a succession of disturbances. Until the present century, she experienced Spanish, Dutch and (very briefly) British rule, with gold and phosphate mining, small plantations and ranches with African and Indian slaves providing a largely subsistence livelihood, supplemented by migration to plantations around the Caribbean Basin during periods of intense drought. A large oil refinery was located on the island in the late-1920s, inducing massive immigration from around the Caribbean, the Americas, and eventually from around the world. This historic process, with populations arriving and departing with the fluctuating economic fortunes of the island, has led to a marked cultural division of labor in Aruba, so that today there are significant correlations between ethnic, sectoral, occupational, geographic and other divisions (Cole, 1993).

In the discussion that follows, households are sub-divided as urban and rural-Arubians, migrants and expatriates, in order to emphasize this last consideration. The native Arubian population is a tight-knit society with strong kinship relations that are relied upon in difficult times. As a generalization, there are distinctive lifestyle differences between the cosmopolitan urban and the traditional rural communities. Again, as a generalization, expatriates are typically wealthier with connections to major businesses, while migrants are typically poorer and socially marginalized and belong to Caribbean-wide social networks. For present purposes, the main point is that each community has distinctive resources and opportunities for dealing with crises, in the short and long-run. It is of note here that the Aruba Calamity Preparedness Committee has adopted a community based approach to disaster management.

The Aruba fuel-electricity-water network

The fuel-electricity-water system in Aruba is treated at the level of individual corporations and its principal customers. Oil is imported into Aruba by the Wickland trans-shipment terminal and a partially re-opened oil refinery operated by Coastal. Both are located in San Nicolas at the extreme East of the island on the site of the former LAGO refinery (subsidiary of Exxon). Fuel oil is piped from Coastal to WEB which is located at the middle-south of Aruba at Balashi. WEB co-produces electricity and water, the latter through distillation from sea water. Electricity and water are sold directly to Wickland and Coastal by WEB. Although in the past WEB provided electricity to LAGO, today WEB is contracted to purchase any excess from Coastal's own co-production facility (CEP, 1991). Electricity is distributed to other users by ELMAR, unlike the water which WEB distributes directly to residences, hotels and commercial users via separate pipelines. This distribution takes place through a series of partially linked regional networks. In addition to a group of water tanks at Balashi, each network is supported by one or more large storage tanks and water towers, including a large tank at the harbor in the capital Oranjestad. Recently, a new tank has been constructed at Alta Vista towards the western end of the island. This region of the island called Noord has seen very rapid commercial and residential development since the shut down of the LAGO refinery, and the trebling of the tourism sector. The principal purpose of the Alta Vista tank was to increase the pressure and provide more water to the rapidly expanding residential and commercial development. But, because of its proximity to the strip, the Alta Vista tank potentially serves as a back-up for the hotels should the primary mains supply, that runs along the Palm Beach via the Oranjestad tanks, fail.

In the past, there have been many problems with the water supply, and costly imports have been made through LAGO, and recently, Coastal (CEP, 1991). In one notorious incident, Exxon tankers were caught stealing water from the Hudson river, after washing their ballast just upstream on one of New York City's major drinking water inlets. Information about the robustness to failure of the present water supply system in Aruba has been provided by WEB in response to an interview and questionnaire. The main water production facilities were installed in 1983-1984 and 1989-1990 with a total capacity of 34,000 m^3 per day, with an average daily output of 20,250 m^3 in 1990. The six Balashi tanks hold about 60,000 m^3, which is roughly equal to all other tanks combined. The Alta Vista tank holds 12,500 m^3. Average daily consumption of water is 10,000 m^3 so if water production should fail completely the tanks hold approximately 6 days supply at regular usage rates. However, WEB estimates that this could be extended to 9 to 10 days with rationing. Water can be shipped in from overseas at a rate of 4000 m^3 per week (with a delay of about one week). In addition many of the older rural homesteads (cunucus) have their own small tanks, and ponds (or tankis) collect run-off from seasonal rainfall, which partially compensate for the somewhat lower tank

capacities in some rural areas. The Santa Cruz area tanks, for example, provide only a 2-3 days supply. The five electricity generating steam turbines at WEB date from 1958 to 1964 and have an installed capacity of 114 MW. Because these generators were originally installed to provide power to LAGO, typically they run well below capacity (in 1990, average production was 35 MW with a peak production of 62 MW). In addition, there is a stand-by generator in case of emergency (CEP, 1991). While the electricity generating system appears to be more robust, the fuel supply lines could be damaged by floods during the hurricane season.

The Aruba tourism sector

Tourism in Aruba is expanding very rapidly and the island's livelihood is increasingly dependent on this sector. The industry comprises a range of hotels with an emphasis on high-rise and low-rise hotels, time-share apartments and a number of smaller condominium complexes. Income from tourism in 1990 was at least Afl 373 million (excluding time share) and hotel employment alone stood at 4,000 (out of a total labor force of around 27,000). It also involves a variety of shopping plazas, casinos (mostly linked to hotels) and other entertainment, eating and sightseeing facilities, providing another 3,000 jobs (CEP, 1991). From 1986-1989 the average annual growth rate of tourist arrivals in Aruba was 24 per cent, compared to 8.5 per cent in the Caribbean as a whole. Hotel capacity is expected to rise from 4000 in 1990 to 7,800 in 1994, compared to 2,400 in 1985 and 2100 in 1980.

While the hotels and tourist facilities themselves are vulnerable to direct damage from natural events, this is not the concern of the present paper. Rather, the concern is the secondary losses arising from a failure of the lifeline system supporting the sector. (The term secondary will be used here for these losses as opposed to other indirect losses in downstream activities to be calculated with the SAM). The financial impact on the hotel trade arising from a loss in water supply varies across hotels and depends on the type of tourist, how the matter is dealt with, and so on. Individual hotels have contingency plans (such as their own short-term back-up supply). Tourists in Aruba come mainly from North America for a 'relaxing week of sun, sand and sea' and tend to become very irritated by inconveniences (Spinrad, 1981). Problems result in early leavers, reimbursements, cancellations by next weeks visitors and non-returns the following year. Besides hotels, other tourist industries such as specialty shops, taxi-tours, restaurants, bars and casinos all loose business. Although the general character of these losses can be described, they are difficult to calculate in a mechanical fashion. The problem of imputing the economic secondary effects of a natural disaster on day-to-day business may be somewhat less tangible than assessing the re-construction costs of damaged physical systems (French and Keown, 1993). The appropriate way to accumulate information is through interviews with hotels managers and others involved in the trade. Again this would be on an hotel-by-hotel basis for the major hotels, and a sample basis for smaller business (similar to Tierney, 1993), and case studies of actual disasters (such as those in Guam, St Croix or south Dade county, Florida).

The Aruba lifeline-tourism SAM

The Aruba lifeline-tourism SAM comprises three components:

1 The core of the Arubian economy and the 'rest-of-the-world' economy, including social distribution across categories of household;
2 the lifeline sectors comprising the oil trans-shipment terminal, the (re-opened but much smaller) oil refinery, the electricity and water production at WEB and the electricity distribution activities of ELMAR; and
3 the tourism sector comprising high- and low-rise hotels, casinos, bars, tourist shops, taxi-and tours, as well as demand from stay-over and cruise-ship visitors.

The combined SAM is shown in Table 1(a). Each entry in the table represents a transaction — the amount paid by one actor (business, sector or household) to another over the course of a year. For example, the Afl 67 million of fuel oil purchased by WEB from the oil refinery appears in the top-left part of the matrix. The columns show the expenditures by each actor, and the rows show their purchases. Total income and expenditures for each actor are approximately equal.

The core economy

The core 1990 matrix was constructed by scaling the previously constructed 1979 Aruba SAM (Cole et al, 1983; NCEER, 1993). The scaling uses multi-proportional RAS procedure that allows new data to be added to the original matrix in a fashion which minimizes

the information loss from the original matrix. The overall level of activity was constrained to match a set of national income and production accounts (NIPA) which were first constructed using a variety of data from the Central Bank of Aruba, the World Bank, IMF and the Aruba Development Plan (1990) and the Aruba Capital Expenditure Plan (CEP, 1991). These national income and product accounts first were organized into a small matrix (in a manner similar to that described by Hanson and Robinson, 1989). Additional information on value added and wages by sector, imports and exports, and public sector activity were then used to scale individual activities and transactions to 1990 levels. These procedures are discussed in detail in NCEER (1993). The supply-side of the economy is sub-divided into the main (1-digit) sectors. The demand side into four classes of household, government, investment, and overseas trade and finance activities. Households are sub-divided as urban and rural Arubians, and expatriates and migrants, each with distinctive income and expenditure patterns. It is this last feature which qualifies the table as a social accounting matrix.

The lifeline network

The lifeline network has been constructed mainly from company reports for WEB and ELMAR, data in the Capital Expenditure Program (CEP, 1991) and the information provided by WEB. The various transactions referred to earlier have been included although a number of inconsistencies between the accounts remain unresolved An effort has been made to allocate co-production costs within WEB between water and electricity, with WEB treated as a vertically integrated corporation producing its own intermediate inputs. This is necessary because of the differences in the potential impacts. For example, a loss in electricity production affects water production far more than the reverse.

The tourism sector

The data for the tourism network also comes from a number of sources. The gross data on tourism revenues comes from the Central Bank of Aruba (1990) and CEP (1991). Details of the allocation of tourist and hotel expenditures between activities comes from Spinrad (1981), Latham (1984) and more recent publications of the Aruba Tourism Board. There is some secrecy with respect to details of the industry (not least, the casino sector). However, the data in the SAM offer a fair impression of the island's tourist industry, and in addition, the

Table 1: Aruba Social Accounts with Tourism and Lifeline Sectors

(a) Social accounts[1]

(A large social accounting matrix is presented, rotated, with the following row categories:)

Sector or activity: Wickland Termina, Coastal Refinery, WEB-Electric, WEB-Water, ELMAR, Transport-Telecom, HighRise Hotels, LowRise Hotels, Tourist Shops, Bars/Cafes, Casino, Taxi/Tours, Industry/Agricultu, Construction, Other Commerce, Other Services, Labor (low edu), Labor (middle edu), Labor (high edu), Depreciation, Local Surplus, Rural Households, Urban Household, Migrant Household, Expatriate House, Firms, Government, Household Capita, Firms Capital, Government Capit, Stayover Tourists, Cruise Ships, Imports, Overseas Finance, Expenditures, Receipts

Column groups: Lifelines (Wick, Coas, WEB, WEBELMA, Tran), Tourist activities (High, LowR, Bars, Tour, Casi, Othe), Other production (Taxi, Indu, Cons, Labo, Othe, Depr, Loca, Labo, Rura, Urba, Migr, Expa), Local factors, Households institutions (Rura, Urba, Migr, Expa, Firm, Gove, Hou, Firm, Gov, Stay, Cru), Capital tourists & overseas (Impo, Over)

(b) Marginal impacts

	Wick	Coas	WEB	WEBELMA	Tran	High	LowR	Bars	Tour	Casi	Indu	Cons	Labo	Othe	Depr	Loca	Rura	Urba	Migr	Expa	Firm	Gove	Hou	Firm	Gov	Stay	Cru
All Lifelines	1.0	1.0	1.8	2.1	1.0	0.3	0.2	0.1	0.2	0.2	0.1	0.2	0.1	0.3	0.1	0.3	0.1	0.3	0.2	0.3	0.1	0.3	0.1	0.1	0.3	0.1	
WEB-Water	0.0	0.0	0.0	0.0	0.0	0.0	0.0	1.1	0.0	0.0	0.0	0.0	0.0	0.1	0.0	0.0	0.1	0.1	0.0	0.0	0.0	0.0	0.0	0.0	0.0	0.1	
Tourism Sector	0.0	0.0	0.0	0.0	0.0	1.1	0.8	1.1	1.1	1.1	0.0	0.0	0.0	0.1	0.0	0.1	0.1	0.1	0.1	1.3	0.1	0.0	1.6	1.0	1.4	0.0	
All Other Sectors	0.0	0.0	0.5	0.9	0.7	0.4	0.5	0.8	0.6	0.8	2.8	2.4	1.5	2.4	0.6	1.5	1.5	1.4	1.3	1.3	1.6	1.6	0.7	1.0	0.3		
Margins	0.0	0.0	0.2	0.4	0.3	0.4	0.3	0.5	0.3	0.5	0.2	0.6	0.3	0.6	0.3	0.4	0.4	0.3	0.3	0.5	0.3	0.3	0.1	0.3	0.1		
Wages	0.0	0.0	0.4	0.5	0.5	0.7	0.8	0.6	0.7	0.8	0.2	0.6	0.3	0.8	1.3	1.7	1.7	1.7	1.6	1.7	0.9	1.5	1.7	0.3	0.4		
All Households	0.0	0.0	0.4	0.8	0.6	0.7	0.8	0.6	0.7	0.8	0.6	0.2	0.6	1.3	0.8	0.4	0.4	0.4	0.5	0.1	0.4	0.5					
Rural	0.0	0.0	0.1	0.1	0.1	0.5	0.1	0.1	0.1	0.1	0.6	0.2	0.1	0.2	0.7	0.4	0.2	1.1	1.7	0.4	0.2	1.1	0.1	0.2	0.1		
Urban	0.0	0.0	0.3	0.7	0.5	0.5	0.4	0.5	0.4	0.5	0.5	1.4	0.5	1.5	1.0	1.2	1.0	1.4	0.4	0.8	1.0	1.2	0.3	0.5	0.3		
Local Value Adde	0.0	0.0	0.1	1.0	0.1	0.8	0.9	0.2	0.9	0.6	1.2	1.4	0.2	0.7	1.8	2.0	1.8	1.8	2.0	0.7	0.9	0.5	0.8	0.3			
Government	0.0	0.0	0.0	0.1	0.1	0.2	0.2	0.1	0.1	0.1	0.2	0.1	0.1	0.2	0.1	0.2	0.2	0.3	0.2	0.2	0.1	0.2	0.1	0.1	0.1		

Notes:

1. Data are from various sources and years. The matrix has been scaled and balanced (see text). Amounts are shown to nearest Afl (1998).

2. Total impacts per unit exogenous change in demand calculated to a 5 year time horizon (see text).

available data allow some individual hotels to be described in the matrix, in a similar fashion to WEB and ELMAR in the lifelines sector. The present division into high and low-rise hotels follows a survey by Spinrad (1981) that differentiates between the class of hotel (high-rise tending to be larger and more luxurious). It also has relevance for their vulnerability to natural disasters, directly and indirectly, since high rise hotels are often more susceptible to hurricane damage, earthquakes and fires, and the two classes of hotels are concentrated at opposite ends of the tourist strip. Thus, breaking down the data in this way, allows the impacts of events on individual parts of the industry, or different events, to be assessed.

Impact assessment using the SAM

The SAM shown in Table 1(a) is a snapshot of the Arubian economy in 1990. Multipliers and impact coefficients calculated from the table may be used to estimate the impact of a change to the economy following a disaster, at a variety of levels of sophistication.

In most cases, the first step is to calculate a set of 'standard impacts' for the economy — that is, the increase in the level of every activity as a result of a unit (say, one Afl) increase in demand for every other activity. This calculation is carried out by 'inverting' the matrix of coefficients obtained from Table 1(a) to obtain a variety of multipliers and total impact coefficients. Table 1(b) shows the impact of unit exogenous shifts in demand on each activity on combinations of activities — lifelines, tourism, other industry, households and government. The table shows, for example, that when indirect and downstream effects are accounted for, a one Afl loss in receipts by high rise hotels leads to an income loss of 2.1 Afl for all production activities (30, 110, and 80 cents from the lifeline, tourism, and other industry sectors respectively), a 67 cent loss to combined households, of which 11 cents and 60 cents go to rural and urban Arubians respectively, and a 19 cent fall in revenues to government.

Multipliers are the ratio of the total economy-wide impact of changes in the level of a given activity, to the original impact. The total impact coefficients shown are the ratio between the level in a given activity (say, household income) arising from a unit change in another activity (such as the level of tourism). Both may be calculated in several ways; most common are Type I or Type II multipliers (Miller and Blair, 1985; Stevens and Lahr, 1988). There are a number of limitations on the use of these multipliers; in particular, the use

of fixed technical coefficients, insufficient attention to price effects, comparative static analysis, and so on. There are several techniques for compensating for such limitations whilst attempting to retain the relative simplicity of the input-output method (Miller and Blair, 1985). A comparison of actual and forecast shifts in employment and income in Aruba over the years 1980 to 1990 suggested that a time-lagged method is likely to give better results (Cole, 1988; NCEER, 1993). Diachronic multipliers and impacts are calculated for all the activities in the SAM with impacts calculated up to a prescribed time horizon using average or marginal coefficients. The multipliers shown in Table 1(b) are calculated up to a five-year time horizon. The calculation may be modified to account for continuous technical change or appropriate discount rates for each activity. Similar considerations also apply when using the results of impact analysis in cost benefit analysis, particularly the question of how to deal with trade-offs between economic and non-economic welfare and the competing needs of interest groups and communities (Laylard, 1980).

A schematic example

Small societies, like Aruba, have a relatively uncomplicated configuration of sectorial and lifeline links, but despite this they have subtle and often contradictory social and economic objectives (to the point that actors may say whether a solution is acceptable, but not why). In this situation, it is obviously important to discuss a range of alternative events, responses and scenarios with different groups within society so as to elicit critical trade-offs and choices, and negotiate compromises. The purpose of the example considered next is partly to confirm existing data in the SAM, but also to reveal the response mechanisms that are implicit in the parameters of any cost-benefit analysis, and are required for a more complete assessment of various events and strategies.

For both purposes it was found useful to begin with the simple calculation that is summarized in Table 2; a serious rupture to the main pipeline from Oranjestad to the Palm Beach, cutting the strip off from the Balashi plant and the Harbor tanks and cutting off the normal water supply to the hotels for as much as five days while repairs are made. It could arise through several causes; a hurricane, an oil spill, an aircraft crash or an earthquake. As a response to this event, the Alta Vista tank is assumed to become the fall-back supply for the hotels. The 'value' of the tank for this

Table 2: Tourism-Lifeline Event Example

Typical Event	Assume a rupture of the main pipeline from Balashi water works and Harbor tanks to Palm Beach hotel strip.	
Determine	Impact on Tourism Revenues and Downstream Income with, and without, the Alta Vista water tank.	
Direct Loss to Tourism Industry	Early leavers/reimbursements - Cancellations (same year) - Non-returns TOTAL	3–4 capacity days lost 1–2 capacity days lost 2 capacity days 7 capacity days (about 2 per cent of annual tourist income)
	Annual tourist income (1990) Potential loss from rupture	Afl 706 million Afl 14 million (US$8 million)
Total Loss	Tourism Multiplier Direct and Indirect Loss	Approx. 2.1 (see text) Approx. Afl 30 million (excluding repairs)
Chance of this Event	Probability over 10 year horizon say 1–5 per cent	
Potential Risk	Likely loss over 10 year horizon about Afl 0.3 to Afl 1.5 million Typical discount horizons Discounted potential loss	3 to 20 years about Afl 0.1 to Afl 0.5 million
Cost of Water Tank	Construction cost	Afl 1.96 million.
Justified Expenditure	Not justified on the basis of this event alone. However, Alta Vista tank has other uses and there are several other contingencies covered by the tank.	

purpose is to be assessed by asking how much damage to the tourism trade is avoided because of this particular use of the Alta Vista tank (noting here that this was not the primary intended purpose for this tank). This event has been hypothesized by the Calamity Preparedness Committee and is taken as typical of the kind of disaster with which we are concerned. It has been used as a basis for discussion with representatives of the Calamity Committee, the tourist industry (AHATA, the Aruba Hotel and Tourism Authority), WEB (the Water and Electric Company) and with several government departments.

In this example, it was assumed that a given loss of water supply to the hotels would lead to a 3 to 4 capacity-day immediate loss in business to this sector as visitors cut short their vacation. In addition, there would be an estimated 1 to 2 capacity-day loss through cancellations (because of uncertainty as to whether the problem will be solved) and a 2 to 3 day capacity-day loss because of non-returning tourists in following years, giving a total of around 7 capacity-days. Thus, should this event occur, the island would lose a total of about Afl 14 million in tourism receipts, since the industry is worth about Afl 700 million annually to the island. Taking a tourist sector multiplier of about two (see above), the total (direct and indirect loss) would be around

Afl 28 million. Fortunately, the likelihood of such a disaster is fairly small. Assuming that the probability over a ten year period of damage of this magnitude is from 1 to 5 per cent, the potential risk (cost of event times the potential loss) would be from Afl 0.3 to 1.5 million. Since the Alta Vista tank cost Afl 1.96 million to install in 1990, its construction would not be justified by this event alone. Moreover, private sector discount horizons in the tourism sector in Aruba are especially short and appear to range between three and six years (compared to twenty to thirty years for the public infrastructure supporting it). Florin-for-florin, for example, income lost from next years' non-returning visitors is worth less than income lost from early-leavers. Discounting the estimate to present value is likely to cut this estimate in half. However, the scenario is only one of many such possibilities with varying probabilities of occurrence, and these should be combined to present an overall potential loss.

Responses and welfare criteria

The implied welfare objective of reducing losses to Aruba's tourism business is only one of several possible goals and may not be the most appropriate for the island as a whole, let alone that of specific communities. But, whatever the goal, there may be ways of reducing the social and economic cost for some or all of the island's community by reallocating the reserves in the Alta Vista tank. This possibility is now explored using the full detail of the social accounting matrix, and suppositions about the response of the island's economy and community to shortfalls in income and water supply. The basic question being asked here is, if the island loses five days of water, how might the cutbacks be distributed in order to minimize the ensuing impacts to selected interests?

For purposes of comparison, we begin by calculating the impacts of an economy-wide six day loss of water supply. The loss of income to activities resulting from this uniform cutback are shown in column (a) of Table 3. In this case, the loss in income is distributed more or less proportionately across all activities; tourism, private sector, households and government. The income lost by the tourism sector is Afl 6.8 million, Afl 44.5 million is lost to local business and Afl 23.4 million by all households. These amounts depend upon the multipliers and cross-impacts for the various sectors. However, this calculation, and those that follow, are subject to several other considerations, now discussed, particularly how costs and trade-offs vary over time and across interests.

The importance of having continuous water supply lifelines varies across businesses (Tierney, 1993). Because of the vulnerability of water supply in Aruba, and its criticality to their own needs, some businesses have their own small reserve supplies usually lasting a few days. Thus, an allocated loss of so many days mains supply implies a smaller net loss. Restaurants and hotels will be impacted more rapidly than taxi services or telecommunications, for example. For most production

activities, a loss of a few days supply will not lead to a pro-rated loss in output since it is usually possible to stretch reduced supplies. The total economic impact on each activity will be determined by the short-term (direct) curtailment of its activities, plus the subsequent indirect loss from other sectors. A poultry farm, for example, may suffer a short-term loss in output (including loss of livestock), followed by decline in orders from hotels and the tourism sector because of early departures by tourists. But, after a few days without water some businesses will be obliged to shut-down temporarily, until service is restored, or suffer cancellations and loss of future business. If the business closes altogether, the potential loss will depend on the economic and human capital of the business, rather than its day-to-day running costs.

For households, the economic costs are almost entirely indirect, arising from loss of wage and entrepreneurial income. Nevertheless, there is direct hardship (non-economic costs) arising from loss of water supply, the disutility of which will eventually exceed that from loss of income. In the very short-run, minimum needs would come from other sources: for example, potable water can be purchased in shops, or waste water used for gardens. But few households, despite the prevalence of water reservoirs in some areas, could be totally without water for a week, even with major usage curtailed. Although supply may always be restored at a cost, the temporary nature of supply cutbacks and the resulting uncertainty makes this a matter of increasing irritation.

Such considerations imply that there is a non-linear relationship between the loss of water supply and the impact on activities, and also on employee income, purchase of inter-

Table 3: Impacts of Uniform and Programmed Allocations

Criteria	(a) Uniform allocat Schedule loss afim		(b) Favor tourism secotr Weight sched. loss afim			(c) Favor local economy Weigh sched. loss afim			(d) Favor all household Weight sched. loss afim			(e) Favor rural household Weight sched. loss afim			(f) Weighted interests Weight sched. loss afim		
Water loss (constraint)	151381		151381														
All lifelines	5.0	53.4		2.2	21.1		1.9	20.2		2.2	22.7		2.2	24.1		2.2	22.1
Tourism sector	5.0	6.8	1	0.6	0.2		1.6	0.8		1.7	1.6		1.7	2.4	2	1.8	1.3
All other sectors	5.0	44.5		1.1	4.9	1	0.3	1.5		3.4	24.2		3.5	40.9	1	2.2	15.2
Wages		11.8			1.1			0.6			4.4			8.5			3.0
Margins		12.1			1.3			0.5			5.5			11.1			3.5
All households	5.0	23.4		6.3	2.2		6.3	1.1	1	5.1	9.6		5.5	18.7		5.7	6.3
Rural	5.0	4.3		7.0	0.4		7.0	0.2		5.7	1.7	1	4.2	3.2	2	4.9	1.2
Urban	5.0	14.7		6.0	1.4		6.0	0.7		6.0	6.1		6.0	23.0	1	6.0	4.0
Local value added		26.7			2.6			1.4			11.0			21.8			7.3
Government	5.0	6.5		0.1	0.5		0.1	0.3		0.1	2.5		0.1	4.3		0.1	1.5
Objective	None		Minimize income loss			Minimize income loss			Minimize weighted welfare loss			Minimize weighted welfare loss			Minimize weighted welfare loss		

Notes: Some criteria and welfare items are mutually exclusive. Schedules are averaged by groups of activities'

mediate goods, household responses and so on. These may be dealt with in a number of ways, most straightforwardly as fixed limits on the number of days that an activity could be without water, before reaching a crisis point, taking into account its own reserves and temporary supplies. These limits stand as surrogates for a variety of the more extreme consequences arising from the event — bankruptcy, illness or death and so on. For the following calculations, the maximum loss of supply is shortest for lifeline and livelihood activities and the hotel sector (2 to 4 days). For most other business activities, the limit is taken to be 5 to 6 days, while for households it is taken to be 6 to 7 days. For some purposes, however, it also is useful to adopt a more explicit trade-off between economic and non-economic components of welfare loss.

Re-allocation of supply to reduce welfare loss

The results of the uniform five-day schedule now are used as a basis for comparison with four programmed responses in which different activities receive favorable treatment, subject to fixed constraints and competing welfare criteria. In addition to those just mentioned, a general constraint on these reallocations is that the *total* loss of supply by volume is the same as with the five-day uniform loss, noting here that the water company WEB applies price differentials by size of business, rental value of homes, amount used, as well as guaranteed supplies or special concessions to some major businesses, including some hotels.

Column (b) in Table 3 shows the revised schedule when cutbacks are designed to minimize the loss of income to the tourist industry. Such a schedule might be adopted in order to protect the interests represented by AHATA. Comparing (b) with (a) shows that this processes reduces the economic impact on all activities greatly. Loss of welfare to businesses is measured as lost income and, in this case, the impact on hotels is almost eliminated, reduced from Afl 23.4 million to Afl 0.2 million. In general, schedules favoring a particular production sector tend to reduce supply to activities with least income loss per unit of water supply. Since households do not generate income, the maximum allowed cutback in supply is passed to households. The outstanding loss is placed successively on activities with higher water utilization, up to the level of the various constraints. All sectors, including the favored sector, tourism, lose some income through indirect effects and will share in the direct cutbacks if this is required to satisfy the overall volume constraint. This pattern is seen also when the schedule favors

business activities in the local economy, shown in the third column (c) of Table 3. The principle change is a shift of financial loss from the local sector to the tourism sector. This shift in priorities might arise for example if the Aruba Chamber of Commerce, which represents local small businesses, could persuade the government that their interests should hold sway over those of AHATA and household interests.

The likelihood in Aruba of a swift reaction, in the media or through Aruba's effective patriarchal political system, might ensure that households would not be treated so arbitrarily. Thus, in contrast to the above, columns (d) to (e) in Table 3 show the result of calculations which favor households. In this case, it is assumed that the welfare loss to households is a trade-off between the loss of household income from employment and entrepreneurship and the irritation at losing water supply for an extended period and the non-economic loss. This is assumed to increase increasingly rapidly as the shortfall in supply is extended and, for purposes of calculation, is assumed to result in household malfunction that can be measured as a proportion of annual income. When all households are favored equally, as in column (d), the schedule tends to push the burden back onto businesses, although the net loss in supply to households is still greater than with uniform allocation. The important trade-off here is between the economic and the social cost — basically, how many days pass before the non-economic loss exceeds the economic loss? The shorter this period, the greater will be the cutbacks forced onto the business sector and the greater will be the loss of income to both businesses and households. When rural households are favored, as in column (e), the schedule tends to push the burden onto other households, and onto the local sector. In this example, some restoration of water supply is preferred at the expense of income. When the schedule favors urban households, the pattern between households becomes similar to case (c), reflecting the dependence of these households on entrepreneurial income from the local economy. Compared to the simple calculation shown in Table 2, these results suggest that particular components of the lifeline system might be used in a more cost-effective way.

Combining events and weighing interests

In the above examples, specific trade-offs have determined the schedule appropriate to particular interests. These interests also may be weighted to establish some broadly acceptable allocation, recognizing that there are several difficulties in balancing economic and non-economic utilities across competing interest groups. The simplest, and most common method is to weigh economic losses to the various interest groups uniformly; for example, by minimizing the loss to domestic value added, or that part of value added that is retained on the island. But if this is done subject to constraints, such as upper limits based on industry and other assessments, then it is evident that non-economic factors are implicitly included. This is equally the case when the future income expectations of the various actors are discounted to their present values at different rates. Thus, even this approach, as a variant of contingent valuation (Haneman, 1995), should be considered to be a multi-criteria (MCA) in the sense of Van der Veen et al (1994), rather than a cost-benefit analysis. In any case, as indicated above, the marginal costs to particular interests may be considered paramount, or deserving of greater weight. In this case, the re-scheduling of supply might necessitate weighing the various interests accordingly. Column (f) of Table 3, for example, illustrates the result of a hypothetical negotiation about how the various interests in Aruba might be traded off. In general, these are difficult issues to address, but reviewing trade-offs in the manner indicated earlier, may reveal preferences that are difficult to ascertain by other means. What matters here is that the final outcomes proposed can be understood by the various parties, and are acceptable to them. Once such trade-offs have been ascertained for several events, or negotiated across interest groups, the same mix of trade-offs can be adapted to determine their response to other events, which also may be reviewed through specific examples such as that shown in Table 2.

As emphasized in the introduction, disasters comprise a series of events and a given event might be assessed in the context of many disaster scenarios. Thus, an interruption in water supply in Aruba might come from a variety of contingencies — hurricanes, oil spills, mechanical breakdowns, all to be mitigated by the Alta Vista tank and other strategies. As long as consistency is maintained between the trade-offs and constraints, then the approach above may be extended to create a composite scenario, resulting from many actual failures and responses to them. To determine the risk value of a strategy, or a specific component of it, sets of events, each with a specified probability, must be combined together to provide an aggregate potential cost. There are here again a number of considerations, such as the treatment of non-additive cumulative effects, when events reinforce each other to create an

especially critical situation (for example, simultaneous damage to components of the supply system) or the assessment of risk for large events, of unknowable uncertainty, that go beyond the scope of the present paper.

In conclusion, it is emphasized that whether any particular response to a disaster is viable depends on technical, economic, political and social considerations. For example, the calculations in this paper suggest a number of ways of dealing with a breakdown in water supply in Aruba through re-allocation of water supply, but this possibility depends on the physical arrangement of mains pipelines, storage tanks and valves. Similarly, while the calculations suggest that major economic loss might be avoided if the burden of water shortage was passed to households, the viability of this would depend on the island's ability to organize emergency supplies for households. The non-economic hardship depends on the balance of essential, versus discretionary, water usage by households and the possibilities for assuring a minimum supply. The prevalence of many household reservoirs in rural areas in Aruba, for instance, suggests these could be used for emergency supplies in rural areas, but this, in turn, would only be effective if it took account of the social networks on the island and the degree of access provided to different communities. Calculations, such as those presented here, can provide information on outcomes that might be used to negotiate a mutually acceptable compromise for contested resources. Thus, although the approach taken in this paper has considered a specific example, this is to be set against the wider considerations for the management of natural disaster preparedness and relief strategies.

Note

1 This research was supported by the National Center for Earthquake Engineering and Research under National Science Foundation grant BCS 90-25010 and New York State Science and Technology Foundation grant NEC-91029. The author is grateful for advice from the Aruba Calamity Preparedness Committee, WEB, and AHATA. Responsibility for the paper remains with the author.

References

Adelman, I., Taylor, S. and Vogel, S. (1988), 'Life in a Mexican Village: A SAM Perspective', *Journal of Development Studies*, Volume 25, Number 1, pp. 5–24.

Berke, P. and Beatley, T. (1992), *Planning for*

Earthquakes: Risk, Politics and Policy, Johns Hopkins University Press, Baltimore.

Boisvert, R. (1992), 'Direct and Indirect Economic Losses from Lifeline Damage', in *Indirect Consequences of a Catastrophic Earthquake*, National Earthquake Hazards Reduction Program, FEMA, Washington, pp. 207–266.

Bon Dia Aruba (1993), *Trembelo di Aruba*, Press Report, January.

Brookshire, D. and McKee M. (1992), 'Indirect Loss Measurement and Computable General Equilibrium', in *Indirect Consequences of a Catastrophic Earthquake*, National Earthquake Hazards Reduction Program, FEMA, Washington, pp. 267–324.

Central Bank of Aruba (1990), *Annual Report*, Oranjestad.

CEP (1991), *Capital Expenditure Plan 1991–1995*, Department of Economic Affairs, Oranjestad.

Chang, S. (1983), 'Do Disaster Areas Benefit from Disasters?', *Growth and Change*, Volume 15, pp. 24–31.

Cochrane, H. (1975), *Natural Hazards and their Distributive Effects*, Monograph Number 3, Institute of Behavioral Studies, University of Colorado.

Cochrane, H. (1992), 'Overview of Economic Research on Earthquake Consequences', in *Forum on Consequences of a Catastrophic Earthquake*, National Research Council, Washington.

Cole, S. (1988), 'The Delayed Impacts of Plant Closures in a Reformulated Leontief Model', *Proceedings of the Regional Science Association*, Volume 65, pp. 135–149.

Cole, S. (1992), 'A Lagrangian Derivation of a General Multi-proportional Scaling Algorithm', *Regional Science and Urban Economics*, Volume 22, pp. 291–97.

Cole, S. (1993), 'Cultural Accounting for Small Economies', *Regional Studies*, Volume 27, Number 2, pp. 121–136.

Cole, S., Opdam, H., Van Veen, B., and Zambrano, R. (1983), 'A Social Accounting Matrix for Aruba', Mimeo, Instituut voor Toegepast Economisch Onderzoek (Department of Economic Development), Oranjestad, Aruba.

Cuny, F. (1983), *Disasters and Development*, Oxford University Press, Oxford.

Doukhan, P. and Leon, J. (1988), 'Parametric Methods for Evaluating Seismic Disturbance', *Revista Tecnica Intevep*, Volume 8, Number 1, pp. 13–22.

Ebert, C. (1982), 'Consequences of Disasters for Developing Nations', *Impact of Science on Society*, Volume 32, Number 1, pp. 93–100.

Ellson, R., Milliman, J. and Roberts, R. (1984), 'Measuring the Regional Economic Effects of Earthquakes and Earthquake Predictions', *Journal of Regional Science*, Volume 24, pp. 561–579.

Freisema, H., Caporaso, J., Goldstein, G., Lineberry, R. and McCleary, R. (1979), *Aftermath: Communities after Natural Disasters*, Sage, Beverly Hills.

French, S. and Isaacson, M. (1984), 'Applying Earthquake Risk Analysis Techniques to Land Use Planning', *Journal of the American Planning Association*, Volume 50, Number 2, pp. 509–522.

French, S. and Keown, S. (1993), 'Earthquake Risk Analysis', in Klosterman, R., Brail, R. and Bessard, R. (eds.), *Spreadsheet Models for Urban and Regional Analysis*, Rutgers University Press, New Brunswick, pp. 271–286.

Guimares, P., Hefner, F. and Woodward, D. (1992), 'Wealth and Income Effects of Natural Disasters: an Econometric Analysis of Hurricane Hugo', *Review of Regional Studies*, Volume 22, pp. 49–54.

Hanemann, W. (1995), 'Are Markets the Solution? Improving Environmental Policy', *Contemporary Economic Policy*, Volume 13, Number 1, January, pp. 74–79.

Hanson, K. and Robinson, S. (1989), *Data, Linkages, and Models*, US Department of Agriculture, Washington.

Jones, B. (1981), *Planning for Reconstruction of Earthquake-stricken Communities*, Peoples Republic of China-United States Joint Workshop, Beijing.

Jones, B. (1989), 'The Need for a Dynamic Approach to Planning for Reconstruction after Earthquakes', Mimeo, National Center for Southgate Engineering Research (NCEER 93-0002), Suny, Buffalo.

Jones, B. and Tomazevic, M. (1981), *Social and Economic Aspects of Earthquakes*, National Science Foundation/Yugoslav Board of Scientific and Technological Cooperation, Bled.

Kreimer, A. and Munasinghe, M. (Eds.) (1990), *Managing Natural Disasters and the Environment*, World Bank, Washington.

Kreimer, A. and Munasinghe, M. (1992), *Environmental Management and Urban Vulnerability*, World Bank, Washington.

Latham, E. (1984), *Direct and Indirect Impacts of Tourism on the Population of Aruba*, Tourism Department, Oranjestad.

Laylard, R. (1980), *Cost Benefit Analysis*, Penguin Modern Economics Readings, London.

Leontief, W. (1970), 'The Dynamic Inverse', in Carter A. and Brody A. (Eds.), *Contributions to Input-Output Analysis*, North-Holland, Amsterdam, pp. 17–46.

McCoy, J. (1990), 'Bauxite Processing and Employment: A Case Study of Jamaica', *Social and Economic Studies*, Volume 39, Number 2, pp. 1–47.

Miller, R. and Blair, P. (1985), *Input-Output Analysis: Foundations and Extensions*, Prentice Hall, New Jersey.

National Earthquake Hazard Reduction Program (NEHRP), (1992), *Indirect Consequences of a Catastrophic Earthquake*, FEMA, Washington.

National Research Council (NRC), (1989), *Estimating Losses from Future Earthquakes*, National Academy Press, Washington.

NCEER (1993), *Social Accounting For Disaster Preparedness and Recovery Planning*, National Center for Earthquake Engineering Research (NCEER 93-0002), SUNY, Buffalo.

Pyatt, G. and Roe, A. (1977), *Social Accounting Matrices for Development Planning with Special Reference to Sri Lanka*, Cambridge University Press, London and World Bank, Washington.

Ray, A. (1984), *Cost-Benefit Analysis: Issues and Methodologies*, World Bank, Washington.

Robinson, M. and Lahr, M. (1993), *A Guide to Sub-*

County Input-Output Modeling, Regional Science Association International, Houston.

Rose, A. and Benavides, J. (1993), *Inter-industry Models for Analyzing the Economic Impacts of Earthquakes and Recovery Policies*, Department of Mineral Economics, Pennsylvania State University.

Spinrad, B. (1981), *The Aruba Tourism Plan*, DECO, Oranjestad.

Stevens, B. and Lahr, M. (1988), 'Regional Economic Multipliers: Definition, Measurement and Application', *Economic Development Quarterly*, Volume 2, Number 1, pp. 88–96.

Taylor, L. (1979), *Models for Development Planning*, MIT Press, Cambridge.

Ten Raa T. (1986), 'Dynamic Input-output Analysis with Distributed Activities', *Review of Economic Statistics*, Volume 68, pp. 300–310.

Tierney, K. (1993), *Urban Seismic Risk Assessment*, Disaster Research Center, University of Delaware.

van der Veen, A., Green, C., Pflugner, W., and Wierstra, E. (1994), 'Appraisal Methods as Tools in Evaluating Responses to Long Term Climatic Changes: Cost Benefit Analysis and Multi-Criteria Analysis', *Journal of Coastal Engineering* (forthcoming).

West, C. and Lenze, D. (1993), *Modeling Natural Disaster and Recovery: An Impact Assessment of Regional Data and Impact Methodology in the Context of Hurricane Andrew*, Bureau of Business and Economic Research, Gainsville, University of Florida.

Part IV
Regional and Economy-Wide Impacts

[13]

JOURNAL OF REGIONAL SCIENCE, VOL. 24, NO. 4, 1984

MEASURING THE REGIONAL ECONOMIC EFFECTS OF EARTHQUAKES AND EARTHQUAKE PREDICTIONS*

Richard W. Ellson, Jerome W. Milliman, and R. Blaine Roberts†

1. INTRODUCTION AND OVERVIEW

The questions of what might be the potential economic effects of a major earthquake and the effects of a credible prediction of such an event have been the focus of considerable recent discussion and research [Cochrane (1974); National Academy of Sciences (1975, 1978); Brookshire and Schulze (1980); Edmonds (1982); Munroe and Ballard (1982); and Wilson (1982)]. In addition, a number of studies have focused upon the nature and magnitude of the long-run economic effects of natural disasters [Dacy and Kunreuther (1969); Cochrane (1975); Haas, Kates, and Bowden (1977); Friesma et al. (1979); Wright et al. (1979); and Wright and Rossi (1981)].

There are methodological deficiencies with each of these studies. Some of the research is defective because of the difficulty of generalizing from a few case studies and because the research does not take place until after the event has occurred. Second, much of the research is marred by the failure to have an adequate baseline forecast for the disaster period and for measuring long-run impacts. The correct comparison is "with and without" rather than a "before and after" look or a simple time-series extrapolation. Third, the economic techniques used for measuring economic effects have been regional economic models (often input-output models) that do not adequately deal with the supply-side constraints in terms of damage to regional capital stocks and transportation systems likely to result from a major earthquake. Fourth, most of the economic impact literature fails to make proper distinctions between measurement of losses and the measurement of longer-run patterns of personal income, employment, and population growth. Finally, much of the research has confused stock and flow concepts in the estimation of losses. Double counting is often involved, and the losses are not estimated in present value terms.

The research we discuss here corrects these deficiencies and presents a methodology for assessing both the short- and long-run regional economic effects—in terms of both loss estimation and long-run growth patterns of income, population, and employment relative to a baseline forecast. These estimates are

*This research has been supported by NSF grant PFR 80-19826 and by the College of Business Administration at the University of South Carolina. Jim Kleckley, Visiting Assistant Professor, University of South Carolina, provided valuable assistance in this project.

†Associate Professor of Economics, University of South Carolina; Professor of Economics, University of Florida; and Professor of Economics, University of South Carolina, respectively.

Date received: March, 1983; revised, July and October, 1983.

560 JOURNAL OF REGIONAL SCIENCE, VOL. 24, NO. 4, 1984

provided within the context of simulations involving an unanticipated quake, an anticipated quake, and also a false-alarm prediction. Without proper measures of expected losses to be averted to compare with extra costs of mitigation, one cannot determine the efficient level of earthquake mitigation. Reduction of earthquake hazards per se as discussed in the Earthquake Hazard Reduction Act of 1977 (Public Law 95-124) is not a proper basis for public policy.

We have developed a regional econometric model that is used to assess the potential economic effects of earthquakes and earthquake predictions. It is clear that traditional demand-oriented regional models are incapable of estimating the effects of a catastrophe that would likely have the greatest impact on supply-side factors. Accordingly, we have made several innovations to the traditional approach. First, we explicitly model such supply-side constraints as capital investment, housing starts, net migration, and transportation. Second, we have incorporated a reasonable degree of spatial disaggregation which shows how the economic consequences will vary across the region. Finally, although most regional models consist of simultaneous equation blocks, our model is fully simultaneous both within an individual county in the region and between the three counties that comprise the Charleston, S.C. SMSA under study.

A critic might point out, however, that our model is estimated from an economic structure (the 1965–1980 period) which does not include a response to a major earthquake or similar disaster. Surely, a major disaster would involve a change in the regional economic structure and, thus, the estimated regional model must be incapable of dealing with such an event. At first blush, this is a damaging criticism. It must be admitted that the criticism is valid for a truly catastrophic event which does dramatically change the economic structure of the region. However, we have examined the best estimates of damages now available for a major earthquake in the United States. It does not appear that the damages likely to be sustained in a large urban area (although substantial in size) are really outside the historical variability of the regional economy in response to more traditional shocks and cyclical fluctuations. For the regions as a whole, earthquake damages to capital and housing stocks are likely to be considerably less than 10 percent. The historical variability of the ratio of gross annual investment to capital stock for the Charleston SMSA has been as high as 23 percent and is expected to average about 14 percent in the baseline projection. Annual variability of housing start ratios to housing stock often exceeds 6 percent. All of the earthquake damages we can reasonably anticipate appear to be within the historical variability of the regional economy in the 1970's and well within the tolerance of the regional economy for replacement.

We report the results of four basic simulations of economic activity for the 1981–1990 period. The four simulations start with a baseline forecast followed by the simulation of an unanticipated quake occurring in 1983 using plausible damage assumptions and the replacement of damages sustained in the years following the event. The third simulation is a false alarm, a prediction without an occurrence. The last simulation is an anticipated quake (a correct prediction) to show the combined effects of dampened investment and net migration before the event along with mitigation followed by the recovery from the prediction and from the event. (Of course, many other simulations were run, but space limitations preclude a more comprehensive discussion here.)

In each simulation we analyzed the long-run growth paths of the regional economic aggregates and calculated the present value of losses relative to the baseline forecast. We specifically attempted to avoid double counting. However, we were forced to use a hybrid measure of stocks and flows because of data limitations.

Our results illustrate the contradictions in prior research. First, the regional economy proved to be quite resilient as long as the exogenous baseline assumptions were maintained. Starting from a point below the baseline trend, the stimulus of recovery can drive employment and personal income beyond the baseline forecast before converging back to it. Our second primary conclusion is that regional losses are still significant in present value terms. These losses are estimated with a combination of differential income flows from nonproperty income plus nonresidential capital income combined with capital stock losses in residential housing and social capital. Losses for each of the three counties comprising the SMSA were also estimated but are not reported here.

We need to point out that we have dealt only with economic losses that are readily measurable. We have not dealt with the social losses from deaths and injuries, nor have we taken into account social losses from trauma or dislocation. However, both the theoretical and empirical approaches we have taken do not conflict with these omissions and could be modified to take them into account if reasonable data are available.

Section 2 describes the Charleston econometric model. Section 3 describes the four basic simulations. Section 4 shows the simulation results in terms of regional population, employment, and income. Section 5 presents our estimates of regional losses for the three quake scenarios. Our concluding remarks appear in Section 6.

2. THE CHARLESTON ECONOMETRIC MODEL

Traditional urban econometric models are specified primarily to estimate the effects of marginal changes in aggregate demand. Following Glickman's (1971, 1977) pioneering work and subsequent enhancement of a model for the Philadelphia metropolitan area, some examples would include Fishkind, Milliman, and Ellson (1978), Rubin and Erickson (1980), and Duobinis (1981). The major contributions of these papers were to disaggregate the economic sectors traditionally modeled, to incorporate additional areas such as finance and resource sectors, and to develop fully simultaneous systems of equations. These efforts provided the framework for an array of urban policy simulations.

However, in situations of catastrophic change such as an earthquake, these models are inadequate for two primary reasons. First, we want to know not only the aggregate economic effects across the region, but the differential effects within the region. Thus, the model must be spatially disaggregated and fully simultaneous both within and between areas in the region. Second, in a natural disaster it is supply-side sectors that will dominate, including such factors as the housing and capital stocks, migration, and transportation. With some limitations, our model incorporates these two elements.

562   JOURNAL OF REGIONAL SCIENCE, VOL. 24, NO. 4, 1984

It is noted above that some researchers have used input-output models with fixed coefficients to estimate earthquake damages. In our view such an approach is inappropriate for the following reasons. First, the supply side of the economy is inadequately portrayed. Second, such models are inherently inflexible. For example, the final demand parameters do not capture the effects of various recovery scenarios. Thus, input-output models will tend to exaggerate losses from the earthquake, and the recovery process will be attenuated. Our results how that a regional economy is significantly more resilient than other studies have shown, and we believe that an econometric approach is necessary to capture this resiliency.

The Charleston (SC) SMSA is composed of three counties: Berkeley, Charleston, and Dorchester. Our model is not one model with three subareas, but three distinct models with appropriate simultaneous linkages. This bottom-up rather than top-down approach allows us to show differential economic effects of an earthquake within the region.

The data base for the model was developed entirely from secondary data sources, and annual observations were obtained from 1965–1980. Due to the changing character of the region, there were missing observations in some series, and these were interpolated with a spline function. The relatively small number of observations necessitated a simple lag structure where appropriate and a rather straightforward specification. The model was estimated with two-stage least squares using principal components. When serial correlation occurred, a Cochrane-Orcutt procedure was employed.

The model for the Charleston SMSA contains 217 equations. One hundred thirty-six of the equations are stochastic and eighty-one are identities. Of the 136 stochastic equations, 44 are for Charleston County, while Berkeley and Dorchester counties each account for 43 equations. The model contains 22 exogenous variables, 11 of which are national, and the remainder are state or regional in character. Three equations comprise the financial sector of the model. Unfortunately, consistent data were available only for savings and loan associations, and accordingly, commercial banks were not included. Finally, three equations estimate transportation flows between counties and within Charleston County.

The basic linkages of the county models are provided in Figure 1. In general, the specification of the model conforms to Fishkind, Milliman, and Ellson (1978). Each county model has (1) an employment block by one-digit SIC with the equations generally conforming to export base specifications, with the exception that manufacturing employment is dependent upon the value of product manufactured and the capital stock; (2) an income block for wage and salary disbursements by one-digit SIC and nonwage transfers, where the explanatory variables are one-digit SIC employment and a wage index; (3) a government block that includes revenues, expenditures and debt, where the equations are primarily based on population, interest rates, and the general level of economic activity.

However, our model also incorporates the following supply-side sectors for each of the counties. Included are: (1) manufacturing investment and capital stock, (2) migration, (3) transportation flows between the counties, (4) financial and capital flows, and (5) the housing sector. The endogeneity of these sectors is crucial to the economic assessment of earthquakes and earthquake predictions. A techni-

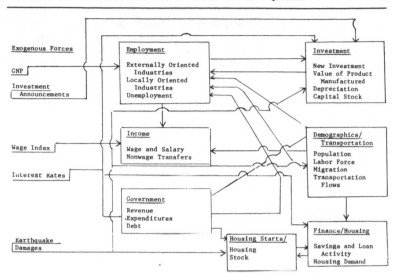

FIGURE 1:   Linkage of County Models.

cal discussion of our econometric model is available from the authors upon request.

3. THE FOUR BASIC SIMULATIONS OF THE CHARLESTON ECONOMETRIC MODEL

In this section we discuss four basic simulations provided by the econometric model—a baseline forecast and three earthquake scenarios for the 1981–1990 period. We simulate the effects of an unanticipated quake in 1983 with assumptions concerning damages and the recovery path. Our third simulation assumes that an event is predicted in 1981 to take place in 1983. The prediction is later declared to be erroneous. This simulation shows the dampening effects on the regional economy of a prediction. Our fourth simulation shows the effects of a prediction in 1981 for 1983 which proves to be correct, so we can see the effects of mitigation on damage reduction.

It is obvious that almost any number of simulations can be run to incorporate differential assumptions about the timing, location, and magnitude of responses and the severity of various quakes. These basic simulations incorporate reasonable assumptions and are generally reflective of the properties of the model.

The Baseline Simulation 1981–1990

The baseline forecast serves as the basis of comparison for the other simulations. It represents a regional forecast of economic activity witout a prediction or a catastrophic event. This is simply a traditional forecast. The forecasted values of the exogenous variables are held constant through the remaining simulations. Briefly, we expect the Charleston economy in the 1981–1990 period to experience a relatively rapid rate of growth given our assumptions of a 3 percent real growth rate in national GNP. In the first four years total employment in the region is predicted to increase at an annual rate of 6 percent, which equals the growth rate in the prior decade. This rate of growth is exceeded in the 1985–1990 period. The capital stock in manufacturing, which rose by 131 percent from 1970–1980, jumps another 205 percent in the next decade. Real total personal income growth is projected to be close to that of the past decade. The average annual growth rate was 6.2 percent from 1970–1980, and it would fall somewhat to 4.1 percent under our assumptions. Population growth in the region, which averaged 2.8 percent annually in the 1970's, would rise to 3 percent in the 1981–1990 period.

The Unanticipated Quake Simulation

In this simulation an earthquake is assumed to strike the region in 1983 with no prior warning. The quake is assumed to be centered in Charleston County and to be roughly of the same magnitude as the 1886 event with an average Modified Mercalli intensity of VII for the three-county region. Damage assumptions and loss estimates for the unanticipated quake simulation are shown in Table 1. In this simulation an optimistic view is assumed about the recovery path in that the damage to the housing stock and to the capital stock sustained in the event is assumed to be fully replaced in 1984, 1985, and 1986 as shown in the replacement ratios in Table 1. Thus, the lost structures are assumed to be cost-effective and will be replaced. This replacement is in addition to investment in housing and capital stock predicted by the model.

The unanticipated quake will have the effect of reducing the stock variables in the model and will also damage the transportation network. We have assumed higher levels of destruction in Charleston County because of the greater age of the building stock, more multifamily housing structures, and the greater vulnerability of the transportation system.

The risk of death in an earthquake varies with the time of occurrence and depends on whether the population is at home or at work. Brookshire and Schulze (1980) quote studies of a major earthquake on the San Andreas fault in Los Angeles with likely deaths as low as 32 per 100,000 population. This would mean a loss of 297 persons. We have assumed higher estimates. Charleston's rate is taken as 100 per 100,000 or 292 deaths. For Berkeley and Dorchester Counties, with lower risk factors, the death rate we use is 50 per 100,000 persons. This results in 52 deaths in Berkeley County and 32 in Dorchester County. Total death loss for the three-county area is 378 persons.

Damage to buildings varies with height, age of building, and type of construction. Single-family woodframe structures are less affected by ground shaking, but those with fireplaces and chimneys suffer more damage. Commercial-industrial structures and multifamily dwellings are more vulnerable. Brookshire and Schulze (1980) estimate that the average ground-shaking intensity of a Mercalli VII for Los Angeles County would give an approximate damage of 3.5 percent of replacement cost to single-family dwellings and a 5 percent damage for commercial structures.

TABLE 1:   Damage Assumptions and Loss Estimates for Two
Unanticipated Quake Scenarios

Death Rate		Deaths
Charleston County	100/100,000	292
Berkeley County	50/100,000	52
Dorchester County	50/100,000	34
		378 total
Housing Stock Damage		Units Destroyed
Charleston County	6.5%	6,754
Berkeley County	4.0%	1,487
Dorchester County	4.0%	945
		9,186 total
Capital Stock Damage		Losses (Millions of Dollars)
Charleston County	8.0%	22.8
Berkeley County	7.0%	103.5
Dorchester County	7.0%	8.4
		134.7 total
Transportation Flows (Annual)		Trips Lost (Thousands)
Charleston County	10.0%	17.6
Berkeley County	5.0%	7.0
Dorchester County	5.0%	1.5
		26.1 total

If replacement of damaged housing and capital stock takes place (The "Replacement" Scenario)

	1984	1985	1986
Capital Stock Replacement (percent)	42	42	16
Housing Stock Replacement (percent)	42	42	16

These are blended rates based on the age of structure, degree of reinforcement, and building height.

For our unanticipated quake scenario in Table 1, we have assumed that damage to housing stock is 6.5 percent in Charleston County and 4 percent in Berkeley and Dorchester Counties. The loss of housing stock in Charleston County is equivalent to 6,754 units. In Berkeley County 1,487 units are lost and 945 units are destroyed in Dorchester County. The total loss of housing is 9,186 units. That compares to a baseline forecast of 164,750 housing units for the three-county region in 1983.

Regarding manufacturing in Table 1, for capital stock, which covers plant, equipment, and inventory, we have assumed that the damages are 8 percent in Charleston County and 7 percent in Berkeley and Dorchester counties. These damage rates are influenced by the presence of a number of wholly or partially reinforced concrete and brick commercial structures in the region. Earthquake-resistant building codes are not in force in the region. The capital stock losses are estimated at $103.5 million in Berkeley County, $22.8 million in Charleston County, and $8.4 million in Dorchester for a total of $134.7 million. Most of the manufacturing plants are located in Berkeley County.

Finally, we assume that damage to the bridges and highways in the area will be severe at least in the short run. We suspect that initial transportation flows within Charleston County will decline 25 percent and the Berkeley to Charleston and Dorchester to Charleston flows will decline 10 percent. However, with repairs to roads, bridges, and overpasses taking place, we assume that on an annual basis, transportation flows within Charleston County will be down 10 percent for all of 1983 and down 5 percent for each of the outlying counties. The trips lost as seen in Table 1 will be largely in Charleston County and are 26,100 for the region as a whole.

The False Alarm: A Prediction Without an Occurrence

The third basic simulation assumes that a prediction is made in 1981 indicating an earthquake will take place in 1983. During the next 24 months following the prediction, revisions and an update of the prediction are assumed to be presented to the public similar to the scenarios in Mileti, Hutton, and Sorrensen (1981). During this period we assume that capital investment in manufacturing, new housing starts, and net migration fall off at an increasing rate as 1983 approaches. We assume that the effects of the prediction on these variables are invariant across counties.

Finally, we assume that late in 1983, the official government agencies decide that the prediction has been based upon incorrect assumptions and that the entire prediction is in error. In effect, an "all clear" signal is given, and people are told to proceed as normal. We assume that the reduced investments in the 1981–1983 period are totally regained in the 1984–1986 period. The rationale for this is that investments are assumed to occur in the region because they are optimal. After the all-clear prediction is made, the investments that were not made become optimal again.

The specific add factors regarding this false-alarm scenario are shown in Table 2.

TABLE 2: Loss and Recovery Estimates—Prediction Without Occurrence

	1981	1982	1983	1984	1985	1986
Capital Investment	(10)	(20)	(40)	30	30	10
Housing Starts	(10)	(20)	(40)	30	30	10
Net Migration	(5)	(15)	(30)	20	20	10

These figures are approximately equal to the percentage changes from the baseline scenario. (They are not exactly percentage changes because of changing bases over time.) In other words, there is a cumulative decline of about 70 percent of annual housing starts in the 1981–1983 period. About 40 percent of the housing starts not made in the 1981–1983 period are added to the 1984 baseline level, with the remainder added in 1985 and 1986.

We do not have any scientific way of verifying the assumptions about the decline in capital investment, housing starts, and net migration for the false-alarm simulation. We have studied the scenario reactions to prediction of an earthquake in California developed by Mileti, Hutton, and Sorrenson (1981), and our numbers are consistent with their description of public and private sector reactions, although more research is needed in this area.

The economic effects of the incorrect prediction are estimated by the model by county and by year. For example, reduced capital investment for the three-county area for the three-year period is estimated at $133.7 million with Berkeley County taking the brunt at $107.6 million. By contrast, new capital investment in Dorchester County is down only $4.2 million.

Total net in-migration for the three-county region is down 3318 persons over the 1981–1983 period. Charleston County net in-migration losses are 1206, Berkeley County losses are 984, and Dorchester County net in-migration is down 1128 persons. Housing starts for the three regions for the 1981–1983 period are off 6137 units.

The Anticipated Quake: A Correct Prediction

This fourth simulation incorporates features of the recovery with replacement from the unanticipated quake plus the mitigation and dampening effects of the prediction from the false-alarm scenario (the third simulation) discussed above. A prediction is made in 1981 for an earthquake to occur in 1983. The specific assumptions regarding reductions in capital investment, housing starts, and net migration are assumed to hold for 1981, 1982, and 1983 because of the prediction. For example, housing starts and new capital investment for 1981, 1982, and 1983 are reduced 10, 20, and 40 percent from the baseline calculations.

After the quake takes place in 1983, the recovery takes place in 1984, 1985, and 1986. The recovery is assumed to compensate for the losses in activity prior to the quake plus the full replacement of damages suffered by the quake in 1983. Thus, the specific assumptions of this scenario exactly track those of the prediction and the unanticipated earthquake with replacement.

TABLE 3: Damage Assumptions for Simulations of Unanticipated Versus Anticipated Earthquake

	Unanticipated Earthquake	Prediction (Mitigation): Anticipated Earthquake
Death Rate		
Charleston County	100/100,000	50/100,000
Berkeley, Dorchester Counties	50/100,000	25/100,000
Housing Stock Damage		
Charleston County	6.5%	5.5%
Berkeley, Dorchester Counties	4.0%	3.0%
Capital Stock Damage		
Charleston County	8.0%	6.0%
Berkeley, Dorchester Counties	7.0%	4.5%
Transportation Flows (Annual)		
Charleston County	10.0%	8.0%
Berkeley, Dorchester Counties	5.0%	4.0%

568   JOURNAL OF REGIONAL SCIENCE, VOL. 24, NO. 4, 1984

TABLE 4:   Selected Damages for Charleston SMSA in Simulations of
           Unanticipated Versus Anticipated Earthquake

	Unanticipated Earthquake	Prediction (Mitigation): Anticipated Earthquake
Deaths		
Charleston	292	145
Berkeley	52	27
Dorchester	378	189
Total	378	189
Housing Stock—Units Destoyed		
Charleston	6,754	5,625
Berkeley	1,487	1,055
Dorchester	945	684
Total	9,186	7,364
Capital Stock—Losses in Millions of Dollars		
Charleston	22.8	17.1
Berkeley	103.5	66.5
Dorchester	8.4	5.4
Total	134.7	89.0
Trips Lost—Thousands		
Charleston	17.6	14.0
Berkeley	7.0	5.6
Dorchester	1.5	1.2
Total	26.1	20.8

During the 1981–1983 period, it is assumed that various mitigation measures are undertaken which will reduce the damage assumptions we used above for the unanticipated quake. Table 3 shows the differences in damage assumptions between the scenarios for the unanticipated quake and the prediction (mitigation) quake or anticipated simulation. The differential damages resulting from these different damage assumptions between an unanticipated quake and an anticipated quake are seen above in Table 4.

Finally, we should point out that the comparisons shown in Table 4 only show the damage effects of the earthquakes themselves—one anticipated and the other unanticipated. But, as we noted above, the effect of a prediction is to reduce economic activity in advance of the predicted event. Thus, despite some increases in expenditures for induced mitigation measures, the prediction itself will dampen housing starts and new capital investment. The net effect on the capital stock depends on the differences in the quake damages between the two events (one anticipated, one not) and the prequake dampening effects on new investment in capital stock and housing units of the prediction.

Table 5 illustrates the seeming paradox of the regional economy at the end of 1983 having less housing stock and less capital investment in the prediction-quake scenario compared to the unanticipated quake simulation. It can be seen that the

TABLE 5: Reductions in Housing and Capital Stock at End of 1983: Unanticipated Versus Anticipated Quake Simulations

	Unanticipated Earthquake	Prediction (Mitigation): Anticipated Earthquake		
		From Prediction	From Quake	Total
Housing Stock (Units)	9,186	6,137	7,364	13,501
Capital Stock (Millons of Dollars)	$134.7	$133.7	$89.0	$222.7

assumed dampening effects of predictions on new expenditures prior to the quake produce reductions in stocks that are almost as large as the physical damages from the quakes themselves. Certainly, the reductions in stock from baseline because of the predictions are greater than the savings from the mitigation measures we have assumed.

There are several comments to make on this apparent paradox. First, it is possible that we have been too severe in our estimates of the dampening effect of a prediction on new investment. This is possible because the damage coefficients we have assumed for the quake (both versions) are relatively small in relation to the annual new investments in capital stock and housing. Second, we also may not have assumed sufficient reduction in damage due to mitigation measures. A third factor is that Table 5 stops the comparison in 1983, and therefore is unfair. What is more relevant is a 1990 comparison. By that time we can take into account the boost to the regional economy which may come about from twin measures: (1) investment pressures for new housing and capital stock postponed by the dampening effects of the prediction; and (2) the pressures and resources for reconstruction and rebuilding of damaged physical plant. The correct perspective should include these two factors.

TABLE 6: Simulation Results for Total Population—Charleston SMSA

Year	Baseline	Unanticipated Quake (With Full Replacement)	Prediction Without Occurrence (With Full Replacement)	Quake Anticipated (With Full Replacement)
1981	439,157	439,157	438,862	438,862
1982	450,995	450,995	449,921	449,921
1983	463,116	461,606	460,265	459,247
1984	475,527	468,932	473,029	467,897
1985	488,384	483,097	486,207	481,898
1986	501,838	497,459	499,178	495,438
1987	516,072	513,449	513,063	510,519
1988	531,226	530,299	527,931	526,564
1989	547,247	547,822	543,706	543,392
1990	564,804	566,616	561,051	561,609

570   JOURNAL OF REGIONAL SCIENCE, VOL. 24, NO. 4, 1984

TABLE 7: Simulation Results for Total Nonfarm Employment—Charleston SMSA

Year	Baseline	Unanticipated Quake (With Full Replacement)	Prediction Without Occurrence (With Full Replacement)	Quake Anticipated (With Full Replacement)
1981	152,714	152,714	152,521	152,521
1982	157,640	157,640	156,743	156,743
1983	164,169	163,742	161,220	160,939
1984	172,587	172,731	168,415	168,587
1985	182,445	186,541	178,330	181,094
1986	194,489	201,596	190,333	195,024
1987	206,688	217,454	204,316	209,982
1988	225,787	235,161	221,080	226,991
1989	246,374	255,682	241,284	246,974
1990	270,698	279,479	265,172	270,324

4. SIMULATIONS OF THE REGIONAL ECONOMY 1981–1990

In this section we compare the effects of the three earthquake simulations with the baseline simulation in terms of the projections of total population, total nonfarm employment, and total personal income for the Charleston SMSA over the 1981–1990 period. Even though the regional losses sustained (as shown in the section below) are substantial, one is struck by the resiliency of the regional economy and its ability to recover from an earthquake disaster and the prediction of one even when pessimistic assumptions are employed. What is clear is that the health of the regional economy is determined more by the assumptions one makes about the national (exogenous) growth factors driving the regional economy than by the disruptive effects of an earthquake whose severe effects are largely temporary and tend to dimish over the longer run.

Although this finding may seem intuitively obvious, it stands in contrast to the existing literature. On the other hand, Cochrane (1975), Edmonds (1982), and

TABLE 8: Simulation Results for Personal Income—Charleston SMSA (Billions of Dollars)

Year	Baseline	Unanticipated Quake (With Full Replacement)	Prediction Without Occurrence (With Full Replacement)	Quake Anticipated (With Full Replacement)
1981	3.441	3.441	3.440	3.440
1982	3.797	2.797	3.788	3.788
1983	4.210	4.205	4.180	4.177
1984	4.684	4.672	4.641	4.636
1985	5.213	5.233	5.172	5.190
1986	5.821	5.866	5.780	5.816
1987	6.511	6.573	6.467	6.514
1988	7.311	7.381	7.262	7.314
1989	8.241	8.315	8.186	8.239
1990	9.303	9.377	9.240	9.293

Munroe and Ballard (1982), all using fixed coefficient input-output models, state that recovery will be slow and difficult. On the other hand, Friesma et al. (1979) and Wright et al. (1979) find that disasters leave no long-run economic effects. However, in these studies the disaster examined did not seriously damage the economic base of the communities involved. Also, all of the findings were derived in ad hoc fashion without the use of structural models of the regional or urban economies involved.

Tables 6, 7, and 8 show the baseline projection for the Charleston SMSA, the unanticipated quake (1983), the prediction without an occurrence, and the anticipated quake (1983) over the 1981–1990 period. In Table 6 the simulation results for total population are given. The baseline projection shows an increase of 125,647 persons over the decade or an average annual increase of about 2.86 percent. For the unanticipated quake simulation the population effects show up in 1983 when there are quake-induced deaths and a slight fall in net migration. In 1984, net migration to the region continues to decline, but in the following years we can see that total population begins to catch up to the baseline figure so that the baseline population is actually exceeded in 1989 and 1990. The reason for this is seen in Tables 7 and 8 which show that the employment and income effects of the recovery from the disaster (which include full replacement of damaged housing and capital stock) drive the economy above the baseline figure.

For the false alarm (prediction without occurrence) and the anticipated quake simulations, Table 6 shows the population differentials compared to the baseline appear in 1981, 1982, and 1983 because of the effects of the prediction on net migration. In both prediction simulations population growth is resumed in 1984. By 1990 all four simulations show a Charleston SMSA population in excess of 560,000 with the difference in the totals from highest to lowest being 5565 persons—approximately 1 percent.

Perhaps the most important Table is 7 because it is regional employment (for the most part) that drives net migration, and it is regional employment that is a major determinant of movements in personal income. The contrasts across the four simulations of total nonfarm employment in Table 7 really tell the tale of the regional economy. By 1990 Table 7 shows that total employment exceeds the baseline employment in the unanticipated quake scenario, just about equals baseline employment in the anticipated quake scenario, and is about 1.8 percent below it in the false-alarm simulation.

What the simulations show is that the dampening effects of the prediction (correct or false) we have assumed over 1981, 1982, and 1983 put brakes on employment not seen in either the baseline or the unanticipated quake simulations. Given these dampening effects, the full replacement assumptions do serve as stimulants to building and reconstruction in 1984, 1985, and 1986, so the economy is pulled toward the baseline simulation. In the anticipated quake simulation, the reconstruction of damaged stock is sufficient to stimulate the economy to make up more than the postponed investment from the false alarm and in fact to put it ahead of the baseline projection in 1986, 1987, and 1988.

The most interesting simulation in Table 7 is the unanticipated quake with full replacement or recovery of damages assumed over the 1984, 1985, and 1986 period. With the stimulus to the economy from repair and replacement of housing and capital stock, employment in this quake simulation is only slightly below the baseline in 1983, and by 1985 it has shot ahead of the baseline employment. Because a prior prediction was not made, the economy started from a higher level when reconstruction began and the amount of reconstruction from the higher damage assumptions is sufficient to stimulate employment to drive it ahead of the baseline very rapidly. Note especially the comparison of employment in the unanticipated quake simulation compared to the baseline employment when the absolute and percentage differences are very large in 1987 and 1988. Also, we can see that the stimulative effects begin to taper off, and by 1990, while the unanticipated quake simulation is still ahead of the baseline, the differences decline, and the regional economy begins to approach its baseline growth path.

At this point, we urge the reader not to jump to the conclusion that the unanticipated quake shows a desirable outcome because it has higher nonfarm employment and somewhat higher total personal income. In the following section we show regional losses. We will show that, despite the stimulus to employment brought about by full replacement of damaged capital stock and housing in the unanticipated quake scenario, regional losses in present value terms (compared to baseline values) substantially exceed the losses of both the anticipated quake and the false-alarm simulation. Also, as expected, the smallest regional losses are seen in the false-alarm simulation which has no earthquake. We need to stress that recovery from earthquakes and their predictions may stimulate employment and construction and drive up labor and business income, but this is not sufficient to offset the very real and substantial income and wealth losses to the region caused by the event. This important point is not made in the literature cited in the first paragraph of this paper. Note also that the social losses in terms of death, injuries, trauma, and dislocation of people, which we have not counted, should also be considered.

Table 8 shows the simulations of personal income for the Charleston SMSA over the 1981–1990 period for the four simulations. In the baseline simulation, personal income growth in real terms rises about 4 percent a year over the decade. The employment effects seen in Table 7 drive up construction salaries, wages, and profits more than enough to offset components of personal income such as interest, rent, and dividends which are adversely affected by the damage sustained in the quake simulations. The net effect is that the personal income path in Table 8 closely follows the employment results seen in Table 7 across the four simulations. However, the differences are less pronounced because personal income figures pick up some losses not shown in employment totals per se.[1]

Tables 9 and 10 illustrate the relation of our damage assumptions to the capital and housing stock at risk and to annual investments in capital plant and equipment and housing. Table 9 shows the relation of gross investment in the

---

[1]We also considered the cases of an unanticipated quake and double damages both without recovery. The growth paths of population, employment, and personal income are not drastically lower compared to the simulations with replacement. This reinforces our belief that the strength of national exogenous forces is the key determinant of recovery.

TABLE 9:   Relation of Gross Investment to Capital Stock and Damage Assumptions

	Gross Investment (Millions of Dollars)	Capital Stock (Millions of Dollars)	Ratio (GI/CS)
1970	78.7	337.4	23.3%
1975	76.9	547.3	14.1
1980	205.8	1,511.4	13.6
1985*	327.4	2,388.2	13.7
1990*	636.3	4,573.1	13.9

Damage Assumptions to Capital Stock		
	Unanticipated Quake	Anticipated Quake
Charleston County	8.0%	6.0%
Berkeley, Dorchester Counties	7.0	4.5

*Baseline forecast

three-county region to capital stock and to the standard assumptions we employed. The damage assumptions to capital we have used for the unanticipated quake are approximately only half of the ratio of estimated annual gross investment to capital stock under normal conditions. Although this is not a conclusive indicator of the resilience of the economy, it is indicative of the fact that the capital stock damage appears on the surface, at least, to be well within the tolerance of the regional economy for replacement.

Table 10 shows the ratio of housing starts (real and estimated) to total units of housing stock. Again, the damage assumptions we have used for the anticipated quake appear to be of approximately the same magnitude. In fact, the cyclical variation in housing starts over a boom-recession cycle is likely to be more than

TABLE 10:   Relation of Housing Starts to Housing Stock and Damage Assumptions

	Housing Starts	Housing Stock (Units)	Starts/Stock
1970	2,971	103,033	2.9%
1975	2,976	124,056	2.4
1980	6,790	151,855	4.5
1985*	11,322	180,958	6.3
1990*	16,313	236,247	6.9

Damage Assumptions to Housing Stock		
	Unanticipated Quake	Anticipated Quake
Charleston County	6.5%	5.5%
Berkeley, Dorchester Counties	4.0	3.0

*Baseline forecast

574   JOURNAL OF REGIONAL SCIENCE, VOL. 24, NO. 4, 1984

TABLE 11:   Present Value of Regional Losses With Full Replacement, Charleston SMSA (Millions of Dollars)

	Unanticipated Quake (Full Replacement)	Anticipated Quake (Full Replacement)	Prediction Without Occurrence (Full Replacement)
Regional Nonproperty Income	(91.641)	81.106	163.388
Labor and Proprietor Income	(149.365)	69.740	194.452
Commuter Income	44.015	14.485	(16.344)
Transfer Payments	13.710	(3.118)	(14.720)
Nonresidential Regional Capital Income	177.562	162.281	130.363
Residential Housing	523.345	415.415	0
Social Capital	391.090	241.331	0
Total	1000.360	900.133	293.751

Note: Totals may not add due to rounding. Gains are in parentheses.

enough to cover the extra damage to the stock of housing, particularly if some allowance is made for a likely influx of construction firms and labor from other regions following the event.

5.   ESTIMATES OF REGIONAL LOSSES FOR FIVE EARTHQUAKE SIMULATIONS

In this section we present estimates of regional losses for the three-county SMSA region as a whole for each of the three earthquake simulations relative to the baseline simulation. We again emphasize that these results depend upon the maintenance of external demands and that the supply of inputs is relatively elastic for the region. Under certain conditions, however, it is plausible that relative costs for the region could increase. In the short run some wage and materials costs could be bid up, but these would be of a transitory nature. A more serious problem is property taxes, which could increase significantly if financial transfers are not forthcoming, but the evidence for the U.S. and most developed nations [Freisma et al. (1979) and Wright et al. (1979)] suggests otherwise. Moreover, regional costs will depend upon the extent of damage relative to the size of the economy. We have shown that the worst case involves less than 15 percent of the capital stocks, and that replacement rates are a significant proportion of expected losses.[2]

The first category of losses as seen in Table 11 is regional nonproperty income which is composed of three parts: labor and proprietor income, commuter income, and transfer payments. Commuter income is the adjustment made in earnings reported by place of residence. Transfer payments are government transfer payments such as social security, welfare, and unemployment benefits.

[2]These issues were raised by our referee who cited the situation at Three Mile Island, Long Island, and potentially the WPSS region. Extraordinary rate increases to consumers will reduce the competitiveness of these regions, particularly for energy-intensive industries. Using an elasticity supplied by our referee, a permanent 10 percent increase in property taxes in the Charleston region will reduce export employment by roughly 120 jobs.

The second category of losses is nonresidential regional capital income. The private nonresidential regional capital stock is estimated to be a constant multiple (5.3) of manufacturing capital. The return on nonresidential regional capital (11.39 percent) is then a blend of the average corporate interest rate and the rate of return on equity. These two categories of income losses reported in Table 11 are losses resulting from the disruption of economic activity and damage to capital stock. These income changes relative to the baseline have been converted to present value terms by a discount rate of 11.39 percent.

The third and fourth categories of loss shown in Table 11 are best estimated directly in terms of capital losses (stocks) rather than income flows. Here the basis of loss is taken to be estimated replacement costs of residential housing units destroyed or damaged and the damage to regional social capital from the quake simulations. Ideally, we would like to measure the willingness to pay for such capital, but this cannot be done so that estimates of replacement cost set an upper bound. Losses of consumer durables are assumed to be 60 percent of housing stock damaged. Social capital in the Charleston region is assumed to be 68 percent of private nonresidential capital.

Again, we emphasize that Table 11 shows the present value of losses over the 1981–1990 period relative to the baseline simulation. Note carefully that numbers in parentheses are thus to be interpreted as *gains*, not losses. Table 11 deserves careful study. First, note the bottom line. The unanticipated quake (with full replacement assumed) has regional losses of $1 billion; the anticipated quake, involving a prediction with dampening effects on investment in 1981, 1982, and 1983 plus a quake in 1983 (with full replacement of investment) has net losses of $900 million; finally, the false-alarm scenario has regional losses of approximately $294 million due to dampening effects upon investment and net migration in 1981, 1982, and 1983 although full replacement over 1984, 1985 and 1986 is assumed.

A study of Table 11 shows that these regional losses are dominated first by capital losses in residential housing, then by losses in social capital, and third by the present value of income losses from nonresidential private capital. This means that one can get a quick notion of regional losses by first looking at these three categories of loss.

For most readers, some explanation of labor and proprietor income will prove interesting. As can be seen in Table 11, labor and proprietor income for the unanticipated 1983 quake is *positive* in present value terms by approximately $149 million. Also, the losses in labor and proprietor income for the anticipated quake are *less* than the losses in labor and proprietor income from an incorrect prediction and no quake at all! How can these apparently strange results be explained?

The answer is that the stimulus to employment and reconstruction stemming from the disaster (with full replacement assumed to take place in 1984, 1985, and 1986) is sufficient to increase labor and proprietor income relative to our rather optimistic baseline projection of employment and income. Cochrane (1975) was quite concerned about the distributive effects of adjustments to natural hazards, and he pointed out that little is known about the distribution impacts of a disaster upon the construction industry. Our simulations provide evidence that destruction of housing and capital stock appear to stimulate labor and proprietor income (we

576   JOURNAL OF REGIONAL SCIENCE, VOL. 24, NO. 4, 1984

TABLE 12: Present Value of Regional Losses With Alternative Replacement and Damage Assumptions, Charleston SMSA (Millions of Dollars)

	Unanticipated Quake (Full Replacement)	Unanticipated Quake (No Replacement)	Double Damages (No Replacement)
Regional Nonproperty Income	(91.641)	105.246	210.720
Labor and Proprietor Income	(149.365)	97.494	195.524
Commuter Income	44.015	10.727	20.760
Transfer Payments	13.710	(2.975)	(3.563)
Nonresidential Regional Capital Income	177.562	308.010	616.117
Residential Housing	523.345	523.345	1046.690
Social Capital	391.090	391.096	782.280
Total	1000.360	1327.7	2655.810

Note: Totals may not add due to rounding. Gains are in parentheses.

earlier saw the effects on regional employment) even though there are net regional losses of substantial amounts.

The full replacement assumption does not deal directly with the question of federal policy and outside aid for relief and reconstruction. We also have not examined the role of insurance. Thus, we do not consider the full range of distribution issues posed by Cochrane (1975).

Table 12 shows the present value of regional losses for the unanticipated quake under full replacement, with no replacement, and with double damages and no replacement. As we should expect, regional losses rise from $1 billion to $1.3 billion (no replacement) to $2.65 billion (with double damages). With less than full replacement, the unanticipated quake now shows losses in labor and proprietor incomes because the stimulus effect to the local economy from reconstruction is much reduced.

Table 12 tells us that policies that encourage rebuilding, such as disaster insurance and special aid, can have a substantial effect on regional income losses and the recovery path. This substantiates the case study findings of Dacy and Kunreuther (1969). In Table 12 we can see that the losses from the no-replacement assumption exceed the losses of the unanticipated quake with full replacement by an amount in excess of 30 percent ($1 billion vs. $1.3 billion). Thus, regional losses from a disaster appear to be very sensitive to assumptions we make about replacement of damage and the recovery path. However, Table 12 also tells us that the bulk of the regional losses (even when income and employment effects of reconstruction are taken into account) are based upon the damage estimates to housing and capital stock assumed to be caused by the event.

In addition, it is important to remember that both Tables 11 and 12 show that the dampening effects of a prediction, which is believed, can have substantial negative effects on regional income and employment. As Table 11 shows, the gains (less losses) of a correct prediction over an unanticipated quake are less than the losses of an incorrect prediction. These results stem, of course, from the rather sharp cutbacks we assumed in investment in housing and capital and in net migration in 1981, 1982, and 1983 because of a credible prediction. Nevertheless, our results do suggest that the dampening effects of a prediction even though it may reduce damages from a correctly predicted event (compared to an unanticipated event) must be carefully considered.

6. CONCLUDING REMARKS

The purpose of this paper is to assess the regional economic effects of a major earthquake and the prediction of one. We have presented the results of three simulations: an unanticipated quake, an anticipated quake, and a false-alarm prediction for the Charleston, SC metropolitan area. We have estimated losses (using care not to double count stocks and flows) in present value terms for the 1981–1990 period. Predictions are made in 1981 for a quake to take place in 1983. All results are compared to a baseline forecast for the 10-year period. We also have tracked the growth path of the regional economy in terms of population (including net migration), employment, and personal income for each of the various simulations. We make distinctions between losses that are incurred and situations where income and employment rise above the baseline simulation in the case of the unanticipated quake.

To accomplish this task we have devised a regional econometric model which explicitly models supply-side constraints such as investment, capital stock, housing stock and starts, net migration, and transportation flows. We have also devised a methodology to correctly measure losses, not only from the disaster itself but also for a prediction including a seven-year recovery period following the event. With the regional model, improved measures of losses, and with 10-year simulations, we believe that we have corrected for the major deficiencies in existing research on the economic effects of a major earthquake. We also have substantially added to the general literature on the long-run economic effects of natural disasters.

Some of the major findings of our study are what one might intuitively expect; other findings seem paradoxical or puzzling at first blush. Despite the shock of a major quake assumed to take place in 1983, we find that the regional economy is quite resilient and that it can recover to baseline levels by 1990—as long as the national forces driving the regional economy (which are assumed in the baseline projection) remain the same. An important factor influencing the long-run growth recovery path is the degree of reconstruction following the event. In fact, under the impetus of reconstruction, labor and proprietors incomes can rise above baseline levels in the recovery. These gains in personal incomes in the post-quake period can offset income lost during the disaster period. With a two-year lead time for a credible prediction, we show that the dampening effects on new investment can have a significant impact on the economy. In some cases this dampening effect can almost equal the losses due to damages to capital stock that are likely to be sustained in the quake.

We have used a hybrid measure of losses combining stock and flow measures because of data limitations. Three categories of losses dominate the totals: residential housing, social capital, and losses in present value of income from nonresidential private capital. One can get a quick notion of regional losses by first

578 JOURNAL OF REGIONAL SCIENCE, VOL. 24, NO. 4, 1984

looking at these three categories of loss. By contrast, it is possible that labor and proprietors income will show gains (not losses) in present value terms when the whole period is examined, due to the stimulus to employment and reconstruction stemming from the disaster. Nevertheless, the regional losses from an unanticipated quake are substantial, even though there may be gains in labor and proprietors income compared to the baseline forecast. These simulations tell us that policies that encourage rebuilding can have a strong impact both on regional income losses and on the recovery path.

We should emphasize again that we have not dealt with social losses of deaths, injuries, trauma, or dislocation. However, the approaches we have taken are not in conflict with these omissions. Second, our econometric model is based upon annual data so that we are unable to show short-run responses. A better model would be based upon quarterly or monthly data. The regional losses we have shown are always in reference to a baseline projection, so improvements in the basic model would be important in affecting possible recovery paths. Third, for the most part we have had to rely upon crude ratios in our estimates of consumer durables, total nonresidential regional capital, and regional social capital. Fourth, although net migration and firm investment are endogenous to the model, we had to use guesses as to how firms and individuals would react to predictions and events. Fifth, we have not dealt with the issue of regional competitiveness following the event. However, there is good reason to believe that losses from a regional perspective will be greater than national losses. This could be dealt with in an interregional framework. Much more could be learned with additional research.

Finally, there are many aspects we have touched upon that deserve further analysis. Our measures of losses are based in theory on aggregate willingness to pay and individual choices based upon state preference theory. However, in a complex economic system it is doubtful that individuals would know what nominal wealth losses would be in the event of an earthquake, and, hence, could not give willingness to pay figures without such estimates. Schemes to elicit willingness to pay are only in their infancy. The entire research area we have studied is full of challenging issues that are relevant to hazard mitigation research and to economic and social theory.

REFERENCES

Brookshire, D. S. and W. D. Schulze. *Methods Development for Valuing Hazards Information.* Laramie, Wyoming: Institute of Policy Research, University of Wyoming, 1980.

Cochrane, Harold C. "Predicting the Economic Impact of Earthquakes," Working Paper No. 15, Institute of Behavioral Science, University of Colorado, Boulder, 1974.

———. *Natural Hazards and Their Distributive Effects.* Boulder, CO: Institute of Behavioral Science, University of Colorado, 1975.

Dacy, D. C. and H. Kunreuther. *The Economics of Natural Disasters.* New York: Free Press, 1969.

Duobinis, Stanley F. "An Econometric Model of the Chicago Standard Metropolitan Statistical Area," *Journal of Regional Science,* 21 (1981), 293–320.

Edmonds, Stahrd. "Economic Recovery from Earthquake Damage," Paper presented at Western Economic Association Meetings, July, 1982, Los Angeles, 1982.

Fishkind, Henry H., Jerome W. Milliman, and Richard W. Ellson. "A Pragmatic Econometric Approach to Assessing Economic Impacts of Growth or Decline in Urban Areas," *Land Economics,* 54 (1978), 442–460.

Friesma, H., J. Caporaso, G. Goldstein, R. Lineberry, and R. McCleary. *Aftermath: Communities After Natural Disasters.* Beverly Hills, California: Sage, 1979.

Glickman, Norman J. "An Econometric Forecasting Model for the Philadelphia Region," *Journal of Regional Science,* 11 (1971), 15–32.

———. *Econometric Analysis of Regional Systems.* New York: Academic Press, 1977.

Haas, J. E., R. Kates, and M. Bowden. *Reconstruction Following Disaster.* Cambridge, MA: MIT Press, 1977.

Mileti, Dennis S., Janice R. Hutton, and John H. Sorrensen. *Earthquake Prediction Response and Options for Public Policy.* Boulder, CO: Institute of Behavioral Science, University of Colorado, 1981.

Munroe, T. and Kenneth Ballard. "Modeling the Economic Disruption of a Major Earthquake in the San Francisco Bay Area—Impact on California," Paper presented at Western Economic Association Meetings, Los Angeles, July, 1982.

National Academy of Sciences. *Earthquake Prediction and Public Policy.* Washington, D.C.: National Academy of Sciences, 1975.

———. *A Program of Studies in the Socioeconomic Effects of Earthquake Predictions.* Washington, D.C.: National Academy of Sciences, 1978.

Rubin, Barry M. and Rodney A. Erickson. "Specification and Performance Improvements in Regional Econometric Forecasting Models: A Model for the Milwaukee Metropolitan Area," *Journal of Regional Science,* 20 (1980), 11–35.

Wilson, R. "Earthquake Vulnerability for Economic Impact Assessments," Working paper, Federal Emergency Management Agency, Washington, D.C., 1982.

Wright, J. D. and P. H. Rossi (eds.). *Social Science and Natural Hazards.* Cambridge, Massachusetts: Abt Books, 1981.

Wright, J. D., P. Rossi, S. Wright, and E. Weber-Burdin. *After the Clean-Up: Long-Range Effects of Natural Disasters.* Beverly Hills, California: Sage, 1979.

[14]

JOURNAL OF REGIONAL SCIENCE, Vol. 37, No. 3, 1997, pp. 437–458

THE REGIONAL ECONOMIC IMPACT OF AN EARTHQUAKE: DIRECT AND INDIRECT EFFECTS OF ELECTRICITY LIFELINE DISRUPTIONS*

Adam Rose

Department of Energy, Environmental, and Mineral Economics, The Pennsylvania State University, University Park, PA 16802, U.S.A.

Juan Benavides

Department of Industrial Engineering, Universidad de Los Andes, Bogota, Colombia

Stephanie E. Chang

EQE International, Inc., Seattle, WA 98101, U.S.A.

Philip Szczesniak

Regional Economics Division, U.S. Bureau of Economic Analysis, Washington, DC 20230, U.S.A.

Dongsoon Lim

Department of Energy, Environmental, and Mineral Economics, The Pennsylvania State University, University Park, PA 16802, U.S.A.

ABSTRACT. This paper develops a methodology to estimate the regional economic impacts of electricity lifeline disruptions caused by a catastrophic earthquake. The methodology is based on specially designed input-output and linear programming models. A simulation of a major earthquake in the New Madrid Seismic Zone near Memphis, Tennessee, indicates the potential production loss over the recovery period could amount to as much as 7 percent of gross regional product. Reallocation of scarce electricity across sectors could reduce the impacts substantially. Additionally, an improved restoration pattern of electricity transmission substations across subareas could reduce losses even more.

*The research contained in this paper was funded by grants from the National Science Foundation and the National Center for Earthquake Engineering Research. An earlier version of the paper was presented at the 41st North American Regional Science Association Meetings, Niagara Falls, Canada, November, 1994. The authors wish to thank Masanobu Shinozuka, Satoshi Tanaka, Howard Hwang, Kathleen Tierney, and the Shelby County Planning Department for access to their data and Steven French for GIS services. The authors also benefited from the helpful suggestions of three anonymous referees. We are, however, responsible for any errors and omissions. The reader is also referred to Shinozuka et al. (1997) for more details of the data and engineering underpinnings of the analysis.

Received October 1995; revised June 1996; accepted August 1996.

438 JOURNAL OF REGIONAL SCIENCE, Vol. 37, No. 3, 1997

1. INTRODUCTION

The literature on regional impact analysis is dominated by models and applications to public policies, business cycles, and large-scale investment projects. Yet there is a major category of even more devastating impacts that stem from natural hazards such as earthquakes, hurricanes, and floods. Unfortunately, very few of these events have been subjected to rigorous regional analysis.

The purpose of this paper is to develop a methodology for evaluating the regional economic impact of a catastrophic earthquake, with special reference to the direct and indirect losses stemming from a disruption of electricity services. Electricity is one of several utilities termed "lifelines," because of their crucial role in sustaining social and economic systems and because of their network characteristics, which make them especially vulnerable to disruption from natural disasters. Although losses from earthquakes are often measured in terms of property damage resulting from the actual ground shaking, the emphasis in this paper will be on the subsequent loss of production of goods and services by businesses directly cut off from electricity service and by businesses indirectly affected because their suppliers or customers are without power.

The methodology is applied to the economy of Memphis, Tennessee. The largest earthquakes in the recorded history of the United States took place during the winter of 1811–1812 in the New Madrid Seismic Zone, near that city. Since then, there have been 17 earthquakes in the Mississippi and Ohio Valleys measuring greater than 5.0 on the Richter scale. Scientists have long considered this area to be capable of generating a catastrophic earthquake at any moment.

This study is the culmination of a multidisciplinary effort to understand key aspects of earthquake events and to improve society's ability to cope with them. Section 3 provides a brief discussion of the Memphis economy, summarizes the work of other researchers in simulating the Memphis Light, Gas, and Water Division's (MLGW) electricity network, and explains how we integrated these engineering results with spatial economic data to provide a pre-earthquake baseline of sectoral electricity demand. In Section 4, we develop estimates of direct economic losses by sector and subregion by combining the above information with survey data that takes into account resiliency to lifeline disruptions. In Sections 5 and 6, we perform a set of economic model simulations to estimate total production losses under a variety of conditions and policies related to the allocation of scarce electricity supplies. First, we show how standard input-output impact analysis must be modified to truly distinguish between direct and indirect impacts of lifeline disruptions. Then, we develop a multi-area linear programming model to show how earthquake losses can be reduced through the reallocation of electricity across sectors and the restoration of lifeline services across areas.

2. LITERATURE REVIEW

Interindustry models were chosen for our analysis because of their ability to reflect the structure of a regional economy in great detail, to trace economic interdependence by calculating indirect effects of lifeline disruptions, and to identify an optimal emergency response. The use of these models to estimate the regional impact of natural hazards dates back to the work of Cochrane (1974). Several standard input-output (I-O) impact analyses of earthquakes have been performed over the past two decades (see, e.g., Wilson, 1982). More recently, several advances have been made in this approach in relation to earthquake damage in general and lifelines in particular. Kawashima and Kanoh (1990), Cole (1996), and Gordon and Richardson (1996) have constructed multiregional I-O models to perform analyses of general earthquake impacts. Cole (1996) has also performed such an analysis at the neighborhood (census tract) level. Cochrane (1997) has recently developed an expert system using IMPLAN input-output data and a set of supply-demand balancing algorithms intended to yield ballpark impact estimates. Aspects of import adjustments in I-O models applied to estimating earthquake impacts were first suggested by Boisvert (1992).

Cochrane's (1974) original work was a linear programming formulation for the economy as a whole, as was a model outlined by Rose (1981) to minimize losses from a utility lifeline disruption by reallocating resources across sectors. Both models were simple formulations of maximizing gross regional product (GRP) subject to only the most rudimentary constraints—constant production technology and limits on primary factors of production. The conceptual models presented by Rose and Benavides (1997) include adjustments in I-O coefficients (including imports), consideration of excess production capacity, minimum final demand requirements for necessities, reallocation of resources over time, and the incorporation of risk (the latter in a "chance-constrained" programming formulation). A recent paper by Cole (1995) utilizes a programming extension of a social accounting matrix to examine the implications of alternative welfare criteria, including giving greater weight to certain socioeconomic or interest groups (see also Cole, 1997).

Of the above research, only Boisvert (1992), Cole (1995), and Rose and Benavides (1997) have explicitly examined the impacts of lifeline disruptions. This paper advances the state-of-the-art in several ways. First, we incorporate into interindustry studies, for the first time, engineering features of electric utility lifelines and their linkage to the economy. Second, we clarify neglected features of I-O impact analysis relating to the estimation of indirect effects, general input supply bottlenecks, the resiliency of production technology to electricity curtailments, and spatial (subregional) differentials in electricity use/availability. Finally, we offer a formal optimization model that incorporates the above features to examine potential policies to alter the restoration pattern

© The Regional Science Research Corporation 1997.

440   JOURNAL OF REGIONAL SCIENCE, Vol. 37, No. 3, 1997

of electricity utility network components across subregions, in addition to the more conventional reallocation of electricity across sectors.

We should note that other approaches to estimating economic impacts of disasters are found in the regional science literature. A major contribution has recently been made by West and Lenze (1994) detailing how to estimate *direct* regional economic losses from natural hazards by piecing together primary and secondary data; however, their study also omits considerations peculiar to lifeline losses. Regional econometric models have been successfully applied to various aspects of actual and simulated disaster impacts by Chang (1983), Ellson et al. (1984), and Guimaraes et al. (1993). However, this approach does not lend itself readily to tracing the linkage between lifelines and the regional macroeconomy. The analysis presented here differs from most of the econometric studies and some of the interindustry studies in that it simulates the impacts of a hypothetical event, as opposed to estimating the impacts of an actual disaster or of the reconstruction spending in its aftermath. The methodology is sufficiently general, however, to undertake both an ex ante and ex post impact analysis, as well as optimal planning. In the ex post context, actual data on lifeline outages can be used instead of engineering simulation data (see Rose and Lim, 1997).

3. ELECTRICITY SERVICE IN MEMPHIS

The core of our economic model is a 21-sector input-output transactions table for Shelby County, Tennessee (the heart of the Memphis Metropolitan Area). The table was derived from the IMPLAN System (U.S. Forest Service, 1993) and modified to explicitly account for electricity purchases from the local distribution network (see Rickman and Schwer, 1995, for a comparative evaluation of IMPLAN and other approaches). The I-O table provides insight into the general structure of the Memphis economy, which is a major commercial and manufacturing center.

Information on physical attributes of the local electricity distribution company, Memphis Light, Gas and Water (MLGW), provides the basic engineering context within which electricity disruption from a major earthquake can be estimated. MLGW imports electricity from the Tennessee Valley Authority (TVA) through gate stations, and it is then transmitted to 23 kv and 12 kv transmission substations.[1] Shelby County itself is divided into 36 Electric Power Service Areas (EPSAs), almost all of which are served by one transmission substation.

To link the engineering analyses with interindustry models, we need to specify baseline electricity demand and disruption levels on a sectoral basis. Our approach is to determine the industrial composition of each EPSA and then

---

[1]Information on substations, lines, buses, etc., has been incorporated in a geographic information system (GIS) and is described in Hwang et al. (1994) and Tanaka (1995).

to map the spatial differentials into our I-O table. Standard census publications only provide information on employment by place of residence. Instead, we utilize an unpublished data source of employment in Shelby County by place of employment, tabulated as part of a special Bureau of Census study undertaken for the Memphis and Shelby County Office of Planning and Development. The spatial delineation included over 500 Traffic Analysis Zones (TAZs) within the County. Employment by EPSA was estimated for us by French (1995) by overlaying TAZs and EPSAs using GIS techniques. Under the assumption of uniform labor productivity within each industry, this data set can be used to represent the spatial distribution of production and energy use within Shelby County.[2]

Network reliability and electricity availability for MLGW following a major earthquake have been estimated by Shinozuka et al. (1995) and Tanaka (1995). Using probabilistic damage models, Monte Carlo simulation with a sample size, $N = 100$, generates a large number of damage and outage realizations for an earthquake of set magnitude and epicentral location. For each substation and the corresponding EPSA, a probabilistic power availability ratio is then computed for each earthquake event (essentially an expected value across the set of magnitude 7.5 earthquake simulations). Results indicate that the region is projected to suffer a severe reduction of electricity availability, reflected in a weighted average of 44.8 percent of baseline availability.

4. ESTIMATION OF DIRECT REGIONAL IMPACTS OF ELECTRICITY DISRUPTION

To estimate the direct impacts of electricity disruption, that is, output losses attributable to electricity outage at the production site, many factors must be considered. In addition to the physical damage affecting electric service, these factors include the basic usage of electricity, the resiliency of productive activities to loss of electricity, and the restoration timeframe of service following the disaster.

Electricity Disruption and Restoration

To estimate the loss of production activities due to electricity disruption, an adjusted usage-based model is developed. Electricity disruption, d_{et}^s, in service areas s at time t, where $0 \leq d_{et}^s \leq 1$, causes a production loss ratio, $l_{ejt}^s (0 \leq l_{ejt}^s \leq 1)$, to industry j in area s at time t according to the following function:

$$(1) \qquad\qquad l_{ejt}^s = (1 - r_{ejt})d_{et}^s$$

where $r_{ejt}(0 \leq r_{ejt} \leq 1)$ represents a "resiliency factor" that reflects industry j's

---

[2]We acknowledge the possibility of the "ecological fallacy" when we perform subregionalizations of our basic data set, which are used in the input-output and linear programming models.

electricity usage and adaptability characteristics. For example, a resiliency factor of 0.1 means that complete disruption of electricity would lead to 90 percent loss in production. For a given industry, this factor may change over time because of the effect of lifeline disruption duration.

Values of the resiliency factor are adapted from results of a recent survey of business vulnerability to lifeline disruption in Shelby County conducted by Tierney and Nigg (1997). These results are used to infer a cumulative distribution of temporary business closures or slowdowns by industry according to duration of electricity disruption for the region as a whole.

Information on estimated electricity outage by EPSA discussed in Section 3 reflects the expected post-disaster availability of electricity based on the probability of malfunction of electric transmission substations. Compared to other components of electric power systems such as power lines and distribution substations, these are the most time-consuming to repair after an earthquake and are therefore typically a controlling factor in the restoration of the entire system. For this reason, the functionality of transmission substations can be used to represent the availability of electric power in a given area.

Results from Shinozuka et al. (1994) were used to group the EPSAs into "impact zones" ranging from one (least impact) to six (greatest impact), as summarized in Table 1. Although the electricity disruption results are presented in probabilistic terms, for purposes of demonstrating the economic impact methodology, it is useful to interpret them as if they represented deterministic disruption ratios.

The restoration of electric power (presented in the last column of Table 1) is modeled on the basis of two main assumptions deriving from experience in past earthquakes. First, restoration proceeds from areas of least damage to areas of heaviest damage. Second, restoration proceeds nonlinearly over time, with most customers having power restored quickly, and proportionally fewer customers being restored as time elapses. The restoration curve was approximated with a nonlinear functional form and calibrated with restoration data from ATC-25 (ATC, 1991) and the Northridge Earthquake (Chang, 1996).

TABLE 1:   Characteristics of Impact Zones

Zone	Probability of Electricity Availability	Number of EPSAs	Percent of Employment	Restoration Time Frame
1	0.5–0.6	17	55.9%	1 week
2	0.4–0.5	6	13.8%	2 weeks
3	0.3–0.4	5	10.7%	2 weeks
4	0.2–0.3	3	2.9%	2 weeks
5	0.1–0.2	4	14.1%	5 weeks
6	0–0.1	1	2.5%	15 weeks

Estimation of Direct Impacts

Direct impacts on each sector are estimated from the integration of all of the factors described above and can be expressed as:

$$\Delta X_{jt} = \sum_s \sum_j l^s_{ejt} w^s_j \overline{X}_j$$

where:

$j(j = 1, \ldots, 21)$ are economic sectors,

$s(s = 1, \ldots, 36)$ are electricity service areas,

X_{jt} is gross output of sector j for the entire region at time t after the earthquake,

l^s_{ejt} is the loss factor for electricity disruption by service area, $0 \le l^s_{ejt} \le 1$,

w^s_j is the fraction of sector j output produced in region s, $\sum_s w^s_j = 1$, and

$\overline{X}_j$ is the gross output of sector j before the earthquake.

The loss factor, l, is determined from Equation (1) and w^s_j from the GIS mapping. These direct impacts do not consider interindustry dependencies.

Estimated direct losses due to electricity disruption in the scenario earthquake are calculated as a percentage of baseline (normal) output. Although all industries suffer significant losses immediately after the earthquake, losses are substantially reduced within two weeks. Industries display differentials in both the initial disruption and recovery depending on location. Overall, petroleum refining, which is concentrated in one, hard-hit EPSA, suffers the largest direct losses from electricity disruption. The figures in column 3 of Table 2 provide a representation of direct losses for the week immediately following the earthquake.

5. ESTIMATION OF TOTAL REGIONAL IMPACTS

I-O Impact Analysis

Indirect impacts can be estimated from direct effects using input-output impact analysis. Assuming no resiliency adjustments for the moment, electricity lifeline disruptions due to earthquakes can be translated into potential output reductions in each sector as follows:

$$(2) \qquad \Delta X_j = \sum_s \sum_j d^s_e w^s_j \overline{X}_j$$

where the variables are as defined previously.

However, for inclusion into an input-output model, we must convert gross output changes into final demand changes because the latter are the conduits

444   JOURNAL OF REGIONAL SCIENCE, Vol. 37, No. 3, 1997

TABLE 2: Final Demand and Gross Output Reductions for Shelby County During First Week of Electricity Disruption (all dollar figures in millions)

Sector	Final Demand (Y) $	Gross Output (X) $	X1 % Reduction without Bottleneck	X2 % Reduction with Bottleneck	Y1 Reduction $	Y2 Reduction $	X1 Reduction $	X2 Reduction $
1. Agriculture	2.715	3.898	40.17	78.71	0.937	2.003	1.565	3.069
2. Mining	0.683	0.763	20.32	78.71	0.128	0.536	0.155	0.601
3. Construction	39.710	47.231	41.14	78.71	15.647	31.259	19.429	37.175
4. Food Products	34.808	41.000	51.68	78.71	16.936	25.686	21.190	32.271
5. Nondurable Manufac	64.235	78.479	54.06	78.71	33.418	47.986	42.423	61.771
6. Durable Manufacturing	41.988	48.821	51.46	78.71	20.932	31.691	25.124	38.427
7. Petroleum Refining	2.888	8.115	78.71	78.71	3.530	1.312	6.388	6.388
8. Transportation	66.800	80.642	40.16	78.71	23.657	48.507	32.390	63.474
9. Communication	3.506	8.765	42.45	78.71	0.339	1.368	3.721	6.899
10. Electric Utilities	1.762	4.171	45.46	78.71	0.322	0.816	1.896	3.283
11. Gas Distribution	0.035	0.208	47.66	78.71	0.000	0.008	0.099	0.163
12. Water & Sanitary Serv	0.610	1.027	47.95	78.71	0.152	0.280	0.492	0.808
13. Wholesale Trade	32.631	41.156	48.66	78.71	14.352	23.158	20.028	32.394
14. Retail Trade	50.419	55.987	48.80	78.71	14.409	23.183	27.321	44.067
15. F.I.R.E.	59.746	75.781	50.74	78.71	17.749	26.625	38.449	59.647
16. Personal Services	10.840	12.338	49.31	78.71	3.760	6.032	6.084	9.712
17. Business & Prof Serv	28.108	57.013	50.92	78.71	11.309	15.972	29.034	44.875
18. Entertainment Services	2.881	3.860	48.93	78.71	0.602	0.946	1.888	3.038
19. Health Services	27.496	37.848	54.54	78.71	8.999	12.143	15.189	21.919
20. Education Services	4.177	4.289	50.03	78.71	0.816	1.266	2.136	3.360
21. Government	53.850	62.098	54.38	78.71	26.532	37.493	33.767	48.877
Total	$529.887	$663.469			$214.524	$338.269	$328.769	$522.217
Weighted Average			49.55%	78.71%	40.48%	63.84%	49.55%	78.71%

Y1: Use of (**I–A**ᵢ) vector and direct output reduction estimates to obtain a new final demand vector.
Y2: Use of (**I–A**ᵢ) vector and largest output reduction rate to obtain a new final demand vector.

through which external shocks are transmitted. A decrease in electricity, d_e, translates into a change in final demand availability ΔY_j, in a given sector, as follows:

$$(3) \quad \Delta Y_j = (I - A_i)\Delta X = (I - A_i)d_e^s \, w^s \, \overline{X} \quad (i = 1\ldots, 21); \quad (s = 1\ldots, 36)$$

where **X** represents the entire vector of gross outputs, A_i is a row vector of **A**, the matrix of technical coefficients, a_{ij}, representing the value of direct input from industry i needed to produce one dollar of output from industry j.[3] Then we utilize the standard I-O impact formula to determine total gross output impacts.

---

[3]Our computations are performed with an I-O table closed with respect to, that is, including households. Those familiar with I-O analysis may find Equation (3) a bit unusual at first glance. The typical conversion of any individual sector's gross output into final demand is done by dividing the former by the element b_{jj}, a diagonal term of the closed Leontief Inverse (see, e.g., Miller and Blair, 1985). However, when more than one element is adjusted, there are interaction effects in the ensuing computations. Therefore, the row vector $(I - A_i)$ is used.

Had we used the original vector of ΔX_j's in place of the ΔY_j's of the standard input-output impact equation, we would have obtained an electricity demand level reduction larger than the disruption level caused by the earthquake (the percentage difference being equivalent to the weighted average of the sectoral multipliers). This would mean that the available electricity would be underutilized in the region, a nonsensical outcome for earthquake disruptions of more than a few days, where firms have time to modify their supplier and customer linkages so as to utilize all available resources. Thus, there may be *no* indirect effects of the utility lifeline disruption over and above the initial estimate of electricity curtailments in each sector and the corresponding gross output reductions. What may appear to be indirect effects are essentially part of the simultaneous direct impacts of electricity disruptions in all industries. "Indirect" effects are artificially created, for computational purposes, because we scale back typically measured impacts into final demand effects (which are *not* equivalent to direct impacts) first and run them through the I-O model. This is done so that we can establish the basic I-O approach to build upon for the more complex cases below.

True indirect effects arise when electricity disruptions in some sectors are much higher than in other sectors and cause supply input *bottlenecks* other than for electricity. This can happen when a sector is heavily concentrated in one subregion that is especially hard-hit by an earthquake. The way to compute this effect is to first note that underlying the I-O model is the concept of the *fixed-coefficient* production function, that is, output is dependent on the most limited input. Thus, we would examine the initial vector of gross output losses due to the earthquake to identify the sector with the largest potential output reduction, which in effect becomes the *constraining* input to other sectors. We would then adjust all of the other X_j's to the constraining sector's output reduction level. Of course, we would need to make sure that the constraining sector was really crucial to production. For example, if the entertainment of personal services sectors had the largest potential output reductions due to an electricity disruption, we would proceed to the sector with the next highest ΔX_j. Effectively, the d_j for the constraining sector is used in Equation (2) for all sectors (except those passed over).[4]

Resiliency bears on the computations in two ways. First, it affects the initial estimates of output reduction in each sector. Second, it means less electricity is needed per unit of output (because of conservation potential, back-up power sources, and so forth) and thus requires a decrease in the electricity input coefficient, which we denote by a_{ej}. As above, let r_{ej} represent the resiliency of sector j to electricity disruption. Thus, we substitute a modified matrix, A^*, for A, by multiplying the electricity input coefficient in each sector,

---

[4]Note that the alternative is to use a *supply-side* input-output analysis (see, e.g., Davis and Salkin, 1984, for an application to water shortages). However, given the dispute over the conceptual soundness and accuracy of this approach (see, e.g., Oosterhaven, 1988; Rose and Allison, 1989), we have chosen to follow the less complicated procedure above.

446   JOURNAL OF REGIONAL SCIENCE, Vol. 37, No. 3, 1997

a_{ej}, by its corresponding $1 - r_{ej}$. These two effects are combined to modify Equation (3) as follows:

$$\Delta Y_j = (\mathbf{I} - \mathbf{A}_j^*)(1 - r_e)\,\mathbf{d}_e^g\,\mathbf{w}^s\,\overline{\mathbf{X}} \qquad (i = 1 \ldots, 21); \qquad (s = 1 \ldots, 36)$$

Analysis of Simulation Results

We applied our basic I-O impact model to the direct disruption estimates in the previous sections, and ran simulations with and without input bottleneck effects. Note that our analysis has not been able to include all of the factors affecting regional economic losses. First, there is likely to be significant damage to buildings, so that even with immediate restoration of electricity services, the economy would not likely revert to baseline production levels. Second, other lifeline services are also likely to be disrupted, and one needs to guard against double-counting. The most extensive damage should be attributed to a "bottleneck" utility lifeline (in a manner analogous to our analysis of bottleneck economic sectors). We have probably understated resiliency by omitting its prospects with regard to the bottlenecked sector and by ignoring the possibility of importing more crucial goods and services. In addition, many sectors can make up lost production by working overtime shifts after electricity is restored. Finally, we have not considered a shortened disruption period due to temporary repair measures. On the other hand, we have underestimated losses by not having data on transmission line and distribution line disruptions. In addition, damage to electric power can cause other types of losses such as gas line explosions and fires, as well as hampering fire fighting and other emergency responses. Overall, many of these factors offset each other, but we surmise that our loss estimates are definitely in the high-end range. Note also that our methodology can readily incorporate most of these omitted factors when data become available, or can do so with some minor adjustments, as in the case of imports (see e.g., Boisvert, 1992; Cochrane, 1996). Natural disaster impacts involve extreme complexities, which we cannot hope to fully understand or model empirically at this time. Still, we hope to provide insight into an important piece of the puzzle.

Preliminary data used in these simulations are akin to those presented in the left-hand portion of Table 2. Note that the final demand and output data are measured on a weekly basis. The changes in gross output column entries differ from period to period because restoration and resiliency changes over time. For example, during the first week (week 0), there was a maximum disruption for the region (no EPSA has had service restored). As shown in Table 2, the bottleneck sector is petroleum refining, which is highly concentrated in an EPSA that suffers the most severe disruption in the County. It is also a sector with a minimum of resiliency with respect to electricity inputs. For the simulation "without bottleneck" effects, gross output losses are the same as the (direct) X1 reduction (as discussed in the previous section) and amount to a total of 49.55 percent ($329 million) of baseline production in Shelby County.

Bottleneck effects raise this disruption to 78.71 percent. Thus, the true indirect effect during week 0 is 29.16 percent of gross output.

Simulation results for additional distinct time periods (not shown) contain some interesting insights. In comparison to week 0, the week 1 impacts "without bottlenecks" are less than the week 0 impacts, but the simulations "with bottlenecks" are greater because of the potential for the bottleneck effect to worsen as resiliency deteriorates over time. Of course, the results signal the wisdom of choosing a new restoration time path, one that favors the EPSA in which the bottleneck occurs. This will be discussed at greater length in Section 5. Non-bottleneck output reductions are reduced even further for the weeks 2–3 results, though the bottleneck results are the same as in week 1. Negative changes in final demand appear in weeks 2–3 stemming from enhanced production levels in various sectors that are not fully synchronized with intermediate output requirements, thus leaving more of the product available for final use. The bottleneck tightens slightly in week 4. However, in weeks 5–15, when power has been totally restored in all but one EPSA, the bottleneck sector changes to nondurable manufacturing. The bottleneck effects are still five times larger than the non-bottleneck results, but they amount to only a 3.70 percent reduction in Gross Output.

The results for the entire 15 week disruption period are presented in Table 3. Note that for this presentation, the final demand and gross output figures are on an annual basis because that is the standard time span for measuring economic changes. The results for the "without bottleneck" case are an overall reduction in final demand and gross output of 1.90 percent and 2.28 percent, respectively. The hardest hit sector in absolute terms is F.I.R.E. (finance, insurance, and real estate), with an output reduction of nearly $100 million (over and above property damage stemming from the earthquake). For the "bottleneck" simulations, the reductions in final demand and gross output are 6.97 percent and 8.95 percent, respectively. This means that indirect effects are 6.31 percent of gross output, or $2.2 billion. Overall, the bottleneck effects are almost four times the direct (and standard total) electricity disruption effects themselves.

6.   OPTIMAL RATIONING OF SCARCE ELECTRICITY

Linear Programming Model

In the previous section, we simulated the economic impact of across-the-board cutbacks (*proportional rationing*) of electricity to each sector in a given EPSA. We now consider the alternative of *differential rationing* of available electricity in order to minimize total economic losses from an earthquake. We will perform two simulations: first, reallocation of electricity across sectors and subregions with our previous restoration pattern and second, reallocation with an optimized restoration pattern.

This problem can be formulated as one of maximizing Gross Regional Product (GRP) given constrained electricity availability, constrained supplies

448
JOURNAL OF REGIONAL SCIENCE, Vol. 37, No. 3, 1997

TABLE 3: Annual Final Demand and Gross Output in Shelby County
Following Electricity Lifeline Disruptions Over All Time Periods
(in millions of dollars)

Sector	Baseline		W/O Bottleneck		W/Bottleneck	
	Final Demand $	Gross Output $	Final Demand $	Gross Output $	Final Demand $	Gross Output $
1. Agriculture	141	203	139	199	130	185
2. Mining	36	40	35	39	32	36
3. Construction	2065	2456	2027	2410	1887	2245
4. Food Products	1810	2132	1783	2097	1664	1949
5. Other Nondurable Manufac	3340	4081	3228	3946	3068	3730
6. Durable Manufacturing	2183	2539	2134	2480	2003	2320
7. Petroleum Refining	150	422	123	389	143	386
8. Transportation	3474	4193	3428	4128	3198	3833
9. Communication	182	456	180	447	175	417
10. Electric Utilities	92	217	91	213	87	198
11. Gas Distribution	2	11	2	11	2	10
12. Water & Sanitary Services	32	53	32	52	30	49
13. Wholesale Trade	1697	2140	1671	2100	1565	1956
14. Retail Trade	2622	2911	2599	2859	2490	2661
15. F.I.R.E.	3107	3941	3059	3845	2956	3602
16. Personal Services	564	642	557	629	529	586
17. Business & Prof Services	1462	2965	1437	2899	1371	2710
18. Entertainment Services	150	201	149	197	144	183
19. Health Services	1430	1448	1405	1409	1361	134
20. Education Services	217	222	216	218	210	203
21. Government	2800	3229	2735	3147	2587	2952
Total (15 weeks)	$27554	$34500	$27031	$33714	$25634	$31535
Weighted Average Reduction			1.90%	2.28%	6.97%	8.59%

of primary factors of production, and fixed technology. The equations are:

$$\max \sum_j \mathbf{Y}_j$$

subject to

(4) $\qquad \mathbf{Y}_i = (\mathbf{I} - \mathbf{A}_{ij})\mathbf{X}_i \qquad (i, j = 1 \ldots, 21)$

(5) $\qquad \sum_j a_{ej}\mathbf{X}_j^s + \mathbf{Y}_e^s \leq \mathbf{X}_e^s \qquad (s = 1 \ldots, 36)$

(6) $\qquad \sum_s \mathbf{X}_j^s = \mathbf{X}_j \qquad (j = 1 \ldots, 21)$

(7) $\qquad \mathbf{Y}_e^s \leq \overline{\mathbf{Y}}_e^s \qquad (s = 1 \ldots, 36)$

(8) $\qquad \mathbf{X}_j^s \leq \overline{\mathbf{X}}_j^s \qquad \begin{pmatrix} s = 1 \ldots, 36 \\ j = 1 \ldots, 21 \end{pmatrix}$

(9) $$\mathbf{Y}_c \geq \alpha \overline{\mathbf{C}}_c \qquad (c = 4, 7 - 9, 19 - 21)$$

(10) $$\mathbf{Y}_e^s \geq \beta \overline{\mathbf{C}}_e^s \qquad (s = 1 \ldots, 36)$$

(11) $$\mathbf{X}_j^s, \mathbf{X}_e^s \geq 0$$

where:

$i, j(j = 1 \ldots, 21)$ are the economic sectors,

$s(s = 1 \ldots, 36)$ are the electricity service areas,

c are necessities,

e is the index of the electricity sector,

$\mathbf{Y}_e^s$ is the final demand of electricity in area s after the earthquake,

$\overline{\mathbf{Y}}_e^s$ is the final of electricity in area s before the earthquake,

$\mathbf{X}_e^s$ is the total electricity available in area s after an earthquake,

$\overline{\mathbf{C}}_c, \overline{\mathbf{C}}_e^s$ are the personal consumption levels for necessities for the region

and electricity by area before the earthquake,

α, β are the desired minimum levels of personal consumption for

necessities and electricty by area after the earthquake,

and other variables are as previously defined.

The objective function maximizes the sum of the final demands over all sectors (equal to gross regional product).[5] Equation (4) reflects the input-output technology matrix. Equation (5) specifies limitations on electricity availability in each serving area, s. Equation (6) sums sectoral gross outputs across all serving areas so the problem can be solved in an economy-wide context. Equation (7) imposes limits on electricity availability to final demand. Equation (8) limits the gross output of each sector in each serving area to not exceed its pre-earthquake level. Given that there are 36 serving areas and 21 sectors, Equation (8) is composed of 756 individual equations! Equations (9) and (10) guarantee minimum levels of necessities (including electricity) for households. Equation (11) is simply the nonnegativity conditions of a linear programming (LP) problem. The LP model minimizes losses by allocating scare electricity in such a way as to favor those sectors that yield the highest contribution to GRP per unit of direct *plus* indirect use of electricity.

Several critical assumptions underlie the implementation of the model. In the absence of further information, we can only assume that productive capacity in each sector was fully utilized in Shelby County. That means that it

---

[5]For examples of other welfare criteria that might be used as the basis for allocating scarce lifeline resources (see Cole, 1995). Note also that the constraints in the model also guarantee necessary amounts of basic necessities such as food and health services.

450   JOURNAL OF REGIONAL SCIENCE, Vol. 37, No. 3, 1997

is not possible for any sector to produce output flows during the recovery period larger than those before the event. Note that given the absence of data at this time, we have also not inserted any capacity reductions, which would stem from damaged factories, for example. The model, however, is sufficiently general to allow for excess capacity or capacity reductions when data are available.

We also assumed that household consumption of electricity by area is bounded from above by the pre-earthquake final demand level. With the information at hand, the vector of final demand of electricity by area is unknown and cannot be consistently estimated as the difference between total utilization by area (computed using peak load information) and total intermediate consumption (computed combining technical coefficients of electricity use from the **A** matrix and output by area). Data come from three different sources, and the combination of simplifying assumptions leads to inconsistencies such as negative figures for final demand in heavily industrialized areas. Thus, the preliminary matrix of electricity flows (including final demand as a sector) sums to the totals given by the I-O information, but does not match total utilization of electricity by area. This rectangular matrix of electricity flows by area and sector is *balanced* by use of the RAS method (Bacharach, 1970) to yield a set of matrices of elements a^s_{ij}.

To impart greater realism into the model, we have added lower bounds for personal consumption in sectors that are crucial during emergency management—*necessities,* as in Rose and Benavides (1997). These sectors are food, petroleum refining, transportation, communication, natural gas, water, health, education, and government. Given that residential use of electricity cannot be transported across areas, the lower bounds for this commodity are area-specific.

Analysis of Simulation Results

Gross regional product in Shelby County was $27.6 billion in 1991, or $529.9 million per week. Recall from Table 2 that for the first week after the scenario magnitude 7.5 earthquake, the reduction in total gross output was 49.6 percent and inclusion of bottleneck effects increase losses to 78.7 percent. In contrast, the linear programming model of electricity reallocation generates a total gross output reduction of $89.5 million during week 0, a 13.5 percent reduction from baseline, and a final demand (GRP) reduction of $66.2 million, a 12.5 percent reduction (see columns 3 and 4 of Table 4). Unlike the basically proportional decrease in electricity use and equivalent percentage production reduction across sectors in the I-O impact analysis, the benefit of the differential allocation is reflected in the fact that a reduction of 1 percent in electricity translates into only a 0.25 percent (12.5 percent ÷ 49.6 percent) reduction in GRP.[6]

---

[6]Note that the optimal reallocation analysis is presented only for the "without bottleneck" case. The results for this case represent a lower absolute level of savings than in the "bottleneck"

TABLE 4:   Final Demand and Gross Output Reductions for Shelby County
After Optimal Electricity Reallocation Across Sectors, Selected Weeks
(in millions of dollars)

	Baseline Levels		Week 0 Reduction		Week 1 Reduction		Week 5–14 Reduction	
Sector	Final Demand $	Gross Output $	Final Demand $	Gross Output $	Final Demand $	Gross Output $	Final Demand $	Gross Output $
1. Agriculture	2.715	3.896	2.715	3.170	0.558	0.726	0.000	−0.004
2. Mining	0.683	0.763	0.000	0.033	0.166	0.191	0.000	0.005
3. Construction	39.710	47.231	0.001	0.576	0.001	0.394	0.001	−0.003
4. Food Products	34.808	41.000	20.808	23.828	12.464	14.490	0.000	0.000
5. Nondurable Manufacturing	64.235	78.479	0.000	3.848	6.590	9.368	1.064	1.155
6. Durable Manufacturing	41.988	48.821	41.988	44.679	19.964	21.323	0.106	0.119
7. Petroleum Refining	2.888	8.115	0.000	0.309	0.000	0.205	0.000	−0.006
8. Transportation	66.800	80.642	0.000	1.647	0.000	1.097	0.000	0.013
9. Communication	3.506	8.765	0.001	0.864	0.001	0.656	0.001	0.009
10. Electric Utilities	1.762	4.171	0.702	1.649	0.620	1.234	0.048	0.155
11. Gas Distribution	0.035	0.208	−0.001	0.037	−0.001	0.026	−0.001	0.005
12. Water & Sanitary Serv	0.610	1.027	−0.001	0.070	−0.001	0.061	−0.001	0.011
13. Wholesale Trade	32.631	41.156	0.001	2.441	0.001	1.469	0.001	0.017
14. Retail Trade	50.419	55.987	0.000	0.357	13.753	14.080	0.000	−0.004
15. F.I.R.E.	59.746	75.781	0.001	1.196	0.001	1.132	0.001	0.004
16. Personal Services	10.840	12.338	0.000	0.249	0.000	0.181	0.000	0.007
17. Business & Prof Serv	28.108	57.013	−0.001	3.041	−0.001	2.616	−0.001	0.050
18. Entertainment Services	2.881	3.860	0.000	0.084	0.000	0.077	0.000	−0.004
19. Health Services	27.496	27.848	0.000	0.001	0.000	0.000	0.000	0.000
20. Education Services	4.177	4.269	0.000	0.028	0.000	0.017	0.000	−0.001
21. Government	53.850	62.098	−0.001	1.348	−0.001	1.108	−0.001	0.039
Total	$529.887	$663.469	$ 66.215	$89.454	$ 54.116	$70.451	$ 1.218	$ 1.565
Weighted Average			12.50%	13.48%	10.21%	10.62%	0.23%	0.24%

Table 4 also presents results for selected other points of the recovery path
that follows from the restoration pattern described in Section 4 over the course
of fifteen weeks. In general, the recovery path is monotonically increasing for
most sectors. However, some major sectoral reallocations do occur. For example, comparing column 4 of Table 4 with column 7 of Table 2, we see that
electricity is shifted away from agriculture, food products, and durable
manufacturing in favor of other sectors during week 0. Note also that the
unfavored sectors change over time as nondurable manufacturing and retail
trade take on that role in week 1.

Total economic impacts of an electric utility lifeline disruption following a
catastrophic earthquake in Shelby County under conditions of electricity

counterpart but a higher percentage improvement. This is because there are more limited
prospects for reallocating electricity to bottlenecked sectors (because of their geographic concentration) than for other sectors in general.

452   JOURNAL OF REGIONAL SCIENCE, Vol. 37, No. 3, 1997

TABLE 5:   Annual Final Demand and Gross Output in Shelby County
Following Electricity Lifeline Disruptions Under Alternative Responses
(in millions of dollars)

Sector	Baseline Levels		Proportional Reduction (I-O)		Optimal Reallocation (LP)		Opt. Realloc. & Restoration (LP)	
	Final Demand $	Gross Output $	Final Demand $	Gross Output $	Final Demand $	Gross Output $	Final Demand $	Gross Output $
1. Agriculture	141	203	139	199	138	199	138	199
2. Mining	36	40	35	39	35	39	35	40
3. Construction	2065	2456	2027	2410	2065	2455	2065	2455
4. Food Products	1810	2132	1783	2097	1777	2094	1780	2098
5. Nondurable Manufac	3340	4081	3228	3946	3311	4042	3340	4075
6. Durable Manufacturing	2183	2539	2134	2480	2102	2452	2121	2473
7. Petroleum Refining	150	422	123	389	150	421	150	422
8. Transportation	3474	4193	3428	4128	3474	4190	3474	4191
9. Communication	182	456	180	447	182	453	182	455
10. Electric Utilities	92	217	91	213	89	211	90	212
11. Gas Distribution	2	11	2	11	2	11	2	11
12. Water & Sanitary Serv	32	53	32	52	32	53	32	53
13. Wholesale Trade	1697	2140	1671	2100	1697	2135	1697	2137
14. Retail Trade	2622	2911	2599	2859	2608	2897	2622	2911
15. F.I.R.E.	3107	3941	3059	3845	3107	3938	3107	3939
16. Personal Services	564	642	557	629	564	641	564	641
17. Business & Prof Serv	1462	2965	1437	2899	1462	2957	1462	2893
18. Entertainment Services	150	201	149	197	150	201	150	201
19. Health Services	1430	1448	1405	1409	1430	1448	1430	1448
20. Education Services	217	222	216	218	217	222	217	222
21. Government	2800	3229	2735	3147	2800	3226	2800	3227
Total	$27554	$34500	$27031	$33714	$27391	$34286	$27457	$34301
Weighted Average Reduction			1.90%	2.28%	0.59%	0.62%	0.35%	0.58%

reallocation are presented in Table 5, along with baseline levels and the results
of other simulations. Overall, on a 52-week basis, final demand (GRP) and gross
output are reduced by 0.59 percent and 0.62 percent, respectively (see columns
5 and 6), in contrast to corresponding losses of 1.90 percent and 2.28 percent
under the (without bottleneck) proportional reduction case (see columns 3 and
4). Moreover, even with the sectoral reallocation, output levels are higher for
each sector than under that case with only three minor exceptions. Overall, the
improvement is 69 percent in final demand and 73 percent in gross output over
proportional reduction.

The restoration of electricity service in each EPSA has thus far followed a
reasonable rule—those substations with the lowest extent of damage are
restored first. This implicitly maximizes the amount of electricity restored per
unit of repair dollar. However, some EPSAs potentially contribute more to GRP

per unit of electricity than others, and this is a superior basis for identifying restoration priorities.

We simulated an optimal restoration pattern by using the shadow prices that stem from the dual of the LP solution referred to above. These shadow prices have the usual economic interpretation that GRP would grow by the amount of the shadow price if one additional unit of electricity were available in the corresponding area and were utilized by the sector with the highest contribution to GRP (directly and indirectly) per unit of electricity.

In week 1, we simply substitute restoration in EPSAs with the highest shadow prices in the original LP, but not exceeding the total megawatts of restored power of the original simulation.[7] This has the effect of yielding a restoration of GRP to 99.97 percent of baseline by weeks 2–3 (in contrast to 98.05 percent in the original LP simulation and 91.96 percent in the I-O simulations of Section 5).

The timepaths for the three different types of responses are presented in Figure 1 and clearly depict the superiority of reallocating electricity both across sectors and across areas. The very nature of the strict concavity of the optimal recovery/restoration timepath is another indicator of its intertemporal optimiz-

---

[7]Note that we have used a consistent regional restoration function throughout our various simulations, that is the same amount of MWs restored per week, rather than a "repair dollar" basis for this simulation because: first, we do not have sufficiently accurate data on repair costs for individual substations, and second, we want all our simulations to have the same basis. Computationally, this means that the $\mathbf{X}_e^s$ term in Equation (5) is increased over time at the same monotonic rate in each case. We are therefore not suggesting that this simulation reflects optimal repair practices under most circumstances, since it omits other pertinent considerations such as constraints on repair dollars (or specialized labor or spare parts). The model is, however, sufficiently general to incorporate these considerations when data are available. For example, to link repair costs and restoration effort one could supplement Equation (5) with:

$$\sum_s a_{re}^s \hat{\mathbf{X}}_e^{st} \le \mathbf{R}$$

$$\mathbf{X}_e^{st} - \hat{\mathbf{X}}_e^{st} = \mathbf{X}_e^{s(t-1)}$$

where $\mathbf{a}_{re}^s$ is the repair cost, $\mathbf{r}$, per MW of electricity restored at a given substation, s; $\hat{\mathbf{X}}_e^{st}$ is the amount of electricity restored in a given EPSA, s, at time t; and $\mathbf{R}$ is total repair cost for a given time period. Thus $\mathbf{X}_e^s$, the electricity available in each EPSA, becomes a choice variable rather than an exogenous variable (likewise $\mathbf{X}_e^s$ would have to be brought over to the left-hand side of Equation (5). However, then the time path of $\mathbf{X}_e^s$ would differ from that of our I-O and first LP analysis. Finally, we acknowledge that without explicit inclusion of repair costs, our numerical results for the second case presented in the second section of Section 6 are likely to involve some redistribution of repair expenses over the recovery period since we have implicitly substituted some restoration effort in "difficult to repair" substations for "simple to repair" substations (we thank one of the reviewers for pointing this out). However, this effect is likely to be minor since the spatial reallocation of electricity in this simulation is not substantial. Also, the bias will be lower the more linear is the repair cost function. If the repair cost function is reasonably linear (also taking account of some indivisibilities), then the "repair dollar" and "time to repair" cases would be equivalent.

454 JOURNAL OF REGIONAL SCIENCE, Vol. 37, No. 3, 1997

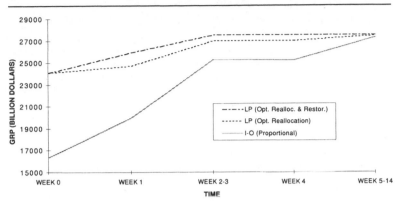

FIGURE 1: Economic Recovery in Shelby County Under
Alternative Responses.

ing capability. The shadow prices of the new LP simulation are in general lower than the shadow prices corresponding to the original LP solution. This is the dual expression of the result that society is better off in terms of GRP (the primal objective function). Note also that in the original LP code, shadow prices increase in several areas between weeks 0 and 1, which indicates that restoration is not optimal in the dynamic sense.

The results on a sector-by-sector basis of the optimal restoration LP case are also presented in the last two columns of Table 5. Note that some significant sector reallocations do take place in that the gross output of business and professional services is lower in the spatial/sectoral reallocation simulations than in the pure sectoral reallocation case. Overall, final demand and gross output losses can be reduced to 0.35 percent and 0.58 percent of annual baseline levels, improvements of 82 percent and 75 percent, respectively. Looked at another way, the GRP improvement is only 0.24 percent, or $66 million and only a modest improvement over the first LP case.[8] However, it is not difficult to imagine cases where this gap is likely to be much higher. Not taking advantage of such opportunities results in losses as devastating as if the earthquake actually toppled the buildings in which the lost production would have originated.

---

[8]The small incremental improvement of our second LP simulation may be surprising at first glance. This is partly due to the spatial configuration of the MLGW electricity network. But more generally, it is due to the fact that the sectoral reallocations of our first LP simulations implicitly capitalize on most of the spatial reallocation possibilities of the problem at hand. We would expect the substation restoration simulations to be more prominent in regions with less sectoral adjustment flexibilities, that is, regions with less uniformly distributed sectors spatially or those with fewer sectors.

Policy Implications

Currently, in the electric utility industry, earthquake recovery plans are at a rudimentary stage with respect to economic criteria. Network managers' experience is limited to less sophisticated prioritization schemes for cases of brownouts or blackouts that do not require maintenance/restoration but orderly switching maneuvers. Given the short duration of the usual restoration efforts, typical contingency plans or algorithms are prioritized according to ease of restoration or size of subarea outage (equivalent to the *direct* impact on output), regardless of location. This would be clearly suboptimal as illustrated by our simulations.

The challenge for utilities such as MLGW is to implement a policy instrument to attain a socially optimal outcome, which we have defined as minimizing gross regional product losses. Implementation requires a mechanism to allocate scarce electricity supplies combining optimal pricing information with a feasible form of load management.

In the basic interruptible service contract, or market, alternative, each customer subscribes to a particular level of capacity *before* the earthquake. The customer pays an interruptibility premium, or capacity charge, for this amount and a usage fee for each unit actually consumed. If usage exceeds subscribed capacity, a circuit breaker, for example, could activate. Because customers differ according to their willingness to pay for electricity, those with a higher demand would ideally buy larger fuse sizes. The utility has two roles in this scheme: to set usage and fuse prices to optimize resource allocation, and to guarantee enough capacity to meet the total required by customers' selections of fuse size. Load management is achieved by a decentralized system in which consumers ration themselves.[9]

In contrast to the above examples of price rationing, an alternative approach that gains significance as the size and duration of the disruption increases is direct quantity rationing. This is sometimes overlooked as an option because of the technological features of electricity lifelines; that is unlike water, where the flow can be reduced, electric power is either on or off. Power

---

[9]This scheme, however, must be supplemented by a contingent rule that will be put into operation when a supply shock reduces capacity beyond the rated fuse sizes of all customers. A simple and realistic modification to this scheme would be to introduce a load control strategy in which a customer continues to self-ration by purchasing a fuse, but the fuses can be activated by the electric utility when a capacity shortage occurs. In practice, however, customers wish to insure some base level of power supply during the emergency. This would require a more complex design (Wilson, 1989), where the customer pays a premium depending on priority class. In general, the optimal allocation of electricity is more complicated than for water, probably the resource for which there has been the most advances in theory and practice in emergency situations (that is, drought), as opposed to local distribution disruptions associated with earthquakes (see, e.g., Howitt et al., 1992; Zarnikau, 1994). Also, the allocation of water to meet broad social objectives is part of standard practice, in part, due to its common property resource characteristics. Both market and centrally administered rationing are found. Generally speaking, electricity lifeline and disaster managers can learn from these experiences.

456   JOURNAL OF REGIONAL SCIENCE, Vol. 37, No. 3, 1997

system shut-off to individual customers is not always feasible, but there are other mechanisms. A good example stems from a recent response to the extreme winter in the eastern United States. In late January, 1994, in Pennsylvania, utilities instituted *rolling blackouts*. In addition, the governor issued a decree (at the request of the utilities) closing state government offices and requiring nonessential industry to close down until the emergency was over.

7. CONCLUSION

We have developed and applied a methodology for estimating the regional economic losses from earthquake-damaged electric utility lifelines. We showed how ordinary input-output impact analysis would overestimate losses for simple cases and underestimate them when production bottlenecks occur elsewhere in the economy. We also showed how losses could be reduced more than threefold by reallocating scarce electricity according to the results of a specially designed linear programming model, and how losses could be reduced more than fourfold by optimizing the sequence of recovery of electricity substations according to the time trend of the LP models shadow prices.

Our models and results should be especially useful to economists, planners, and engineers in making decisions on mitigation measures and implementing recovery policies. Although our analysis was applied to an earthquake in Memphis, Tennessee, it can be readily generalized to other regions and to other types of natural hazards.

REFERENCES

Advanced Technology Council (ATC-25). 1991. *Seismic Vulnerability and Impact of Disruption of Lifelines in the Coterminous United States,* Federal Emergency Management Agency, Washington, DC: USGPO.

Bacharach, Michael. 1970. *Biproportional Matrices and Input-Output Change,* Cambridge, UK: Cambridge University Press.

Billinton, Roy and Ronald Allan. 1992. *Reliability Evaluation of Engineering Systems: Concepts and Techniques* (2nd ed.), New York: Plenum Press.

Boisvert, Richard. 1992. "Indirect Losses from a Catastrophic Earthquake and the Local, Regional, and National Interest," in *Indirect Economic Consequences of a Catastrophic Earthquake,* Washington, DC: National Earthquake Hazards Reduction Program, FEMA, pp. 207–265.

Chang, Semoon. 1983. "Disasters and Fiscal Policy," *Urban Affairs Quarterly,* 18, 511–523.

Chang, Stephanie. 1996. "Estimating Direct Losses from Electricity Lifeline Disruptions," in Masanobu Shinozuka, Adam Rose, and Ronald Eguchi (eds.), *Engineering and Socioeconomic Analysis of a New Madrid Earthquake,* Buffalo, NY: National Center for Earthquake Engineering Research.

Chang, Stephanie, Hope Seligson, and Ronald Eguchi. 1996. *Estimation of the Economic Impact of Multiple Lifeline Disruption: Memphis Light, Gas, and Case Study,* Buffalo, NY: National Center for Earthquake Engineering Research.

Cochrane, Harold. 1974. "Predicting the Economic Impact of Earthquakes," in Harold C. Cochrane, J. Eugene Haas, Martin J. Bowden, Robert W. Kates (eds.), *Social Science Perspectives on the Coming San Francisco Earthquake,* Natural Hazards Research Paper No. 25, NHRAIC, Boulder: U. of Colorado.

Cochrane, Harold. 1997. "Indirect Economic Losses," in *Development of Standardized Earthquake Loss Estimation Methodology Vol. II,* Menlo Park, CA: Risk Management Solutions, Inc., forthcoming.

Cole, H. Sam. 1995. "Lifelines and Livelihood: A Social Accounting Matrix Approach to Calamity
    Preparedness," *Journal of Contingencies and Crisis Management,* 3, 1–11.
Cole, H. Sam. 1997. "The Socio-Economic and Inter-Regional Impacts of an Earthquake," in
    Masandou, Shinozuka, Adam Rose, and Ronald Eguchi (eds.), *Engineering and Socioeconomic
    Analysis of a New Madrid Earthquake,* Buffalo, NY: National Center for Earthquake Engineer-
    ing Research.
Davis, H. Craig and E. Leonard Salkin. 1984. "Alternative Approaches to the Estimation of
    Economic Impacts Resulting from Supply Constraints," *Annals of Regional Science,* 18, 25–34.
Eguchi, Ronald and Susan Pelmulder. 1991. "Indirect Economic Impacts of Energy Network," in
    Indirect Economic Consequences of a Catastrophic Earthquake, Washington, DC: Federal Emer-
    gency Management Agency, pp. 143–206.
Ellson, Richard W., Jerome W. Milliman, and R. Blaine Roberts. 1984. "Measuring the Regional
    Economic Effects of Earthquakes and Earthquake Prediction," *Journal of Regional Science,* 24,
    559–79.
Gordon, Peter and Harry Richardson. 1996. "The Business Interruption Effects of the Northridge
    Earthquake," Lusk Center Research Institute, University of Southern California, Los Angeles.
Guimaraes, Paulo, Frank L. Hefner, and Douglas P. Woodward. 1993. "Wealth and Income Effects
    of Natural Disasters: An Econometric Analysis of Hurricane Hugo," *Review of Regional Studies,*
    23, 97–114.
Howitt, Richard, Nancy Moore, and Rodney T. Smith. 1992. *A Retrospective on California's 1991
    Emergency Drought Water Bank,* Sacramento: Department of Water Resources.
Hwang, Howard, H. Lin, and T. Chou. 1994. "GIS Data Sets of MLGW Electric Transmission
    System," Center for Earthquake Research and Information, The University of Memphis, Mem-
    phis.
Kawashima, Kazuhiko and Takashi Kanoh. 1990. "Evaluation of Indirect Economic Effects Caused
    by the 1983 Nohonkai-chubu, Japan, Earthquake," *Earthquake Spectra,* 6, 739–56.
Miller, Ronald E. and Peter D. Blair. 1985. *Input-Output Analysis: Foundations and Extensions,*
    Englewood Cliffs, NJ: Prentice-Hall.
Oosterhaven, Jan. 1988. "On the Plausibility of the Supply-Driven Input-Output Model," *Journal
    of Regional Science,* 28, 203–217.
Rickman, Daniel S. and R. Keith Schwer. 1995. "A Comparison of the Multipliers of IMPLAN,
    REMI, and RIMS II: Benchmarking Ready-Made Models for Comparison," *Annals of Regional
    Science,* 29, 363–380.
Rose, Adam. 1981. "Utility Lifelines and Economic Activity in the Context of Earthquakes," in J.
    Isenberg (ed.), *Social and Economic Impact of Earthquakes on Utility Lifelines,* New York:
    American Society of Civil Engineers.
Rose, Adam and Tim Allison. 1989. "On the Plausibility of the Supply-Driven Input-Output Model:
    Empirical Evidence on Joint Stability," *Journal of Regional Science,* 29, 451–58.
Rose, Adam and Juan Benavides. 1997. "Interindustry Models for Analyzing the Economics
    Impacts of Earthquakes and Recovery Policies: Illustrative Examples," in B. Jones (ed.), *Ad-
    vances in Social Science Analysis of Earthquakes,* Buffalo, NY: National Center for Earthquake
    Engineering Research.
Rose, Adam and Dangsoon Lim. 1997. *The Economic Impact of Electricity Lifeline Disruptions
    Stemming from the Northridge Earthquake,* Final Report to the National Science Foundation,
    Department of Energy, Environmental, and Mineral Economics, The Pennsylvania State Univer-
    sity, University Park, PA.
Shelby County (Tennessee) Planning Department. 1995. "Census Tabulations of Sectoral Employ-
    ment for Traffic Area Zones," (computer diskette) Memphis.
Shinozuka, Masanobu. 1995. "Interaction of Lifeline Systems under Earthquake Conditions,"
    unpublished manuscript, Princeton University, Princeton.
Shinozuka, Masanobu, Adam Rose, and Ronald Eguchi (eds.). 1997. *Engineering and Socioeco-
    nomic Analysis of a New Madrid Earthquake,* Buffalo, NY: National Center for Earthquake
    Engineering Research.

458   JOURNAL OF REGIONAL SCIENCE, Vol. 37, No. 3, 1997

Shinozuka, Masanobu, Satoshi Tanaka, and Hiromichi Koiwa. 1994. "Interaction of Lifeline Systems Under Earthquake Conditions," *Proceedings of the 2nd China-Japan-U.S. Trilateral Symposium on Lifeline Earthquake Engineering,* pp. 43–52.

Tanaka, Satoshi. 1995. "Lifeline Seismic Reliability Analysis," Ph.D. Dissertation, Waseda University, Tokyo.

Tierney, Kathleen and Joann Nigg. 1997. "Urban Seismic Risk Assessment—Assessing Earthquake Impacts on Business Activity in the Greater Memphis Area," in Shinozuka, Masanobu, Adam Rose and Ronald Eguchi (eds), *Engineering and Socioeconomic Analysis of a New Madrid Earthquake,* Buffalo, NY: National Center for Earthquake Engineering Research.

U.S. Forest Service. 1993. *Micro IMPLAN: A User's Guide,* Rocky Mountain Experiment Station, Ft. Collins, CO.

USC Planning Institute. 1992. *The Business Interruption Effects of a Catastrophic Earthquake on the Newport-Inglewood Fault Zone,* Los Angeles: University of Southern California.

West, Carol T. and Douglas G. Lenze. 1994. "Modeling the Regional Impact of Natural Disaster and Recovery: A General Framework and an Application to Hurricane Andrew," *International Regional Science Review,* 17, 121–50.

Wilson, Robert. 1982. "Earthquake Vulnerability Analysis for Economic Impact Assessment," Information Resources Management Office, Federal Emergency Management Agency, Washington, DC.

Wilson, Robert. 1989. "Efficient and Competitive Rationing," *Econometrica,* 57, 1–40.

Zarnikau, Jay. 1994. "Spot Market Pricing of Water and Efficient Means of Rationing Water during Scarcity," *Resource and Energy Economics,* 16, 189–210.

[15]

JOURNAL OF REGIONAL SCIENCE, VOL. 41, NO. 1, 2001, pp. 39–65

INTEGRATING TRANSPORTATION NETWORK AND REGIONAL ECONOMIC MODELS TO ESTIMATE THE COSTS OF A LARGE URBAN EARTHQUAKE*

Sungbin Cho and Peter Gordon

School of Policy, Planning, & Development,University of Southern California, Los Angeles, CA 90089 U.S.A. E-mail: sungbinc@usc.edu and pgordon@usc.edu

James E. Moore II

Department of Civil and Environmental Engineering, University of Southern California, Los Angeles, CA 90089, U.S.A. E-mail: jmoore@usc.edu

Harry W. Richardson

School of Policy, Planning, & Development, University of Southern California, Los Angeles, CA 90089, U.S.A. E-mail: hrichard@usc.edu

Masanobu Shinozuka

Department of Civil and Environmental Engineering, University of Southern California, Los Angeles, CA 90089, U.S.A. E-mail: shino@usc.edu

Stephanie Chang

Department of Geography, University of Washington, Seattle, WA 98195, U.S.A. E-mail: sec@u.washington.edu

ABSTRACT. In this paper we summarize an integrated, operational model of losses due to earthquake impacts on transportation and industrial capacity, and how these losses affect the metropolitan economy. The procedure advances the information provided by transportation and activity system analysis techniques in ways that help capture the most important ecomonic implications of earthquakes. Network costs and origin-destination requirements are modeled endogenously and consistently. Indirect and induced losses associated with direct impacts on transportation and industrial capacity are distributed

*The research was supported by National Science Foundation, Award CMS 9633386 (EHM). This work has contributed to ongoing investigations supported by NSF Award CMS 9812503 (ISMHR), by the Earthquake Engineering Research Centers Program of the NSF under Award Number EEC-9701568, and by the Institute for Civil Infrastructure Systems. We are grateful for this support, and for the substantive guidance and assistance provided by three anonymous *Journal of Regional Science* referees. This research is a highly collaborative effort. We thank our research assistants, Seongkil Cho, Shin Lee, Junghoon Ki, and Gang Yu of the USC School of Policy, Planning, and Development; and Xue Dong, and Yue Yue Fan of the USC Department of Civil and Environmental Engineering. Their intellectual investment in this work matches our own. The authors remain responsible for any errors or omissions.

Received December 1999; revised June 2000; accepted August 2000.

40   JOURNAL OF REGIONAL SCIENCE, VOL. 41, NO. 1, 2001

across zones and ecomonic sectors. Preliminary results are summarized for a magnitude 7.1 earthquake on the Elysian Park blind thrust fault in Los Angeles.

1. INTRODUCTION

Some of the most dramatic changes in regional economic and infrastructure capacity follow natural disasters. These events result in substantial economic losses associated with the disruption of the urban economy. Despite this, the existing literature on the cost of earthquakes is largely restricted to the measurement of structure and contents losses.

Three research questions motivate this work: first, to integrate regional economic, transportation, bridge performance, and other structural response models in a way that respects feedback relationships between land use and transportation; second, to apply such integrated, operational models to the problem of estimating the full costs of a large earthquake, and the benefits of proposed mitigation measures; and finally, because mitigation measures for public infrastructure are the result of a political process, and "all politics are local," we describe these costs and benefits at the submetropolitan level. To meet these objectives we have specified and operationalized a computable model of the Los Angeles economy that includes both spatial and sectoral detail.

Regional scientists have invested much time examining interindustry models. The detailed intersectoral linkages in these models are useful for exploring regional economic structure. However, this approach does not permit adequate treatment of transportation costs, not all of which are transacted because most roads are publicly provided. Recently this problem was addressed at the national level by the Bureau of Transportation Statistics effort to create Transportation Satellite Accounts (U.S. Department of Transportation, 1998, 1999).

Regional scientists are particularly interested in the spatial dimension of regional economic performance. Spatial elaborations of input-output and related approaches require explicit treatment of the resources consumed by flows between origin-destination pairs (Moses, 1955; Okuyama, Hewings, and Sonis, 1997). In these multiregional-level approaches, explicit representation of the transportation network is usually not necessary. Line-haul costs dominate congestion costs. It is another matter at the intrametropolitan level.

Intrametropolitan input-output analysis has rarely been operationalized in spatial detail. Richardson et al. (1993) provide one approach, combining a metropolitan-level input-output model with a Garin-Lowry model to spatially allocate induced economic impacts. Their model has a number of limitations including the absence of an explicit transportation network and associated congestion effects.

Adding a transportation network to this type of model provides important opportunities. For example, distance decay relationships (destination choice) can be endogenized, permitting spatial allocation of indirect economic impacts as well as induced impacts. Further, the integration of input-output and transportation network models makes it possible to better understand the economic consequences of changes in network capacity. More recently, social science based research on earthquakes has addressed the measurement of business interruption costs (Boarnet, 1998; Gordon, Richardson, and Davis, 1998; Kawashima and Kanoh, 1990; Rose and Benavides, 1998; Rose et al., 1997). Yet, there are still few studies of the role of infrastructure and its interactions with the metropolitan economy.

In this paper we report a model that traces the effects of an earthquake on the Los Angeles economy, including its impact on the transportation services delivered by the highway network. To do this, we develop an integrated framework and methodologies for evaluating the effects of earthquakes on the services delivered by the transportation network. Specifically, we integrate bridge and other structure performance models, transportation network models, spatial allocation models, and interindustry (input-output) models.

Previous Research

Reporting less than two months after the Northridge earthquake, Kimbell and Bolton (1994) relied upon a "historical analogies approach." The nature of that approach is not clear in the report except that they used data on the effects of prior earthquakes and disasters, including the Loma Prieta quake, the Whittier quake, the Oakland fires, and the Los Angeles riots. They found 29,300 immediate job losses for Los Angeles County, with an additional 6,400 jobs lost outside the County. The authors report net positive impacts because of reconstruction later in 1994, but nevertheless, there is a long term negative impact of 18,500 jobs lost.

Using a survey approach, Boarnet (1998) sought information on the impacts of freeway damage from the Northridge earthquake. He found that 43 percent of all firms reporting any losses mentioned that some of these were because of transportation problems. Eguchi et al. (1998) reported on their application of EQE International's Early Post-Earthquake Damage Assessment Tool (EPEDAT), a GIS-based model, to the problem of estimating Northridge losses. They calculated that these losses were in excess of 44 billion dollars.

Chang (1995) introduced multivariate techniques for post-event assessments of lifeline related losses versus those resulting from nonlifeline factors. She applied these methods to an assessment of the economic effects of lifeline disruptions in the Hanshin earthquake. Railroad capacity losses were found to be more consequential than highway losses. Rose and Benavides (1998) also applied interindustry models as a means of measuring regional economic impact analysis, emphasizing indirect costs. The authors traced and recorded the intersectoral ripple effects associated with the full impacts of electricity disruptions expected from a hypothetical 7.5 magnitude earthquake in the Memphis area. A seven percent loss of Gross Regional Product was forecast over the first 15 weeks after the event. Rose and Lim (1997) applied the same model to an analysis of the Northridge earthquake's effects. Rose et al. (1997) developed a methodology for integrated assessment of the regional economic impacts of earthquake-induced electricity lifeline disruptions.

Cochrane (1997) elaborated on the nature of indirect economic damages, including problems with backward and forward linkages. He demonstrated that the receipt of disaster assistance matters in a full accounting of regional impacts—even though these are simply transfers within the larger national context. In addition, any resulting indebtedness merely shifts the burden to future generations. Cochrane also introduces the NIBS (National Institute of Building Standards) model to account for net regional losses and gains after all transfer payments and possible debt payments are included. Among other things, he found that indirect (nonstructure) losses are inversely proportional to the size of the sector shocked.

Okuyama, Hewings, and Sonis (1997) developed a closed interregional input-output model that emphasizes distributional effects. The approach is also sequential and applicable to earthquake-type events where there may be drastic quarter-to-quarter changes in demand and capacity. The model is applied to the Kobe earthquake. Four types of model coefficients are manipulated to simulate the disaster.

Kim et al. (1998) suggested how the Leontief and Strout (1963) multi-regional input-output model can be combined with Wilson's (1970) entropy function. Kim et al. suggested an approach that focuses on the incentives to return an interregional (substate) transportation system to pre-earthquake conditions. They discussed a procedure for matching post-earthquake flows to pre-earthquake flows as a mechanism for imputing changes in final demands.

Gordon, Richardson, and Davis (1998) applied an input-output model (Southern California Planning Model version 1, SCPM1) of the Southern California region to the problem of estimating business interruption costs of the 1994 Northridge earthquake. Their analysis found that business interruption accounted for 25–30 percent of the full costs of the earthquake. Conventional loss estimation studies focused on structure losses (what earthquake engineers refer to as "direct losses"), thereby omitting many significant costs.

As this summary indicates, there has been limited attention given to the socioeconomic impacts of earthquakes. Most of the research on earthquakes is in engineering and geology. Progress in economic impact research is more recent. Earthquake engineering is a challenging field, but exploring and integrating the economic impacts of earthquakes with engineering models is especially challenging.

Impact Models and the Southern California Planning Model Version 1 (SCPM1)

As demonstrated above, the most widely used models of regional economic impacts are versions of interindustry models. These attempt to trace intra-regional and interregional shipments, usually at a high level of industrial disaggregation. Being demand driven, they only account for losses via backward linkages.

The Southern California Planning Model version 1 (SCPM1) was developed for the five-county Los Angeles metropolitan region, and has the unique capability to allocate all impacts, in terms of jobs or the dollar value of output, to 308 subregional zones, mostly municipalities. This is the result of an integrated modeling approach that incorporates two fundamental components: input-output and spatial allocation. The approach allows the representation of estimated spatial and sectoral impacts corresponding to any vector of changes in final demand. Exogenous shocks treated as changes in final demand are fed through an input-output model to generate sectoral effects that are then introduced into the spatial allocation model.

An early version of this model was developed to analyze the spatial-sectoral impacts of the South Coast Air Quality Management District's Air Quality Management Plan and has since been applied to other Los Angeles metropolitan-area policy problems. Our work on Northridge earthquake business interruption effects uses SCPM1. That model is driven by reduced demand by damaged businesses, as ascertained in a survey of businesses.

The first model component is built upon the Regional Science Research Corporation input-output model. This model has several advantages. These include:

a high degree of sectoral disaggregation (515 sectors);

anticipated adjustments in production technology;

an embedded occupation-industry matrix enabling employment impacts to be identified across ninety-three occupational groups: this is particularly useful for disaggregating consumption effects by income class and facilitates the estimation of job impacts by race;

an efficient mechanism for differentiating local from out-of-region input-output transactions using Regional Purchase Coefficients (RPC); and

the identification of state and local tax impacts.

The second basic model component is used for allocating sectoral impacts across 308 geographic zones in southern California. The key was to adapt a Garin-Lowry style model for spatially allocating the induced impacts generated by the input-output model. The building blocks of the SCPM1 are the metropolitan input-output model, a journey-to-work matrix, and a journey-to-nonwork-destinations matrix. This is a journey-from-services-to-home matrix that is more restrictively described as a "journey-to-shop" matrix in the Garin-Lowry model.

The journey-from-services-to-home matrix includes any trip associated with a home based transaction other than the sale of labor to an employer. This includes retail trips and other transaction trips, but excludes nontransaction trips such as trips to visit friends and relatives. Data for the journey-from-services-to-home matrix includes all of the trips classified by the Southern

44   JOURNAL OF REGIONAL SCIENCE, VOL. 41, NO. 1, 2001

California Association of Governments as home-to-shop trips, and a subset of the trips classified as home-to-other and other-to-other trips.

The key innovation associated with the SCPM1 is to incorporate the full range of multipliers obtained via input-output techniques to obtain detailed economic impacts by sector and by submetropolitan zone. The SCPM1 follows the principles of the Garin-Lowry model by allocating sectoral output (or employment) to zones via a loop that relies on the trip matrices. Induced consumption expenditures are traced back from the workplace to the residential site using a journey-to-work matrix and from the residential site to the place of purchase or consumption through a journey-to-services matrix. See Appendix A for a further summary of SCPM1.

Incorporating the Garin-Lowry approach to spatial allocation makes the transportation flows in SCPM1 exogenous. They are also relatively aggregate, defined at the level of political jurisdictions. With no explicit representation of the transportation network, SCPM1 has no means to account for the economic impact of changes in transportation supply and demand. Earthquakes are likely to induce such changes.

2. APPROACH

In the present work, we focus on a hypothetical earthquake, a magnitude 7.1 event on the Elysian Park blind thrust fault. Figure 1 is a map of the Los Angeles metropolitan area described in terms of the transportation network.

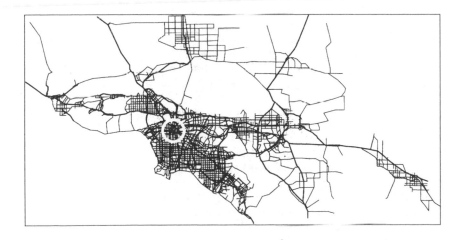

FIGURE 1: The Los Angeles Metropolitan Area Transportation Network, Consisting of 19,601 Links and 1,534 Traffic Analysis Zones.

The circle includes Elysian Park and downtown Los Angeles. The Elysian Park fault runs East Southeast from the center of the circle. Results of structure damage to businesses, as developed by EQE's EPEDAT model of structure damage, were used to drive a new version of SCPM, SCPM2, that has been improved to include the regional transportation network. EQE's EPEDAT is a GIS-based earthquake loss estimation program that estimates ground motion, structural damage, and direct business interruption losses associated with a specific earthquake (Eguchi et al., 1997; Campbell, 1997).

The building damage models in EPEDAT are based on ground motion, structural type, number of stories, and building use category. These models incorporate expert judgment and empirical damage data from previous earthquakes. The EPEDAT data for Los Angeles incorporate building inventory data and experience from previous disasters. The EPEDAT models do not include measures of construction quality. Detailed building inventory data on construction quality is generally nonexistent.

EPEDAT predicts, among other values, the lengths of time for which firms throughout the region will be nonoperational. This allows the calculation of exogenously prompted reductions in demand by these businesses. These are introduced into the interindustry model as reductions in final demand (Isard and Kuenne, 1953). Explicit treatment of the transportation network makes it possible to model the concurrent impact of transportation cost changes on the activity system, including reductions in regional network capacity resulting from large numbers of bridge failures.

Figure 2 summarizes our approach. Engineering models predict damage to transportation structures by location for the Elysian Park scenario. EPEDAT predicts spatial loss of industrial function. The I-O model translates this production shock into direct, indirect, and induced costs, and the indirect and induced costs are spatially allocated in terms consistent with the endogenous transportation behaviors of firms and household.

Implementing this approach is a data intensive effort that builds on the data resources assembled for SCPM1. SCPM2 results are computed at the level of the Southern California Association of Governments' (SCAG) 1,527 traffic analysis zones, and then aggregated to the level of the 308 political jurisdictions defined for SCPM1. These jurisdictional boundaries routinely cross traffic analysis zones. Results for traffic analysis zones crossed by jurisdictional boundaries are allocated in proportion to area. Like SCPM1, SCPM2 aggregates to 17 the 515 sectors represented in the Regional Science Research Corporation's PC I-O model Version 7 (Stevens, 1996) based on the work of Stevens, Treyz, and Lahr (1983). This research extended SCPM1 by treating the transportation network explicitly, endogenizing otherwise exogenous Garin-Lowry style matrices describing the travel behavior of households, achieving consistency across network costs and origin-destination requirements. SCPM2 makes distance decay and congestion functions explicit. This allows us to endogenize the spatial allocation of indirect and induced economic losses by endogenizing choices of

46   JOURNAL OF REGIONAL SCIENCE, VOL. 41, NO. 1, 2001

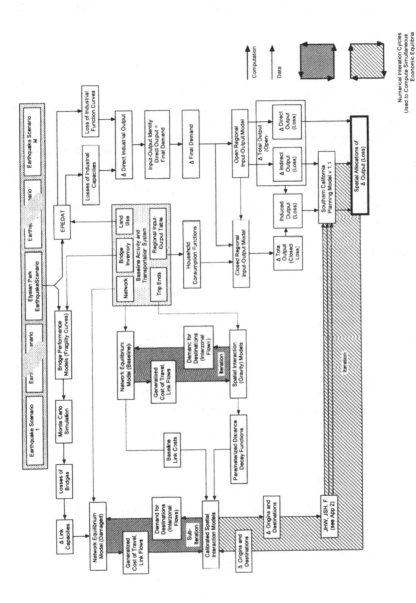

FIGURE 2:   Summary of the Southern California Planning Model-2 (SCPM2).

route and destination. This better allocates indirect and induced economic losses over zones in response to direct earthquake losses to industrial and transportation capacity.

Establishing a Baseline

Our goal is to model the effects of earthquakes on industrial capacity and system-wide transportation demand and supply. As for as possible we also measure the economic impacts associated with both of these effects. Our first step is to compute a pre-earthquake baseline that is consistent with respect to equilibrium network costs, network flows, and interzonal flows and origin-destination requirements.

SCPM1 includes work and shopping (including service) trips, but not other nonwork travel and freight flows. The SCAG origin-destination data includes requirements for work and nonwork trips, but not freight flows. We map the five-county, 1,527-zone SCAG transportation network to the five-county, 308-zone SCPM activity system. This expresses the scaled interzonal flows associated with the regional transportation network in terms of flows between SCPM zones.

Each element in the SCPM1 journey-from home to-work matrix **JHW** describes the proportion of workers residing in zone i who work in zone j relative to the total employment in zone j. Each element of the SCPM1 journey-from-services-to-home matrix **JSH** describes the proportion of purchasers residing in zone i who transact for services in zone j relative to total to the total number of purchasers transacting in zone j. The SCPM1 **JHW** matrix is based on spatial distributions extracted from the Census Transportation Planning Package (CTPP) made available to SCAG by the U.S. Bureau of Transportation Statistics (U.S. Department of Transportation, 1994). The SCPM1 version of the **JSH** matrix is the result of a gravity model estimation. In the SCPM2 extension developed in this research, the elements of the **JHW** and **JSH** matrices are endogenized as a simultaneous function of network costs and estimated gravity model parameters.

Some of the model's 17 economic sectors involve freight flows. We account for these in four categories: nondurable manufactured goods, durable manufactured goods, mining (including petroleum), and wholesale. Freight flows include intermediate flows to production facilities, as well as flows to final demand sites inside and outside the region. This includes import and export flows, but not flows to and from residential sites. Most of these latter flows correspond to shopping trips. Export flows satisfy final demand outside the region. Some import flows satisfy final demand within the region, and some are inputs to production processes. Some import and export flows also appear as throughputs. Data on the area's trade flows is assembled from a variety of sources. This presented some difficulties because imports and exports are reported for the Customs District, an area larger than the metropolitan area. Also, some of these reported flows are simply transshipped via the Los Angeles area. Consequently, we also rely on 1996 international export sales for the five-county area (U.S. Bureau of the Census, 1997). These data are tabulated in the Metro Area Exporter Location (EL) file (*www.ita.doc.gov/*).

Given the SCPM input-output relationships describing input requirements per unit of output, and given baseline jobs by economic sector and zone from the CTPP, the next step is to compute the total requirements of output i in zone z

(1) $\qquad D_i^z = \sum_j a_{i,j} X_j^z +$ sector i shipments to zone z from

transshipment zones (imports) and from other zones
to accommodate lodal final demand not associated
with households

where $X_j^z =$ the total output of commodity j in zone z given base year
employment in sector j and zone z,

and

$\qquad a_{i,j} =$ is the i,jth element of the matrix of value demand coefficients
for the (open) input-output model **A**. This is the flow from i to j
per unit output of j.

The first term on the right-hand side of Equation (1) accounts for interindustry shipments out of all zones by aggregate freight sector i. This summation applies to the open input-output model so D_i^z excludes most shipments to households. In the open model, households generate local final demands but no intermediate demands. Most shipments associated with this final demand are treated as shopping trips. D_i^z is the total flow of commodity i supplied from everywhere to all nonfinal demand activities in zone z.

Similarly, we compute total supply of output i furnished by zone z,

(2) $\quad O_i^z = \sum_j b_{i,j} X_i^z +$ sector i shipments to transshipment zones from

zone z to accommodate nonlocal final demand (exports)
and to other zones to accommodate local final demand
not associated with households

where $X_i^z =$ the total output of commodity i in zone z given base year
employment in sector i and zone z,

and

$\qquad b_{i,j} =$ is the i,jth element of the matrix of value supply coefficients
for for the (open) input-output model **B**. This is the flow from i
to j per unit output of i.

The first term on the right-hand side of Equation (2) accounts for interindustry shipments out of zone z by aggregate freight sector i. Like D_i^z, O_i^z excludes most shipments to households. As in the case of Equation (1), these shipments consist of shopping trips. O_i^z is the total flow of aggregate freight commodity i supplied from zone z to all activities everywhere.

Value flows O_i^z supplied by activity i and originating in zone z and value flows D^z_i demanded from activity i and terminating in zone z must be translated into freight trip productions P_i^r and attractions A_i^s associated with activity i in zone z. Using conversion factors constructed from the 1993 Commodity Flow Survey (CFS, U.S. Department of Transportation, 1997), we convert all value flows D_i^z and O_i^z dollar values to truckload equivalents. The CFS describes freight flows in terms of dollars per ton for the major industrial sectors. The 1992 census of transportation (U.S. Bureau of the Census, 1993) describes tons per truck. This permits calculation of a coefficient η_i relating the value of shipments to zonal transportation requirements, typically passenger car units (PCU)

$$(3) \qquad\qquad\qquad P_i^r = \eta_i O_i^z$$
$$= \text{trip production of commodity } i \text{ in origin zone } z = r$$

and

$$(4) \qquad\qquad\qquad A_i^s = \eta_i D_i^z$$
$$= \text{trip attraction of commodity } i \text{ to destination zone } z = s$$

Based on available network equilibrium costs $c_{SCAG}^{r,s}$ and the trip production and attraction vectors determined previously, we calibrate thirteen separate spatial interaction models. These include the four classes of commodity flows listed above and nine flows involving people: home-to-work, work-to-home, home-to-shop, shop-to-home, home-to-other, other-to-home, work-to-other, other-to-work, and other-to-other. We estimate each of these thirteen matrices of interzonal flows separately, but in response to a common measure of network equilibrium costs. The structure of interzonal flows in each of these matrices influences network equilibrium costs. Thus this baseline calibration required iteration between the network assignment model and the set of gravity models. The objective of these baseline gravity model calibrations is the estimation of distance decay parameters (Wilson, 1970). These distance decay parameters are used to predict travel demand following an earthquake. Once estimated, the home-to-work matrix is converted to the **JHW** matrix by striking proportions in columns, that is, relative to the total number of trips terminating in zone j. The home-to-shop matrix is added to a subset of flows from the home-to-other and other-to-other matrices; and then converted to be **JSH** matrix, also by striking proportions in columns.

We rely on a singly-constrained gravity model formulation in the case of freight because we do not have trip interchange matrices for freight sectors. The

50   JOURNAL OF REGIONAL SCIENCE, VOL. 41, NO. 1, 2001

parameters of the singly-constrained formulation are calibrated based on the
following criteria (Putnam, 1983)

(5)
$$\text{Min}_{\beta_i} \sum_r \left| P_i^r(\beta_i) \ln\left(P_i^r\right) - \sum_r P_i^r(\beta_i) \ln\left[P_i^r(\beta_i)\right] \right|$$

where β_i = distance decay coefficient for sector i;

$P_i^r(\beta_i)$ = estimated trip production of commodity i in origin zone r

$$= \sum_s A_i^s \left[B_i^r \exp\left(-\beta_i c^{r,s}\right) \Big/ \sum_r B_i^r \exp\left(-\beta_i c^{r,s}\right) \right]$$

$c^{r,s}$ = generalized cost of transportation from origin zone r to
destination zone s;

P_i^r = trip production of commodity i in origin zone r;

A_i^s = trip attraction of commodity i to destination zone s; and

B_i^r – constant specific to sector i and origin zone r, the square
root of the number of total employees in origin zone r.

We construct production and attraction vectors for each freight sector using
Equations (1), (2), (3), and (4). Given initial values for transportation costs and
gravity model parameters, we proceed by estimating inter-zonal flows for sector
i and calculating trip productions implied by these flows. Trip attractions are
fixed. For each sector, the value of β_i is adjusted to move the estimated values
$P_i^r(\beta_i)$ toward the target values P_i^r.

We have more information about people flows, namely, SCAG's empirically
estimated trip interchange tables for the nine classes of flows described above.
The availability of these interchange matrices makes it possible to estimate
distance decay parameters for a doubly-constrained gravity model

$$t_i^{r,s}(\beta) = P_i^r A_i^s \left[B_i^r H_i^s \beta_{0,i} \exp\left(-\beta_{1,i} c^{r,s}\right) c^{r,s^{(\beta_{2,i})}} \right]$$

where

$\beta_{0,i}$, $\beta_{1,i}$, and $\beta_{2,i}$ = elements in a vector of distance decay coefficients for
sector i;

$c^{r,s}$ = generalized cost of transportation from origin zone r
to destination zone s;

P_i^r = trip production of flow i in origin zone r;

A_i^s = trip attraction of flow i to destination zone s;

B_i^r = constant specific to sector i and origin zone r

$$= \left[\sum_s A_i^s H_i^s \beta_{0,i} \exp\left(-\beta_{1,i} c^{r,s}\right) c^{r,s(-\beta_{2,i})} \right]^{-1}$$

and

$$H_i^s = \text{constant specific to sector } i \text{ and origin zone } rs$$

$$= \left[\sum_r P_i^r B_i^r \beta_{0,i} \exp\left(-\beta_{1,i} c^{r,s}\right) c^{r,s(-\beta_{2,i})} \right]^{-1}$$

Calibration is accomplished by adjusting the vector β to match the observed travel distribution, which in turn depends on the observed flows $t_i^{r,s}$ and the equilibrium network costs $c^{r,s}$.

In all cases, equilibrium transportation costs $c^{r,s}$ are initialized as $c_{SCAG}^{r,s}$, based on estimated link flows and costs provided by the Southern California Association of Governments. The parameters that minimize Equation (5) and match the travel time distributions for observed flows also produce a set of 13 trip interchange matrices. Summing the 13 trip interchange matrices provides a new set of flows, expressed in PCUs, and associated equilibrium network costs $c^{r,s}$. These costs are fed back into each of the gravity models. The matrix of equilibrium network costs **c** and the vector of distance decay parameters β are iteratively adjusted until consistent travel demands and travel costs are computed. The end result is a matrix of equilibrium link costs $c^{*r,s}$ consistent with a corresponding set of equilibrium trip interchange matrices consisting of elements $t_i^{*r,s}$.

Status Quo: Earthquake Impacts Without Mitigation

The information needed to model the baseline with the internal consistency described here is sufficient to treat changes in configuration of the network and the activity system. Following an earthquake, there will be losses of network capacity and simultaneous losses of industrial capacity. The former reduces transportation capacity and raises costs. The latter reduces demands imposed on the network. The building fragility curve analysis provided by EPEDAT and the bridge performance models ascribe consistent losses of both types to particular earthquake scenarios. The spatial interaction elements of our approach make it possible to capture the changes in transportation requirements associated with changes in network performance. These changes and changes resulting from earthquake damage to industrial facilities are treated simultaneously and consistently.

3. AN APPLICATION: THE ELYSIAN PARK SCENARIO EARTHQUAKE

SCPM2 is applied to the Los Angeles metropolitan area for the scenario defined by a maximum credible earthquake (magnitude 7.1) on the Elysian Park thrust ramp. This Elysian Park scenario was selected on the basis of its potential to cause major damage and casualties. Like the 1994 Northridge earthquake, the Elysian Park scenario occurs on a blind thrust fault. Although the maximum size earthquakes that seismologists believe are possible on the blind thrust faults are lower than those on, for example, the San Andreas Fault, they are

52   JOURNAL OF REGIONAL SCIENCE, VOL. 41, NO. 1, 2001

expected to have the potential to cause severe damage due to their proximity to metropolitan Los Angeles. The planar earthquake source representation for the Elysian Park event varies in depth from 11 to 16 kilometers below the surface. The surface projection of this source includes a broad, densely populated area of central Los Angeles County, including downtown Los Angeles.

Bridge Fragility Curves

Bridge fragility curves (Shinozuka, 1998; Shinozuka et al., 2000) give the probability distribution of bridge damage states conditioned by bridge type and earthquake event in the case the Elysian Park scenario. These damage states are defined in terms of a bridge damage index (BDI) ranging from zero (no damage) to unity (collapse). See Table 1.

The qualitative labels for bridge damage states are standard in the earthquake engineering field, but the functionality of a damaged bridge remains subjective. Yet, the earthquake and transportation engineering literatures remain silent on the question of how to translate qualitative characterizations such as "moderate damage" or "severe damage" into traffic capacity. A moderately damaged bridge might well be used before the bridge is repaired or replaced by, for example, restricting its use to automobiles, restricting the right of way to the least damaged portions of the bridge deck, suppressing vibrations by instituting very low speed limits for larger vehicles, metering access to the bridge to ensure low density volumes, or temporarily reinforcing the bridge. However, operations personnel from several State Departments of Transportation (DOTs) indicate that the liability and safety risks associated with extracting service from a damaged bridge suppresses the likelihood that these options would be implemented. If there is a substantive risk of injury or death from post earthquake failures, the current operational perspective is that the bridge should be closed. The California Department of Transportation appears somewhat more risk tolerant in this respect than DOTs in the midwest, but we conclude that this reflects the California perspective that earthquakes are not rare events, and a particularly sophisticated view of the importance of network management. Still, from a network management perspective the key operational question for all State DOTs is "At what bridge damage index value should bridge closure occur?" Our approach makes it possible to systematically investigate the cost implications of alternative bridge closure criteria.

TABLE 1: Bridge Damage Indices and Bridge Damage States[a]

Bridge Damage State	Representative Bridge Damage Index (BDI)	Approximate Interval of Bridge Damage Index Values
No Damage	0.000	0.000–0.050
Minor Damage	0.100	0.050–0.200
Moderate Damage	0.300	0.200–0.525
Major Damage	0.750	0.525–0.875
Collapse	1.000	0.875–1.000

Note: [a]Cho et al. (1999).

The approximate midpoints of the bridge damage index intervals associated with moderate and severe damage states are 0.30 and 0.75, respectively. We treat these values as the most conservative and riskiest BDI thresholds that transportation authorities are likely to accept as bridge closure criteria. A conservative, safety-oriented policy will close moderately damaged structures to traffic, including bridges with a damage index ≥ 0.30. This will increase delay and other transportation costs. A less risk averse policy emphasizing an emergency focus on maintaining regional economic function will leave moderately damaged structures open, closing only bridges with a damage index ≥ 0.75. No authority will open the most dangerous structures.

Modeling Losses

Earthquakes induce changes in industrial production due to effects on building stocks, particularly factories, warehouses, and office buildings. Damage to production facilities is translated into an exogenous change in final demand. Building damage causes direct loss in industrial production. EPEDAT's loss-of-function curves convert damage to building stocks to loss of production by zone and sector. The loss-of-function curves relate structural damage states to business closure times and direct business interruption (production) losses. Inputs are commercial and industrial building damage estimates from EPEDAT, expressed as the percent of structures in each of four damage states by use class and by each of the 308 SCPM zones. Outputs are estimates of direct business interruption loss for the region by industry, month (over the first year following the earthquake), and SCPM zone.

EPEDAT projects structure losses in the five-county Los Angeles metropolitan region of between 21.7 billion dollars and 36.2 billion dollars for the Elysian Park event. If building contents are included, property damage is estimated at 33.9 dollars to 56.6 billion dollars. Residential damage accounts for approximately two-thirds of the total. About 72 percent of the structural damage is estimated to occur in Los Angeles County.

A corresponding change in final demand drives SCPM2, ultimately provides changes in output and employment for 17 sectors across 308 zones. This is an iterative calculation. Direct changes are exogenous and already spatially identified. SCPM2 allocates indirect and induced changes in a way that respects both observed travel behavior and new network costs. A core contribution of this research is the ability to more completely endogenize submetropolitan freight and passengers flows and destinations. In this case nine classes of passenger flows are combined with four classes of freight and loaded on a common network. Details of this procedure appear in Appendix B.

Results for the Elysian Park Scenario Earthquake

Aggregate results. Bridge damage results are generated for 200 Monte Carlo simulations of the Elysian Park scenario earthquake. The bridge damage index achieved by any specific structure varies across each simulation, but each

54   JOURNAL OF REGIONAL SCIENCE, VOL. 41, NO. 1, 2001

outcome is drawn from the fixed stochastic process corresponding to the Elysian Park scenario. Collectively, these simulations correspond to a distribution of damaged transportation networks. Each network is characterized (in part) by a vector of dimension 2,810 bridges, each assigned a BDI value. The alternative bridge closure criteria (BDI $\geq$ 0.30, BDI $\geq$ 0.75) are applied to every bridge in every network in this set, producing two new distributions. The transportation networks in these distributions are still characterized by a vector of 2,810 bridges, but each bridge is now open (1), or closed (0).

Our model of the Los Angeles economy is convergent. We implement an improved version of the Frank-Wolfe algorithm that relies on an application of the dual simplex method to complete shortest path calculations. Preliminary comparisons with commercial codes indicate substantial computational advantage with respect to large scale network flow estimates. Yet, it is still computationally infeasible to exhaustively investigate each network state represented in these distributions. Instead, we select representative members of each. The 200 simulations are rank ordered in terms of the baseline vehicle-miles that would otherwise be traveled across the damaged links. This rank ordering makes it possible to identify those simulations that are maximally disruptive with respect to baseline transportation flows, and representative in a median sense. Figures 3 and 4 identify maximal and median outcomes, respectively, for a conservative, safety-oriented bridge closure criterion of BDI $\geq$ 0.3.

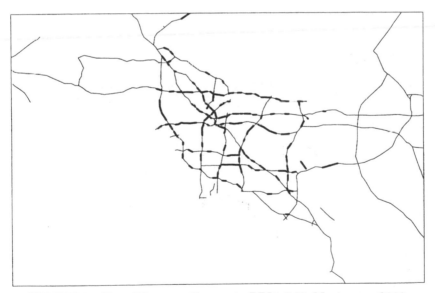

FIGURE 3: Closed Freeway Segments, BDI $\geq$ 0.75, Maximum of 200 Simulations.

An example of preliminary simulation results describing the full costs of a magnitude 7.1 Elysian Park event are summarized in Table 2. Row A reflects the midpoint of the range of structure damage predicted by EPEDAT, 45.25 billion dollars including 29 billion dollars in structure losses. This is the unamortized replacement (or repair) cost of buildings and contents. This value excludes the cost of replacing bridges. Row B is the sum of direct, indirect, and induced losses computed by the I-O model of the five-county, Los Angeles metropolitan area. This sum is 46.7 billion dollars. These aggregate values are identical across all other simulations (Cho et al., 1999). These costs are a cumulative impact over one year of economic activity. Row C summarizes the post-earthquake network equilibrium transportation costs in light of reduced production and reduced network capacity. These values vary across all simulations. These costs are also cumulative over one year of economic activity. Table 2 corresponds to maximum simulated disruption of baseline transportation combined with a conservative, safety-oriented bridge closure criterion. This results in a substantial reduction in transportation network capacity, and an associated increase in transportation costs of almost 43 billion dollars. The full costs of the earthquake are estimated to be almost 135 billion dollars, close to 20 percent of Gross Regional Product (GRP), although direct (business interruption) costs account for about six percent. In this case, transportation costs account for a little less than one-third of the full cost of the earthquake. The full costs for the

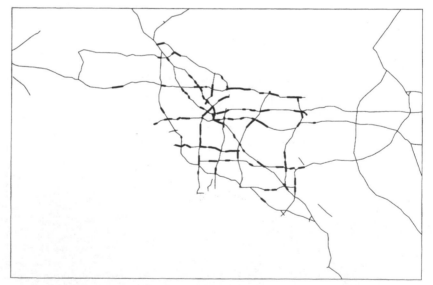

FIGURE 4: Closed Freeway Segments, BDI ≥ 0.30, Median of 200 Simulations.

56 JOURNAL OF REGIONAL SCIENCE, VOL. 41, NO. 1, 2001

TABLE 2: Total Loss ($Billions): Elysian Park Magnitude 7.1 Earthquake, Maximum Simulated Disruption to Baseline Transportation (Closure at BDI $\geq$ 0.30)

Loss Type	Baseline		Elysian Park Scenario: Conservative Bridge Closure Criterion	
A Structure Loss[a]			$45.250 billion (33.5 percent of total)	
Business Loss				
Direct Loss[b]			28.155	
Indirect Loss[c]			9.627	
Induced Loss[d]			8.955	
B Business Loss Subtotal			46.737 billion (34.6 percent of total)	
Network Costs[e]	PCU Minutes	$ Billions	PCU Minutes	$ Billions
Personal Travel Cost	85,396,813.	21.290	225,830,486.	56.300
Freight Cost	10,298.781.	4.550	28,285,954.	12.495
Total Travel Cost	95,695,594.	25.839	254,116,440.	68.795
Network Loss = Δ Network Costs			PCU Minutes	$ Billions
Δ Personal Travel Cost			140,433,673.	35.010
Δ Freight Cost			17,987,173	7.946
C Δ Total Travel Cost			158,420,846.	42.956 (31.8 percent of total)
Loss Total = A + B + C			$134.943 billion	

Notes: [a]Midpoint of the range of structure damage predicted by EPEDAT, EQE International.
[b]EPEDAT.

[c]RSRI Model.

[d]Difference between the RSRI solution with the processing sector closed with respect to labor and the RSRI solution with the processing sector open with respect to labor.

[e]Network cost is the generalized total transportation cost associated with a simultaneous equilibrium across choice of destinations and routes. These estimates reflect 365 travel days per year, an average vehicle occupancy of 1.42 for passenger cars, 2.14 passenger car units per truck, a value of time for individuals of 6.5 dollars per hour, and 35 dollars per hr for freight.

median case in 200 simulations are 102.332 billion dollars. Slightly more than ten percent of the median value consists of increased travel costs.

One way to interpret the full cost of the earthquake is as the true of cost of damage to economic stocks, expressed as the sum of replacement and repair costs and the net present value of future losses due to diminished production and transportation stocks. The loss-of-function curves used in this research describe production capacity over a one-year period following the earthquake. Production capacity is predicted by EPEDAT to approach pre-earthquake levels within six months. Restoration of transportation network capacity is less well accounted for at this point. Bridges are assumed to remain closed for one year following the earthquake. During this period they are repaired or replaced. Other assumptions or empirical relationships can be accommodated to further refine these preliminary results. Damage to Los Angeles freeways was repaired very quickly after the Northridge earthquake. Repairs in the San Francisco Bay Area took significantly longer than one year following the Loma Prieta earthquake. State DOT officials provide very different expert estimates of the time required for repair following extensive damage.

Summary of spatially disaggregated results. SCPM2 provides unprecedented disaggregation of economic impacts over metropolitan space. Tabular results for this research and corresponding maps are available on our website (*http://www.usc.edu/schools/research/research2.html*). A summary of the disaggregate results indicates the following:

Nonstructural direct economic (business interruption) losses are 28.2 billion dollars, or 3.65 percent of the I-O model GRP baseline. Most of these losses are in Los Angeles County, where the finance, insurance and real estate (FIRE) sector account for 15 percent of the total losses.

The region's five largest cities (Los Angeles, Long Beach, Anaheim, Santa Ana, and Irvine) suffer the largest business interruption losses in absolute terms. This is as expected, that is, the largest cities are likely to accrue the largest losses.

Of the twenty cities (subareas in the case of the City of Los Angeles) that suffer the greatest proportionate business interruption impacts, the five cities and subareas most heavily affected lose slightly less than six percent of their GRP (5.46 to 5.83 percent). The twenty proportionally hardest hit cities and subregions are located mainly in the central and east-central areas of the region. Nine of the top twenty are subareas of the city of Los Angeles, mostly located toward the east. The only westside cities among the top twenty are Beverly Hills and West Hollywood.

Regional, nonstructural indirect economic losses are 9.6 billion dollars, accruing mostly in Los Angeles County. Regional induced economic losses are 8.9 billion dollars, also mostly to Los Angeles county. Total economic losses given no network damage are 46.8 billion dollars, or 6.05 percent of GRP. This implies an overall multiplier between direct and total impacts of 1.66. Most regional indirect economic losses are in the manufacturing (nondurable) and FIRE sectors. Most regional induced economic losses are in the same sectors, but the FIRE sector is more heavily affected than the nondurable manufacturing sector.

Corresponding results are calculated for other representative bridge-closure simulations. All of these results include the change in network costs associated with reductions in the supply of transportation services. The resulting redistribution of economic activities are just one source of local (city-level) losses. Increases in network transportation costs are another significant source of local impacts. These costs are more difficult to disaggregate. There is insufficient information to reliably allocate these transportation costs to economic sectors, but these costs can be geographically distributed to traffic origins and destinations. These new network costs may also influence the distribution of indirect and induced economic losses through the distance decay relationship between travel cost and destination choice. However, in all our simulations the overall GRP changes associated with indirect and induced economic losses remain modest. Differences in spatially distributed impacts are also modest.

The Southern California region has a highly redundant road and highway system, and these findings corroborate the economic importance of the regional transportation network's high levels of redundancy. The high level of travel endogeneity associated with the travel choices represented in SCPM2 is explained by the redundancy of the Los Angeles regional transportation network. The various bridge closure simulations affect between 84 and 326 directional network links, including freeway and arterial links. The representation of the network contained in SCPM2 includes 16,946 links. Bridge closures do affect total travel cost and route choice. A comparison of our simulations indicates that the cumulative value of increased network cost can be significant, but the day-to-day increase does not induce profound changes in destination choice, and thus does not have a pronounced impact on the spatial distribution of economic losses.

4. CONCLUSIONS

Summary of Results

These research results permit us to assess the earthquake risk to the transportation system and the urban economy by accounting for a wide range of outcomes associated with damage to bridges and production facilities. This approach has three elements; specifying an integrated model, assembling data from disparate sources, and achieving computability. Our results are preliminary, and we continue to pursue improvements in all three dimensions. Our estimate that the full cost of an Elysian Park earthquake will account for 20 percent of GRP is plausible in light of the available literature. Structure losses account for approximately one-third of this total. Modeling business interruption costs is essential for estimating full regional economic losses.

Our integration of seismic, transportation network, spatial allocation, and input-output models permits the study of how the economic impacts of industrial and transportation structure loss are distributed over metropolitan space. Some of this loss is produced directly by the earthquake, which destroys industrial capacity. The procedure accounts for the effect of industrial structure losses and resulting direct production losses. The model computes further indirect and induced losses, and makes the spatial distribution of these losses sensitive to increases in network costs resulting from transportation structure losses.

Research Extensions

Policy tests: earthquake impacts with alternative mitigation measures. We can execute this procedure for any relevant earthquake, mitigation, or reconstruction scenario. The baseline exercise describes pre-earthquake conditions. The simulations described above summarize post-earthquake outcomes conditioned on present levels of mitigation. These results should be contrasted with results that include mitigation measures. The difference between these full-cost results measures the benefits of the mitigation, to be compared against the costs of implementing the mitigation. Importantly, the benefits measured in this manner are provided at the local submetropolitan level. This includes municipalities, and in the case of the City of Los Angeles, city council districts. If all politics are indeed local, then results like this are critically important to policy implementation.

However, these sorts of comparisons remain difficult. SCPM2 provides a good starting point. SCPM2 can determine a distribution of costs associated with a given earthquake scenario. More fundamental information is needed to apply SCPM2 to policy evaluation. Bridge fragility curves have been estimated for unretrofitted structures, but are not available for retrofitted facilities. Consequently the additional post-earthquake transportation capacity that would be made available by retrofit programs is difficult to model.

Even as improved engineering models are made available, rational prioritization of facilities for retrofit will remain a challenge. Retrofit, repair, and reconstruction options are probably best described as a special case of the network design problem, and large-scale network design problems are difficult. SCPM2 makes it possible to model the system states associated with conventional attacks on the network design problem, but even our most efficient computing procedures are too expensive to allow the problem to be addressed optimally. Further, retrofit programs do not consist of projects dedicated to individual bridges. Large-scale bridge retrofit and reconstruction programs involved defining projects consisting of several proximate facilities bundled to reduce equipment and traffic diversion costs.

Improving SCPM2. Our results suggest several hypotheses relating to the relationships accounted for by SCPM2 and the way these relationships are parameterized.

First, this application of SCPM2 remains incomplete. The loss-of-function curves apply only to production activities. The impact on households, that is, on the production of labor, has not yet been accounted for, and changes in the spatial distribution of activities and losses does not reflect the impact of changes in household consumption.

Second, destination choice may be more sensitive to post-earthquake travel costs than to pre-earthquake costs. The distance decay functions in SCPM2 are estimated with pre-earthquake data. Post-earthquake responses to travel cost may be different. Travelers may be more risk averse than the distance decay functions in SCPM2 imply.

Third, travelers may diminish trip frequencies in response to the cost of travel. In SCPM2, demand for freight transportation changes as a result of the earthquake, but passenger trip generation rates remain unchanged. If trip generation rates are endogenized, some longer passenger trips will be removed from these results, which will intensify changes in the geographic distribution of activities and losses.

In addition to the obvious data difficulties, there are a variety of inevitable theoretical omissions at this stage of our research. The procedure does not account for the impact of transportation structure losses on final demand. The employment consequences of residential structure losses are not considered in this procedure. Input-output approaches emphasize backward linkages but ignore forward linkages. The reduced demand associated with damaged industrial facilities is included, but the consequences of constraints on industrial capacity are overlooked. We did not attempt to account for the many nonmaterial costs inflicted on the victims of earthquakes. However, we hope to add a feedback from increased freight costs to reduced household final demand.

Treating the Los Angeles metropolitan region in isolation from the rest of the world inevitably distorts the local economic impact of a Los Angeles earthquake. Cochrane (1997) and others suggested that regions affected by earthquakes are likely to increase their imports to make up for local shortfalls, and undamaged firms within the region may seek export markets outside the region if local demands are reduced. SCPM2's I-O framework does not accommodate these adjustments well, and these may be important, particularly with respect to transportation costs. While interregional import and export changes will reduce production losses, these interregional changes also tend to increase demand for transportation, and intensify transportation costs.

Perhaps most importantly, the interindustry core of SCPM2 does not account for the role of price changes. Price adjustments are crucial resource allocation mechanisms, especially in areas afflicted by natural disasters. In addition to addressing the points listed above, our current research activity will extend SCPM2 to account for endogenous price adjustments.

REFERENCES

Boarnet, Marlon. 1998. "Business Losses, Transportation Damage and the Northridge Earthquake," *Journal of Transportation and Statistics*, 1, 49–64.

Campbell, Kenneth W. 1997. "Empirical Near Source Attenuation Relationships for Horizontal and Vertical Components of Peak Ground Acceleration, Peak Ground Velocity, and Pseudo-Absolute Acceleration Response Spectra," *Seismological Research Letters*, 68, 154–179.

Chang, Stephanie E. 1995. "Urban Economic Impact of Transportation Disruption: Evidence from the January 17, 1995 Hyogo-ken Nambu Earthquake," paper presented at the 14th Conference of the Pacific Regional Science Association, Taipei.

Cho, Sungbin, Peter Gordon, James E. Moore II, Harry W. Richardson, M. Shinozuka, and Stephanie E. Chang. 1999. "Effect of Earthquakes on Urban Highway Infrastructure Productivity, Volume 2: Integrating Transportation Network and Regional Economic Models to Estimate the Costs of A Large Earthquake," Technical Report to the National Science Foundation, Award CMS 9633386 (EHM), School of Policy, Planning & Development, and Department of Civil & Environmental Engineering, University of Southern California (http://www.usc.edu/sppd/research/research2.html).

Cochrane, Harold C. 1997. "Forecasting the Economic Impact of a Midwest Earthquake," in B. G. Jones (ed.), *Economic Consequences of Earthquakes: Preparing for the Unexpected*. Buffalo: NCEER.

Eguchi, Ronald T., James D. Goltz, Craig E. Taylor, Stephanie E. Chang, Paul J. Flores, Lauie A. Johnson, Hope A. Seligson, and Neil C. Blais. 1998. "Direct Economic Losses in the Northridge Earthquake: A Three-Year Post Event Perspective," *Earthquake Spectra*, 14, 245–264.

Eguchi, Ronald T., James D. Goltz, H. A. Seligson, P. J. Flores, N. C. Blais, T. H. Heaton, and E. Bortugno. 1997. "Real-Time Loss Estimation as an Emergency Response Decision Support System: The Early Post-Earthquake Damage Assessment Tool," *Earthquake Spectra*, 13, 815–832.

Gordon, Peter, Harry W. Richardson, and Bill Davis. 1998. "Transport-Related Impacts of the Northridge Earthquake," *Journal of Transportation and Statistics*, 1, 21–36.

Isard, Walter and Robert E. Kuenne. 1953. "The Impact of Steel Upon the Greater New York-Philadelphia Industrial Region," *Review of Economics and Statistics*, 35, 289–301.

Kawashima, Kazuhiko and Takashi Kanoh. 1990. "Evaluation of Indirect Economic Effects Caused by the 1983 Nohonkai-chubu, Japan, Earthquake," *Earthquake Spectra*, 6, 739–756.

Kim, T. John, David E. Boyce, Heejoo Ham and Yasuhide Okuyama. 1999. "Implementation of an Integrated Transportation Network and Input-Output Model for Assessing Economic Impacts of Unexpected Events: A Solution Algorithm and Issues," paper presented at the Northeast Regional Science Conference, Ithica.

Kimbell, Larry J. and Nancy Bolton. 1994. "The Impact of the Northridge Earthquake on the Economies of Los Angeles and California," paper presented to the Seismic Safety Commission of the State of California, Burbank.

Leontief, Wassily and Alan Strout. 1963. *Multiregional Input-Output Analysis*, Second Edition. New York: Oxford University Press.

Moses, Leon N. 1955. "The Stability of Interregional Trading Patterns and Input-Output Analysis," *American Economic Review*, 45, 803–832.

Okuyama, Yasuhide and Geoffrey H.D. Hewings, and Michael Sonis. 1997. "Interregional Analysis of an Unscheduled Event," paper presented at the 44th North American Meetings of the Regional Science Association International, Buffalo.

Putnam, Steven H. 1983. *Integrated Urban Models: Policy Analysis of Transportation and Land Use*. London: Pion.

Richardson, Harry W., Peter Gordon, Myun-JinJun, and Moon H. Kim. 1993. "PRIDE and Prejudice: The Economic Impacts of Growth Controls in Pasadena," *Environment and Planning A*, 25, 987–1002.

Rose, Adam and Julian Benavides. 1998. Regional Economic Impacts, in M. Shinozuka, A. Rose, and Ronald T. Eguchi (eds.), *Engineering and Socioeconomic Impacts of Earthquakes: An Analysis of Electricity Lifeline Disruptions in the New Madrid Area*. Buffalo: MCEER.

Rose, Adam, Juan Benavides, Stephanie E. Chang, Philip Szczesniak, and Dongsoon Lim. 1997. "The Regional Economic Impact of an Earthquake: Direct and Indirect Effects of Electricity Lifeline Disruptions," *Journal of Regional Science*, 37, 437–458.

Rose, Adam and Dongsoon Lim. 1997. "The Economic Impact of Electricity Lifeline Disruptions Stemming from the Northridge Earthquake," Final Report to the National Science Foundation, Department of Energy, Environmental, and Mineral Economics. The Pennsylvania State University.

Shinozuka, Masanobu. 1998. "Development of Bridge Fragility Curves," *Proceedings of the Joint U.S.-Italy Workshop on Seismic Protective Systems for Bridges*, New York: Columbia University.

62 JOURNAL OF REGIONAL SCIENCE, VOL. 41, NO. 1, 2001

Shinozuka, Masanobu., Maria Q. Feng, Hokyung Kim, Tetsushi Uzawa, and Takayuki Ueda 2000. "Statistical Analysis of Fragility Curves," Technical Report to the Multidisciplinary Center for Earthquake Engineering Research, Federal Highway Administration Contracts DTFH61-92-C00112 (Task 106-E-7.3.5.) and DTFH61-92-C00106 (Task 106-E-7.3.6), Department of Civil & Environmental Engineering, University of Southern California.

Stevens, Benjamin H. 1996. *PC I-O Version 7.* Heightstown, NJ: Regional Science Research Corporation.

Stevens, Benjamin H., George Treyz, and Michael Lahr. 1983. "A New Technique for the Construction of Non-Survey Regional Input-Output Models," *International Regional Science Review,* 8, 271–286.

U.S. Bureau of the Census, Economics and Statistics Administration. 1993. *1992 Economic Census: Census of Transportation, Communication, and Utilities—1993 Commodity Flow Survey,* TC92-CF-52. Washington, DC: U.S. Department of Commerce.

U.S. Bureau of the Census. 1997. *Statistical Abstract of the United States: 1997,* 117th Edition. Washington, DC: U.S. Department of Commerce.

U.S. Department of Transportation, Bureau of Transportation Statistics. 1994. *Census Transportation Planning Package: Urban Element,* BTS-CD-15-31 Los Angeles, CA, Special Tabulations of the 1990 Census Data. Washington, DC.

———. 1997. *1993 Commodity Flow Survey: U.S. Highlights.* Washington, DC.

———. 1998. "The Economic Importance of Transportation Services: Highlights of the Transportation Satellite Accounts," *TranStats,* BTS98-TS-4R. Washington, DC.

———. 1999. *Transportation Satellite Accounts: A New Way of Measuring Transportation Services in America,* BTS99-R-01. Washington, DC.

Wilson, Alan G. 1970. *Entropy in Urban and Regional Modeling.* London: Pion.

APPENDIX A

Southern California Planning Model Version 1 (SCPM1)

The generic structure of SCPM1 is summarized as follows. First, beginning with a vector of final demands, $\mathbf{v(d)}$, total outputs from the open and closed input-output (I-O) models are calculated as

$$\mathbf{v(o)} = (\mathbf{I} - \mathbf{A_o})^{-1}\,\mathbf{v(d)}$$

and

$$\mathbf{v(c')} = (\mathbf{I} - \mathbf{A_c})^{-1}\,\mathbf{v(d)}$$

where $\mathbf{A_o}$ and $\mathbf{A_c}$ are matrices of technical coefficients for the open and closed I-O models respectively, and where $\mathbf{v(o)}$ and $\mathbf{v(c')}$ are the corresponding vectors of total outputs. The notation $\mathbf{c'}$ indicates that the household sector is included. We use $\mathbf{v(c)}$ to represent the vector of total output from the closed model for all but the household sector. By definition, $\mathbf{v(c)}$ may then be reexpressed as the sum of three types of output; direct ($\mathbf{d}$), indirect ($\mathbf{i}$), and induced ($\mathbf{u}$).

(A1)
$$\left. \begin{aligned} \mathbf{v(c)} &= \mathbf{v(d)} + \mathbf{v(i)} + \mathbf{v(u)} \\ \mathbf{v(i)} &= \mathbf{v(o)} - \mathbf{v(d)} \end{aligned} \right\} \quad (17 \times 1)$$

and

$$\mathbf{v(u)} = \mathbf{v(c)} - \mathbf{v(o)}$$

Equation (A2) is the spatial counterpart to Equation (A1)

(A2) $$\mathbf{Z}(\mathbf{c}) = \mathbf{Z}(\mathbf{d}) + \mathbf{Z}(\mathbf{i}) + \mathbf{Z}(\mathbf{u}) \quad (308 \times 17)$$

where in each case $\mathbf{Z}(\bullet)$ is a matrix of impacts both by spatial unit (zone) and by sector. The matrices $\mathbf{Z}(\mathbf{d})$, $\mathbf{Z}(\mathbf{i})$, and $\mathbf{Z}(\mathbf{u})$ are all specified or derived in different ways. The most straightforward of these is $\mathbf{Z}(\mathbf{d})$, which is defined exogenously, such as by an earthquake. SCPM1 allocates indirect outputs according to the proportion of employees in each sector by zone. Specifically

$$\mathbf{Z}(i) = \mathbf{P}\text{Diag}[\mathbf{v}(\mathbf{i})]$$

where $\mathbf{P}$ is a (308×17) matrix indicating the proportion of employees in each zone. The "Diag" operator diagonalizes the indicated vector into a (17×17) matrix.

The spatial allocation of induced impacts is somewhat more involved because the induced output must be traced via household expenditure patterns. Two separate origin – destination matrixes are employed, journey-from-services-to-home $\mathbf{JSH}$ and journey-from-home-to-work $\mathbf{JHW}$ based on spatial distributions extracted from the Census Transportation Planning Package (CTPP). Essentially, employees are traced home from work through $\mathbf{JHW}$ and then from home we take them back further to their shopping destinations, thereby indirectly accounting for the spatial allocation of that increment of sectoral output satisfying induced household expenditures. This may be expressed more succinctly in terms of matrix notation as

$$\mathbf{Z}(\mathbf{u}) = \mathbf{JSH} \times \mathbf{JHW} \times \mathbf{P} \times \text{Diag}[\mathbf{v}(\mathbf{u})] \quad (308 \times 308)^2 \, (308 \times 17) \, (17 \times 17)$$

The output from SCPM1 is a (308×17) matrix of impacts by 17 economic sectors and 308 geographic zones.

APPENDIX B

Endogenizing Transportation Flows: Southern California Planning Model Version 2 (SCPM2)

SCPM2 is initialized by allocating indirect impacts to zones in proportion to baseline data by applying a modified version of SCPM1. SCPM1 relies on the proportion of workers in each traffic analysis zone to establish the spatial distribution of economic activities. The modified version of SCPM1 applied here relies instead on a 1527×17 matrix of indices constructed from economic flows into and out of each traffic analysis zone, the elements of which are initialized as

$$F_i^z = \left[O_i^z + D_i^z \middle/ \sum_z \left(O_i^z + D_i^z \right) \right]$$

where O_i^z and D_i^z are the baseline values given by Equations (1) and (2).

64   JOURNAL OF REGIONAL SCIENCE, VOL. 41, NO. 1, 2001

Given an initial matrix $\mathbf{F}$, a matrix of baseline equilibrium path costs $\mathbf{c}$, baseline interzonal shipments, baseline journey-from-home-to-work $\mathbf{JHW}$ and journey-from-services-to-home $\mathbf{JSH}$ matrices, a matrix $\mathbf{V(d)}$ of direct impacts by sector and municipality from EPEDAT, disaggregated using GIS over traffic analysis zones, and vectors of $\mathbf{v(i)}$ and $\mathbf{v(u)}$ of indirect and induced impacts by sector from the RSRI input-output model, we establish an interative sequence that spatially allocates the vectors $\mathbf{v(i)}$ and $\mathbf{v(u)}$ over the traffic analysis zones. This creates matrices $\mathbf{V(i)}$ and $\mathbf{V(u)}$. Set

$$^{k=0}D_i^z = D_i^z$$
$$^{k=0}O_i^z = O_i^z$$
$$^{k=0}F_i^z = F_i^z$$
$$^{k=0}\mathbf{V(i)} = {}^{k=0}\mathbf{F}\mathrm{Diag}\big[\mathbf{v(i)}\big]$$

and

(A3) $^{k=0}\mathbf{V(u)} = {}^{k=0}\mathbf{JSH}^T \times {}^{k=0}\mathbf{JHW} \times {}^{k=0}\mathbf{F} \times \mathrm{Diag}[\mathbf{v(u)}]$

where k is an iteration counter. This initialization associates indirect and induced impacts with employment locations. The induced impacts are then distributed across residential locations and then commercial locations using the journey-from-home-to-work and journey-from-home-to-shop matrices. The total impact by zone at any iteration k is

(A4) $^k\mathbf{V}^z = {}^k\mathbf{V(d)}^z + {}^k\mathbf{V(i)}^z + {}^k\mathbf{V(u)}^z$

Unlike the corresponding elements of SCPM1, the matrices $\mathbf{JSH}, \mathbf{JHW}$, and $\mathbf{F}$ are endogenous. They are updated iteratively to search for a spatial allocation of indirect and induced impacts that produces mutually consistent travel demand and network costs given simultaneous reductions in transportation demand and transportation supply. Define

$$\Delta^k D_i^z = \sum_j a_{i,j}{}^k V_j^z$$
$$\Delta^k O_i^z = \sum_j b_{i,j}{}^k V_i^z$$

These changes represent decrements in economic activity due to impact of the earthquake. They are subtracted from baseline values. Update $^kD^z_i$ and $^kO^z_i$ by defining

$$^{k+1}O_i^z = {}^kO_i^z - \Delta^k O_i^z$$

and

$$^{k+1}D_i^z = {}^kD_i^z - \Delta^k D_i^z$$

Update $^k\mathbf{F}$ by defining

$$^{k+1}F_i^z = \left[{}^{k+1}O_i^z + {}^{k+1}D_i^z \middle/ \sum_z \left({}^{k+1}O_i^z + {}^{k+1}D_i^z \right) \right]$$

Convert these updated values $^{k+1}D_i^z$ and $^{k+1}O_i^z$ to marginal distributions of trip productions and attractions in PCUs

$$^{k+1}P_i^r = \eta_i \times {}^{k+1}O_i^z$$

and

$$^{k+1}A_i^s = \eta_i \times {}^{k+1}D_i^z$$

In SCPM1, the network is not explicit and trip making is exogenous. In SCPM2, the trip interchange matrices are adjusted subiteratively. The entries of the thirteen interchange matrices describing four classes of freight flows and nine passenger trip types are determined by applying the baseline gravity model coefficients and network costs to the set of updated trip production and attraction elements $^{k+1}P_i^r$ and $^{k+1}A_i^s$. In the case of freight flows

$$t_i^{r,s} = A_i^s \left[B_i^r \exp\left(-\beta_i c^{r,s}\right) \middle/ \sum_r B_i^r \exp\left(-\beta_i c^{r,s}\right) \right]$$

In the case of labor, shopping, and other flows involving people

$$t_i^{r,s} = P_i^r A_i^s \left[B_i^r H_i^s \beta_{0,i} \exp\left(-\beta_{1,i} c^{r,s}\right) c^{r,s\left(\beta_{2,i}\right)} \right]$$

Collectively, these interzonal flows combine with the earthquake damaged configuration of the transportation network to imply new endogenous network flows and costs different from the values of $c^{r,s}$. This provides an opportunity for further iteration. Given fixed trip production and attraction vectors, and fixed gravity model parameters, the feedback between network costs the trip interchange matrices attenuates. Trip distribution and network flows converge to consistent values.

The resulting trip interchange matrices imply new values for the matrices $^{k+1}\mathbf{JHW}$ and $^{k+1}\mathbf{JSH}$, which, along with $^{k+1}\mathbf{F}$, update $^k\mathbf{V(i)}$ to $^{k+1}\mathbf{V(i)}$ via Equation (A3) and $^k\mathbf{V(u)}$ to $^{k+1}\mathbf{V(u)}$ via Equation (A4).

[16]

A General Equilibrium Analysis of Partial-Equilibrium Welfare Measures: The Case of Climate Change

By MARY F. KOKOSKI AND V. KERRY SMITH*

This paper uses computable general equilibrium models to demonstrate that partial-equilibrium welfare measures can offer reasonable approximations of the true welfare changes for large exogenous changes. With consistency in the size and direction of the indirect price effects associated with large shocks, single-sector partial-equilibrium measures will exhibit small errors. Otherwise the errors can be substantial and difficult to sign.

The purpose of this paper is to evaluate the errors in partial-equilibrium measures of the welfare changes resulting from large multisector, exogenous shocks to an economic system. It would not be surprising to any economist to find that partial-equilibrium welfare measures would perform poorly in such cases. However, general answers to the questions of what is a large change, or how many sectors need to be involved before partial-equilibrium methods break down, are not available. We begin the process of developing answers by illustrating a new use for computable general equilibrium (CGE) models—one that has been largely overlooked in the extensive literature that uses these models to evaluate the implications of domestic tax or international trade (for example, tariff) changes.[1] More specifi-

cally, we impose exogenous changes on the unit costs of producing commodities in several sectors with a CGE model of a developed economy, and compare partial-equilibrium welfare measures of their impact with the "true" general equilibrium measures. Our application also has independent interest. It is the first general equilibrium evaluation of the economic effects of a carbon dioxide (CO_2) induced climate change.

Based on estimates of the atmospheric concentration of CO_2 around the start of the industrial revolution in comparison with the 1983 measurements, CO_2 levels have increased approximately 22 percent. The CO_2 absorbs long-wave terrestrial radiation. This leads to increased resistance to the upward radiative transfer of heat and increases in the mean global temperature—the so-called "greenhouse effect." With a doubling in atmospheric CO_2, mean temperatures are expected to rise 1°C to 3°C, with greater increases at the poles. Melting of the polar ice caps and uncovering of land or ocean are expected to change wind and precipitation patterns. Our analysis focuses on scenarios designed to represent a 50 percent increase in CO_2 (over the industrial revolution levels). This corresponds to an increase likely to arise in under fifty years.[2]

*Economist, Division of Price and Index Number Research, U.S. Bureau of Labor Statistics, Washington, D.C. 20212, and Centennial Professor of Economics, Vanderbilt University, Nashville, TN 37235, respectively. Support for Kokoski's research was provided by the Lurcy Fellowship at the University of North Carolina-Chapel Hill, and we both acknowledge the Climate Dynamic Program of the National Science Foundation, grant nos. ATM 8217303 and ATM 8317619. Thanks are due John Shoven and John Whalley for assistance in locating related literature, Knox Lovell and three anonymous referees for constructive comments on earlier drafts of this paper, and to participants at the Microeconomics Workshop at Vanderbilt University, the NBER Applied General Equilibrium Workshop at Stanford University, and the Economics Workshop at Oak Ridge National Laboratory for comments.

[1] For a detailed overview of the results of these studies, see John Shoven and John Whalley (1984).

[2] For summary of the evidence on the accumulation of CO_2 and the climatic effects of CO_2 and other trace gases, see F. Kenneth Hare (1985, pp. 52–59) and John Firor and Paul Portney (1982, pp. 182–99).

Our results can be used to address two issues—partial-equilibrium welfare measurement and the potential economic impacts of climate change. On the first of these, the findings suggest that fairly large single-sector impacts (with as large as a 42 percent unit cost increase in one sector) can be adequately measured using a single-market partial-equilibrium measure of compensating variation. However, smaller multisector changes (in terms of the unit cost increases implied for each sector) exhibit large errors in single market, partial-equilibrium (*PE*) welfare measures. Moreover, none of our attempts to extend the *PE* measures to include several markets either "vertically" or "horizontally" was consistently superior to the other alternatives.

The results for the second issue—the economic impacts of CO_2 increase—are intended to be illustrative only. Our model is a small approximation of a developed economy, parameterized with U.S. data. The scenarios are also approximate descriptions of the types of impacts thought to arise from CO_2 induced climatic change. The specific findings depend on the effects specified to arise in sectoral production patterns as part of the scenario design. Two interesting features were consistently observed for all the scenarios we considered. The scenarios used to represent a CO_2 induced climate change can produce large and mixed price (and output) effects with both increases and decreases. Thus, partial appraisals of selected sectors can give a misleading view of the full economic impacts of such changes. Equally important, the policies did not uniformly affect low- and high-income households.

I. Background and Outline of the Analysis

A. *Background*

Two sets of research have considered problems related to general equilibrium welfare measurement. The first involves descriptions of the rules a government should use when evaluating the efficiency gains from public projects in a tax distorted economy. Much of this work is summarized in W. Erwin Diewert (1983). All of the analyses

have tended to accept a Harberger-type measure of efficiency gains or losses,[3] and consider only differential changes resulting from a proposed policy action (usually defined as a tax change). They ignore indirect price and income changes from other markets on the market affected by the policies under evaluation. Robin Boadway's 1975 synthesis of Arnold Harberger's 1971 general recommendations for applied welfare analysis together with his specific suggestions for the factor prices used in public projects, given distorted markets (Harberger, 1969), and the Diamond-Mirrlees (see Peter Diamond and James Mirrlees, 1971a,b) arguments for the use of producer prices, all highlight this assumption.

The second set of research is more closely related to our objectives. It consists primarily of two papers. The first (John Whalley, 1975) evaluated simple, Harberger-type, partial-equilibrium (*PE*), extended partial-equilibrium (*EPE*), and general equilibrium (*GE*) measures of the efficiency implications of the removal of the distortionary U.K. capital income taxation system (with total tax receipts held constant). Whalley's analy-

---

[3] Diewert (1985) has recently compared two alternative measures of the efficiency losses from tax distortions in a general equilibrium context. They include a quantity index and price index. The quantity measure holds each individual at his initial, tax distorted utility level, and considers the number of multiples of the reference (i.e., associated with the tax distorted equilibrium) vector the economy can produce without these distortions. He attributes this measure to Maurice Allais (1943) and Gerard Debreu (1951). The price measure of efficiency loss is (minus) the sum of the Hicksian equivalent variations over all consumers with the Pareto optimal prices as the reference point. He also proposed a differential approach to sensitivity analysis in general equilibrium models. This approach is implemented by differentiating the loss measure with respect to second-order parameters characterizing either demand or supply features of the economy. His analysis suggests that the Allais-Debreu measure of inefficiency increases with increased substitution on either the demand or supply side of the economy. While this is an interesting alternative to the use of numerical methods in gauging the sensitivity of general equilibrium results to alternative parameterizations, it is not relevant to our objectives because we seek to evaluate the performance of approximations when aspects of the general equilibrium solution have been ignored.

sis used a CGE model of the U.K. economy and three estimates of the change in the value of the total product to gauge these efficiency gains. His *PE* scheme holds all prices but capital constant and used linearized marginal product schedules for capital in each sector together with an iterative price adjustment scheme to estimate the common, post-tax-removal price for capital. The sum of the changes in the areas under marginal product schedules (for capital in each sector) was used to measure the change in value of aggregate output. The *EPE* collapses the economy to a two-commodity framework and used a simple capital allocation and price adjustment procedure to measure the changes in the value of output. The last measure calculates it using his nine-sector, seven-household class CGE model for the U.K. economy. All three approaches were used in several scenarios varying the assumptions on the production elasticities of substitution. The results uniformly suggest that the *PE* and *EPE* measures were unreliable approximations of the true changes in the value of output.

The second study of this type by Lee Edlefsen (1983) confirmed Whalley's findings. He found that the Harberger deadweight loss triangle can overstate welfare losses above a general equilibrium equivalent variation measure by a factor of 2 to 4. Moreover, his results suggested that the majority of this error can be due to the indirect effects. They were based on a four-equation demand and supply model with functions specified to be linear in price ratios (i.e., three commodities were assumed to capture general equilibrium effects). From his description it appears that the model does not reflect the influence of price changes on income by revaluing endowments. To capture all these effects requires a CGE model that takes account of commodity and factor markets, including the roles of their respective prices for the value of consumers' endowments.

B. Specification of the CGE Model

To evaluate the performance of partial-equilibrium welfare measures, a fairly simple nine-commodity CGE model was designed to represent a developed economy. Parameter values for the model were derived from U.S. data sources. Because it is a small-scale model, it was not intended to be capable of offering policy insights for the U.S. economy. Rather, the use of actual data for the prototype economic structure provides one strategy for dealing with the parameterization issues raised in judging results obtained from CGE models. Shoven and Whalley (1984) acknowledge this issue, noting that the results of CGE models are quite sensitive to model parameterization, especially the selection of elasticity values. Unfortunately, systematic sensitivity analyses with simple models (see Glenn Harrison and Lawrence Kimbell, 1983) have not uncovered general conclusions. Our approach limits the set of feasible parameter values to those estimated for an existing economic structure.

The nine-commodity economy includes: labor, land, capital, energy, chemicals, consumer durables, construction, services, and agriculture. These commodity definitions were the result of a compromise strategy. The model sought to identify important sectors in the economy and identify sectors likely to be affected by a CO_2 induced climate change. The model includes three consumers (with each intended to reflect specific groups of households). Two are domestic and one specified to represent the foreign sector. The domestic households were differentiated by income. Consumers were endowed with land, labor, and capital. Labor was specified so that a work-leisure choice is a part of household decisions.

Each of the produced commodities in each model was assumed to be derived from a nested Cobb-Douglas CES cost function with constant returns to scale as in

$$(1) \quad C_j = \prod_{k=1}^{N_j} \left[\sum_{i=1}^{m} \left(a_{jik} P_i \right)^{r_{kj}} \right]^{\alpha_{kj}/r_{kj}}$$

where C_j = average cost for the jth produced commodity;

P_i = price of the ith factor input;

N_j = number of CES subfunctions (i.e., aggregate factors) in the production process for the jth commodity;

m = potential number of factor inputs (8 in principle, if all commodities served as inputs and final goods);

a_{jik}, α_{kj}, r_{kj} = production parameters (with $\sum_k \alpha_{kj} = 1$ and $\sum_i a_{jik} = 1$).

The domestic household's utility functions were specified to follow a Stone-Geary form as in (2). The foreign sector had a Cobb-Douglas form:

$$(2) \qquad U_t = \prod_{i=1}^{m+1} (Q_{it} - \gamma_{it})^{\beta_{it}}$$

with $\beta_{it} > 0$, $\sum_i \beta_{it} = 1$, $Q_{it} > \gamma_{it}$,

where U_t = utility level for household t;

Q_{it} = consumption of commodity i by household t;

β_{it} = marginal budget share for commodity i by household t;

γ_{it} = threshold consumption level of commodity i by household t.

Two aspects of our specification of the domestic household utility functions are potentially important to the welfare analysis. In contrast to the frequently used CES formulations, income elasticities will not be equal (and unity) across commodities. Equally important, the definition of the compensating variation (CV) must be adjusted from conventional expressions with this utility function (see G. W. McKenzie, 1983, p. 40) to reflect the effects of price changes on income changes resulting from changes in the value of household endowments as well as on earnings through revisions in the labor-leisure choice (see our 1985b paper for discussion of the implications of these adjustments), as in

$$(3) \quad CV = (R-1)\overline{M}^0 + \sum_i \left(P_i^1 - RP_i^0\right)\gamma_i$$
$$+ \overline{Q}_k \left(RP_k^0 - P_k^1\right) - d\overline{M},$$

where $\overline{M}$ = income associated with an individual's endowments, where there is no "own consumption demand"; the superscript 0 designates the initial value;

$d\overline{M}$ = the change in this exogenous income as a result of the change in the prices of these endowments;

$\overline{Q}_k$ = endowment of labor time (Q_k);
$R = \prod_i (P_i^1/P_i^0)^{\beta_i}$.

C. Parameterization of the Model

The year 1972 was the base year for our characterization of consumer demand and the distribution of income between the two domestic households. The parameters for the utility functions were taken from estimates reported by D. Eastwood and J. Craven (1981) for the extended linear expenditure system, with two adjustments. Their model did not include a labor/leisure choice so we assumed (following Shoven and Whalley, 1972) that leisure comprised 3/7 of total labor time and calculated the budget share for leisure as 3/7 of the share of labor income. The *LES* subsistence parameters for all commodities but leisure were adjusted for each of the two domestic households using estimates in C. Lluch et al. (1977) to reflect the effect of income level. The low-income consumers' source of income and share of national income were specified based on the lower three quintiles and the higher that of the top two quintiles. The third consumer group represents the foreign sector with foreign sector income defined as the sum of exports to the United States in 1972. The shares of imports of total expenditures on these commodities determined the parameters of the function.

The parameters for the sectoral cost functions were obtained from a variety of sources —cost shares primarily from Census of Manufacturers, Mining or Construction in 1972. Substitution elasticities were selected based on examination of a range of studies, including the detailed results reported in Michael Hazilla and Raymond Kopp (1982). The specification of the cost function allowed some flexibility in assignment of substitution elasticities by grouping factors into separate subfunctions. Panel A of Table 1 reports the composition of these subfunctions for each of the six production sectors in the model by indicating the Allen gross elasticities of substitution for the pairs of inputs in each, and by specifying the non-zero input cost shares in the five rows below this.

TABLE 1—PRODUCTION AND DEMAND PARAMETERIZATION FOR THE CGE MODEL

	Sector/Commodity					
	Energy	Durables	Agriculture	Chemicals	Construction	Services
A. Production						
1) Gross Substitution Elasticity[a]						
I	–	–	–	–	$\sigma_{12}=.50$	$\sigma_{13}=.25$
II	$\sigma_{23}=2.0$	$\sigma_{13}=.10$	$\sigma_{14}=\sigma_{15}=$ $\sigma_{15}=-2.0$	$\sigma_{34}=2.0$	$\sigma_{34}=-1.0$	–
2) Cost Shares						
Labor	.15	.33	.15	.25	.42	.69
	(.16)	(.42)	(.14)	(.27)	(.36)	(.60)
Land	.20	–	.80	–	.38	–
	(.10)		(.80)		(.43)	
Capital	.65	.57	.05	.38	.20	.11
	(.74)	(.50)	(.03)	(.67)	(.14)	(.20)
Energy	–	.10	.00	.38	.00	.20
		(.08)	(.01)	(.06)	(.07)	(.20)
Chemicals	–	–	.00	–	–	–
			(.02)			
3) Capital-Labor Ratio						
Benchmark	4.63	1.19	.21	2.48	.45	.33
Base Case Solution	4.36	1.70	.33	1.47	.47	.16
B. Demand Elasticities						
1) Eastwood-Craven Own-Price[b]	−.49	−.82	−.23	−.73	−.65	−.54
2) Base Case Solution Own-Price						
Low Income	−.951	−.957	−.641	−.960	−.705	−.865
High Income	−.923	−.933	−.539	−.972	−.763	−.972
Income						
Low Income	1.157	1.159	.734	1.183	.787	1.034
High Income	1.060	.992	.594	1.135	.832	1.126

[a] s_i = Share of total costs associated with ith factor. Subscript i corresponds to the row labels for commodities in each model (i.e., developed and less developed).

σ = Gross (holding output constant) elasticity of substitution. In terms of parameters of equation (1) $\sigma = [r_k - (1 - \alpha_k)]/\alpha_k$, where k corresponds to the kth CES nest. Both factors must be members of the same CES nest for this equation to be valid. $(1 - r_k)$ designates the net elasticity of substitution for any pair of factors in the k nest.

[b] These elasticities correspond to estimates reported for closely related commodity categories. For a discussion of our adjustments to derive the values for our definitions, see Kokoski (1984).

Following the substitution elasticities we report some information on how well the base case solution reproduced the initial features of the data used to parameterize the production side of the model. These results will be affected by the interaction of the production and the demand specifications. Consequently, they need not reproduce the values of the data used to parameterize each component of the model.[4] Our summary includes both the cost shares for factor inputs and the capital-labor ratios from the benchmark data versus those implied by the model's base case. For example, the energy sector was specified to have three inputs— labor, land (to designate primary materials inputs), and capital. Capital and land were

[4] Most CGE models have been parameterized by calibrating the models (see A. Mansur and Whalley, 1984). That is, a subset of the parameters are set so the model reproduces a base case expenditure pattern. As

Diewert (1985) observed, this procedure usually implies that preferences and technology sets are reasonably well approximated to the first-order but not to the second-order. In the past, use of restrictive functional forms, such as the CES, to characterize both preferences and technology have limited the distortions to second-order properties induced by these calibration techniques.

included in one subfunction and labor in another. The cost shares implied by the base solution are given first and then those used in the parameterization are shown below in parentheses. Thus, labor was specified to account for 16 percent of total costs of energy production while the base case solution implied 15 percent.

Panel B of Table 1 reports some comparable information for the demand side of the model. The approximate own-price elasticities from Eastwood and Craven are compared with the calculated values at the base case for the low- and high-income households and the base case calculated values of the income elasticities. In this case we would not expect close comparability because the Eastwood-Craven study did not provide estimates for households at different income levels and it did not incorporate a labor/leisure choice. Our estimates for the base solution reflect the adjustments made. Nonetheless, the overall results indicate a reasonably good correspondence for both sides of the economy. Of course, the match need not be exact since our objectives require only an economically plausible description of a developed economy.

D. Scenario Design

A CO_2 induced climate change will have at least two important features—a temperature increase and a precipitation change. The direction of the change in precipitation has not been as clear as the effect on temperature. Our scenarios have been designed recognizing the range of possibilities for these physical changes and using the available information on the effects of climate by sector to postulate the percentage changes in unit costs of production for each of a set of sectors.

It is reasonable to expect that the climate changes associated with a 50 percent increase in atmospheric CO_2 will impact several sectors simultaneously. Nonetheless, to provide information to judge the quality of partial-equilibrium welfare measures, we have specified single- and multiple-sector impacts of varying sizes. The single-sector scenarios involve effects only on agriculture while the

multiple-sector effects involve from two to four sectors simultaneously. Our overall analysis has considered a large number of scenarios (and several specifications for the CGE economies).[5] However, we have limited the results presented here to seven cases.

The connection between a postulated change in temperature and precipitation and sectoral costs is probably best for agriculture. Our scenarios should be treated as judgmental summaries of the estimated effects from past studies of similar hypothesized climate changes. For example, using the case of agriculture, several studies have considered crop and area-specific analyses of changes comparable to those implied by our smallest impact cases. Early analyses of a 1°C temperature increase and 10 percent decline in precipitation implied a 26 percent reduction in the yields of corn (Wilfred Bach et al., 1981), 10 percent decline in wheat yields, and 26 percent decline in soybeans (Louis Thompson, 1975) for a weighted (by share of U.S. crop production) decline of about 22 percent. More recent evidence discussed by Paul Waggoner in the National Academy of Sciences report *Changing Climate* (1983) indicates two sets of estimates —one based on regression yield models and a second on a simulation of yield changes due to climate. The first implies the same climate change from about 2 to 13 percent decline for these same crops (with a weighted average close to 10 percent). By contrast, the second has a larger effect—about a 24.5 percent decline. We selected estimates at the higher end of this range (22 percent) to indicate the maximum impact and ignored adjustments in input mix or technology that might reduce the effect.

Table 2 defines the seven scenarios we report. In each case we report the features of the postulated climate change that provides the basis for selecting the unit cost impacts. The results in this table and in Table 3 provide a basis for gauging the implications of these changes for economic activities com-

---

[5] See Kokoski (1984) and our paper (1985a) for a more detailed discussion of some of this work.

TABLE 2—CLIMATE IMPACT SCENARIOS AND THEIR EFFECTS ON PRICES

Scenario Design			Percent Change in Commodity Prices								
	Climate Parameters	Increase in Unit Costs (percent)	La-bor	Land	Cap-ital	Ener-gy	Chemi-cals	Dur-ables	Const.	Ser-vices	Agric.
A. Single Sector											
1) Agriculture	1^0, +10%p	+4	−.5	+.2	−.5	−.5	−.5	−.5	−.3	−.3	+4.0
2) Agriculture	1^0, −10%p	+22	−3.0	+1.1	−2.8	−2.1	−2.4	−2.8	−1.4	−2.7	+22.0
3) Agriculture	2^0, −20%p	+42	−5.7	+2.2	−5.3	−4.1	−4.8	−5.3	−2.7	−5.1	+42.0
B. Multiple Sector											
4) Agriculture	1^0, −10%p	+22	−5.8	−.5	−.1	+3.7	0.0	−1.6	−2.6	−3.2	+20.5
Energy		+5									
5) Agriculture	2^0, −20%p	+42	−7.8	−1.4	−4.9	−4.8	−5.6	+3.5	−4.9	−7.0	+38.3
Durables		+10									
6) Agriculture	1^0, −10%p	+22	6.8	−6.0	+2.0	+3.7	+.5	−.8	−4.8	+1.1	+23.9
Energy		+5									
Services		+5									
7) Agriculture	2^0, −20%p	+42	−12.8	−4.8	−.6	+5.0	−1.4	+5.4	−7.4	+1.1	+38.9
Energy		+9									
Durables		+10									
Services		+10									

TABLE 3—A COMPARATIVE ANALYSIS OF PARTIAL-EQUILIBRIUM WELFARE MEASURES

Scenario	Laspeyre's Price Index	CV Relative to Income		Proportionate Error in Approximate Welfare Measures[a]				
		Low	High	PE	VPE	HPE	ΣPE	$\overline{HPE}$
A. Single Sector								
1) Agriculture	1.001	.025	.014	.000	.487	−.564	–	
2) Agriculture	1.003	.128	.072	.045	.627	−.657	–	–
3) Agriculture	1.006	.231	.125	.081	.688	−.691	–	–
B. Multiple Sector								
4) Agriculture	1.006	.170	.113	−.325	.449	–	−.191	−.184
Energy								
5) Agriculture	1.015	.303	.284	−.411	.141	–	−.259	−.256
Durables								
6) Agriculture	1.012	.219	.197	−.466	.245	–	−.349	−.341
Energy								
Services								
7) Agriculture	1.029	.421	.416	−.631	.004	–	−.393	−.386
Energy								
Durables								
Services								

[a] These partial-equilibrium welfare measures are distinguished according to single-market analyses (PE); vertically integrated analyses (VPE) involving the product market and relevant factor markets; or horizontally connected analyses involving the directly affected final goods markets ($\overline{HPE}$). ΣPE = the sum of the partial-equilibrium estimates.

puted to take place under each set of conditions in relationship to the baseline solution. Table 2 also reports the percentage change in each commodity's price, while Table 3 summarizes the overall price level impact with a Laspeyres price index. Table 3 includes the correctly calculated compensating variation relative to household incomes at the base case for the low- and high- income households.

II. Welfare Measures

Our analysis of partial-equilibrium measures of welfare change due to the specified effects of a climate change focuses on the price changes from the base solution, computed to arise with our CGE model. The welfare measures considered are defined as the Hicksian compensating variation (CV) for alternative price changes. Our partial-equilibrium CV measures are specified by varying the number of commodities whose price changes are recognized. As Table 2 indicates, each scenario (single and multiple sector) leads to changes in the vector of commodity prices. Assume, for example, the change is from $(P_1^0, P_2^0, \ldots, P_9^0)$ to $(P_1^1, P_2^1, \ldots, P_9^1)$. If we designate $E(\cdot)$ as the Hicksian expenditure function consistent with our utility function, then a single-sector, partial-equilibrium measure, CV_{PE}, would change only that sector's price, holding all others at the initial price levels as defined (for sector 1) in

$$(4) \quad CV_{PE} = E\left(P_1^0, P_2^0, \ldots, P_9^0, U^0\right)$$
$$- E\left(P_1^1, P_2^0, \ldots, P_9^0, U^0\right).$$

We have considered three types of partial-equilibrium measures: 1) single-market (PE) analysis described above; 2) a multiple-market analysis with a vertically integrated version of extended partial-equilibrium analysis (VPE), where the prices of the specified consumption good and all of its inputs change to reflect the impacts of the climatic change; and 3) a multiple-market analysis with a horizontal connection of markets with the directly affected commodities prices changing for the welfare measurement. These last two measures follow from Richard Just et al.'s suggestions (1982). The last was formulated in two ways. For our scenarios that have direct changes in only one sector we specified it to involve all final consumption goods (HPE). When the scenarios imply simultaneous impacts on several sectors, it was defined to include only the directly affected final goods' prices ($\overline{HPE}$).

Before discussing the results we should acknowledge that while this approach does allow an evaluation of the importance of all the indirect effects for welfare measurement, it also places the partial-equilibrium welfare measures selected for evaluation in their "best light."[6] This is so because it assumes knowledge of *both* the correct expenditure function (for the welfare measures) and the correct price changes for all commodities that are considered in the analysis. In practice, as Whalley's 1975 study illustrated, we must estimate both the price change and a function to describe consumer preferences as a part of the partial-equilibrium modeling. Thus there are additional sources of error from each of these tasks. We do not consider them here. Rather we propose to gauge the importance of these indirect effects without the potential confounding errors introduced by other measurement tasks.

Table 3 reports the proportionate error found by comparing each partial-equilibrium measure of the welfare change (for each scenario) to the correct general equilibrium measure in the aggregate (i.e., summed across the two domestic households in each economy). That is, if CV_{PE}^k designates the compensating variation measured using a subset of the prices for scenario k, and CV_{GE}^k the correct general equilibrium measure, then our index of the error, EI_k, is given as

$$(5) \quad EI_k = \left(CV_{GE}^k - CV_{PE}^k\right)/CV_{GE}^k.$$

The results for the single-sector scenarios indicate a clear preference for the partial-equilibrium, single-sector measure. Even with large unit cost impacts in that sector, the error in the partial-equilibrium measure represented a small understatement of the effect (i.e., less than 10 percent). By contrast, the extended partial-equilibrium measures have very large errors, even for *small* unit cost changes. However, we should emphasize that

---

[6] Of course, our proposed partial-equilibrium measures are just a sample of the possibilities. Each model will ultimately reflect the analyst's judgments in an attempt to best represent the important general equilibrium within a more restricted framework.

these findings are specific to the CGE model and scenarios we formulated.

Our overall work in this area (see our paper, 1985a) has considered several specifications for CGE models. In one case, with a model of comparable size and detail to the one reported here but for a less developed economy, the single-sector measures were uniformly worse (for comparable exogenous impacts) than the extended partial-equilibrium measures. Moreover, the magnitude of the errors were larger, often exceeding a 100 percent understatement of the welfare impacts with the single-sector *PE* measures. Given these discrepancies, it is essential to consider the features of the model's structure and of the scenarios that may have led to these results.

The first potential feature can be understood by referring to the results in Table 2. For the benchmark solution, agriculture accounts for about 14 percent of domestic output in this model. Nonetheless, the indirect effects of the climate impacts on other consumer commodities are calculated to be small in relationship to the primary effect on agriculture. Equally important, they are all the same sign and about the same magnitude. Thus, the set of consumer goods can be approximately treated as a Hicksian composite commodity. Under this assumption the use of a *PE* measure would largely represent a mistake in the magnitude specified for the change in price of the agriculture commodity *relative* to this composite good. If this interpretation is reasonable, we would expect welfare measurement errors to be related to the direction and magnitude of the error in the specified relative price change and it is. Using this framework, a single-sector *PE* approach would understate the increase in the relative price of agriculture goods. Thus, we would expect the *PE* welfare measure to understate the *CV* change. This is exactly what our results suggest.

In our analyses with the other CGE model referred to earlier, the economic sectors were more closely interconnected (with several produced commodities serving as intermediate inputs in multiple sectors). Moreover, in this case agriculture is more than twice as large a contributor to domestic output, accounting for about 30 percent. As a consequence, single-sector changes of comparable size in agriculture had larger indirect effects across the final consumption commodities. The sign and magnitude of the price impacts were not consistent across sectors. Consequently, the same Hicksian composite commodity assumptions would not be upheld in this case. Single-sector, partial-equilibrium measures would have been expected to be flawed, but the exceptionally large errors could not have been anticipated a priori.

This same framework also helps to understand our findings with the multiple-sector scenarios. In two cases (scenarios 4 and 6) the price effects (both the direct changes and approximate size of the indirect changes) are similar to those for one of the single-sector cases (scenario 2). The importance of the change as a fraction of the domestic households' incomes is also similar. Yet, the errors in the single-sector *PE* welfare measures range from 30 to nearly 50 percent overstatements. A part of the answer may well lie in the disparity in the directions of the indirect effects across sectors. Prices do not move in the same direction. In addition, while the average absolute magnitude of the percentage price change is about comparable to that experienced with the second scenario, the disparity across sectors is substantially greater.

Unfortunately, there does not appear to be a clear explanation for the performance of the extended partial-equilibrium measures. Presumably the answers to the performance of each measure lie in the patterns of relative price change in each scenario and importance of each commodity in the domestic households' expenditures in relationship to the definition of the commodities involved in the respective partial-equilibrium extensions.

On the second aspect of our application —its implications for economic impact analyses of a climate change—our findings should be interpreted only in qualitative terms because the model was not intended to authentically represent a specific economy. Nonetheless, they provide the first (to our knowledge) evidence of potentially large and mixed price effects of a CO_2 induced climate change. Consequently, they (especially the multiple-sector scenarios) imply that focusing on selected sectors may give a very misleading description of the economic impacts of such a large scale change in the environmental conditions affecting production activities. In addition, they identify the possibility that the distributional implications of such changes may also be important; though clearly our results follow from the fact that climatic change affects the price of a commodity that is a large fraction of the low-income household's budget and the assumed patterns maintained for ownership of the CGE economy's resources across households.

III. Implications

Our results have confirmed a priori intuition with respect to the impacts of economy-wide shocks on the performance of single-sector, partial-equilibrium welfare measures. Since our explanations of the conditions leading to the cases of both the good and the poor performance are largely qualitative, one must consider the "value-added" from exercises such as this one. We believe there are at least two potential contributions of our approach. First, an important assumption in recent theoretical analyses of general equilibrium measures of welfare losses is proportionality in distortion changes. Diewert (1985), for example, found that if all distortion vectors increase proportionately then the approximate loss (measured with an Allais-Debreu index) increases quadratically. Our scenarios clearly indicate that proportionality in price movements in response to economywide impacts (or distortions) may in itself be a quite restrictive assumption.

Second, while qualitative judgments on the performance of partial-equilibrium welfare measures have clearly been a part of applied welfare economics for two decades, quantitative information on the exact magnitude of the errors introduced by ignoring indirect effects has been largely nonexistent. Our analysis suggests that the errors associated with these effects can be quite large for plausible scenarios and therefore it moti-

vates further research to isolate the specific economic features that lead to these large effects.

Of course, it is also clear that the CGE framework provides a simple laboratory for evaluating a number of aspects of the practices of applied microeconomics, and thereby of adding a more precise quantitative basis for the judgments that are inherent in virtually all applied work.

REFERENCES

Allais, M., *A La Recherch d'une Discipline Economique*, Vol. I, Paris: Imprimerie Nationale, 1943.

Bach, Wilfred, Pankrath, Jurgen and Schneider, Stephen H., *Flood-Climate Interactions*, Boston: D. Reidel, 1981.

Boadway, Robin W., "Cost-Benefit Rules in General Equilibrium," *Review of Economic Studies*, July 1975, *42*, 361–74.

Debreu, G., "The Coefficient of Resource Utilization," *Econometrica*, July 1951, *19*, 273–92.

Diamond, P. A. and Mirrlees, J. A., (1971a) "Optimal Taxation and Public Production I: Production Efficiency," *American Economic Review*, March 1971, *61*, 8–27.

_____ and _____, (1971b) "Optimal Taxation and Public Production II: Tax Rules," *American Economic Review*, June 1971, *61*, 261–78.

Diewert, W. Erwin, "Cost-Benefit Analysis and Project Evaluation: A Comparison of Alternative Approaches," *Journal of Public Economics*, December 1983, *22*, 265–302.

_____, "The Measurement of Waste and Welfare in Applied General Equilibrium Models," paper presented at NBER Applied General Equilibrium Workshop, Stanford University, April 12–13, 1985.

Eastwood, D. and Craven, J., "Food Demand and Savings in a Complete Extended Linear Expenditure System," *American Journal of Agricultural Economics*, August 1981, *63*, 544–49.

Edlefsen, Lee E., "The Deadweight Loss Triangle as a Measure of General Equilibrium Welfare Toss: Harberger Reconsidered," unpublished paper, University of

Washington, 1983.

Firor, John W. and Portney, Paul R., "The Global Climate" in P. R. Portney, ed., *Current Issues in Natural Resource Policy*, Baltimore: Johns Hopkins University Press, 1982.

Harberger, Arnold C., "Professor Arrow on the Social Discount Rate" in G. G. Somers and W. D. Woods, eds., *Cost-Benefit Analysis of Manpower Policies*, Kingston: Industrial Relations Centre, Queens University, 1969, 81–88.

_____, "Three Basic Postulates for Applied Welfare Economics: An Interpretive Essay," *Journal of Economic Literature*, September 1971, *9*, 785–97.

Hare, F. Kenneth, "Climate Variability and Change" in R. W. Kates et al., eds., *Climate Impact Assessment*, SCOPE, Vol. 27, New York: Wiley & Sons, 1985.

Harrison, Glenn W. and Kimbell, Lawrence, "How Reliable is Numerical General Equilibrium Analysis?," unpublished manuscript, University of Western Ontario, January 1983.

Hazilla, Michael and Kopp, Raymond J., *Substitution Between Energy and Other Factors of Production: U.S. Industrial Experience, 1958–74*, Vol. 1, Final Report to the Electric Power Research Institute, Washington: Resources for the Future, August 1982.

Just, Richard E., Hueth, Darrell L. and Schmitz, Andrew, *Applied Welfare Economics and Public Policy*, Englewood Cliffs: Prentice-Hall, 1982.

Kokoski, Mary F., "A General Equilibrium Analysis of the Measurement of the Economic Impacts of Climatic Change," unpublished doctoral dissertation, University of North Carolina-Chapel Hill, 1984.

Kokoski, Mary F. and Smith, V. Kerry, (1985a) "A General Equilibrium Analysis of Partial Equilibrium Welfare Measures," discussion paper, Vanderbilt University,

1985.

_____ and _____, (1985b) "General Equilibrium Welfare Measurement: A Cautionary Note," Working Paper No. 85-W-21, Vanderbilt University, April, 1985.

Lluch, C., Powell, A. and Williams, R., *Patterns in Household Demand and Saving*, New York: Oxford University Press, 1977.

McKenzie, G. W., *Measuring Economic Welfare: New Methods*, New York: Cambridge University Press, 1983.

Mansur, A. and Whalley, J., "Numerical Specification of Applied General Equilibrium Models: Estimation, Calibration and Data," in H. Scarf and J. Shoven, eds., *Applied General Equilibrium Analysis*, Cambridge: Cambridge University Press, 1984.

Scarf, Herbert, *The Computation of Economic Equilibria*, New Haven: Yale University Press, 1973.

Shoven, John and Whalley, John, "General Equilibrium Calculation of the Effects of Differential Taxation of Income from Capital in the U.S.," *Journal of Public Economics*, Nos. 3/4, 1972, *1*, 281–321.

_____ and _____, "Applied General Equilibrium Models of Taxation and International Trade," *Journal of Economic Literature*, September 1984, *22*, 1007–51.

Thompson, Louis M., "Weather Variability Climatic Change, and Grain Production," *Science*, May 1975, *188*, 535–41.

Waggoner, Paul E., "Agriculture and a Climate Changed by More Carbon Dioxide," in *Changing Climate: Report of the Carbon Dioxide Assessment Committee*, Washington: National Academy Press, 1983, ch. 6.

Whalley, John, "How Reliable is Partial Equilibrium?," *Review of Economics and Statistics*, August 1975, *57*, 299–310.

National Academy of Sciences, *Changing Climate: Report of the Carbon Dioxide Assessment Committee*, Washington: National Academy Press, 1983.

Part V
Role of Forecasting in Reducing Disaster Impacts

[17]

A CASE STUDY IN THE ECONOMICS OF INFORMATION AND COORDINATION
THE WEATHER FORECASTING SYSTEM *

RICHARD R. NELSON
and
SIDNEY G. WINTER, JR.

The economics of information and coordination long has occupied a paradoxical position in the structure of economic thought as a whole. In both the classical and modern discussion of the allocative efficiency of a system of prices and markets, great emphasis has been put on the economy of information, communication and coordination that such a system may achieve. Yet, with few exceptions, the rigorous formulations of the theory of such a system do not contain reference to any real costs of information processing. Business firms and consumers are assumed to *have* all relevant information. The computations that enable firms to make optimum choices of technique and output are assumed to require no investment of time or resources; the process of maximizing utility does not itself involve disutility; the markets where supply and demand are balanced function without benefit of land and buildings, clerical assistance, telephones, and so forth; the price changes generated by market adjustment are costlessly known by all and summarize all of the information firms and consumers need to know to make their decisions. Thus the analysis of the ability of a price and market system to achieve economies of information-processing typically has been carried on in a context of assumptions which makes information a free good, the processing of it costless, and the attempt to economize it pointless.

For many reasons it is important to attempt a more careful and systematic treatment of the economics of information and coordination. It must be recognized that prices are not the only information

*Any views expressed in this paper are those of the authors. They should not be interpreted as reflecting the views of The RAND Corporation or the official opinion or policy of any of its governmental or private research sponsors. Papers are reproduced by The RAND Corporation as a courtesy to members of its staff.

THE WEATHER FORECASTING SYSTEM   **421**

of economic significance. The costs of generating, sending, and processing information must be considered. There are special problems relating to information as a commodity which require special treatment.

Some beginnings on the construction of a framework capable of dealing with certain aspects of information and coordination have been made in recent years on foundations contributed largely by statistical decision theory. Of particular importance is the work of J. Marschak,[1] R. Radner,[2] C. B. McGuire[3] and others on the economic theory of "teams" — a "team" being defined as an organization composed of individual decision-makers all of whom share a single common objective. T. Marschak has examined the effects of speed of information processing on economic organization.[4] G. Stigler[5] and R. Nelson[6] have explored other aspects of the economics of information.

But very little has been done in the way of studies of particular applied problems in the economics of information and coordination to test the usefulness of the theory and to indicate areas where it needs strengthening. In the present paper, we adapt the concepts of the emerging economic theory of information to examine some particular problems involving the dissemination, use, and evaluation of weather information. The theoretical framework follows closely that of Marschak and Radner in the works referred to earlier. The example we use is more than an illustration, but less than a full-scale case study. While it originally was designed as part of a

1. J. Marschak, "Towards an Economic Theory of Organization and Information," in *Decision Processes*, Thrall, Davis and Coombs (eds.), (New York: John Wiley, 1954); "Elements for a Theory of Teams," *Management Science*, Vol. 1 (Jan. 1955), pp. 127–37; "Theory of an Efficient Several-Person Firm," *American Economic Review*, L (May 1960), 541–48.

2. R. Radner, "The Linear Team: An Example of Linear Programming Under Uncertainty," *Proceedings of the Second Symposium on Linear Programming*, (Washington: National Bureau of Standards, 1955); " The Application of Linear Programming to Team Decision Problems," *Management Science*, Vol. 5 (Jan. 1959), pp. 143–50; "The Evaluation of Information in Organizations," *Proceedings of Fourth Berkeley Symposium on Mathematical Statistics and Probability* (Berkeley: University of California Press, 1961), pp. 491–533; "Team Decision Problems," *The Annals of Mathematical Statistics*, Vol. 33 (Sept. 1962), pp. 857–81.

3. C. B. McGuire, "Some Team Models of a Sales Organization," *Management Science*, Vol. 7 (Jan. 1961), pp. 101–30. Also, "Comparisons of Information Structures," Cowles Foundation Discussion Paper No. 71, April 1959 (unpublished).

4. T. Marschak, "Centralization and Decentralization in Economic Organizations," *Econometrica*, Vol. 27 (July 1959), pp. 399–430.

5. G. Stigler, "The Economics of Information," *Journal of Political Economy*, LXIX (June 1961).

6. R. Nelson, "Uncertainty, Prediction and Competitive Equilibrium," this *Journal*, LXXV (Feb. 1961), 41–62.

study examining some aspects of the weather forecasting system per se,[7] this case is presented here in the belief that examination of a real problem should shed some light on the economies of information generally. In particular, we believe it raises some important questions which hitherto have gone unnoticed.

I. The General Framework

In trying to deal with the economics of weather forecasting, we were forced to modify in some respects the framework developed in connection with the theory of teams, but nevertheless found that framework a useful one.

Looking first at the user of information, we consider a single decision-maker whose problem is to make a choice of an *action a* from some set A of possible actions. From this choice the decision-maker will derive a utility u which depends in some known way upon the "true state of the world," w, where w is an element of a set W of possible true states of the world. That is

$$u = \gamma(a, w) \qquad a \in A, w \in W.$$

In the case where A and W are finite sets, the function v can, of course, be displayed as a "payoff matrix" of the type made familiar by statistical decision theory and the theory of games.

The decision-maker does not in general know the true state of the world, w. But an information source supplies him with some "message," y, where y is an element of a set Y of possible messages.[8] There exists some joint probability distribution $\pi(y, w)$ over the sets, Y and W, of messages and true states of the world, and we assume that this distribution is known to the decision-maker. We further assume that the decision-maker will, upon receiving message y, choose that action a which maximizes expected utility for the conditional probability distribution of w given y.[9] The

7. We should like to acknowledge our indebtedness to R. Rapp, D. Sartor, and L. Kolb for their cooperation in the study which produced these "case studies." The original study from which the case is drawn is our "Weather Information and Economic Decisions: A Preliminary Report," RAND RM-2620-NASA, August 1960.

8. We will assume that the set Y is defined in such a way that the message y is the *only* information the decision-maker receives. Thus the "information source" may consist in part of the decision-maker's own activities. In the formal framework this is merely a convention, but in our case studies we will turn it into a genuine assumption by ignoring any information the decision-maker has that is not supplied by the weather forecaster.

9. Of course, on the modern view of utility, the question of the validity of this behavioral assumption is more properly a question about the existence of the utility function.

function $\hat{a}$ which associates with each possible message y the action a which maximizes $E(u/y)$ is the decision-maker's best (Bayesian) *decision rule*, or strategy. Thus

$$a = \hat{a}(y).$$

Given the conditional probability distribution of w for each y, and the marginal probability distribution of y, and assuming the optimum decision rule is used, over-all utility is:

$$E(\hat{u}) = E_y \, E_{w/y} \, \gamma \, [\hat{a} \, (y), \, w].$$

Turning next to analysis of the information source; we regard the activities of this source as involving two stages. First there is an observation stage, in which some element z of a set Z of possible observations is observed. There is assumed to be a joint probability distribution, $\phi(z, w)$ over the sets, Z and W, of possible observations and true states of the world. This joint distribution is not necessarily known to the decision-maker, but it is known to the manager of the information source. Secondly, there is a *communication* stage, in which the message y is determined as a function of the observation, z, $y = \eta \, (z)$, and the message is made available to the decision-maker. Following J. Marschak, we call the function η the *information structure*.[1]

The probability distribution ϕ and the information structure η obviously determine between them the joint probability distribution π of messages and true states of the world. Both ϕ and η are to some extent subject to choice by the manager of the information source.[2] The distribution ϕ is determined by decisions relating to what shall be observed and how these things shall be observed, as well as by the distribution of true states of the world.[3] As for the information

1. Actually, in the typical team theory formulation, the information structure is a mapping from the set of states of the world to the set of messages. At the purely formal level, it is not necessary to hypothesize a set of possible observations distinct from the set of states of the world, since such problems as errors in observations can always be handled by supposing the values of error terms to be included in a complete description of the true state of the world. However, it is often convenient to hypothesize a separate observation stage, for the distinction between observation and transmission of information corresponds to an obvious distinction between the types of equipment and skills involved in different stages of the total information acquiring-and-transmitting process. We have found this split convenient in our study.

2. Both our ϕ and η would be regarded as determinants of the information structure in the usual team theory formulation, and the choice of an information structure would therefore comprise choices with respect to both functions.

3. To take an example which illustrates the connection between these concepts and ordinary statistical decision problems, let w be a parameter of some probability distribution of known form. Let the observation z be a statistic computed from a sample drawn from a population with this distribution, but with the parameter w shifting from one time period to the next.

structure, there may exist possibilities of communicating z itself, of communicating only the sign of z, or of partitioning the range of values of z into intervals and communicating a signal which tells the interval in which z falls. In the examples to be considered subsequently, our primary focus will be on the problem of choosing η, with ϕ being taken as given.

In many instances, it will be a satisfactory approximation to assume that utility is linear in money, since the amount the decision-maker has at risk in any particular confrontation with his decision problem may be small relative to his total capital. We then lack only a determination of a zero point to permit us to define the value of a particular information structure (with ϕ taken as given) to the decision-maker. We follow Marschak and Radner in defining

$$V(\eta) = E(\hat{u}) - \underset{a}{\text{Max }} E_w\ \gamma(a,w)$$
$$= E_y\ E_{w/y}\ \gamma(\hat{a}(y),\ w) - E_w\ \gamma(\hat{a},w).$$

That is, we assign the value 0 to the information structure which provides no information at all to the decision-maker, assuming that in this case the decision-maker knows the probability distribution of true states of the world (a special case of his knowing the distribution π) and that he always takes the action which maximizes expected payoff relative to that probability distribution. The quantity $V(\eta)$ is the value of the information structure to the decision-maker in the sense of demand price, when the only alternative available is no information at all. Obviously, the other alternatives available and the costs of all of the alternative information structures are also determinants of the value of an information structure in the sense of the demand price of that particular information service.

There are several different types of applications for the foregoing analysis. It may serve as the basis of a positive theory of behavior under uncertainty and of the value of information. Or it may be regarded as a normative theory, pointing the way toward the determination of best decision rules and best information structures in particular situations. Or the theory of the behavior of the decision-maker may be regarded as descriptive, while the remainder of the analysis is regarded as normative guidance for the manager of the information source. It is the latter point of view that we take in our subsequent discussion of the principles that should guide a "public forecaster" (e.g., the Weather Bureau).

(footnote 3 continued)
Then the joint distribution ϕ is obviously influenced by the statistic chosen and by the sampling method and sample size.

THE WEATHER FORECASTING SYSTEM 425

II. The Use of Weather Information [4]

We turn now to an application of the general framework in which we identify w, the true state of the world, with some future weather condition, the observation z with the meteorological information available to a weather forecaster, and the message y with a weather forecast of some sort. (This last identification involves an assumption that the weather forecast is the decision-maker's sole source of weather information.) The assumption that the decision-maker knows the probability distribution of true states of the world, even if he has no other information, translates into an assumption that the decision-maker has accurate climatological information for those weather events which are relevant to his problem; i.e., he knows the relative frequencies with which these events will occur given the time of the year, but, in the absence of weather forecasts, cannot predict better than this.

Our example is representative of a wide class of real world decision problems which can, without too much violence to reality, be reduced to the following simple structure: the decision-maker must choose between taking or not taking some specific protective action against a future unfavorable weather condition; taking the protective action involves some cost with certainty; not taking it involves escaping that cost but incurring a certain loss if the unfavorable weather condition does in fact occur.

Thus a newspaper distributor, who has a standard routine for distribution, can wrap his papers in wax paper to protect them from rain. A storekeeper can tape his windows to protect them from a threatening hurricane. A citrus grower can light smudge pots to protect his fruit from frost.

4. We should emphasize at this point that we are by no means the first to apply some sort of statistical decision theory framework to the problems of making, responding to and evaluating weather forecasts. Among the prior contributions in this field we may cite, I. Gringorten, "Probability Estimates of the Weather in Relation to Operation Decisions," *Journal of Meteorology*, Vol. 16 (Dec. 1959), pp. 663–71; and "On the Comparison of One or More Sets of Probability Forecasts," *Journal of Meteorology*, Vol. 15 (June 1958), pp. 283–87. Also, J. C. Thompson and G. L. Brier, "The Economic Utility of Weather Forecasts," *Monthly Weather Review*, Vol. 83 (Nov. 1955), pp. 249–53; J. C. Thompson, "On the Operational Deficiencies in Categorical Weather Forecasts," *Bulletin of the American Meteorological Society*, Vol. 33 (June 1952), pp. 223–26. The latter papers consider in particular the simple "protect — don't protect" problem which serves as our main example. Our own treatment casts this example in a more general framework and also provides a particular illustration of it. The present paper draws in part on our own earlier work on the subject, reported in "Weather Information and Economic Decisions: A Preliminary Report," The RAND Corporation, RM-2620-NASA, August 1, 1960.

We will examine here a decision problem that confronts the dispatcher of a fleet of trucks.

The schedule requires that all loading be accomplished on the day or evening before dispatch so that the trucks can leave early in the morning. All of the trucks are "flat racks" (uncovered trucks), and the merchandise carried is seldom of a sort which will be damaged significantly by light rain. It is customary to ship such merchandise — building material, canned goods, etc. — unprotected or protected only by normal packaging, if the chances of rain are judged to be slim.

However, a moderate or heavy rain can cause considerable damage even to cargo usually considered quite unperishable. The top layers of the goods may be completely soaked. Cardboard packaging may be weakened to the point of being worthless. Labels, for example on canned goods, may be loosened and even soaked off. A reasonable figure for the average damage resulting from a moderate or heavy rain is $500 per truckload of unprotected merchandise.

If a significant amount of rain is expected, the dispatcher can direct his crews to "tarp the trucks" (cover the merchandise with a tarpaulin) after loading them. The cost of doing this job, including labor time plus wear and tear on the tarping on an average trip, may be put at about $20 a truck. To permit an early morning departure, tarping must be done the prior evening.

For the purposes of this study we consider any amount of rain in excess of .15 inches as "heavy," and assume that if rain is less than this amount no damage will result. Each evening the dispatcher must decide whether or not to tarp the trucks. Clearly it would be good policy to tarp the trucks only on evenings preceding bad days and at no other times, but in the absence of perfect forecasts this is impossible. In the absence of perfect information, the dispatcher bases his decision on the weather forecast he receives from a private weather consultant. If the forecast is for rain, the trucks are tarped, but otherwise not.

In the Los Angeles area, the site of our example, the climatological probability of rain in excess of .14 inches is .09 during the winter rainy season, the period of our example. It is obvious that if the dispatcher has to make his daily decisions on this information alone and aims to minimize expected cost, he should order the trucks tarped every evening, thus incurring a daily cost of $20 per truck. The alternative, never tarping the trucks, would work out well on an average of 91 days out of 100, but on an average of 9 days out of 100 the company would incur a loss of $500 per truck, an average daily loss of $45 per truck. (We assume, not perfectly accurately, that regardless of how the weather looks on the *morning* of departure, no makeshift protective measures can be taken and the trucks must depart on schedule.)

Let us now consider the forecasts the decision-maker receives from a private weather consultant. In our trucking example the forecast received by the decision-maker is either a prediction that weather state w_1 = "heavy rain" will occur — call this forecast y_1 — or a forecast that weather state w_2 (= less than .15 inches rain) will occur — call this forecast y_2. Records show that out of 100 forecasts made during a four month period, 18 were predictions of rain, and 82 were predictions that it would not rain. The no-rain forecasts were very reliable; on only two days did rain occur when none was forecast. This high accuracy of the y_2 forecasts was achieved because the forecaster always predicted rain whenever there was any doubt in his mind. His y_1 forecasts, therefore, were not very reliable. Indeed, on 11 out of the 18 days that he forecast rain, it did not rain. It will be demonstrated later that this low accuracy of the y_1 forecasts, rather than reflecting adversely on the forecaster, is an indication that he was sensibly tailoring his forecasts to his customer's needs.

The forecasts thus define the following two-by-two contingency table:

TABLE I

FORECAST

		y_1	y_2	Total
Observed	w_1	7	2	9
	w_2	11	80	91
Total		18	82	100

The entry in any column and row gives the number of days out of 100 in which a specific forecast was made, and a specific weather state occurred. From this table we will subsequently derive the distribution $\pi(y, w)$ for this example.

Instead of proceeding directly to find the value to the trucking company of the forecasts just described, let us set up the "protect — don't protect" problem more generally, find a general solution, and then substitute in the specific numbers that relate to our example.

The following notation will prove convenient. Let

π_1 = the relative frequency of forecast y_1, the forecast of unfavorable weather;

$\pi_2 = 1 - \pi_1 =$ the relative frequency of forecast y_2, the forecast of favorable weather;

$\pi_{11} =$ the conditional probability of unfavorable weather, given that forecast y_1 is made;

$\pi_{21} = 1 - \pi_{11} =$ the conditional probability of favorable weather, given that forecast y_1 is made;

$\pi_{12} =$ the conditional probability of unfavorable weather, given that forecast y_2 is made;

$\pi_{22} = 1 - \pi_{12} =$ the conditional probability of favorable weather, given that forecast y_2 is made.

Thus in the π_{ij}'s above, the first subscript refers to the weather state while the second refers to the forecast. Note that these are *conditional* probabilities, not joint probabilities.

We now determine the value of an information structure characterized by the above probabilities when the payoff function $\gamma(a, w)$ is of the type displayed in the following table:

TABLE II

WEATHER

		y_1	y_2
	a_1	$v(a_1,\ w_1) = -C$	$v(a_1,\ w_2) = -C$
Action			
	a_2	$v(a_2,\ w_1) = -L$	$v(a_2,\ w_2) = 0$

Thus C is the cost of protection and L the loss incurred if adverse weather occurs and no protective action is taken. We naturally assume $C < L$, since otherwise the problem is completely trivial.

It is convenient in this problem to work in terms of minimizing cost (disutility) rather than maximizing payoff (utility). So we set $c(a, w) = - v(a, w)$. If the decision-maker receives forecast y_1, his expected cost if he chooses action a_1 is C, while his expected cost if he chooses a_2 is $\pi_{11} L$. Hence

$$\hat{a}(y_1) = \begin{cases} a_1 & \text{if } C < \pi_{11}\ L \\ a_1 \text{ or } a_2 & \text{if } C = \pi_{11}\ L \\ a_2 & \text{if } C > \pi_{11}\ L \end{cases}$$

and $E(\hat{a}|y_1) = \text{Min} \ (C, \pi_{11}\ L)$.

Similarly, when he receives forecast y_2, he chooses a_1 or a_2 depending on whether C or $\pi_{12} L$ is smaller:

$$\hat{a}(y_2) = \begin{cases} a_1 & \text{if } C < \pi_{12}\ L \\ a_1 \text{ or } a_2 & \text{if } C = \pi_{12}\ L \\ a_2 & \text{if } C > \pi_{12}\ L \end{cases}$$

THE WEATHER FORECASTING SYSTEM   **429**

and $E(\hat{a}|y_2) = \text{Min } (C, \pi_{12} L)$.

The equations above determine the decision-maker's best decision rule, and the expected minimized cost for each of the two forecasts. The over-all expected cost under the best decision rule is given by

$$E(c) = \pi_1 \text{ Min } (C, \pi_{11} L) + \pi_2 \text{ Min } (C, \pi_{12} L).$$

Let us look at the problem from another point of view. There are four decision rules connecting the two messages with the two possible actions. These are displayed in Table III.

TABLE III

FORECAST

		y_1	y_2
	a_1	a_1	a_1
Decision	a_2	a_1	a_2
Rule	a_3	a_2	a_2
	a_4	a_2	a_1

Of these four rules, the last may be ruled out by an assumption that the forecasts are correctly labeled. Thus rain is not more likely after a no rain forecast than after a rain forecast.

For the remaining possibilities,

$$\hat{a} = \begin{cases} a_1 \text{ if } C < \pi_{11} L \text{ and } C < \pi_{12} L \\ \qquad \text{i.e., if } \dfrac{C}{L} < \pi_{12} \ (< \pi_{11}) \\ a_2 \text{ if } \pi_{12} < \dfrac{C}{L} < \pi_{11} \\ a_3 \text{ if } \pi_{12} < \pi_{11} < \dfrac{C}{L} \,. \end{cases}$$

The climatological probability of unfavorable weather is $\pi^1 = \pi_1 \pi_{11} + \pi_2 \pi_{12}$, which is obviously between π_{12} and π_{11}. Hence a_1 is the best rule on the basis of climatological information alone if $\dfrac{C}{L} < \pi^1$ and a_3 is the best rule on the basis of climatological information alone if $\dfrac{C}{L} > \pi^1$; Thus it is only in the case $\pi_{12} < \dfrac{C}{L} < \pi_{11}$ that the optimal response to the forecasts differs from the optimal action that would be taken on the basis of climatological information alone, and it is only in this case that the forecasts can have any value to the decision-maker. This condition means that unless the weather forecaster is able to better climatology by a certain finite amount (determined by $\frac{C}{L}$) his forecast will have no value at all.

Assuming the forecasts are good enough to have some value

$$E(c) = \pi_1 C + \pi_2 \pi_{12} L.$$

To determine the value of the information structure which provides forecasts characterized by the indicated probabilities, we must compare this expected cost with the expected cost which would result if climatological information alone were available. The latter is Min $(C, \pi^1 L)$; the best action is to protect all the time if $\frac{C}{L} < \pi^1$, and to run the risk of a loss L occurring if $\frac{C}{L} > \pi^1$. Thus, the value of the information structure — the saving in expected cost that the forecast makes possible — is given by

$$V(\eta) = \text{Min} \ (C, \pi^1 L) - \pi_1 C - \pi_2 \pi_{12} L$$

or

$$V(\eta) = \begin{cases} \pi_2 \ (C - \pi_{12} \ L) & \text{if } \dfrac{C}{L} \le \pi^1 \\[2ex] \pi_1 \ (\pi_{11} \ L - C) & \text{if } \dfrac{C}{L} \ge \pi^1. \end{cases}$$

To apply this result to our trucking example, we use the experience recorded in Table I as the basis for estimates of the various probabilities. We find

$$\pi_1 = \frac{18}{100} \qquad \pi_{11} = \frac{7}{18} \approx .389$$

$$\pi_2 = \frac{82}{100} \qquad \pi_{12} = \frac{2}{82} \approx .0244$$

and $\qquad \pi^1 = \frac{9}{100}$.

We also have $\dfrac{C}{L} = \dfrac{20}{500} = .04$. Since the condition $\pi_{12} < \dfrac{C}{L} < \pi_{11}$ is satisfied, the trucks will be tarped if and only if the forecast is for rain, and the forecasts have value. Since the climatological probability of rain exceeds $\dfrac{C}{L}$, the best action in the absence of forecasts would be to protect all the time, and the value of the forecasts is given by $\pi_2(C - \pi_{12} L)$, or \$6.40 per truck per day.

We have chosen the value of climatological information as the zero point in our value scale for information structures; but it is also of interest to compare a particular information structure with a hypothetical perfect forecasting system. (The possibility of achieving such a system obviously depends on the probability distribution ϕ as well as on the function η.) In our example, perfect forecasting would mean that favorable weather would be forecast $1 - \pi^1 = .91$ of the time, and the forecasts would always be right, so $\pi_{12} = 0$. Therefore the value of perfect forecasts would be $.91\ C$, or $18.20 per truck per day.

III. The Making of Forecasts: Optimal Information Structures

We now turn to the problem of determining how the weather forecaster should summarize the information in his observations if he wishes to make the decision-maker's expected payoff as large as possible. That is, taking as given the observations z and their joint distribution ϕ with the true state of the world, we wish to determine the information structure η that has the largest possible value, $V(\eta)$.

Much of the forecaster's knowledge of present and future weather states relates to weather variables which have no direct relevance to economic activity. For example, few if any activities are directly affected by atmospheric pressure. A decision-maker whose best decision depends on the amount of rain has no interest in the atmospheric pressure except insofar as it provides information about the probability distribution of the amount of rain. Not only is much of the forecaster's information irrelevant from the point of view of the decision-maker — much of it is incomprehensible (to raise a problem in semantics we will examine in more detail later). Thus, not only on grounds of cost saving (assuming it is less costly to send less information than more) but on grounds of decoding capacity of the receiver, the weather forecaster must summarize his information, and, in general, translate it.

We shall consider here the problem of determining an optimal information structure for the simple protect-don't protect problem discussed in the previous section. Turning to ϕ, let $p(z)$ be the probability that "unfavorable" weather will occur the day after the forecaster's observation is z. Let η^* be the *identity* information structure; the information structure that provides z itself to the decision-maker. Thus $y = \eta^*(z) = z$. It is clear that (abstracting from the decoding or semantics problem) if the information structure is the identity information structure η^* (all of the forecaster's information is sent on to the decision-maker), the optimal decision rule is as follows: [5]

5. In the following equation and elsewhere there is the minor problem

$$\hat{a}(\eta^*(z)) = \begin{array}{l} a_1 \text{ if } C \leqq p(z) \ L \\ a_2 \text{ if } C \geqq p(z) \ L \ . \end{array}$$

Further, any information structure η which has the property that each observation z is associated with a unique message y differs only superficially (again abstracting from semantics) from the identity information structure. It is clear that there is no information structure which can have a higher value than η^*. But η^* may be very costly.

We shall call any information structure that has the same value as η^* a sufficient information structure; each of the signals y provided by such a system must be a sufficient statistic in the sense that it conveys all the information bearing on the decision problem that z itself contains. In the case where the decision-maker has n possible actions it is easily seen that there exists a sufficient information structure involving no more than n messages.[6] If the cost of η is related to the number of possible signals "the minimal message sufficient information structure" is of considerable interest.

For the protection problem, the information structure

$$\hat{\eta}(z) = \begin{array}{l} y_1 \text{ ("unfavorable") if } p(z) \geqq \dfrac{C}{L} \\ \\ y_2 \text{ ("favorable") if } p(z) \leqq \dfrac{C}{L} \end{array}$$

is sufficient. It will have positive value provided that the function $p(z)$ is not everywhere greater than, or everywhere less than, the critical ratio $\dfrac{C}{L}$ (in which case either y_1 or y_2 could never be sent). Thus for this particular problem an information structure involving only two different messages can be as good as any information structure, in particular as good as the (possibly very costly) identity structure.

We may illustrate these ideas by applying them to the determination of the minimum-message sufficient information structure

that if the decision rule (or information structure is to be a *function*, some arbitrary choices must be made to resolve the borderline cases; in this equation, the case $C = p(z) \ L$. We will not bother to treat this minor difficulty with precision, on the grounds that the returns from such a change in the information structure we are providing to the reader would not cover the costs.

6. We can simply let the message η (z) be y_i whenever z is an observation such that $\hat{a}(z)$ is a_i; then clearly $\hat{a}(y_i)$ is a_i also, and the decision-maker responds to each of the messages $y_1, \ldots y_n$ just as he would if he had full information about z. To put it another way, if n different messages can be given to the decision-maker, there exists an information structure such that he will never take an action which is inferior to the action he would take given complete knowledge of z.

THE WEATHER FORECASTING SYSTEM 433

for the truck protection problem considered earlier. As the meteorological input to the analysis, we take J. C. Thompson's objective scheme for forecasting rainfall in the Los Angeles area.[7] In this scheme, the implications for the probability distribution of rain of several different meteorological observations are summarized in the value of a single variable, designated Y_2 in the Thompson article but identified here as z. The first two columns of Table IV give the absolute frequency distribution for z, and the cumulative relative frequency distribution derived from it. The third column gives the number of days that rain in excess of .15 inches fell after the z value in the indicated interval was observed, and the fourth column is

TABLE IV

z Interval [1]	Number of Days	Cumulative Relative Frequency [2]	Days of Rain (rain > .15") for z in Interval	Relative Frequency of Rain; Given z in Interval
Less than 0	54	.151	0	.00
0 to 10	55	.304	0	.00
10 to 20	60	.472	0	.00
20 to 30	45	.598	1	.02
30 to 40	54	.749	3	.06
40 to 50	36	.849	3	.08
50 to 60	21	.907	6	.29
60 to 70	14	.947	4	.36
70 to 80	9	.972	6	.67
Over 80	10	1.000	8	.80
Total	358		32	(.09)

[1] Intervals are inclusive of their upper bounds, exclusive of their lower bounds.
[2] To upper bound of indicated interval.

column three divided by column one — the conditional relative frequency of rain for z observations in the indicated interval. As can be seen, the greater the observed z, the greater the probability of rain.

In Figures I and II, smooth curves have been fitted (freehand) to the relative frequency data. We will interpret these curves as giving true "population" values of the probabilities, since our framework has no place for the problems raised by imperfect knowledge of the basic probability distribution ϕ.

The curve for $p(z)$ in Figure II indicates that a probability of

7. J. C. Thompson, "A Numerical Method for Forecasting Rainfall in the Los Angeles Area," *Monthly Weather Review*, Vol. 78 (July 1950), pp. 113–24. Table IV was obtained by counting points in the scatter diagram, Fig. 5, p. 118 of Thompson's article.

434   QUARTERLY JOURNAL OF ECONOMICS

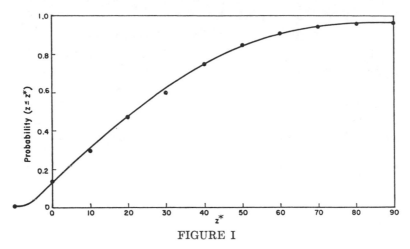

FIGURE I

$$\frac{20}{500} = .04 = \frac{C}{L}$$ is associated with a z value of about 31. Hence a sufficient, minimum-message information structure for the truck protection problem would be to forecast "rain" whenever z exceeds

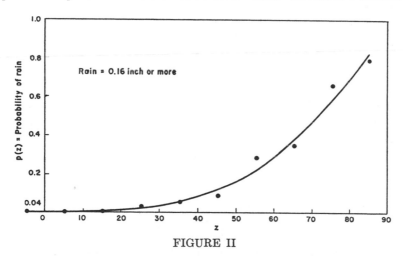

FIGURE II

31 and to forecast "no rain" otherwise. From Figure I, values of z giving rise to the no rain forecast would arise about .63 of the time, so $\pi_2 = .63$. Figure III shows the conditional probabilities of rain given that z is less than any particular "cutoff value," z^*. For $z^* = 31$, this probability is about .006, so $\pi_{12} = .006$. Since the climatological probability of rain is .09, the value of this sufficient information structure is given by

$$V(\eta) = \pi_2 \ (C - \pi_{12} \ L)$$
$$= .63 \, [20 - (.006) \, 500] = \$10.40/\text{truck/day}.$$

It is interesting to note that the problem of determining a sufficient information structure and its value can, in this case at least, be cast into a transformation curve — indifference curve framework. We may consider information structures to be characterized by the accuracy of the no rain forecast and the frequency with which it is made.[8] The expression given above for the value of an information

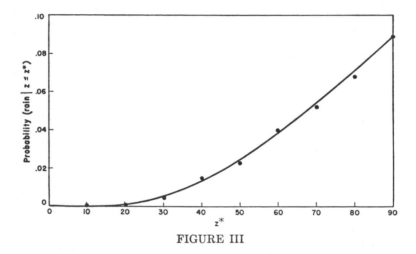

FIGURE III

structure can be rewritten to read $V = \pi_2 \ (C - (1 - \pi_{22}) \ L)$; it then tells us how these two characteristics can be traded off from the point of view of the consumer of the information: For any given value of V, we can plot the combinations of values of π_2 and π_{22} that yield that value of V.

On the "production" side, there is also a possibility of trade-off between the accuracy and the frequency of the forecast. Greater and greater accuracy in the forecast of no rain can be achieved by insisting on more and more unequivocal evidence of fair weather, but this unequivocal evidence is available less frequently, and consequently the forecast can be made less often. To put the matter in different terms, the forecaster can obviously take any cutoff value z^* and choose to forecast no rain if z is less than that value. For any z^* so chosen, Figure I shows the frequency with which the no rain forecast will be made, and one minus the ordinate in Figure

8. This is equivalent to characterizing them in terms of the "Type I and Type II errors," π_{12} and π_{21}.

III gives the accuracy. Plotting the accuracy — frequency pairs for all possible values of z^* gives us the transformation curve between accuracy and frequency.[9]

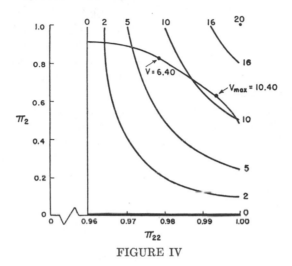

FIGURE IV

Figure IV shows the resulting transformation and indifference curves. The optimum previously identified is now associated, of course, with tangency between the indifference curves and the transformation curve. The actual information structure discussed in Section II is seen to be on the transformation curve (the forecaster either is using the Thompson framework or something as good), but the "optimal" η is more than 60 per cent more "valuable" than the actual η. The actual η utilizes a lower accuracy of the no rain forecast than is optimal. Nevertheless, that accuracy is significantly higher than would be achieved if the forecast did not "discriminate" in favor of forecasting rain in doubtful cases. If the forecaster forecast the weather most likely to occur (so that $p(z^*) = .5$), the accuracy of the no rain forecast would be only .95, and the forecasts would have no value at all.

IV. OTHER PROBLEMS OF COST

Our concern with "minimum message sufficient information structures" stems from the conjecture that the greater the number

---

9. It might be noted here that an improvement in meteorological observation and analysis, an improvement in ϕ, would shift the transformation curve out. Choice among alternative ϕ would have to be made by repeating this analysis for each one.

THE WEATHER FORECASTING SYSTEM   **437**

of messages, the greater the cost. If the cost of an information structure depends *only* on the number of messages, no information structure can be optimal that involves more messages than there are actions. Of course, it may be optimal to use an information structure which involves less than n messages. Before one can determine the optimal number of messages to use, one must determine the optimal way to use any given number of messages. This is not a simple matter in general but the following principle provides some guidance: Let η be an information structure involving n-k messages, and having a value as great as that for any such structure. Then for any observation z, the action taken in response to the message η (z) yields an expected payoff at least as great as that yielded by the action that would be $k + $ 1st best given complete knowledge of z. The case $k = 0$ of this proposition is the statement that an n-message structure must be sufficient if it is to be optimal. If $k = 1$, the proposition says that in no state of the world will an action be taken that is worse than second best in that state of the world, and so on.

Clearly, the assumption that the cost of an information structure depends only on the number of messages is a very special one. An alternative simple assumption would be that the cost is proportional to the number of *signals* actually sent.

Any signal may be interpreted as a message and *no signal* also may be interpreted as a *message*. Let s be the cost of a signal. Then, in the protection problem the expected cost of the information structure, $K(\eta)$, is given by

$$K(\eta) = s \text{ Min } (\pi_1, \pi_2).$$

If the cost function has this form, the minimum message sufficient information structure discussed above is not generally optimal in the sense of maximizing $R(\eta) = V(\eta) - K(\eta)$. In fact, it is optimal only in the case $s = 0$, when information structures involving more than the minimum number of messages are also optimal.

To see the reason for this conclusion, consider the sufficient information structure discussed above, where $\pi_1 = .37$ and $\pi_2 = .63$. Obviously, the message y_2 (no rain) should be conveyed by "no signal." But now consider a value of z such that $p(z)$ exceeds very slightly the critical ratio $\dfrac{C}{L} = .04$. For such a value of z, it makes almost no difference which action the decision-maker takes. And if $p(z)$ is close enough to .04, the improvement the signal permits in the decision-maker's expected payoff will not be sufficient to cover the cost s of sending the signal. Thus the forecaster should send the rain forecast somewhat less often when there is a positive cost associated with sending it than is required by the sufficient information structure.

Under these circumstances, the forecaster should actually choose the value of z such that $p(z) = \dfrac{C + s}{L}$ as his cutoff value, forecasting rain only if z exceeds this value. For whenever the rain forecast is made, both the protection cost C and the signal cost s will be incurred with certainty, while if the no rain forecast is made the expected cost is still $p(z)\ L$.[1]

More complicated problems of cost arise when the decision-maker has more than two possible actions. These problems, and others as well, face a central weather bureau which serves several different decision-makers with the same set of signals and we shall examine them here in this broader context. These broader problems involve both difficulties with respect to institutional arrangements, and with respect to semantics.

To an increasing extent, large companies whose operations are affected by the weather are hiring private meteorological firms to forecast the weather for them, rather than relying on the services of the Weather Bureau.[2] These firms rely in general upon the data obtained by the Weather Bureau's network of reporting stations, and they typically do not rest the case for the value of their services upon an alleged superiority in scientific skill relative to the Weather Bureau. What they do offer is, in our terms, a superior information structure: they provide more information about the weather dimensions which affect the client's operations; they concentrate on forecasting events in the space and time frame of interest to the client; and, it appears that they sometimes take into account the risks associated with the alternative actions open to the decision-maker and "slant" their forecasting accordingly. It is interesting, therefore, to examine the question of what the appropriate division of

---

1. It is the other way around, of course, if the rain forecast is made more than half the time; the cutoff value should then be the z such that $p(z) = \dfrac{C - s}{L}$. In the general case, it is necessary to make an explicit comparison of the two alternatives $p(z^{*}) = \dfrac{C + s}{L}$ (no signal = no rain), and $p(z^{*}) = \dfrac{C - s}{L}$ (no signal = rain) to determine which is better.

2. See the article, "How's the Weather," *The Wall Street Journal*, March 19, 1963, p. 1, where it is reported that private weather forecasters are expected to do $15 million worth of business in 1963 as against $10 million in 1961, and that the number of private meteorological firms in the United States is 35, up from 27 two years ago.

labor is between a public information source such as the Weather Bureau and the private firms which supplement the services it provides to particular decision-makers.

Let us continue, for the moment, to assume that the only relevant weather states from the point of view of any decision-maker are rain and no rain. But any decision-maker may have m possible choices of degrees of protective action. If the probability of rain is high, it may be optimal to take quite expensive protection; if there is little chance of rain, less protection. Given m possible actions, we know that each may be optimal for a given range of rain probability, and thus to provide sufficient information to the decision-maker may require as many as m possible messages. If there are N decision-makers, all of whom are to receive the forecast, as many as $\sum_{k=1}^{N} m_k$ signals may be required for a sufficient information structure. Clearly, this might be very costly and, if the cost of the structure were dependent upon the number of possible forecasts, undoubtedly a system involving less than sufficient information would be optimal.

Clearly, this is the type of situation where private weather consultants, drawing on weather bureau basic information, but tailoring their forecasts to the needs of a particular client, can play a useful role. This institutional arrangement makes economic sense if the major problem in having a central weather bureau provide information of sufficient detail to be useful to all lay in the costs of having an information structure with such a large number of possible messages.

However, in many instances it would not appear that the number of possible messages has much to do with the transmission costs of the information structure. The problem of structures involving many messages, at least in the weather forecasting case, lies in the added difficulty of decoding or understanding the messages, rather than in the costs of sending them. In the example we have studied the problem is one of semantics, not of channel capacity. We have not until now attached significance to the exact words or numbers used to convey the signal to the decision-maker. We have assumed that the decision-maker knows the true relation between the signals he receives and the probabilities of the weather states, presumably through long experience with the forecasts. But the question of how the labeling of the forecasts may affect their value cannot be pushed aside in a discussion of how the forecaster's knowledge of the weather should be conveyed to decision-makers. Intelligibility is obviously an important consideration. Or, to put it another way, we must not ignore the costs of information processing which the labeling of the forecast imposes upon the decision-maker, or the possibility that the decision-maker may be unaware of the relevance of the signals to his problem if the labeling is inconvenient.

If the number of decision-makers served by the forecasts and the number of actions open to each are small, or if the decision problems are virtually identical, it may be possible to construct a suggestive set of verbal labels for the small number of forecasts required for a sufficient information structure — slight chance of rain, etc. But the most obvious practical solution to the labeling problem in this case is for the forecaster simply to provide the probability $p(z)$ itself, to whatever degree of accuracy may be warranted by the state of knowledge of the joint distribution of z and w.[3] A major advantage of this solution is that the forecaster does not need to have detailed knowledge of all of the decision problems in order to provide a sufficient information structure (or a close approximation thereto).

As compared with the more typical alternatives of providing some "categorical" forecast, or a vague verbal description of the forecaster's uncertainty, probability forecasts offer a much closer approximation to sufficiency. The benefits from this can be very large when, as in the case of the Thompson objective scheme, different observations provide different degrees of certainty that certain weather states will or will not occur. Much of the forecaster's information about future weather is kept from the decision-maker when high certainty situations are lumped with much more doubtful situations in an information structure which involves a small number of distinct signals. For example, a system of forecasts which merely described the weather state most likely to occur involves such a drastic summarization of the forecaster's information as to wipe out, for many decision-makers, the information value potentially derivable from the forecaster's observations. If some of these decision-makers then turn to private forecasters who charge a positive price to supply information which they do not produce and which has a very small transmission cost, only a part of the social loss resulting from oversummarization can be recouped.

Forecasts of rain stated in probability terms are not standard in several American cities, and our discussion above suggests that

3. Here we must recognize as a practical matter that knowledge of the distribution ϕ is less than perfect. Clearly, if $p(z)$ can be any real number in the $0 - 1$ interval, the task of communicating its precise value is going to be formidable.

the extension of this practice is desirable. However, this does not begin to answer the question of how the public forecaster should operate.

For the Weather Bureau to provide close to sufficient information to all would necessarily be very costly. While many decision problems can be adequately treated by distinguishing only "rain" and "no rain" as weather states, for other problems the decision-maker will want to know a great deal more about the probability distribution of amounts of rain than the probability concentrated at the origin. Still other problems depend on events in other weather dimensions — wind and temperature, type of precipitation, and so forth — and different decision-makers will in general be interested in events in different localities. Also, when it is recognized that taking action is generally time consuming and that predictions of the weather at a future time t will improve as t gets closer, it becomes clear that many decision-makers face problems whose solution depends in principle upon the joint distribution of weather states and forecasts over time. Without violence to the complexity of real world decision problems, the amount of detail that a sufficient-for-everybody information structure would provide can be regarded as essentially infinite. Therefore, constraints on communication and information processing cannot be disregarded indefinitely. The public forecaster *must* provide an information structure that is less than sufficient for some decision-makers, and the question is what amounts and types of detail it is the function of the public forecaster to provide, and what should be left to private forecasters.

Clearly, the answer is that the public forecaster's choice of an information structure should reflect the importance of the different weather dimensions as determined by the number and types of decision problems faced and the sensitivity of the payoff to the action taken, and in those dimensions the information provided about the probability distribution should reflect any clustering of "critical points" that may exist — whether these are critical points for probabilities, for the expectations of certain quantities, for the time that will elapse before certain events occur, or something else. But it is equally clear that considerable progress will have to be made in the economic theory of information before the vague proposition just stated can be made precise.

RAND Corporation
University of California, Berkeley

[18]

A DECISION MODEL FOR ADJUSTING TO NATURAL HAZARD EVENTS WITH APPLICATION TO URBAN SNOW STORMS

Charles W. Howe and Harold C. Cochrane*

I. Introduction

THE purpose of this paper is to present a decision model which, while relatively simple in structure, has proven valuable in structuring the elements of a rather wide variety of decision situations involving man's individual or collective adjustment to natural events such as weather phenomena. It is felt that the model may be useful in the formulation and solution of still other types of problems. A case study of adjustment to snow hazard is used to illustrate the direct empirical application of the model to an urban decision problem.

Time seems to divide itself conveniently into two spans for decision purposes: the oft-mentioned short and long runs. While there may exist a spectrum of responses over time to a perceived stimulus, most economic decisions take place within systems which have design capacities for response outside of which response is more difficult or costly than when system design capacity can be adjusted. The economic theory of the firm with its many elaborations is a perfect illustration.

The long run-short run distinction seems to hold well also for decision situations which are more accurately characterized as adjustment to natural conditions or environment. In adjusting to floods, the long run holds the possibilities of constructing dams, levees, floodproof buildings, and changing locations, while short run response is restricted to warnings, evacuation, movement of furnishings, etc. There exist other natural hazard situations which are nicely characterized by a similar dichotomy of responses: tornadoes, hurricanes, hail, frost, and snow.

The present model was initially constructed to help understand decision processes relating to weather conditions and to assist in valuing changes in the accuracy of weather forecasts. Where weather is an important part of the environment of a production process (including such activities as recreation), there are usually long and short run forms of adjustment. There are also two corresponding types of information: climatological data collected over long time periods, and weather forecasts which reach from the present to perhaps five days in the future. While climatological parameters may be quite stable, particular weather events occur randomly and the forecasts of those events are subject to error. Weather information can thus be capsulated in the joint probability distribution of weather events and forecasts.[1]

The model is constructed to minimize the expected value of the sum of the costs of adjustment and residual damage. In our opinion, therefore, it deals with repetitious, non-catastrophic natural events.

The structure of this model is similar to the basic framework of Nelson and Winter (1964). The major differences between the two formulations are that the present model includes both short run and long run responses to the distribution of weather events by the weather information user, but it does not analyze the problem of the transmission of weather information from the weather forecaster's point of view. Nelson and Winter were able to characterize analytically the value of a forecast for cases involving a small number of discrete actions and forecast values. Perhaps more importantly,

Received for publication May 28, 1974. Revision accepted for publication December 30, 1974.

* This work was started under NSF Grant GA-31298, "User Needs and Dissemination Requirements for Weather Information," made to the University of Colorado in 1970. The application to snow hazard was worked out as part of the "Assessment of Research on Natural Hazards" project under NSF Grant GI-32942 to the University of Colorado.

[1] The marginal distribution of weather events would be constructed from the climatological record.

they introduced the concept of the sufficiency of a forecast message for the purpose of a specified weather information user; that is, that the forecast message contains all of the information possessed by the forecaster which is relevant to the user's decision problem. The Nelson and Winter formulation thus sheds light on the form and information content of forecast messages. While they were unable to draw clear-cut conclusions regarding these matters for the case when the forecaster is serving a diverse clientele, they were able to structure the problem quite clearly.

A classic application of the Nelson and Winter model is Lave's (1963) investigation of the value of better weather information to the raisin industry. A partial equilibrium determination of the value per acre of perfect three week forecasts was carried out, supplemented by an analysis of the impacts that the resultant increases in output would have on industry profits.

II. Model Development

To motivate the elements of the model, we shall refer to the snow hazard case which is empirically investigated at the end of this paper. A municipal authority is pictured as facing two decisions with respect to snow-removal capability: (1) the snow removal capability of equipment and associated manpower owned and held ready by the city; (2) the short run decision to call up privately owned equipment and crews from outside to help handle a snow event. The public equipment inventory is relatively fixed and heavily dependent upon climatological factors. The call-up of outside equipment is a decision made in light of the existing equipment inventory and is heavily dependent upon current short term weather forecasts. Naturally, the two decisions are not independent and the optimal values of the equipment stock and the parameters of the decision rule should, ideally, be determined simultaneously.

Figure 1 symbolically depicts the elements of this model. We let x represent the level of long run response, assumed to be constant once set within a given decision setting. The level of short run response is designated y, and the

decision rule for y relating it to the short term forecast z is assumed to take the following form:

$$y = 0 \text{ if } z < \alpha x$$
$$y = \beta (z - \alpha x) \text{ if } z \geqslant \alpha x. \qquad (1)$$

The parameter α is thus referred to as the "triggering level" with respect to x, and β is the "strength of response" parameter in the decision rule.

Damages due to the disruption of the natural event in any one period are a function of the long and short run adjustment levels and the actual value of the natural event, s:

$$D(s, x, y) = \begin{cases} \text{(a)} \quad 0 & \text{if } s \leqslant x \\ \text{(b)} \quad g(s-x, 0) & \text{if } \begin{cases} s > x \\ z \leqslant \alpha x \end{cases} \\ \text{(c)} \quad g(s-x, y) & \text{if } \begin{cases} s > x \\ z > \alpha x. \end{cases} \end{cases}$$
$$(2)$$

The formulation of this damage function might differ somewhat among problem applications. The above seems natural for the snow case, where s represents the 24-hour accumulation and $(s-x)$ represents how much the accumulation exceeds the in-house removal capability. In the flood damage case where x represents, say, floodwall height, it might be more appropriate to write segments (b) and (c) as $g(s,o)$ and $g(s,y)$ since, once the floodwall is topped, the actual flood height is the relevant determinant of damage.

The joint density function of the events and forecasts is given by $f(z,s)$ which could be derived empirically from the climatological record, $h_1(s)$, and the recorded value of forecasts which had been made for particular events, $h_2(z|s)$:

$$f(z, s) = h_2(z|s) \cdot h_1(s). \qquad (3)$$

Cost data are assumed to take the form of an annualized cost of the long run measures, $C_1(x)$, and a "per-event" cost of activating the short run response, $C_2(y)$. Relating these cost functions in a clear manner requires a precise statement of what one means by an "event" and how many events can occur within the life of the assets represented by x. In the snow case, we can let N represent the number of days when snow is possible (presumably taken

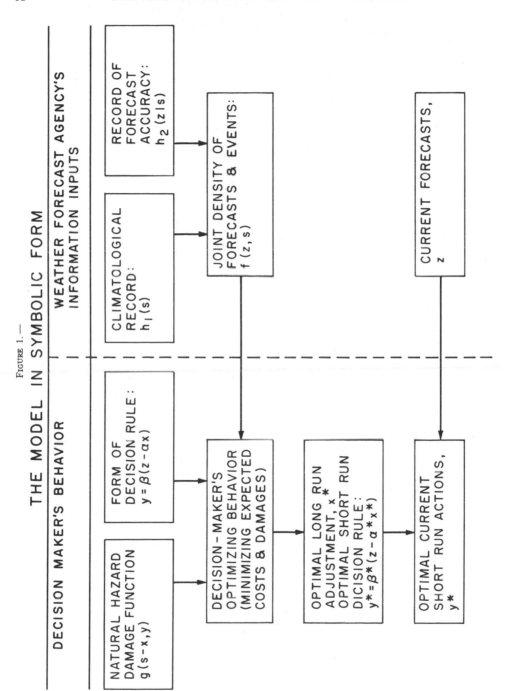

FIGURE 1. —

THE MODEL IN SYMBOLIC FORM

from historical record), s being the 24-hour accumulation (ranging from zero upward).

The expected annual costs of short run adjustment are given by

$$E(C_2(y)) = N \int_0^\infty \int_{ax}^\infty C_2 \left(\beta(z - \alpha x)\right)$$
$$f(z,s)dzds, \qquad (4)$$

while the expected annual residual damages are given by

$$E(D(s,x,y)) = N \int_x^\infty \int_0^{ax} g \ (s - x, 0)$$
$$f(z,s)dzds$$
$$+ N \int_x^\infty \int_{ax}^\infty g((s - x),$$
$$\beta(z - \alpha x)) \ f(z,s)dzds. \quad (5)$$

The objective then is to find the values of x, α, and β which serve to:[2]

$$\min \{\phi(x, \alpha, \beta) = C_1(x) + E[C_2(y)]$$
$$+ E[D(s,x,y)]\}. \qquad (6)$$

It is assumed that only non-negativity constraints apply to the selection of the optimum values x^*, α^*, and β^*. The Kuhn-Tucker conditions for a minimum point are then given by:[3]

$$\frac{\partial \phi}{\partial x} \equiv C'_1(x)$$

$$- N\alpha\beta \Big[\int_0^\infty \int_{ax}^\infty C'_2(\beta(z - \alpha x))$$
$$f(z,s)dzds$$
$$+ \int_x^\infty \int_{ax}^\infty \frac{\partial g(u,y)}{\partial y} \cdot f(z,s)dzds\Big]$$
$$- N\Big[\int_x^\infty \int_0^{ax} \frac{\partial g(u,o)}{\partial u} \cdot f(z,s)dzds$$
$$+ \int_x^\infty \int_{ax}^\infty \frac{\partial g(u,y)}{\partial u} f(z,s)dzds\Big] \geq 0; (7a)$$

$$\frac{\partial \phi}{\partial \alpha} = - Nx\beta$$

$$\cdot \Big[\int_x^\infty \int_{ax}^\infty \frac{\partial g(u,y)}{\partial y} \cdot f(z,s)dzds$$
$$+ \int_x^\infty \int_{ax}^\infty C'_2(y) \ f(z,s)dzds\Big] \geq 0; \quad (7b)$$

[2] From the viewpoint of mathematical tractability, it is to be hoped that $C''_1(x) \geq 0$, $C''_2(y) \geq 0$, $\dfrac{\partial^2 g(u,y)}{\partial u^2} \geq 0$, $\dfrac{\partial^2 g(u,y)}{\partial u \partial y} < 0$, and $\dfrac{\partial^2 g(u,y)}{\partial y^2} < 0$.

[3] To simplify notation, let $u \equiv s - x$ and recall that $y = \beta(z - \alpha x)$ when $y > 0$.

$$\frac{\partial \phi}{\partial \beta} = N \Big[\int_x^\infty \int_{ax}^\infty (z - \alpha x)$$

$$\cdot \frac{\partial g(u,y)}{\partial y} \cdot f(z,s)dzds$$

$$+ \int_x^\infty \int_{ax}^\infty (z - \alpha x)C'_2(y)f(z,s)dzds\Big] \geq 0;$$
$$(7c)$$

and whenever "strictly greater than zero" holds, the corresponding decision variable value must be zero.

Since x^*, α^*, and β^* can each potentially be zero or positive, eight possible classes of solutions are possible.

When (7a) holds with equality, the interpretation of the terms is straightforward: x should be increased until its marginal cost, $C'_1(x)$, just equals the rate of reduction in the cost of y, less the increase in damages due to the slower activation of y, plus the rate of reduction in damages due to the less frequent exceedance of x.

It will be noted that whenever (7b) holds with equality, the first bracketed expression in (7a) drops out. In particular, whenever $\alpha^* > 0$ (so that (7b) must hold with equality), then $C'_1(x^*)$ should equal the rate of reduction of damages stemming directly from larger x. When (7b) holds with equality, α^* has been adjusted until the increase in damages due to slower activation of y just equals the cost saving from less frequent activation of y.

When (7c) holds with equality, β^* has been adjusted until the marginal expected cost of y just equals the rate of reduction of damages due to increased y.

III. An Application to Urban Snow Hazard

We would now like to present an application of the model to actual urban snow hazard situations. These cases will bring out the problems encountered in implementing the model, but they will also demonstrate the usefulness of the model in solving practical problems. This section will develop the model inputs for a sample of four cities. The cities chosen represent a wide range of climatic conditions: from Nashville, Tennessee in the South, to Worcester, Massachusetts, in the Northeast; with Rockford, Illinois, and Evansville, Indiana, in between. A more pragmatic reason for selecting these cities was that a considerable data base had already been established; their climate, damage functions, and cost functions had been analyzed by Baumann and Russell (1969) in their investigation of the urban snow hazard. It is our opinion that the functions available in the Baumann-Russell report are adequate for testing the optimizing model and determining its general properties.

To develop the density function, $h_1(s)$, the hourly rate of fall used by Baumann and Russell was summed to obtain the 24-hour accumulation. Because of the small sample of high accumulation snow falls, it was necessary to complete the statistical record by using the gamma distribution. This distribution has been found to be a good fit for zero-bounded continuous variables, and has been used extensively with precipitation data.

In addition to $h_1(s)$, the length (in days) of the snow season, N, and the probability of snow occurring on any particular day had to be determined. Again, the climatological record provided by Baumann and Russell was used. To determine the length of the snow season, the numbers of days from first to last snow were counted and averaged for a five-year period (1964–1969). The probability of snow occurring is directly obtained from the number of "snowdays" and the length of the snow season. It is recognized that the probability of snow is variable depending upon the time of the season, but this complicating factor is neglected. The results for each city are shown in table 1.

TABLE 1. — LENGTH OF SNOW SEASON

City	Average Number of Days in Snow Season, N	Probability of Snow Occurring on Any Day of the Snow Season
Evansville	80	.11
Nashville	50	.09
Rockford	130	.19
Worcester	130	.23

Information on snow forecast accuracy is difficult to obtain, although it is a very important ingredient in an assessment of the value of snow warnings. Fortunately, it has been possible to procure the actual forecasts provided by a private meteorological consulting firm for three cities. These forecasts were coded and compared with the actual accumulations as recorded by nearby observation stations as reported in the Local Climatological Data Summary for each station. The results for the three cities were aggregated and are shown in the form of a contingency table in table 2. An estimate of the conditional density function $h_2(z/s)$ was derived from frequencies appearing in each column. The joint density function included in the model is the product of $h_1(s)$ previously derived, and $h_2(z/s)$.

The costs of adjustment consist of maintaining equipment inventories, $C_1(x)$, and the cost of procuring supplemental equipment and crews

TABLE 2. — CONTINGENCY TABLE OF FORECASTS AND ACTUAL SNOWFALLS

	Actual Snowfall										Marginal Totals
	0	T	2	4	6	8	10	12	14	16	
0[a]	389	95	27	6	1						518
T[b]	20	55	24	4	1						104
2	11	25	23	4	1						64
4	1	13	11	10	1			1			37
6		2	2	7	4						15
8		1			3						4
10			1		1	1				1	4
12										1	1
14											
16									1		1
Marginal Totals	421	191	88	31	12	1		1	1	2	748

Note: Frequencies are aggregated for 3 cities for 2 snow seasons.
[a] 0 means that no forecasts were made.
[b] T means trace.

when forecasts warrant. The basic cost functions are given below.[4]

$$C_1(x) = g\ .232x^{0.715} \qquad (8)$$

$$C_2(y) = 1000\ y^2 \qquad (9)$$

The cost function $C_1(x)$ exhibits increasing returns to scale. $C_2(y)$ was assumed in the absence of actual data, reflecting decreasing returns to scale because of problems of coordinating supplemental equipment.

The damage function relates worker absenteeism, tardiness, losses from slowing commercial traffic, and losses from slowing and preventing worker travel to the level of uncleared snow. To quantify its effects, we have to make certain assumptions about society's willingness to forego mobility, and consideration must be given to the spatial transference or temporal deference of lost sales or production. Since federal funds play a negligible part in adjustment to the snow hazard, we will consider a local stance for loss accounting and assume no transference or deference of such losses. Our strategy has been to use the basic damage model developed by Baumann and Russell[5] and to construct for each city in our sample a linear relationship between damages and level of uncleared snow. The resulting functions employed in the model are shown in table 3.

TABLE 3. — DAMAGE FUNCTIONS

City	Damage Function
Evansville	$D = 18,000\ (s - x - y)$
Nashville	$D = 25,000\ (s - x - y)$
Rockford	$D = 2,100\ (s - x - y)$
Worcester	$D = 278,000\ (s - x - y)$

IV. Results

The optimal values of α, β, and x could, under appropriate conditions, be obtained for

[4] These relationships were derived in part from Baumann and Russell (1969). The estimates of cost provided in their report are based upon rate of removal whereas our estimate is related to capacity to remove 24-hour accumulations. In order to bridge this difference, a relationship between daily accumulation and hourly rate of fall was estimated from data provided by Baumann — $p = 0.36s^{0.5}$ — where p is the rate of fall and s is accumulation. The factor g in (8) reflects average annual snowfall and miles of streets maintained: 152,880 for Evansville, 86,000 for Nashville, 341,880 for Rockford, and 831,490 for Worcester.

[5] Baumann and Russell (1969), based upon American Public Works Association data (1965).

each city by solving equations (7a), (7b), and (7c) simultaneously. Because of nonlinearities in the cost functions (especially the increasing returns to scale in $C_1(x)$) and the necessity of using a contingency table to represent forecast accuracy, it was decided that the optimal solutions could more readily be derived numerically by computer.

The data that have been developed for each city are: (1) total expected annual cost as a function of α, β, and x; (2) long run adjustment levels; (3) average optimal short run adjustment levels; (4) cost of protecting when no protection is needed; and (5) damages when protection is needed but no protection is provided. A set of tables taken from computer print-out that depict the snow removal situation in Rockford is presented as table 4. The upper left-hand side of each table would correspond to frequent use of short run measures, the triggering limit being set for a relatively small predicted snow accumulation, while the strength of application (β) is great. This may also be interpreted as an area of risk aversion — at least as far as short term measures are concerned. The lower righthand corners of the tables correspond to high trigger limits and a low level of application of the short run measure.

The top table incorporates the sum of the adjustment costs and the residual damages. For Rockford, the minimum cost solution appears to lie at $\alpha = 1.8$ and $\beta = 0.4$. It appears best to apply equipment supplements (y) only weakly and only when very severe conditions are forecast. The solutions for the other cities investigated demonstrate much the same type of behavior. This would indicate that, with present snow forecast accuracy, nothing would be gained from convincing snow removal authorities to be more sensitive toward available forecast information. Table 5 presents α^*, β^*, and x^* for the four cities.

These normative results appear quite similar to actual practice as determined by the Baumann-Russell study. When asked about the type of actions undertaken to prepare for a forecasted storm, one of the four managers indicated that no action was instituted, the other three admitted some form of action, but

56   THE REVIEW OF ECONOMICS AND STATISTICS

TABLE 4. — REGULAR FORECAST: ROCKFORD

Total Expected Cost (thousands of dollars) per year: $E[TC(\alpha, \beta, x^*)]$[a]

(α)										
.0	397	361	333	305	285	269	257	250	245	241
.2	379	346	321	298	279	265	255	248	243	240
.4	359	330	309	290	274	261	253	247	242	240
.6	340	315	296	282	269	258	250	245	241	239
.8	320	300	285	272	263	254	248	243	240	237
1.0	301	285	273	263	257	250	245	241	238	236
1.2	283	270	262	255	250	245	241	238	235	234
1.4	265	256	251	246	243	240	237	235	233	233
1.6	248	243	241	238	237	235	234	233	232	231
1.8	234	232	232	232	232	231	231	231	[230]	231
(β)	2.0	1.8	1.6	1.4	1.2	1.0	.8	.6	.4	.2

Optimal Adjustment Level (inches of snow), x^*, y^*
Long Run: $x^*(\alpha, \beta)$

(α)										
.0	2	3	3	4	4	4	4	4	4	4
.2	2	3	3	4	4	4	4	4	4	4
.4	3	3	3	4	4	4	4	4	4	4
.6	3	3	3	3	4	4	4	4	4	3
.8	3	3	3	3	4	4	4	4	3	3
1.0	3	3	3	3	3	3	3	3	3	3
1.2	3	3	3	3	3	3	3	3	3	3
1.4	3	3	3	3	3	3	3	3	3	3
1.6	3	3	3	3	3	3	3	3	3	3
1.8	3	3	3	3	3	3	3	3	[3]	3
(β)	2.0	1.8	1.6	1.4	1.2	1.0	.8	.6	.4	.2

Short Run: $y^*(\alpha, \beta)$

(α)										
.0	202	162	127	78	55	38	26	17	11	7
.2	182	146	114	70	50	34	23	16	10	6
.4	162	130	102	63	44	30	21	14	9	6
.6	141	114	89	70	39	26	18	12	8	13
.8	121	97	76	60	33	23	16	10	16	11
1.0	101	81	63	50	39	30	23	17	13	10
1.2	81	65	51	40	31	24	19	14	10	8
1.4	61	49	39	30	23	18	14	10	8	6
1.6	40	32	25	20	16	12	9	7	5	4
1.8	20	16	13	10	8	5	5	3	[3]	2
(β)	2.0	1.8	1.6	1.4	1.2	1.0	.8	.6	.4	.2

[a] This table is one of many generated and contains the minimum $E(TC)$, \$230 at $\alpha = 1.8$, $\beta = 0.4$.

limited in scope. One of the four indicated that a blizzard forecast would be a sufficient warning to dispatch all men and equipment. These results suggest that there is a reluctance on the part of municipalities to incur cost for a storm that may fail to materialize, and that a weak response which is insensitive to forecasts frequently is actual practice. The model results suggest that this represents optimal behavior from an economic viewpoint.

V. Improvements in Forecast Accuracy

A test was performed with the model, substituting perfect forecasts for the contingency table developed in section III. In this case, the probability of forecasting anything but the correct snow accumulation was zero.

As one might suspect, the minimum cost solution shifts considerably. Instead of a heavy

TABLE 5. — OPTIMAL DECISION SETS FOR NORMAL FORECASTS

	a^*	Normal Forecast Accuracy β^*	x^*
Evansville	1.8	1.6	7
Nashville	0.0 to 1.8	1.0	19
Rockford	1.8	.4	3
Worcester	1.8	1.6	19

ADJUSTING TO NATURAL HAZARD EVENTS   57

TABLE 6. — PERFECT FORECAST: ROCKFORD

Total Expected Cost (thousands of dollars) per year									
(α)									
.0	135	131	126	122	117	113	114	115	123	140
.2	133	129	125	121	117	115	116	117	128	144
.4	131	127	124	121	119	118	110	121	133	149
.6	129	126	125	127	122	120	122	128	139	154
.8	129	128	127	126	124	123	126	138	146	159
1.0	131	130	129	128	128	127	134	143	153	165
1.2	133	133	132	132	133	137	144	152	161	172
1.4	137	136	137	141	145	149	155	162	170	178
1.6	147	150	153	156	159	162	166	171	178	179
1.8	163	163	164	165	167	169	172	175	180	182
(β)	2.0	1.8	1.6	1.4	1.2	1.0	.8	.6	.4	.2

fixed capacity, x, and a limited response to forecasts, y, the best action is to employ short run measures as the weather forecast dictates, reducing investment in fixed snow-removal capability. Replacement of the long run inventory by forecast-induced supplementary equipment is beneficial. See tables 6 and 7.

TABLE 7. — OPTIMAL DECISION SETS UNDER PERFECT FORECASTS

	a^*	β^*	x^*
Evansville	0	1.4	2
Nashville	0	1.4	12
Rockford	0	1.0	1
Worcester	0	1.4	14

The new solution is highly sensitive to forecasts ($\alpha^* = 0$) and strong in response ($\beta^* \geq 1$). The total expected cost of snow fighting could be reduced by 50% if such forecasts and the related user behavior were forthcoming (i.e., $231,000 to $113,000 annually). Similar results were observed for the other 3 cities in the study. The optimum values are shown in table 7.

To further probe the properties of the model, the following sensitivity analyses were performed:

1. a change in the damage function;
2. a decreased cost of y, given normal forecast accuracy; and
3. increased cost of y, given perfect forecast accuracy.

The change in the damage function was assumed to represent the effect of increased adoption of snow tires and took the form of truncating the damage function for all levels of un-

removed snow below one inch. The strategy of requiring snow tires or chains on main roads during snow is a widespread practice. The result of this change was a 10% reduction in total expected cost — the entire reduction being concentrated in residual damages. Again, short run measures were relatively ineffective.

An increased cost of y had little effect on the solutions, given "normal" forecasts, and had the effect of raising the triggering point, given perfect forecasts. A decreased cost of y also had little effect on the optimum decision rule under normal forecasts.

VI. Conclusions

Two conclusions can be drawn from this application of the model. First, the observed reluctance on the part of snow removal authorities to be sensitive to any but very severe forecasts in making operating decisions agrees with the optimum strategy derived from the model. The expected cost surface around the optimum is, however, relatively flat, indicating that there is a range of decisions which will cause only small differences in the expected total cost of snow fighting. Second, perfect forecasts would have the effect of reducing total cost by as much as 50%. Although the possibility of eliminating forecast error is very remote, there are large potential benefits from improved accuracy and increased sensitivity to those improved forecasts.

Further applications of the model would include flood hazards which can be handled with the same general formulation but with appropriately amended damage functions. From the weather forecaster's viewpoint, such models permit the evaluation of benefits stemming from increased accuracy. There has been a sharpened interest in the past few years on the part of government in the application of benefit-cost analysis to various parts of the U.S. weather forecast program. For example, see Thompson (1966), Day (1966, 1970).

It has been assumed in this analysis that the joint distribution of forecasts and weather events, $f(z,s)$, is known to the user, so that a particular forecast in effect permits the user to deduce the appropriate conditional distribution of weather events, $f_2(s/z)$, for decision-making purposes. Depending upon the sophistication of the user, $f(z,s)$ may or may not be known. If not, then the forecast itself may be the only information possessed by the user, and it would be of value to have the forecasts contain some detail of the probabilities of events of different severity. These issues warrant further research.

REFERENCES

American Public Works Association, *Snow Removal and Ice Control in Urban Areas*, Research Project no. 114 (Chicago: American Public Works Association, 1965).

Baumann, D. D., and C. S. Russell, Interviews conducted in Worcester, Massachusetts; Nashville, Tennessee; Utica, New York; Rockford, Illinois; and Evansville, Indiana, in connection with *Urban Snow Hazard: Economic and Social Implications*, 1969.

Day, H. J., "A Study of the Benefits Due To The U.S. Weather Bureau River Forecast Service," Civil Engineering Department, Carnegie Institute of Technology, June 9, 1966.

———, "Flood Warning Benefit Evaluation-Susquehanna River Basin (Urban Residences)," ESSA Technical Memorandum WBTM Hydro 10, Silver Springs, Maryland, March 1970.

Lave, L. B., "The Value of Better Weather Information to the Raisin Industry," *Econometrica*, 31 (Jan.–Apr. 1964), 151–164.

Nelson, R. R., and S. G. Winter, Jr., "A Case Study in the Economics of Information and Coordination: The Weather Forecasting System," *Quarterly Journal of Economics*, 78 (Aug. 1964), 420–441.

Thom, H. C. S., "Some Methods of Climatological Analysis," World Meteorological Organization, Geneva, Switzerland. TN no. 81, 1966.

Thompson, J. C., "The Potential Economic and Associated Values of the World Weather Watch," World Weather Watch Planning Report no. 4, World Meteorological Organization, Geneva, 1966.

The Decision to Seed Hurricanes

On the basis of present information, the probability
of severe damage is less if a hurricane is seeded.

R. A. Howard, J. E. Matheson, D. W. North

The possibility of mitigating the destructive force of hurricanes by seeding them with silver iodide was suggested by R. H. Simpson in 1961. Early experiments on hurricanes Esther (1961) and Beulah (1963) were encouraging (1), but strong evidence for the effectiveness of seeding was not obtained until the 1969 experiments on Hurricane Debbie (2). Debbie was seeded with massive amounts of silver iodide on 18 and 20 August 1969. Reductions of 31 and 15 percent in peak wind speed were observed after the seedings.

Over the last 10 years property damage caused by hurricanes has averaged $440 million annually. Hurricane Betsy (1965) and Hurricane Camille (1969) each caused property damage of approximately $1.5 billion. Any means of reducing the destructive force of hurricanes would therefore have great economic implications.

Decision to Permit Operational Seeding

In the spring of 1970 Stanford Research Institute began a small study for the Environmental Science Service Administration (ESSA) (3) to explore areas in which decision analysis (4, 5) might make significant contributions to

Dr. Matheson and Dr. North are with the decision analysis group, Stanford Research Institute, Menlo Park, California 94025. Dr. Howard is with the department of engineering-economic systems, Stanford University, Stanford, California 94305, and is a consultant to the decision analysis group, Stanford Research Institute.

ESSA, both in its technical operations and in its management and planning function. At the suggestion of Myron Tribus, Assistant Secretary of Commerce for Science and Technology, we decided to focus the study on the decision problems inherent in hurricane modification (6).

The objective of the present U.S. government program in hurricane modification, Project Stormfury, is strictly scientific: to add to man's knowledge about hurricanes. Any seeding of hurricanes that threaten inhabited coastal areas is prohibited. According to the policy currently in force, seeding will be carried out only if there is less than a 10 percent chance of the hurricane center coming within 50 miles of a populated land area within 18 hours after seeding.

If the seeding of hurricanes threatening inhabited coastal areas is to be undertaken, it will be necessary to modify the existing policies. The purpose of our analysis is to examine the circumstances that bear on the decision to change or not to change these existing policies.

The decision to seed a hurricane threatening a coastal area should therefore be viewed as a two-stage process: (i) a decision is taken to lift the present prohibition against seeding threatening hurricanes and (ii) a decision is taken to seed a particular hurricane a few hours before that hurricane is expected to strike the coast. Our study is concentrated on the policy decision rather than on the tactical decision to seed a particular hurricane at a particular

time. It is also addressed to the experimental question: What would be the value of expanding research in hurricane modification, and, specifically, what would be the value of conducting additional field experiments such as the seedings of Hurricane Debbie in 1969?

Our approach was to consider a representative severe hurricane bearing down on a coastal area and to analyze the decision to seed or not to seed this "nominal" hurricane. The level of the analysis was relatively coarse, because for the policy decision we did not have to consider many geographical and meteorological details that might influence the tactical decision to seed. We described the hurricane by a single measure of intensity, its maximum sustained surface wind speed, since it is this characteristic that seeding is expected to influence (7). The surface winds, directly and indirectly (through the storm tide), are the primary cause of the destruction wrought by most hurricanes (8). The direct consequence of a decision for or against seeding a hurricane is considered to be the property damage caused by that hurricane. (Injuries and loss of life are often dependent on the issuance and effectiveness of storm warnings; they were not explicitly included in our analysis.)

However, property damage alone is not sufficient to describe the consequence of the decision. There are indirect legal and social effects that arise from the fact that the hurricane is known to have been seeded. For example, the government might have some legal responsibility for the damage caused by a seeded hurricane (9). Even if legal action against the government were not possible, a strong public outcry might result if a seeded hurricane caused an unusual amount of damage. Nearly all the government hurricane meteorologists that we questioned said they would seed a hurricane threatening their homes and families—if they could be freed from professional liability.

The importance of the indirect effects stems in large part from uncertainty about the consequences of taking either decision. A hurricane is complex and highly variable, and at present meteor-

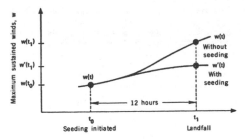

Fig. 1. Maximum sustained winds over time.

stems in large part from uncertainty about the consequences of taking either decision. A hurricane is complex and highly variable, and at present meteorologists cannot predict accurately how the behavior of a hurricane will evolve over time. The effect of seeding is uncertain also; consequently, the behavior of a hurricane that is seeded will be a combination of two uncertain effects: natural changes and the changes induced by seeding.

The seeding decision would remain difficult even if the uncertainty were removed. Suppose that, if the hurricane is not seeded, the surface wind intensifies as shown by the curve $w(t)$ in Fig. 1 and that, if the hurricane is seeded, the behavior of the wind is that shown by the curve $w'(t)$. The effect of the seeding has been to diminish the wind, thus reducing property damage, yet the wind speed $w'(t_1)$ when the hurricane strikes land at time t_1 is higher than the wind speed when the seeding was initiated at time t_0. Even if the decision-maker were certain of $w(t_1)$ and $w'(t_1)$, he would still have a difficult choice. If he chooses not to seed, the citizens may have more property damage. On the other hand, if he chooses to seed, the citizens may not perceive themselves as better off because of his decision. Instead, they may perceive only that the storm became worse after the seeding and they may blame the decision-maker for his choice. The trade off between accepting the responsibility for seeding and accepting higher probabilities of severe property damage is the crucial issue in the decision to seed hurricanes.

Decision under Uncertainty

The decision to seed a threatening hurricane would be taken about 12 hours before the hurricane is predicted to strike the coast. At this time the con-

sequences are uncertain for both alternatives; the decision-maker does not know what amount of property damage will be sustained if the hurricane is seeded or is not seeded. We may illustrate the situation facing him in the form of a decision tree, as shown in Fig. 2. The decision-maker must select one of the two alternatives, seeding or not seeding. The decision cannot be avoided for inaction is equivalent to selecting the alternative of not seeding. Each alternative leads to a set of possible consequences: property damage caused by the hurricane and the responsibility incurred by the government. These consequences are, in turn, related to the intensity of the hurricane and whether or not it was seeded. The consequences for each alternative are uncertain at the time the decision is made; the uncertainty will be resolved after the decision-maker selects his choice. This decision under uncertainty may be examined according to the usual procedures of a decision analysis. We use the information that is currently available to develop a probability distribution over changes in the intensity of the hurricane as measured by its maximum sustained surface wind speed for each of the two decision alternatives. Then we use data from past hurricanes to infer a relation between wind speed and property damage. By assessing the consequences in property damage and government responsibility and the probability that these consequences will be achieved, we are able to determine which of the decision alternatives is the preferred choice.

Uncertainty in Hurricane Wind Changes

We began our analysis by considering the change in maximum sustained surface winds over a 12-hour period for a hurricane that is not seeded. If enough data had been available on the changes

in hurricane wind speeds with time, a probability distribution for wind changes could have been based largely on these past data. Wind-change data were not available, but data were available for changes over time in the central pressure of hurricanes. The central pressure and the maximum wind speed of a hurricane are closely related; Holliday has shown that the available data can be summarized fairly well by a linear relation (*10*). We combined this relation with observations of the change in central pressure over a 12-hour period, using the assumption that the discrepancies from the Holliday relation are independent over a 12-hour period and independent of the change in central pressure. These assumptions imply a probability distribution on wind changes over a 12-hour period that is normal with a mean of zero and a standard deviation of 15.6 percent (*11*).

Therefore, present information is consistent with rather large natural changes in hurricane intensity over a 12-hour period. There is about one chance in six that a hurricane whose maximum sustained wind speed is 100 miles per hour will intensify over a 12-hour period to a maximum wind speed of over 115 miles per hour; there is also about one chance in six that the winds would naturally diminish to less than 85 miles per hour. In assessing these probabilities only general historical and meteorological information has been used. In a specific hurricane situation additional meteorological information might indicate that the hurricane would be more likely to intensify or more likely to diminish.

Effect of Seeding

The next step is to develop a probability distribution for the wind speed if the hurricane is seeded. The change in wind speed over 12 hours would then be a combination of the natural change occurring in the hurricane and the change caused by seeding. With the limited data available it is reasonable to assume that the two effects would be independent of each other and act in an additive fashion; for example, if the natural change is an intensification such that the maximum sustained wind speed is increased from 100 to (100 + x) percent, and if the effect of seeding is to diminish the maximum sustained wind speed from 100 to (100 − y) percent, the net observed change over 12 hours is from 100 to $(100 + x - y)$ percent. A probability distribution has already been assigned for natural changes; we need to assign a probability distribution for the change caused by seeding. In developing this probability distribution it is necessary to distinguish between the effect of seeding on one hurricane and the average effect of seeding on many hurricanes. The effect of seeding on a particular hurricane might be quite different from its average effect.

After discussion with meteorologists associated with Project Stormfury, we concluded that the major uncertainty about the effect of seeding would be resolved if we knew which of the following mutually exclusive and collectively exhaustive hypotheses described the effect of seeding:

1) H_1, the "beneficial" hypothesis. The average effect of seeding is to reduce the maximum sustained wind speed.

2) H_2, the "null" hypothesis. Seeding has no effect on hurricanes. No change is induced in maximum sustained wind speed.

3) H_3, the "detrimental" hypothesis. The average effect of seeding is to increase the maximum sustained wind speed.

The scientific basis for the "beneficial" hypothesis, H_1, had its origins in the original Simpson theory (*1*). It has been modified and strengthened by Project Stormfury studies involving a computer model of hurricane dynamics (*1*, *12*). This hypothesis, in fact, motivated the formation of the Project Stormfury research program. A possible basis for the "null" hypothesis, H_2, is that seeding does not release enough latent heat to affect the dynamics of the hurricane. The "detrimental" hypothesis, H_3, has been added to complete the set. Meteorologists do not have a basis in physical theory for H_3 that is comparable to that for H_1 or H_2.

Even if we know which of the hypotheses is true, there remain uncertainties about the effects of seeding. We now describe the approach we followed in creating a model to formalize existing knowledge about these uncertainties. Then we shall return to the hypotheses.

Let us suppose we have access to a clairvoyant who can tell us which hypothesis, H_1, H_2, or H_3, represents the actual effect of seeding on hurricanes. What probability would we assign to the 12-hour change in the maximum sustained

tained winds of a seeded hurricane for each of his three possible answers? If the clairvoyant says H_2 is true, the assignment process is simple. Seeding has no effect, and the same probabilities are assigned to the wind speed w' if the hurricane is seeded as to the wind speed w if the hurricane is not seeded (*13*).

$$P(w'|H_2) = P(w) = f_N(100\%, 15.6\%) \quad (1)$$

If H_1 is the clairvoyant's answer, the process is more difficult. The average effect is known to be a reduction in storm intensity, but the amount of this average reduction is uncertain. The Simpson theory and the computer studies indicate that a reduction of 10 to 20 percent in wind speed should be expected, with 15 percent as the most likely value. This information was summarized by assigning to the change in wind speed a normal probability distribution with a mean of -15 percent and a standard deviation of 7 percent. An average reduction greater than 15 percent is considered as likely as an average reduction less than 15 percent, and the odds are about 2 to 1 that the average reduction will lie between 22 and 8 percent rather than outside this interval.

The effect of seeding on an individual hurricane would be uncertain even if the average effect of seeding were known. Odds of about 2 to 1 were considered appropriate that the effect of seeding would not differ from the average effect by more than about 7 percent; thus, a normal distribution centered at the average value with a standard deviation of 7 percent was judged an adequate summary of the information available on fluctuations in seeding effects. Combining the uncertainty about fluctuations with the uncertainty about the average effect leads to a probability distribution for the effect of seeding a specific hurricane that is normal with a mean equal to -15 percent and a standard deviation of 7 percent (*14*).

Adding the natural change in the hurricane over a 12-hour period to the change resulting from seeding gives the total 12-hour change if hypothesis H_1 is true. The probability distribution assigned to w' is then normal with a mean of 85 percent and a standard deviation of 18.6 percent (*15*):

$$P(w'|H_1) = f_N(85\%, 18.6\%) \quad (2)$$

The development of a probability distribution for w', if it is considered that H_3 is true, proceeds in a similar way. The average change effected by seeding is described by a normal probability distribution with a mean of $+10$ percent and a standard deviation of 7 percent. The fluctuations expected when an individual hurricane is seeded are normally distributed around the average with a standard deviation of 7 percent. Combining these uncertainties

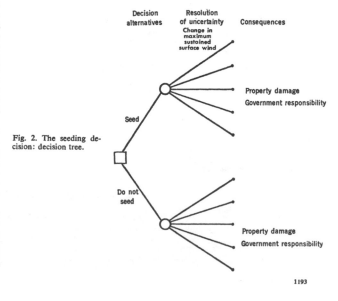

Fig. 2. The seeding decision: decision tree.

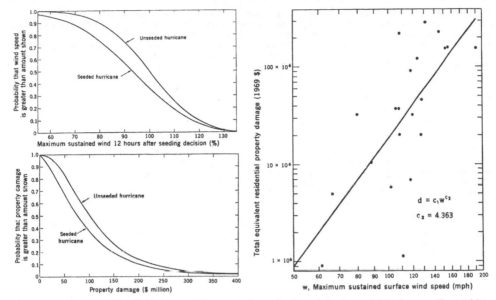

Fig. 3 (upper left). Probability distributions on 12-hour wind changes for the seeded and unseeded hurricane.   Fig. 4 (right). Property damage plotted against maximum sustained wind speed.   Fig. 5 (lower left). Probability distributions on property damage for the seeded and unseeded hurricane.

with the uncertainty about the natural change in the hurricane over a 12-hour period, we obtain a probability distribution for w' that is normal with a mean of 110 percent and a standard deviation of 18.6 percent:

$$P(w'|H_a) = f_N(110\%, 18.6\%) \quad (3)$$

We have now developed probability distributions for the wind speed w' over a 12-hour period following the initiation of seeding for each of the three hypotheses. To obtain the probability distribution for w' that represents present information about the change in a seeded hurricane, we multiply each of the above distributions by the probability that is presently assigned to each of the hypotheses being true and sum over the three hypotheses:

$$P(w') = \sum_{i=1}^{3} P(w'|H_i)P(H_i) \quad (4)$$

Assigning Probabilities
to the Hypotheses

The last element in developing a probability distribution for w' is to assign the probabilities $P(H_1)$, $P(H_2)$, and $P(H_3)$. These probabilities should

1194

take into account both present meteorological information and meteorological information before the results of the 1969 Debbie experiments. The models we have just constructed allow us to examine the effect of experimental observations, such as the Debbie results, in revising the probabilities assigned to the three hypotheses. If a wind speed $w' = u$ has been observed after a seeding experiment, the posterior probabilities $P(H_i|u)$ are related to the probabilities $P(H_i)$ assigned before the experiment by Bayes' equation (5, 16, 17):

$$P(H_i|u) = \frac{P(u|H_i)P(H_i)}{P(u)} \quad (5)$$

where the denominator is

$$P(u) = P(w' = u) =$$
$$\sum_{i=1}^{3} P(w' = u|H_i)P(H_i) \quad (6)$$

The extension to several independent experiments is straightforward. The Debbie results are considered as two independent experiments in which reductions of 31 and 15 percent in wind speed were observed over a 12-hour period. The posterior probabilities assigned to the hypotheses are computed by multiplying together the appropriate

values of two normal probability density functions. The probability density function for the Debbie results if hypothesis H_i is true, $P(u_1 = 69 \text{ percent}, u_2 = 85 \text{ percent}|H_i)$, is

$$P(69\%, 85\%|H_1) = 1.50 \times 2.14 = 3.21$$
$$P(69\%, 85\%|H_2) = 0.372 \times 1.64 = 0.61$$
$$P(69\%, 85\%|H_3) = 0.195 \times 0.886 = 0.173 \quad (7)$$

These numbers can be used to compute the posterior probabilities appropriate after the Debbie results from any set of probabilities assigned to the hypotheses before the Debbie results were known. For example, suppose that before the Debbie experiments the three hypotheses H_1, H_2, and H_3 were considered to be equally likely, that is, each had a probability of 1/3. Then, after the Debbie results are incorporated through Bayes' equation, the corresponding posterior probabilities assigned to the hypotheses are

$$P(H_1|\text{Debbie}) =$$
$$\frac{3.21 \times 1/3}{3.21 \times 1/3 + 0.61 \times 1/3 + 0.173 \times 1/3}$$
$$= .81$$

$$P(H_2|\text{Debbie}) = .15$$
$$P(H_3|\text{Debbie}) = .04 \quad (8)$$

However, meteorologists did not believe that H_1, H_2, and H_3 were equally likely before the Debbie experiments. They thought that seeding was unlikely to have any effect but that, if seeding did have an effect, it was more likely to be a reduction in wind speed than an increase, because a reduction was expected from both the Simpson theory and the computer model studies. Further, the four field experiments that were conducted before Debbie all led to no change or to reductions in the maximum wind speeds (1).

We determined probability assignments for the three hypotheses to reflect present information by two conditions: (i) Before Debbie, meteorologists believed that H_1 was more likely than H_3 if seeding had any effect on a hurricane. (ii) Since Debbie, meteorologists believe that H_1 and H_2 are equally likely.

These conditions led us to use the probabilities

$$P(H_1) = .49$$
$$P(H_2) = .49 \qquad (9)$$
$$P(H_3) = .02$$

in our analysis. These posterior probabilities correspond to the pre-Debbie probabilities

$$P(H_1) = .15$$
$$P(H_2) = .75 \qquad (10)$$
$$P(H_3) = .10$$

This set of probability assignments implies that prior to Debbie the odds were 3 to 1 that seeding would have no effect but that, if seeding did have an effect, the odds were 3 to 2 for wind reduction rather than wind intensification. Since the Debbie results, the chance of seeding causing an average intensification of hurricanes is assessed at 1 in 50, and the "null" hypothesis, H_2, of no effect and the "beneficial" hypothesis, H_1, of an average reduction are judged equally likely.

The probability assignments (Eq. 9) representing present information were reviewed with Project Stormfury officials before being used in the analysis. However, the results of the analysis are not particularly sensitive to the specific numbers, as we discuss below.

Probability Distributions on Wind Speed

We now can compute the probability distributions on wind speed for the seeding and not-seeding alternatives (from Eqs. 1–4 and Eq. 9). These distributions are plotted in Fig. 3 as complementary cumulative distribution functions. By reading the ordinate values corresponding to an initial wind intensity of 100 percent, we find that the probability assigned to intensification if a hurricane is seeded is .36; if the hurricane is not seeded, the probability is .50. The probability of intensification by 10 percent or more is .18 if a hurricane is seeded and .26 if it is unseeded. For any particular wind speed, the probability that this speed will be exceeded is always greater if the hurricane is unseeded than if it is seeded because the complementary cumulative distribution function for the not-seeding alternative is always above the curve for the seeding alternative. This result is called stochastic dominance of the seeding alternative.

We have now specified the uncertainties about the outcome of the decision to seed. The same methods could be applied if the outcome were specified by several variables rather than simply by the relative change in maximum sustained wind speed. Much of the uncertainty in the outcome is the result of uncertainty about the natural change in hurricane behavior, not about the effect of seeding. This characteristic holds even more strongly if other aspects of hurricane behavior are examined, such as the trajectory of a hurricane or the precipitation it generates. Although it is considered unlikely that seeding would have a significant effect on these features of hurricanes, substantial variations may occur from natural causes.

The uncertainty about the natural behavior of a hurricane makes the issue of government responsibility of paramount importance. The intensification after seeding illustrated in Fig. 1 is a distinct possibility. Even if further experiments confirm that the "beneficial" hypothesis, H_1, is true, there would still be about one chance in ten that a seeded hurricane will intensify by 10 percent or more. Meteorological advances and improved computer models may eventually allow many of the natural changes in a hurricane to be predicted accurately, but this capability may require many years to achieve.

Wind Changes and Property Damage

The winds of a hurricane cause property damage directly and indirectly, the latter by creating a high storm tide that can flood low-lying coastal areas. The data available for past hurricanes do not distinguish wind and storm-tide damage; consequently, a detailed basis is lacking for a causal model relating wind and property damage. In our analysis, we assumed a general power law of the form

$$d = c_1 w^{c_2} \qquad (11)$$

where d is property damage in millions of dollars, w is the maximum sustained wind speed in miles per hour, and c_1 and c_2 are empirical constants to be determined from historical data on hurricanes. We estimated c_2 from data obtained from the American Red Cross on residential damage from 21 hurricanes. Since the Red Cross data were available for counties, we could isolate the damage caused by precipitation-induced flooding rather than by the wind or the storm tide by assuming that such damage occurred well inland. (The Red Cross data are the only statistics available that permit even this crude distinction between causes of damage.) Corrections for construction cost inflation and population growth were included, and c_2 was determined as 4.36 by a linear least-squares fit of the logarithms (Fig. 4). Thus, a change in the wind speed by a factor x implies a change in property damage by the factor x to the power 4.36. If x is 0.85, corresponding to a 15 percent reduction in maximum wind speed, the corresponding reduction in property damage is 51 percent (18).

The approximations of this method and the limited data indicate that broad limits are appropriate in a sensitivity analysis. If c_2 is 3, the reduction in damage corresponding to a 15 percent reduction in wind speed is 39 percent; if c_2 is 6, the corresponding damage reduction is 62 percent.

Since the probability assignments to wind changes were made on relative rather than absolute changes in maximum sustained wind speeds, the scaling factor c_1 can be assigned as the last step in the analysis. We assume a nominal hurricane whose maximum wind speed at the time of the seeding decision is such that, if no change occurs in the 12 hours before landfall, the property damage will be $100 million. The analysis for a more or a less severe hurricane can be obtained by a suitable change in scale factor (19).

Using this relationship between property damage and maximum wind speed, we can develop the probability distributions for property damage for the nominal hurricane, whether seeded or unseeded. Figure 5 shows that the seeding alternative stochastically dominates the not-seeding alternative: the probability of exceeding a particular amount of property damage is always greater if the hurricane is not seeded than if it is seeded. Hence, if property damage is the criterion, the better alternative is to seed.

Further Analysis of the
Decision to Seed

The decision to seed is shown in the form of a decision tree in Fig. 6. The decision to seed or not to seed is shown at the decision node denoted by the small square box; the consequent resolution of the uncertainty about wind change is indicated at the chance nodes denoted by open circles. For expository clarity and convenience, especially in the later stages of the analysis, it is convenient to use discrete approximations to the probability distributions for wind change (20) (Table 1).

As a measure of the worth of each alternative we can compute the expected loss for each alternative by multiplying the property damage for each of the five possible outcomes by the probability that the outcome will be achieved and summing over the possible consequences. The expected loss for the seeding alternative is $94.33 million (including a cost of $0.25 million to carry out the seeding); the expected loss for the not-seeding alternative is $116 million; the difference is $21.67 million or 18.7 percent.

These results should be examined to see how much they depend on the specific assumptions in the model. Stochastic dominance is a general result that does not depend on the specific form of the relationship between property damage and maximum wind speed (see Eq. 11); rather, it depends on the probabilities assigned to hypotheses H_1, H_2, and H_3. The probability of H_3 must be raised to .07 before stochastic dominance no longer holds. Even if the probability of H_3 is raised much higher, seeding still results in the least expected property damage. If $P(H_1)$ is .40, $P(H_2)$ is .40, and $P(H_3)$ is .20, the expected loss for the seeding alternative is $107.8 million—7 percent less than for the not-seeding alternative. Variation of the exponent c_2 from 3 to 6 does not change the decision: if c_2 is 3, the expected property damage with seeding is 14 percent less; if c_2 is 6, the expected reduction in damage is 22 percent. If the criterion of expected cost is replaced by a nonlinear utility function reflecting aversion to risk, the relative advantage of the seeding alternative is even greater (21). The results of extensive sensitivity analysis may be summarized as follows: The expected loss in terms of property damage appears to be about 20 percent less if the hurricane is seeded. Varying the assumptions of the analysis causes this reduction to vary between 10 and 30 percent but does not change the preferred alternative.

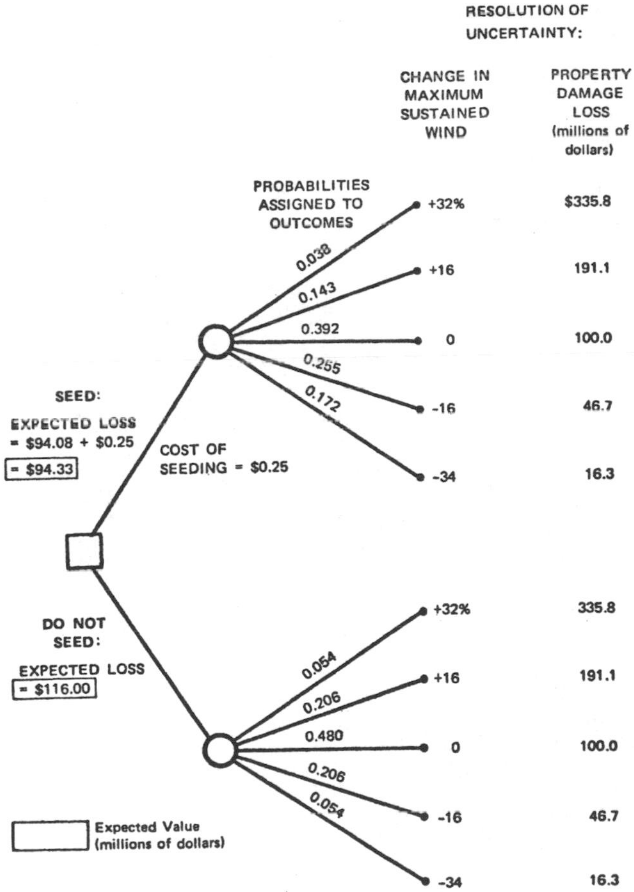

Government Responsibility

The analysis in the section above indicates that, if minimizing the expected loss in terms of property damage (and the cost of seeding) is the only criterion, then seeding is preferred. However, an important aspect of the decision—the matter of government responsibility—has not yet been included in the analysis. We have calculated a probability of .36 that a seeded hurricane will intensify between seeding and landfall and a probability of .18 that this intensification will be at least 10 percent. This high probability is largely the result of the great natural variability in hurricane intensity. It is advisable to consider both the legal and the social consequences that might

Fig. 6. The seeding decision for the nominal hurricane.

occur if a seeded hurricane intensified.

The crucial issue in the decision to seed a hurricane threatening a coastal area is the relative desirability of reducing the expected property damage and assuming the responsibility for a dangerous and erratic natural phenomenon. This is difficult to assess, and to have a simple way of regarding it we use the concept of a government responsibility cost, defined as follows. The government is faced with a choice between assuming the responsibility for a hurricane and accepting higher probabilities of property damage. This situation is comparable to one of haggling over price: What increment of property-damage reduction justifies the assumption of responsibility entailed by seeding a hurricane? This increment of property damage is defined as the government responsibility cost. The government responsibility cost is a means of quantifying the indirect social, legal, and political factors related to seeding a hurricane. It is distinguished from the direct measure—property damage—that is assumed to be the same for both modified and natural hurricanes with the same maximum sustained wind speed.

We define the government responsibility cost so that it is incurred only if the hurricane is seeded. It is conceivable that the public may hold the government responsible for not seeding a severe hurricane, which implies that a responsibility cost should also be attached to the alternative of not seeding. Such a cost would strengthen the implication of the analysis in favor of permitting seeding.

The assessment of government responsibility cost is made by considering the seeding decision in a hypothetical situation in which no uncertainty is present. Suppose the government must choose between two outcomes:

1) A seeded hurricane that intensifies 16 percent between the time of seeding and landfall.

2) An unseeded hurricane that intensifies more than 16 percent between the time of seeding and landfall. The property damage from outcome 2 is x percent more than the property damage from outcome 1.

If x is near zero, the government will choose outcome 2. If x is large, the government will prefer outcome 1. We then adjust x until the choice becomes very difficult; that is, the government is indifferent to which outcome it receives. For example, the indifference

16 JUNE 1972

Table 1. Probabilities assigned to wind changes occurring in the 12 hours before hurricane landfall. Discrete approximation for five outcomes.

Interval of changes in maximum sustained wind	Representative value in discrete approximation (%)	Probability that wind change will be within interval	
		If seeded	If not seeded
Increase of 25% or more	+32	.038	.054
Increase of 10 to 25%	+16	.143	.206
Little change, +10 to −10%	0	.392	.480
Reduction of 10 to 25%	−16	.255	.206
Reduction of 25% or more	−34	.172	.054

point might occur when x is 30 percent. An increase of 16 percent in the intensity of the nominal hurricane corresponds to property damage of $191 million, so that the corresponding responsibility cost defined by the indifference point at 30 percent is (.30) ($191 million), or $57.3 million. The responsibility cost is then assessed for other possible changes in hurricane intensity.

The assessment of government responsibility costs entails considerable introspective effort on the part of the decision-maker who represents the government. The difficulty of determining the numbers does not provide an excuse to avoid the issue. Any decision or pol-

icy prohibiting seeding implicitly determines a set of government responsibility costs. As shown in the last section, seeding is the preferred decision unless the government responsibility costs are high.

Let us consider an illustrative set of responsibility costs. The government is indifferent, if the choice is between:

1) A seeded hurricane that intensifies 32 percent and an unseeded hurricane that intensifies even more, causing 50 percent more property damage.

2) A seeded hurricane that intensifies 16 percent and an unseeded hurricane that causes 30 percent more property damage.

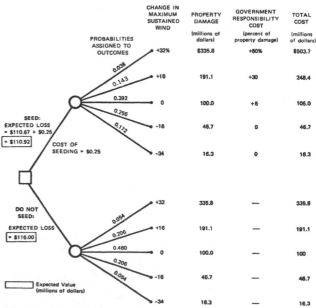

Fig. 7. The seeding decision for the nominal hurricane (government responsibility cost included).

3) A seeded hurricane that neither intensifies nor diminishes (0 percent change in the maximum sustained wind speed after the seeding) and an unseeded hurricane that intensifies slightly, causing 5 percent more property damage.

4) A seeded hurricane that diminishes by more than 10 percent and an unseeded hurricane that diminishes by the same amount. (If the hurricane diminishes after seeding, everyone agrees that the government acted wisely; thus, responsibility costs are set at zero.)

The analysis of the seeding decision with these government responsibility costs included is diagramed in Fig. 7. Even with these large responsibility costs, the preferred decision is still to seed.

The responsibility costs needed to change the decision are a substantial fraction of the property damage caused by the hurricane. For the $100-million hurricane chosen as the example for this section, the average responsibility cost must be about $22 million to change the decision. If the hurricane were in the $1-billion class, as Camille

(1969) and Betsy (1965) were, an average responsibility cost of $200 million would be needed. In other words, an expected reduction of $200 million in property damage would be foregone if the government decided not to accept the responsibility of seeding the hurricane.

The importance of the responsibility issue led us to investigate the legal basis for hurricane seeding in some detail. These investigations were carried out by Gary Widman, Hastings College of the Law, University of California. A firm legal basis for operational seeding apparently does not now exist. The doctrine of sovereign immunity provides the government only partial and unpredictable protection against lawsuits, and substantial grounds for bringing such lawsuits might exist (22). A better legal basis for government seeding activities is needed before hurricane seeding could be considered other than as an extraordinary emergency action. Specific congressional legislation may be the best means of investing a government agency with the authority to seed hurricanes threatening the coast of the United States.

Value of Information

One of the most important concepts in decision analysis is the value of information: How much it would be worth to make the decision after rather than before uncertainty is resolved? In the case of hurricane modification, how much should be the government pay to learn which of the three hypotheses, H_1, H_2, or H_0, is actually true (23)? We imagine that the government has access to a clairvoyant who has this information and is willing to sell it to the government, if he is paid before he makes the information available. It is easiest to understand the calculation in terms of the decision to seed one hurricane threatening a coastal area.

Let us consider the choice between the two decision situations shown in Fig. 8. The government can choose to buy the information and make the decision after it has learned which hypothesis is true, or it can choose not to buy the information and can make the seeding decision on the basis of the present uncertainty.

Let us, for the moment, consider only property damage and the cost of seeding and disregard government responsibility costs. If H_1 is true, the preferred decision is to seed because the expected

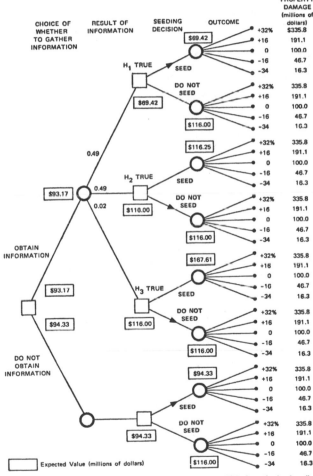

Fig. 8. Expected value of the clairvoyant's information—which hypothesis describes the effect of seeding? (There is no government responsibility cost.)

loss is $69.42 million compared with a loss of $116.00 million for the alternative of not seeding. If H_2 is true, then by choosing not to seed, the government saves the $0.25-million cost of seeding; the loss expected from property damage is the same for both alternatives: $116.00 million. If H_3 is true, seeding is a poor choice; the expected loss from property damage is $167.61 million, $51.61 million more than for the alternative of not seeding. At the present time, the government does not know what the clairvoyant will say, but probabilities have been assigned to his answers:

$$P(H_1) = .49$$
$$P(H_2) = .49 \qquad (12)$$
$$P(H_3) = .02$$

The expected loss corresponding to the decision situation in Fig. 8 is then computed by multiplying the probability of each of the clairvoyant's answers by the expected loss associated with that answer and summing over the three possible answers:

$$(.49)\,(\$69.42) + (.49)\,(\$116.00) +$$
$$(.02)\,(\$116.00) = \$93.17 \text{ million} \quad (13)$$

Comparing this with the expected loss for the best alternative (seed) without the clairvoyant's information, which was $94.33 million, we see that it is $1.16 million less. This difference represents the expected value of the clairvoyant's information in allowing the government to make a better decision. It is a relatively small number compared with the expected losses because the information is not expected to be of much value—the probability assignments indicate that seeding is already a good idea. Without the clairvoyant's information the government should seed; with the clairvoyant's information, with probability .49, the government will save the cost of seeding ($0.25 million), and with the low probability .02 it will avert the potentially disastrous intensification expected from H_3, saving $167.61 million − $116 million = $51.61 million. By this reasoning we get the same answer as before for the value of information

$$(.49)\,(\$0.25) + (.02)\,(\$51.61) =$$
$$\$1.16 \text{ million} \quad (14)$$

and we can see that the value is very sensitive to the small probability assigned to H_3.

Now suppose that the government responsibility costs assumed previously are included. The expected value of perfect information is then much higher

because, if H_2 is true, the government responsibility costs can be saved by not seeding. If the decision without perfect information is to seed, the expected saving from engaging the clairvoyant is

$$(.49)\,(\$0.25 + \$23.28) +$$
$$(.02)\,(\$51.61 + \$53.57) =$$
$$\$13.63 \text{ million} \quad (15)$$

This figure represents 11.75 percent of the expected property damage if the alternative of not seeding is taken for the nominal hurricane.

The value of information largely derives from the fact that it allows the government to avoid the responsibility for seeding if seeding turns out to have no effect. The large increase over the value computed in Eq. 13 is due to the contribution of the government responsibility costs. Most of the increase of $12.47 million, namely $11.41 million, comes from the first or H_2 term.

The value of information depends on the extent to which the government is willing to assume responsibility for seeding a hurricane. If responsibility were not an issue, the government would seed operationally now, and information would have a comparatively low value in the context of this decision. The value of information is greatest when the government responsibility costs are large enough to make the decision essentially even between seeding and not seeding. Still higher responsibility costs cause the value of information to decrease (24).

Value of Further Seeding Experiments

The analysis of the value of a seeding experiment is similar to the determination of the value of the clairvoyant's information. The difference is that the resolution of uncertainty is only partial. The information obtained in the experiment is used in Bayes' equation (Eq. 5) to revise the prior probability assignments to the hypotheses. The original decision is then reevaluated with the posterior probabilities (Fig. 9). The result of the experiment is uncertain when the decision to experiment is made; consequently, the value of experimentation must be computed as an expectation over the possible posterior decision situations. The situation can be diagramed in tree form as shown in Fig. 9.

The analysis for two experimental seedings is given in Table 2 (25). The values assumed above for the govern-

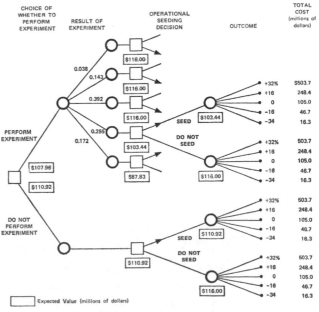

Fig. 9. Value of a seeding experiment (government responsibility cost included).

ment responsibility costs have been used. The expected value of the experiment in improving one operational seeding decision is $5.39 million, slightly less than twice the value of a single experimental seeding and more than ten times the assumed experimental cost, $0.50 million. This value represents 4.7 percent of the expected property damage if the alternative of not seeding is taken. In the discrete version used in the analysis, one of five possible values (see Table 1) is taken as representative of the observed change in hurricane intensity over a 12-hour period following seeding: -34, -16, 0, $+16$, and $+32$ percent. The order in which the results are obtained is not significant, and a total of 15 pairs of results could be obtained with two experiments (Table 2). These pairs might be placed in three groups: favorable, unfavorable, and mixed results. The probability of obtaining a pair of favorable results (-34, -34; -34, -16; -34, 0; and -16, -16 percent) (26) in the two experimental seedings is .327; a pair of results in this group would provide substantial confirmation of hypothesis H_1.

For example, a repetition of the pair

of results obtained with Debbie in 1969 (-34, -16 percent in the discrete approximation) would lead to posterior probabilities of .89 for H_1, .11 for H_2, and less than .005 for H_3. A probability of .075 is computed for a pair of strongly unfavorable results (0, $+32$; $+16$, $+16$; $+16$, $+32$; $+32$, $+32$ percent); in this case the probability assigned to H_1 would be revised strongly downward. The remaining mixed pairs of results do not significantly confirm or deny H_1, and these results have a total probability of .595. Within this group a small probability (.055) is accorded to conflicting results in the two experiments (-34, $+16$; -34, $+32$; -16, $+16$; -16, $+32$ percent).

Another Approach to Determining the Value of Seeding Experiments

The preceding discussion indicates that the value of experiments is sensitive to the government responsibility costs that are assumed in the analysis. We may wish to determine the value of experiments in a different manner in which the issue of government responsibility is treated implicitly.

Suppose that operational seeding will be permitted only after another successful result is obtained in a pair of experiments of the Debbie type. This approximation gives a lower bound to the value of experiments because only a successful experimental result is regarded as valuable. Even if wind reductions are not observed, knowledge gained about the effects of seeding may have implications for future successful operational seeding.

The probability of a favorable pair of results in two experimental seedings of a hurricane was computed as .327. If favorable experimental results are obtained and a subsequent hurricane is seeded operationally, the expected reduction in property-damage losses is $37.88 million. Even if government responsibility costs are included, the reduction in expected losses is $26.80 million. Since these reductions occur with a probability of .327, the expected value of the experiment in improving one operational decision is $12.40 million if only the property damage is considered and $8.77 million if the decrease in property damage is partially offset by the government responsibility costs. The figures $8.77 million and $12.40 million represent 7.6 and 10.7 percent, respectively, of the $116-million property damage expected from the not-seeding alternative in the seeding decision for the nominal hurricane.

We see that the value of experiments is considerably higher than the values computed earlier. This difference results from the high responsibility costs implicit in the decision not to seed on the basis of present information. It may be a reasonable assumption that a bad outcome for the first seeding of a hurricane threatening a coastal area would have much less severe legal and social consequences if it were preceded by another successful experiment. Therefore, lowering the government responsibility costs may be appropriate after another successful field experiment.

Generalizing the Value of Additional Information

The preceding discussions are directed specifically toward updating our information about which hypothesis, H_1, H_2, or H_3, describes the effect of seeding on the maximum sustained wind speed of a hurricane. The analysis has been done for a single seeding decision for a moderately intense hurricane threatening a coastal area. Per-

Table 2. Evaluation of a future experiment with two (independent) experimental seedings. Government responsibility cost is included.

Observed change in wind speed		Prior probability of observation	Posterior probability of hypotheses			Subsequent operational seeding decision expected values (million dollars)		
u_1	u_2		H_1	H_2	H_3	Loss with seeding alternative	Loss with the better alternative	Posterior value of perfect information
-34	-34	.0441	.97	.03	$<.005$	79.87	79.87	0.80
-34	-16	.1009	.89	.11	$<.005$	84.67	84.67	2.68
-34	0	.1140	.77	.22	$<.005$	92.11	92.11	5.64
-16	-16	.0684	.69	.30	$<.005$	97.08	97.08	7.53
		.3274						
-34	$+16$	.0324	.65	.34	.01	100.16	100.16	9.06
-34	$+32$	.0078	.60	.37	.03	105.27	105.27	12.10
-16	0	.1915	.49	.51	.01	110.25	110.25	12.78
-16	$+16$	.0651	.34	.64	.02	120.07	116.00	13.05
0	0	.1610	.28	.70	.02	123.37	116.00	10.81
-16	$+32$	.0167	.29	.65	.06	126.05	116.00	11.15
0	$+16$	.1229	.18	.79	.03	131.35	116.00	6.78
		.5974						
0	$+32$	.0332	.14	.77	.09	138.02	116.00	5.51
$+16$	$+16$	.0251	.10	.83	.07	138.62	116.00	3.98
$+16$	$+32$	.0145	.08	.75	.17	148.37	116.00	3.02
$+32$	$+32$	.0024	.05	.59	.36	165.72	116.00	1.98
		.0752						

Value of seeding decision with prior information	110.92
Expected value of seeding decision with seeding experiments	105.53
Value of experiment	5.39
Cost of experiment	0.50
Net expected value of experiment	4.89

1200

fect information applies not only to a single hurricane but to all hurricanes that might be seeded operationally. The numerical results for the single nominal hurricane are summarized in the extreme left column of Table 3 and are extended to multiple hurricanes in the remaining columns.

Even if only half the hurricanes could be seeded because of tactical considerations having to do with precipitation, hurricane trajectory, and so on, the expected annual benefit from perfect information is $26 million. If we assume that only half the hurricanes could be seeded, and discount the expected benefits of perfect information for all future hurricane seasons at a discount rate of 7 percent, we arrive at $370 million. This figure represents the value of a "perfect" experiment that would determine whether H_1 is true.

A single repetition of the 1969 Hurricane Debbie experiment has an expected value of $5.39 million in the context of the nominal hurricane, or about 4.7 percent of expected property damage. For the decision to seed a single hurricane in the billion-dollar range, the expected value of the experiment is ten times as high, about $50 million. For one hurricane season the value is 4.7 percent of $220 million, or $10.2 million (it is assumed again that various tactical considerations might preclude seeding in half of the cases). For all future hurricane seasons, with a discount rate of 7 percent, the value is $146 million compared with an experimental cost of about $500,000. The benefit to cost ratio is therefore about 300. Even if only a single hurricane season is considered, the expected benefits are 20 times greater than the cost of the experiment and ten times the present annual budget for Project Stormfury.

Experimental Capability Decision

The occurrence of hurricanes is a random phenomenon. Therefore, it is uncertain whether there will be an opportunity for an experimental seeding before the arrival of a threatening storm that might be operationally seeded. Opportunities for experimental seeding have been scarce. In the last few years there have been only six experimental seedings, and these have been conducted on three hurricanes, Esther (1961), Beulah (1963), and Debbie (1969) (7). Experimental seedings have been limited to a small region

Table 3. Summary of the value of additional information on the effect of seeding. Only the 50 percent of hurricanes that are assumed to be possible candidates for seeding on the basis of tactical considerations are considered. If all hurricanes are assumed to be candidates for operational seeding, the figures of the last two columns should be doubled.

Item	Nominal hurricane used in analysis		Single hurricane season (million dollars)	All future hurricane seasons, discounted at 7% (million dollars)
	Million dollars	Percentage		
Expected property damage without seeding	116.0	100	220.0	3142
Expected value of perfect information	13.6	11.8	26.0	370
Expected value of a field experiment consisting of two experimental seedings	5.4	4.7	10.2	146
Expected value of field experiments: * With government responsibility costs	8.8	7.6	16.6	238
Government responsibility costs = 0	12.4	10.7	23.5	335

* If it is assumed that prior operational seeding is not permitted.

of the Atlantic Ocean accessible to aircraft based in Puerto Rico, and few hurricanes have passed through this region.

There are many other regions of the ocean where hurricanes might be found that satisfy the present criterion for experimental seeding—that is, the hurricane will be seeded only if the probability is less than .10 that it will come within 50 miles of a populated land area within 18 hours after seeding. However, a decision to expand the present experimental capability of Project Stormfury would need to be made well before the experiment itself. Whereas the seeding itself requires only that an aircraft be fitted with silver iodide pyrotechnic generators, the monitoring of the subsequent development of the hurricane requires other aircraft fitted with the appropriate instrumentation. The requirements in equipment, crew training, and communications and support facilities are substantial. In addition, permission may be needed from nations whose shores might be threatened by the seeded hurricane. The experimental decision, then, involves an investment in the capability to perform an experimental seeding. Whether an experiment is performed depends on the uncertain occurrences of hurricanes in the experimental areas.

The expected time before another experimental opportunity for Project Stormfury's present capability is about one full hurricane season. There was no opportunity during 1970. Preliminary estimates of the cost of a capability to seed hurricanes in the Pacific are about $1 million (27). The incidence of experimentally seedable hurricanes in the Pacific appears to be more than twice that in the Atlantic (28). Therefore, it appears advisable to develop a

capability to conduct experimental hurricane seeding in the Pacific Ocean since the benefits expected from this capability outweigh the costs by a factor of at least 5 (29).

Conclusions from the Analysis

The decision to seed a hurricane imposes a great responsibility on public officials. This decision cannot be avoided because inaction is equivalent to a decision not to permit seeding. Either the government must accept the responsibility of a seeding that may be perceived by the public as deleterious, or it must accept the responsibility for not seeding and thereby exposing the public to higher probabilities of severe storm damage.

Our report to the National Oceanic and Atmospheric Administration recommended that seeding be permitted on an emergency basis. We hope that further experimental results and a formal analysis of the tactical decision to seed a particular hurricane will precede the emergency. However, a decision may be required before additional experimental or analytical results are available. A hurricane with the intensity of Camille threatening a populous coastal area of the United States would confront public officials with an agonizing but unavoidable choice.

The decision to seed hurricanes can not be resolved on strictly scientific grounds. It is a complex decision whose uncertain consequences affect many people. Appropriate legal and political institutions should be designated for making the hurricane-seeding decision, and further analysis should be conducted to support these institutions in carrying out their work.

Role of Decision Analysis

The results of a decision analysis depend on the information available at the time it is performed. Decision analysis should not be used to arrive at a static recommendation to be verified by further research, rather it should be used as a dynamic tool for making necessary decisions at any time. Various sensitivity analyses included here indicate how new information might be expected to influence policy recommendations. However, the advent of a severe hurricane will necessitate a decision on the basis of the information then available.

The analysis of hurricane modification points up a difficulty that is common in public decision-making on complex technological issues. When the consequences of deploying new technology are uncertain, who will make the choice? While many individuals or groups may share responsibility, decision analysis conceptually separates the roles of the executive decision-maker, the expert, and the analyst. The analyst's role is to structure a complex problem in a tractable manner so that the uncertain consequences of the alternative actions may be assessed. Various experts provide the technical information from which the analysis is fashioned. The decision-maker acts for society in providing the basis for choosing among the alternatives. The analysis provides a mechanism for integration and communication so that the technical judgments of the experts and the value judgments of the decision-maker may be seen in relation to each other, examined, and debated. Decision analysis makes not only the decision but the decision process a matter of formal record. For any complex decision that may affect the lives of millions, a decision analysis showing explicitly the uncertainties and decision criteria can and should be carried out.

References and Notes

1. R. H. Simpson and J. S. Malkus, *Sci. Amer.* 211, 27 (Dec. 1964).
2. R. C. Gentry, *Science* 168, 473 (1970).
3. Now incorporated in the National Oceanic and Atmospheric Administration.
4. R. A. Howard, *Proceedings of the Fourth International Conference on Operational Research* (Wiley, New York, 1966).
5. ———, *IEEE Trans. Syst. Sci. Cybern.* 4 (1968), p. 211.
6. A detailed discussion of the research is to be found in the project's final report [D. W. Boyd, R. A. Howard, J. E. Matheson, D. W. North, *Decision Analysis of Hurricane Modification* (Project 8503, Stanford Research Institute, Menlo Park, Calif., 1971)]. This report is available through the National Technical Information Service, U.S. Department of Commerce, Washington, D.C., accession number COM-71-00784.
7. The meteorological information leading to this

approximation is discussed in detail in the SRI project final report (6), especially appendix B. Meteorologists connected with Project Stormfury believe it highly improbable that seeding will cause any substantial change in the course of the hurricane, and other important consequences of seeding are not foreseen at this time. We wish to stress that our role in the decision analysis of hurricane modification has been to provide the methodology for analyzing a complex decision with uncertain consequences. The specific assumptions have been provided by the hurricane meteorologists associated with Project Stormfury and by other experts in relevant fields. Because of space limitations these assumptions cannot be discussed in detail in this article; the interested reader is advised to consult the project's final report or communicate directly with the authors. The type of seeding is assumed to be the same as that used in the Hurricane Debbie experiments: massive multiple seeding of the clouds in the outer eyewall region with silver iodide. During September 1971, Project Stormfury conducted seeding experiments of a different type on Hurricane Ginger (R. C. Gentry, internal communication, National Oceanic and Atmospheric Administration, October 1971). The Ginger experiment involved the seeding of clouds in the rain bands well outside the eyewall region. This "rainsector" experiment was selected because Ginger had a large and poorly formed eyewall and was judged not to be a good subject for eyewall-region seeding. Although some changes in cloud structure and wind field occurred at a time when they might have been caused by seeding, these changes were minor compared with the dramatic changes that occurred in Hurricane Debbie after seeding. Because of the difference in type of seeding, the Ginger results do not imply a need for revision of the analysis or data presented in this article.

8. In some hurricanes, such as Diane (1955) and Camille (1969), precipitation-induced inland flooding has also been an important cause of property damage. Seeding might cause some increase in precipitation. In considering the policy decision to permit seeding we ignored these precipitation effects, but they might sometimes be important in the decision to seed a specific hurricane.
9. Throughout the analysis it is assumed that seeding would be authorized and carried out by some agency of the federal government.
10. C. Holliday, *Technical Memorandum WBTM SR-45* (Environmental Science Service Administration, Washington, D.C., 1969).
11. The details of the derivation of this probability distribution are given in appendix B of (6). The indirect approach of using the Holliday relation combined with pressure-change observations was first suggested by R. C. Sheets of the National Hurricane Research Laboratory.
12. S. L. Rosenthal, *Technical Memorandum ERLTM-NHRL 88* (Environmental Science Service Administration, Washington, D.C., 1970). See also *Project Stormfury Annual Report 1970* (National Hurricane Research Laboratory, Miami, 1971).
13. A probability distribution on an uncertain quantity x will be denoted $P(x)$ whether x takes on discrete or continuous values. If x is discrete, $P(x)$ will be the probability mass function; if x is continuous, $P(x)$ will be the probability density function. A probability distribution of the normal or Gaussian family specified by its mean m and standard deviation σ will be denoted $f_N (m, \sigma)$.
14. The average effect of seeding and the fluctuation from the average may be regarded as (independent) normal random variables whose sum represents the effect of seeding on a specific hurricane. According to well-known results in probability theory, this sum will be normally distributed with a mean equal to the sum of the two means and a standard deviation equal to the square root of the sum of the squares of the two standard deviations.
15. The effect of seeding and the natural change in the storm are described as independent normal random variables and the total change is their sum. The independence assumption is judged an appropriate summary of present knowledge; sensitivity to this assumption is examined in (6). Important assumptions such as this one were reviewed with Project Stormfury meteorologists. A letter to us from R. C. Gentry (October 1970) stated, "while seeding may affect different hurricanes by differ-

ent amounts, we are not yet prepared to predict these differences." The assumption of independence does not deny that there may be a relationship between the natural change occurring in a hurricane and the effect of modification. When information about this relationship becomes available, it should be incorporated into the analysis and the independence assumption should be withdrawn.

16. H. Raiffa, *Decision Analysis: Introductory Lectures on Choices Under Uncertainty* (Addison-Wesley, Reading, Mass., 1968); M. Tribus, *Rational Descriptions, Decisions, and Designs* (Pergamon, New York, 1969).
17. D. W. North, *IEEE Trans. Syst. Sci. Cybern.* 4 (1968), p. 200.
18. The details of the calculation of c_2 are given in (6). Similar relationships between maximum sustained wind speed and property damage have been stated by other investigators [R. L. Hendrick and D. G. Friedman, in *Human Dimensions in Weather Modification*, W. R. Derrick Sewell, Ed. (Univ. of Chicago Press, Chicago, 1966), pp. 227–246]. In November 1971, D. G. Friedman communicated to us some results from analyzing insurance claim data. He finds an exponent of 6.7; this value would lead to much larger reductions in property damage than were assumed in our analysis. Other investigators have suggested an equation of the form $d = c_1 (w - w_0)^2$, where c_1 and w_0 are empirical constants (R. C. Gentry, private communication). This equation would give results essentially equivalent to ours.
19. This procedure is an approximation, which depends on the fact that seeding costs are small compared with costs of property damage.
20. It is shown in (6) that the results are not sensitive to the discrete approximation.
21. For example, if an exponential utility function with a risk aversion coefficient of $\gamma = 0.001$ is used, the difference between the certain equivalents for the two alternatives increases from $21.67 million to $24.2 million. Because of stochastic dominance, any risk attitude will always leave seeding as the preferred alternative. Further discussion on risk preference may be found in (5) and (17).
22. These issues are discussed in detail in appendices E and F of (6).
23. In answering this question we assume that the government is willing to pay up to $1 to avoid $1 of property damage.
24. It is possible for the responsibility costs to be so high that a hurricane would not be seeded even if it were certain that H_2 is true. This amount of responsibility cost implies that the government would prefer an unseeded hurricane to a seeded hurricane that caused only half as much property damage.
25. For these calculations a system of computer programs for evaluating large decision trees, developed by W. Rousseau of Stanford Research Institute, was used.
26. These discrete outcomes correspond to a reduction of 10 percent or more. The discrete approximation simplifies the analysis by restricting the number of possible experimental results. Earlier we considered the revision of probabilities based on the results of the 1969 Hurricane Debbie experiments. There the discrete approximation was not used, but it would have given equivalent results.
27. R. C. Gentry, personal communication. In arriving at this figure it was assumed that military aircraft based in the Pacific could be used in the seeding.
28. *Project Stormfury Annual Report 1968* (National Hurricane Research Laboratory, Miami, 1969).
29. The details of this calculation are given in (6).
30. This article summarizes research performed for the National Oceanic and Atmospheric Administration, U.S. Department of Commerce, contract 0-35172; the project leader is D. W. North. The authors acknowledge the substantial contribution of Dr. Dean W. Boyd. The authors also wish to acknowledge Professor Gary Widman of Hastings College of the Law, University of California, San Francisco, for legal research supporting the project and Dr. Cecil Gentry, Dr. Robert Simpson, Dr. Joanne Simpson, and many others who have been associated with Project Stormfury for their assistance and cooperation. The findings and conclusions presented are the sole responsibility of the authors and do not necessarily reflect the views of the U.S. government or any of the individuals mentioned above.

28 April 1978, Volume 200, Number 4340

SCIENCE

Hail Suppression and Society

Assessment of future hail suppression technology
reveals its development should be sizable or ignored.

Stanley A. Changnon, Jr., Barbara C. Farhar, Earl R. Swanson

Scientific knowledge about the effectiveness of hail suppression is incomplete and conflicting (1, 2). Limited use of this potentially beneficial technology for relieving hail losses to crops and property has continued in the face of the current uncertain status. These technological models were then coupled to social, economic, and legal variables to derive future adoption levels in the nation. The social impacts of these adoption patterns were established and eval-

Summary. An interdisciplinary assessment of hail suppression in the past, present, and future has shown it to be currently scientifically uncertain but a potentially beneficial future technology. An established suppression technology would be widely adopted in the Great Plains, providing benefits to agriculture and secondarily to the American consumer. Development of a reliable technology will require a sizable long-term federal commitment to atmospheric and social research. Subcritical funding would be a mistake. Orderly future usage of hail suppression, with its scientific complexities and regional character, will necessitate development of governmental regulations, evaluation procedures, interstate arrangements, and means for compensating those who lose from modification.

scientific uncertainty about whether or how it works (3, pp. 10–15). Public controversy over its use has erupted in several areas and the legal implications of this uncertain technology have been under study (4–6). We performed a technology assessment to address the future of hail suppression in the nation (7). The effort required an interdisciplinary research team drawn from various physical and social sciences as well as from legal and business communities (8).

Evaluation in depth of all past and present aspects of hail suppression became the basis from which our research group projected the technologies into an uncertain future. Initially, the national hail problem was dimensionalized, and all social and environmental questions raised by hail suppression were identified. Three models of hail suppression's future capability were extrapolated from

uated. They served as the basis for identifying related policy issues, for drawing conclusions, and for making recommendations. We have drawn together the major findings of this technology assessment.

The Hail Problem

The key characteristic of hail in the United States is its enormous variability in both time and space. Most locales in the nation experience only two or three hailstorms a year (Fig. 1) and only 5 to 10 percent of these hailstorms may ever produce seriously damaging hail (9). During the warm season of the year (about April through October), crop-damaging hail falls somewhere in the eastern two-thirds of the United States on almost every day. On 20 days in an

average year, crop losses from hail exceed $1 million. These infrequent but large loss events represent 5 percent of the hail loss days but 39 percent of the national loss to hail.

The most damage from hail is done to crops, averaging $773 million annually (1975 dollars); in addition, property is damaged at a cost of $75 million each year (10). The $773 million crop loss from hail represents about 1 percent of cash receipts from national marketing of farm products. Half of all hail losses occurs in the Great Plains, that is, from Texas to North Dakota, where hailstorms are intense (Fig. 1). Intensity is a function of hailstone sizes and frequencies plus attendant wind speeds. Crops most severely damaged by hail are wheat, cotton, corn, soybeans, and tobacco; about 25 percent of these crops is usually insured. The amount of food lost to the nation is equivalent to that needed to feed about 2 million Americans a normal diet for 1 year.

Insurance is the only current alternative response to the problem of hail; it serves to spread the burden of loss without reducing the losses themselves. Although hail suppression is at present a much more uncertain solution to the hail problem than insurance, the latter is not a complete solution. In areas where the loss is high, losses are sufficiently frequent and substantial so that many farmers are unable to afford insurance and the insurance industry finds it difficult to price coverage at a profitable level (11).

Hail Suppression Hypotheses and Evidence

In 1946, Schaefer discovered that Dry Ice dropped into supercooled water vapor in a laboratory cold box caused the rapid formation of ice crystals (9). The crystals that formed in the home freezer he was using for his experiments were like those of the natural atmosphere (12) and could serve to change the amounts

S. A. Changnon, Jr., is the head of the Atmospheric Sciences Section of the Illinois State Water Survey and a professor of geography at the University of Illinois, Urbana 61801. B. C. Farhar is a research associate at the Institute of Behavioral Science of the University of Colorado, Boulder 80302. E. R. Swanson is a professor of agricultural economics at the University of Illinois, Urbana 61801.

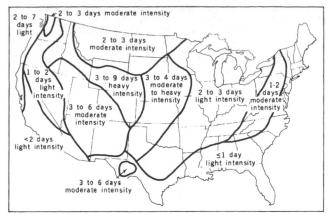

Fig. 1. Hail regions in the United States showing the average annual number of days with hail at any point in a region and the average intensity of hail.

of water and ice in the colder upper parts of clouds. The implications of the discovery were enormous. Schaefer conducted the first "cloud-seeding" flight before the end of 1946. Soon after, it was found that silver iodide could be substituted for Dry Ice with about the same effect, and this substance became the seeding agent most frequently used in contemporary weather modification efforts.

Modern weather modification has a history of almost 30 years of parallel thrusts in experimentation and usage without clear proof of effectiveness. Cloud seeding has been conducted to seek increases in rainfall and snowfall, to suppress lightning and dissipate fog, and to mitigate hurricanes and hailstorms. Conceivably, there are many ways to modify hailstorms, but the extensive attempts, either in field experiments or in commercial operational (nonexperimental) projects, have been based on the use of silver iodide to alter microphysical processes inside the cold upper parts of thunderstorms. Two basic approaches involving conceptual hypotheses are followed: the introduction of silver iodide either for "competition" or for "glaciation." The glaciation hypothesis involves relatively heavy seeding in an attempt to convert all the supercooled cloud water above the freezing level into ice crystals so that no hail can form. However, if only part of the supercooled water is transformed into ice, the storm could actually be worsened because growth by accretion is especially rapid in an environment composed of a mixture of supercooled drops and ice crystals. To be successful, this approach requires the

massive seeding to take place well in advance of the first hailstone formation. It is the approach that has been used in a Canadian experiment and in a South African operational project (2).

The competition hypothesis involves the development of fewer, but still many, hail embryos (ice nuclei) that compete for the available water and thus minimize hailstone growth in the zone of maximum liquid water content. This approach has been used in major field experiments in North Dakota and Colorado and in commercial projects in Texas, South Dakota, and North Dakota. A major uncertainty with each approach is whether the desired amount of silver iodide is delivered and distributed at the right time and in the proper volume within a storm.

Results from the Canadian experiment suggest (i) success in suppression of hail in the smaller, less complex storms, but (ii) no success in the more organized, larger, multicellular hailstorms. Results of a 4-year experimental project in North Dakota indicate a 60 percent reduction in crop hail loss that is marginally significant at the .92 confidence level. The National Hail Research Experiment in Colorado, ended after 3 years of experimentation, showed that seeding neither decreased nor increased hail. The operational hail suppression projects in the Dakotas and Texas that are based on the competition hypothesis have yielded results suggesting moderate success, although scientifically suitable proof cannot be derived (2).

As a result, hail suppression in the United States since the 1950's has been marked by confusion, by scientific un-

certainty, and sometimes by public controversy (3). Agriculturists utilized the services of commercial weather modification firms for operational projects before experimental results on the effectiveness of the technology were available. The three North American field experiments involving statistical controls and the collection of data on relevant atmospheric properties adequate to allow scientific evaluation that have been conducted in recent years have yielded mixed and inconclusive results. In the typical private or state-supported operational project little or no data to allow an in-depth scientific evaluation of its effects have been collected. Over the 15-year period from 1958 to 1975, 357 cloud-seeding field operational projects and experiments were conducted. Of these, approximately 17 percent (or 61) involved hail suppression, and many of them were located in the Great Plains area of the United States. The public's experience with hail suppression remains limited (13).

Evaluation of all available information regarding the current status of hail suppression revealed that three different positions appear in describing the current status (2). One view is based on the results of evaluations of six hail suppression projects. Five of the projects suggested the existence of a hail suppression capability with decreases in hail loss ranging from 20 to 48 percent, but the results were not statistically significant at the 5 percent level. In general, these results would be classed by atmospheric scientists as "optimistic." Another view of hail suppression is that afforded by the various recent scientific reviews of weather modification (14). These generally suggest a position that may be characterized as guarded optimism, but with no indication of definitive proof of hail suppression. The third view might best be labeled as the average scientific belief. The results of two surveys of scientific opinion show a wide range of opinion on the readiness of hail suppression for operational application. A majority of experts on weather modification indicated no belief in a hail suppression capability, but a sizable minority indicated that a moderate (more than 20 percent) reduction in hail damage was a current capability. At best, average scientific belief must be labeled "we don't know" (15, 16). These three views of the current status of hail suppression—optimistic, slightly optimistic, and pessimistic—reflect the wide range of opinions and results, and clearly the current status of hail suppression may be described as one of uncertainty (1).

Use of Hail Suppression:

Past and Present

Case history material and public survey data taken in areas with weather modification projects reveal several factors associated with public acceptance or rejection of hail suppression in the past (*3, 17*).

1) The first such factor is the area's heterogeneity of weather needs. That is, within a weather modification project area differing requirements for beneficial weather may exist. For example, some crops at certain time periods benefit from additional rainfall, whereas others suffer damage if rainfall occurs at that time. Heterogeneity of weather needs is the basis for potential conflict at the community or regional level with regard to planned intervention in weather processes.

2) If a drought develops or deepens while hail suppression is being conducted, grass roots opposition groups may develop because it is perceived that the seeding to suppress hail is also accidentally suppressing rainfall.

3) The lack of scientific consensus about the readiness of hail suppression technology for operational application impedes its social acceptance.

The decision to adopt hail suppression has necessarily been reached in a context of uncertainty about its effectiveness and possible side effects. The uncertainty implies that a degree of risk is involved, and, in general, risk-takers prefer to take their own risks, rather than to have such decisions made for them. Thus, the degree of public participation in the decision to implement a hail suppression project may have an influence on whether or not the project finds ultimate acceptance in the community.

Adoption of hail suppression has tended to occur in areas of high loss where hail destroys up to 20 percent of the crop. Those interested in using hail suppression have included irrigating barley and lettuce growers; cotton, grain, and wheat farmers; and fruit growers. Where adoption did not occur even though hail losses were significant (mostly in the tobacco areas of the mid-Atlantic region), growers were generally unaware of the technology and did not perceive hail as a serious problem. Most of them relied on insurance to cope with crop loss to hail (*18*). As the technical performance of cloud seeding improved, as it began to depend more on public funding, and as it was used over more extensive land areas, awareness increased that the activity had implications for entire communities and regions. Adoption of weather

Table 1. Preferred decision-making regarding cloud seeding. The question: Who do you think should decide whether or not a hail or rain experiment will be started (or continued)?*

Response	Percentage of number of respondents			
	Illinois 1974 (*N* = 274)	Colorado 1974 (*N* = 221)	South Dakota 1974 (*N* = 293)	South Dakota 1976 (*N* = 430)
Local	54	56	59	50
Nonlocal	46	44	41	50

*Questions were phrased slightly differently in each state.

modification thus became a collective decision, requiring action on the part of a community or larger social aggregate in order for it to be adopted. A slow rate of adoption of innovations may be considered quite normal (*19*). Thus, widespread adoption of hail suppression technology can be expected to require at least the remainder of this century, provided that an effective technology is developed (*20*).

Results of surveys in agricultural areas on citizen attitudes, knowledge, and belief concerning weather modification have shown that belief in the technology's effectiveness in increasing rainfall and decreasing hail is a key predictor of favorability to having a cloud-seeding project (*4, 21*). About 40 percent of those sampled have consistently expressed concern about the unknown risks involved in human intervention in weather processes. However, many respondents have favored trying to control the weather for the benefit of man. In general, environmental concern does not appear to be a basis of opposition to cloud seeding in agricultural areas of the country.

Survey findings have been notable for their marked consistency and comparability. Public response to cloud-seeding projects is far more dependent on citizen observation of actual project effects than on their initial favorability or unfavorability toward a project (*4*). If community members attribute beneficial weather events to cloud seeding, acceptance is likely. If they think weather modification causes detrimental events (as in the relatively frequent argument that hail suppression causes drought), then social rejection of the project is likely.

The majority of citizens interviewed in various parts of the nation have expressed a preference for local decision control over implementation of weather modification (Table 1). In one recent survey, the majority of respondents called for a vote to decide the matter. Widespread citizen preference for local control over cloud seeding is often in direct conflict with scientific and governmental agency desires to retain decision control

over weather modification. This issue between officials and citizens has played a role in more than one community dispute over weather modification (*22*).

Nevertheless, given the popularity of participative mechanisms and their increasingly extensive use, it seems unlikely that public participation in weather modification decision-making will decline. The active and forceful participation of representatives of groups, such as attentive minorities, having a direct stake in the outcomes of public decision processes can be expected (*23*).

Up until now, weather modification projects have been implemented with a minimum of public involvement in the decision process. Since scientists and agency officials generally wish to retain control of the decisions concerning when, where, how, and for what purposes to conduct weather modification projects, and since citizens in the areas wish to have a voice in these decisions, the conflict between them requires resolution by means of an adequate decision mechanism—an institutionalized procedure that is socially acceptable. Extensive public participation should minimize the potential for community polarization (*24*).

Weather modification, and thus hail suppression, is now regulated primarily at the state level, with 60 percent of the states having enacted a relevant statute (*25, 26*). The federal government requires only that all weather modification activity in the nation be reported to the National Oceanic and Atmospheric Administration (NOAA).

States vary with respect to the complexity and degree of regulation that they impose on weather modification activity. Several states require weather modifiers to show competence and obtain a license; they may also require a permit for the conduct of each field project. In general, the federal government considers itself not answerable to state law; therefore, some federal weather modification projects have operated without any external regulatory control whatsoever.

Statutes in six states make it manda-

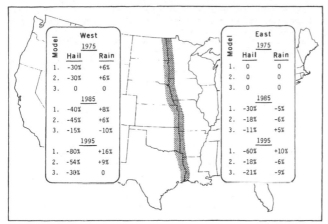

Fig. 2. Areas projected to adopt hail suppression as a result of varying hail and rain modification capabilities (technological models).

tory that public hearings be held prior to the granting of a permit to conduct field operations, while in several other states hearings are optional. Three states provide for funding of state-sponsored cloud seeding through general fund appropriations; however, most states provide minimal budgets for administration of weather modification statutes. Thus, proper evaluation of operational projects, including the required reports, is unlikely to occur.

Major lawsuits involving weather modification have numbered 15. Of the 13 that have been decided, the defendants (weather modifiers) have won 11. The two that they lost included a Texas case in which a temporary injunction against cloud seeding was issued, and a Pennsylvania case of criminal prosecution for hail suppression seeding (6). Generally, plaintiffs in court have been unable to prove the causal relation between the harm alleged by them and the cloud seeding on a given day (25).

Studies of the effects of cloud seeding on the environment, both in terms of silver iodide (the seeding agent most commonly employed) and of weather effects themselves (for example, the effect of increased precipitation on natural ecological processes) suggest a general finding of minimal measurable short-term environmental effects (27). However, environmental researchers hesitate to make definitive statements because they perceive that serious environmental effects of silver iodide and precipitation changes might occur and too little research has been accomplished. Although it is unlikely that serious adverse environmen-

tal impacts would result from widespread adoption of hail suppression, the possibility of adverse effects cannot yet be discounted.

Future Technological Models

Since an established hail suppression technology does not currently exist, we projected future capabilities. Three such projections, called technological models, were developed. Each was based on one of the three different scientific views about current capabilities in hail suppression: optimistic, slightly optimistic, and pessimistic (15).

The three numbered models are presented in Fig. 2. A capability was estimated for each of three levels for the eastern and western United States, a distinction made necessary because of the great differences in hailstorms and because more experimentation has occurred in the western part of the country. Estimates for future hail in the models are based on season-long averages over a seeded area (typically more than 2000 square kilometers), and they are expressions of average seasonal changes achieved in property and crop hail damages. Since a capability to suppress hail will probably affect the amount of rainfall an area receives, the estimated rainfall effects presented in the models are those anticipated as a result of the hail suppression activity itself. The lack of any information on the possible effects of hail suppression on hail or rain beyond the area of suppression activities (called the "downwind" area by atmospheric

scientists) led us to exclude such effects from the models. Each model reflects a series of reasonable and probable technical developments and could best be described as scientific estimates.

Model 1 starts from a slightly optimistic assessment of the current capability in the West, and from no capability in the East (Fig. 2). Its future is characterized by relatively extensive concurrent usage and experimentation, with a major scientific breakthrough by 1995. Such a breakthrough might occur in the understanding of cloud behavior, in improved storm forecasting, and in better approaches to nocturnal storm seeding, and is expected to make possible the high level of effectiveness predicted for 1995 (with as much as 80 percent reduction of hail damage in the West).

Model 2 involves intermittent applications and experimentation with moderate advances. This model also begins with a slightly optimistic view of the current state-of-the-art in the West. Moderate advances in technical skill would occur, but no major scientific breakthrough would be achieved. By 1995, these activities would lead to a capability of reducing hail damage by about 50 percent in the West, and by about 20 percent in the East (Fig. 2).

Model 3 involves little usage anywhere in the nation and has instead an experimental focus. It is based on a pessimistic view of current capabilities for both West and East. Decreases in rainfall associated with hail suppression in the western half of the country would minimize usage, but moderate research would ultimately lead to a very modest capability (30 percent reduction of hail damage in the West) by 1995.

In the Great Plains where usage of hail suppression exists and is projected to continue, a 50 percent decrease in hail loss results in an 11 percent increase in average net income per harvest acre. If this shift in hail loss were accompanied by a 10 percent decrease in rainfall, the net effect would be a 1 percent income decrease, whereas a rain increase of 10 percent with a 50 percent hail decrease would bring an income increase of 22 percent. The relatively greater importance of rainfall modification is shown by the fact that a 10 percent rain increase alone is equivalent to a 50 percent decrease in hail loss.

Future growth of hail suppression activities will require management systems with several key program elements including design, field operations, evaluation of effects, and public information systems (20, 28). The probable regional nature of future programs (in response to the broad spatial distribution of hail-producing weather systems) will necessitate sophisticated program designs. Areas of effective future operations, from a technological standpoint, would be from 10,000 to 40,000 square kilometers in extent. Operational efforts will potentially involve three types of seeding systems (aircraft dispensing material at cloud base or inside storms, and a less likely use of surface rockets). Highly skilled storm-forecasting and storm-monitoring facilities will be necessary, and all components of the system will require specially trained staff. Costs for all aspects of a well-conducted future hail suppression program will reach $1 per planted acre (in 1975 dollars).

Future Adoption of Hail Suppression

Given the three alternative models of hail suppression's potential development, the research group projected future adoption patterns on the basis of several important economic, legal, and sociopolitical variables. Adoption referred to the commercial use of hail suppression technology in an area. Data on the social variables were integrated by crop-producing regions of the United States for each technological model at 1985 and 1995 (20). This analysis was a key integrative effort in the assessment project, making possible the ensuing evaluation of economic and other social impacts.

Seven variables were developed and utilized in the adoption analysis. First was an economic incentive index based on an analysis of individual farm operators and regional weather-crop relations. The second variable was a legal receptivity index based on data concerning the extent of legal regulation of hail suppression and of state governmental support of weather modification through appropriations, the extent and direction of trends in administrative law, and the occurrences of litigation and their outcomes. Indices on the social incentive to adopt hail suppression, based on each region's severity of hail losses and drought and on the importance of agriculture in the area's economy, were employed. Another index included heterogeneity of weather needs in each region, with respect to rain and hail, to represent an area's conflict potential. Other variables included (i) the political stance of each region as represented by statute wording, (ii) an estimate of the level of scientific consensus associated with each technological model, and (iii) an estimate of the social acceptability of each mod-

el's effects. Values for these variables were defined for each crop-producing region and for each model for the years 1985 and 1995. If the summarized value exceeded a predetermined threshold value, adoption was predicted. Threshold values were determined by examining the data in relation to the actual adoption of hail suppression.

Results should be viewed as projections or forecasts of adoption by crop-producing regions. These results are conditional on the occurrence of the capabilities in the technological models. As can be seen on the maps of projected adopting areas (Fig. 3), the most extensive adoption predicted was for the highest level of technology (model 1, 80 percent reduction in hail damage accompanied by a 16 percent enhancement of rainfall) in 1995. The Great Plains area of the nation would be the area most heavily involved in hail suppression, with a few scattered projects in California and the Pacific Northwest.

Hail suppression was not projected to occur in the Midwest or in East Coast areas. A low-level technology (model 3) would result in virtually no adoption in the nation in 1995.

Impacts on Agriculture

Our study of impacts resulting from future use of hail suppression established agriculture as the main impacted activity. Given the adoption patterns projected for the nation with the three technological models, a prime question was "What will be the savings in resources required to meet projected domestic and foreign demand for crops in future years?" Resource savings were defined as reductions from hail suppression in the costs of production and transportation for eight principal crops.

In conducting the analyses of the national economic impact of hail suppression, a national linear programming computer model was used (29). National modeling calculations included the cost for operations, expenditures for future research and evaluation, the extent of adoption, and the future demands for food.

As is shown in Table 2, the high-level hail suppression capability (model 1) would result in a resource savings of 1 percent in 1985 and 3 percent in 1995. The low-level capability (model 3) has such minimal adoption that no resource saving would occur on a national scale. In fact, the costs of attaining model 3 (including $1 per acre for operations) outweigh the benefits of hail suppression in

1995, leading to a $2 million increase in costs. The annual benefit (resource savings) derived from the high-level technology (model 1) by 1995 was calculated to be $493 million. This value is nearly twice the benefit obtained with the moderate technology (model 2 at $263 million).

In a sense, hail suppression technology can be viewed as a substitute for land. Because yields per acre increase, less farmland is required to meet projected demands. Therefore, land rents and land values tend to decline slightly in nonadopting areas, but they increase in adopting areas. The overall effect at the national level is estimated to be a slight reduction in land rents.

The adoption of hail suppression would also affect the comparative market advantage of the crops in various regions. The resulting changes in location of crop production would not appear substantial when compared to recent year-to-year changes in crop acreages by state.

Another agricultural impact question concerned which of the three alternative routes of technological development (models) promises to be the best investment for public funds. In the benefit-cost analysis performed, the benefits were based on the resource savings accomplished by the predicted adoption. The costs included the requisite research, development, and information system expenses estimated to be associated with each model. Using an 8 percent discount rate, the high-level technology (model 1) was found to have an estimated benefit-cost ratio of 14.6:1 (Table 3); the moderate technology (model 2) had a ratio of 16.6:1; and the low-level technology (model 3) had a ratio of −0.4:1. Use of substantially higher discount rates did not affect the relative ranking of the models, although it did reduce the benefit-cost ratios.

Although the benefit-cost ratio is highest for model 2 (because of lower predicted expenses for research and development than in model 1), the total benefits produced by model 1 are much greater. Comparison of model 1 and 2 values in Table 2 shows the difference between the benefits of models 1 and 2 is $1124 million and their difference in costs is $91 million. Thus, the benefit-cost ratio of going from model 2 to model 1 is 12.3:1, indicating that model 1 would be the best choice.

The benefit-cost ratios for models 1 and 2 appear high for two reasons. First, previous expenditures for research have provided a knowledge base for the expected future development, and second, there was no risk discounting to reflect the uncertainty of obtaining the specified technology level, given the funding level.

As we have noted, agriculture is the primary stakeholder in an effective hail suppression capability. If high-level technology (model 1) is developed, one major effect will be on the income of crop producers in adopting areas. These producers would receive immediate economic benefits from increased farm output. After an adjustment period, however, the national prices for these commodities would reflect the increased production, and some of the income advantage of producers in the first regions to adopt would be lost, but these producers would still benefit from increased stability of production. In contrast, producers of the same crops in nonadopting regions would receive neither output increases nor greater production stability and therefore would be economically disadvantaged relative to the adopters. In adopting areas, to the extent that farm income stability is increased, farmers should have less need for emergency loans, less need to default on loans, and be able to obtain new loans more easily and on better terms. There would probably be some alteration of cropping patterns caused by readjustments in the market prices of farm products.

Four social impacts of a high capability in hail suppression (model 1) were judged significant by the research team. As noted, agriculture would experience the most significant national effects of an advanced hail suppression capability. Producers in early adopting areas would receive immediate benefits from increased farm output. After a period of adjustment, the economic advantage would be decreased somewhat, but increased stability of income would remain.

Probable effects of successful hail suppression on the hail insurance industry would include benefits caused by increased purchases of insurance (as risk is reduced in high-loss areas) and increased profits because premium reductions would be slower than actual loss reductions. Problems would include shifts in methods of recording losses and the emergence of hail suppression liability insurance. On balance, there would be a slight benefit to the hail insurance industry from an effective suppression capability.

Consumers of agricultural products would benefit through slightly lowered prices. Although the economic benefit to any one individual would be small, the number of individuals benefited would be very large.

Government agencies involved in regulating hail suppression activity, in supporting research and development, and in working out interstate arrangements would experience pressure for implementing these changes. New government entities would develop in these functional areas and in response to the design, operational, and evaluation activities.

Finally, an increased stature for weather modification in general would result from favorable experience with hail suppression in adopting areas. All other impacts of an advanced hail suppression capability were judged minor.

Table 2. Future changes in national agricultural production costs due to hail suppression having different capabilities.

Year	Basic cost of production	Reduction in annual cost					
		Model 1		Model 2		Model 3	
		Dollars*	Percent	Dollars*	Percent	Dollars*	Percent
1985	$15,840	206	1	152	1	0	0
1995	15,850	493	3	263	2	−2	0

*Dollar cost in millions

Table 3. Present values of benefits and costs with various hail suppression capabilities.

Item	Model 1	Model 2	Model 3
Present value of benefits (million dollars)	+2,840.233	+1,715.870	−7.555
Present value of costs (million dollars)	+194.186	+102.758	20.839
Benefit-cost ratio	14.6:1	16.6:1	−0.4:1

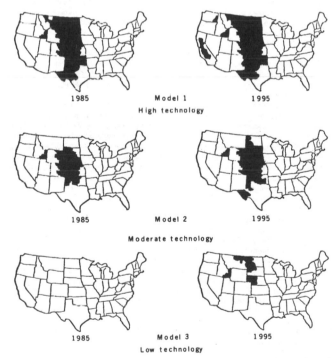

Fig. 3. Three future technological models (1, 2, and 3) with capabilities for hail suppression and modification of rainfall resulting from hail suppression in the western and eastern United States.

Policy Issues

With regard to hail suppression, the most significant policy question at all levels of government is the extent of financial and institutional support for the development of hail suppression technology. Assuming that national goals of ensuring adequate food supplies for the entire population while maintaining environmental quality and other social values are served by (or at least not violated by) an effective hail suppression technology, then the removal of the scientific and technical uncertainties is the major policy action addressed (20).

Removing these uncertainties will require (i) orderly federal management and adequate long-range funding with a lead agency addressing the modification of severe convective storms, and (ii) a scientific research group dedicated to a well-designed program of basic and applied research. The utilization of hail suppression technology will probably not await the final resolution of all scientific uncertainties. Application, discouragement, encouraging research results, scientific argument, and fairly prolonged debate will probably characterize the technology's scientific and technical development.

Four important policy questions were identified in the assessment study.

The first of these concerned the sources of funding. In general, federal funding of research and user funding of operations have been prevailing patterns. However, policy options can involve federal funding of the evaluation of operational projects and taxpayer funding of operations.

A second policy question is whether compensation should be provided for the losers and if so, how. The question of causation has been a substantial barrier to the development of a compensation mechanism, but this difficulty will be overcome with technological and scientific improvements. Several policy options with regard to this question may be considered, but no workable arrangement for compensation has yet been institutionalized.

The third issue concerns the appropriate division of responsibility, between the states and the federal government, in regulating hail suppression. Throughout our study, the atmosphere was considered a common property resource, and thus public regulation of intentional weather modification has been viewed as inevitable. Heretofore, regulation has resided with the state governments; however, regulation might also arise in conjunction with financial regulation in

support of hail suppression design, operation, and evaluation.

The fourth issue deals with monitoring, record keeping, and evaluation. Where operational programs are conducted, a contribution to scientific knowledge can be achieved by adequate data collection, analysis, and evaluation. Policy decisions are needed on who should fund and conduct these evaluations.

In general, policy decisions on hail suppression revolve around two basic issues (i) whether or not to stimulate the further development of hail suppression technology, and (ii) how to handle the implications concomitant with its development and application.

Public Policy Recommendations

The federal government should attempt to develop hail suppression with an approach that will lead to a technology having a high level of effectiveness. Most of the research and development should be the responsibility of a single federal agency having broad control over the whole federal program on planned weather modification. Support of hail suppression research should be at a level of at least $3 million annually and should be sustained for at least 20 years or until it is clear that a highly useful technology is developed or cannot be developed. Low-level support is not warranted.

Operational hail suppression programs should be permitted only under conditions of full disclosure to a governmental agency. Full disclosure includes revelation of all advertising, contract, and promotional material, as well as reports on project effects. Operational projects should be required by law to provide sufficient data to independent government agencies (on a cost-reimbursement basis) so that monitoring and evaluation of project effects will be expedited.

For the present, regulation of hail suppression projects should continue to be a state responsibility. However, federal standards for monitoring and evaluation should be developed and incorporated into state regulations. States should appropriate more funds for the administration of weather modification statutes, especially to allow a more extensive analysis of current records.

The decisions to authorize, interrupt, or discontinue any hail suppression effort should be made at the local and state levels. Such decisions should involve active participation of potentially affected groups and, if tax funds are to be used, it

is possible that all of the citizens within the potentially affected areas should vote on a referendum.

Some type of compensation mechanism is needed to provide for payment to those with legitimate damage claims. Discretion to develop such compensation mechanisms should be left to the states.

Research Recommendations

Advancement of the capability to suppress hail can be wisely accomplished through a two-pronged scientific effort. First, a well-defined experimental analytic research program must be conducted, with strong continuity and a focus on all the atmospheric science issues. It should include efforts to monitor closely and to evaluate operational hail suppression projects, and should also include a continuing program to integrate the findings from both efforts. Second, the storm modification hypotheses of the future must consider the whole convective storm process, to attempt to suppress hail and to reduce associated strong surface winds. These hypotheses should include a simultaneous goal and study of producing no change or an increase in rainfall and to address downwind effects.

Within this recommendation, certain specific basic and applied research activities should be followed including (i) in-cloud measurements throughout the lifetime of storms, (ii) sufficient regional and climatic sampling to ensure transferability of results, and (iii) a study of weather forecasting issues, to improve design and operation of future programs.

The technical aspects of integrating the advanced understanding of atmospheric processes achieved through the studies recommended above should be developed. Aspects such as seeding technologies and delivery systems need further development. A technology assessment of the modification of precipitation should be conducted, since rainfall effects were found to be more important than hail effects in economic and sociopolitical impacts.

Along with research, a comprehensive study of potential compensatory mechanisms that would be economically feasible as well as socially and legally acceptable is needed, to refine further the parameters of feasible and socially acceptable decision-making mechanisms. Work should be continued on the development of a model weather modification law for interested states, and research into possible federal standards for program monitoring and evaluation should be launched.

The specific environmental studies recommended include (i) the effects of altered precipitation on ecosystems; (ii) basic studies on plant and microorganism adaptation to seeding agents; (iii) the potential for combination of seeding agent silver with other metals, pesticides, power plant emission products, and other pollution sources; (iv) tracer studies of nucleants in seeded storm cells to locate their deposition in the environment; and (v) long-term monitoring of silver levels and dynamics in the soil-plant-aquatic environment before and after cloud-seeding activities.

Several of our findings indicate that scientific research and policy research efforts should be continued as well as monitoring and reevaluation of effects. A continuing assessment of the nation's hail suppression capability should occur in the years ahead.

References and Notes

1. D. Atlas, *Science* **195**, 139 (1977).
2. S. Changnon, *Bull. Am. Meteorol. Soc.* **58**, 20 (1977).
3. B. Farhar, Ed., *Hail Suppression: Society and Environment* (monograph 24, Institute of Behavioral Science, University of Colorado, Boulder, 1977).
4. _____ and J. Mewes, *Social Acceptance of Weather Modification: The Emergent South Dakota Controversy* (monograph 23, Institute of Behavioral Science, University of Colorado, Boulder, 1976), pp. 10-15.
5. J. Mewes and B. Farhar, in (*3*), pp. 35-45; M. Smith, B. Farhar, J. Mewes, R. Davis, S. Cox, in *ibid.*, pp. 124-155; S. Cox and S. Hernandez, in *ibid.*, pp. 156-170; S. Hernandez and T. Toll, in *ibid.*, pp. 171-188; G. Fletcher, in *ibid.*, pp. 189-195; R. Davis, in *Weather and Climate Modification*, W. Hess, Ed. (Wiley, New York, 1974), pp. 767-786.
6. J. Mewes, in (*3*), pp. 80-95 and 103-116.
7. G. H. Stever, Phi Beta Kappa Lecture, Washington, D.C., 18 May 1973; S. Changnon, *Bull. Am. Meteorol. Soc.* **56**, 27 (1975); *ibid.* **57**, 234 (1976).
8. The other major contributors to this assessment study, with their specialty areas in parentheses, were R. Davis (law), E. Fosse (crop insurance), D. Friedman (property insurance), J. Haas (sociology), T. Henderson (weather modification practices), J. Ivens (science writer), M. Jones (technology assessment), D. Klein (ecology), D. Mann (political science), G. Morgan (meteorology), S. Sonka (economics), C. Taylor (economics), and J. Van Blokland (economics).
9. S. Changnon, *J. Appl. Meteorol.* **16**, 837 (1977).
10. L. Boone, *Estimating Crop Losses due to Hail* (Agricultural Economics Report 267, U.S. Department of Agriculture, Washington, D.C. 1974), pp. 4-40; S. Changnon, *J. Appl. Meteorol.* **11**, 1128 (1972); E. Fosse, *Impacts of Effective Hail Suppression on Crop Insurance Industry and Probable Policy Action Response* (Report of Crop-Hail Insurance Actuarial Association, Chicago, 1976), pp. 4-41; D. Friedman, *Hail Suppression Impact Upon Property Insurance* (Report of the Travelers Insurance Company, Hartford, Conn., 1976), pp. 1-69.
11. W. Brinkmann, *Severe Local Storm Hazard in the United States: A Research Assessment* (Institute of Behavioral Science, University of Colorado, Boulder, 1975), pp. 1-154.
12. V. Schaefer, *J. Weather Mod.* **8**, 5 (1976).
13. B. Farhar, thesis, University of Colorado, Boulder (1975).
14. Committee on Atmospheric Science, *Weather and Climate Modification, Problems and Progress* (National Academy of Sciences, Washington, D.C., 1973) pp. 100-106; *Bull. Am. Meteorol. Soc.* **54**, 694 (1973); L. Grand and J. Reid, *Workshop for an Assessment of the Present and Potential Role of Weather Modification in Agricultural Production* (Atmospheric Sciences Paper 236, Colorado State University, Fort Collins, 1975), pp. 38-236.
15. S. Changnon and G. Morgan, *J. Weather Mod.* **8**, 164 (1976).
16. B. Farhar and J. Clark, in preparation. Scientific opinion could have changed since these 1975 cross-sectional surveys [see also (*15*)], as a result of maturation and developments in the field. However, it is unlikely that it would have changed sufficiently to define hail suppression as a currently feasible and certain technology.
17. J. Haas, *Bull. Am. Meteorol. Soc.* **54**, (No. 7), 647 (1973); B. Farhar, *Mass Emergencies* **1**, 313 (1976).
18. D. Pfost, in (*3*), pp. 117-123.
19. E. Rogers and F. Shoemaker, *Communication of Innovations* (Free Press, New York, 1971); B. Farhar, "Public reaction to weather modifica-

tion," paper presented National Science Foundation Advisory Panel Meeting, Boulder, Colo., 14 July 1975.
20. S. Changnon *et al.*, *Hail Suppression Impacts and Issues* (Report of Illinois State Water Survey, Urbana, 1977), pp. 1-442.
21. S. Krane, *Social Implications of the National Hail Research Experiment: A Longitudinal Study* (Human Ecology Research Services, Boulder, Colo., 1976); B. Farhar and J. Mewes, *Weather Modification and Public Opinion: South Dakota, 1973, Second Interim Report* (Institute of Behavioral Science, University of Colorado, Boulder, 1974).
22. B. Farhar, "The locus of control of weather modification: scientists vs. citizens," paper presented at the Midwest Sociological Society Meeting, Minneapolis, 15 April 1977.
23. D. Mann and B. Farhar, in (*3*), pp. 196-218.
24. B. Farhar, R. Rinkle, G. Johnson, "Cloud seeding in California: risk, control and citizen response," paper presented at the Pacific Sociological Society Meetings, Sacramento, 21 April 1977.
25. R. Davis, *Hydrology and Water Resources in Arizona and Southwest* (Proceedings 1975 Meeting of AWWA and Hydrology Section of Arizona Academy of Sciences, Tucson, 1976), vol. 6, pp. 48-64.
26. R. Davis, paper presented at National Convention of American Society of Civil Engineers, Denver, 10 December 1975.
27. D. Klein, *J. Appl. Meteorol.* **14**, 673 (1975); C. Cooper, *Modifying the Weather, A Social Assessment* (University of Victoria, Victoria, British Columbia, 1973), pp. 99-134.
28. S. Changnon, paper presented at the AAAS Annual Meeting, Denver, 22 February 1977.
29. C. Taylor and E. Swanson, *The Economic Impact of Selected Nitrogen Restrictions* (AERR-133, Department of Agricultural Economics, University of Illinois, Urbana, 1975); C. Taylor, P. Van Blokland, E. Swanson, K. Frohberg, *Two National-Equilibrium Models of Crop Production* (AERR-147, Department of Agricultural Economics, University of Illinois, Urbana, 1977).
30. We thank R. Davis, J. Haas, J. Ivens, M. Jones, D. Klein, D. Mann, G. Morgan, S. Sonka, C. Taylor, and J. Van Blokland. Many others gave support and critical reviews, including W. Ackermann and 34 attendees at a user's workshop; and the members of the advisory panel including S. Borland, E. Bollay, J. Fivor, W. Fowler, W. Thomas, and C. Wolf. Many students contributed to the background research, and two theses based on various elements of the study were awarded at the University of Illinois. This work was supported by grant ERP 75-09980 from the National Science Foundation and by the State of Illinois.

Part VI
Reducing Risks through Self-Protection

[21]

Market Insurance, Self-Insurance, and Self-Protection

Isaac Ehrlich

University of Chicago and Tel-Aviv University

Gary S. Becker

University of Chicago

The article develops a theory of demand for insurance that emphasizes the interaction between market insurance, "self-insurance," and "self-protection." The effects of changes in "prices," income, and other variables on the demand for these alternative forms of insurance are analyzed using the "state preference" approach to behavior under uncertainty. Market insurance and self-insurance are shown to be substitutes, but market insurance and self-protection can be complements. The analysis challenges the notion that "moral hazard" is an inevitable consequence of market insurance, by showing that under certain conditions the latter may lead to a reduction in the probabilities of hazardous events.

The incentive to insure and its behavioral implications have usually been analyzed by applying the expected utility approach without reference to the indifference curve analysis ordinarily employed in consumption theory. In this paper insurance is discussed by combining expected utility and an indifference curve analysis within the context of the "state preference" approach to behavior under uncertainty (the preferences in question relating to states of the world).[1] We use this framework to restate

Becker's contribution was primarily an unpublished paper that sets out the approach developed here. Ehrlich greatly extended and applied that approach and was primarily responsible for writing this paper. We have had many helpful comments from Harold Demsetz, Jacques Drèze, Jack Hirshleifer, and members of the Labor Workshop at Columbia University and the Industrial Organization Workshop at the University of Chicago.

[1] An approach originally devised by Arrow (1963–64) and worked out in application to investment decisions under uncertainty by Hirshleifer (1970).

and reinterpret in a simpler and more intuitive way some familiar propositions concerning insurance behavior; more important, we derive a number
of apparently new results, especially those concerned with self-insurance
and self-protection. Our approach separates objective opportunities
from "taste" and other environmental factors, which facilitates an independent investigation of each class of factors analytically as well as
empirically. In addition, we consider not only the incentive to insure,
but also how much insurance is purchased under varying "opportunities"[2]
and in view of the existence of the alternatives of self-insurance and self-
protection. We use the basic analytical tools employed throughout traditional consumption and production theory.

It has been argued that insurance is different from "ordinary" goods
and services because it is not desired per se, but as a means of satisfying
more basic needs.[3] Recent developments in consumption theory[4] suggest,
however, that the distinction between goods and services purchased in the
market and more basic needs they satisfy is not a unique characteristic of
insurance, but applies to all goods and services. The demand for the
latter is also derived from the needs they satisfy, just as the demand for
factors of production in ordinary production theory is derived from their
contribution to final products.

The basic needs underlying the purchase of insurance will be identified
with consumption opportunities contingent upon the occurrence of various
mutually exclusive and jointly exhaustive "states of the world."[5] Market
insurance in this approach redistributes income and, consequently, consumption opportunities, toward the less well-endowed states. Self-insurance,
however, redistributes income similarly, self-protection has a related
effect, and either might be pursued when market insurance was not available. Moreover, optimal decisions about market insurance depend on the
availability of these other activities and should be viewed within the context of a more comprehensive "insurance" decision.

----

[2] Theorems concerning optimal insurance decisions have been derived in two recent
contributions by Smith (1968) and Mossin (1968). Our approach differs not only in
form but also in substance; for example, in the analysis of the interaction between
market insurance, self-insurance, and self-protection.

[3] For example, Arrow (1965) says, "Insurance is not a material good . . . its value
to the buyer is clearly different in kind from the satisfaction of consumer's desires
for medical treatment or transportation. Indeed, unlike goods and services, transactions involving insurance are an exchange of money for money, not money for
something which directly meets needs" (p. 45).

[4] See, for example, Becker and Michael (1970).

[5] By consumption opportunities in each state of the world is meant command over
commodities, C_i, produced by combining market goods, X_i, time spent in consumption,
t_i, and the "state environment," E_i, via household production functions (for the latter
concept see Becker and Michael 1970): $C_{ij} = f_{ij}(X_{ij}, t_{ij}, E_i)$ $j = 1, \ldots, m$ where j
refers to different commodities. If the production functions fully incorporate the effects
of environment, the utility function of commodities would not depend on which state
occurred. In particular, for an aggregate commodity C, $U(C_0) = U(C_1)$ if $C_0 = 1$,
where 0, 1 denote different states.

The first part of this paper spells out a model of market insurance and discusses the effects of changes in terms of trade, "income," and other environmental factors on optimal insurance decisions. Self-insurance, self-protection, and a simultaneous determination of the full insurance decision are then discussed in the second and more original part.

I. Market Insurance

We assume for simplicity that an individual is faced with only two states of the world $(0, 1)$ with probabilities p and $1 - p$, respectively, and that his real income endowment in each state is given with certainty by I_o^e and I_1^e, where $I_1^e - I_o^e$ is the prospective loss if state 0 occurs. If income in state 1 can be exchanged for income in state 0 at the fixed rate

$$-\frac{dI_1}{dI_0} = \pi, \tag{1}$$

π can be called the "price of insurance" measured in terms of income in state 1. The amount of insurance purchased in state 0 can be defined as the difference between the actual and endowed incomes:[6]

$$s = I_0 - I_0^e. \tag{2}$$

The expenditure on insurance measured in terms of state 1's income is

$$b = I_1^e - I_1 = s\pi. \tag{3}$$

Substituting (2) in (3) gives the opportunity boundary

$$I_1^e - I_1 = \pi(I_0 - I_0^e), \tag{4}$$

or the line $\overline{AB}$ in figure 1.[7] It is assumed that the individual chooses the optimal income in states 1 and 0 by maximizing the expected utility of the income prospect,

$$U^* = (1 - p)\, U(I_1) + p\, U(I_0),[8] \tag{5}$$

subject to the constraint given by the opportunity boundary. The first-order optimality condition is

$$\pi = \frac{p\, U_0'}{(1 - p) U_1'}, \tag{6}$$

---

[6] Note that insurance is defined not in terms of the liability "coverage" of potential losses, as in Smith's (1968) and Mossin's (1968) papers, but in terms of "coverage minus premium," or the net addition to income in state 0.

[7] In figure 1, the opportunity boundary $\overline{AB}$ is drawn as a straight line. This assumes that the same terms of trade apply to both insurance and "gambling," that is, to movements to the right and to the left of E, the endowment position. In practice, the opportunity boundary may be kinked about the endowment point.

[8] For analytical simplicity we ignore the time and environment inputs and assume only a single aggregate commodity in each state. Then the output of commodities can be identified with the input of goods and services, or with income.

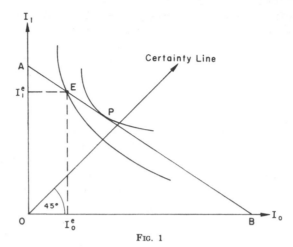

FIG. 1

where $(pU_0')/(1-p)U_1'$ is the slope of the indifference curve (defined along $dU^* = 0$), and π is the slope of the budget line. In equilibrium, they must be the same (see point P).

One can more completely separate tastes from environmental factors by dividing $p/(1-p)$ through in (6) to obtain

$$\bar{\pi} = \frac{1-p}{p}\ \pi = \frac{U_0'}{U_1'}. \tag{7}$$

Further, $\bar{\pi}$, the price of insurance deflated by the actuarially "fair"[9] price, $p/(1-p)$, is a measure of the "real" price of insurance because a fair price is "costless" to the individual (see the second paragraph below). Equation (7) thus implies that, in equilibrium, the real price of insurance equals the ratio of the marginal utility of I_0 to that of I_1, the ordinary result in consumer demand theory.

The second-order condition requires that the indifference curve be convex to the origin at the equilibrium point, or

$$D = -p\,U_0'' - \pi^2\,(1-p)\,U_1'' > 0. \tag{8}$$

A sufficient condition is that the marginal utility of income is strictly declining.[10]

An immediate implication of equation (7) is that insurance would be

[9] An actuarially fair exchange is an exchange of $p/(1-p)$ units of income in state 1 for an additional unit of income in state 0, where $p/(1-p)$ is the odds that state 0 would occur.

[10] Hirshleifer (1970, p. 233) points out that although diminishing marginal utility of income is not a necessary condition for equilibrum at any given point, it is a necessary condition for the indifference curve to be convex at all points.

demanded—some I_1 would be traded for I_0—if the slope of the indifference curve exceeded the price of insurance at the endowment point, E:

$$\bar{\pi} < \frac{U'(I_0{}^e)}{U'(I_1{}^e)}. \qquad (9)$$

If the opposite were true, "gambling" would be demanded, provided similar terms of trade apply in redistributions of income toward state 1. Note that gambling can occur without increasing marginal utility of income if the opportunities available are sufficiently favorable. Therefore, inferences about attitudes toward risk cannot be made independently of existing market opportunities: a person may appear to be a "risk avoider" under one combination of prices and potential losses and a "risk taker" under another.[11]

If the price of insurance were actuarially fair, equation (7) would reduce to $1 = U_0'/U_1'$: incomes would be equalized in both states of the world if the marginal utility of income were always diminishing. This is "full insurance" in the sense that a person would be indifferent as to which state occurred.[12] In particular, for small changes around the equilibrium position, he would act as if he were indifferent toward risk and interested only in maximizing his expected income. Indeed, his income in each state would equal his expected income;[13] therefore, fair insurance can be regarded as costless to him.[14]

---

[11] Indeed, when faced with several independent hazards, a person might "gamble" and "insure" at the same time, provided the different hazards were associated with different opportunities. For example, given a fair price of theft insurance, he may fully insure his household against theft and at the same time engage in a risky activity if his expected earnings there were greater than his earnings in alternative "safe" activities (see Ehrlich 1970).

[12] Full insurance can be identified with full coverage of potential losses, since the equation $I_1 = I_0$ implies that $I_1{}^e - b = I_0{}^e + d - b$, where d is the gross coverage and b is the premium. Clearly, then, $d = I_1{}^e - I_0{}^e$. By the same reasoning, since an "unfair" price of insurance $\bar{\pi} > 1$ implies that $I_1 > I_0$, it also implies necessarily less than full coverage of potential losses.

[13] If $I_0 = I_1 = I$ that is, $I_1 = I_1{}^e - s\,\pi = I_0 = I_0{}^e + s$, where $\pi = p/(1-p)$, then $I = p\,I_0{}^e + (1-p)\,I_1{}^e$.

[14] Although the model has been developed for two states of the world, the analysis applies equally well to n states. We define the state with the highest income—say, state n—as the state without hazard and define all the states with hazard ($h = 1, \ldots, n-1$) relative to that state. Denoting by p_h the probability of state h, by

$$p = 1 - \sum_{h=1}^{n-1} p_h$$

the probability of state n, and by π_h the implicit terms of trade between income in state n and income in state h, it can easily be shown that if the terms of trade were fair ($\bar{\pi}_h = [p/p_h]\,\pi_h = 1$) s_h would be chosen to equalize incomes in all states of the world and losses would be "fully covered." If the real terms of trade were unfair but

A. Substitution Effects

The effect of an exogenous increase in the price of insurance on the demand for I_0, with the probability of loss and the initial endowment being the same, can be found by partially differentiating the first-order optimality condition with respect to π:

$$\frac{\partial I_0}{\partial \pi} = \frac{1}{D} \left[-(1-p)\, U_1' + (I_0 - I_0{}^e)\, \pi\, (1-p)\, U_1'' \right]. \quad (10)$$

Since the denominator D has already been shown to be positive, the sign of equation (10) is the same as the sign of the numerator, or negative if $I_0 > I_0{}^e$, since we are assuming $U_1'' \lessgtr 0$. An increase in the relative cost of income in state 0 necessarily decreases the demand for income in this state. Moreover, it also reduces the amount of insurance purchased, since $I_0{}^e$ remains unchanged: $\partial s/\partial \pi = \partial I_0/\partial \pi - \partial I_0{}^e/\partial \pi = \partial I_0/\partial \pi$.

Similarly, the effect of an increase in π on I_1, and thus on the amount spent on insurance, is

$$\frac{\partial I_1}{\partial \pi} = \frac{1}{D} \left[(1-p)\, U_1'\, \pi + (I_0 - I_0{}^e)\, p\, U_0'' \right]. \quad (11)$$

Here the result is ambiguous since U_1' is positive whereas

$$(I_0 - I_0{}^e)\, p U_0'' = s p U_0''$$

is negative if $U_0'' < 0$ and $s > 0$. The result is ambiguous because, although an increase in π reduces the amount of insurance purchased, each unit purchased becomes more expensive. Consequently, the amount spent on insurance would decline only if the price elasticity of demand for insurance exceeded unity[15] (a proof is obvious).

Equations (10) and (11) do not isolate a "pure" substitution effect because an increase in π lowers the opportunities available (if $s > 0$). If both I_1 and I_0 are superior goods, the income and substitution effects both reduce the demand for I_0, whereas they have opposite effects on the demand for I_1. Diagrammatically, as the opportunity boundary changes from $\overline{AB}$ to $\overline{CD}$ (see fig. 2), the equilibrium point shifts from P to Q. If I_0 were a superior good, Q must be to the left of P'. Even if I_0 were an inferior good, however, a "pure" (that is, expenditure-compensated) increase in the terms of trade must always reduce the demand for I_0 and increase I_1: the equilibrium must shift from P to a point to its left, like S.

---

constant ($\bar{\pi}_h = \pi = 1 + \lambda > 1$ for all h), s_h would be chosen to equalize incomes in states with hazard only, that is, we would achieve what has been called full insurance above a deductible (for a definition of this concept and an alternative proof see Arrow 1963).

[15] This analysis, therefore, also shows that the effect of a change in π on the "fullness" of insurance (the difference $I_1 - I_0$) and thus on the degree of gross coverage is generally not unambiguous.

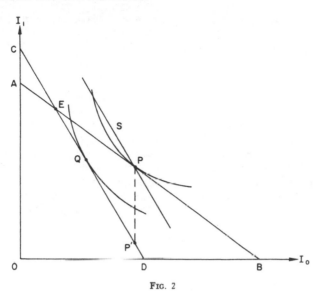

FIG. 2

B. Income Effects

Equation (4) can be written as

$$I_1^e + \pi I_0^e = W = I_1 + \pi I_0, \tag{12}$$

where W is a measure of the total opportunities available. (This is shown in fig. 1 by the intercept $\overline{OA}$ on the I_1 axis.) The effect of a change in the endowments on the income demanded in each state can be determined by differentiating the first-order condition:

$$\frac{\partial I_0}{\partial W} = \frac{\partial I_0}{\partial I_0^e} = \frac{\partial I_0}{\partial I_1^e} \frac{\partial I_0^e}{\partial W} = -\frac{D_{31}}{D}$$

$$\frac{\partial I_1}{\partial W} = \frac{\partial I_1}{\partial I_0^e} = \frac{\partial I_1}{\partial I_1^e} \frac{\partial I_0^e}{\partial W} = -\frac{D_{32}}{D} \tag{13}$$

where $D_{31} = \pi(1 - p)U_1''$, and $D_{32} = pU_0''$. The income demanded in each state necessarily increases with opportunities if the marginal utility of income is falling. Hence, an increase in each state's endowment increases the demand for income in other states as well. The effects on the demand for insurance are more complicated, however, since they depend on how different endowments change. For example, if I_1^e alone increased,

$$\frac{\partial s}{\partial I_1^e} = \frac{\partial I_0}{\partial I_1^e} > 0, \tag{14}$$

and the demand for insurance would increase. Similarly, if $I_0{}^e$ alone increased,

$$\frac{\partial s}{\partial I_0{}^e} = \frac{\partial I_0}{\partial I_0{}^e} - 1 < 0,^{[16]} \tag{15}$$

and the demand for insurance would decrease. Equations (14) and (15) imply that if the difference in endowed income—the endowed loss from the hazard—increased either because $I_0{}^e$ decreased or $I_1{}^e$ increased, the demand for insurance would increase. Put differently, a person would be more likely to insure large rather than small losses (see Lees and Rice 1965).[17] The effects of a change in total opportunities on the demand for insurance cannot be derived without knowledge of the way opportunities change essentially because insurance is a "residual" that bridges the gap between endowed and desired levels of income in different states of the world.[18]

For example, if both endowments (and hence the size of the loss) are changed by the same percentage, then

$$(\varepsilon_{sW} - 1) = \frac{I_0}{s}\,(\eta_0 - 1), \tag{16}$$

where $\varepsilon_{sW} = \partial s/\partial W \cdot W/s$ and $\eta_0 = \partial I_0/\partial W \cdot W/I_0$ are the opportunity elasticities of demand for s and I_0, respectively.[19]

Equation (16) incorporates the rather obvious conclusion that the effect of a change in opportunities on the demand for insurance depends on the effects on the income demanded in each state. If the slopes of the indifference curves are constant along a given ray from the origin (the indifference curves are like EPF and GQ_1H in fig. 3)—there is constant

---

[16] According to equation (13), $\partial I_0/\partial I_0{}^e = [-\pi^2\,(1-p)\,U_1{}'']/[-pU_0{}'' - \pi^2\,(1 - p)\,U_1{}''] = \delta$, where clearly $0 < \delta < 1$ if $U_1{}''$ and $U_0{}'' < 0$. But since $s = I_0 - I_0{}^e$, $\partial s/\partial I_0{}^e = \delta - 1 < 0$.

[17] Similarly, he would be less likely to take large gambles (see the discussion in Hirshleifer 1966). Of course, if insurance is fair he will fully insure all losses, large or small.

[18] Note the analogy between insurance and savings: the latter bridges the gap between "endowed" and desired levels of consumption at different points in time.

[19] Given $s = I_0 - I_0{}^e$ and $I_1{}^e = \gamma I_0{}^e$, then $(\partial s/\partial W)(W/s) = (ds/dI_0{}^e)(I_0{}^e/s) = \eta_0\,(I_0/s) - (I_0{}^e/s)$; by collecting terms, we get equation (16). Since $I_0 \geqslant s$, $\varepsilon_{sW} \geqslant 1$ if $\eta_0 \geqslant 1$.

If the loss is unaffected by an equal increase in endowments, that is, if $I_0{}^e = I_1{}^e - L$ where L is a constant, then $\varepsilon_{se} = (ds/dI_1{}^e)(I_1{}^e/s) = (I_0/s)\eta_0\,(d\log W)/(d\log I_1{}^e) - (I_1{}^e/s)$. This implies that

$$\varepsilon_{se} \gtrless 0 \quad \text{as} \quad \eta_0 \gtrless \frac{W}{I_0(1+\pi)} \geqslant 1 \quad (\text{if } I_1 \geqslant I_0). \tag{16a}$$

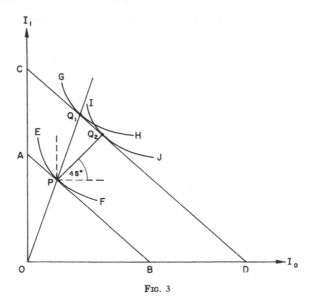

FIG. 3

relative risk aversion[20]—then all equilibrium positions lie on a given ray from the origin, as P and Q_1 do in figure 3, and $\eta_0 = \eta_1 = 1$. An equal proportional increase in all endowments would then increase the demand for insurance by the same proportion. If the slopes of the indifference

[20] Note that

$$\frac{d \text{ slope}}{dI_0} = \frac{d}{dI_0} \left[\frac{pU_0'}{(1-p)U_1'} \right]$$

subject to $I_1 = \gamma I_0$ *is* $\gtreqless 0$ as $-(U_1''/U_1') \; \gamma \gtreqless -(U_0''/U_0')$; the latter defines increasing, constant, or decreasing relative risk aversion. Similarly

$$\frac{d}{dI_0} \left[\frac{pU_0'}{(1-p)U_1'} \right]$$

subject to $I_1 - I_0 = L$ is $\gtreqless 0$ as $-(U_1''/U_1') \gtreqless -(U_0''/U_0')$; the latter defines increasing, constant, or decreasing absolute risk aversion (see Pratt 1964, Arrow 1965). (Diagramatically, constant absolute risk aversion implies that the slopes of the indifference curves are constant along any 45° line joining two equilibrium positions—the indifference curves are like EPF and IQ_2J in fig. 3.) Equation (16a) in n.19 implies that increasing relative risk aversion, $\eta_0 > 1$, is compatible with decreasing absolute risk aversion, $\epsilon_{se} < 0$, only if $\eta_0 < W/I_0(1 + \pi)$.

curves increase along a given ray from the origin, as shown by *EPF* and *IQ₂J* in figure 3, there is increasing relative risk aversion, and η_0 and thus ε_{sw} would exceed unity. Increasing relative risk aversion implies that the elasticity of substitution between I_0 and I_1 tends to decline as opportunities increase.[21] Regardless of the shape of preferences elsewhere in the preference space, however, relative (and absolute) risk aversion remains constant along the certainty line. This constancy always characterizes choices when the price of insurance is actuarially fair (see fig. 4).

C. Rare Losses

An inspection of the necessary conditions for insurance given in equation (9) shows that changes in p, the probability of loss, do not affect the incentive to insure as long as the real price of insurance is independent of p. If insurance were actuarially fair, the real price would always equal unity, and thus would be independent of p.

The deviation from a fair price, or the "loading" in insurance terminology, can be defined from the identity

$$\pi \equiv \frac{(1+\lambda)\,p}{1-p}, \tag{17}$$

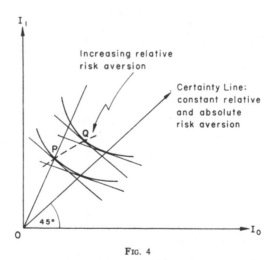

Fɪɢ. 4

---

[21] Since the slopes of the indifference curves necessarily are constant along the "certainty line" and by assumption become increasingly steep toward I_0 along other rays from the origin, a given percentage deviation of the price of insurance from the fair price results in smaller percentage changes in the ratio I_1/I_0 at higher indifference levels. That is, $\sigma = (d \log I_1/I_0)/d \log \pi$ decreases at higher indifference levels when π equals the fair price.

where λ is the "loading factor." If λ were independent of p, so also would be the real price of insurance and p would have no effect on the incentive to insure. In particular, there would *not* then be a greater incentive to insure "rare" losses of a given size.[22]

Since, apparently, rare losses are more frequently insured,[23] λ is presumably positively related to p, perhaps because processing and investigating costs increase as p increases.[24] (An alternative explanation is provided by the interaction between market and self-insurance analyzed in the next section.) Even if the *incentive* to insure were independent of p, the *amount* insured would decline and the expenditure on insurance would increase as p increased.[25]

II. Self-Insurance and Self-Protection

Two alternatives to market insurance that have not been systematically analyzed in the literature on insurance are self-insurance—a reduction in the size of a loss—and self-protection—a reduction in the probability of a loss.[26] For example, sprinkler systems reduce the loss from fires; burglar alarms reduce the probability of illegal entry; cash balances reduce fluctuations in consumption; medicines, certain foods, and medical

---

[22] This result appears to contradict one by Lees and Rice (1965) because they define the loading factor in terms of the gross rather than net amount paid in claim; that is by λ' in $\pi = [(1 + \lambda') \, p]/[1 - (1 + \lambda') \, p]$. A reduction in p, λ' held constant, would reduce λ—our definition of the loading factor—and thus would increase the incentive to insure.

[23] Some evidence is presented in Lees and Rice (1965).

[24] Let the amount a that is spent processing and investigating each claim be the only administrative cost of providing insurance. In a zero profit equilibrium position, the unit price of insurance would equal the ratio of the total amount collected in premiums in state 1 (including administration costs) to the difference between the net amount paid in claims in state 0 and administration costs: $\pi = (p \, d + p \, a)/[d \, (1 - p) - p \, a]$, where d is the amount covered by insurance. The degree of loading defined by $\lambda = [(1 - p)/p] \, \pi - 1 = (d + a)/[d - p \, a/(1 - p)] - 1 = a/[d - p \, (d + a)]$ would be larger the larger p was if d were fixed (d would tend to decrease as p increased, and this would increase λ even further).

[25] Generally, the effect of an increase in p on the optimal values of I_0 and I_1, assuming that $\pi = [(1 + \lambda) \, p]/(1 - p)$ and that λ, I^e_0, and I^e_1 are constant, is given by

$$\frac{\partial I_0}{\partial p} = \frac{1}{D} \left[U_1'' s \, \pi \, \frac{1 + \lambda}{1 - p} \right] < 0$$

$$\frac{\partial I_1}{\partial p} = \frac{1}{D} \left[U_0'' s \, \pi \, \frac{1}{1 - p} \right] < 0$$

provided $U'' < 0$. An increase in p would then lower the optimal amount of insurance $s = I_0 - I_0{}^e$ and increase the optimal expenditure on insurance $b = I_1{}^e - I_1$.

[26] These have been called "loss protection" and "loss prevention," respectively (see Mehr and Commack 1966, pp. 28–29).

checkups reduce vulnerability to illness; and good lawyers reduce both the probability of conviction and the punishment for crime. As these examples indicate, it is somewhat artificial to distinguish behavior that reduces the probability of a loss from behavior that reduces the size of a loss, since many actions do both. Nevertheless, we do so for expository convenience and because self-insurance clearly illustrates the insurance principle of redistributing income toward less favorable states.

A. Self-Insurance

Assume that market insurance is unavailable and write the loss to a person as $L = L(L^e, c)$, where $L^e = I_1{}^e - I_0{}^e$ is the endowed loss, c is the expenditure on self-insurance, and $\dfrac{\partial L}{\partial c} = L'(c) \leqslant 0$. The expected utility can be written as

$$U^* = (1 - p)\, U(I_1{}^e - c) + p\, U(I_1{}^e - L(L^e, c) - c).^{27} \quad (18)$$

The value of c that maximizes equation (18), c^0, satisfies the first-order condition

$$-\frac{1}{L'(c^0) + 1} = \frac{p\, U_0'}{(1 - p)\, U_1'}. \quad (19)$$

This maximizes expected utility if the marginal utility of income and the marginal productivity of self-insurance are decreasing, that is, if the indifference curves are convex and if the production transformation curve between income in states 1 and 0 (TN in fig. 5) is concave to the origin.[28] A necessary condition for a positive amount of self-insurance obviously is $-L'(c^0) > 1$, or that there be a net addition to income in state 0. A sufficient condition, if the transformation and indifference curves do not have kinks, is that

$$-\frac{1}{L'(L^e, 0) + 1} < \frac{p\, U'(I_0{}^e)}{(1 - p)\, U'(I_1{}^e)}.^{29} \quad (20)$$

An increase in the unit cost of self-insurance, measured by the marginal

---

[27] For analytical convenience we assume that $I_0{}^e$ alone is affected by c, although, of course, both endowments may be affected. Moreover, the assumption that $\partial L/\partial c \leqslant 0$ is not always true: an individual could increase $I_1{}^e$ and reduce $I_0{}^e$ by deliberately exposing himself to hazards; for example, by committing a crime or engaging in a risky legal occupation (see Ehrlich 1970). The condition $\partial L/\partial c > 0$ can be said to define "negative self-insurance."

[28] See equation (A5). Note that the transformation curve may be kinked at the endowment point.

[29] If the opposite were true, there would be an incentive to increase the loss by increasing I_1 and reducing I_0 (see n. 27 above).

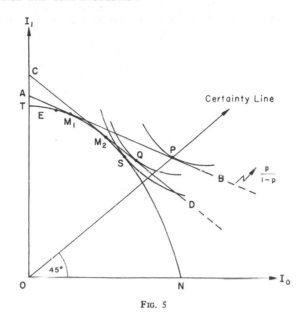

FIG. 5

productivity of self-insurance, would reduce the demand for self-insurance, measured by c^0:[30]

$$\frac{\partial c^0}{\partial \alpha} < 0,^{31} \tag{21}$$

where α is a parameter that reduces the absolute value of L' for a given c. Similarly, a reduction in I_0^e would increase the demand for self-insurance:

$$-\frac{\partial c^0}{\partial I_0^e} > 0.^{32} \tag{22}$$

Equation (20) shows clearly that the incentive to self-insure, unlike the incentive to use market insurance, is smaller for rare losses. The reason is that the loading factor of self-insurance is *larger* for rare losses because

---

[30] Although c denotes the expenditure on self-insurance rather than the reduction in the size of the loss, there is a one-to-one relationship between expenditure and insurance because $-L'(c) > 1$.

[31] By differentiating equation (19) with respect to α—p, I_0^e and I_1^e held constant—one obtains $\partial c^0/\partial \alpha = (pU_0'/U^*_{cc})(\partial L'/\partial \alpha) = (+)/(-) < 0$, where $U^*_{cc} = \partial^2 U^*/\partial c^2 < 0$ (see Appendix A), and by assumption $\partial L'/\partial \alpha > 0$.

[32] By differentiating equation (19) with respect to $I_0^e - I_1^e$, p and L' held constant, one obtains $-\partial c^0/\partial I_0^e = \partial c^0/\partial L^e = -\{pU_0''[L'(c) + 1]/U^*_{cc}\} \ \partial L/\partial L^e = (-)/(-) > 0$, where by assumption $\partial L/\partial L^e > 0$.

its price, unlike the price of market insurance, can be presumed to be independent of the probability of loss.[33]

An increase in endowed incomes that resulted from investment in human capital would probably be associated with an increase in the marginal productivity of self-insurance.[34] Therefore, the effect on self-insurance of a change in income has to be separated from the effect of the associated change in marginal productivity.

If market and self-insurance were both available, values of c and s would be chosen simultaneously to maximize the expected utility function,

$$U^* = (1 - p) \, U(I_1{}^e - c - s \, \pi) + p \, U(I_1{}^e - L(L^e, c) - c + s). \tag{23}$$

If the price of market insurance were independent of the amount of self-insurance, the first-order optimality conditions would be

$$- (1 - p) \, U_1{}' \, \pi + p \, U_0{}' = 0. \tag{24}$$

$$- (1 - p) \, U_1{}' - p \, U_0{}' [L'(c) + 1] = 0.$$

By combining these equations we get

$$\pi = - \frac{1}{L'(c) + 1}. \tag{25}$$

In equilibrium, therefore, the "shadow price" of self-insurance would equal the price of market insurance.

Clearly, market insurance and self-insurance are "substitutes" in the sense that an increase in π, the probability of loss being the same, would decrease the demand for market insurance and increase the demand for self-insurance.[35] For example, a change in the market insurance line from $\overline{AB}$ to $\overline{CD}$ in figure 5 would increase self-insurance by the horizontal distance between M_1 and M_2 and reduce market insurance by the horizontal distance between Q and P. In particular, the purchase of market insurance would reduce the demand for self-insurance—compare points S and, say, M_1.

When market insurance is available at a fair price, the equilibrium condition (25) becomes

$$- \frac{1}{L'(c) + 1} = \frac{p}{1 - p},$$

or   (26)

---

[33] The price of self-insurance is given by $\pi = - 1/[L'(c) + 1]$, where $L'(c)$ presumably does not depend on p. The loading factor is then given by $\lambda = - \{1/[L'(c) + 1]\} \, [(1 - p)/p] - 1$. Hence $\partial \lambda / \partial p < 0$.

[34] That is, not only would $\partial I_i{}^e / \partial E > 0$ $i = 0, 1$ where E is the stock of human capital, but probably also $\partial^2 L / \partial c \partial E < 0$.

[35] A mathematical proof can be found in Appendix A.

$$- L'(c) = \frac{1}{p},$$

precisely the condition that maximizes expected income.[36] Even with diminishing marginal utility of income, a person would act as if he were risk neutral and choose the amount of self-insurance that maximized his expected income. Consequently, apparent attitudes toward risk are dependent on market opportunities, and real attitudes cannot easily be inferred from behavior.

More generally, even if the price of market insurance were not fair, the optimal amount of self-insurance would maximize the market value of income (given by W in equation [12]), and would not depend on the shape of the indifference curves or even on the probability distribution of states.[37] Geometrically, optimal self-insurance is determined by moving along the transformation curve in figure 5 to the point of tangency between this curve and a market insurance line; since the market value of income is the intercept on the y-axis, that intercept would be maximized at such point of tangency.

The effects of specific parameters on the demand for market and self-insurance when both are available often are quite different from their effect when market insurance or self-insurance alone is available. For example, although an increase in the endowed loss increases the demand for self- or market insurance when either alone is available since an increase in market insurance itself reduces self-insurance, and vice versa, the indirect effects can offset the direct effects when both market and self-insurance are positive (see Appendix A for an example of this). Similarly, because a decrease in the probability of loss with no change in the market loading factor reduces the demand for self-insurance, it increases the demand for market insurance. Therefore, people may be more likely to use the market to insure rare losses not necessarily because of a positive relation between the probability of loss and the loading factor (see the discussion in Section IC), but because of a substitution between market and self-insurance.

B. *Self-Protection, Subjective Probabilities, and "Moral Hazard"*

Self-insurance and market insurance both redistribute income toward hazardous states, whereas self-protection reduces the probabilities of these states. Unlike insurance, self-protection does not redistribute income, because the amount spent reducing the probability of a loss decreases income

---

[36] Equation (26) can be derived by maximizing $(1 - p) \ (I_1{}^e - c)$ $+ p \ [I_1{}^e - L(L^e, c) - c]$ with respect to c.

[37] Equation (25) can be derived by maximizing $W = (I_1{}^e - c) + \pi \ [I_1{}^e - L(L^e, c) - c]$ with respect to c. We are indebted to Jacques Drèze for emphasizing this point.

638   JOURNAL OF POLITICAL ECONOMY

in all states equally, leaving unchanged the absolute size of the loss (its relative size actually increases).

Studies using the states-of-the-world approach to analyze decision making under uncertainty have assumed that the probability of a state is entirely determined by "nature" and is independent of human actions. With this approach there is no such thing as self-protection; the activities we call by this name would be subsumed under self-insurance. It has been claimed that states can always be defined to guarantee the independence of their probabilities from human actions,[38] but we deny that this can be done in a meaningful way. Consider, for example, the probability that a given house will be damaged by lightning.[39] Since this probability can be reduced by the installation of lightning rods, independent state probabilities could be obtained only by using a more fundamental state description: the probability of a stroke of lightning itself. If control of the weather is ruled out, the probability of lightning can be assumed to be unaffected by human actions. We are concerned, however, about the probability of damage to the house—we do not care about the probability of lightning per se—and the probability of damage is affected by lightning rods.

In other words, although an appropriate definition of states would produce state probabilities that are independent of human actions, it would not produce a probability distribution of outcomes—the relevant probability distribution—that is independent of these actions. Since one of the main purposes of the state-of-the-world approach is to equate the probability distribution of outcomes with the probability distribution of states, a search for state probabilities that are independent of human actions would be self-defeating.

To look at the difference between self-protection and self-insurance from the viewpoint of outcomes, assume the probability distribution of endowed outcomes given by AB in figure 6. Self-insurance, by contracting the distribution to, say, CD, lowers the probability of both high and low outcomes, thereby unambiguously reducing the dispersion of outcomes. Self-protection, on the other hand, by shifting the whole distribution to the left to, say, EF, reduces the probability of low outcomes and raises the probability of high ones and does not have an unambiguous effect on the dispersion.[40]

Since the preceding discussion shows that self-insurance is to be distinguished from self-protection, we develop a formal analysis of the latter. Let us assume that the probability of a hazardous state can be reduced by

---

[38] The only explicit discussion is by Hirshleifer (1970, p. 217).

[39] This example is discussed by Hirshleifer (1970).

[40] The effect of the introduction of self-protection on the variance of income, $p(1-p)(I_1^e - I_0^e)^2$, can be found by differentiation $v'(r) \equiv \partial \operatorname{Var}(I^e)/\partial r = (1-$

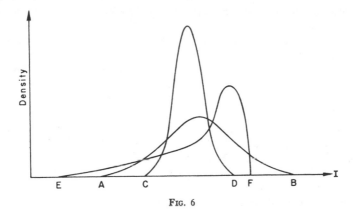

FIG. 6

appropriate expenditure: $p = p(p^e, r)$, where p^e is the endowed probability of hazard, r is the expenditure on self-protection, and $\partial p/\partial r = \mathrm{p}'(\mathrm{r}) \leqslant 0$. If no market or self-insurance were available, the optimal expenditure on self-protection would maximize

$$U^* = [1 - p(p^e, r)] \, U(I_1^e - r) + p(p^e, r) \, U(I_0^e - r); \qquad (27)$$

the optimality condition is

$$- p'(r^0) \, (U_1 - U_0) = (1 - p) \, U_1' + p \, U_0'. \qquad (28)$$

The term on the left is the marginal gain from the reduction in p; that on the right, the decline in utility due to the decline in both incomes, is the marginal cost. In equilibrium, of course, they must be equal.

The second-order optimality condition requires that

$$U^*_{rr} = - p''(r^0) \, (U_1 - U_0) + 2p'(r^0)(U_1' - U_0')$$

$$+ (1 - p) \, U_1'' + p \, U_0'' < 0. \quad (29)$$

Decreasing marginal utility of income is neither a necessary nor a sufficient condition. If $p''(r^0) > 0$, equation (29) is always satisfied if the marginal utility of income is constant and may or may not be satisfied if the marginal utility is decreasing or increasing. This shows that the incentive to self-protect, unlike the incentive to insure, is not so dependent

---

$2p) \; (I_1^e - I_0^e)^2 \, p'(0)$, where r is the expenditure on self-protection. Clearly $v'(r) \gtreqless 0$

as $p \gtreqless 1/2$.

on attitudes toward risk, and could be as strong for risk preferrers as for risk avoiders.

As with market and self-insurance, the effect of a change in incomes on the demand for self-protection depends on the source of the change as well as on preferences.[41] A decline in I_0^e alone might not increase the demand for self-protection, even if the marginal utility of income were falling, because a decline in I_0^e would increase the marginal cost of self-protection.[42]

A decline in the marginal productivity of self-protection—an increase in the shadow price of protection—always decreases the demand for self-protection regardless of attitudes toward risk.[43] Therefore, if the endowed probabilities and incomes were the same, more efficient providers of self-protection would have lower equilibrium probabilities of hazard. Consequently, different persons use different probabilities in their decision-making process not only because of differences in "temperament," or optimism, but also because of differences in productivity at self-protection. As suggested in the last section, differences in productivity, in turn, may be attributed to differences in education and other forms of "human capital."

If market insurance and self-protection were jointly available, the function

$$U^* = [1 - p(p^e, r)] \, U(I_1^e - r - s\,\pi(r)) + p(p^e, r) \, U(I_0^e - r + s) \tag{30}$$

would be maximized with respect to r and s; the first-order optimality conditions are

$$- (1 - p) \, U_1' \, \pi + p \, U_0' = 0 \tag{31}$$

$$- p'(r^*)(U_1 - U_0) - (1 - p) \, U_1'[1 + s^* \pi'(r^*)] - p \, U_0' = 0. \tag{32}$$

The term $\pi'(r^*)$ measures the effect of a change in self-protection on the price of market insurance through its effects on p and the loading factor λ. From the definition of π in equation (17) we obtain:

$$\frac{\partial \pi}{\partial r} = \pi'(r) = \pi'(p) \, p'(r) + \pi'(\lambda) \, \lambda'(r). \tag{33}$$

---

[41] An equal proportional increase in endowments $(I_1^e = \gamma I_0^e)$ would increase the demand for self-protection if $(dr^0/dI_0^e) = (1/U^*_{rr})[p'(r^0)(U_1'\gamma - U_0')$ $+ (1 - p) \, U_1'' \gamma + p \, U_0''] > 0$. A sufficient condition if $U'' < 0$ is $(U_1'/U_0')(I_1^e/I_0^e) \geqq 1$, or that the "average relative risk aversion" between I_0^e and I_1^e be sufficiently greater than one.

[42] That is, $-\partial r^0/\partial I_0^e = [p'(r^0) \, U_0' - p U_0'']/U^*_{rr} \gtreqqless 0$ as $-[p'(r^0)]/p \gtreqqless -U_0''/U_0'$.

[43] That is, $\partial r^0/\partial \beta = [(U_1 - U_0)/U^*_{rr}] \, (\partial p'/\partial \beta) = (+)/(-) > 0$, where by assumption $\partial p'/\partial \beta < 0$.

The effect of market insurance on the demand for self-protection has generally been called "moral hazard." In particular, moral hazard refers to an alleged deterrent effect of market insurance on self-protection[44] that increases the actual probabilities of hazardous events (Arrow 1962). Consequently, moral hazard is said to be "a relevant cost of producing insurance that is imposed by the insured on the insurance company" (Demsetz 1969, p. 7) and to provide a "limit to the possibilities of insurance" (Arrow 1962, p. 612). We showed in the last section that market insurance does reduce self-insurance, but no one has shown rigorously why, or under what conditions, market insurance reduces self-protection.

Market insurance has two opposite effects on self-protection. On the one hand, self-protection is discouraged because its marginal gain is reduced by the reduction of the difference between the incomes and thus the utilities in different states (see equation [28]); on the other hand, it is encouraged if the price of market insurance is negatively related to the amount spent on protection through the effect of these expenditures on the probabilities. Consider the relative importance of these opposite effects in two extreme cases:

If market insurance were always available at an actuarially fair price regardless of the amount spent on self-protection, then $\pi = p/(1 - p)$, and equation (31) implies that the optimal amount of market insurance (s^*) equalizes income in both states of the world. There is still an incentive to spend on self-protection, however, because π is negatively related to these expenditures (r):

$$\pi'(r) = \frac{p'(r)}{(1 - p)^2}. \tag{33a}$$

Substituting $U_1 = U_0$ and $U_1' = U_0'$ into equation (32), and using equation (33a) and the fact that $s^* = (1 - p)(I_1^e - I_0^e)$, we get

$$p'(r^*) = -\frac{1 - p}{s^*} = -\frac{1}{I_1^e - I_0^e}, \tag{34}$$

precisely the condition to maximize expected income. As with self-insurance, a fair price of market insurance encourages an expenditure on self-protection that maximizes expected income. Consequently, moral hazard would not then increase the real cost of insurance, reduce an economy's technical efficiency, or limit the development of market insurance since an

---

[44] See, for example, Arrow (1962, pp. 612, 613, 616; 1963, pp. 945, 961). Some writers have viewed moral hazard, in part, as a moral phenomenon related to fraud in the collection of benefits (see, for example, Mehr and Commack 1966, p. 174): a fire insurance policy, for example, may create an incentive for arson as well as for carelessness. Our analysis deals explicitly only with the effects of market insurance on self-protection, although implicitly it applies also to the effects on fraud.

642   JOURNAL OF POLITICAL ECONOMY

amount of market insurance equalizing income in all states would be chosen.

Even more important is that, contrary to the moral hazard argument, the optimal expenditure on self-protection, r^*, can be *larger* than the amount spent in the absence of market insurance, r^0. By equations (34) and (28), and the condition $p'(r) < 0$, r^* would be larger than r^0 if

$$\frac{U(I_1{}^e - r^0) - U(I_0{}^e - r^0)}{I_1{}^e - I_0{}^e}$$

$$= \bar{U}' < (1 - p) \, U'(I_1{}^e - r^0) + p \, U'(I_0{}^e - r^0), \quad (35)$$

which is likely provided p is not very small and U is concave. Indeed, if utility were a quadratic function of income, r^* would be larger than r^0 if p were larger than one-half.[45] Not only are market insurance and self-protection complements in the sense that the availability of the former could increase the demand for the latter, but also in the sense that an increase in the productivity of self-protection or a decrease in the real cost of market insurance would increase the demand for both (see Appendix B).

Suppose, at the other extreme, that the price of market insurance was independent of expenditures on self-protection—the loading factor increased sufficiently to offset exactly the reduction in the probability of loss. Self-protection would then usually be discouraged by market insurance—moral hazard would exist—because the main effect of introducing market insurance would be to narrow the differences between incomes in different states.[46] Moreover, since the demand for market insurance is negatively related to the degree of loading, it would be negatively related to expenditures on self-protection. Consequently, for those kinds of market insurance with prices that are largely independent of expenditures on self-protection, one should observe either a large demand for insurance and a small demand for self-protection, or the converse. In our judgment, this

---

[45] If $U = a\,I + b\,I^2$, with $b < 0$, equation (35) becomes $[p - (1/2)]\,I_1{}^e - [p - (1/2)]\,I_0{}^e > 0$. Since $I_1{}^e > I_0{}^e$, this implies that $p > 1/2$.

[46] If $\pi'(r) = 0$, the optimality condition for r, given the value of s, is from equation (32): $-p'(r^*)\,[U(I_1{}^e - r^* - s\,\pi) - U(I_0{}^e - r^* + s)] - (1 - p)\,U'\,(I_1{}^e - r^* - s\,\pi) - p\,U'\,(I_0{}^e - r^* + s) = 0$. Self-protection would be discouraged by market insurance if an exogenous increase in the latter always reduced the optimal value of r^*; that is, if $dr^*/ds < 0$, or $dr^*/ds = \{p'(r^*)\,[U_1{}'\,(-\pi) - U_0{}'] + [(1 - p)\,U_1{}''\,(-\pi) + p\,U_0{}'']\}/U^*{}_{rr} < 0$, where $U^*{}_{rr} < 0$. The first term in the numerator is necessarily positive since $p'\,(r^*)$ is negative and π, $U_0{}'$ and $U_1{}'$ are all positive. Therefore, a sufficient condition for the inequality to hold is that the second term be nonnegative, or since $\pi = [(1 + \lambda)\,p]/(1 - p)$, that $U_0{}'' \geqslant (1 + \lambda)\,U_1{}''$. If $\lambda \geqslant 0$—no negative loading—this latter inequality necessarily holds provided U'' and $U''' \leqslant 0$; for example, if U were the quadratic function $a\,I + b\,I^2$, with $b \leqslant 0$. Of course, it *might* hold even if $U''' > 0$.

is the major reason why certain kinds of hazards, like failure in business, are not considered insurable by the market.

Since the price of self-insurance is independent of the probability of hazard (see the discussion in Section IIA) and thus of expenditures on self-protection, our analysis of market insurance implies that self-insurance is likely to create a moral hazard. That is to say, the availability of self-insurance would discourage self-protection and vice versa. Moreover, technological progress in the provision of one would tend to discourage the other.

This analysis of moral hazard applies not only to the relation between self-protection and insurance as ordinarily conceived, but also to the relation between protection and insurance for all uncertain events that can be influenced by human actions. For example, do unemployment compensation, relief, or negative income tax rates increase the probability that someone becomes unemployed? Does the presence of underground shelters increase the probability that a country goes to war, the use of seat belts the probability of an automobile accident, or generous parental support the probability that children become "irresponsible"?

Since each of these, in effect, relates a form of insurance to a form of protection, our answers are not necessarily "yes," and depend on how responsive the cost of insurance is to the amount spent on protection. Shelters and seat belts are ways to self-insure, and have costs that are essentially unrelated to the probability of the hazards; therefore they would tend to reduce (perhaps only slightly) the incentive to avoid a war or an automobile accident. On the other hand, if the cost—in time, embarrassment, etc.—of applying for relief, unemployment compensation, or parental support were sufficiently positively related to its frequency, the answers might well be "no": the availability of insurance might encourage the insured to make his own efforts.

Appendix A

Self-Insurance and Market Insurance

If both self-insurance and market insurance are available, the expected utility is

$$U^* = (1 - p)\, U(I_1{}^e - c - s\,\pi) + p\, U(I_1{}^e - L(L^e, c) - c + s). \quad \text{(A1)}$$

The values of c and s that maximize this function must satisfy the first-order optimality conditions

$$U^*{}_s = -(1 - p)\, U_1{}'\,\pi + p\, U_0{}' = 0 \quad \text{(A2)}$$

$$U^*{}_c = -(1 - p)\, U_1{}' - p\, U_0{}'[L'(c^*) + 1] = 0. \quad \text{(A3)}$$

Clearly, equation (A3) would be satisfied only if $\delta = [L'(c^*) + 1] < 0$: only if expenditures on self-insurance increased the net income in the hazardous state.

Second-order optimality conditions are

$$U^*_{ss} = (1 - p)\, U_1'' \pi^2 + p\, U_0'' < 0 \tag{A4}$$

$$U^*_{cc} = (1 - p)\, U_1'' + p\, U_0'' \delta^2 - p\, U_0'\, L'' < 0 \tag{A5}$$

$$\Delta = U^*_{ss}\, U^*_{cc} - (U^*_{sc})^2 > 0. \tag{A6}$$

Equations (A4) and A5) are obviously satisfied if everywhere $U'' < 0$ and $L'' = \partial^2 L/\partial c^2 > 0$, that is, if the marginal utility of income and the marginal productivity of self-insurance are both decreasing. These assumptions are also sufficient to satisfy equation (A6) since

$$U^*_{sc} = (1 - p)\, U_1'' \pi - p\, U_0'' \delta < 0. \tag{A7}$$

Utilizing the first-order condition $\pi \delta = -1$, we can write

$$\Delta = - p(1 - p)\, U_0'\, U_1''\, L''\, \pi^2 - p^2\, U_0'\, U_0''\, L'',$$

which is positive if $U'' < 0$ and $L'' > 0$.

A. Terms of Trade Effects

The effect of an increase in π on the optimal values of s and c—I_1^e, L^e, and p held constant—can be found by differentiating equations (A2) and (A3) with respect to π. By Cramer's rule,

$$\frac{ds^*}{d\pi} = \frac{A_1 U^*_{cc} - A_2 U^*_{sc}}{\Delta} = \frac{1}{\Delta} [(1 - p)^2 U_1' U_1'' + p(1 - p) U_1' U_0'' \delta^2$$

$$- p(1 - p) U_0' U_1' L'' + p(1 - p) U_0' U_1'' s^* \pi L''] = \frac{(-)}{(+)} < 0 \tag{A8}$$

where $-A_1 = -(1 - p) U_1' + (1 - p) U_1'' s^* \pi$ and $-A_2 = (1 - p) U_1'' s^*$ are the partial derivatives of (A2) and (A3) with respect to π. Similarly,

$$\frac{dc^*}{d\pi} = \frac{A_2 U^*_{ss} - A_1 U^*_{sc}}{\Delta} = \frac{1}{\Delta} [- (1 - p)^2 U_1' U_1'' \pi$$

$$+ p(1 - p) U_1' U_0'' \delta] = \frac{(+)}{(+)} > 0. \tag{A9}$$

Hence, market insurance and self-insurance can be considered substitutes.

By similar reasoning, the effect of an increase in p on the optimal values of s and c, given that λ in $\pi = [(1 + \lambda)p]/(1 - p)$, I_1^e and I_1^e are constant, is found to be

$$\frac{ds^*}{dp} = \frac{B_1 U^*_{cc} - B_2 U^*_{sc}}{\Delta} = \frac{1}{\Delta} [U_0' U_1'' L'' s^* \pi^2 + (1 - p) U_1' U_1'' \pi$$

$$+ (1 - p) U_0' U_1'' - p U_1' U_0'' \delta + p U_0' U_0'' \delta^2] = \frac{(-)}{(+)} < 0; \tag{A10}$$

also

$$\frac{dc^*}{dp} = \frac{B_2 U^*_{cc} - B_1 U^*_{sc}}{\Delta} = \frac{1}{\Delta} [-(1-p)U_1'U_1''\pi^2$$

$$-(1-p)U_0'U_1''\pi - pU_1'U_0'' + pU_0'U_0''\delta] = \frac{(+)}{(+)} > 0$$

$$(A11)$$

where $-B_1 = (1-p)U_1''s^*\pi'(p)\pi$, $-B_2 = U_1' - U_0'\delta + (1-p)U_1''s^*\pi'(p)$, and $\pi'(p) = \partial\pi/\partial p = \pi/[p(1-p)]$.

B. An Endowment Effect

The effect of a decrease in $I_0^e = I_1^e - I.^e - I_1^e$, π, p, and L' held constant—can be shown to be

$$-\frac{ds^*}{dI_0^e} = \frac{-p^2 U_0'U_0''L''}{\Delta} \frac{\partial L}{\partial L^e} = \frac{(+)}{(+)} > 0, \qquad (A12)$$

where, by assumption, $\partial L/\partial L^e > 0$; and

$$-\frac{dc^*}{dI_0^e} = \frac{-pU_0''\delta U^*_{ss} - pU_0''U^*_{sc}}{\Delta} \frac{\partial L}{\partial L^e} = 0, \qquad (A13)$$

since by equations (A7) and (A8) $U^*_{sc} = -\delta U^*_{ss}$. If the change in I_0^e also changed L', the results would be different.

Appendix B

Self-Protection and Market Insurance

If both market insurance and self-protection are available, the expected utility is

$$U^* = [1 - p(p^e, r)]U(I_1^e - r - s\,\pi(r)) + p(p^e, r)U(I_0^e - r + s). \qquad (B1)$$

The first-order optimality conditions are

$$U^*_s = -(1-p)U_1'\pi + pU_0' = 0 \qquad (B2)$$

$$U^*_r = -p'(r^*)(U_1 - U_0) - (1-p)U_1'[1 + s^*\pi'(r)] - pU_0' = 0 \qquad (B3)$$

where $p'(r^*) < 0$ and $\pi'(r^*) \leqslant 0$.

Second-order conditions are that

$$U^*_{ss} = (1-p)U_1''\pi^2 + pU_0'' < 0 \qquad (B4)$$

$$U^*_{rr} = -p''(r^*)(U_1 - U_0) + (1-p)U_1''[1 + s^*\pi'(r^*)^2 + pU_0'' \qquad (B5)$$

$$+ 2p'(r^*)\{U_1'[1 + s^*\pi'(r)] - U_0'\} - (1-p)U_1's^*\pi''(r^*) < 0. \qquad (B6)$$

$$\Sigma = U^*_{ss}U^*_{rr} - (U^*_{sr})^2 > 0.$$

Equations (B4) and (B5) would be satisfied if $U'' < 0$, if both $p''(r^*)$ and $\pi''(r^*) > 0$, and if $D = 2p'(r^*)\{U_1'[1 + s^*\pi'(r^*)] - U_0'\}$ (which is positive if $U'' < 0)$[47] were small in absolute value relative to the other terms in equation (B5). These conditions are also sufficient to satisfy equation (B6) if, in particular, $D < (1 - p)U_1' s^* \pi''(r^*) + p''(r^*)(U_1 - U_0)$.

Since $\pi = [(1 + \lambda)p]/(1 - p)$, the effect of an increase in r on π would be

$$\pi'(r) = \frac{(1 + \lambda)p'(r)}{(1 - p)^2} + \frac{p\lambda'(r)}{(1 - p)}, \tag{B7}$$

where $\lambda'(r)$ gives the effect on the loading of an additional expenditure on self-protection and is generally assumed to be positive.[48]

If insurance were always available at an actuarially fair price, then $\lambda(p) = 0$ for all p; hence

$$\pi = \frac{p(r)}{1 - p(r)}, \quad \pi'(r) = \frac{p'(r)}{(1 - p)^2}, \quad \text{and}$$

$$\pi''(r) = \frac{p''(r)}{(1 - p)^2} + \frac{2[p'(r)]^2}{(1 - p)^3} > 0.$$

Equation (B2) reduces to

$$U_1' = U_0', \tag{B8}$$

and equation (B3) to

$$p'(r^*) = -\frac{(1 - p)}{s^*}. \tag{B9}$$

Therefore, $\pi'(r^*) = -1/[s^* (1 - p)]$ and $1 + s^* \pi'(r^*) = -\pi$.

A. Terms of Trade Effects

If an initially fair price $\pi = [p(r^*)]/[1 - p(r^*)]$ were increased by an increase in the loading with no change in $\pi'(r)$,[49] the change in the optimal values of s and r would be given by

$$\frac{ds^*}{d\pi} = \frac{C_1 U^*_{rr} - C_2 U^*_{sr}}{\Sigma} = \frac{C_1 \left[\dfrac{2U_1'}{s^*} - (1 - p)U_1's^*\pi''(r) \right]}{\Sigma}$$

$$= \frac{(-)}{(+)} < 0,^{50} \tag{B10}$$

[47] According to equations (B2) and (B9) and the condition $U'' < 0$, $U_1'[1 + s^* \pi'(r^*)] < U_0'$ if $\pi \geqslant p/1 - p)$.

[48] One can write $\lambda'(r) = (\partial\lambda/\partial p)(\partial p/\partial r)$, where $\partial p/\partial r < 0$. Hence, $\lambda'(r) > 0$ only if $\partial\lambda/\partial p < 0$. (But see our discussion in Section IC.)

[49] According to equation (B7), an increase in λ due to an exogenous factor θ would not change $\pi'(r)$ if, and only if, $[p'(r)/(1 - p)][\partial\lambda(r, \theta)/\partial\theta] = -p[\partial\lambda'(r, \theta)/\partial\theta]$. This assumption is made to separate an autonomous change in the price of insurance from an autonomous change in the effect of self protection on the price of insurance.

[50] Using equations (B8) and (B9) and the second-order optimality conditions

INSURANCE AND SELF-PROTECTION   647

$$\frac{dr^*}{d\pi} = \frac{C_2 U^*_{ss} - C_1 U^*_{sr}}{\Sigma} = \frac{-2(1-p)U_1'U^*_{sr}}{\Sigma} = \frac{(-)}{(+)} < 0,$$

$$\tag{B11}$$

where

$$-C_1 = U^*_{s\pi} \Big]_{\substack{s^*,\, r^*,\, p,\, \pi'(r^*) \\ \text{constant}}} = -(1-p)U_1' + (1-p)U_1''s^*\pi$$

and

$$-C_2 = U^*_{r\pi} \Big]_{\substack{s^*,\, r^*,\, p,\, \pi'(r^*) \\ \text{constant}}}$$

$$= p'(r^*)U_1's^* + (1-p)U_1''s^*[1 + s^*\pi'(r^*)]$$

$$= -(1-p)U_1' - (1-p)U_1''s^*\pi$$

(from equation [B9]). Hence, if the price of insurance increased from an initially fair level, the demand for both self-protection and market insurance would decrease.

If the price of insurance were always actuarially fair, the effect of an exogenous increase in the productivity of self-protection on s^* and r^* with no change in the endowed probabilities and in the endowed incomes would be given by

$$\frac{ds^*}{d\beta} = \frac{D_2 U^*_{sr}}{\Sigma} = \frac{(+)}{(+)} > 0 \tag{B12}$$

and

$$\frac{dc^*}{d\beta} = \frac{-D_2 U^*_{ss}}{\Sigma} = \frac{(+)}{(+)} > 0, \tag{B13}$$

where $D_2 = -U_1'[s/(1-p)]\partial p'/\partial\beta$ and, by assumption $\partial p'/\partial\beta < 0$. Technological improvements in self-protection are thus seen to increase the demand for both market insurance and self-protection.

B. The Effect of Exogenous Changes in p and L

If insurance were provided at an actuarially fair price, and if the endowed probability increased due to an exogenous factor γ with no change in $p'(r)$, then

----

discussed above, it follows that $U^*_{rr} = (1-p)\ U_1''\pi^2 + pU_0'' + 2U_1'/s^* - (1-p)\ U_1's^*\pi''\ (r) < 0$; $U^*_{sr} = -(1-p)\ U_1''\pi^2 - pU_0'' > 0$; and

$$\Sigma = U^*_{ss}\left[\frac{2U_1'}{s^*} - (1-p)U_1's^*\pi''(r)\right] > 0.$$

Since by equation (B4) $U^*_{ss} < 0$, $2U_1'/s^* - (1-p)\ U_1's^*\pi''\ (r)$ must be negative in order for Σ to be positive.

$$\frac{ds^*}{d\gamma} = \frac{\left[-(1-p)U_1''s^*\pi\,\pi'(p) \right]\left[\frac{2U_1'}{s} - (1-p)U_1's^*\pi''(r) \right]}{\Sigma}$$

$$\cdot \frac{\partial p}{\partial \gamma} = \frac{(-)}{(+)} < 0 \tag{B14}$$

where, by assumption, $\partial p/\partial \gamma > 0$, and

$$\frac{dr^*}{d\gamma} = \frac{(1-p)U_1''s^*\pi\,\pi'(p)[U^*_{ss} + U^*_{sr}]}{\Sigma}\frac{\partial p}{\partial \gamma} = 0, \tag{B15}$$

since $U^*_{ss} = -U^*_s$.[51] The last result is intuitively obvious since a fair price of insurance implies that $-p'(r^*) = 1/(I_1^e - I_0^e)$; therefore, r^* is independent of p provided that $p'(r)$ is unaffected by changes in $p\gamma$. By the same reasoning one can show that an increase in the size of the prospective loss increases the optimal values of both s and r.

References

Arrow, K. J. "Economic Welfare and the Allocation of Resources for Invention." In *The Rate and Direction of Inventive Activity: Economic and Social Factors*, edited by National Bureau Committee for Economic Research. Princeton, N.J.: Nat. Bur. Econ. Res., 1962.
——. "Uncertainty and the Welfare Economics of Medical Care." *AER* 53 (December 1963):941–73.
——. "The Role of Securities in the Optimal Allocation of Risk Bearing." *Rev. Econ. Studies* (April 1964):91–96.
——. *Aspects of the Theory of Risk Bearing.* Helsinki: Yrgö Jahnssonin Säätio, 1965.
Becker, G. S. "Uncertainty and Insurance, a Few Notes." Unpublished paper, 1968.
Becker, G. S., and Michael, R. T. "On the Theory of Consumer Demand." Unpublished paper, March 1970.
Demsetz, H. "Information and Efficiency: Another Viewpoint." *J. Law and Econ.* 12, no. 1 (April 1959): 1–22.
Ehrlich, I. "Participation in Illegitimate Activities: An Economic Analysis." Ph.D. dissertation, Columbia Univ., 1970.
Hirshleifer, J. "Investment Decision under Uncertainty: Applications of the State Preference Approach." *Q.J.E.* 80 (May 1966):252–77.
——. *Investment, Interest and Capital.* Englewood Cliffs, N.J.: Prentice-Hall, 1970.
Lees, D. S., and Rice, R. G. "Uncertainty and the Welfare Economics of Medical Care: Comment." *A.E.R.* 55 (March 1965):140–54.
Mehr, R. I., and Commack, E. *Principles of Insurance.* 4th ed. Homewood, Ill.: Irwin, 1966.
Mossin, J. "Aspects of Rational Insurance Purchasing." *J.P.E.* 76 (July/August): 1968):553–68.
Pratt, J. W. "Risk Aversion in the Small and in the Large." *Econometrica* 32, nos. 1–2 (January–April 1964):122–36.
Smith, V. L. "Optimal Insurance Coverage." *J.P.E.* 76 (January/February 1968): 68–77.

[51] See equation (B4) and the footnote following equation (B10).

[22]

JOURNAL OF ENVIRONMENTAL ECONOMICS AND MANAGEMENT 16, 209–223 (1989)

Self-Insurance against Natural Disasters[1]

TRACY LEWIS

Department of Economics, University of California—Davis, Davis, California 95616

AND

DAVID NICKERSON

*Faculty of Commerce, University of British Columbia, Vancouver,
British Columbia, Canada V6T 1Y8*

Received April 7, 1986; revised January 12, 1988

Expenditures on self-insurance to mitigate the effects of natural disasters on the value of private assets are examined in a model where individuals are partially insured against financial loss by a public relief program and where private insurance is unavailable. The model predicts that optimal private expenditures on self-insurance will be excessive or insufficient according to the nature of the technology by which individuals protect their assets. The comparative static effects of variations in the level of public compensation, individual wealth, and attitudes toward risk and the degree of environmental uncertainty on self-insurance expenditures and on the magnitude and frequency of public compensation are also characterized and their implications for remedial government policies are examined. © 1989 Academic Press, Inc.

1. INTRODUCTION

The occurrence of natural disasters has traditionally elicited public financial compensation, through grants and subsidized loans, to victims of the disasters.[2] Such compensation influences the care individuals exercise to protect their property from damage. Public insurance programs with strict eligibility requirements, making aid to victims contingent on adequate individual care, cannot be considered credible since the provision of aid has often been compelled by social and political considerations.[3] As a consequence, the government exhibits a commitment to compensate

---

[1] We thank Jim Brander, Marsha Courchane, Joseph Harrington, Bill Keeton, Todd Sandler, Dave Weimer, Dick Zeckhauser, two anonymous referees, and seminar participants at the 1986 North American Summer Meetings of the Econometric Society, the 1986 Risk Theory Seminar at the University of South Carolina, the 1984 NSF Conference on "The Economics of Natural Hazards and Their Mitigation" at the University of Florida, the Federal Reserve Bank of Kansas City, the University of British Columbia, and the University of Washington for their helpful comments, correspondence, and discussion. Partial research support for David Nickerson was provided by the Federal Reserve Bank of Kansas City and by UBC-SSHRC Research Grant 5-57707. The usual disclaimer applies.

[2] Comprehensive descriptions of public disaster relief programs in the United States appear in Clary [2], Cohen [3], Kunreuther *et al.* [14], Sorkin [24], and elsewhere.

[3] Pauly *et al.* [20], Rubin [21], and Warner [25] discuss the issue of credibility and examine political influences on the provision of disaster relief. Clary [2] and Goodisman [8] describe the influence of flood-plain regulations and other ex ante eligibility criteria on compensation for financial loss from disasters.

209

disaster victims regardless of the disincentives created by this commitment for efficient self-insurance.

The divergence between socially efficient and privately optimal levels of self-insurance created by the government provision of disaster relief and the ensuing condition of moral hazard have significant implications for economic theory and public policy. Theoretical comparisons of the optimal and efficient levels of self-insurance are sensitive to alternative environments in which the insurance decision is made.[4] Historical documentation of private underinsurance with respect to natural disasters has been used as evidence against the hypotheses of expected utility maximization and consumer rationality and to support the direct regulation of private insurance decisions.[5]

This paper compares those alternative levels of self-insurance expenditures which are optimal and which minimize the expected costs of public compensation in the context of a simple expected-utility model of the individual decision to self-insure under conditions of limited liability for financial loss. We focus on the influence of two important factors on this decision. The first factor is the degree of uncertainty with which the individual perceives the occurrence and severity of a disaster and his concomitant attitudes toward risk. The second factor is the nature of the technology by which individuals protect their assets.

Each of these factors influences the divergence between optimal and cost-minimizing levels of self-insurance. The technology of asset protection is described by the relation between the marginal return to expenditures on self-insurance and the random severity of a natural disaster. Investment in such protection is "risk-reducing" when the marginal return to expenditures on self-insurance varies directly with the severity of a disaster and is "risky" when the marginal return to such expenditures varies inversely with disaster severity. Optimal private expenditures on self-insurance are found to be inadequate (excessive), relative to the cost-minimizing level, when investment in protection is risk-reducing (risky). Increases in individual wealth, reductions in individual aversion to risk, and increased uncertainty about the potential severity of an impending disaster are also all found to exacerbate this divergence.

The paper is organized as follows. The formal model of the individual decision to self-insure under limited liability is presented in Section 2. An analysis of the effects on this decision of variations in initial wealth, aversion to risk, the value of public compensation, and environmental uncertainty is made in Section 3. The implications of this analysis for the design of government policies to induce less socially costly levels of private expenditures on self-insurance are discussed in Section 4. Conclusions appear in the final section.

---

[4]Kunreuther [12] and Kunreuther *et al.* [14] examine models employing decision criteria other than expected-utility maximization and find that private self-insurance expenditures are likely to be inadequate relative to the efficient level. Ehrlich and Becker [6] and Marshall [16] demonstrate, in expected-utility models in which individuals bear full liability for financial loss, that self-insurance expenditure will be excessive in the absence of market insurance. Marshall [16] also shows that optimal private expenditures on self-protection by an agent with rational price expectations will be inadequate (excessive), relative to the efficient level, when the probability of a potential disaster is high (low).

[5]Kunreuther *et al.* [14] extensively document the incidence of private underinsurance against natural disasters and argue that such evidence severely compromises the realism of the expected utility hypothesis. They recognize the possibility that limited liability effects could account for such underinsurance but make no attempt to model this. Kunreuther [13] discusses the case for the direct regulation of private insurance decisions on the basis of consumer irrationality.

2. A MODEL OF SELF-INSURANCE EXPENDITURES

2.1. Assumptions

Consider a regional economy in which each resident is endowed with an exogenous value of monetary wealth, W, and a physical asset or property which is subject to damage from fires, floods, earthquakes, or other natural disasters. The effect of the environment on property value is measured by a function, $H(q, z)$. This function depends on q, the level of expenditures by the representative individual on self-insurance to protect his property from damage, and on the state of nature, z, which measures the random severity of a natural disaster. Individual beliefs about the distribution of the random variable z are represented by the arbitrary cumulative density function $F(z)$ defined over the support $[\underline{z}, \bar{z}]$.

Since both the severity of a disaster and expenditures on self-insurance may vary continuously, $H(q, z)$, which measures property value net of self-insurance expenditures, is assumed to be twice-continuously differentiable in each argument. Also, since measures designed to protect property are likely to exhibit diminishing returns, H is assumed to be strictly concave in insurance expenditures q. Finally, smaller realizations of z are assumed to correspond to relatively more severe disasters, so that $H_z > 0$.[6]

The marginal return to expenditures on property, $H_q(q, z)$, will vary with the severity z of a disaster. Based on the technological relation between q and z, we consider two alternative types of such expenditures:[7]

Risk-reducing expenditures ($H_{qz} < 0$). Marginal returns to expenditures on property are higher in more adverse states of nature. Self-insurance reduces the variation in the value of property in this case since marginal returns to protection are positively correlated with the severity of a disaster.[8]

Risky expenditures ($H_{qz} > 0$). Marginal returns to expenditures on protection, as well as to ordinary investment in property improvement, are higher in more benign states of nature. Expenditures on property increase the variation in its value in this case since marginal returns to such expenditures are negatively correlated with disaster severity.[9]

The marginal return H_q is assumed to be strictly monotonic over the support of the state of nature z in our analysis. This assumption can be relaxed to one of only

---

[6] Partial derivatives are denoted by subscripts throughout the text (e.g., $H_z = (\partial H / \partial z)$).

[7] If the state of nature z and self-insurance expenditures q are regarded as inputs in the production of net property value $H(q, z)$, the risk-reducing and risky cases, respectively, correspond to situations in which z and q are substitutes and complements. Corresponding to this interpretation, we assume $q \geq 0$.

[8] Examples of protective measures which may exhibit this relationship in at least a significant portion of the interior of the support of z include smoke detectors, vaccination against epidemics, automobile airbags, and auxiliary generators for use in blackouts. These measures appear to be increasingly valuable in more adverse states of nature.

[9] Examples of protective measures which may exhibit this relationship in at least a significant portion of the interior of the support of z include the installation of fire retardants in fabrics, reinforcement of building foundations against earthquakes and soil shifting, and the erection of dikes and levees. These measures are most effective in more benign states of nature. It should be noted that, while previous studies which consider economies with only two states of nature necessarily restrict self-insurance to be a risk-reducing activity, consideration of a continuum of states allows the relation between H_q and z to define self-insurance as either a risky or a risk-reducing activity.

monotonicity without qualitatively changing our conclusions. Those types of property expenditure which feature variation in the sign of H_{qz} in the interior of the support of z are not considered for reasons of mathematical tractability.[10]

Individual liability for financial loss due to a natural disaster is limited by compensation from the program of public disaster relief. Private decisions to invest in self-insurance are made contingent on a knowledge of this program and prior to an observation of the severity of an impending disaster. On the basis of empirical realism, and in order to portray the effects of limited individual liability for loss in as simple and explicit a manner possible, we assume the program of compensation ensures that the net value of property after the occurrence of a disaster does not fall below some minimal value M.[11] This value is realistically assumed to be set in advance of the private decision to self-insure and at a level determined by social and political considerations, rather than by considerations of economic efficiency.[12]

Individuals who suffer losses due to a disaster sufficient to reduce their property value, $H(q, z)$, equal to or below M qualify for public compensation.[13] Final wealth for such individuals will consequently be bounded below by $M + W$, where W is the value of exogenous individual wealth.[14] The effect of the government compensation program on final wealth is depicted in Fig. 1. Although individuals self-insure by their selection of expenditure q, we assume that private disaster insurance is

[10] For example, $H_{qz} = 0$ could occur at the upper or lower end of the support of z, where either the environment is so benign or so adverse that small variations in the environment are inconsequential. The possibility that H_{qz} changes sign in the interior of the support of z will, however, render any comparative statics results ambiguous since it will preclude signing changes in the expected marginal utility of self-insurance expenditures, unless restrictive assumptions on preferences or the property value function H are made. Those types of property expenditures for which H_{qz} does change sign in the interior of the support of z require a local, rather than global, interpretation of the comparative static results displayed in Table I.

[11] The possibility that the government only insures some fraction of personal asset losses when $H(q, z)$ falls below M would not compromise the essence of our results, which simply requires that the individual's liability for property loss changes at the level of M. We concentrate on the case of full insurance instead of co-insurance since this assumption appears to characterize most public compensation programs in the United States, including those described in the Disaster Relief Act of 1969 and the Federal Disaster Relief Act Amendments of 1974. See Clary [2], Cohen [3], Sorkin [24], and FEMA Publications DR&R-2 and DR&R-3 [7] for descriptions of this legislation and compensation schedules under current programs of disaster relief.

[12] Descriptions of public disaster relief programs in Clary [2], Cohen [3], Goodisman [8], Sorkin [24], and Warner [25] make clear that compensation schedules are not set on a strategic basis but rather on the bases of equity and political considerations. This implies, in the context of our model, that the government does not condition its choice of M on the optimal or cost-minimizing levels of self-insurance expenditures.

[13] Two alternative programs of public relief would make compensation contingent on total ex post individual wealth, $H + W$, or on the gross property value after a disaster, $K = H + q^*$. Adopting the first assumption changes only those comparative static results which describe a change in exogenous wealth, as noted in Table I. Adopting the second assumption shifts the focus of the analysis to assessing the sign of $K_q = H_q + 1$, the gross marginal return to self-insurance expenditures. However, all of the comparative static results for the case of risky investment remain unchanged while those of the risk-reducing case are also invariant, provided the magnitude of $U''(W + M - q^*)F(z)$, the change in expected marginal utility over the lower portion of the support of z, is sufficiently small.

[14] By assuming that the government can accurately measure H, we abstract from some potentially significant monitoring problems involved in administering disaster relief programs. A description of the method by which H is measured after actual disasters appears in FEMA Publication DR&R-7 [7].

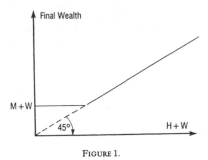

FIGURE 1.

either unavailable or is unpurchased over the relevant range of public compensation levels. This assumption has been extensively documented for a variety of disasters.[15]

2.2. Optimal and Cost-Minimizing Expenditures

Individuals choose a level of expenditures on self-insurance to maximize their expected utility from final wealth over all potential states of nature, conditional on the program of public disaster relief.[16] The individual is assumed to possess a standard strictly concave utility function, $U(\cdot)$, defined over the value of final wealth and it is further assumed that his expected utility from final wealth over all states of nature, $V(\cdot)$, is strictly concave in expenditures q on self-insurance. The optimal private level of expenditure on self-insurance selected by the individual is the solution to

$$\max_q V = \max_q \left[U(M + W)F(\hat{z}) + \int_{\hat{z}}^{\bar{z}} U(H(q, z) + W)\, dF(z) \right], \quad (1)$$

$$H(q, \hat{z}) = M. \quad (2)$$

The variable $\hat{z}$, which appears in (2), is that threshold state of nature, endogenously defined by the program of disaster relief and by private expenditures on self-insurance, at which the individual qualifies for public compensation.[17]

Equation (1) clearly illustrates the limit on individual liability for financial loss imposed by the public program of disaster relief. The first term in (1) reflects the minimal level of final wealth guaranteed to the individual by government compensa-

---

[15]Requirements of private co-insurance are frequently not made or enforced in many cases of disaster compensation, as discussed in Cohen [3], Goodisman [8], and Kunreuther *et al.* [14]. Our analysis could, however, accommodate the case where the government provides only partial compensation for all levels of property damage, up to some limit M, without substantively changing our results. The important aspect of our analysis of public compensation programs is that there exists a critical point at which the individual accepts only a limited liability for financial loss to his property.

[16]Conceptual problems with the expected utility approach to modeling human behavior are discussed in Kahnemen and Tversky [9], Kunreuther *et al.* [14], Chew [1], and elsewhere.

[17]Since considerations of equity appear to govern the design of disaster relief programs, the threshold state of nature, $\hat{z}$, is not treated as a strategic variable by the government but is determined as a residual by M and q^* through (1) and (2), and by M and q_m through (2) and (4).

tion in all adverse states of nature where $z \leqslant \hat{z}$. Of course the individual remains fully liable for the value of his property in more benign states of the world, as reflected by the second term in (1). Since the individual is aware of the limit on his liability for loss in adverse states of nature, his optimal expenditures on self-insurance, q^*, satisfy the condition[18]

$$V_q = \int_{\hat{z}}^{\bar{z}} U' H_q(q^*, z) \, dF(z) = 0. \tag{3}$$

Equation (3) indicates that the individual purchases self-insurance up to the point where the marginal utility he receives from such expenditures equals zero over those states of nature for which he assumes full financial liability.

While the government is committed to a program of disaster relief, it is also realistically assumed to desire to minimize the expected costs of such a program.[19] The expected cost C of providing disaster relief to the representative individual is defined by

$$C = \int_{z}^{\hat{z}} [M - H(q, z)] \, dF(z), \tag{4}$$

where the threshold level of disaster severity, $\hat{z}$, is again described by (2) and where the government shares the common belief that $F(z)$ represents the cumulative distribution of z. Expected costs depend in (4) on M, the minimum property value guaranteed by public compensation, and on private expenditures for self-insurance.

According to (4), the government provides sufficient compensation to disaster victims so that their minimum property value after a severe disaster is at least M. The level of self-insurance expenditure which minimizes the expected costs of compensation to the government, q_m, satisfies[20]

$$-C_q = \int_{\hat{z}}^{\hat{z}} H_q(q_m, z) \, dF(z) = 0. \tag{5}$$

Equation (5) indicates that the expected costs of disaster relief are minimized by a level of self-insurance expenditures which makes the marginal return to such expenditures zero over those states of nature for which the government assumes partial liability for individual financial loss.

---

[18] The condition (3) is also sufficient to determine a unique value of q^* for the system defined by (1) and (2) since we have assumed that the value function V is strictly concave with respect to expenditures q. This assumption is equivalent to assuming that H_{qq} and U'' are negative and relatively large in absolute value. The assumption of strict concavity of V in q is also sufficient to guarantee uniqueness of the comparative static results in part a of Table I.

[19] Clary [2], Kunreuther [13], and Sorkin [24] describe the increasing concern government officials display about minimizing the expected costs of providing disaster relief. Since the absence of private insurance markets implies that the private level of risky investments will not be socially efficient, programs of disaster relief can have the effect of partially remedying the lack of private insurance and so possibly improve the incentives for such investment. The minimization of expected compensation costs, while empirically realistic, will not in general be a second-best policy for the government to pursue this case.

[20] The condition (5) is also sufficient to determine a unique value of q_m for the system defined by (2) and (4) because of the strict concavity of H in q.

SELF-INSURANCE   215

TABLE I

	Risky investment: $H_{qz} > 0$ ($q^* > q_m$)				Risk-reducing investment: $H_{qz} < 0$ ($q^* < q_m$)			
	q^*	q_m	C	$F(z)$	q^*	q_m	C	$F(\hat{z})$
M	+	+	+	+	−	−	+	+
Degree of risk aversion[a]	−	−	−	+		−	−	
W^b	+	+	+	+	−		+	+
Degree of uncertainty[c]	+	−	$+^d$	$+^d$	−	+	$+^d$	$+^d$

[a] One utility function, U^1, exhibits a greater degree of risk aversion than another, U^2, if U^1 can be expressed as a strictly concave function of U^2.

[b] These results assume that individuals exhibit decreasing absolute risk aversion. The signs may be indeterminate if compensation is based on total wealth rather than on H.

[c] We consider only that family of changes in the cumulative distribution function F to the cumulative distribution function G represented by $L(z)$, $G = F + L$, where L is a function of bounded variation defined over the compact support $[\underline{z} - \varepsilon, \bar{z} + \varepsilon]$ for $\varepsilon > 0$ and which satisfies

$$\int_{\underline{z}}^{y} H_q(q, z)\, dL(z) \leqslant 0 \quad \text{for } H_{qz} < 0 \quad \text{and} \quad \int_{\underline{z}}^{y} H_q(q, z)\, dL(z) \geqslant 0 \quad \text{for } H_{qz} > 0,$$

for all arbitrary y such that $\hat{z} \leqslant y \leqslant \bar{z} + \varepsilon$ (see Meyer–Ormiston [18]). When $F(z)$ is the cumulative uniform distribution, a mean-preserving spread in the support of z represents an example of such a change.

[d] These results are derived for the case of a uniform distribution in which $\hat{z} < (\underline{z} + \bar{z})/2$, so that the threshold state of nature is less than the mean. This seems reasonable since disaster relief does not occur with great frequency.

3. COMPARATIVE STATIC ANALYSIS

Optimal private expenditures on self-insurance, q^*, are described, in Eqs. (2) and (3), in terms of M, the minimum property value guaranteed by the public program of disaster relief; W, the value of exogenous individual wealth; $F(z)$, the cumulative density function which represents individual beliefs about the distribution of the severity of a potential disaster; and $U(\cdot)$, which incorporates the degree of individual aversion to risk. Expenditures on self-insurance which minimize the expected costs of compensation, q_m, are also described, in Eqs. (2) and (5), in terms of these variables. Table I summarizes the effects of variations in these variables on the optimal and cost-minimizing values of property expenditures.[21]

The first result exhibited in Table I is the reversal in ranking between q^* and q_m, depending on whether expenditures on property are characterized as risky or risk-reducing. This conclusion is important for two reasons. First, it provides a rigorous theoretical explanation, fully consistent with the expected utility hypothesis, for the historical evidence that individuals overinvest in ordinary (noninsuring) improvements to property which is exposed to the effects of natural disasters while simultaneously underinvesting in measures specifically designed to protect their

---

[21] Derivation of the results in Table I is available from the authors upon request.

property from potential damage.[22] Second, it indicates that private expenditures on self-insurance could be excessive from the government's perspective, if the marginal return to such expenditures is inversely correlated with the severity of a disaster, and will be inadequate otherwise.

This conclusion follows directly from the limit placed on individual liability for financial loss and from the relation between H_q, the marginal return to self-insurance, and the state of nature z. When $H_{qz} > 0$, marginal returns to self-insurance are highest for disasters of only modest severity. Inspection of Eqs. (3) and (5) reveals that, because of the program of disaster relief, the individual is only interested in marginal returns in relatively benign states of nature ($\hat{z} < z \leqslant \bar{z}$) where H_q tends to be higher, while the government is interested in marginal returns in relatively adverse states ($\underline{z} \leqslant z \leqslant \hat{z}$) where H_q tends to be smaller. Optimal private expenditures on self-insurance are excessive, relative to the cost-minimizing level, because, for a given q, the marginal return to the individual is greater than the marginal return perceived by the government. When $H_{qz} < 0$, the difference in marginal returns perceived by the individual and by the government are reversed, leading to the conclusion that optimal private expenditures are inadequate.

Comparing parts a and b of Table I, it can be seen that increases in individual wealth, reductions in individual aversion to risk, and increasing environmental uncertainty all contribute to a greater divergence between the optimal and cost-minimizing levels of expenditure, as reflected in increases in the expected cost, C, and frequency, $F(z)$, of public compensation. Although inefficient decisions to self-insure are manifested differently according to the technology of property protection, in both cases the magnitude of the divergence is affected in similar ways by common factors. For example, when $H_{qz} > 0$, expenditures on property are regarded by the individual as a risky investment. Consequently, a decrease in his aversion to risk or an increase in his exogenous level of wealth will increase his expenditures. This serves, however, to exacerbate the existing divergence between q^* and q_m because private expenditures are already excessive in this case. When $H_{qz} < 0$, expenditures on property are a risk-reducing investment. Consequently, an increase in wealth or a decrease in aversion to risk serves to reduce private expenditures, which in this case are already less than the cost-minimizing level.

An increase in environmental uncertainty is reflected in our model by a change in the cumulative distribution function of the state of nature z which is consistent with the conditions of Meyer and Ormiston [18].[23] One example of such an increase

---

[22] Ordinary property improvements include all those risky investments which are primarily intended to increase the market value of property without significantly adding to the protection of the property from potential damage. Classifying those investments which simultaneously add to property protection while significantly increasing its market value as risky or risk-reducing depends on the net sign of the derivative H_{qz}.

[23] As pointed out in Propositions 1–3 of Meyer and Ormiston [18], the general class of changes in risk for which determinate comparative statics results can be obtained in models like ours is exceedingly narrow. The conditions of Theorem 1 in Meyer and Ormiston [18] restrict us to consider only that family of changes in the cumulative distribution function F to the cumulative distribution G represented by $L(z)$, $G = F + L$, where the support of G is in the closed interval $[\underline{z} - \varepsilon, \bar{z} + \varepsilon]$, for $\varepsilon > 0$, and where L, which is a function of bounded variation over the support $[\underline{z} - \varepsilon, \bar{z} + \varepsilon]$, satisfies

$$\int_{\underline{z}}^{y} H_q(q, z)\, dL(z) \leqslant 0 \quad \text{for } H_{qz} < 0 \quad \text{and} \quad \int_{\underline{z}}^{y} H_q(q, z)\, dL(z) \geqslant 0 \quad \text{for } H_{qz} > 0,$$

proceeds from the assumption that the function $F(z)$ represents the cumulative uniform distribution. An increase in uncertainty can, in this case, be represented by a mean-preserving spread, in the form of an expansion of the compact support of z to $[z - \varepsilon, z + \varepsilon]$, for an arbitrary $\varepsilon > 0$. According to Table I, the individual responds to greater uncertainty about the severity of a potential disaster by increasing (decreasing) his expenditures on property when such expenditures are a risky (risk-reducing) investment.

This behavior by the individual may seem counterintuitive. For example, when expenditures on self-insurance constitute a risky investment, a decline in these expenditures might be expected to occur in response to greater uncertainty in the environment. The intuition for this behavior comes, however, from recognizing that because of the program of disaster relief, the individual is insulated against an increase in the probability of relatively more adverse states of nature when variation in z increases. The existence of public compensation for disasters of severity greater than $\hat{z}$ implies that an increase in the variation in z has the effect of improving the distribution of states of nature over which the individual bears full liability for financial loss. It may be immediately deduced from this that expenditures on property will increase (decrease) when $H_{qz} > 0$ (< 0). Analogously, the existence of public compensation also implies that an increase in the variation of z worsens the distribution of states of nature relevant to the government. Consequently, q_m, the cost-minimizing level of expenditures, will decrease (increase) when $H_{qz} > 0$ (< 0). The conflict of interest between minimizing the expected costs of government compensation and maximizing the welfare of potential disaster victims increases when environmental uncertainty worsens.

As expected, an increase in M, the minimum property value guaranteed by public compensation, increases both the expected costs and frequency of such compensation. Two factors contribute to the increased costs associated with more generous programs of disaster relief. There is a direct effect: ceteris paribus, more generous compensation, reflected by an increase in the value of M, costs more to finance. The second contributing factor is the effect on individual incentives to self-insure: an increase in M reduces the individual's liability for damage, leading to greater inefficiency in private expenditures on self-insurance.

Increases in M have qualitatively similar effects on q^* and q_m. It may seem paradoxical that, as the government assumes more liability through an increase in M, its preferred level of expenditures on self-insurance declines when $H_{qz} < 0$. The explanation for this is that, as the government assumes more liability, it becomes concerned with the return from self-insurance expenditures in marginally better states of nature, where H_q tends to be smaller. The expected marginal return from self-insurance over all states of nature relevant to the government decreases, which reduces the cost-minimizing level of self-insurance expenditures.

4. POLICY IMPLICATIONS

Our analysis is based on the premise that social and political considerations commit the government to offer financial aid to victims of natural disasters in an

---

for all arbitrary y such that $\hat{z} \leqslant y \leqslant \bar{z} + \varepsilon$, where $\hat{z}$ is evaluated at q^* through (2), and for all q in a neighborhood of q^*. The uniform distribution is the most salient example of a distribution in which a mean-preserving spread representing an increase in uncertainty satisfies these requisite conditions for determinate comparative static results.

amount sufficient to guarantee a minimum value for their damaged property. Expectations of the provision of aid after a disaster has occurred affect the decision of individuals to self-insure prior to the occurrence of the disaster. While committed to the provision of disaster aid, the government has also been realistically assumed to desire to minimize the expected costs of providing such aid to disaster victims.

The implications of our analysis for government policies which induce less costly levels of private expenditures on self-insurance are examined below. Three types of policies often discussed in previous literature are considered: (a) the direct regulation of expenditure on property; (b) imposition of taxes and subsidies on property expenditures; and (c) the dissemination of information by government about the severity of a potential disaster. While the simplicity of our analysis precludes a complete evaluation of each of these policies, it does reveal, through inspection of Table I, certain strengths and weaknesses of each approach.

a. Direct Regulation

The direct regulation of private expenditures on property is warranted either when individuals are misinformed about the probability and consequences of a potential disaster or when the government is more adept at collecting and processing information about disasters, and also when the relative costs of implementing and monitoring insurance standards are low. When the government possesses superior information, an alternative to the direct regulation of rational individual decisions is for the government to disseminate its information. This alternative is discussed below. When the government has no informational advantage, the effectiveness of direct regulation depends on the feasibility of monitoring and enforcement.

The feasibility of controlling private expenditures on property varies with the type of natural disaster to which such property is exposed. Mandatory compliance with building codes and restrictions on flood-plain development, enforced by on-site inspections and coupled with economic incentives such as access to subsidized insurance, is an example of one method of controlling private property expenditures which has met with mixed success.[24] However, even when monitoring and enforcement are relatively inexpensive, direct regulation of property expenditures may be politically infeasible. One example suggested by our model is the obvious infeasibility of preventing individuals from spending too much to protect their property from disasters, a case which could occur when the marginal return to self-insurance varies inversely with the severity of a disaster ($H_{qz} > 0$).

b. Taxes and Subsidies

The use of taxes or subsidies is an alternative means for inducing preferred levels of private expenditure on property. When such expenditures constitute a risk-reducing investment, so that private expenditures are inadequate, imposition of a discrete tax or mandatory public insurance premium on each property owner would both induce a greater level of private expenditure by reducing individual wealth and could finance the public program of disaster relief. Alternatively, a per-unit subsidy

[24]See Clary [2] for a discussion of the effectiveness of programs regulating construction in flood-plains.

for self-insurance would also induce larger private expenditures, although this would be at least partially offset by the positive wealth effect such a subsidy would produce.

When expenditures on property constitute a risky investment, so that private expenditures are excessive, imposition of a discrete tax or premium to finance the relief program will again reduce the divergence between optimal and cost-minimizing levels of private expenditure. A per-unit tax on the purchase of protective measures would also reduce private expenditures on self-insurance through both price and wealth effects by increasing the cost of protection. As in the case of direct regulation of risky investment, however, it is difficult to imagine popular support for a policy like a tax that discourages expenditures by individuals to protect their property.

c. Information Dissemination

A popular explanation for the observed underexpenditure on self-insurance by property owners has been that these individuals systematically underestimate both the probability of natural disasters and the effectiveness of protective measures.[25] If the government has a cost advantage in collecting and processing information about these phenomena, one remedial policy might involve the dissemination of its information to individual property owners. Such a policy might serve as an alternative to the direct regulation of private expenditures on self-insurance.

Assuming that the ability of individuals to make efficient decisions is at least as great as that of the government, two strategic issues arise in the evaluation of a policy of information dissemination. The first issue concerns the credibility of the information issued by the government and the response of individuals to such information. Individuals with rational expectations may be suspicious of information if they believe it is self-serving for the government to publish it or if they are unable to verify its accuracy after repeated trials. For example, the government might attempt to minimize the expected costs of disaster relief by adopting a strategy of repeatedly announcing that a natural disaster was imminent. The credibility individuals place on such information would presumably decline after many such announcements unless its accuracy could somehow be independently confirmed.[26] The second issue concerns the ability of the government to manipulate private decisions to self-insure, assuming that it adopts a strategy of disseminating only complete accurate information about disasters and that this accuracy is common knowledge.[27] If the latter situation exists, the efficacy of a policy of information dissemination in our model depends on whether the information possessed by the government concerns the effectiveness of protective measures, as

[25] For an example see Kleindorfer and Kunreuther [11].

[26] See Malueg [15] for a general characterization of the phenomenon of moral hazard in repeated games, and Nickerson and Sandler [19] for an example in a differential game.

[27] Crawford and Sobel [5] consider the class of games of strategic information transmission in which the accuracy of information is common knowledge. Rational expectations equilibria in such games are characterized by the transmission of a signal which is an element of the partition of the support of the probability distribution of the variable that represents the private information held by one player in the game.

measured by the marginal return to self-insurance expenditures, or the severity of a natural disaster, as measured by a translation or partition of the support of the random state of nature z. While analysis of the former case is straightforward, general conclusions about a strategy of disseminating information about disaster severity in our model are precluded, for the reasons discussed in Meyer and Ormiston [18], unless further restrictions are imposed on either the curvature of the asset value function $H(q, z)$ or the cumulative density function $F(z)$. Below we first analyze the dissemination of information about the effectiveness of self-insurance. We then consider two empirically relevant examples of the dissemination of information about disaster severity, each based on the assumption that $F(z)$ represents the cumulative uniform distribution.

If, as has been alleged, individuals systematically underestimate the effectiveness of protective measures, the publication of more accurate information would cause the function H_q, which describes the marginal return to self-insurance perceived by individuals, to rise. Such a rise would induce an increase in private expenditures on self-insurance. This would reduce the expected costs of disaster relief when property expenditures are a risk-reducing investment, since such expenditures are inadequate in this case. When property expenditures are a risky investment, however, the government might choose to suppress information about H_q to avoid further increases in private expenditures.

It has also been alleged that individuals systematically underestimate the potential severity of a natural disaster. Assume, for simplicity, that individuals mistakenly perceive that the state of nature z is uniformly distributed over the support $[\underline{z} + \varepsilon, \bar{z} + \varepsilon]$, for $\varepsilon > 0$. When property expenditures are a risky (risk-reducing) investment, inspection of Eq. (3) reveals that individuals increase (decrease) their property expenditures as their underestimation of disaster severity, represented by the value of ε, increases.[28] Provision of more accurate information about disaster severity would induce individuals to translate their perception of the true support of the state of nature z to the left, resulting in a reduction in both the expected costs and frequency of public compensation.

Finally, consider the incentive for the government to disseminate an accurate forecast of the severity of an imminent disaster. Again assume for simplicity that individuals perceive the state of nature z to be uniformly distributed over the support $[\underline{z}, \bar{z}]$ and that the government forecast takes the form of a refinement of the support within which the state of nature will occur to some subinterval $[z_{j-1}, z_j]$, where $\underline{z} < z_{j-1} < z_j \leqslant \bar{z}$.[29] Publication of such a forecast will generally reduce the expected costs and frequency of public compensation and at worst will leave the welfare of both individuals and the government unchanged. Consider the case in which property expenditures are a risky investment. While no change in private property expenditures will occur if only individual perceptions of the lower bound of the support are changed by the government forecast, a reduction in perceptions of the upper bound of the support will, by Eq. (3), cause individuals to

---

[28]It can be seen from Eq. (3) in this case that $dq^*/d\varepsilon$ has the same sign as $U'H_q(q^*, \bar{z} + \varepsilon)$, and so is positive (negative) when H_{qz} is positive (negative).

[29]Such a forecast, which represents a partition of the support of the state of nature z, would be an optimal strategy for the government to adopt in this strategic game of information transmission, as shown in Crawford and Sobel [5]. Derivation of the results in this case are available from the authors upon request.

revise downward their expected marginal utility from property expenditures over those states of nature which are relevant in light of the government forecast. This revision will induce them to lower their property expenditures, which will also, by Table I, reduce the expected costs and frequency of public compensation. An analogous argument may be used when property expenditures are a risk-reducing investment.

5. CONCLUSION

Over the past 3 decades, the occurrence of natural disasters has frequently elicited public compensation payments to victims of the disaster. The limited liability for financial loss created by such compensation creates a divergence between optimal private levels of expenditure on self-insurance and that level which would minimize the expected costs and frequency of compensation borne by government. As a consequence, there is a need to rigorously analyze the individual decision to self-insure under conditions of limited liability and to examine both the compatibility of this analysis with observed patterns in private behavior and its implications for the design of remedial government policies. This paper has examined a simple model of the individual decision to self-insure when market insurance is unavailable and when expectations of public compensation limit the individual's liability for financial loss. Public compensation effectively truncates the range of disaster severity with which the individual is concerned and so creates a divergence between those levels of expenditure on property which are optimal for individuals and for the government.

Two important implications arise from our model. First, empirical evidence that individuals overinvest in ordinary improvements to property exposed to the effects of natural disasters and underinvest in measures designed to protect such property from damage is rigorously explained in terms of the maximization of expected utility from wealth by individuals. Such behavior in our model is a consequence of the limited liability provided by government programs of disaster relief. Second, whether private expenditures on self-insurance are regarded as excessive or inadequate by the government has been shown to depend on the nature of the technology by which individuals protect their property. Further, increases in individual wealth, reductions in risk aversion, and increased environmental uncertainty are also all found to increase the divergence between private and cost-minimizing levels of self-insurance expenditures.

While the simplicity of our model and our usage of the expected utility hypothesis requires our results to be viewed as exploratory, our analysis suggests at least three areas for further research. First, alternative models of decision making under uncertainty should be investigated for their implications regarding individual self-insurance against natural disasters. Second, the importance of the technology of protection in determining expenditures on self-insurance suggests a need for an empirical examination of the relationship between the marginal return to expenditures on methods of self-insurance and the severity of recurrent disasters, particularly for those types of disasters for which private insurance is unavailable. Third, a more general examination should be made of government policies involving the collection and dissemination of information about the occurrence and consequences

222   LEWIS AND NICKERSON

of natural disasters. We have examined certain cases where the dissemination of more precise information about disasters would benefit individuals and the government. Further analysis is needed to design a policy of information dissemination under more general conditions, where the government's predictions about future disasters may be subject to error and where individuals may be limited to their ability to interpret and act on the new information they receive.

REFERENCES

1. S. H. Chew, A generalization of the quasilinear mean with applications to the measurement of income inequality and decision theory resolving the Allais paradox, *Econometrica* 51, 1047–1065 (1983).
2. B. Clary, Evolution and structure of natural hazard policies, *Public Admin. Rev.* 45(Special Issue), 20–28 (1985).
3. L. Cohen, "A Public Policy Approach to the Study of Optimal Compensation Systems: The Case of the Price–Anderson Act," Kennedy School of Government Discussion Paper 61D (1979).
4. L. Cohen and R. Noll, The economics of building codes to resist seismic shock, *Public Policy* 29(1), 1–29 (1981).
5. V. Crawford and J. Sobel, Strategic information transmission, *Econometrica* 50, 1431–1452 (1982).
6. I. Ehrlich and G. Becker, Market insurance, self-insurance and self-protection, *J. Polit. Econom.* 80, 623–648 (1972).
7. FEMA, "Disaster Response and Recovery Series," Publications DR&R-2, 3, and 7, Federal Emergency Management Administration, Printing and Publications Division, Washington, DC (1981).
8. L. Goodisman, Budgeting and field discretion in disaster relief, *Public Budgeting Finance* 3, 89–102 (1983).
9. D. Kahnemen and A. Tversky, Prospect theory: An analysis of decision under risk, *Econometrica* 47, 263–291 (1979).
10. W. Keeton and E. Kwerel, Externalities in automobile insurance and the underinsured driver problem, *J. Law Econom.* 27, 149–179 (1984).
11. P. Kleindorfer and H. Kunreuther, Descriptive and prescriptive aspects of health and safety regulation, *in* "The Benefits of Health and Safety Regulations" (A. Ferguson and R. Leveen, Eds.), Ballinger Press, Cambridge, MA (1981).
12. H. Kunreuther, "Behavioral Insights for Public Policy: Ex Ante/Ex Post Considerations," Wharton School Discussion Paper 84-05-02 (1984).
13. H. Kunreuther, The changing societal consequences of risks from natural hazards, *Ann. Amer. Acad. Polit. Soc. Sci.* 443, 104–116 (1979).
14. H. Kunreuther, R. Ginsberg, L. Miller, P. Sagi, P. Slovic, B. Borkan, and N. Katz, "Disaster Insurance Protection: Public Policy Lessons," Wiley-Interscience, New York (1978).
15. D. Malueg, Efficient outcomes in a repeated agency model without discounting, *J. Math. Econom.* 15(3), 217–230 (1986).
16. J. Marshall, Moral hazard, *Amer. Econom. Rev.* 66, 880–890 (1976).
17. J. Marshall, Insurance as a market in contingent claims: Structure and performance, *Bell J. Econom. Management Sci.* 5, 670–682 (1974).
18. J. Meyer and M. Ormiston, The comparative statics of cumulative distribution function changes for the class of risk-averse agents, *J. Econom. Theory* 31, 153–169 (1983).
19. D. Nickerson and T. Sandler, Intertemporal incentive allocation in simple hierarchies, *Math. Soc. Sci.* 7, 33–57 (1984).
20. M. Pauly, H. Kunreuther, and J. Vaupel, "Public Protection against Misperceived Risks: Insights from Positive Political Economy," Wharton School Discussion Paper 83-04-05 (1983).
21. C. Rubin, Managing recovery from a natural disaster, *Management Inform. Service Rep.* 14(2), 1–15 (1982).
22. P. Slovic, B. Fischoff, S. Lichtenstein, B. Corrigan, and B. Combs, Preference for insuring against probable small loss: Implications for the theory and practice of insurance, *J. Risk Insur.* 44, 237–258 (1977).

SELF-INSURANCE 223

23. P. Slovic, H. Kunreuther, and F. White, Decision processes, rationality and adjustment to natural hazards, *in* "Natural hazards: Local, National and Global," (G. White, Ed.), Oxford Univ. Press, London/New York (1974).

24. A. Sorkin, "Economic Aspects of Natural Hazards," Lexington Books, Lexington, MA (1982).

25. E. Warner, Federal disaster relief: Edging toward disaster, *Inst. Socioeconom. Stud. J.* **8**, 23–35 (1983).

26. M. Wheeler, The use of criminal statutes to regulate product safety, *J. Legal Stud.* **13**(3), 593–618 (1984).

[23]

JOURNAL OF ENVIRONMENTAL ECONOMICS AND MANAGEMENT **20**, 1–15 (1991)

Risk, Self-Protection, and Ex Ante Economic Value*

Jason F. Shogren

Department of Economics, Iowa State University, Ames, Iowa 50011

AND

Thomas D. Crocker

Department of Economics, University of Wyoming, Laramie, Wyoming 82071

Received July 6, 1989; revised November 14, 1989

We develop three propositions about the ex ante value of reduced risk. If there is a continuous outcome distribution and if self-protection influences outcome probability and severity, then (1) unobservable utility terms cannot be eliminated from the ex ante value expressions; (2) knowledge of the convexity or the nonconvexity of dose–response functions is insufficient to sign changes in these expressions; and (3) self-protection expenditures need not be a lower bound measure of these expressions. Therefore, many restrictions applied in recent empirical work on the economic value of risk changes are not immediately transferable to settings where endogenous risks prevail. © 1991 Academic Press, Inc.

1. INTRODUCTION

Public agencies now feel considerable pressure to reduce risks to individuals' health and welfare through additional provision of security, personnel safety, fire and flood prevention, auto safety, product safety, environmental protection, and emergency planning. Persons who might suffer harm from exposure to hazards can reduce their expected ex post costs by purchasing market insurance. However, Arrow [1] and Shavell [31] show that moral hazard compels private insurers to defray only a fraction of these costs. Moreover, adverse selection and nonindependence of risks causes contingent claims markets to be incomplete. Finally, many individuals are thought to be " ... psychologically unable to cope with risk" (Oi [25]), causing them to misperceive it systematically. Collective attempts to overcome these limits to decentralized allocations and resolutions of risk can be more efficient if accurate estimates are available of individuals' choices and the ex ante economic values of risk reductions that these choices imply.

The empirical risk valuation literature typically assumes that (i) risks are independent of individual actions, and (ii) individuals require progressively increasing compensation if they are to maintain constant expected utility when confronted by increasing risk. Jones-Lee *et al.* [16], for example, embodies both conditions. These conditions could be excessively restrictive in the sense that they excise common and plausibly significant features of the individual's decision

---

*This research was partly supported by the Wyoming Water Research Center. The comments of Tim Perri, Fred Sterbenz, and two anonymous referees have improved the paper.

1

problem. We investigate the structure of functions representing the individual's willingness to pay to reduce risk when these two restrictions are set aside.

Two bits of theoretical and empirical evidence suggest that the two restrictions lead to misleading results. First, Marshall [22] shows that exogenous risk requires a complete set of Arrow–Debreu contingent claims contracts. Because the writing of contracts is costly, complete contracts rarely, if ever, exist: the individual must therefore choose between contractually defining states of nature or making an effort to alter states of nature. Spence and Zeckhauser [37] demonstrate that the ability to influence states of nature enhances both the ex ante and the ex post gains from adaptation. Ehrlich and Becker [10], Laffont [19], and Crocker [5] allow individual prior actions to influence ex post gains. Shogren and Crocker [33] show in a set of controlled experiments that these prior actions influence the individual's ex ante willingness-to-pay for collective risk reduction efforts.

Second, in a contingent valuation study of the risk valuations attached to hazardous waste exposures, Smith and Desvousges [34, 35] report increasing marginal valuations with decreasing exogenous risk. This finding is but the latest in a 15-year-long parade of analytical (Starett [40], Winrich [45]) and empirical (Crocker [6], Repetto [28]) papers which use prior information on physical dose–response relations, individual abilities to process information about these relations, or individual perceptions of the relations to produce an increasing marginal valuation result for more of a desirable commodity. However, when risk is endogenous, no one has yet asked whether convexity of the marginal value of risk follows when cognition is not an issue.

Berger et al. [2] appear to be among the first to consider endogenous risks in the context of human health. Our treatment differs from their seminal effort in two significant ways. First, though they state the general continuous distribution case of risks to human health, they examine ex ante value only in a world of two mutually exclusive and independent states of nature: survival or death. We extend the ex ante value concept to the general continuous case, while presuming that individuals recognize that outcomes are stochastically related to actions, implying that predictions of behavior and the relative values that motivate it depend not only on preference orderings over outcomes, but also on preference orderings of lotteries over outcomes.[1]

Second, Berger et al. [2] model only probability-influencing self-protection. They disregard the severity of the health outcome being risked, even though they concede that prior self-protection can influence both ex ante probability and ex post severity. Similarly, Lewis and Nickerson [21] work with self-insurance that influences ex post severity but they do not allow the individual to affect ex ante probabilities. Ehrlich and Becker [10] point out that the distinction between self-protection that influences probability and self-protection that influences severity is somewhat artificial. The distinction is often made for theoretical convenience (see, for example, Hiebert [13]). In contrast, we model the effects of self-protection that influences both the probability and the severity of the undesired state, and consider the effects on the ex ante value of reduced risk. This allows us to develop

---

[1]The ability of our individuals to take intervening actions implies that we are working within the "temporal risk" context of Spence and Zeckhauser [37]. Because we directly incorporate these intervening actions into our model, we do not violate the independence axiom of expected utility theory.

three propositions:

(1) Given moral hazard, when self-protection influences the probability, the severity, or both of an undesirable state, unobservable utility terms cannot be eliminated from the individual's ex ante valuation expression. Consequently, empirical studies that attribute differences across groups in ex ante value estimates solely to unobserved differences in household health production technologies are misplaced.

(2) With moral hazard and self-protection, knowledge of the convexity or nonconvexity of physical dose–response relations is insufficient to sign unambiguously the change in an individual's ex ante marginal valuation for a reduction in the level of the hazard, even when consumer cognition is perfect. Therefore, we do not support the traditional argument that those individuals exposed to greater risk with greater income must place a higher value on a given risk reduction.

(3) With moral hazard, an increase in the level of the environmental hazard does not necessarily lead to an increase in the level of self-protection. Therefore, self-protection expenditures are not a consistent lower bound of the ex ante value a risk averse individual attaches to a reduction in risk.

These three statements imply that several propositions originally developed for cases of exogenous risk and which form the analytical basis for most recent empirical work on the value of health risk changes are not immediately transferable to settings where endogenous risks prevail.

2. SELF-PROTECTION AND RISK

Psychologists agree that individuals perceive that they have substantial control over uncertain events (Perlmuter and Monty [26]). Stallen and Tomas [38] conclude that "... the individual is not so much concerned with estimating uncertain parameters of a physical or material system as he is with estimating the uncertainty involved in his exposure to the threatening event and in opportunities to *influence* or *control* his exposure" (emphasis added). Starr [39], an engineer, makes much of the difference between voluntary (endogenous) and involuntary (exogenous) exposures to risk. Indeed, rare is the noneconomic discussion of risk that does not consider "... measures that modify events or reduce the vulnerability to loss" (Kates [18, p. 7]). People move or reduce physical activities when air pollution becomes intolerable, they buy bottled water if they suspect that alternative supplies are polluted, they chelate children who have high blood lead concentrations, and they apply sunscreen to protect their skins from UV radiation. Finally, if one sets aside its risk valuation component, endogenous risk considerations are abundant in technical economic discourse.[2]

At the policy level, the success of collective safety mandates often depends upon individual choices. Auto seat belts, when worn, reduce both the probability and the severity of injury but their mandatory installation cannot guarantee that passengers

[2]For example, the moral hazard literature deals with the effect of insurance on an individual's incentives to self-protect, the bidding literature recognizes that the probability of winning depends upon the bid submitted, and the resource depletion literature accounts for the effect that the amount extracted has upon knowledge of additional reserves.

4   SHOGREN AND CROCKER

will choose to wear them. Workplace safety initiatives involving personal protective gear (e.g., hard hats) have the same problem. Highway speed limits are yet another example. In each case, individual decisions influence both the chance and the magnitude of harm.[3]

Individuals often substitute self-protection that is expected to reduce hazard probability or severity or both for collectively supplied safety programs. Burton *et al.* [3] enumerate numerous examples including the use of higher-strength building materials in response to prospective tornado, storm surge, and earthquake hazards, more thorough weeding and crop storage in response to the prospect of drought, sand bagging and evacuation in anticipation of floods, and improved nutrition and exercise regimens to cope with health threats. These and similar private coping strategies reduce the individual's chance of having a threat realized and its magnitude if it is realized.

Finally, recognition of the frequently endogenous nature of risk raises questions about the assessment–management bifurcation now common in scientific and policy discussions about environmental risks to human health and property. Broadly, risk assessment, because it defines what risk levels are, is considered to be the exclusive domain of the natural and the biomedical sciences, while risk management is left to the law, politics, philosophy, economics, and the sciences (National Academy of Sciences [24]). However, endogenous risk implies that observed risks are functions of natural science parameters and the self-protection decisions of individuals. Alternatively stated, the risks on the basis of which people make decisions will differ across individuals with the relative marginal productivities of their self-protection efforts, even though the properties of the natural phenomena that trigger these efforts may apply equally to everyone. It follows that attempts to assess observed risk levels solely in natural science terms may be highly misleading: costly self-protection is endogenous and may thus vary systematically in the observed risk data. Economic parameters enter and the manner in which they do so depends upon the relative values that people assign them. Some properties of these values for the case of endogenous risk are established in the next section.

3. THE MODEL

Consider an individual who is involuntarily exposed to a health risk under a particular liability regime. Assume the risk is created by exposure to an ambient concentration of given duration of an environmental hazard, r, taken from the real interval, R:

$$R = [\underline{r}, \bar{r}].$$ (1)

Because of moral hazard, the individual cannot acquire enough market insurance to avoid the risk completely. If he were able to do so, the risk would be exogenous (Marshall [22]). The individual must decide from a real interval, S, how much self-protection, s, to undertake:

$$S = [\underline{s}, \bar{s}].$$ (2)

---

[3]The folk truth that "you can lead a horse to water but you can't make it drink" seems appropriate.

RISK, SELF-PROTECTION, AND VALUE   5

Given exposure to the hazard, the individual is uncertain as to where in a continuum of health outcomes, h, he will be. Let $h(s, r)$ denote the outcome space, where outcomes are the individual's human health capital returns ordered from smallest to largest, given the individual's genetic and development history.

Let $f(h; s, r)$ denote the probability of a particular outcome occurring given that self-protection, s, is undertaken and that the exposure level to the environmental hazard is r. Assume the following about $f(\cdot)$:

Assumption 1. $f(h; s, r) > 0$ for every $s \in S$ and $r \in R$.

Let $F(h; s, r)$ denote the corresponding distribution function defined over the support $[a, b]$,

$$F(h; s, r) = \int_a^b f(h; s, r)\, dh, \tag{3}$$

where a and b are the minimum and maximum health outcomes.[4] We assume the following about $F(\cdot)$:

Assumption 2. $F(h; s, r)$ is twice continuously differentiable in $s \in S$ and $r \in R$ for every health outcome.

Assumption 3. $F_s(h; s, r) \leq 0$ for every $s \in S$ and $r \in R$ and every health outcome in the sense of first-order stochastic dominance, where a subscript denotes a partial derivative.[5]

Assumption 4. $F_r(h; s, r) \geq 0$ for every $s \in S$ and $r \in R$ and every health outcome in the sense of first-order stochastic dominance.

Assumption 5.   No restrictions are placed on the convexity of the distribution function in the immediate neighborhood of an optimal level of self-protection, s^*, for all $s \in S$ and $r \in R$ and for every health outcome.

The individual is risk averse with a von Neumann–Morgenstern utility index over wealth W, $U(W)$. The following assumptions are made about $U(W)$:

Assumption 6. U is defined over the real interval $[\overline{W}, \infty]$, where $\overline{W}$ is 0.

Assumption 7. $\mathrm{Lim}_{W \to \overline{W}}\, U(W) = -\infty$.

Assumption 8. U is strictly increasing, concave, and thrice continuously differentiable.

For each health outcome the individual might realize, he selects a minimum cost combination of medical care and foregone work and consumption. Let

$$C = C(h; s, r) \tag{4}$$

be his ex ante expectation of realized costs which depend on the uncertain health

---

[4]The $[a, b]$ interval could also be influenced in subsequent periods by self-protection. We disregard this issue.

[5]The distribution $G(h)$ first-order stochastically dominates the distribution $F(h)$ when $G(h) \leq F(h)$ for all $h \in [a, b]$, which is equivalent to obtaining $G(h)$ from $F(h)$ by shifting the probability mass to the right.

6   SHOGREN AND CROCKER

outcome, self-protection, and the exposure level to the hazard. Assume the
following about $C(\cdot)$:

Assumption 9. C is strictly decreasing, convex, and thrice continuously differentiable in $s \in S$ for every health outcome such that $C_s < 0$, $C_{ss} > 0$, and $C_{sh} \neq 0$
for all h.

Assumption 10. C is strictly increasing and thrice continuously differentiable in
$r \in R$ for every health outcome such that $C_r > 0$, and $C_{rh} \neq 0$. No restrictions,
however, are placed on C_{rr} for all h.

Given incomplete insurance purchases, intertemporally separable utility, and
constant expected prices for medical care, the individual's choice problem is then

$$\underset{s \in S}{\text{Max}} \left[\int_a^b U(W - C(h; s, r) - s) \, dF(h; s, r) \right]. \tag{5}$$

Note that the price of self-protection has been normalized to unity.

Given the model, we are now able to develop the propositions stated in the
introduction.

4. EX ANTE VALUE AND WILLINGNESS-TO-PAY

4.1. Endogenous Risk

A few very recent refinements to the willingness-to-pay approach to valuing
environmental hazards have acknowledged the frequently endogenous form of the
problem. For example, Rosen [30], Berger et al. [2], and Viscusi et al. [41] note that
self-protection affects survival or injury probabilities, while Shibata and Winrich
[32] and Gerking and Stanley [11] allow self-protection to influence the severity of
ex post damages. In a nonstochastic world or in an uncertain world with only two
feasible states, these studies demonstrate that marginal willingness to pay can be
expressed solely in terms of the marginal rate of technical substitution between
hazard concentrations and self-protection. This result cannot be generalized to a
continuous world with endogenous risk.

PROPOSITION 1. *Given the model assumptions, when self-protection influences
either the probability or the severity of health outcomes or both, the individual's
marginal willingness to pay for reduced risk cannot be expressed solely in terms of the
marginal rate of technical substitution between ambient hazard concentrations and
self-protection. In particular, unobservable utility terms cannot be eliminated from
expressions for the ex ante value of reduced risk.*

Proof. To show that for a continuous distribution the individual's compensating
variation statement of willingness to pay for reduced risk includes the unobservable utility terms, we examine self-protection that influences either the probability
distribution or the severity (costs) of the health outcomes or both.

First, maximize the expected utility index (5) by selecting an optimal level of
self-protection $s^* \in S$ yielding the first-order condition for an interior solution

$$EU_w = -E[U_w C_s] + \int_a^b U_w C_h F_s \, dh. \tag{6}$$

RISK, SELF-PROTECTION, AND VALUE   7

The left-hand side of (6) represents the marginal cost of increased self-protection in terms of the utility of foregone wealth. The right-hand side reflects two types of marginal self-protection benefits: the first term is the direct utility effect of enhanced wealth resulting from reduced expected ex post costs; the second term is the indirect utility effect of a stochastically dominating change in the distribution of health outcomes.

The indirect effect was derived by integrating by parts the effect of self-protection on the distribution

$$\int_a^b U(\cdot)\, dF_s(\cdot) = UF_s\big|_a^b + \int_a^b U_w C_h F_s\, dh$$

$$= \int_a^b U_w C_h F_s\, dh,$$

since $F_s(a; \cdot) = F_s(b; \cdot) = 0$. Assume that improved health outcomes will decrease the ex post costs, $C_h < 0$.

Solve for the compensating variation statement of the willingness-to-pay for reduced risk by totally differentiating the expected utility index (5), and then applying the first-order condition (6). When self-protection influences both the probability and the severity of health outcomes such that $F_s < 0$ and $C_s < 0$, the willingness-to-pay expression is

$$\frac{dW}{dr} = -\left[\frac{\int U_w C_h F_r\, dh - \int U_w C_r\, dF}{\int U_w C_h F_s\, dh - \int U_w C_s\, dF}\right] > 0, \qquad (7)$$

where all integrals are evaluated over the support $[a, b]$. Obviously, the unobservable utility indexes cannot be removed from the individual's willingness-to-pay expression (7).

Even the assumption of a simple two-state world fails to remove the utility terms from (7). For example, let $\pi(s, r)$ and $(1 - \pi(s, r))$ respectively represent the subjective probabilities of healthy and of sick states. Let $U_0(W - s)$ and $U_1(W - s - C(s, r))$ be the expected utility of being healthy or sick, where $U_0 > U_1$. The individual thus chooses $s \in S$ to maximize

$$EU = \pi(s, r)U_0(W - s) + (1 - \pi(s, r))U_1(W - s - C(s, r)). \qquad (8)$$

Following the same steps as before, the willingness-to-pay expression is

$$\frac{dW}{dr} = -\left[\frac{\pi_r[U_0 - U_1] - (1 - \pi)U_1'C_r}{\pi_s[U_0 - U_1] - (1 - \pi)U_0'C_s}\right] > 0, \qquad (9)$$

where $\pi_r < 0$, $\pi_s > 0$, $U_1' = \partial U_1/\partial W$, and $U_0' = \partial U_0/\partial W$. Again, utility terms cannot be removed irrespective of state independence or dependence.

Next allow, as do Gerking and Stanley [11], self-protection to influence the severity, $C_s < 0$, but not the probability, $F_s = 0$, of health outcomes. Further assume that $F_r = 0$ which, with $F_s = 0$, implies that neither collective nor individual actions will influence the probability of a particular health outcome, i.e., hazard concentrations resemble sunspots or the phases of the moon. With these assumptions, expression (7) reduces to

$$\frac{dW}{dr} = -\frac{E[U_w C_r]}{E[U_w C_s]} = -\left[\frac{EU_w EC_r - \mathrm{cov}(U_w, C_r)}{EU_w EC_s - \mathrm{cov}(U_w, C_s)}\right] > 0. \qquad (10)$$

For the unobservable utility terms to be absent from (10), the two covariance expressions must be zero; however, our model assumptions do not allow them to be zero. Therefore the two utility terms cannot be removed.

Finally, assume, as does Rosen [30], that self-protection affects probability, $F_s < 0$, but not severity, $C_s = 0$. In Rosen's [30] terms, one cannot be more severely dead. For similar reasons, $C_r = 0$. Under these conditions, expression (7) reduces to

$$\frac{dW}{dr} = -\frac{\int U_w C_h F_r \, dh}{\int U_w C_h F_s \, dh}, \qquad (11)$$

and again the willingness-to-pay expression cannot be rid of the unobservable utility terms, which concludes the proof.

We could examine additional cases. For example, self-protection might influence only the probability of a health outcome, but hazard concentrations could affect probability and severity, or vice versa. The results would not change: utility terms would loom up in the willingness-to-pay expressions, implying empirical efforts that use observed behavior data, and that policy efforts to aggregate across individuals and to account simultaneously for the reality of probability and severity, unavoidably involve interpersonal utility comparisons.[6]

Given the assumptions of the model and our above development of it, the sufficient conditions under which Proposition 1 would *not* hold can be stated as a corollary.[7]

COROLLARY 1. *Utility terms will not appear in ex ante willingness-to-pay expressions for endogenous risk changes if and only if at least one of the following conditions is true*:

(a) *A two-state world exists where ex ante self-protection affects only ex ante probability*;

(b) *A two-state world exists where ex ante self-protection affects only ex post severity, and the marginal utilities between states are equal*;

(c) *States are discrete, ex post severity is independent of ex ante self-protection, and a unique self-protection activity exists that exerts no cross-partial effects across states.*

---

[6]Assumptions of a risk-neutral individual with an identity map of ex post costs would eliminate the unobservable utility terms. These assumptions seem excessively restrictive. Alternatively, one might eliminate the utility terms by using the pointwise optimization technique that Mirrlees [23] and Holmstrom [14] employ. However, pointwise optimization evaluates self-protecting choices individually at each and every health state rather than in terms of lotteries over health states. It thus adopts an ex post rather than an ex ante perspective.

[7]Proofs of this and of subsequent corollaries are available from the authors upon request.

Corollary 1a clearly fits some stark life and death situations. In addition, self-protection can reduce the probability of diseases like cancer without changing its severity. Substantial imagination is required to think of real situations corresponding to 1b. Corollary 1c might apply where there are multiple forms of a disease like cancer. It requires that actions taken to avoid skin cancer, for example, do not change the probability of lung cancer.

4.2 Nonconvex Dose-Response Relations

Proposition 1 poses hurdles to procedures which use observed behavior data or which would establish a social risk–benefit test by summing unweighted compensating or equivalent variations across individuals.[8] Yet another problem for these procedures is the ambiguous effect that a change in hazard concentrations has on the sign of compensating variation.

An individual's marginal compensating variation can be shown to be ambiguous in sign even if the strongest possible case for negative effects of increased hazard exposure is imposed. To illustrate, define strong convexity as follows.

DEFINITION 1. Strong convexity of risk is defined as: convex ex post cost, $C_{rr} > 0$; convexity of the distribution function, $F_{rr} > 0$; and declining marginal productivity of self-protection, $C_{sr} > 0$, $C_{hr} > 0$, $C_{sh} > 0$ and $F_{sr} > 0$.

Strong convexity describes the conditions most favorable for the traditional argument that increased risk requires progressively increasing compensation to maintain a constant level of expected utility. Increased exposure increases the probability and the expected ex post costs of undesirable health outcomes to the hazard at an increasing rate; moreover, the marginal productivity of self-protection is decreasing across the board.

The opposite case is strong nonconvexity. Strong nonconvexity defines the weakest case for negative effects of increased exposure to the hazard.

DEFINITION 2. Strong nonconvexity of risk is defined as nonconvex ex post cost, $C_{rr} < 0$; concavity of the distribution function, $F_{rr} < 0$; and increasing marginal productivity of self-protection, $C_{sr} < 0$, $C_{hr} < 0$, $C_{sh} < 0$, and $F_{sr} < 0$.[9]

The following proposition states the result:

PROPOSITION 2. *Even in the absence of cognitive illusions or failure to consider all scarcity dimensions of the risk-taking problem, a maintained hypothesis of strong convexity of risk is insufficient to guarantee that increased exposure to a hazard requires progressively increasing compensation to maintain a constant level of expected utility. Similarly, strong nonconvexity is insufficient to guarantee progressively decreasing compensation.*

The proposition is supported by Dehez and Drèze [8, p. 98], who show that the sign of the marginal willingness to pay for safety given an increase in the probability of death is generally ambiguous. Drèze [9, p. 172] concludes that any

---

[8]See Polemarchakis *et al.* [27] for recent thinking on aggregation under exogenous risk.

[9]Rogerson [29] assumes that the distribution function must generally satisfy the convexity of the distribution function condition (CDFC). Therefore, the assumption of a concave distribution in *r* and *s* is perhaps restrictive. As shown by Jewitt [15], however, the CDFC assumption is not universally required in that it satisfies very few of the standard distributions set forth in statistics textbooks.

assertions about this sign given a change in safety "... must be carefully justified in terms of underlying assumptions".

Proposition 2 contradicts the argument of Weinstein *et al.* [44] and others that individuals at greater risk must have a greater demand for safety. Consequently, contrary to Rosen [30], individuals at greater risk with greater wealth cannot necessarily be weighted more heavily when risk reductions are valued. Similarly, the assertions by Kahneman and Tversky [17] and Smith and Desvousges [35] that increasing marginal willingness to pay for reduced risk constitutes a lapse from rational economical behavior are not supported.[10]

Proof. To demonstrate that an increase in hazard concentration has an ambiguous effect on an individual's compensating variation, differentiate the compensating variation in expression (7) with respect to the hazard exposure,

$$
\frac{d(dW/dr)}{dr} = -\frac{1}{\Omega}\left[E[U_{ww}C_r^2 - U_wC_{rr}] - 2\int[U_{ww}C_rC_h - U_wC_{hr}]F_r\,dh \right.
$$
$$
\left. + \int U_wC_hF_{rr}\,dh \right]
$$
$$
+ \frac{\Delta}{\Omega^2}\left[E[U_{ww}C_sC_r - U_wC_{sr}] + \int[U_wC_{hr} \quad U_{ww}C_hC_r]F_s\,dh \right.
$$
$$
\left. + \int[U_{ww}C_sC_r - U_wC_{sr}]F_r\,dh + \int U_wC_hF_{sr}\,dh \right], \qquad (12)
$$

where

$$
\Omega = \int U_wC_hF_s\,dh - \int U_wC_s\,dF > 0,
$$
$$
\Delta = \int U_wC_hF_r\,dh - \int U_wC_r\,dF < 0,
$$

and all integrals are evaluated over the support $[a, b]$.

The terms on the right-hand side of (12) can be defined in terms of direct and indirect utility effects given an increase in exposure to a hazard. $\Omega > 0$ and $\Delta < 0$ represent the combined first-order direct and indirect utility effects of s and r. The first and fourth terms in (12) represent second-order direct utility effects on expected costs with an increase in exposure. Given strong convexity, the sign of the first term is negative. The sign of the fourth term is ambiguous in the sense that alternative parameterizations are conceivable in which either $U_{ww}C_sC_r$ or U_wC_{sr} dominates in absolute magnitude. The second, fifth, and sixth terms are second-order direct and indirect utility effects weighted by the marginal effect on the distribution of either s or r. Given strong convexity, the signs of all three terms are

---

[10]Close inspection of the Smith and Desvousges [35, pp. 110–111] questionnaire reveals that respondent opportunities to influence the chance of death and the time to death were not fully controlled. Given the enhanced adjustment opportunities that self-protection provides, the exogenous risk valuations that Smith and Desvousges [35] presume they are reporting would be underestimates of risk reduction values and overestimates of risk increase values. Effects on changes in *marginal* willingness-to-pay depend upon the manner in which the marginal productivity of self-protection varies with risk.

ambiguous in the above sense. Without prior information on the magnitude of the marginal effects on the expected cost function, there is no reason to expect one term to dominate. The third and seventh terms represent the second-order indirect and cross-indirect utility effects of increased exposure. By the definition of strong convexity, the sign on both terms is negative. Without the relative magnitudes of all the direct and indirect utility effects being known, however, strong convexity is insufficient to sign (12) unambiguously. Likewise, the assumption of strong non-convexity is also insufficient to sign (12). Whether one imposes strong convexity or strong nonconvexity the sign of (12) is ambiguous. Although numerous sufficient conditions for increasing or decreasing marginal willingness to pay can be determined, there is, in the absence of prior information or simple ad hoc assumptions, no reason to expect that one or two terms will dominate expression (12). This concludes the proof.

Intuitively, the results occur because a changed exposure that induces self-protection may have productivity effects on probability that differ from those on severity. The only clear cut sufficient condition for signing (12) is the absence of all severity effects. This is stated as Corollary 2.

COROLLARY 2. *Assuming no severity effects ($C_s = C_r = 0$), the assumption of strong convexity is sufficient to guarantee increasing marginal ex ante valuations with increasing exposures.*

Again, diseases such as cancer or events such as death seem the only apt examples that clearly fit the corollary.

4.3. Self-Protection Expenditures as a Lower Bound

Consideration of self-protection has not been limited to problems of ex ante valuation under uncertainty. A substantial literature has emerged, e.g., Courant and Porter [4], and Harrington and Portney [12], which demonstrates that under perfect certainty the marginal benefit of a reduction in a health threat is equal to the savings in self-protection expenditures necessary to maintain the initial health state. This result cannot be extended to the uncertainty case when self-protection influences both ex ante probability and ex post severity.

PROPOSITION 3. *Neither strong convexity nor strong nonconvexity of risk is sufficient to sign the effect of a risk change upon self-protection expenditures. Therefore these expenditures cannot be used alone to determine the welfare effect of a risk change.*

Proposition 3 contradicts Berger *et al.*'s [2] argument that if increased exposure increases the marginal productivity of self-protection, $F_{sr} < 0$, then self-protection will increase with exposure. Consequently, Berger *et al.*'s [2, p. 975] sufficient conditions for "plausible" results do not hold when self-protection influences both probability and severity.

Proof. To demonstrate that strong convexity is insufficient to determine the effect increased hazard exposure has on self-protection, take the first-order condition in Eq. (6) and apply the implicit function theorem. The effect of

12   SHOGREN AND CROCKER

increased exposure on self-protection is

$$\frac{ds}{dr} = -\left[E[U_{ww}C_r(1 + C_s) - U_wC_{rs}] + \int[U_wC_{sh} - U_{ww}C_h(1 + C_s)]F_r\,dh\right.$$

$$\left. + \int[U_wC_{hr} - U_{ww}C_rC_h]F_s\,dh + \int U_wC_hF_{sr}\,dh\right]\Big/ D, \tag{13}$$

where

$$D \equiv E[U_{ww}C_s(1 + C_s) - U_wC_{ss}] + 2\int[U_wC_{sh} - U_{ww}C_hC_s]F_s\,dh$$

$$- \int U_{ww}C_hF_s\,dh + \int U_wC_hF_{ss}\,dh < 0 \tag{14}$$

and all integrals are evaluated over the support $[a, b]$. D is the second-order sufficient condition of the maximization problem (5), and is assumed to hold whenever (6) holds.

Given $D < 0$, the sign of (13) depends on the sign of its right-hand-side numerator. The first term in the numerator of (13) is the direct utility effect of increased exposure on expected costs. Given strong convexity of risk and $(1 + C_s) > 0$ from the first-order condition, the sign of the first term is negative. The second term reflects the indirect utility effect of increased exposure on the distribution. Given strong convexity, its sign is ambiguous in the earlier defined parameterization sense. The third term is a direct utility effect weighted by the marginal effect of self-protection on the distribution ($F_s < 0$), and its sign is also ambiguous. The signs for the second and third effect are ambiguous since there is no a priori reason to believe that any one set of terms dominates the others. The fourth term in the numerator is the cross-indirect utility effect of increased exposure. Given strong convexity, its sign is negative. Therefore, without prior information on the relative magnitudes of the four direct and indirect utility effects, strong convexity is insufficient to sign (13) unambiguously. Given the conditions most favorable to the traditional argument that increased risk will increase self-protection, we still require prior information on the impact that increased exposure has on the marginal productivity of self-protection to support the argument.

Following the logic above, an assumption of strong nonconvexity of risk leads to a similar conclusion of an ambiguous effect of increased exposure on self-protection. Consequently, since self-protection may decrease as exposure to a hazard increases, self-protection expenditures cannot be considered a consistent lower bound on the ex ante value a risk averse individual attaches to a reduction in risk. This concludes the proof.

The only clear cut cases in which these expenditures would be a lower bound can be stated as a corollary.

COROLLARY 3. *Sufficient conditions for self-protection expenditures being a lower bound on the ex ante value of risk reductions include:*

(a) $C_{sr} < 0$, *which is true under strong nonconvexity, and* $F_s = F_r = 0$.

(b) $F_{sr} > 0$, *which is true under strong convexity, and* $C_s = C_r = 0$.

Examples of Corollary 3a are not obvious; cancer and death provide the best examples for Corollary 3b.

5. CONCLUSIONS AND IMPLICATIONS

Individuals and policymakers use self-protection activities to influence both their ex ante risks and their expected ex post consequences. Given, as we have argued, that both forms of self-protection jointly occur in practice with great frequency, the implications of this for efforts to value risks to human health and property are unequivocally negative. Only the corollaries provide a rather pinched basis for optimism about the efficiency of traditional risk valuation efforts. With a parsimonious model in which only wealth provides direct utility, we show that unobservable utility terms cannot be eliminated from marginal willingness-to-pay expressions, implying that empirical efforts which identify marginal rates of substitution with willingness to pay are misdirected. We also show that even under the most favorable restrictions increased risk need not imply progressively increasing levels of compensation in order to restore initial utility levels. Consequently the traditional argument that those who are exposed to greater risk and have greater wealth must value a given risk reduction more highly does not follow. Finally, we demonstrate that increased risk need not imply increased self-protection expenditures; thus changes in these expenditures may not bound the value of a risk change.

Some succor for risk valuation efforts could be obtained by stepping outside professional boundaries to draw upon prior information from psychology, biomedicine, and other disciplines. Insight might therefore be gained into the signs and the relative magnitudes of many terms in expressions (12) and (13). It is odd that the field of economics which explicitly recognizes the policy relevance of incomplete markets has historically been reluctant to use information from other disciplines in order to simulate the valuation results of a complete market. We recognize that there is a growing tendency to incorporate restrictions about structure, functional forms, and parameter values from other disciplines into the behavioral postulates of economic models.[11] The results of this paper suggest that the incorporation process should be accelerated. With nonexperimental data, the Bayesian diagnostic techniques of Leamer [20] could be used to establish systematically the restrictions to which estimates of (12) and (13) are especially sensitive. Controlled experiments could be used for the same purpose. We report elsewhere (Shogren and Crocker [33]) results of controlled experiments showing empirically that self-protection increases the willingness to pay for risk reduction, where, by definition, the reductions are collectively *and* self-supplied. Although this result conforms neatly to the Le Chatelier principle as well as to Spence and Zeckhauser [37], similar empirical rather than purely theoretical analyses are likely to be required if the complexities offered by the three propositions in this paper are to be overcome.

Incorporation and more empirical analysis will not overcome, however, the aggregation problems posed by the presence of utility terms in individuals' willingness-to-pay expressions. Approaches to aggregate risk–benefit analysis do exist

[11]See Warneryd [42], Weinstein and Quinn [43] and Smith and Johnson [36], for example.

14   SHOGREN AND CROCKER

other than the mechanical summation of consumer surpluses calculated from the singular value judgement that social welfare and aggregate total income are synonymous. Given that individual consumer surpluses can be estimated, one possibility is to draw upon the extensive equivalence scale literature, e.g., Deaton and Muellbauer [7], in order to weight each individual or household. Tradeoffs can then be evaluated using an explicit social welfare function which recognizes that personal health is in part self-produced and inalienable. Alternatively, utilities might be calculated directly.

REFERENCES

1. K. Arrow, Uncertainty and the welfare economics of medical care, *Amer. Econom. Rev.* **53**, 941–969 (1963).
2. M. Berger, G. Blomquist, D. Kenkel, and G. Tolley, Valuing changes in health risk: A comparison of alternative measures, *Southern Econom. J.* **53**, 967–983 (1987).
3. S. Burton, R. W. Kates, and G. F. White, "The Environment as Hazard," Oxford Univ. Press, New York (1979).
4. P. Courant and R. Porter, Averting expenditures and the cost of pollution, *J. Environ. Econom. Management* **8**, 321–329 (1981).
5. T. D. Crocker, Scientific truths and policy truths in acid deposition research, *in* "Economic Perspectives on Acid Deposition Control" (T. D. Crocker, Ed.), pp. 65–80, Butterworth, Boston (1984).
6. T. D. Crocker, On the value of the condition of a forest stock, *Land Econom.* **61**, 244–254 (1985).
7. A. S. Deaton and J. Muellbauer, On measuring child costs: With applications to poor countries, *J. Polit. Economy* **94**, 720–744 (1986).
8. P. Dehez and J. H. Drèze, State-dependent utility, the demand for insurance and the value of safety, *in* "Premium Calculation in Insurance" (de Vylder, Goovaerts, and Haezendonck, Eds.), D. Reidel, Boston (1984).
9. J. H. Drèze, "Essays on Economic Decision under Uncertainty," Cambridge Univ. Press, New York (1987).
10. I. Ehrlich and G. Becker, Market insurance, self-insurance, and self-protection, *J. Polit. Economy* **80**, 623–648 (1972).
11. S. Gerking and L. Stanley, An economic analysis of air pollution and health: The case of St. Louis, *Rev. Econom. Statist.* **68**, 115–121 (1986).
12. W. Harrington and P. Portney, Valuing the benefits of health and safety regulation, *J. Urban Econom.* **22**, 101–112 (1987).
13. L. Hiebert, Self insurance, self protection, and the theory of the firm, *Southern Econom. J.* **50**, 160–168 (1983).
14. B. Holmstrom, Moral hazard and observability, *Bell. J. Econom.* **10**, 74–91 (1979).
15. I. Jewitt, Justifying the first-order approach to principal–agent problems, *Econometrica* **56**, 1177–1190 (1988).
16. M. W. Jones-Lee. M. Hammerton, and P. R. Philips, The value of safety: Results of a national sample survey. *Econom. J.* **95**, 49–52 (1985).
17. D. Kahneman and A. Tversky, Prospect theory: An analysis of decision under risk, *Econometrica* **47**, 263–291 (1979).
18. R. W. Kates, "Risk Assessment of Environmental Hazard," Wiley, New York (1978).
19. J. J. Laffont, "Essays in the Economics of Uncertainty," Harvard Univ. Press, Cambridge, MA (1980).
20. E. E. Leamer, "Specification Searches: Ad Hoc Inference with Nonexperimental Data," Wiley, New York (1978).
21. T. Lewis and D. Nickerson, Self-insurance against natural disasters, *J. Environ. Econom. Management* **16**, 209–223 (1989).
22. J. Marshall, Moral hazard, *Amer. Econom. Rev.* **66**, 880–890 (1976).
23. J. Mirrlees, Notes on welfare economics, information, and uncertainty, *in* "Essays on Economic Behavior under Uncertainty" (Balch, McFadden, and Wu, Eds.), pp. 118–124, North-Holland, Amsterdam (1974).

24. National Academy of Sciences, "Risk Assessment in the Federal Government: Managing the Process," National Academy Press, Washington, DC (1983).

25. W. Oi, The economics of product safety, *Bell J. Econom. Management Sci.* **4**, 3–28 (1973).

26. L. Perlmuter and R. Monty, "Choice and Perceived Control," Erlbaum, Hillsdale, NJ (1979).

27. H. M. Polemarchakis, L. Seldent, P. Zipkin, and L. Pohlman, Approximate aggregation under uncertainty, *J. Econom. Theory* **38**, 189–210 (1986).

28. R. Repetto, The policy implications of non-convex environmental damages: A smog control case study, *J. Environ. Econom. Management* **14**, 13–29 (1987).

29. W. Rogerson, The first-order approach to principal–agent problems, *Econometrica* **53**, 1357–1367 (1989).

30. S. Rosen, Valuing health risk, *Amer. Econom. Rev. Pap. Proceed.* **71**, 241–245 (1981).

31. S. Shavell, On moral hazard and insurance, *Quart. J. Econom.* **93**, 541–562 (1979).

32. H. Shibata and J. S. Winrich, Control of pollution when the offended defend themselves, *Economica* **50**, 425–437 (1983).

33. J. F. Shogren and T. D. Crocker, "Risk Reduction Mechanisms and Risk Valuation: An Experimental Study," Working Paper, Dept. of Economics, University of Wyoming, Laramie (1989).

34. V. K. Smith and W. Desvousges, Asymmetries in the valuation of risk and the siting of hazardous waste disposal facilities, *Amer. Econ. Rev. Pap. Proceed.* **76**, 291–294 (1986).

35. V. K. Smith and W. Desvousges, An empirical analysis of the economic value of risk change, *J. Polit. Economy* **95**, 89–115 (1987).

36. V. K. Smith and F. R. Johnson, How does risk perception respond to information: The case of radon, *Rev. Econom. Statist.* **70**, 1–18 (1988).

37. A. M. Spence and R. Zeckhauser, The effect of the timing of consumption decisions and the resolution of lotteries on the choice of lotteries, *Econometrica* **40**, 401–403 (1972).

38. P. Stallen and A. Thomas, Psychological aspects of risk: The assessment of threat and control, *in* "Technological Risk Assessment" (Ricci, Sagan, and Whipple, Eds.), pp. 211–229, Nijhoff, The Hague (1984).

39. C. Starr, Benefit–risk studies in sociotechnical systems, *in* "Perspectives on Benefit–Risk Decision-making," National Academy Press, Washington, DC (1972).

40. D. Starett, Fundamental nonconvexities in the theory of externalities, *J. Econom. Theory* **4**, 180–199 (1972).

41. W. K. Viscusi, W. A. Magat, and J. Huber, The rationality of consumer valuations of multiple health risks, *Rand. J. Econom.* **18**, 465–479 (1987).

42. K. E. Warneryd, Economic and psychological approaches to the study of economic behavior: Similarities and differences, *in* "New Directions in Research on Decision Making" (Brehmer, Jungerman, Lourens, and Sevon, Eds.), pp. 48–66, North-Holland, New York (1986).

43. M. Weinstein and R. Quinn, Psychological consideration in valuing health risk reductions, *Nat. Resour. J.* **23**, 659–674 (1983).

44. M. C. Weinstein, D. S. Shepard, and J. S. Pliskin, The economic value of changing mortality probabilities: A decision-theoretic approach, *Quart. J. Econom.* **94**, 373–396 (1980).

45. J. Winrich, Convexity and corner solutions in the theory of externality, *J. Environ. Econom. Management* **9**, 29–41 (1982).

Part VII
Structural Mitigation Measures

[24]

Public Policy Volume 29 No. 1 (Winter 1981)

THE ECONOMICS OF BUILDING CODES
TO RESIST SEISMIC SHOCK

LINDA COHEN AND ROGER NOLL

This paper applies economic analysis to the problem of evaluating building codes that are designed to mitigate the damaging effects of earthquakes. Earthquake damage is a probabilistic event, and the best technology for mitigating it entails increasing the capital costs of threatened structures. Consequently, selecting an optimal seismic resistivity for buildings is a problem in optimal investment planning when returns are risky. Most types of disasters and the defenses against them have these general characteristics. The methods used in this paper therefore apply to evaluating defenses against all such disasters, ranging from flood control projects to emergence core cooling systems for nuclear reactors. Nevertheless, each form of disaster has unique technical characteristics that are of potentially great empirical importance. Hence, this paper eschews generality and deals explicitly with the problem of selecting optimal building standards in seismically active areas.

For the most part, seismic codes apply to new structures. The codes specify minimum design features that new structures must match or exceed. The codes are designed so that a conforming structure will be able to withstand a specified intensity of violent ground motions without collapsing, although building to code also diminishes the damage to the structure from earthquakes that are not severe enough to cause the building to collapse. In some instances, new information about the vulnerability of structures or

Part of the costs of preparing this manuscript were financed by a grant from the National Aeronautics and Space Administration and part by a grant from the National Science Foundation program of Research Applied to National Needs, grant no. A0I75-16566A01. We are grateful to George Housner, Paul Joskow, James Rosse, and anonymous referees for comments on an earlier draft.

the nature of the threat of an earthquake in a particular area leads local governments to adopt codes for existing buildings as well as new structures. For example, the Field Act in California, passed after the damaging Long Beach earthquake of 1934, required that all schools in the state, old and new, be made strong enough to withstand a major earthquake. In the aftermath of the 1971 San Fernando earthquake, measures have been adopted or proposed that would require retrofitting of particularly hazardous structures, such as dams, public meeting halls, and theaters, to bring them up to the standards required of new structures.

The primary economic justification for seismic building codes is that the structural soundness of a building has a social value that is not likely to be taken into account by its owner.[1] If a building collapses during an earthquake, the owner suffers a financial loss equal to the value of the structure. But the collapse of a building can have a higher social cost than simply its asset value. First, occupants of the building or persons in its immediate vicinity may be killed or maimed by the collapsing structure. Second, other capital assets, such as adjacent buildings or vehicles, may be damaged by its collapse. Third, government resources are used to clean up part of the damage of an earthquake and to maintain order in damaged areas.

The owner of a building lacks the incentive to consider the full social cost of the collapse of a building, even if the owner is liable to compensate persons who suffer damage when the building collapses. For several reasons, complete compensation is unlikely to be paid, and so the owner will not be led to minimize the sum of the costs of earthquake defenses and expected liability for earthquake related damages. First, the collapse of a building may bankrupt its owner. In any event, the wealth of the owner, whether an individual or a corporation, represents the legal limit to compensation. Second, since an important element of the damage of an earthquake is loss of life and serious injuries, compensation is likely to be, at best, arbitrary, if not systematically too small. Third, whatever their merit as policies, governmental

---

[1] The analysis in this paper ignores arguments for building codes and other public policies related to disasters that presume people are unable to calculate accurate probabilities of disasters or to behave rationally when confronted by low probability, catastrophic contingencies.

disaster relief programs are, in effect, social insurance policies that pay a substantial part of the costs of a disaster. These programs affect incentives to defend against disasters, creating a type of moral hazard problem.[2] Fourth, in a major earthquake the cause of a particular part of the damage is likely to be difficult if not impossible to ascertain. If a block of buildings collapses, it is difficult to determine which would have withstood the earthquake if others had not collapsed, and which individuals and vehicles in the surrounding area were damaged by which building.[3]

Much of the damage associated with earthquakes is so-called secondary damage—destruction caused not by the earthquake directly, but by other problems that arise because of the earthquake. For example, more than 90 percent of the damage and deaths associated with the 1906 San Francisco earthquake were directly attributable to the ensuing fire.[4] If the collapse of one building is accompanied by fire, at what point does fire damage cease to be the responsibility of the owner of the collapsed structure? In New York State, for example, in the case of a fire resulting from negligence, liability is limited to damage to the structures that are adjacent to the structure in which the fire started. Owners of all other damaged structures have no claims against the negligent party or owners of structures through which the fire passed.[5] Although there are economically sound historical reasons for this policy, its perverse incentives *vis-a-vis* earthquake-resistant construction practices are clear.

---

[2] Linda Cohen, "A Public Policy Approach to the Study of Optimal Compensation Systems: the Case of the Price-Anderson Act," Kennedy School of Government Discussion Paper No. 61D, Harvard University, February 1979.

[3] This paper does not systematically examine taxation according to the seismic vulnerability of a structure as an alternative to codes. Obviously, basing taxes in part on seismic risk categories may be a desirable policy, although it has certain problems owing to the uncertainties associated with the likelihood that an earthquake will occur, the actual seismic resistivity of any particular method of construction before a structure has been subjected to seismic shock, and the fact that earthquake damage is sometimes difficult to attribute to any particular building or structural feature.

[4] Charles Boden, "San Francisco's Cisterns," *California Historical Quarterly, 15*(4) (1937): 1–13.

[5] Marc Franklin, *Tort Law and Alternatives: Injuries and Remedies* (The Foundation Press, Mineola, NY, 1971), pp. 170–171.

In sum, determining who is liable for the damages suffered by each person as a result of an earthquake is an all but impossible task, and probably fruitless in any event because some who are ultimately held responsible for the damage will be unable to compensate the victim. Seismic building codes are one mechanism for dealing with this problem. A properly designed code can effect an approximate internalization of the social costs of earthquake damage.

The next section develops a simple theoretical model of the choice of an optimal building code, given that differing codes imply differing cost increments for structures and provide differing degrees of protection from seismic shock. The purpose of the section is to derive equations that can be estimated using the limited data now available. Several important simplifying assumptions are employed; these are relaxed in Section III.

The second section examines the rudimentary data that are available to examine the extent to which building codes might be said to be economically optimal. Because the benefits of codes include savings in human lives and injuries that are difficult, if not impossible, to evaluate, no definitive judgment on codes is offered. Instead, the second section contains a calculation of the magnitude of these benefits that would rationalize existing and proposed codes.

The third section provides a theoretical analysis of the effects of changes in the expected frequency of earthquakes on decisions about optimal seismic resistivity. This analysis is useful for gaining insights about the likely effect of the development of techniques for predicting earthquakes.

I. A Simple Theoretical Framework

The problem of devising an optimal seismic building code is regarded here as equivalent to the problem of minimizing the costs of a long-lived capital investment, including the expected damage of earthquakes. The extent to which this random event undermines the value of the asset depends upon the amount of defensive expenditure made at the time the investment was made.

Henceforth, the following notation will be adopted:

ECONOMICS OF BUILDING CODES   5

> K = investment in the structure that yields income, including investment in the contents of the structure.
>
> x = the additional investment in a structure for the purpose of increasing its resistivity to seismic shocks, measured as a percent of K; the total investment in the structure is then $(1 + x)K$.
>
> $p(t)$ = the probability that an earthquake will occur at time t that causes structural collapse if $x = 0$.
>
> i = a measure of the intensity of ground shaking associated with an earthquake, with $i_0 \leqslant i \leqslant I$.
>
> r = the market rate of interest.
>
> v = the rate of depreciation of the structure.
>
> N = the useful life of the structure.
>
> $q(i)$ = the probability that shaking of intensity i will occur at the site of the structure, given that a major earthquake occurs in the area.
>
> $f(K,x,i)$ = the proportion of the income-earning investment in the structure, K, that would be destroyed by ground shaking of intensity i if defensive expenditures xK have been made on the structure.

The damage function, f, is assumed to depend on K; that is, a given percentage increment in costs for a structure has a different protective effect on buildings of differing costs. In general, larger structures are more likely to be damaged by an earthquake. In reality, of course, other structural features of a building, such as height and construction materials, determine in part the relationship between the amount of damage suffered and the expenditures on defense against seismic shocks. Nevertheless, as a general proposition, bigger structures are more prone to damage given any intensity i (e.g., $f_K > 0$) and benefit more from defensive expenditures ($f_{Kx} < 0$). Since $f(K,x,i)$ must be bounded above by one and below by zero, at least for large values of K and x, $f_{KK} \leqslant 0$ and $f_{xx} \geqslant 0$.

The earthquake probability function, $p(t)$, would normally be estimated from historical frequencies of damaging earthquakes, although in the future reliable earthquake predictions may be possible. Because damage from ground motion diminishes as one moves away from the center of an earthquake, $p(t)$ varies from location to location.

The characterization of ground shaking used in this model is greatly simplified from reality, but is sufficient to capture the policy problem at issue. The probability that an earthquake of sufficiently large magnitude to impose uncompensated losses will occur at time t is denoted by $p(t)$. Because the principal external costs of earthquakes arise only when structural collapse occurs, small earthquakes that cause some private losses are ignored. Moreover, earthquakes are assumed here to be sufficiently infrequent that at most one damaging earthquake will occur during the planned life of the structure.

The expected life of a structure is assumed to be independent of the amount of seismic resistivity built into it. In reality, the type of reinforcing that makes a building more earthquake resistant also increases its durability. If N is large, as is the case for nearly all buildings, the discounted present value of the income stream added because of the building code is small, and the analysis is greatly simplified if it is ignored.

The problem of picking an optimal building code is regarded as equivalent to picking an optimal value of x, the proportion of the capital investment that is attributable to additional seismic resistivity over that which would normally be built into the structure as a matter of standard practice, even if the structure were located in an area with no seismic risk. Of course, a modern structure is naturally resistant to earthquakes because design features that add to its longevity, insulation from wind resistance (in the case of tall structures), and other desirable structural characteristics also make the building somewhat resistant to seismic shock. The variable x measures expenditures specifically for the purpose of providing added seismic resistivity.

This particular formulation of the problem presumes that building codes are suboptimized, i.e., that they call for the maximum seismic resistivity available at the cost of implementing the codes. For most types of building codes, this would be a facetious assumption, because the point of many codes is to protect particular product and labor inputs; however, in the case of building codes in seismically threatened areas, the assumption probably is not violently wrong. Academic structural engineers play a major role in designing and evaluating seismic codes and receive no

ECONOMICS OF BUILDING CODES 7

economic benefits from the effects of the codes on the choice of building inputs. Moreover, the codes are based in part on experimental and theoretical engineering research that is widely published in the professional literature, and subject to disinterested professional scrutiny. Thus, it is not likely that, for any given degree of seismic resistivity contemplated in a code, an alternative technology is readily available that could provide the same protection at significantly lower cost. Of course, it may still be the case that the extent of seismic resistivity that is implicit in the code is not optimal.

The firm's optimal choice of x is that value that minimizes private costs, i.e., the sum of the initial investment and expected earthquake damage. The latter is the depreciated cost of the investment at the time of the earthquake, so some specific time path of the building's market value—a depreciation rate v—must be incorporated into the analysis. Thus, the cost-minimization problem is as follows:

$$\min_{x} \left\{ K(1+x) + \int_{i_0}^{I} \int_{0}^{N} K\,p(t)\,f(K,x,i)\,e^{-(r+v)t}\,q(i)\,dt\,di \right\}. \tag{1}$$

In this formulation, the frequency of earthquakes is assumed to be sufficiently low so that no more than one will occur during the life of a building. Consequently, after an earthquake occurs, no additional value is derived from expenditures xK on seismic resistivity. Moreover, the term representing earthquake damage is simplified to represent the expected damage from the possibility of precisely one earthquake during the N years of a structure's life.

The first order condition for cost minimization is

$$K + K \int_{0}^{N} p(t)e^{-(r+v)t}\,dt \int_{i_0}^{I} f_x(K,x,i)\,q(i)\,di = 0. \tag{2}$$

If the further assumptions are made that v can be approximated by $1/N$ and that the probability of an earthquake is uniformly distributed with respect to time, eq. (2) with the integration performed and rearranged reduces to:

8   *Public Policy*

$$1 + p\left(\frac{1-e^{-(r+1/N)N}}{r+1/N}\right) \int_{i_0}^{I} f_x(K,x,i)\,q(i)\,di = 0. \qquad (3)$$

The integral

$$\int_{i_0}^{I} f_x(K,x,i)\,q(i)\,di$$

is the expected value of f_x over i, and is denoted by $G(f_x(K,x,i))$.

In nearly all cases, the value of N is very large. Consequently, expression (3) can be simplified by use of the following approximation:

$$\left(\frac{1-e^{-(r+1/N)N}}{r+1/N}\right) = \frac{1}{r}.$$

In the analysis to follow, this simplification will be used rather than estimating the true value of N and evaluating the complicated exponential.

To generalize the cost-minimization problem to account for external costs, another element is added to the optimization problem that represents the costs of earthquake damage that are not borne by owners of a structure. Two additional terms must be defined:

$E(K,i) =$ the external costs caused by ground shaking of intensity i at a structure of size K, if it were constructed without account being taken of earthquake risks.

$g(K,x,i) =$ the proportion of loss $E(K,i)$ that is suffered if xK is spent on defense.

The function $E(K,i)$ covers a multitude of damages, running from the easily monetizable (e.g., government disaster relief expenditures to clean up rubble) to the dubiously monetizable (e.g., pain, suffering, and death of persons in or around the collapsed structure). Again, for ease of exposition, these damages are assumed not to be time-dependent.

The external damage function is included here for the purpose of examining qualitatively its implications in the optimization problem, not because there is much hope of estimating the function empirically. Here $E(K,i)$ is assumed to rise as K increases be-

ECONOMICS OF BUILDING CODES   9

cause larger buildings affect more people and a wider area when they collapse; e.g., $E_K(K,i) > 0$.

The function $g(K,x,i)$ serves the same purpose as did $f(K,x,i)$ in the private cost-minimization problem. It is assumed that expenditures on defense against earthquakes reduce external costs and are more important in large structures. Moreover, because $g(K,x,i) \in [0,1]$, the function must for some range become less sensitive to further increases in K and x (e.g., for $K \geqslant$ some value K^* and $x \geqslant x^*$). These requirements can be expressed as follows:

$$
\begin{aligned}
g_K &\geqslant 0 \\
g_L &\leqslant 0 \\
g_{KK} &\leqslant 0 \text{ for } K \geqslant K^* \\
g_{xx} &\geqslant 0 \text{ for } x \geqslant x^* \\
g_{xK} &\leqslant 0.
\end{aligned}
$$

The assumption that the same x enters $f(K,x,i)$ and $g(K,x,i)$ presumes an identity of actions to protect buildings and measures to protect people. While this presumption may be generally correct, there may be exceptions. For example, flexible high-rise structures may be more resistant to seismic shocks than rigid buildings, but the people at the top of flexible buildings may be injured by being flung about as the structures sway in response to a seismic shock. The analysis in this paper ignores any potential conflicts between saving lives and protecting buildings.

Social welfare maximization entails including the external costs of an earthquake in the private optimization problem, thereby arriving at the following cost-minimization problem:

$$
\min_{x} \left\{ K(1+x) + \int_{i_o}^{I} \int_{0}^{N} \left[Kf(K,x,i)e^{-(r+v)t} + E(K,i)g(K,x,i)e^{-st} \right] \right.
$$
$$
\left. \times\, p(t)q(i)\,dt\,di \right\} ,
$$

where s is the social discount rate.

The second of the two terms in brackets represents the external costs of earthquakes, and the entire integrand represents the expected social loss in a time interval. The social discount rate, s, is not necessarily the same as the rate, r, used in the rest of the objective expression. Writing these rates as different parameters avoids taking an explicit stand on the appropriate discount rate to apply to irreversible events, such as the loss of life. Whether $s = r$, $s = 0$, or $0 < s < r$ is not germane to the purposes of this paper because no attempt will be made to evaluate the social externalities associated with an earthquake.

As is readily apparent, the first-order condition for this problem contains the terms in the first-order condition for private cost minimization, plus an additional term reflecting external costs. Making the same assumptions as were made in the preceding analysis, this term reduces to

$$\frac{p}{r} \int_{i_0}^{I} E(K,i) g_x(K,x,i) di,$$

in which the integral is the expected external damage if a damaging earthquake occurs, which is henceforth written as $H(E, g_x)$. The assumptions on functional forms imply that this expression will be negative as long as further effective earthquake defenses are available. Hence, the value of x that satisfies (3) (and thereby minimizes private costs) will be too small to minimize social costs. The equilibrium condition for minimizing social cost can be written as

$$\frac{p}{r} [G(f_x) + H(E, g_x)] = 0. \tag{3'}$$

II. Empirical Application

The strategy of this section is to provide a crude index of the extent to which private profits are not maximized. If building codes require an investment in earthquake defenses that diverges from the optimal private value of x, then expression (3) will not be satisfied. However, expression (3) minimizes only private structural costs. If society is choosing optimal building codes, the disequilibrium will indicate the social valuation of the nonstructural costs of earthquake damage; that is, the actual value of $-(p/r) G(f_x)$ is the value that $(p/r) H(E, g_x)$ must take to minimize social costs.

ECONOMICS OF BUILDING CODES   11

Thus, the extent to which the expenditures on defenses diverge from the cost-minimizing equilibrium provides a measure of the value of the external effects of earthquakes that is embodied in the codes, that is, an estimate of the social valuation of

$$\frac{p}{r} \int_{i_0}^{I} E(K,i)g_x(K,x,i)\,di.$$

The desirability of a code can then be viewed as a subjective assessment of whether this implicit valuation of external effects is reasonable.

The empirical analysis to follow must be a crude approximation to reality. One source of difficulty is due to the fact that each structure is to some degree unique. The likelihood that a structure will collapse in an earthquake depends upon the location of the structure relative to the epicenter, the magnitude of the earthquake, the orientation of the axes of the structure in relation to the direction of ground motion due to the earthquake, the composition of the ground on which the structure is built, and numerous other features that are specific to the site, the structure, and the nature of the earthquake threat that it faces. The problem of designing an optimal degree of seismic resistivity into a structure is, therefore, unique to each building. A uniform building code is intrinsically inefficient in that it requires some degree of uniformity among structures that is not strictly desirable. As local government has become more sophisticated about the nature of the threat of earthquakes, building codes have begun to move in the direction of design standards based on the characteristics of a building site that affect its seismic vulnerability.[6] Nevertheless, given the costs of writing and enforcing a unique code for each structure, the least costly strategy is likely to be to maintain considerable uniformity of treatment among buildings. In most localities, the movement away from uniform codes is only begin-

[6] For example, in Long Beach, California, old commercial structures and apartment houses are assigned to a "seismic hazard" category. Each design feature that is related to seismic vulnerability is assigned a score, and the total score for the structure determines its risk category. Owners are given a fixed amount of time to improve the seismic resistivity of the structure or remove it, with the amount of time being shorter for greater risks. Owners can stretch this period by repairing part of the hazard and causing the building to move to a lower risk category.

12   *Public Policy*

ning. Consequently, an empirical analysis must be a fictional representation of conditions for a "representative" structure.

Expression (3) has minimal data requirements. In order to determine whether equation (3) is satisfied for a particular type of structure, one need only know: (1) the annual probability of an earthquake; (2) the proportion of the area exposed to different amounts of ground shaking intensity, given a major earthquake; (3) the life of the structure if no earthquake occurs; (4) the long-term interest rate; and (5) the expected reduction in the proportion of damage to the investment due to a given intensity of ground shaking that was accomplished by the last percentage point increase in the fraction of building costs that is attributable to seismic resistivity.

EARTHQUAKE FREQUENCIES AND INTENSITIES

One inescapable data requirement for estimating the appropriate amount of seismic defenses in the manner implied by the preceding model is information about the frequency of damaging earthquakes. Perhaps surprisingly, little information is available about the frequency of earthquakes in specific locations. Damaging earthquakes are very rare events, even in seismically active areas, and meaningful data on the intensity of earthquakes has been collected only for about the last hundred years. Two measures of earthquake intensity are commonly used: Richter Magnitude (RM) and Modified Mercalli Intensity (MMI). The former is a measure of the energy released during the peak of an earthquake at its epicenter, and the latter is a crude categorization scale based upon the effects of the earthquake at a particular point.

The Mercalli measure is made at each location affected by an earthquake, and varies from one location to another according to distance from the epicenter of the earthquake and ground conditions. Because the concern here is with structural damage, the MMI scale is the appropriate measure. That is, the function $p(t)$ will denote the frequency of earthquakes that measure at least some minimally damaging value of MMI. The maximum intensity of ground shaking due to an earthquake is commonly denoted by MMI_0.

ECONOMICS OF BUILDING CODES   13

Table 1 shows the surprisingly vague standard definitions of the twelve categories of the Mercalli intensity. MMI VIII represents the threshold at which structural collapse of modern buildings occurs. As Table 1 shows, MMI VIII is also the minimum intensity at which any substantial number of modern buildings will suffer heavy damage. Accordingly, $p(t)$ will measure the frequency of ground shaking of at least MMI VIII.

The frequency of intense ground shaking due to earthquakes varies according to location, and so empirical application of the general method developed in this paper must be site-specific. The data used here are from California where information about earthquakes has been systematically gathered for the longest period of time.[7] The estimate of $p(t)$ is necessarily crude, because data on major earthquakes are extremely scarce, even in California. The lowest magnitude Southern California earthquake that has a recorded intensity of MMI VIII measured 5.8 on the Richter scale.[8] Earthquakes of roughly this magnitude occur about every two years, but most often are centered in unpopulated areas and, therefore, cause no significant damage. Great earthquakes causing widespread damage are sufficiently infrequent that few have been observed. But this does not make the major earthquakes necessarily of lesser importance. The more intense the earthquake, the larger the area affected by it. A magnitude 6.0 earthquake will cause severe ground motion and serious structural damage in an area with a radius of about 15 miles, but is unlikely to cause structural collapse of modern buildings; the area of damaging shaking has a radius of about 50 miles for a magnitude 7.0 earthquake and of about 90 miles for a magnitude 8.2, although in both instances the area in which structural collapse will occur is much

---

[7] In part, California has better data because it is in an active seismic region, but this is not the only explanation. Major earthquakes are roughly as great a threat in several other parts of the United States—notably Alaska, parts of the Rocky Mountain Area, Missouri, Tennessee, and Eastern Massachusetts. Another factor contributing to the richer data base in California is the extent and quality of research on seismology at the U.S. Geological Survey offices in California and at the state's major universities, notably Caltech, University of California at Berkeley, and Stanford. The modern science of geophysics was, for the most part, invented in California, and California had the first extensive seismic network for measuring earthquakes.

[8] S. T. Algermissen et al., *A Study of Earthquake Losses in the Los Angeles, California Area* (U.S. Government Printing Office, Washington, D.C., 1973).

Table 1. MODIFIED MERCALLI INTENSITY CATEGORIES

I. Not felt except by a very few under especially favorable circumstances.

II. Felt only by a few persons at rest, especially on upper floors of buildings. Delicately suspended objects may swing.

III. Felt quite noticeably indoors, especially on upper floors of buildings, but many people do not recognize it as an earthquake. Standing motor cars may rock slightly. Vibration like passing of truck. Duration estimated.

IV. During the day felt indoors by many, outdoors by few. At night some awakened. Dishes, windows, doors disturbed; walls made creaking sound. Sensation like heavy truck striking building. Standing motor cars rocked noticeably.

V. Felt by nearly everyone; many awakened. Some dishes, windows, etc., broken; a few instances of cracked plaster; unstable objects overturned. Disturbance of trees, poles, and other tall objects sometimes noticed. Pendulum clocks may stop.

VI. Felt by all; many frightened and run outdoors. Some heavy furniture moved; a few instances of fallen plaster or damaged chimneys. Damage slight.

VII. Everybody runs outdoors. Damage negligible in buildings of good design and construction; slight to moderate in well-built ordinary structures; considerable in poorly built or badly designed structures; some chimneys broken. Noticed by persons driving motor cars.

VIII. Damage slight in specially designed structures; considerable in ordinary substantial buildings with partial collapse; great in poorly built structures. Panel walls thrown out of frame structures. Fall of chimney, factory stacks, columns, monuments, walls. Heavy furniture overturned. Sand and mud ejected in small amounts. Changes in well water. Disturbs persons driving motor cars.

IX. Damage considerable in specially designed structures; well-designed frame structures thrown out of plumb; great in substantial buildings, with partial collapse. Buildings shifted off foundations. Ground cracked conspicuously. Underground pipes broken.

X. Some well-built wooden structures destroyed; most masonry and frame structures destroyed with foundations; ground badly cracked. Rails bent. Landslides considerable from river banks and steep slopes. Shifted sand and mud. Water splashed (slopped) over banks.

XI. Few, if any, (masonry) structures remain standing. Bridges destroyed. Broad fissures in ground. Underground pipe lines completely out of service. Earth slumps and land slips in soft ground. Rails bent greatly.

XII. Damage total. Waves seen on ground surfaces. Lines of sight and level distorted. Objects thrown upward into the air.

Source: S. T. Algermissen et al., *A Study of Earthquake Losses in the Los Angeles, California Area,* (U.S. Government Printing Office, Washington, D.C., 1973).

ECONOMICS OF BUILDING CODES   15

smaller.[9] Housner has estimated the frequency of earthquakes in California by Richter magnitude and the area of severe shaking associated with each magnitude. The results are summarized in Table 2. The Housner radius includes shaking of intensity MMI VII or greater.

Using these data and Housner's calculation regarding the area affected by earthquakes of varying magnitudes, the size of the areas affected by earthquakes of each range of magnitudes can also be estimated, as is shown in Table 2. The last column sums to approximately 400,000 square miles; considering that California contains approximately 150,000 square miles and that nearly all of the State is seismically active, these data imply that a particular seismically active location can expect to experience severe ground shaking about once every thirty to forty years.

Ground shaking of a severity postulated in the calculations shown in Table 2 does not necessarily lead to structural collapse. Table 3 compares RM and MMI for 23 Southern California earthquakes that occurred from 1907 to 1973 for which estimates of both intensity measures have been made. The Housner calculation is intended to include areas of serious structural damage that falls

[9] G. W. Housner, "Vibration of Structure Induced by Seismic Waves: Part I—Earthquakes," in M. Harris and E. Crede, *Shock and Vibration Handbook,* Vol. 3 (McGraw-Hill, New York, 1961).

Table 2. PROBABLE NUMBER OF EARTHQUAKES AND AREA OF SEVERE
GROUND MOTION PER CENTURY BY RICHTER MAGNITUDE
FOR STATE OF CALIFORNIA

Richter Magnitude	Number of Earthquakes per 100 Years	Area in Square Miles Subject to Severe Ground Shaking per Earthquake	Total Area in Square Miles Affected by all Earthquakes of Magnitude Class
6.0 – 6.3	46	1,000	46,000
6.4 – 6.7	27	3,000	81,000
6.8 – 7.3	19.3	8,000	154,000
7.4 – 7.9	5.6	15,000	84,000
8.0 – up	1.1	25,000	28,000

Source: Based upon data and calculations in G. W. Housner, ftn. 9.

16 *Public Policy*

Table 3. RELATIONSHIP BETWEEN RICHTER MAGNITUDE
AND MODIFIED MERCALLI INTENSITY: 1907–1973

Range of Magnitude	Number of Earthquakes	Number with MMI VIII or above
5.8 – 6.1	11	3
6.2 – 6.5	8	4
6.6 – up	4	4

Source: S. T. Algermissen et al., *A Study of Earthquake Losses in the Los Angeles, California Area* (U.S. Government Printing Office, Washington, D.C., 1973).

short of collapse, as is evident by the inclusion of magnitude 6.0–6.3 earthquakes in the calculations. These earthquakes are rarely associated with the collapse of modern structures, or with large nonstructural costs, as is shown below.

Wiggins and Moran have presented a formal representation of the relationships among Mercalli intensity, Richter magnitude, and the distance (d) from the epicenter of the earthquake as follows[10] :

$$MMI = 4.7 + 1.04RM - 3.14 \log d.$$

This equation should not be taken too seriously. Wiggins and Moran provide no justification for the functional form nor any measures of the statistical significance of either the individual variables or the equation as a whole. Thus, whether the relation is even remotely accurate for large earthquakes, which lay at the extreme values covered by the data being analyzed and which necessarily constitute a small part of the sample owing to their infrequency, remains in doubt but seems unlikely. In any event, the equation suggests that the MMI VIII region for a magnitude 8.0 earthquake constitutes about half of the total area that suffers significant damage, according to Housner's definition. The implication is that less than half of the areas included in the calculations in Table 3 are shaken severely enough so that heavy structural damage or collapse is a possibility. If so, the frequency of shaking

[10] J. H. Wiggins and D. H. Moran, *Earthquake Safety in Long Beach Based on the Concept of Balanced Risk* (J. H. Wiggins, 1971) (mimeo).

of intensity MMI VIII or greater at a given location is half the frequency of major earthquakes, or, at most, once every sixty to eighty years. Thus, in estimating expression (9), values of p less than 0.02 are appropriate.

Values of $q(i)$ are even more uncertain than for $p(t)$. Table 2, the Wiggins-Moran relation, and other data on the relative frequencies of various degrees of shaking intensity suggest that for earthquakes that may cause structural collapse, more than half the area shaken is subject to MMI VIII and about one-fourth to MMI IX. The remainder is subject to even more severe ground shaking.

RELATING EARTHQUAKE INTENSITY TO DAMAGES

An estimate of the proportion of the investment lost due to ground shaking is dependent on the nature of the structure. Whitman et al. have estimated the probabilities of varying degrees of damage to 8 to 13-story structures of a particular design, given the Mercalli intensity of the earthquake at the site of the structure. Table 4 defines the damage categories used by Whitman et al. Of course, because larger buildings are more vulnerable to earthquakes, the figures in Table 4 would be substantially smaller for one or two-story structures. An important element of this table is its demonstration of the fact that the damage to a structure must be fairly severe before many of the occupants of the structure are likely to be hurt.

Table 5 shows the effect on the probability that the hypothetical 8 to 13-story structure will suffer each damage state of different values of the Mercalli intensity of the earthquake and differences in the seismic resistivity of the structure. Three seismic codes are shown: UBC 0-1 corresponds to the construction of modern buildings without reference to the seismicity of the site; UBC 3 corresponds to the codes now in force in most localities in which the threat of earthquakes is greatest within the United States, such as California; and UBC S represents new standards that have been developed during the 1970s that would make buildings more resistant to earthquakes than do the old UBC 3 codes.

18   *Public Policy*

Table 4. RELATIONSHIP OF STRUCTURAL DAMAGE TO DEATH AND INJURY

Damage State	Fraction of Structure Lost	Fraction of Occupants Killed	Fraction of Occupants Injured
Moderate	0.05	0	0.01
Heavy	0.30	0.0025	0.02
Total	1.00	0.01	0.10
Collapse	1.00	0.20	1.00

Source: R. V. Whitman, J. M. Biggs, J. E. Brennan III, C. A. Cornell, R. L. deNeufville, and E. H. Vanmarcke, "Seismic Design Decision Analysis," *Journal of the Structural Division, American Society of Structural Engineers* (May 1975), p. 1077.

EVALUATING SEISMIC CODES

In order to estimate the value of

$$\int_{i_0}^{I} f_x\,(K,x,i)\,q\,(i)\,di = G\,(f_x\,(K,x,i))$$

in expession (3), information must be obtained on the changes in expected losses for each relevant intensity level, i, and in construction costs due to a change in building codes. The ratio, $\triangle f/\triangle x$, of these two changes can be used to estimate $G\,(f_x\,(K,x,i))$. Tables 2, 4, and 5 provide the information necessary to estimate the change in expected losses. Multiplication of the damage estimates for each type of structure in Table 4 and the probabilities of damage states, given the occurrence of an earthquake, in Table 5, produces the expected loss from each intensity of earthquake for each type of structure. If these entries are then multiplied by the relative frequencies of each intensity level of earthquake and the products are summed for each category of structure, the results are the expected damage to each type of structure, conditional on the occurrence of a damaging earthquake. The value to a building owner of a movement from UBC 3 to UBC S, which is the relevant choice in most communities in seismically active areas, can be estimated by comparing these expected losses. The result of these calculations is that the change in building codes makes a measurable difference to

ECONOMICS OF BUILDING CODES   19

building owners only in the two situations in which the code substantially affects the probability of total loss: MMI VIII and MMI IX. The expected loss under UBC S differs from the loss under UBC 3 by 5 and 24 percent, respectively, for these two intensities. According to the preceding calculations on the likelihood of severe earthquakes, the relative frequencies of these states are one-half for MMI VIII and one-fourth for MMI IX. Thus, the expected gain to a building owner of building to UBC S instead of UBC 3 is approximately 9 percent of the value of the structure, conditional on the occurrence of an earthquake that produces MMI VIII or higher shaking at the site. Of course, society would derive additional benefits from this change in codes. The most important element of the additional social gain is the increase in the proportion of buildings that are destroyed but that do not collapse, as building collapse is the principal threat to life as well as the principal disrupting event to the normal life of the community.

The second element entering into the estimate of $G(f_x(K,x,i))$ is the cost of adopting UBC S compared to UBC 3. Whitman et al. have performed an engineering design study of the cost of constructing certain "pilot" or particular buildings to satisfy

Table 5. PROBABILITY OF DAMAGE STATE FOR VARIOUS
EARTHQUAKE INTENSITIES AND SEISMIC BUILDING CODES

Code	Damage State	*Mercalli Intensity of Earthquake*				
		MM VII	MM VIII	MM IX	MM X	MM XII
UBC 0–1	Moderate	0.33	0.20	0	0	0
	Heavy	0.04	0.41	0	0	0
	Total	0	0.34	0.75	0.25	0
	Collapse	0	0.05	0.25	0.75	1.00
UBC 3	Moderate	0.25	0.53	0.20	0	0
	Heavy	0	0.21	0.52	0	0
	Total	0	0.01	0.23	0.80	0
	Collapse	0	0	0.05	0.20	1.00
UBC 5	Moderate	0.21	0.52	0.30	0	0
	Heavy	0	0.08	0.58	0	0
	Total	0	0	0.02	0.90	0
	Collapse	0	0	0	0.10	1.00

Source: Whitman et al., p. 1077.

various building codes, and their results are summarized in Figure 1. As the figure makes clear, moving from UBC 3 to UBC S increases the cost of a structure by 1 to 5 percent, depending upon the type of structure. The effect on the value of the contents is ignored.

Based upon these calculations, in the range of UBC 3 and UBC S, the value of $G\left(f_x\left(K,x,i\right)\right)$ can be placed within the range of -2

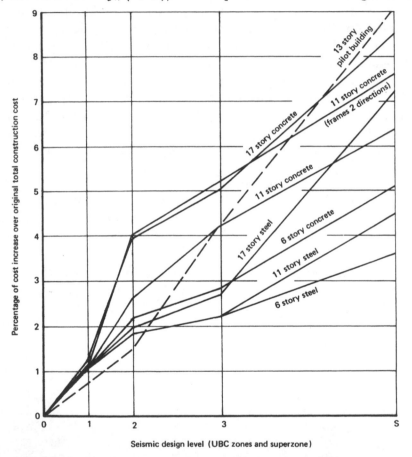

Seismic design level (UBC zones and superzone)

Figure 1. COSTS OF ALTERNATIVE SEISMIC RESISTIVITY CODES.

Source: R. V. Whitman, J. M. Biggs, J. E. Brennan III, C. A. Cornell, R. L. deNeufville, and E. H. Vanmarcke, *Methodology and Pilot Application,* SSDA Report No. 10 (Department of Civil Engineering, Massachusetts Institute of Technology, 1974) (mimeo).

and -9. Armed with this information, expression (3) can now be crudely estimated.

Table 6 shows calculated values of the left side of (3) based on several values of p, $G(f_x)$, and r that are possible candidates for the "correct" value for a particular structure. Comparison of the results for different values of these parameters provides a sensitivity analysis of the model. At the point of minimization of expected private costs, (3) would equal zero. Positive entries in the matrix correspond to combinations of values of the variables in (3) that indicate that UBC S requires strengthening beyond the degree of seismic resistivity that minimizes the private cost function that includes seismic risks. Negative entries correspond to situations in which even UBC S falls short of the best design to protect the private investment in the structure.

For the pilot building in the Whitman et al. study, which was the basis for calculating Tables 4 and 5, the costs of moving from UBC 3 to UBC S are about 5 percent of total costs, so that the value of $f_x(K,x)$ is approximately -1.8. For a discount rate of 0.10 and a probability equal to 0.01 that shaking of MMI VIII or greater will occur, the value of (3) is 0.8. More generally, realistic values of the variables—e.g., (f_x) less than 9, r near 0.10 or higher, and p less than 0.02—produce a pattern of positive entries.

This means that UBC S involves more resistivity than owners of structures would freely pick—a happy result in terms of verifying the model used herein, because owners are now observed rarely to adopt UBC S on their own.[11] These results also confirm the view that the principal purpose of codes is to internalize external effects, rather than to offset irrationality or ignorance. One can readily compute the value of the external costs that are implicit in UBC S. In order for (3′) to be zero (given r and p), $G(f_x) + H(K,g_x)$ would have to be -10. For this to be the case, the costs of moving from UBC 3 and UBC S would have to total 0.9 percent of the costs of the structure rather than about 5 percent. To force the pilot building to satisfy UBC S is, implicitly, to value the avoidance of damage other than to the structure that UBC S

---

[11] Whitman et al. (1975) note that at the time of the 1971 San Fernando earthquake, the Los Angeles building stock was vulnerable because most buildings were not being built to this standard. They also make a similar observation about Boston.

Table 6. VALUES OF $1 + p\,G(f_x(K,x,i))/r$

| | r = 0.05 | | | | r = 0.10 | | | |
	p = 0.1	p = 0.02	p = 0.01	p = 0.005	p = 0.1	p = 0.02	p = 0.01	p = 0.005
$G(f_x) = -1$	-1.0	0.6	0.8	0.9	0	0.8	0.9	0.95
$G(f_x) = -2$	-3.0	0.2	0.6	0.8	-1.0	0.6	0.8	0.9
$G(f_x) = -4$	-7.0	-0.6	0.2	0.6	-3.0	0.2	0.6	0.8
$G(f_x) = -7$	-13.0	-1.8	-0.4	0.3	-6.0	-0.4	0.3	0.65
$G(f_x) = -10$	-19.0	-3.0	-1.0	0.0	-9.0	-1.0	0	0.5
$G(f_x) = -50$	-29.0	-5.0	-2.0	-0.5	-14.0	-2.0	-0.05	0.25

Source: Calculations in text.

makes possible at about 4.5 times the value of the savings to the building from adopting UBC S. According to the calculations based on Tables 4 and 5, the latter is approximately 9 percent, so the bottom line of the calculations is that, given an earthquake of damaging intensity, the savings from UBC S other than to the owner must equal about 40 percent of the value of the building.

The preceding calculations are offered as illustrations of the uses of which the analysis and data summarized in this paper can be put. Forty percent of the cost of a 13-story building may or may not be a good estimate of the savings in terms of external costs that would accrue, given a damaging earthquake, if the buildings were built to UBC S specifications instead of UBC 3. Whatever the answer to this loaded question, the type of analysis provided in this paper provides a mechanism for collapsing the debate about seismic building codes into the rather simple framework of whether the expected savings are worth the cost. Moreover, the process of making these calculations is instructive because it encounters many relatively difficult data problems along the way. In particular, information on the underlying events that give rise to seismic codes—namely, the intensity of shaking from earthquakes that can be expected during the life of a structure—is too poor to make more than crude empirical efforts possible.

III. The Effects of Earthquake Predictions

In this section a more general investment problem is analyzed. that of maximizing the (nonzero) returns of a capital investment. The asset is threatened by a random event that, if it occurs, will reduce the earnings potential of the asset. This formulation is not useful for empirical purposes, because it assumes data regarding the expected revenue stream from a structure as a function of the amount of investment made in it. A more general formulation is valuable for deriving theoretical results. The model formulated here is used to investigate changes in investment patterns that will result from improved earthquake prediction technology.

Define $R(K)$ to be the annual income earned from an investment K if the structure has not yet been damaged by an earthquake.[12] The revenue function, $R(K)$, is assumed to exhibit positive marginal revenue of capital ($R_K > 0$) for at least some $K > 0$, but with declining marginal revenue for all values of K (e.g., $R_{KK} < 0$). Revenues are assumed to be the same in each year, an assumption that greatly simplifies the theoretical exposition. The revenue function is not assumed to be linear, for locational factors are likely to produce an optimal K for each site. Of course, this does not imply noncompetitive behavior—for each K, the builder can be a price taker, but face a given functional relationship between K and R that allows a single choice of K and x that produces non-negative profits. Let $F(t)$ be the probability that an earthquake that would cause structural collapse if $x = 0$ will occur by time t in the area of seismic risk in which the structure is located, with time $t = 0$ the date of construction of the structure. In the notation of Section I, $p(t) = F'(t)$.

A convenient minimum value, m^*, for the magnitude of earthquakes considered here is one that causes some modern buildings to suffer collapse if they are not constructed to withstand seismic shocks, i.e., if $x = 0$. The same earthquake causes moderate to heavy damage in some of the structures further from the center of the earthquake fault. The probability density function (pdf), $q(i)$, distinguishes between areas subject to different degrees of ground shaking. If $F(t,m)$ is the cumulative distribution function (CDF) from time zero to time t of an earthquake of magnitude $m \geqslant m^*$, and if $q(i|m)$ is the conditional pdf of intensity $i \geqslant i_0$, given a magnitude m earthquake, then:

$$F(t) = \int_{m \geqslant m^*} F(t,m)\,dm,$$

and

$$q(i) = \frac{\displaystyle\int_{m \geqslant m^*} q(i|m)\,F(t,m)\,dm}{\displaystyle\int_{m \geqslant m^*} F(t,m)\,dm}.$$

---

[12] The revenue may depend on x as well, assuming centers can tell the seismic resistivity of a structure by examining it. Making x an argument of R greatly complicates the manipulations to follow, but it does not change the qualitative theoretical results or the implications for empirical work.

ECONOMICS OF BUILDING CODES   25

Within this framework, the profit-maximization problem of a private investor contemplating an investment in a building is

$$\max_{K,x} \left\{ \int_{t=0}^{N} R(K)e^{-(r+v)t}\, dt - (1+x)K \right.$$
$$\left. - \int_{i=i_0}^{I} \int_{t=0}^{N} R(K)f(K,x,i)F(t)q(i)e^{-(r+v)t}\, dt\, di \right\} .$$

The first term is the discounted present value of the stream of revenues from the structure, the second term is the total cost of the structure (including defensive costs built into the building), and the third term represents the discounted present value of expected revenue loss due to earthquakes.

The necessary conditions for a maximum for this profit expression are

$$R'(K)\left(\frac{1-e^{-(r+v)N}}{r+v}\right) - (1+x)$$

$$- \int_{i=i_0}^{I} \left\{ \left[R'(K)f(K,x,i) + R(K)f_K(K,x,i) \right] q(i) \int_{t=0}^{N} F(t)e^{-(r+v)t}\, dt \right\} di = 0.$$

$$\tag{4}$$

$$K + \int_{i=i_0}^{I} \left\{ R(K)f_x(K,x,i)q(i) \int_{t=0}^{N} F(t)e^{-(r+v)t}\, dt \right\} di = 0. \tag{5}$$

The integral of the discounted CDF

$$\int_{t=0}^{N} F(t)e^{-(r+v)t}\, dt,$$

will be written as J. The second-order conditions are as follows:

$$R''(K)\left(\frac{1-e^{-(r+v)N}}{r+v}\right)$$

$$-J \int_{i=i_0}^{I} \left[R''(K)f(K,x,i) + 2R(K)f_K(K,x,i) + R(K)f_{KK}(K,x,i) \right]$$

$$q(i)\,di \leqslant 0. \qquad (6)$$

$$J \int_{i=i_0}^{I} R(K)f_{xx}(K,x,i)\,q(i)\,di \leqslant 0. \qquad (7)$$

$$1 + J \int_{i=i_0}^{I} \left[R'(K)f_x(K,x,i) + R(K)f_{Kx}(K,x,i) \right] q(i)\,di < 0. \qquad (8)^{13}$$

These conditions, especially (4) and (5), permit some exploration of the effects of the introduction of prediction technology by use of a conventional comparative statistical analysis. A valid earthquake prediction can be expressed as an increase in $F(t)$, and hence J, for values of t near zero. Conversely, the absence of a prediction supports the negative inference that, for t near zero, $F(t)$ is less than the historical frequency of seismic shocks.

Total differentiation of (4) and (5) produces the following conditions:

$$\frac{dx}{dJ} \left[i + J \int_{i_0}^{I} \left\{ R'(K)f_x(K,x,i) + R''(K)f_{Kx}(K,x,i) \right\} q(i)\,di \right]$$

$$= \frac{dx}{dJ} \left[R'(K) \left\{ \frac{1 - e^{-(r+v)N}}{r+v} \right\} - J \int_{i_0}^{I} \left\{ R''(K)f(K,x,i) + 2R'(K) \right. \right.$$

$$\times \left. f_K(K,x,i) + R(K)f_{KK}(K,x,i) \right\} q(i)\,di \right]$$

$$- \left[\int_{i_0}^{I} \left\{ R'(K)f(K,x,i) + R(K)f_K(K,x,i) \right\} q(i)\,di \right]. \qquad (9)$$

$$\frac{dx}{dJ} \left[R(K)J \int_{i_0}^{I} f_{xx}(K,x,i)\,q(i)\,di \right]$$

[13] The actual condition on this term is that it be less than a strictly negative term involving expressions (6) and (7); however, only the weaker version in (8) will be used below.

$$= -\frac{dx}{dJ} \left[1 + J \int_{i_0}^{I} \left\{ R'(K)f_x(K,x,i) + R(K)f_{Kx}(K,x,i) \right\} q(i)\,di \right]$$

$$+ R(K) \int_{i_0}^{I} f_x(K,x,i)q(i)\,di . \tag{10}[14]$$

From the second-order conditions and the assumptions about the functional forms of $R(K)$ and $f(K,x,i)$, all of the terms (9) and (10) can be signed, and the following established.

Proposition 1. If an earthquake is predicted (i.e., $dJ > 0$), the optimum expenditure on capital structures, K, will decline and the optimum expenditure proportion devoted to protection, x, will increase; conversely, the absence of a prediction will have the opposite effects.

The invention of reliable prediction technology will, then, have an indeterminate effect on the safety of buildings, depending on the form predictions take and the frequency of prediction. At one extreme, predictions might be certain, and may foresee some fraction, α, of all earthquakes. Because earthquakes that affect any given locality are extremely rare events, in nearly all years this prediction technology would forecast no event.

In these years, the expected probability of a damaging earthquake would be $(1-\alpha)h$, where h is the historical frequency, and $F(t)$ would be correspondingly reduced. Only rarely would $F(t)$ be increased in the next very few years, and so, according to Proposi-

---

[14] It is assumed that $q(i)$ is insensitive to changes in J, e.g., a positive prediction raises the probability of all large earthquakes occurring. Given the current state of knowledge on the relation between intensity and ground shaking for very large earthquakes, the total area affected increases with magnitude but the ratio of land suffering heavy damage to land suffering total damage remains roughly the same (see Section II). However, a prediction might narrow the variance of the expected magnitude of the earthquake. If it predicts an increased change of a major earthquake but rules out a great earthquake, dq/dJ might be negative. The left sides of both (9) and (10) then include the term

$$-J R(K) \int_{i_0}^{I} f_x(K,x,i)\frac{dq}{dJ}(i)\,di$$

which is indeterminate in sign.

tion 1, the net effect over time of the introduction of prediction technology would be to reduce the strength of most structures.

At the other extreme, a prediction technique might detect conditions that are only weakly associated with earthquakes but that occur frequently. Letting δ represent the increment to h that makes $(h + \delta)$ the probability of a damaging earthquake when the condition is present, as long as the condition is observed sufficiently frequently the impact of the prediction could be to raise the mean strength of buildings, depending on the exact shape of $R(x)$ and $f(K,x,i)$.

Proposition 1 holds for any source of change in the value of J. In addition to changes in the CDF of major earthquakes, J also depends on N (the life of the structure) and r (the interest rate). Thus, by the same reasoning applied to changes in $F(t)$ due to predictions, the following proposition can also be established (as well as its converse):

Proposition 2. A fall in the interest rate or an increase in the durability characteristics of structures that is unrelated to seismic resistivity will lead to an increase in defenses against earthquakes.

Table 6 in Section II provides some further insight into the consequences of long-term earthquake predictions. If r is 0.10 and $G(f_x(K,x,i))$ is -2, consider the effect of a prediction that an earthquake was certain to occur in, say, the next ten years. In this case, p would equal 0.1, and the value of expression (3) would become strongly negative. In fact, for any time horizon under twenty years, the UBC S code would be less stringent than the standard calculated to minimize private costs. Alternatively, suppose a prediction technology indicates that for the next decade the chance of an earthquake has been halved, from a normal 0.01 to 0.005. Because of discounting, this eliminates most of the present-value benefits of a stronger structure and would cause UBC S to become even less attractive to owners of buildings. Indeed, requiring UBC S in the face of such a prediction, given $r = 0.10$ and $g(f_x) = -2$, implies a social benefit equal to about nine times the expected benefits to the structure, rather than the fourfold relationship that would justify UBC S without a prediction.

ECONOMICS OF BUILDING CODES 29

IV. Conclusions

By casting the problem of optimal seismic resistance as a standard problem of optimal investment under uncertainty, two useful results have emerged. First, a method has been developed that enables the analyst to use engineering cost information and other available data to estimate the minimum social benefits that a strengthening of the code must provide to be worthwhile. Second, the same method permits an estimation of the effects of changes in information about the frequency of earthquakes, such as valid predictions, on the private choice of seismic resistivity and on the implicit social benefit that justifies a particular code. Because of negative inferences from the absence of predictions, the introduction of a prediction method has an indeterminate but potentially important effect on incentives to defend against seismic shocks.

JOURNAL OF ENVIRONMENTAL ECONOMICS AND MANAGEMENT **29,** 304–320 (1995)

Alternatives for Managing Drought:
A Comparative Cost Analysis*

ANTHONY FISHER, DAVID FULLERTON, NILE HATCH, AND PETER
REINELT

*Department of Agricultural and Resource Economics, University of California at Berkeley,
Berkeley, California 94720*

Received July 11, 1993; revised October 29, 1993

The question addressed by this study is how a large urban water district can best respond
to a drought. Using a computer model of a representative district, we find that a combination
of conjunctive use and water marketing is well over an order of magnitude cheaper than the
traditional alternative of constructing new storage capacity. The indicated cost saving can be
explained by the intermittent nature of the transfer, corresponding to the intermittent
demand. Comparing costs to benefits, the consumer-surplus loss otherwise entailed by raising
prices to cut back on consumption in the event of a drought, we find that construction of new
storage does not pass a benefit/cost test, but introduction of conjunctive use/water marketing does. © 1995 Academic Press, Inc.

I. INTRODUCTION

The problem addressed by this study is how to determine the least-cost combination of alternatives to meet periodic water shortages. A solution to this problem
may involve demand management strategies and/or supply augmentation. Supply
augmentation approaches may be purely structural (such as developing new local
storage capacity) or a mix of structural and nonstructural (such as "conjunctive
use" of surface and groundwater supplies combined with water exchanges or sales).
The application is to the East Bay Municipal Utility District (EBMUD), which
includes large portions of Alameda and Contra Costa counties on the east side of
the San Francisco Bay, but the concepts and methods (and some of the findings)
will be relevant to other districts.

Other analyses of drought-contingent water transfers investigate the benefits of
interruptible irrigation in low-flow years to maintain hydropower supply reliability
[10, 12]. Michelson and Young [13] examine interruptible irrigation "water-supply
option contracts" to satisfy municipal water demands during drought. Our approach is similar but expands on the options considered. Thus, while they assume
that the need for additional drought water supply is determined a priori, we
consider the effective welfare costs of demand-reduction strategies as well as the
costs of supply augmentation in the form of expansion of surface storage or of
effectively storing water underground. They focus on purchase of water rights and
drought option contracts which are comparable to still another option that we
consider—intermittent water marketing. Our results can easily be converted into

* This research has been supported by a grant from the Water Resources Center of the University of
California. We are grateful to Robert Deacon, Michael Hanemann, and three reviewers for helpful
comments on an earlier draft.

304

Michelson and Young's "present value of the benefit of an option contract" by recouping the present-value cost of each of our options and subtracting the present-value cost of the water-marketing option (their option exercise cost).

In order to compare the costs of the various combinations of options, a computer program has been developed to model the operation of the EBMUD system under a wide variety of environmental and management scenarios. Separate cost estimates for construction and operation of the supply-side options are calculated with engineering data from EBMUD and other sources. The next section describes the computer model. In Section III, supply-side cost estimation procedures are described and cost estimates are presented, in terms of dollars per af of water provided in drought years, for key reservoir options under consideration. The same approach to a range of conjunctive-use/water-marketing options is applied in Section IV. Finally, in Section V the cost estimates are compared to the benefit of averting or mitigating a shortfall, the loss in surplus that would be entailed by restricting consumption through higher prices.

II. THE EBMUD SYSTEM AND OPERATIONS MODEL

A. The EBMUD System

The main features of the EBMUD system are two large reservoirs on the upper Mokelumne River (approximately 80 miles to the northeast of the service district), three aqueducts to bring water to the district, five local or terminal reservoirs, and six local treatment plants. Of the two reservoirs on the river, just Pardee, the upper, smaller of the two, with a capacity of 211 thousand acre-feet (kaf), is currently connected to the aqueducts. The larger (430 kaf) Camanche Reservoir is used for supplying senior water rights (mainly agricultural users in the reservoir area), stream flow regulation, and flood control. Terminal storage capacity is about 150 kaf. These reservoirs serve a district of about 350 thousand households or 1.1 million people. Before the current drought, annual consumption had reached a maximum of about 240 kaf, which is equivalent to an average over the year of 220 million gallons per day (mgd). EBMUD is entitled to a substantially larger amount of Mokelumne water, about 360 kaf or 325 mgd.

The issue that motivates this study is whether the district needs an addition to terminal storage, both to help it get through periods of shortage and to protect against sudden outage due to disruption of the aqueducts at their most vulnerable point, where they traverse the Sacramento River Delta, by a natural disaster such as an earthquake or flood. EBMUD began an in-house planning process to address this issue in early 1987 and solicited public input over the next couple of years. Findings and recommendations are given in a final EIR [7]. The main recommendation is for construction of a large, new local reservoir, preferably in Buckhorn Canyon, just to the east of the existing Upper San Leandro Reservoir. The proposed Buckhorn Reservoir would have a capacity of 145 kaf, making it almost as large as all of the existing local reservoirs combined. A variant of this plan would involve cooperation with the adjacent Contra Costa Water District (CCWD) in construction of a new reservoir, Los Vaqueros, to serve both districts. As it appears CCWD intends to go ahead with Los Vaqueros in any event, the issue for EBMUD is whether to join in an expanded effort.

EBMUD argues that a new reservoir, preferably a 145 kaf Buckhorn, would best meet the objectives of averting both drought-related shortfalls and sudden disruptions. However, EBMUD's own engineering data reveal that separate solutions for each threat, namely, construction of an earthquake-secure aqueduct and a smaller 55 kaf Buckhorn reservoir (which is the amount of storage EBMUD analysis requires for the drought problem alone), result in lower costs, as we show in the more detailed report on which this paper is based [8]. Moreover, as we show in this paper, once the earthquake-security and drought problems are decoupled, drought-relief options other than terminal storage can be considered which have orders of magnitude lower unit costs.

B. Structure of the Model

The computer program is a mass balance model, allocating water flowing down the Mokelumne River to downstream releases, storage, transport, or consumptive use. In each run of the model, a static (constant average use) EBMUD system is subjected to a sequence of variable runoff patterns. Shortage patterns (frequency and severity) can then be estimated for each planning scenario. The model is highly parameterized, allowing examination of a wide variety of physical and operational scenarios.

A flow file contains assumed inflows to Pardee Reservoir by month, based on U.S. Geological Survey records from October 1927 through September 1989. Clearly, past flow patterns will not recur in the future. However, use of the historical patterns provides a reasonable starting point for estimating the frequency of shortages under various assumptions. Synthetically generated flow patterns could also be used. For example, if the changes in precipitation patterns resulting from global warming can be estimated, synthetic flows could be generated to indicate how a given system would perform under the new conditions.

Key physical parameters include seepage losses in the river and evaporation from the reservoirs. The important structural parameters are size of existing storage reservoirs (for example, how much of the bottom storage in existing reservoirs could be extracted during a shortage), integration of new storage reservoirs (such as Buckhorn and Los Vaqueros), and capacity of conveyance facilities. Operational parameters include maximum acceptable demand reductions in drought (25 to 39% in EBMUD planning), storage levels, releases for downstream water-rights holders and for environmental purposes, and water-transfer/conjunctive-use programs.

With respect to storage levels, a critical parameter is the October carryover target (i.e., the amount of total storage to be carried into the next water year). Current EBMUD practice, adopted in this study, appears to call for a target carryover of about 1.2 times annual demand or use. It is important to recognize that this is not a particularly "economic" approach in that no attempt is made to optimize reservoir operation with respect to water inventory; we rely on the existing "rules of thumb" of carryover targets and allowable supply reductions to address the trade-off between supplying current period needs and providing drought security for future periods. A recent survey on planning procedures for drought at local water agencies finds that most agencies "plan for enough water for

normal times and for a reserve to guard against drought and other problems ..."
[9] with no explicit or implicit consideration of balancing the current and future
benefits of releasing the last unit of water. In the water-resource literature, models
have been developed that account for the stochastic nature of hydrological inflows.
However, stated objectives are almost uniformly based on proximity and variation
from some specified target storage volume [11].

With respect to water transfers, one way to increase water supplies during
drought is to reduce releases from Camanche Reservoir for downstream water-
rights holders, in turn allowing EBMUD to keep more water in Pardee Reservoir
for transmission through the aqueducts. This could be done by purchase or as part
of a conjunctive-use program in which reduced surface water deliveries are
compensated by pumping extra groundwater. Both options will be considered here.

A working file takes information from the flow and parameter files and operates
the system on a month-by-month basis; distributing and releasing water, calling for
demand reductions in time of drought, and so on. The output from this file is a
detailed record of hypothetical operations over the period chosen. Each month
begins with a set of initial values for the system. Inflows are drawn from the flows
file while demand is drawn from the parameter file. Demand will be reduced if
drought reductions are in effect. Aqueduct flows from Pardee are drawn so that
demand and target terminal-storage levels are met if possible. Next, releases from
Camanche for downstream commitments, flood control, or other purposes
(e.g., spillage) are computed. Finally, Pardee releases are computed. Now, new
Camanche and Pardee storage levels can be computed.

The month of April is treated separately in the model. This is when basic
decisions are made about how the system will be operated over the next year. April
is chosen because by April 1 most of the winter's precipitation has already fallen
and the snowpack has been assessed. Thus, the runoff for that water year is known
with a fair degree of certainty. In April, predictions are made about the storage
levels in EBMUD reservoirs which will exist on October 1. If storage levels will be
adequate, then the system operates normally. If October 1 storage falls below
acceptable carryover minimums, then a drought response will be necessary. The
model requires conservation as needed to ensure that the October 1 carryover level
is met—until the maximum acceptable conservation level is reached. Thereafter,
storage is allowed to fall below acceptable carryover minimums.

III. COST ESTIMATION OF RESERVOIR OPTIONS

To determine the effective unit cost of water supplied by the proposed projects,
we use three variants: (1) unit cost calculated over the defined planning horizon,
(2) unit cost calculated over the approximated lifetime of reservoir projects, and
(3) unit cost of a perpetuity (a project that provides benefits "forever"). The
concept most often employed in the comparison of different possible capital
expenditures is that of economic equivalent unit cost over a defined planning
horizon. This is the standard method employed by the California Department of
Water Resources (DWR); see, for example, [5]. EBMUD has defined its planning
horizon to be 30 years. However, reservoir projects under consideration have
expected lifetimes of between 50 and 100 years. Since EBMUD presents some data

308   FISHER ET AL.

for an 80-year operation period, this time span will be used as an approximation of the lifetime of various projects.

The economic equivalent unit cost of a project is the ratio of the equivalent annual cost to the annual "water-supply accomplishments." To calculate the equivalent annual cost, the sum of the present value of the costs for each year, or equivalently the total present-value cost, of the project is multiplied by the capital recovery factor (see Riggs and West [16]; details of our computational formula are available on request). Since the objective of the project is to create a standby water supply capable of alleviating hardships during drought, rather than a yearly or even daily online supply, the water-supply accomplishments are defined to be the water actually delivered in drought years that otherwise would be unavailable. Thus, the water-supply accomplishments of each project are evaluated using the 62-year hydrological record for the Mokelumne River watershed, and a yearly average is calculated to obtain the annual water-supply accomplishments.

In the present analysis of reservoir options, we restrict our attention to Buckhorn and Los Vaqueros, the principal proposals in EBMUD's final EIR [7]. The water-supply accomplishments of additional storage are calculated using the model described in the preceding section. Figure 1 is an example of one run. The bars extending down from the top of the graph indicate an occurrence of a water shortage below the nominal demand level, and the oscillating line across the middle of the graph represents the total amount of water in storage at any time over the 62-year hydrological data set.

Predicted total water-supply shortages over the course of a 62-year hydrological cycle for a range of demand levels for the current reservoir system (zero additional storage) and for an augmented reservoir system with 50, 100, or 145 kaf of additional capacity are shown in Table I. At the 210 mgd demand level, any of the additional storage capacities results in no shortages; in particular, the 1977 short-

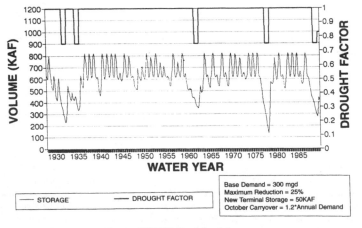

FIG. 1.   EBMUD demand and storage.

ALTERNATIVES FOR MANAGING DROUGHT   309

TABLE I

Total Supply Reductions and Total Water Supply Accomplishments
under Various Reservoir Options

Demand level (mgd)	Additional storage (kaf)	Acceptable percent supply reduction (kaf)			
		39%		25%	
		Total supply shortage	Total water supply accomplishment	Total supply shortage	Total water supply accomplishment
300	0	788.6		517.6	
	50	627.6	161.0	478.0	39.6
	100	488.5	300.1	404.3	113.3
	145	332.8	455.8	238.8	278.8
270	0	377.9		251.0	
	50	232.1	145.8	75.7	175.3
	100	118.0	259.9	75.7	175.3
	145	118.0	259.9	75.7	175.3
240	0	104.9		67.3	
	50	104.9	0.0	67.3	0.0
	100	67.3	37.6	67.3	0.0
	145	0.0	104.9	0.0	67.3
210	0	65.9		58.8	
	50	0.0	65.9	0.0	58.8
	100	0.0	65.9	0.0	58.8
	145	0.0	65.9	0.0	58.8

age is avoided. However, at the 240 mgd demand level, the 1977 shortage still occurs with an additional 50 kaf of storage, is ameliorated somewhat with 100 kaf of additional storage with 39% acceptable reductions, and is completely eliminated with 145 kaf of additional storage. At the 270 mgd demand level, additional storage eliminates most of the shortages other than that of 1977; this shortage still occurs because the reservoir system enters the year 1977 with a lower inventory than it would under a lower demand.

To summarize, water-supply accomplishments are monotonically increasing with respect to storage capacity at *any* demand level. Also, for fixed storage capacity, the ability to alleviate any particular drought-induced shortfall (and thus produce water-supply accomplishments for that year) decreases monotonically with respect to demand level. However, the number of years in which shortfalls occur (and thus the potential to produce water-supply accomplishments) increases monotonically with respect to demand level. Therefore, water-supply accomplishments are *not necessarily* monotonic with respect to demand level.

The costs for the various reservoir options are derived from estimates in the EBMUD final EIR [7] and supporting documents. Table II lists the capital costs, initial filling costs, and estimated annual operating expenses which include refilling costs for Buckhorn and Los Vaqueros Reservoirs (specified capacity dedicated to EBMUD). For the planning horizon and approximate lifetime equivalent unit cost calculations, a three-year construction period followed by one year for initial filling of the reservoir is assumed. To establish a lower bound on unit water costs, in the

TABLE II

Capital Costs, Initial Filling Costs, and Estimated Annual Operating and
Maintenance Expenses: Various Reservoir Options

	Buckhorn Reservoir		
Capacity (kaf)	Capital costs (million dollars)	Initial fill costs (million dollars)	Estimated annual operating and maintenance costs (million dollars)
50	83	7	.418
100	133	12	.627
145	160	18	.794
Dedicated EBMUD capacity (kaf)	Los Vaqueros Reservoir Capital costs (million dollars)	Initial fill costs (million dollars)	
50	124	4	
100	159	8	
145	187	11	

perpetuity calculation, the construction time and filling time are neglected and it is assumed that benefits derive from the projects immediately.

The resulting unit costs for the range of reservoir options under consideration are presented in Table III. For a 39% acceptable reduction, an 80-year lifetime, a 4% real interest rate, and 210 mgd demand (the demand level in the table closest to the historic high of 220 mgd), the cost per af for a 145 kaf reservoir at Buckhorn Canyon is $8,265.83. Of course, the cost is lower at higher demand levels; at 300 mgd, for example, it falls to just $1,195.12. One apparent anomaly is the high cost of water at the 240 mgd demand level; however, this can be explained by the same argument presented above describing the water-supply accomplishments. At the 240 mgd demand level, additional storage will slightly or not at all alleviate the 1977 shortage; whereas, at higher demand levels, the 1977 shortage is not alleviated but other shortages not occurring at the 240 mgd level are alleviated and, at lower demand levels, the 1977 shortage is totally eliminated.

It is clear that Los Vaqueros water would be more expensive than Buckhorn water for the reservoir capacity options investigated, presumably because the terrain at Buckhorn—a relatively narrow canyon—is better suited to dam construction. On the other hand, given that Los Vaqueros will be built even without EBMUD's participation, the environmental impacts associated with EBMUD's participation in Los Vaqueros are likely to be less than those resulting from construction at both sites. Also significant are the high costs of dam extensions if a smaller capacity Buckhorn reservoir is initially constructed. If weather patterns change significantly from those of the recent past, the option of maintaining the Buckhorn site for a full-size reservoir, i.e., not constructing a smaller reservoir now, may be quite valuable.

The most striking feature of this analysis, the very high cost of water per af under any of the options considered, points to the difficulty and expense of attempting to solve an intermittent problem (drought) with a permanent increment

TABLE III
Buckhorn Reservoir: Unit Cost of Water Supplied
(Dollars per af)

Demand level (mgd)	Additional storage (kaf)	Acceptable supply reduction 39%						Acceptable supply reduction 25%					
		Method of calculation						Method of calculation					
		Perpetuity		80-year lifetime		30-year planning horizon		Perpetuity		80-year lifetime		30-year planning horizon	
		Discount Rate		Discount Rate		Discount Rate		Discount Rate		Discount Rate		Discount Rate	
		3%	4%	3%	4%	3%	4%	3%	4%	3%	4%	3%	4%
300	50	1,185.32	1,540.38	1,373.21	1,719.81	2,028.82	2,316.90	4,819.16	6,262.53	5,580.99	6,989.53	8,245.19	9,415.84
	100	1,016.46	1,332.23	1,177.22	1,476.63	1,743.82	1,992.62	2,592.32	3,502.24	3,118.62	3,911.86	4,619.63	4,657.02
	145	824.31	1,071.88	953.77	1,195.12	1,411.19	1,611.53	1,487.42	1,831.84	1,559.29	1,953.86	2,307.11	2,634.64
270	50	1,308.89	1,700.97	1,516.25	1,898.95	2,240.15	2,558.21	1,201.55	1,478.87	1,261.47	1,579.88	1,863.76	2,128.36
	100	1,173.68	1,526.75	1,359.19	1,704.90	2,013.38	2,300.63	1,920.60	2,366.20	2,015.46	2,528.08	2,985.54	3,411.44
	145	1,445.63	1,879.80	1,672.74	2,096.34	2,474.97	2,826.33	2,365.62	2,913.38	2,480.40	3,108.08	3,670.02	4,190.96
240	50	∞	∞	∞	∞	∞	∞	∞	∞	∞	∞	∞	∞
	100	8,112.79	10,553.39	9,402.03	11,793.35	13,927.35	15,914.50	6,151.92	7,588.60	6,462.77	8,098.27	9,562.49	10,919.68
	145	3,581.69	4,657.43	4,146.78	5,196.06	6,135.53	7,006.43	3,532.15	4,408.98	3,761.86	4,711.27	5,557.88	6,346.92
210	50	2,895.85	3,763.22	3,354.89	4,201.64	4,956.61	5,660.46	5,725.86	7,054.36	6,010.34	7,538.86	8,903.13	10,173.12
	100	4,628.85	6,021.15	5,360.12	6,723.35	7,939.96	9,072.85						
	145	5,701.38	7,413.54	6,596.64	8,255.83	9,760.31	11,146.02	8,906.13	8,685.68	7,396.86	9,268.44	10,944.30	12,497.71

312   FISHER ET AL.

to storage. As we show in the next section, an intermittent solution to an intermittent problem can be much more cost effective. In other words, if the extra water is needed only occasionally, it may be cheaper to rent than to buy.[1]

IV. COST ESTIMATION OF CONJUNCTIVE-USE / WATER-EXCHANGE OPTIONS

Conjunctive-use options combined with water exchanges or water marketing address the intermittent nature of the drought problem. Since nearby irrigation districts, most importantly the Woodbridge Irrigation District (WID), and also some riparian users, have both groundwater reserves and surface water entitlements, the idea is to work out an agreement in which one or more of these agencies or individuals pump additional groundwater in dry years, thereby freeing some of their surface entitlements. EBMUD might then purchase the surface water. Alternatively, EBMUD might pay the costs of pumping groundwater and also subsidize groundwater recharge during normal or wet years.

Three program options are investigated in this section. The list is not all-inclusive, but a plausible range of possibilities is considered. The specific options are hypothetical at this point but are based on what we understand EBMUD is looking at in a general way. The first two options specifically address the issue of groundwater depletion in San Joaquin County, in particular groundwater depletion in the vicinity of the Mokelumne River. The conjunctive-use programs that we consider are, in essence, underground water banks with WID acting as the banking intermediary. In wet years EBMUD makes deposits in the WID aquifer, and in dry years EBMUD makes withdrawals of surface water dedicated to WID at Pardee Reservoir. Over the course of the hydrological cycle, these programs must meet the stipulation that the annual groundwater deficit in Eastern San Joaquin county is not exacerbated. In both options, water-right holders downstream from Camanche Reservoir reduce their use of surface water in dry years and make up the deficit by pumping groundwater. EBMUD covers the cost of acquisition of groundwater for farmers. The two options explored here diverge only in the proposed EBMUD investment in the acquisition of water for the farmers. In the first, existing wells are utilized and EBMUD subsidizes the energy cost of pumping the water to the surface. In the second, EBMUD subsidizes in addition the cost of constructing new wells and annual maintenance. In either case, in wet years EBMUD provides excess water to the downstream agricultural users to supplant existing groundwater use and/or to enhance groundwater recharge. The third option is direct water purchases by EBMUD from downstream water-right holders (or others) in dry years.

In all of the options, both parties to the agreement are better off after the agreement is in place. In all, as we shall show, EBMUD obtains water that it can

---

[1] The California Department of Fish and Game has recommended increased flows (above current minimum levels) in the Mokelumne River to protect instream uses. Incorporating these increased flows into the model results in a substantial increase in the frequency and severity of shortages, in turn reducing the cost per af of water delivered from new storage. Some simulated results are presented in Fisher *et al.* [8]. We should note, however, that in these scenarios, reservoir levels can be drawn down nearly to zero. This is certainly unrealistic; the model's operating criteria would probably need to be altered to provide some minimum carryover.

deliver to its customers during droughts at far lower cost than is possible from the reservoir options. In the first two options, the downstream right holders receive the same amount of water. The only difference is that groundwater is substituted for surface water. Additionally, the local groundwater aquifer is enhanced, reducing future pumping costs. In the third option, the farmers receive a payment for the water which they are willing to accept; farmers will only be willing to accept a payment which fully compensates them for the expected profit that will be lost if they forgo the use of some quantity of water. The local groundwater aquifer could also be enhanced in this option, if farmers choose to leave some land fallow in dry years. However, if farmers replace the transferred surface water with groundwater, the aquifer will deteriorate at a greater rate. Therefore, for the third option to be feasible given the groundwater deficit problem in San Joaquin county, some land must be left fallow in dry years.

The model is employed to assess the first two options with an additional operational criterion which supersedes all others to determine the years in which water transfers occur. The water-transfer decision criterion is based on the predicted October 1 reservoir system carryover as calculated on April 1 and is triggered by the level of Camanche Reservoir. The system goal is to keep Pardee Reservoir full. If it is predicted that Camanche will become too low and thus water will have to be drawn from Pardee, then the water transfer is instituted. The volume of the transfer is calculated to be the maximum possible up to the point where instream flow requirements will be violated. This maximum volume derives from the quantity of downstream water rights which, in turn, are based on the type of year (wet or dry) that actually does occur. The transfer volumes represent the difference between the releases that would be necessary to satisfy downstream water rights and the releases necessary only to satisfy flow requirements. These transfer volumes assume 40% transit losses resulting from seepage and illegal diversions. Some surface water may still be available to farmers, depending on the nature of the flow requirements. In particular, if flow requirements are higher between Camanche Reservoir and agricultural diversion locations than they are further downstream, the difference may still be diverted for agricultural use. After a transfer occurs, the criteria are the same as before; incur a shortage and then allow the carryover to fall below 1.2 times annual demand.

An example of the model output is given in Fig. 2. The dark bars extending up from the bottom of the graph indicate the volume of water transfer that occurs for the given year. The total supply shortage and water-supply accomplishments over the 62-year hydrological record for the conjunctive-use program are presented in Table IV. In Table V the reduction in releases resulting from the transfer program and the actual water transfers (60% of release reduction) are shown. Note, in comparing Tables IV and V, that the total reduction in releases is greater than the total water-supply accomplishments. This disparity occurs because the transfers are instituted as of April 1 based on predictions of carryover volume for October 1. Therefore, the total reduction in releases may not translate directly into water-supply accomplishments if, for example, runoff or rainfall after April 1 is greater than predicted.

Table V also shows that EBMUD could meet the stipulation that the groundwater deficit problem not be exacerbated. Over the 62-year period, total water transfers are between 45.6 and 193.2 kaf. Given that EBMUD is entitled to 360 kaf annually, which is available "in most years" (EBMUD [7], p. III-16), and that

314   FISHER ET AL.

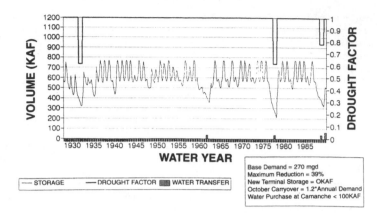

FIG. 2.   EBMUD demand, storage, and transfers.

annual consumption has not exceeded 240 kaf, clearly the stipulation can be met. This excess water, in fact, provides the means to supplant existing groundwater use in wet years and also for spreading operations to augment groundwater recharge should this be desired.

To complete the calculation of the unit cost of water, the costs associated with each transfer mechanism must be determined. In the first option, where existing wells are used and EBMUD subsidizes the pumping costs, the following assumptions are made: (1) the approximate average depth to groundwater in the area concerned is 65 ft. (derived from Brown and Caldwell [4]); (2) the average well pump energy consumption is 1.75 kilowatt hours (kwh) per af per foot raised (Brown and Caldwell [4], supporting data); (3) the average cost of energy is $0.0633125 per kwh (average summer price based on Pacific Gas and Electric (PG & E) agricultural rate schedule AG-5B, a reasonable assumption reflecting the

TABLE IV

Total Supply Reductions and Water Supply Accomplishments of
a Conjunctive Use Option and 39% Acceptable
Supply Reduction Policy

Demand level (mgd)	Water transfers (yes or no)	Total supply shortage (kaf)	Total water supply accomplishments (kaf)
300	n	788.6	
	y	585.5	203.1
270	n	377.9	
	y	300.2	77.7
240	n	104.9	
	y	104.9	0.0
210	n	65.9	
	y	0.0	65.9

TABLE V

Total Reductions in Releases and Total Water Transfers

Demand level (mgd)	Number of years out of 62, water transfer to EBMUD	Total reduction in releases (kaf)	Total water transfer to EBMUD (60% of total reductions) (kaf)
300	7	322	193.2
270	4	180	108.0
240	4	180	108.0
210	2	76	45.6

unknown excess capacity of existing wells); and (4) planning and administrative costs of 15% are added (following standard engineering/economic cost accounting practice).

Resulting unit costs based on these assumptions and calculated over a 30-year planning horizon are presented in Table VI. Since expected costs and benefits are utilized and it is assumed that a shortage can occur in any given year with equal probability based on historical averages, the unit costs of water are independent of the discount rate for the first option. The striking result is that unit costs are far lower—by as much as two to three orders of magnitude—than corresponding reservoir costs. For a 39% acceptable reduction, a 4% real interest rate, and 210 mgd demand, the cost per af under the first option is just $5.73.

For the second option, five additional assumptions are necessary: (1) the cost of construction of a well, including a pump rated at 2,000 gallons per minute, is $25,000 (based on inquiries of local drillers and pump distributors); (2) each pump undergoes a major overhaul every five years costing $2,500 (based on inquiries of pump distributors); (3) if each pump is operated an average of approximately 18 hours per day for 6 months of the year, then 33 wells are required to extract the maximum transfer capacity; (4) the cost of energy is $0.03907 (based on the summer off-peak rate from PG&E agricultural rate schedule AG-5B; the off-peak rate is utilized because a preliminary calculation revealed that a greater number of pumps operating in only off-peak hours is less expensive than fewer pumps

TABLE VI

Unit Cost of Water Supplied for Conjunctive Use Options Based
On 39% Acceptable Supply Reduction Policy Calculated
for 30-Year Planning Horizon (dollars per af)

Demand level (mgd)	Option 1, pumping energy costs, discount rate		Option 2, all well costs, discount rate	
	3%	4%	3%	4%
300	7.88	7.88	36.07	38.03
270	11.51	11.51	88.68	93.79
240	∞	∞	∞	∞
210	5.73	5.73	99.72	105.75

operating continuously); and (5) annual operation and maintenance costs per well are, net of energy and overhaul costs, $1,000 per well. Resulting unit costs of water based on these additional cost assumptions for the second conjunctive-use option are also presented in Table VI. In reality, an intermediate option, where wells are jointly financed and used, is likely to evolve because, in the second option, the new wells are only used in dry years. Again, however, the costs are strikingly lower—by one to two orders of magnitude—than for the reservoirs. For the low-demand scenario (210 mgd), the cost per af is $105.75.

The third option, as noted above, is direct water purchases by EBMUD from the downstream right holders. How large a payment might they require in order to be willing to give up the water? We have just seen that one alternative to the use of the foregone surface water, namely, pumping additional groundwater, would entail costs ranging (approximately) from $5 per af to $105, depending on what one assumes about the need for new wells. If these cost estimates are reasonable, then an offer of not less than $105 per af ought to be sufficient to induce substantial sales. In this case the farmer has the option of taking the money and using it to simply replace the surface water with groundwater. Of course, farmers (or districts) without access to groundwater might require a larger payment. They, and for that matter some farmers with access to groundwater, might let at least a portion of their land lie fallow for a year. Others might switch to less water-intensive crops, and still others might adopt water-saving irrigation methods. These adjustments, which do not involve additional pumping of groundwater, may in fact be socially preferred, as they would not aggravate the overdraft problem.

Here, we need to mention a recent institutional innovation. In 1991 a State Water Bank was created, for the purpose of facilitating transfers from those districts with water to sell to those who want to buy. The Bank set the prices, $125 per af to sellers, and $175 per af to buyers. It is interesting to note that the price to sellers was calculated to "yield a net income to the farmer similar to what the farmer would have earned from farming plus an additional amount to encourage the farmer to enter into a contract with a new and untried Water Bank" (DWR [6], p. 5). The price to buyers did not include conveyance costs (the energy costs of pumping the water from the Delta for State Water Project contractors, and the energy costs plus a facilities fee for noncontractors). That is, buyers would have to pay $175 per af plus conveyance costs. Assuming the Bank operates in future drought years, and the price schedule remains the same, the downstream right holders on the Mokelumne River could sell water for $125 per af. Similarly, EBMUD could buy water for $175. Conveyance costs would presumably be low, as EBMUD has a pumping station at the western edge of the Delta, where the aqueducts emerge. However, an alternative marketing arrangement might be made between EBMUD and the downstream right holders directly, i.e., without the intermediation of the Bank. A direct transfer at any price between $125 and $175 plus conveyance costs would, in theory, leave both buyer and seller better off. The opportunity for a mutually beneficial transaction will exist so long as there is a difference between the buying and selling prices set by the Bank, since the transfer is accomplished simply by leaving additional water in Pardee Reservoir.

However the conjunctive-use/water-transfer arrangement works, it is evident that the much lower unit costs of water obtained in this fashion result both from the intermittent nature of the arrangement and the disparity in cost between, on the one hand, pumping groundwater and, on the other, building and maintaining

TABLE VII
Summary of Welfare Losses

Authors	Time horizon of elasticity	Change in marginal price per ccf[a]	Welfare loss per af due to 25% cutback
Agthe, Billings, Dobra,	long-run	$0.185	$40.22
and Raffiee [2]	short-run	$0.317	$68.85
Agthe and Billings [1]	long-run	$0.335	$72.94
	short-run	$0.465	$101.25
Billings and Day [3]	mixed[b]	$0.238	$51.81
	mixed[b]	$0.320	$69.54
Moncur [14]	long-run	$0.482	$104.98
	short-run	$0.628	$137.03
Nieswiadomy and Molina [15]	short-run[b]	$0.259	$42.27
Schefter and David [17]	long-run[b]	$0.719	$156.80
Weber [18]	mixed	$0.827	$179.97

[a] Base price for January 1, 1987 = $0.666 per ccf.
[b] Not stated by the author(s) but determined by the nature (time series or cross section) of the data.

surface reservoirs for the first two options, as well as from the disparity in the (marginal) value of water to farmers and to urban users for the third option.[2]

V. CONSUMER-SURPLUS LOSS DUE TO A PRICE-INDUCED REDUCTION IN WATER CONSUMPTION

Thus far, we have considered a variety of techniques to supplement water supplies during periods of drought. One important alternative available to water district managers—the one in fact chosen by EBMUD during recent droughts—is to reduce demand through higher prices. The associated consumer-surplus loss can be regarded as the benefit from mitigating the drought through the construction of new storage capacity or operation of a conjunctive-use/water-marketing program. No definitive study has yet been done for EBMUD, but there have been many studies of residential demand for water in other regions. It is possible to use the estimated elasticities to compute the loss in surplus associated with a price-induced cutback of 25% in consumption in the EBMUD service area. Table VII shows the range of estimates, on an af basis, produced using a selection of recent studies that, in our judgment, most effectively address the econometric problems.[3] The range

[2] We have also studied the implications of increased flow requirements for the conjunctive-use/water-transfer arrangements. The cost per af remains about the same for the first option, and actually falls for the second, since well construction costs are spread over a larger volume of water transfers. For details, see Fisher *et al.* [8].

[3] These problems mostly derive from the nonlinear price structure produced by rising or falling block rates. Two key questions, in our judgment not fully resolved in the literature, are: (1) What is the appropriate measure of price—average, marginal, or something else? and (2) How should one deal with the simultaneity that results when the price faced by consumers is affected by their choice of quantity? The now widely used Taylor–Nordin specification includes both marginal price and a variable accounting for the difference between what was paid and what would have been paid if the marginal price were constant over quantities.

$40–$180 per af is below that for the reservoir options but similar to or above that for conjunctive use.[4]

VI. SUMMARY AND CONCLUSIONS

The problem posed at the outset of this paper was, how can a large urban water district best respond to a drought? What is the least-cost combination of alternatives to meet periodic shortages? We hypothesized that an answer might involve what we call nonstructural, or marketing, approaches, as well as the conventional approach of adding to storage capacity by building new reservoirs. The hypothesis was tested in application to EBMUD, a large district serving 1.1 million people on the east side of San Francisco Bay.

Our findings by and large confirm the hypothesis. The cost per af of water delivered was estimated for a range of capacities for each of the new reservoir options identified in the EBMUD planning process, Buckhorn and Los Vaqueros. Buckhorn, which EBMUD would build and use by itself, appears to be somewhat cheaper than Los Vaqueros, which would be a joint project with the Contra Costa Water District. Our more detailed cost calculations therefore were carried out for Buckhorn. Summarizing the sensitivity analyses for variants of the Buckhorn project, we found a range of costs running from about $1,000 per af to about $12,000 per af. The low cost is for a reservoir with a capacity of 145 thousand kaf, EBMUD's preferred alternative, demand at the top of the range of estimates, namely, 300 mgd, and a management regime that would, in the absence of the new reservoir, accept a shortage of up to 39% of normal deliveries (one of EBMUD's planning alternatives). The high cost is for a reservoir with the same capacity, demand at the low end of the range of estimates (210 mgd), and an acceptable shortage of 25% (EBMUD's other planning alternative). Our best estimate would be somewhere in the middle of this range, between $4,000 and $8,000 per af. It is worth noting (though that is all we do in the present study) that Los Vaqueros, though somewhat more expensive, would be preferred on environmental grounds. This is because CCWD will almost certainly proceed here regardless of EBMUD participation, so that development of the Buckhorn site would mean two impacts instead of one.

A prime alternative to reservoir construction that we identified was a combination of conjunctive use and water transfer. One variant of the approach would have EBMUD pay the costs of increased groundwater pumping by downstream (from the EBMUD dams) water-right holders in dry years, and perhaps also undertake low-cost groundwater recharge activities in wet years, in exchange for the right holders' not taking some or all of their surface water entitlements, which would be left behind the dams for EBMUD use. Another variant would have EBMUD simply pay for this water, leaving to the sellers the decision on how to adjust to reduced surface water supplies. We calculated that the costs of increased groundwater pumping would range from $5 per af to $105, depending on whether new wells are required. The higher figure might also represent the sale price of the surface water, since the sellers would have the option of taking the payment and

---

[4] The change in output can be associated also with a change in producer surplus. Since we do not know the EBMUD cost curve, we do not attempt to compute this. The change in consumer surplus can, therefore, be regarded as an approximation to the welfare loss.

using it to replace the surface water with groundwater. The cost saving, as compared to the reservoir alternatives, is dramatic. It can be explained by the intermittent nature of the conjunctive use/transfer, the disparity in cost between pumping groundwater and building a surface reservoir, and the disparity in the (marginal) value of water to farmers and urban users.

One difficulty with the conjunctive-use/transfer approach is that it would probably not yield enough water, by itself, to compensate fully for projected EBMUD shortages. The next most promising alternative appears to be participation in the new State Water Bank, if this continues in operation. Founded in 1991, the Bank bought water for $125 per af and sold it for $175 plus conveyance costs. In fact, assuming the Bank continues, the downstream right holders would have the option of selling to it, rather than to EBMUD directly. A mutually beneficial exchange might then involve EBMUD paying the right holders some amount greater than the $125 they could get from the Bank, but less than the $175 plus conveyance costs it would have to pay the Bank for water.

Finally, we compared the costs of new storage or conjunctive-use options to the benefits, the averted consumer-surplus loss otherwise entailed by raising prices to cut back consumption in the event of a shortage. The loss in consumer surplus associated with the price increase required to achieve a 25% cutback falls within a range of approximately $40–$180 per af, depending on the demand elasticity. This is well below the range of reservoir cost estimates but, for the most part, above the cost of conjunctive use/water marketing. Construction of new storage capacity thus does not pass a benefit/cost test, but introduction of conjunctive use and water marketing does.

REFERENCES

1. D. E. Agthe and R. B. Billings, Dynamic models of residential water demand, *Nat. Resour. Res.* **16**, 476–480 (1980).
2. D. E. Agthe, R. B. Billings, J. L. Dobra, and K. Raffiee, A simultaneous equation demand model for block rates, *Water Resour. Res.* **22**, 1–4 (1986).
3. R. B. Billings and W. M. Day, Demand management factors in residential water use: The southern Arizona experience, *J. Amer. Water Works Assoc.*, 58–64 (1989).
4. Brown and Caldwell, "Eastern San Joaquin County Groundwater Study" (October 1985).
5. DWR, "Kern Water Bank, First-Stage Kern Fan Element," Feasibility Report and EIR (December 1990).
6. DWR, "The 1991 Drought Water Bank," Report, Department of Water Resources, The Resources Agency, State of California, Sacramento (1991).
7. EBMUD, "Water Supply Management Program, Volume II: Final EIR" (January 1989).
8. A. Fisher, D. Fullerton, N. Hatch, and P. Reinelt, "Optimal Response to Periodic Shortage: Engineering/Economic Analysis for a Large Urban Water District," University of California, Department of Agricultural and Resource Economics, Working Paper 629, Berkeley (1992).
9. N. S. Grigg, Planning for raw water supplies for drought conditions: An overview, *in* "Water Resources Planning and Management," Proceedings of the 16th Annual Conference, American Society of Civil Engineers, New York (1989).
10. J. R. Hamilton, N. K. Whittlesey, and P. Halverson, Interruptible water markets in the Pacific Northwest, *Amer. J. Agr. Econom.* **71**, 63–75 (1989).
11. D. P. Loucks, J. R. Stedinger, and D. A. Haith, "Water Resource Systems Planning and Analysis," Prentice Hall, New Jersey (1981).
12. B. A. McCarl and G. H. Parandvash, Irrigation development versus hydroelectric generation: Can interruptible irrigation play a role? *Western J. Agr. Econom.* **13**, 267–276 (1988).

13. A. M. Michelson and R. A. Young, Optioning agricultural water rights for urban water supplies during drought, *Amer. J. Agr. Econom.* **75**, 1010–1020 (1993).
14. J. E. T. Moncur, Urban water pricing and drought management, *Water Resour. Res.* **23**, 393–398 (1987).
15. M. L. Nieswiadomy and D. J. Molina, Comparing residential water demand estimates under decreasing and increasing block rates using household data, *Land Econom.* **65**, 280–289 (1989).
16. J. L. Riggs and T. M. West, "Engineering Economics," McGraw–Hill, New York, 1986.
17. J. E. Schefter and E. L. David, Estimating residential water demand under multi-part tariffs using aggregate data, *Land Econom.* **61**, 272–280 (1985).
18. J. A. Weber, Forecasting demand and measuring price elasticity, *J. Amer. Water Works Assoc.* **81**, 57–65.

[26]

WATER RESOURCES RESEARCH, VOL. 22, NO. 1, PAGES 5-14, JANUARY 1986

Risk Costs for New Dams:
Economic Analysis and Effects of Monitoring

M. Elisabeth Paté-Cornell and George Tagaras

Department of Industrial Engineering and Engineering Management, Stanford University, Stanford, California

This paper presents new developments and illustrations of the introduction of risk and costs in cost-benefit analysis for new dams. The emphasis is on a method of evaluation of the risk costs based on the structure of the local economy. Costs to agricultural property as well as residential, commercial, industrial, and public property are studied in detail. Of particular interest is the case of sequential dam failure and the evaluation of the risk costs attributable to a new dam upstream from an existing one. Three real cases are presented as illustrations of the method: the Auburn Dam, the Dickey-Lincoln School Project, and the Teton Dam, which failed in 1976. This last case provides a calibration tool for the estimation of loss ratios. For these three projects, the risk-modified benefit-cost ratios are computed to assess the effect of the risk on the economic performance of the project. The role of a warning system provided by systematic monitoring of the dam is analyzed: by reducing the risk costs, the warning system attenuates their effect on the benefit-cost ratio. The precursors, however, can be missed or misinterpreted: monitoring does not guarantee that the risks to human life can be reduced to zero. This study shows, in particular, that it is critical to consider the risk costs in the decision to build a new dam when the flood area is large and densely populated.

1. INTRODUCTION

The trade-offs between failure risks and economic benefits in the decision to build a new dam are not currently considered in cost-benefit analysis. Although well-engineered dams do not fail, the fact is that at the stage of planning and construction decisions, uncertainties remain about the future performance of the structures. In urban areas, in particular, the failure of a dam could destroy many times the benefits of the project. The necessity of introducing risk costs in the cost-benefit analysis has been emphasized in the past [*Mark and Stuart-Alexander*, 1977; *Rose*, 1978]. A probabilistic method was proposed in which the expected value of the failure costs over the lifetime of the project are subtracted from the benefits and the initial benefit-cost ratio is modified by a risk-benefit factor [*Baecher et al.*, 1979, 1980; *Paté*, 1984a]. This method presents some challenges.

The first one is the assessment of a failure probability for a given single dam. In the absence of better analytical tools accounting for the characteristics of individual projects, we adopt here estimates (or default values) based on past statistical observations [*Gruner*, 1963; *Babb and Mermel*, 1968; *Shah and Franzini*, 1979; *Baecher et al.*, 1980]. This procedure, obviously, does not do justice to a better than average project. Recent publications have emphasized this point (see, for example, *Serafim* [1981]). It simply reflects our uncertainty at the time of planning about which ones are better than average among the large, engineered dams which are considered here [*Paté*, 1984a]. The default values, however, can be adjusted by the judgment of experts to account for special features and circumstances [*Peck*, 1980].

The evaluation of the risks of failure of sequential dams poses particular problems: if both dams are new, the possibility of their individual and joint failures has to be considered in the risk assessment, including probabilistic dependencies among these events. If the proposed project is only one of two sequential dams, the relevant figure is the marginal risk cost corresponding to the addition of the new project (the same

marginal analysis applies to the benefits of the project). We propose here a simple Bayesian treatment of this problem.

The evaluation of failure consequences poses another type of question, although the assessment of failure losses is less controversial than the study of failure probabilities because the analysis can be site-specific. The method of analysis of potential failure losses proposed here is based on detailed study and forecasts of the structure of the population and the economy downstream. Their expected growth over the lifetime of the project is considered in the model.

Finally, it was pointed out in the literature that the potential loss of human lives could be greatly decreased by a careful and systematic monitoring of dams [*Vanmarcke*, 1974; *Fanelli*, 1979; *Dolcimascolo*, 1980; *Serafim*, 1981]. The problem, of course, is that no warning system is perfect and that for many reasons, including human errors, signals may be missed and response may be only partial [*Paté*, 1984b, 1985]. Also, false alerts can be issued that may decrease the future willingness of the people to evacuate the area promptly when required to do so [*ICOLD*, 1976]. Yet, monitoring, early warnings, and evacuation do reduce the expected losses. We propose here a Bayesian analysis of such a warning system. In the final analysis, the potential loss of human lives thus has to be included in the risk cost. As with many other manmade structures and technological systems, the residual risk must first of all be acceptable to those who are exposed to it [*Slovic*, 1979]. Once this constraint is satisfied, it must be verified that the residual risk is compensated by a sufficient economic benefit. To account for the value of human safety ("value of life" multiplied by the residual risk), we perform a sensitivity analysis over the range of figures implied by other regulatory and individual decisions [*Linnerooth*, 1975; *Acton*, 1973; *Buehler*, 1975; *Zeckhauser*, 1975; *Bailey*, 1980; *Graham and Vaupel*, 1981]. We compare these (conservative) results to those obtained by ignoring human safety in the risk costs, which means in effect giving it a zero value. All costs (including risk costs) and benefits of a given project are discounted to reflect societal opportunity costs, including those of other life saving options [*Arrow*, 1976; *Page*, 1977; *Freeman*, 1977; *Lind et al.*, 1982; *Keeler and Cretin*, 1983; *Paté*, 1984c].

In spite of these analytical difficulties, introducing risk costs in the economic evaluation of a new project is necessary. An

Paper number 5W0673.
0043-1397/86/005W-0673$05.00

intuitive perspective is to consider the risk cost as an insurance premium. Including this insurance premium in the benefit-cost ratio for a new dam means that in the national accounting, the long-term benefits of all water resources projects are required to exceed their global costs, including failure costs. From a more theoretical perspective, in the framework of decision theory, the risk costs computed as expected value of future losses simply reflect the maximization of the public planner's expected utility, assuming risk indifference. Indeed, if he is risk averse, the risk costs which involve large amounts, will carry a still heavier weight in the project's cost effectiveness.

In the following sections, we present first an extension of the method of risk costs computation to the particular case of sequential dams, then a method of analysis of the failure costs followed by three applications representative of different types of projects and different magnitudes of risk costs. The first case of application is the Teton Dam (Idaho) that failed in 1976. It provides a point of reference for the evaluation of losses and in particular, for the calibration of loss ratios. The second illustration is the planned Dickey-Lincoln School Project (Maine), a large project in a rural area. The third illustration is the Auburn Dam (California) first proposed in 1961 and since then the object of a controversy because it is located in a seismic area, upstream of the large urban zone of Sacramento. For each illustration we study the sensitivity of the results to failure probability and to the chosen "value of human life." The case of the Auburn Dam raises the question of risk reduction by monitoring of the dam. We use a Bayesian analysis of failure precursors [*Benjamin and Cornell*, 1970] to show to what extent a warning system can reduce the risk costs. The detail of the computations can be found in the original reports [*Paté*, 1981; *Paté and Tagaras*, 1985].

2. SEQUENTIAL DAMS

The probability of failure for a system of two dams built within a short distance on the same river is different from the probability of failure of a dam standing alone. Whereas the probability of failure of the upper dam is the same as if it were isolated, the probability of failure of the lower dam is modified by the existence of the upper one. On one hand, failure of the upper dam may cause the failure of the lower one; on the other hand, the upper dam may protect the lower one from overtopping by retaining excessive flow. The final effect depends on the relative size of the reservoirs, the distance between the two dams, and the shape of the intermediate river valley. We examine here two cases: construction of two new dams and construction of a new dam upstream from an existing one.

The notations are as follows.

F_1 failure of the lower dam;
F_2 failure of the upper dam;
$\bar{}$ negation of event;
p annual failure probability of the upper dam ("default value") $p = p(F_2)$;
q probability that the lower dam fails, given that the upper dam fails $q = p(F_1|F_2)$;
r factor of reduction of the annual failure probability for the lower dam due to the existence of the upper dam and given that the upper dam does not fail.

The annual probability that the upper dam fails alone is

$$p(\bar{F}_1, F_2) = p(F_2) \times p(\bar{F}_1|F_2) = p \times (1 - q) \qquad (1)$$

The annual probability that the lower dam fails alone is

$$p(F_1, \bar{F}_2) = p(\bar{F}_2) \times p(F_1|\bar{F}_2) = (1 - p)rp \qquad (2)$$

The annual probability that both dams fail is

$$p(F_1, F_2) = p(F_2) \times p(F_1|F_2) = p \times q \qquad (3)$$

The annual (marginal) failure probability of the lower dam is thus

$$p(F_1) = p(F_1, F_2) + p(F_1, \bar{F}_2) = pq + (1 - p)pr$$
$$= p(q + (1 - p)r) \approx p(q + r) \qquad (4)$$

Indeed, depending on q and r, the existence of the upper dam may either increase or decrease the probability of failure of the lower dam.

For the year t, let $C_{F_1}(t)$ be the cost of failure of the lower dam alone, $C_{F_2}(t)$ be the cost of failure of the upper dam alone, and $C_{F_{12}}(t)$ the cost of failure of both dams. The expected value of costs of total or partial failure of the two-dam system ($\bar{C}_F(t)$) is

$$\bar{C}_F(t) = p(1 - q)C_{F_2}(t) + (1 - p)rpC_{F_1}(t) + pqC_{F_{12}}(t) \qquad (5)$$

In the case where a new dam is constructed upstream from an existing one, the risk costs associated with the new project are due (1) to the potential failure of the new dam and (2) to the variation of the failure probability of the old one, given the existence of the new one. We therefore make the difference between $p(\bar{F}_2, F_1)$, the probability of failure of the downstream dam and no failure of the upstream one, and $p_0(F_1)$, which is the probability of failure of the downstream dam before (or without) construction of the upstream dam. This probability is assumed to be equal to p, the default value for the annual failure probability of large, engineered dams. Let $\Delta \bar{C}_F(t)$ be the additional risk cost associated with the new project:

$$\Delta \bar{C}_F(t) = p(1 - q)C_{F_2}(t) + (1 - p)rpC_{F_1}(t)$$
$$+ pqC_{F_{12}}(t) - pC_{F_1}(t) \qquad (6)$$

This is the case of the Auburn Dam project, which is planned to stand above the Folsom Dam. For Auburn Dam, however, the failure probabilities are increased by the possibility of earthquakes.

External events such as earthquakes modify the risk costs in the following way. Assume for simplicity that the local effects of earthquakes are captured entirely by the peak ground acceleration; assume also that in any year, if failure occurs, it is associated with the maximum peak ground acceleration for the year, which is noted $a(t)$. When $a(t)$ is equal to zero, the failure probabilities are the standard ones; otherwise, they increase with a. There is no protection of the lower dam by the upper dam for all significant, positive values of a; therefore $r(a)$ is equal to 1 for $a > 0$. Let $f_A(a)$ be the probability density function of the random variable A. The risk costs associated with a two-dam project in a seismic area are

$$\bar{C}_F(t) = \int_a \{p(a)[1 - q(a)]C_{F_2}(t) + [1 - p(a)]r(a)p(a)C_{F_1}(t)$$
$$+ p(a)q(a)C_{F_{12}}(t)\}f_A(a)\,da \qquad (7)$$

The increase of risk costs attributable to the construction of a new dam upstream from an existing dam in a seismic area is therefore

$$\Delta \bar{C}_F(t) = \int_a \{p(a)[1 - q(a)]C_{F_2}(t) + [1 - p(a)]r(a)p(a)C_{F_1}(t)$$
$$+ p(a)q(a)C_{F_{12}}(t) - p(a)C_{F_1}(t)\}f_A(a)\,da \qquad (8)$$

3. ANALYSIS OF FAILURE CONSEQUENCES

The analysis of failure consequences involves three elements: identification of the flood zones, the estimation of the

TABLE 1.   Population at Risk in the Three Projects Considered

Hypothetical Dam(s) Failure	Population Year	Population	
		Wave Path	Inundation Zone
Teton	1976	12,000	120,000
Lincoln-School alone	1978	1000	5000
Dickey alone	1978	no population between dams	
Dickey and Lincoln School Lakes	1978	10,000	40,000
Auburn alone	1978	no population between dams	
Folsom alone	1961	190,000	360,000
Auburn and Folsom	1978	?60,000	500,000

downstream occupancy, and the assessment of the loss ratios (damage ratio and casualty ratio). To identify the flood zones, we need to use the maps drawn by specialists in order to determine the wave path (zone 1) and the inundation area (zone 2). These areas, however, may vary with the level of water in the reservoir [*Burkham*, 1978].

To assess the loss ratios, we first assume that no warning is issued. We then study the effect of a warning system on the risk costs in section 5. The loss ratios are defined as follows: the damage ratio is the proportion of the initial property value to be spent to restore the area to its initial use; the casualty ratio is the proportion of inhabitants who might be killed if the dam fails, assuming a weighted average of night and day occupancy. The damage ratio was estimated at 90% on the path of the wave, and 10-15% in the inundation area. These figures were derived from previous disasters, and in particular from damage in the failure of the Teton Dam, where the losses were estimated in 1976 dollars between $700 million [*Mark and Stuart-Alexander*, 1977] and $900 million [*Serdar*, 1979].

The casualty ratio is more difficult to calibrate. In the absence of a warning, and considering the losses in such sudden failures as that of the Malpasset Dam in France in 1959, it was assessed at 50% on the path of the wave. This figure is based on the assumption that depending on the time of the day, some regular inhabitants of that zone may be out of the area. It was also estimated that there would be no casualties in the flooded zone.

The assessment of downstream occupancy assumes a growth rate for the population and another growth rate for the property at risk. The population at risk in the initial year (year 0) is estimated using Census of Population data.

The property at risk consists of residential, commercial, industrial, agricultural, and public property. Only the value of residential property can be calculated with accuracy for a particular geographic region, using population census, the mean number of persons per household, and the median value of housing units. In further computation involving this value, the mean is approximated by the median, which is the only available data. The value of other types of property is related to the value of residential property (RP) through ratios that vary from place to place.

The value of commercial and industrial property (CI) is estimated by its ratio to the value of residential property for places where the information is directly available (e.g., Sacramento County). For other places, this ratio was derived by assuming that in general, CI is proportional to the value added by manufacturing and that RP is proportional to the population.

The value of public property was divided (generally in equal parts) between value of public buildings (PB) and value of infrastructures (railroads and highways). The ratio PB/RP was obtained from public records in places where the information is available (Sacramento County) and extended to other places

by considering the structure of the economy (rural versus urban).

The value of agricultural property is computed using the following information: number of farms, acreage, value of land and buildings, value per acre, balance sheet of farming sector in the United States, and farm marketing. The first step in the analysis of the statistical data is the computation of some general ratios for the farming sector:

(Nonreal estate)/(total real and nonreal estate) = 22%
(buildings and equipment)/(total value of land and buildings) = 30%
(livestock and crops)/(value of land and buildings) = 11%

These ratios are used to determine the total value of agricultural property and the proportion of this property that corresponds to land only. The data on agricultural land per county are used to specify the acreage of agricultural land in the two damage zones. The damage to the agricultural property caused by the failure of a dam is then assessed as the sum of damage to agricultural buildings, machinery, equipment, livestock, and stored crops, as well as the loss of farm products marketing for 1 year. The loss of land, which does occur but is difficult to estimate, was considered negligible. Thus the total agricultural loss was, in this respect, slightly underestimated.

4.   THREE ILLUSTRATIONS: EFFECTS OF RISK COSTS ON THE B/C RATIO

4.1.   Teton Dam

Teton Dam was built in Idaho between 1972 and 1975 by the U.S. Bureau of Reclamation. It was constructed on the Teton River, 3 miles northeast of Newdale. The Teton Dam and Reservoir were the principal features of the Teton Basin project, a multipurpose project which, when completed, served the objectives of flood control, power generation, recreation, and irrigation. The reservoir had a total capacity of 355 million cubic meters. The dam failed on June 5, 1976, killing 14 persons and destroying roughly $700-$900 million in property [*Mark and Stuart-Alexander*, 1977; *Serdar*, 1979].

All costs and benefits were calculated by the Bureau of Reclamation in 1969. The original figures are converted here into 1978 dollars in order to make all costs and benefits comparable with those of the other two examples.

Annual estimated benefits	$5.16 million
Annual costs	$3.38 million
Benefit-cost ratio	1.52
Discount rate	6⅜%
Economic horizon	50 years

The reason for considering Teton Dam is that the actual losses are known and provide a basis for cost calibration.

Using the method described above, the population at risk and the property at risk for the three illustrative cases are shown respectively in Table 1 and Table 2. The details of the computation can be found in the original report [*Paté and Tagaras*, 1985].

TABLE 2.   Property Damage Evalutation

Hypothetical Failures	Damage Year	Damage in Wave Path*	Damage in Inundation Zone*
Teton	1976	336	3360
Lincoln-School alone	1978	22	110
Dickey alone	1978	no property between dams	
Dickey and Lincoln School	1978	220	880
Auburn alone	1978	no property between dams	
Auburn and Folsom	1978	6650	12,780

TABLE 3.   Growth Rates for the Three Regions Considered

Region	Population Growth Rate	Property Growth Rate
Teton Dam	2.5%	4%
Dickey-Lincoln School Project	1%	2%
Auburn Dam	2%	4%

The total damage in the case of failure of Teton Dam is estimated, using the method described in section 3, to be $800 million (1978 dollars), which coincides fairly well with the actual damage observed in 1976 ($700–$900 million). By contrast, by our method, the number of casualties are estimated to be 6000, which is far greater than the losses (14 casualties) of the 1976 failure. The computed results assume instantaneous and total collapse of the dam. The actual number of casualties in the 1976 collapse was much lower due to slower failure mechanism and timely evacuation. It is therefore essential to include the effect of a warning system on losses. We propose a method for doing it in section 5 of this paper.

The growth rates (property and population) used for the three illustrative cases are shown in Table 3. The results and the sensitivity analysis are shown in Table 4. The annual failure probability is noted P_{F1} for years 1–5, and P_{F2} from year 6 to the end of the planned life of the dam. For high failure probabilities ($P_{F1} = 10^{-2}$ or 10^{-3}, $P_{F2} = 10^{-3}$) the expected losses exceed the benefits ($\alpha > 1$) when a value of life is taken into consideration. Although Teton Dam had been built in a rural area and the estimated number of casualties was relatively small, the factors are sensitive to both the failure probability and the value of life. It is only for low failure probabilities ($P_{F1} = 10^{-4}$, $P_{F2} = 10^{-5}$) that the benefit-cost ratio is practically not affected by the introduction of risk and cost of failure. This is explained by the small scale of the project: the total discounted value of benefits is only $80 million (1978 dollars), and the total discounted value of costs is only $52 million (1978 dollars). Therefore even low figures for the cost of failure have a significant effect on the original benefit cost ratio of 1.52.

It is interesting to notice that for the "base case" annual failure probabilities ($P_{F2} = 10^{-3}$, $P_{F2} = 10^{-5}$) and with a value of life of $1 million the benefit-cost ratio falls to 0.81. If these numbers had been considered for a risk-cost-benefit analysis, the project would thus have been considered unacceptable on economic grounds.

4.2. Dickey-Lincoln School Lakes Project

This is a proposed multipurpose project planned by the U.S. Corps of Engineers that turned out to be controversial

for environmental and economic reasons. The project is located on the upper part of the Saint John River, in Aroostook County, Maine. It consists of two dams, associated reservoirs, and hydroelectric generation plants. Dickey Dam is the larger of the two dams, with a reservoir capacity of 9.5 billion cubic meters. It is planned immediately above the joining of the Saint John and Allagash Rivers, near the town of Allagash, 45 km upstream from Fort Kent. The Lincoln School Dam is the smaller of the two dams, with a reservoir capacity of 1.06 million cubic meters. It is planned 18 km downstream from the Dickey Dam at the town of Saint Francis.

The sources of benefits from this project are mainly electrical production (96% of the benefits) and also flood protection and recreation. The economic evaluation was performed in 1978 by the Corps of Engineers [*U.S. Army Corps of Engineers*, 1976, 1977a, b; 1978] with the following results:

Annual estimated benefits	$79 million
Annual estimated costs (spread over the 50-year lifetime of the project)	$65 million
Benefit-cost ratio	1.22
Discount rate	$6\frac{5}{8}$%
Economic horizon	50 years

The size of the Dickey Dam (DD) reservoir is almost 30 times the size of the downstream Lincoln School Dam (LSD) reservoir (9.5 billion cubic meters versus 1.06 million cubic meters). Given this relative size of the two reservoirs it was estimated that the probability that LSD fails given that DD fails is $q = 0.8$. From our computations, it follows that the annual failure probability of LSD, alone or not, is $1.3p$.

The models described in sections 2 and 3 are used to determine the property damage and number of casualties in the case of LSD failure only, as well as in the case of failure of both DD and Lincoln School Dam. The results are as follows: (1) if LSD fails alone, the estimated property damage is $36 million and the number of casualties 850, and (2) if both DD and LSD fail, the estimated property damage is $330 million and the estimated number of casualties 8,400.

Considering the probability of failure of LSD computed in section 2 as the relevant probability because it is the one that may cause most of the losses, the property damage is derived as follows:

$$D(0) = \tfrac{5}{13} \times 36 + \tfrac{8}{13} \times 330 = \$215 \text{ million}$$

Similarly, the estimated number of casualties is

$$L(0) = \tfrac{5}{13} \times 850 + \tfrac{8}{13} \times 8,400 = 5,500 \text{ persons}$$

TABLE 4.   Teton Dam: Results and Sensitivity Analysis

Annual Failure Probability		Total Risk Costs			Risk Modified B/C Ratio			Risk-Benefit Factor		
Years 1–5 P_{F1}	Years 6–50 P_{F2}	(L_0) C_{F0}	(L_1) C_{F1}	(L_2) C_{F2}	(L_0) $(B/C)_{F0}$	(L_1) $(B/C)_{F1}$	(L_2) $(B/C)_{F2}$	(L_0) α_0	(L_1) α_1	(L_2) α_2
10^{-2}	10^{-3}	70	152	481	0.19	<0	<0	0.88	>1	>1
10^{-3}	10^{-3}	25	49	143	1.06	0.60	<0	0.30	0.61	>1
10^{-3}	10^{-4}	7	15	48	1.41	1.25	0.61	0.07	0.18	0.60
10^{-3}	10^{-5}	5	12	38	1.44	1.31	0.81	0.05	0.14	0.47
10^{-4}	10^{-4}	2.5	5	14	1.49	1.44	1.26	0.02	0.05	0.17
10^{-4}	10^{-5}	0.7	1.5	5	1.52	1.51	1.44	0	0.01	0.05

All figures are in (1978) million dollars; benefits: $5.16/year; costs: $3.38/year; total discounted value of benefits: $80; total discounted value of costs: $52; initial B/C ratio: 1.52; rate of discount: $6\frac{5}{8}$%; property growth: 4%/year; population growth: 2.5%/year; lifetime: 50 years. Value of life: L_0, not included; L_1; $200,000; L_2, $1,000,000.

TABLE 5. Dickey-Lincoln School Lakes: Results and Sensitivity Analysis

Annual Failure Probability		Total Risk Costs			Risk Modified B/C Ratio			Risk-Benefit Factor		
Years 1–5 P_{F1}	Years 6–50 P_{F2}	(L_0) $\bar{C}_{F0}$	(L_1) $\bar{C}_{F1}$	(L_2) $\bar{C}_{F2}$	(L_0) $(B/C)_{F0}$	(L_1) $(B/C)_{F1}$	(L_2) $(B/C)_{F2}$	(L_0) α_0	(L_1) α_1	(L_2) α_2
10^{-2}	10^{-3}	113	168	388	1.10	1.05	0.83	9.8	13.9	32
10^{-3}	10^{-3}	27	42	100	1.19	1.17	1.12	2.5	4.1	8.2
10^{-3}	10^{-4}	12	18	40	1.20	1.20	1.18	1.3	1.3	3.3
10^{-3}	10^{-5}	10	16	33	1.21	1.20	1.18	0.5	1.3	3.3
10^{-4}	10^{-4}	3	4	10	1.21	1.21	1.20	0.5	0.5	1.3
10^{-4}	10^{-5}	1.2	2	4	1.21	1.21	1.21	0.5	0.5	0.5

All figures are in (1978) million dollars; benefits: $79/year; costs: $65/year; total discounted value of benefits: $1223; total discounted value of costs: $1006; B/C ratio: 1.22; rate of discount: $6\frac{5}{8}$%; property growth: 2%/year; population growth: 1%/year; lifetime: 50 years. Value of life: L_0, not included; L_1; $200,000; L_2, $1,000,000.

Here again, the issue of whether or not evacuation can occur is a critical one, and the results can be reexamined using the model described in section 5, assuming the existence of a warning system.

The results of the sensitivity analysis for the case of the Dickey-Lincoln School Lakes project are shown in Table 5. Note that the probabilities of failure P_{F1} and P_{F2} are multiplied by 1.3. This modification is justified by the possibility of joint failures as explained in section 2: the sensitivity analysis is performed for the basic annual failure probability of a dam standing alone in general, and transposed for the probability of sequential failures.

From Table 5 one can conclude that the influence of the risk to human life on the benefit-cost (B/C) ratio is not significant. This is due to the location of the dams in a rural area and to the high costs and benefits of the project. The large scale of the project is also the reason for the small effect of the change in the failure probability on the benefit-cost ratios. The original benefit-cost ratio is 1.22 and the adjusted one falls below 1 only in the case of very high failure probabilities ($P_{F1} = 10^{-2}$, $P_{F2} = 10^{-3}$) and a value of life of $1 million. Note that the benefit-cost ratios would be even more insensitive to the risk costs if the conditional probability of failure of Lincoln School Dam, given the failure of Dickey Dam, were lower, i.e., if the larger reservoir were the lower one.

4.3. Auburn Dam

Auburn Dam is another controversial case for safety and economic reasons. It was planned by the U.S. Bureau of Reclamation in a seismic area (the Sierra Nevada) 65 km upstream from the city of Sacramento on the American River in California. It was first proposed in 1961 and was authorized in 1965 for irrigation, water supply, hydroelectric power, flood control, recreation, and fish and wildlife enhancement. The possibility of an earthquake (one occurred 65 km away in August 1974 at Oroville, California) made further investigations necessary. The project was redesigned and reevaluated in 1977–1978. Funding has been withheld until the final conclusions of the investigations become available.

There is some controversy about the benefits attributable to Auburn Dam because a portion of the benefits can also be attributed to the already existing Folsom Dam. The evaluation performed in 1960 by the U.S. Bureau of Reclamation [U.S. Bureau of Reclamation, 1960] converted into 1978 dollars, yielded the following results:

Annual estimated benefits	$29.8 million
Annual estimated costs	$15.3 million
Benefit-cost ratio	1.95

Discount rate	$3\frac{1}{4}$%
Economic horizon	50 years

After the redesign of the project, the benefits and also the costs escalated dramatically, resulting in a benefit-cost ratio close to 1.

The escalation of costs was due to three factors: (1) additional costs were incurred for the redesigning of the dam, (2) the scale of the project increased relative to the scale proposed in 1961, and (3) the costs were severely underestimated in the evaluation performed in 1961. On the other hand, the benefits increased with the scale of the project.

Finally, the different discount rates used in the calculation had a significant effect on the benefit-cost ratio: the new rate of $6\frac{5}{8}$% (as opposed to $3\frac{1}{4}$% in 1961) decreased considerably the present value of long-term benefits.

The calculations contained in the 1977 review by the U.S. Department of the Interior (converted here to 1978 dollars) show a significant difference from the previous figures:

Annual estimated benefits	$88 million
Annual costs	$87 million
Benefit-cost ratio	1.01
Discount rate	$6\frac{5}{8}$%
Economic horizon	50 years

The size of the Auburn Dam reservoir is 2.3 times the size of the downstream Folsom Dam reservoir (2.84 billion cubic meters versus 1.23 billion cubic meters). A quote from the Auburn Folsom-South Central Valley Project review by the U.S. Department of the interior refers implicitly to the probability q for this case: "A sudden and complete collapse of the [Auburn] dam when the reservoir was full would imperil the lives of 750,000 persons...Folsom Dam immediately downstream from Auburn, would fail...". Given the relative size of the two reservoirs and the preceding quote, a probability $q = 0.5$ was selected as the appropriate probability of failure of Folsom Dam conditional on the collapse of the Auburn Dam. This probability may look relatively low, but it accounts for the fact that the Auburn reservoir may not be full and that early signs of weakness may allow one to lower its level in an emergency. According to the computation above, the annual probability that Auburn Dam fails alone is $0.5p$; the annual probability that both dams fail is then also $0.5p$. The total annual probability that Auburn Dam fails (alone or not) is therefore equal to p. The annual failure probability p is greater a priori for the Auburn dam than for a dam constructed in a

TABLE 6. Auburn Dam, 1961 Evaluation: Results and Sensitivity Analysis

Annual Failure Probability		Total Risk Costs			Risk Modified B/C Ratio			Risk-Benefit Factor		
Years 1–5 P_{F1}	Years 6–50 P_{F2}	(L_0) $\bar{C}_{F0}$	(L_1) $\bar{C}_{F1}$	(L_2) $\bar{C}_{F2}$	(L_0) $(B/C)_{F0}$	(L_1) $(B/C)_{F1}$	(L_2) $(B/C)_{F2}$	(L_0) α_0	(L_1) α_1	(L_2) α_2
10^{-2}	10^{-3}	318	1149	4474	1.15	<0	<0	0.41	>1	>1
10^{-3}	10^{-3}	149	485	1830	1.57	0.73	<0	0.19	0.63	>1
10^{-3}	10^{-4}	32	115	448	1.87	1.66	0.83	0.04	0.15	0.57
10^{-3}	10^{-5}	20	78	309	1.90	1.75	1.17	0.03	0.10	0.40
10^{-4}	10^{-4}	15	49	183	1.91	1.83	1.49	0.02	0.06	0.24
10^{-4}	10^{-5}	3	11	45	1.94	1.92	1.84	0.01	0.02	0.06

All figures are in (1978) million dollars; benefits: $29.8/year; costs: $15.3/year; total discounted value of benefits: $779; total discounted value of costs: $440; initial B/C ratio: 1.95; rate of discount: $3\frac{1}{8}$%; property growth: 4%/year; population growth: 2%/year; lifetime: 50 years. Value of life: L_0, not included; L_1, $200,000; L_2, $1,000,000.

nonseismic area. We do not attempt here to use results of seismic risk analysis of the dam; for lack of better information, the seismic effect can be examined from the sensitivity of the results with respect to the annual failure probability.

In the case of Auburn Dam, only the losses caused by the failure of Auburn Dam itself are relevant to the current decision to build or not build this dam, because Folsom Dam already exists downstream. Because there is virtually no property at risk between the two dams, the event of interest is a failure of Auburn Dam which results in the collapse of Folsom Dam as well. Using the 1977–1978 data, the losses assuming failure at year 1978 are estimated to be

$$D = \$7.9 \text{ billion}$$

$$L = 130,000$$

The modification of the benefit-cost ratio by the risk costs is studied first for the original 1961 figures, at the time when the Auburn Dam was first proposed; these results are then recomputed using the 1978 economic analysis of the project. Using a 4% annual growth rate for property in the Sacramento County and data from the 1960 Census of Population, the losses assuming failure at year 1961 are estimated to be

$$D = \$4.05 \text{ billion (1978 dollars)}$$

$$L = 95,000$$

The risk-modified benefit-cost ratios and the sensitivity analysis for Auburn Dam are shown in Table 6 and Table 7: one set of data corresponds to the first proposal of the project in 1961 and the other to the reevaluation of the project in 1977–1978. The social rate of discount required for water resources projects was $3\frac{1}{8}$% in the early 1960's and $6\frac{5}{8}$% in 1978. The model described above is used, accounting for the special

features of this case: the annual failure probabilities are adapted to the situation of sequential dams. The results are the corresponding probability of failure of Auburn Dam alone, and of both Auburn and Folsom Dams. In the former case, the cost of failure consists only of the stream of lost benefits; in the latter case, it includes expected damage and casualties as well as the stream of lost benefits. There is great controversy about the benefits that are attributable to each dam [*House Committee on Appropriations Hearings*, 1978]. Comparisons found in the Water and Power Development Hearings [*House Committee on Appropriations Hearings*, 1978] lead to the assumption that the benefits from each dam are roughly equal.

From Table 6 (1961 data) the general conclusion is that both the annual probability of failure and the value of life are important factors. For high failure probabilities ($P_{F1} = 10^{-2}$ and 10^{-3}, $P_{F2} = 10^{-3}$) the expected losses exceed the benefits ($\alpha > 1$) when the value of life is taken into account. However, the original benefit-cost ratio is high (1.95), and this explains the economic desirability of the project for annual failure probabilities lower than $P_{F1} = 10^{-3}$, $P_{F2} = 10^{-4}$.

Table 7 shows the overwhelming importance both of the failure probability and of the value of life given the 1978 economic evaluation of Auburn Dam. The original benefit-cost ratio which is then 1.01 makes the project only marginally acceptable. The introduction of risk in the computation of the B/C ratio thus makes the project clearly unacceptable in almost all cases. For the "base case" of annual failure probabilities, for example, the B/C ratio is 0.93 for a value of life of $200,000, and 0.72 for a value of life of $1 million.

The significant downstream occupancy accounts for the critical decrease in the risk-adjusted B/C ratios, despite the great benefits of the project. The decrease would have been

TABLE 7. Auburn Dam, 1978 Evaluation: Results and Sensitivity Analysis

Annual Failure Probability		Total Risk Costs			Risk Modified B/C Ratio			Risk-Benefit Factor		
Years 1–5 P_{F1}	Years 6–50 P_{F2}	(L_0) $\bar{C}_{F0}$	(L_1) $\bar{C}_{F1}$	(L_2) $\bar{C}_{F2}$	(L_0) $(B/C)_{F0}$	(L_1) $(B/C)_{F1}$	(L_2) $(B/C)_{F2}$	(L_0) α_0	(L_1) α_1	(L_2) α_2
10^{-2}	10^{-3}	437	1313	4817	0.69	0.04	<0	0.32	0.96	>1
10^{-3}	10^{-3}	142	390	1372	0.91	0.72	<0	0.10	0.29	>1
10^{-3}	10^{-4}	44	132	482	0.98	0.91	0.65	0.03	0.10	0.36
10^{-3}	10^{-5}	34	106	393	0.99	0.93	0.73	0.02	0.08	0.29
10^{-4}	10^{-4}	14	39	133	1.00	0.98	0.91	0.01	0.03	0.10
10^{-4}	10^{-5}	4	13	43	1.01	1.00	0.98	0	0.01	0.03

All figures are in (1978) million dollars; benefits: $88/year; costs: $87/year; total discounted value of benefits: $1362; total discounted value of costs: $1347; initial B/C ratio: 1.01; rate of discount: $6\frac{5}{8}$%; property growth: 4%/year; population growth: 2%/year; lifetime: 50 years. Value of life: L_0, not included; L_1, $200,000; L_2, $1,000,000.

even more dramatic if Folsom Dam had not already been built downstream of the Auburn site. The existence of Folsom Dam, to the extent that it may contain the flooding in cases of rupture of the Auburn Dam, reduces the probability of catastrophic inundation of the city of Sacramento; it therefore decreases the risk costs that would otherwise be attributed to the Auburn Dam.

5. BENEFITS OF DAM MONITORING

When the failure probability of dams and the loss estimates are discussed, it is often pointed out that an appropriate warning system could greatly decrease the number of expected casualties. As mentioned in a 1976 ICOLD report [*ICOLD*, 1976]; "France in 1970 and the USA in 1972 have each passed acts requiring a particular governmental authority to inspect all existing dams of significant size." Yet, "such warning systems are not favored in other countries" for fear of the adverse effects of false alarms. Indeed, warning systems of this type cannot be expected to perform without errors, missed signals, and false alerts.

The costs of false alerts include not only the direct costs of unnecessary risk reduction measures, but also a decrease in the public confidence and in the percentage of the population responding to subsequent alerts. The "cry-wolf" effect and its consequences on the overall performance of a warning system have been studied elsewhere [*Paté*, 1985]; the results can be incorporated in the analysis and optimization of any warning system. The optimization problem, in the general case, is to find the level of sensitivity of the alert system which on one hand does not miss the signals too often and on the other hand does not issue too many false alerts. The optimization is performed on the long-term effectiveness of the system and includes the memory effect in the response. Our general model thus requires a dynamic study of the signal model and of the human response model. Similar models of response to flood forecasts have been developed elsewhere [*Krzysztofowicz and Davis*, 1984].

What we propose here is a simplified version of a general model, using a Bayesian analysis in order to assess the effect of monitoring on the risk costs [*Paté*, 1984a]. We do not treat explicitly the problem of false alerts, except indirectly in the results of an evacuation model expressed as the proportion of people saved who would have been killed without the warning system. The cry-wolf effect is to decrease the number of people who respond (and therefore of the people saved) by a factor that can be considered constant in a stationary situation in which the rate of false alerts is itself constant. The system performance can then be studied for one time unit (e.g., 1 year).

5.1. Elements of the Model

The Bayesian analysis of monitoring of dams that is proposed here includes the following elements: (1) failure modes, (2) signals, (3) lead time, (4) corrective actions to prevent dam failure, (5) and evacuation model (proportions of people saved). The results of this analysis include the probability that a failure that would have occurred otherwise is avoided by appropriate actions following a warning, the expected value of avoided property damage by preventing the collapse of the dam, and the expected proportion of avoided casualties by evacuation following a warning. The risk costs as computed above can then be reevaluated to include the existence of the considered warning system. The risk-adjusted benefit-cost ratio is recomputed along with the new risk-benefit ratios to check whether or not the existence of a warning system can

truly affect on economic grounds the decision to build or not to build the proposed dam. A preliminary analysis of the risk costs according to the method described above is necessary to determine whether or not they make any difference in the benefit-cost ratio, and whether or not reduction of these losses can make a difference in the decision to build. The 1978 economic evaluation of Auburn dam shows such a narrow margin of net benefits that decreasing the risk costs by a fraction can hardly change the *B/C* results except, perhaps, to make the project marginally acceptable for a $200,000 value of life, and a very low failure probability. This is not true a priori for the 1961 evaluation of Auburn Dam; then, a warning system might make a difference in the acceptability of the risk costs. We use this case as an illustrative example of a probabilistic method of analysis of the benefits of monitoring.

Figure 1 represents a decision tree [*Raiffa*, 1968] to address the question of whether or not one should adopt a warning system of given characteristics for a hypothetical earth dam. The performance of the warning system is assessed by difference of risk costs with and without the considered monitoring system. What has not been included in this evaluation is the actual cost of false alerts (not only financial but also psychological) and the fact that false alerts may erode the people's confidence in subsequent warnings.

5.2. Failure modes and signals

The efficiency of a warning system depends on several factors [*Paté*, 1984b]: (1) the probability of appearance of early signals given that failure later occurs; (2) the probability that these signals are detected and properly interpreted given that they appear at all; (3) the lead time of these signals; and (4) the expected proportion of the population that can actually be evacuated given the lead time. It is assumed here that property damage cannot be significantly reduced by warnings, except by actions that actually prevent the failure of a dam that would otherwise have occurred.

5.2.1. *Failure modes.* Statistical information on failure causes can be found in the literature (see, for example, *USCOLD* [1975]). It should be noted first that the actual failure cause is not always clear, and second, that there may be more than one cause involved in a given accident. From leading causes, one can derive statistics about the failure modes of earth dams, considering failure mechanisms and external stimuli: (1) overtopping: 20% of cases; (2) internal erosion (e.g., piping or seepage): 40% of cases; (3) embankment slide: 30% of cases; and (4) other external causes such as acts of war or earthquakes: 10% of cases. In a first approach, it can be considered that conditional on failure occurrence, these percentages represent the probability of each possible failure mode.

5.2.2. *Signals.* The next step is to relate the occurrence of precursor signals to the failure modes. Three types of signals each related to one failure mode are considered here. They reveal a potentially serious situation that may require evacuation (W. A. Marr, personal communication, 1980). These signals are (1) the appearance of significant cracks in the embankments, (2) the appearance of water springs carrying soil particles, and (3) the forecast of an extreme storm.

The appearance of large cracks may be a precursor of an embankment slide. Immediate actions can include drawing down the reservoir, plugging the cracks to prevent inflow of surface water and, depending on conditions, stabilizing the slope by placing material downstream. The lead time for such signals can range from less than an hour to months. Most often, it ranges between a few hours and few days, possibly a month. Immediate evacuation is appropriate if a slide devel-

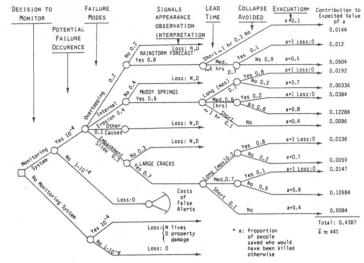

Fig. 1.   Probabilistic analysis of a monitoring system: illustrative example for an earth dam.

ops that removes the crest of the dam, and water seeps out of the slide zone. Immediate evacuation seems appropriate if a slide develops during a severe storm which reduces freeboard.

The appearance of muddy springs along the downstream slope or on the flat ground below may be an indicator of piping, and therefore a precursor of failure by internal erosion. The key issue is to detect whether or not the spring water carries away soil particles, in which case there is an imminent hazard. Internal erosion may worsen with time: as the phenomenon progresses, the gradient (change of "total head") that causes particles movement, increases.

Immediate actions to be taken include, as in all cases, lowering the water level in the reservoir. The next possible step is to construct an outside filter that could retain the soil while letting the water escape. Later, one can construct drains or improve the core by injection of chemicals (colloidal chemicals, cements, or clay).

The lead time is in the order of a few days, although signals can appear earlier (e.g., Teton Dam). The problem is to properly interpret the spring signal because a spring of water that does not contain soil particles is much more frequent and of much less concern. Clearly, a large and growing muddy spring, carrying away a lot of material, requires immediate evacuation.

Extreme rainstorms can lead to overtopping. Their forecast can be a reason for evacuation in examples of the following type: the spillway capacity is adequate for 10-year return period storms; a 5000-year storm is a few miles away. Clearly, the dam cannot withstand it and is going to be overtopped.

Immediate actions are to remove as much water as possible from the reservoir and evacuate the downstream area. Lead times are short, typically up to 6 hours.

Other external mechanisms are difficult to detect in advance. If and when earthquake prediction becomes a possibility, it will be possible to evacuate the zone downstream from a dam, when an earthquake is predicted with a larger magnitude than the design magnitude of the dam. Unfortunately, such a system is not yet developed and cannot be relied upon to eliminate the risk of human loss from dam failure in earthquakes. A landslide in the reservoir can also cause overtopping and be observed with short lead time. Finally, as in the illustrative case, a failure of a dam upstream can also lead to the failure of a dam downstream, again leaving a very short lead time for evacuation.

5.3.   *Probabilistic analysis of monitoring of an earth dam*

The case studied in Figure 1 concerns an earth-filled embankment dam and assumes regular monitoring. The expected performance of the warning system relies on the probability that the signals appear, are observed, and are interpreted given the occurrence of each failure mode. Assumptions have been made about the performance of that hypothetical system and the efficiency of the measures taken, inluding an evacuation model.

The result, for each possible scenario, is its contribution to the expected proportion of avoided casualties. It is obtained by multiplying the conditional probabilities along each branch of the event tree, thus obtaining the joint probability of the different sequences of events, and multiplying this probability by the corresponding proportion of inhabitants that are protected, either by avoiding the failure, or by evacuation.

Property damage is avoided to the extent that failure of the dam is avoided. The probability that failure is avoided by appropriate actions following a warning, is computed by adding the probabilities of all such scenarios. Probabilities and results of the evacuation model are indicated on Figure 1. The costs due to false alerts have not been included because their expected value appears to be negligible in the economic analysis of the dam. A false alert, however, could also cause a subsequent real alert to be ignored. A simplification made in this model has been to assume that consecutive alerts are independent. Finally the value of the information provided by the warning system is the expected value of the avoided losses [*Howard*, 1966; *Raiffa*, 1968].

For the illustrative case described in Figure 1, one obtains the following results: (1) there is a 0.12 probability that a failure that would have occurred otherwise will be avoided because of timely warning and appropriate actions; (2) the

TABLE 8. Effect of Dam Monitoring on the Risk-Modified Benefit-Cost Ratio Illustration: Auburn Dam; 1961 Evaluation with $6\frac{3}{8}$% Discount Rate

Annual Failure Probability		Total Risk Costs			Risk Modified B/C Ratio			Risk-Benefit Factor		
Years 1–5 P_{F1}	Years 6–50 P_{F2}	(L_0) C_{F0}	(L_1) C_{F1}	(L_2) C_{F2}	(L_0) $(B/C)_{F0}$	(L_1) $(B/C)_{F1}$	(L_2) $(B/C)_{F2}$	(L_0) α_0	(L_1) α_1	(L_2) α_2
				Without Warning System						
10^{-2}	10^{-3}	136	573	2,329	0.89	<0	<0	0.29	>1	>1
10^{-3}	10^{-3}	46	177	700	1.12	0.78	<0	0.10	0.38	>1
10^{-3}	10^{-4}	14	58	233	1.21	1.09	0.63	0.03	0.13	0.50
10^{-3}	10^{-5}	10	45	186	1.22	1.13	0.75	0.02	0.10	0.40
10^{-4}	10^{-4}	5	18	70	1.23	1.20	1.06	0.02	0.04	0.15
10^{-4}	10^{-5}	1	6	23	1.24	1.23	1.19	0.01	0.02	0.05
				With Warning System						
10^{-2}	10^{-3}	120	365	1,348	0.93	0.28	<0	0.26	0.78	>1
10^{-3}	10^{-3}	40	113	406	1.14	0.95	0.17	0.09	0.24	0.86
10^{-3}	10^{-4}	12	37	135	1.22	1.15	0.89	0.02	0.08	0.29
10^{-3}	10^{-5}	9	29	108	1.22	1.17	0.96	0.02	0.06	0.23
10^{-4}	10^{-4}	4	11	40	1.24	1.22	1.14	0.01	0.02	0.09
10^{-4}	10^{-5}	1	4	13	1.24	1.24	1.21	0.01	0.01	0.03

All figures are in (1978) million dollars; benefits: $29.8/year; costs: $23.8/year; total discounted value of benefits; total discounted value of costs; initial B/C ratio: 1.25; rate of discount: $6\frac{3}{8}$%; property growth: 4%/year, population growth: 2%/year; lifetime: 50 years. Value of life: L_0, not included; L_1, $200,000; L_2, $1,000,000.

number of casualties can be reduced by 44% of what it would be without warning system; and (3) the property damage that would occur otherwise can be reduced by 12% (the probability of avoided failure).

5.4. Reduction of the risk costs and effect on the risk adjusted B/C ratio

Assume that the Auburn Dam is replanned as an earth dam and that it can be shown that proper monitoring will actually take place. The previous method can be used to analyze the reduction of risk costs. This, in turn, modifies their reduction effect on the benefit-cost ratio.

Using as an illustration the 1961 evaluation of Auburn dam but with the rate of discount of $6\frac{3}{8}$% that is currently applied, the risk-modified benefit-cost ratio was recomputed for all values of life and all failure probabilities previously considered. The question is to know under what circumstances this modification could reverse the decision to undertake the project. In fact, the effect of the monitoring system is insufficient to modify for any value of life, the threshold of failure probabilities below which the project is acceptable (see Table 8). For example, for a value of life of $1 million, the failure probability has to be below 10^{-4} for the entire life of the project in order to make it economically acceptable. In this case, the economic effect of the monitoring system is merely to make the project a little more attractive in all cases.

6. CONCLUSIONS

Introducing risk costs in benefit-cost analysis is a way of introducing societal risk into the process of deciding to build a dam. The results and the sensitivity analysis performed on three real cases shows that under some circumstances, the decision to accept a project indeed could be reversed by the introduction of risk costs in the cost-benefit ratio. This shift depends on the societal value of human safety, and the annual probability of failure that characterizes the project a priori. The human component of the risk is particularly important in urban areas where human lives, in particular if valued at $1 million each, dominated property damage.

In cases of sequential dams, the relative size of the two reservoirs affects the risk-adjusted benefit-cost ratio through the probability of failure of the whole system of the two dams.

What matters, when considering the addition of a dam, is the variation of the risk cost of the system with respect to the risk cost of the original dam alone.

The safety of dams can be improved by the existence of a reliable warning system. It is important, however, to recognize that signals can be missed or false alerts can be issued. Whereas monitoring can definitely improve individual safety (e.g., by 50%), this risk reduction may be insufficient to reduce significantly the effects of risk costs on the benefit-cost ratio in the considered range of failure probabilities.

Acknowledgments. This study was partially funded by NSF Grant PFR-7815898 and by the Stanford Institute for Energy Studies whose support is gratefully acknowledged. The authors greatly benefited in this study from discussions with W. A. Marr from Geocomp Corporation.

REFERENCES

Acton, J. P., Evaluation of public programs to save lives: The case of heart attacks, *Rep. R-950-RC*, Rand Corp., Santa Monica, Calif., 1973.
Arrow, K. J., The rate of discount for long-term investment, in *Energy and the Environment: A Risk-Benefit Approach*, edited by Holt Ashley, Richard Rudman, and Christopher Whipple, pp. 113–140, Pergamon, New York, 1976.
Babb, A. O., and T. W. Mermel. Catalog of dam disasters, failures, and accidents, *Rep. NTIS PB179234*, U.S. Bur. of Reclam., Springfield, Va., 1968.
Baecher, G., M. E. Paté, R. de Neufville, NED cost determination for probability of dam failure, technical report, U.S. Water Resour. Counc., Washington, D.C., 1979.
Baecher, G., M. E. Paté, and R. de Neufville, Risk of dam failure in benefit-cost analysis, *Water Resour. Res.*, *16*(3), 449–456, 1980.
Bailey, J. M., *Reducing Risks to Life: Measurement of the Benefits*, American Enterprises Institute for Public Policy Research, Washington, D.C., 1980.
Benjamin, J. R., and C. A. Cornell, *Probability, Statistics, and Decisions for Civil Engineers*, McGraw-Hill, New York, 1970.
Buehler, B., Monetary values of life and health, *J. Hydraul. Div.*, Am. Soc. Civ. Eng., *101*, 29–47, 1975.
Burkham, D. E., Accuracy of flood mapping, *J. Res. U.S. Geol. Surv.*, *6*(4), 515–527, 1978.
Dolcimascolo, A., Safety inspection of dams, *Int. Water Power Dam Constr.*, *32*(10), 32–37, 1980.
Fanelli, M., Automatic observation for dam safety, *Int. Water Power Dam Constr.*, *31*(11), 106–110, 1979.
Freeman, A. M., III, Equity, efficiency, and discounting: The reasons for discounting intergenerational effects, *Futures*, *9*(5), 375–376, 1977.

Graham. J. D., and J. W. Vaupel, Value of a life: What difference does it make?, *Risk Anal.*, *1*(1), 89–95, 1981.

Gruner, E. C., *Catalog of Dam Disasters*, Gruner Brothers, Basle, Switzerland, 1963.

Howard, R. A., Information value theory, *IEEE Trans. Sys. Sci. Cyber.*, *SSC-2*(1), 22–26, 1966.

ICOLD, Committee on risks to third parties from large dams, technical report, Mexico City, 1976.

Keeler, E. B., and S. Cretin, Discounting of life saving and other nonmonetary effects, *Manage. Sci.*, *29*(3), 300–306, 1983.

Krzysztofowicz, R., and D. R. Davis, Toward improving flood forecast-response systems, *Interface*, *14*(3), 1–14, 1984.

Lind, R. C., K. J. Arrow, G. R. Corey, P. Dasgupta, A. K. Sen, T. Stauffer, J. E. Stiglitz, J. A. Stockfisch, and R. Wilson, *Discounting for Time and Risk in Energy Policy*, Resources for the Future, Washington, D.C., 1982.

Linnerooth, J., The evaluation of life saving: A survey, *Rep. IIASA PR-75-21*, Int. Inst. for App. Sys. Analy., Laxenburg, Austria, 1975.

Mark, R. K., and D. E. Stuart-Alexander, Disasters as a necessary part of benefit-cost analysis, *Science, 197*, 1160–1162, 1977.

Page, T., Discounting and intergenerational equity, *Futures, 9*(5), 377–382, 1977.

Paté, M. E., Risk-benefit analysis for construction of new dams: Sensitivity study and real case application, *Res. Rep. R81-26*, Dep. of Civ. Eng., Mass. Inst. of Technol., Cambridge, Mass., 1981.

Paté, M. E., Warning systems: Application to the reduction of risk costs for new dams, edited by J. L. Serafim, pp. 73–83, Balkema, Rotterdam, Holland, 1984a.

Paté, M. E., Probabilistic assessment of warning systems: Signals and response, *Pap. 13*, Cent. for Econ. Policy Res., Stanford Univ., Calif., 1984b.

Paté, M. E., Discounting in risk analysis: Capital vs human safety, in *Risk, Structural Engineering and Human Error*, edited by M. Grigoriu, pp. 18–32, University of Waterloo Press, Waterloo, Ont., 1984c.

Paté, M. E., Warning systems and risk reduction, in *Risk Analysis in the Private Sector*, edited by C. Whipple and V. Covello, pp. 469–482, New York, Plenum, 1985.

Paté, M. E., and G. Tagaras, Risks of failure in cost-benefit analysis for dams: Update and applications, *Res. Rep. TR85-3*, Dep. of Ind. Eng. and Eng. Manage., Stanford Univ., Stanford, Calif., 1985.

Peck, R., Where has all the judgement gone?, paper presented at The Laurits Bjerrum Memorial Lecture, Norwegian Geotechnical Institute, Oslo, Norway, May, 1980.

Raiffa, H., *Decision Analysis*, Addison-Wesley, Reading, Mass., 1968.

Rose, D., Risk of catastrophic failure of major dams, *J. Hydraul. Div. Am. Soc. Civ. Eng., 104(HY7)*, 1011–1026, 1978.

Serafim, J. L., Safety of dams judged from failures, *Int. Water Power Dam Constr., 33*(12), 32–35, 1981.

Serdar, L., The decision to build and site a dam: Sensitivity to probability of failure, Master's thesis, Dep. of Civ. Eng., Mass. Inst. of Technol., Cambridge, Mass., 1979.

Shah, H. D., and J. P. Franzini, Dam failure risk analysis, in Proceedings of the Third Engineering Mechanics Division Specialty Conference, American Society of Civil Engineers, New York, 1979.

Slovic, P., Dam safety and judgement under uncertainty, technical report, Decis. Res., Eugene, Oreg., 1979.

U.S. Army Corps of Engineers, Dickey-Lincoln School Lakes, *Design Memo. 3*, Waltham, Mass., 1976.

U.S. Army Corps of Engineers, Dickey-Lincoln School Lakes, *Design Memo. 4A*, Waltham, Mass., 1977a.

U.S. Army Corps of Engineers, Dickey-Lincoln School Lakes, *Design Memo. 4B*, Waltham, Mass., 1977b.

U.S. Army Corps of Engineers, Report on Dickey-Lincoln School Lakes Project, technical report, Waltham, Mass., 1978.

U.S. Bureau of Reclamation, Auburn Unit, Central Valley Project, California: A Report on the feasibility of water supply development, technical report, Washington, D.C., 1960.

USCOLD, Committee on Failures and Accidents to Large Dams in the U.S. Lessons from dam incidents USA, technical report, Am. Soc. Civ. Eng., New York, 1975.

U.S. Congress, Public Works for Water and Power Development and Energy Research Appropriation Bill, 1978, Committee on Appropriations Hearings, U.S. House of Representatives, 95th Congress, 1st Session, 1977.

Vanmarcke, E. H., Decision analysis in dam safety monitoring, paper presented at Proceedings of the Engineering Foundation Conference on Safety of Small Dams, New England College, Henniker, N. H., August, 1974.

Zeckhauser, R., Procedures for valuing lives, Pub. Pol., *23*(3), 419–464, 1975.

M. E. Pate-Cornell and G. Tagaras, Terman Engineering Center, Department of Industrial Engineering and Engineering Management, Stanford, University, CA 94305.

(Received July 8, 1985;
revised August 15, 1985;
accepted August 20, 1985.)

Risk Analysis, Vol. 18, No. 4, 1998

Risk Analysis and Management of Dam Safety

Lester B. Lave[1,3] and Tunde Balvanyos[2]

1. INTRODUCTION

Dams offer major benefits to society, including flood control, electricity generation, water for irrigation, recreation, urban use, and benefits (and disbenefits) to ecology. Dams offer flood control through providing storage capacity to impound flood water. Small floods are impounded, but larger floods contain more water than can be impounded and so the excess must be spilled downstream. Careful management of the dam during a medium sized flood could enable the dam to lower the peak flow downstream, lowering flood damage, even when the dam was not able to impound all the flood.[1]

As with any built structures, dams also pose potential risks. High hazard dams are those that pose large potential threats to people or property. If these dams fail catastrophically, they can result not only in large loss of property, including the dam itself, but also in deaths.

Nearly 9000 high hazard dams have been built in the U.S. They exhibit wide ranges of potential risks and benefits. At one extreme Hoover Dam offers vast benefits in terms of flood protection, power generation, and recreation with relatively little risks to health and property. (A series of large storms forced Hoover Dam to spill water, flooding downstream property since it could not contain the floods fully).[2] At the other extreme are dams that were classified as unsafe during a national inspection ordered by President Carter in 1977.[3] In some cases, these dams posed extreme risks to people and property, sometimes with little benefits.

Dam failures have killed thousands of people and caused billions of dollars of property damage.[4] These incidents have given rise to two quite different approaches to making dams safe. The first approach in-

volves professional judgment or statistical analysis to estimate a design flood for a site. The second approach is to weight the costs, benefits, and risks in order to arrive at a socially desirable outcome. Government regulators have turned to professional societies for guidance on what is acceptable safety for dams.

The dominant approach to dam safety criteria is to choose a design flood that the dam must be able to survive without major damage. Professional judgment is used to choose a "probable maximum flood" (PMF), the design flood for a high hazard dam. The PMF is "the flood that may be expected from the most severe combination of critical meteorological and hydrologic conditions that are reasonably possible in the region."[3] The magnitude of a PMF comes from professional judgment as to what is "the most severe combination of critical meteorological and hydrologic conditions" in a region and what "reasonably possible" means.

Not surprisingly, experts differ in their interpretation of these criteria. For example, experts have revised the PMF upward in the last several decades.[3] Since high hazard dams are supposed to be able to pass a PMF, these upward revisions led the Army Corps of Engineers and Bureau of Reclamation to request funding to retrofit the dams that no longer satisfied the safety criterion.[3] Regulatory authorities also demanded that privately owned dams meet the criterion. Congress resisted appropriating the funds for these retrofits.

The alternative approach is to set dam safety goals using benefit-cost analysis. A large project has enormous implications for the regional economy, environment, recreation, transportation, and water supply, as well as for government expenditures. Since the 1930s, Congress has required that waterway projects be subject to a benefit-cost analysis and that only projects with net benefits be built. Professional engineers have also recognized the need to balance the potentially large costs of safety retrofits with the social benefit. In particular, a 1985 report of the National Research Council[3] has as its first recommendation: "To the extent practicable, reservoir

[1] Graduate School of Industrial Administration and Department of Engineering and Public Policy, Carnegie Mellon University, Pittsburgh, Pennsylvania.
[2] Department of Civil and Environmental Engineering, Carnegie Mellon University, Pittsburgh, Pennsylvania.
[3] To whom all correspondence should be addressed.

455

0272-4332/98/0800-0455$15.00/1 © 1998 Society for Risk Analysis

Failure Vs. Age

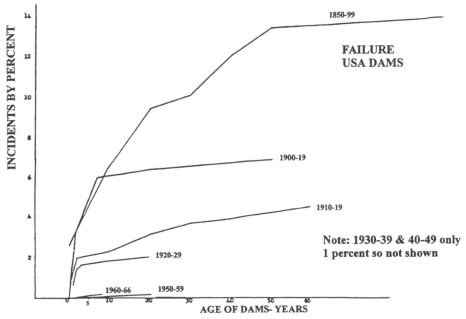

Fig. 1. Historical data of dam failures.

safety evaluations should strike a balance among such considerations as project benefits, construction costs, social costs, and public safety, including the possible consequences of dam failure due to major earthquakes and floods. (While achieving such balance is the ideal, currently available technology does not permit this balancing with full confidence in the results.)''

The 1985 report of the National Research Council[3] backs away from immediate implementation of this recommendation on the basis of the difficulty and social controversy associated with estimating the social benefits of retrofit. In particular, the report recognizes the difficulty of estimating the frequency of extremely large, infrequent, floods. The report also shies away from placing a dollar value on preventing premature deaths due to dam failure. Both of these issues were recognized in the dam design community long before the report and are viewed as major obstacles to estimating the benefits of increasing dam safety.

We show that neither an accurate estimate of the peak flow distribution nor placing a dollar value on premature death pose problems. Statistical hydrologists can construct sufficiently good estimates of the peak flow distribution with currently available data and methods. Deaths from floods can be all but eliminated and so there is no need to place a dollar value on premature deaths. (Some government agencies have adopted procedures for placing monetary values on premature deaths.)[5,6]

2. CURRENT SAFETY CRITERIA ARE DESIGNED TO PROTECT DAMS

2.1. Causes of Dam Failures

A historical record of dam failures in the U.S. (1975), shown in Fig. 1, does not support the current emphasis on protecting dams from overtopping.[7] Many failures occur when the reservoir is being filled for the first time.[8] Failure occurs for a variety of reasons, from seepage failure to structural failure to overtopping (due to mud slides and storms) and other hydraulic failure.

Lave, Resendiz-Carrillo, and McMichael[9] point out that the risk of dam failure from overtopping is small compared to the safety risks to dams from other hazards. Overtopping seems to be particularly visible and thus the subject of great attention, even though it is the cause of only 13% of all failures. For other failure modes, such as piping (36% of all failures) and structural failure (about 30% of all failures), there is less attention, even though there are more failures.[8] A primary reason for this concern is that hundreds of high hazard dams failed to pass the national inspection ordered by President Carter. Not being able to pass a PMF meant that these dams must be drained or retrofitted.

2.2. Protecting Dams from Overtopping

Dam professionals distinguish between damage and deaths caused by a flood and those caused by dam failure. They regard the latter as their primary responsibility. Few people at risk from floods recognize this distinction. People assume, and often are assured, that flood control dams will protect them for all floods. With this assurance, they build in the flood plain. To flood plain residents, flood damage is no more acceptable when it results from water deliberately spilled than when it results from dam failure.

Without an adequate spillway to pass water that cannot be impounded, a large flood would overtop the dam causing catastrophic failure and increasing the peak flow downstream. Safety discussions center on the size of the spillway and its ability to spill the water of large floods so that the dam does not fail by being overtopped.

Large floods are extremely rare. With much greater frequency, medium sized floods pass over the spillway damaging downstream property and threatening lives. Focusing on having a spillway capable of passing large, infrequent floods means that dam professionals are focusing on the safety of the dam rather than on preventing property damage and deaths downstream.

3. THE DESIGN FLOOD

The current approach to safety for high hazard dams is to design the spillway to pass a design flood, the PMF. The initial approach to estimating a PMF for

a location was to look for historical records of peak flow and to estimate the probable maximum precipitation (PMP) for a storm in this area. Hydrologists then route this storm to the waterway, defining the PMF. A PMF has never been recorded at a site in the U.S., despite the fact that about 600,000 site-years have been observed (tens of thousands of sites observed over time periods of up to 100 years).[10,11] A histogram of observed peak flows suggests that the PMF is not a 10,000 or even 500,000 year event.

Some hydrologists reject the PMF approach and attempt to estimate the peak flow from peak flow data using extreme value distributions.[12] In few cases are there 100 years of peak flow data for an area and often much less than that. Statistical hydrologists find that a number of extreme value distributions fit the data equally well, but have very different implications for the size of extremely rare events.[13]

Since there are a large number of plausible peak flow distributions and since there is little data, the estimation cannot provide confident estimates of floods that have return periods of 10,000 years or larger. The data do allow confident estimates of floods with return periods of 50–100 years.

Annual data for a site can be supplemented by analyzing the data for a number of sites in the same geographic area.[12] While adding watersheds increases the number of peak flow observations, interpreting the analysis requires stringent assumptions about the relationships among areas.

Events, such as cutting or planting trees and other vegetation and paving areas cause changes in land cover which result in changes in runoff. Constricting river channels also contributes to the change in peak flow for a given storm. Since the U.S. landscape is continually being changed, data from more than 100 years ago is of limited relevance in predicting peak flows.

"The classic approach in flood frequency analysis is hampered by the lack of sufficient data. This is especially true when the interest is in estimates of events of large return periods (hundred years or more). . . . Regional analyses can to some extent compensate for the lack of temporal data, but introduce a spatial dimension which is not always well understood. Classical flood frequency analysis, be it at-site or regional, has been criticized for lacking balance, for putting too much emphasis on mathematical rigor while completely neglecting the understanding of the physical factors that cause flood events."[12] We agree.

Thus, statistical hydrology is able to estimate the 50–100 year flood with confidence, but no techniques are likely to estimate the 10,000 year flood with confidence. We suggest giving less attention to finding the "best" peak flow distribution.

4. WARNINGS TO PROTECT PEOPLE

Flood waters that endanger people are inevitable, even when there are flood control dams. Saving lives requires getting people out of harm's way. Brown and Graham (1988)[14] and others have shown that even as little as 90 minutes of warning can all but eliminate flood deaths. Krzysztofowicz[15] gives a more elegant derivation of a two-step process for warning of possible dam failure.

This formulation gets closer to the current system of warning about hurricanes. Current hurricane warnings start as soon as a tropical depression is observed. As more information becomes available about the size and strength of the hurricane and where it might strike land, people are continually updated. People have different attitude toward risks with some fleeing days in advance of a possible hurricane landing. Others wait until the storm is only a few hours away and uncertainty is almost eliminated. For low lying cities, such as New Orleans, or islands where evacuation is time consuming, evacuation must be started when the uncertainty is still large. People have learned to interpret the information and to react according to their personal risk aversion. The hurricane warning system has greatly reduced deaths in the past decade.

Similar to hurricane warnings, forecasters predict the possibility of large storms and conditions that would lead to large floods. In the midst of a large storm, there is increasing data on the amount of rain fall and peak flows. Still later, water in the flood control reservoir rises and the dam operator gets still better data to predict how much water will be spilled and whether the dam is likely to be overtopped. Finally, even when the dam starts to be overtopped and failure is inevitable, there is still an hour or more of warning time before the dam fails and the flood reaches downstream areas. A warning system could provide this information with updates beginning 12 or more hours before possible dam failure and provide ever more confident warnings. Like the hurricane warning system, it seems reasonable to assume that such a warning system would all but eliminate flood deaths.

The length of warning time sufficient to get people out of danger depends on whether they believe the warning, whether they are prepared to leave, and how far they must travel. In a rural area with advanced warning of possible floods, the warning time can be short. If a densely populated area is involved, the warning time might have to be more than 24 hours. As with warnings of hurricanes, tornadoes, and other extreme weather events, people should learn to understand flood warnings and to act appropriately.

Pate-Cornell[4] focuses on the ill-effects of false warnings, since people cease to react to someone crying "wolf" when there is none. DeKay and McClelland[16] examine the issue by a survey and analysis. They find that people would prefer to be warned when the probability of a flood is extremely low. DeKay and McClelland[16] also reason that, if the warnings are rare, people will not cease to react because of false positives.

The literature on warning shows that it is effective and will not lose effectiveness if most warnings are false, as long as the warnings are infrequent.[16] This literature suggests that loss of life due to dam failure can be removed as a major concern. If the dam manager sets up a warning system and provides the warnings, the risk of flood deaths will be small.

Assuming the risks of flood deaths can be reduced to near zero, there is no need to put a dollar value on premature death. The problem reduces to optimizing spillway size to trade off spillway cost against expected property damage. As shown below, this reformulation of the problem means that PMF changes should rarely lead to retrofitting the spillway.

5. ESTIMATING THE NET BENEFITS OF A DAM

As quoted above, the *Blue Book*[3] states the social goal of maximizing the net benefit (benefits minus costs) from building a dam:

$$B - C - R$$

B is the benefits from flood control, electricity, irrigation, recreation, C is the costs of construction and operation, and R is the risks of flooding. We assume we are examining a socially valuable dam whose economic benefits greatly exceed its costs. Thus, we focus on minimizing the sum of construction (and operation) costs and flood damage. For a sufficiently large expenditure on construction (for example, building a dam as high as the terrain will allow in containing the flood), flood damage could be greatly reduced, but the sum of the two costs would be large. In contrast, a much smaller expenditure on construction would leave higher expected flood damage, but the sum of construction costs and flood damage would be much smaller.

To estimate expected flood damage, we integrate the product of the probability function and the loss function. In practice, however, the calculation is uncertain because the peak flow distribution becomes progressively more uncertain for larger floods.

We propose to deal with the uncertainty by choosing the estimated peak flow distribution with the largest right hand tail. Although the distribution is uncertain, choosing the most conservative estimated distribution is likely not to understate flood losses. As calculated below, the estimated occurrence probability for a given peak flow or larger floods would have to be more than a factor of 10 or even 100 too low to change the nature of our conclusion.

6. IMPLEMENTING BENEFIT-COST ANALYSIS: MOHAWK DAM

We apply these concepts to a particular dam, Mohawk Dam on the Walhonding River.[17] Assuming the risk of premature death is removed, the problem is simplified to be minimizing the sum of flood losses and cost of the dam. For any location, the relationship between flood damage and peak flow can be estimated. This relationship for the Mohawk dam is shown in Fig. 2. For floods large enough to damage property, in general, doubling peak flow will lead to less than a doubling of property damage. Even when the flow is large enough to overtop the dam and cause catastrophic failure, the flow is already so large that the increased flow does not cause much additional damage.

The expected damage function is shown as a cumulative distribution in Fig. 3. The figure shows that large floods contribute little to the damage curve; although the damage is very great, the likelihood of flooding is so small that the expected value is small.

For example, Resendiz-Carrillo and Lave[17] find that, although property damage from a large flood (10,000 m^3 or more per sec) at the Mohawk Dam in Ohio could reach $600 million, the likelihood of these extreme floods is extremely small. They estimate four extreme value distributions with the Walhonding River data and find that the smallest return period for the PMF is 2.2 million years. While we cannot be confident of this return period, we can be confident that the PMF would be extremely rare at this site. Assuming that the PMF has a return period of 2.2 million years, the expected cost of this or a larger flood can be calculated by multiplying the probability of these floods by the amount of damage. If so, the expected cost of a flood of 10,000

m^3 per sec or larger is only about $300. Note that the peak flow distribution would have to be underestimating the occurrence rate for these large floods by more than a factor of 100 in order for these large floods to contribute substantial expected loss. Such underestimation seems unlikely, if not impossible, given the constraints on a probability distribution and assuming that it accurately estimates the floods with return periods of 100 years or less.

In contrast to the estimated PMF, using the most conservative peak flow distribution estimated at Mohawk Dam for a 10,000 year flood leads to a flood loss of $200 million (the highest peak flow among the distributions estimated) and an expected loss of $20,000 (assuming a log Pearson 3 distribution). This sort of calculation is shown in ASCE Task Committee on Spillway Design Selection (1987, p. 60)[18] and ASCE Task Committee on the Reevaluation of the Adequacy of Spillways (1973, p. 357).[19] According to the Corps of Engineers data, the Mohawk dam is one where there is no downstream flooding for a peak flow of less than 3000 m^3 per sec, which is almost a 1000 year flood.

Funds available to build or retrofit dams are limited. At present, large resources are devoted to building or retrofitting spillways to pass a PMF. We conclude that society would be better served by using more of the available funds in order to lower losses from small and medium sized floods than to protect the dam from extremely rare floods.

7. SUMMARY

The current safety criteria for a high hazard dam focus on protecting the dam during a large flood. While protecting the dam does help to protect downstream people and property, the two objectives are not the same. Instead, the criteria should focus on lowering property damage (including damage to the dam) and preventing flood deaths.

High hazard dams must survive a design flood in the current safety criteria. However, experts don't agree on the size of the peak flow that meets this criteria.

Statistical hydrologists have proposed an alternative to using professional judgment to specify the design flood. Unfortunately, peak flow distributions cannot be estimated with confidence for extreme floods given available data.

A major safety goal is to prevent deaths from floods. Preventing deaths is a major reason for constructing the spillway to handle extreme floods so that the dam

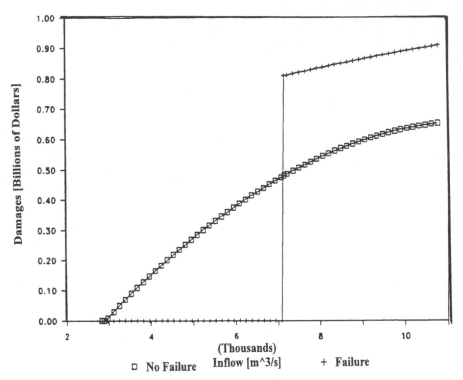

Fig. 2. Downstream flood damage as a function of peak flow.

doesn't fail due to overtopping. However, even if the dam doesn't fail, the spilled floods could cause many deaths. A better approach is to warn people to get them out of harm's way if a flood is coming.

Retrofitting existing dams that could pass a "probable maximum flood" (PMF) when built is almost never a good use of funds. Instead, funds would be spent better by focusing on preventing damage from small floods, lowering the damage from medium-sized floods, and warning people in the event of a flood that could pose risks to life.

8. CONCLUSIONS: A PROPOSED MANAGEMENT PLAN

The public and Congress are concerned with saving lives in the event of severe floods and with protecting property from flood damage. Currently engineering prac-

tice addresses these two goals but both goals could be achieved better with a reallocation of current expenditures. We agree with Orwig and Fodrea[1] that protecting property is best done by focusing on lowering damage from small and medium size floods. Protecting people requires getting them out of harm's way for large floods. Current engineering practice confuses protecting the dam with the two real goals: protecting property and getting people out of harm's way in a flood. The confusion is greatest on retrofit decisions where the PMF has been increased. Our analysis shows little or no additional benefits from retrofitting the spillway to pass the new PMF. Greater social benefit would be realized by raising the height of the dam to decrease damage from small and medium-sized floods.

The current difficulties in safety goals for high hazard dams stem from current engineering practice. The dams can serve society's interests better by changing engineering practice without having to convince mem-

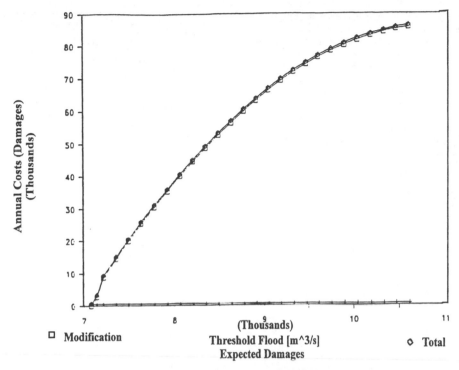

Fig. 3. Annual costs as a function of threshold flood.

bers of Congress or the general public to change their goals. Catastrophic dam failure due to overtopping is thought to put many lives at risk. The concern that dam failure not cause death has led to highly conservative estimates of the PMF and the increase in the PMF over time. Disagreements among experts led to the search for a more systematic approach, such as statistical hydrology. However, it has become clear that observed peak flow data cannot lead to confident estimates of an extremely rare event, such as a 10,000 year flood. Dam professionals have worried too much about the uncertainties associated with determining the PMF, estimating the peak flow distribution, and not having to place a dollar value on premature death. We recommend that dam professionals focus their attention on warning systems to get people out of harm's way, on computing the expected flood loss in order to conduct a benefit-cost analysis, and on other failure modes.

In designing flood control dams, the principal issue is generating net social benefits, the benefits of flood control, plus benefits of power generation, recreation, etc., minus the costs of the dam and the costs of flood losses and injuries. No flood control dam can guarantee zero risk or even lower risk from large floods. Dams are designed to spill large peak flows and will fail catastrophically in a flood larger than a PMF.

To protect lives, better warning systems and public education are needed. Hurricane warnings show that high quality warnings and public education can essentially eliminate deaths by getting people out of harm's way. For large floods, there is ample time to warn people of the dangers of flooding and thus there is no reason for flood-related deaths.

By eliminating risks to lives, the design decision for a flood control dam is greatly simplified. The dam should be designed to contain small floods and lower the peak flow on medium-sized ones. Since the dam can do nothing to protect property against large floods, people should be informed about long term risks and warned about immediate danger. Flood control benefits depend more on the ability to impound small floods and lessen the peak flow of medium size floods than they do on the size of the spillway and catastrophic failure for the largest floods. The peak flow distribution for small and medium-sized floods can be estimated with reasonable confidence. The distribution for large floods cannot be estimated with confidence, but the many statistical analyses indicate that the return period for large floods can be approximated. The implication of these analyses is that the expected loss from large floods seems to be much smaller than the expected loss from uncontained small floods. Although the property loss might be large, the likelihood of the flood is so low that the expected value is small. The analysis suggests that current spillway sizing criteria are highly conservative. Determining the optimal spillway size by the expected value criteria would lead to little or no retrofitting of dams that could pass a PMF when they were built, but which cannot pass a revised PMF.

We conclude that officials responsible for dam safety should:

1. Focus on lowering expected flood damage.
2. Improve warning systems and educate the public to get them out of harm's way.
3. Shift their attention to failure modes other than overtopping.
4. Size the spillway by stopping when the incremental expansion cost is just equal to the expected loss prevented by the expansion.

REFERENCES

1. C. E. Orwig and D. J. Fodrea, Jr., "Real-Time Operations in the Willamette river System Using the SSARR model with Meteorological Uncertainty," in T. E. Unny and E. A. McBean (eds.), *Experience in Operation of Hydrosystems* (BookCrafters, Inc., Chelsea, Michigan, 1981), pp. 153–175.
2. G. B. Freeny, "Managing Conflicts on the Lower Colorado river System" in G. H. Toebes and A. A. Shepherd (eds.), *Proceeding of the National Workshop on Reservoir System Operation* (ASCE, New York, NY, 1979), pp. 450–480.

3. Committee on Safety Criteria for Dams, *Safety of Dams: Flood and Earthquake Criteria* (National Research Council, National Academy Press, Washington, D.C., 1985).
4. M. E. Pate-Cornell, "Warning Systems and Risk Reduction," in C. Whipple and V. Covello (eds.), *Risk Analysis in the Private Sector* (Plenum, New York, 1985).
5. J. K. Virjling, Some Considerations of an Acceptable Level of Risk in the Netherlands, Report, Work Group 10, Technical Advisory Committee for Dikes and Flood Definitions, Delft, Netherlands (1987).
6. W. K. Viscusi, *Fatal Tradeoffs: Public and Private Responsibilities for Risk* (Oxford University Press, New York, 1992).
7. Committee on Failures and Accidents to Large Dams, *Lessons from Dam Incidents, USA*, USCOLD (ASCE/USCOLD, New York, 1975).
8. Committee on the Safety of Existing Dams, *Safety of Existing Dams: Evaluation and Improvement* (National Research Council, National Academy Press, Washington, D.C., 1983).
9. L. B. Lave, D. Resendiz-Carrillo, and F. C. McMichael, "Safety Goals for High-Hazard Dams: Are Dams Too Safe?," *Water Res. Rese.* **26**, 1383–1391 (1990).
10. K. L. Bullard, Comparison of Estimated Probable Maximum Flood Peaks with Historical Floods, U.S. Department of the Interior, Bureau of Reclamation, Denver, CO (1986).
11. W. L. Baldewicz, "Dam Failures: Insights to Nuclear Power Risks," in R. Waller and V. Covello (eds.), *Low-Probability/High Consequence Risk Analysis* (Plenum, New York, 1984).
12. B. Bobee, and P. F. Rasmussen, "Recent Advances in Flood Frequency Analysis," *Rev. Geophys.* (Suppl.), 1111–1116 (1995).
13. I. D. Cluckie and M. L. Pessoa, "Dam Safety: An Evaluation of Some Procedures for Design Flood Estimation," *Hydrol. Sci.* **35**, 547–565 (1990).
14. C. A. Brown, and W. J. Graham, "Assessing the Threat to Life from Dam Failure," *Water Res. Bull.* **24**, 1303–1309 (1988).
15. R. Krzysztofowicz, Choice of Actions Based on the Probability of a Flash Flood, University of Virginia School of Engineering and Applied Science, Department of System Engineering, Report to the Office of Hydrology, National Weather Service, Silver Spring, MD (1985).
16. M. L. DeKay and G. H. McClelland, Setting Decision Thresholds for Dam Failure Warning: A Practical Theory-Based Approach, Center for Research on Judgment and Policy, University of Colorado, CRJP Report 328, 12–31 (1991).
17. D. Resendiz-Carrillo and L. B. Lave, "Evaluating Dam Safety Retrofits with Uncertain Benefits: The Case of Mohawk Dam (Walhonding River, Ohio)," *Water Res. Rese.* **25**, 1093–1098 (1990).
18. Evaluation Procedures for Hydrologic Safety of Dams, Task Committee on Spillway Design Flood Selection, Surface Water Hydrology Committee of the Hydraulics Division of the ASCE (1987).
19. Task Committee on the Reevaluation of the Adequacy of Spillway of Existing Dams of the Committee on Hydrometeorology of the Hydraulics Division, Reevaluating Spillway Adequacy of Existing Dams, Proceedings of the ASCE (1973).

Name Index

The International Library of Critical Writings in Economics